WORLD HEALTH ORGANIZATION

INTERNATIONAL AGENCY FOR
RESEARCH ON CANCER

UNITED NATIONS

ENVIRONMENT PROGRAMME

ENVIRONMENTAL CARCINOGENS SELECTED METHODS OF ANALYSIS

VOLUME 8 – Some Metals:
As, Be, Cd, Cr, Ni, Pb, Se, Zn

EDITORS

I.K. O'NEILL, P. SCHULLER & L. FISHBEIN

IARC Scientific Publications No. 71

INTERNATIONAL AGENCY FOR RESEARCH ON CANCER

LYON

1986

The International Agency for Research on Cancer (IARC) was established in 1965 by the World Health Assembly, as an independently financed organization within the framework of the World Health Organization. The headquarters of the Agency are at Lyon, France.

The Agency conducts a programme of research concentrating particularly on the epidemiology of cancer and the study of potential carcinogens in the human environment. Its field studies are supplemented by biological and chemical research carried out in the Agency's laboratories in Lyon and, through collaborative research agreements, in national research institutions in many countries. The Agency also conducts a programme for the education and training of personnel for cancer research.

The publications of the Agency are intended to contribute to the dissemination of authoritative information on different aspects of cancer research.

Distributed for the International Agency for Research on Cancer by
Oxford University Press, Walton Street, Oxford OX2 6DP, UK

London   New York   Toronto
Delhi   Bombay   Calcutta   Madras   Karachi
Kuala Lumpur   Singapore   Hong Kong   Tokyo
Nairobi   Dar es Salaam   Cape Town
Melbourne   Auckland

Oxford is a trade mark of Oxford University Press

Distributed in the United States
by Oxford University Press, New York

ISBN 92 832 1171 5
ISSN 0300-5085

© International Agency for Research on Cancer 1985
150 cours Albert Thomas, 69372 Lyon Cedex 08, France

PRINTED IN SWITZERLAND

ENVIRONMENTAL CARCINOGENS – SELECTED METHODS
OF ANALYSIS
VOLUME 8 – SOME METALS: As, Be, Cd, Cr, Ni, Pb, Se, Zn

In order to ensure that future volumes in this series meet the needs of workers in this field, we would be pleased if you could return this questionaire.

1) How did you get to know of this publication?

....

2) Why did you decide to obtain it?

....

3) What is your main interest in this book?

Methods.. Chapters...

4) Does this book meet your needs?

....

5) Do you have any suggestions to improve content, format or presentation?

....

6) Do you know of or use other volumes in this Manual series?

Volume..

7) Do you have suggestions for further volumes?

....

8) Other comments...

....

Name...

Address...

Thank you for returning this page to

Dr I.K. O'Neill
International Agency for Research on Cancer
150 cours Albert Thomas
69372 Lyon Cedex 08
France

IARC MANUAL SERIES:

ENVIRONMENTAL CARCINOGENS – SELECTED METHODS OF ANALYSIS

Volume 1 (1978)
Analysis of volatile Nitrosamines in Food (IARC Scientific Publications No. 18), International Agency for Research on Cancer, Lyon

Volume 2 (1978)
Methods for the Measurement of Vinyl Chloride in Poly (Vinyl Chloride), Air, Water and Foodstuffs (IARC Scientific Publications No. 22), International Agency for Research on Cancer, Lyon

Volume 3 (1979)
Analysis of Polycyclic Aromatic Hydrocarbons in Environmental Samples (IARC Scientific Publications No. 29), International Agency for Research on Cancer, Lyon

Volume 4 (1982)
Some Aromatic Amines and Azo Dyes in the General and Industrial Environments (IARC Scientific Publications No. 40), International Agency for Research on Cancer, Lyon

Volume 5 (1982)
Some Mycotoxins (IARC Scientific Publications No. 44), International Agency for Research on Cancer, Lyon

Volume 6 (1982)
N-*Nitroso Compounds (IARC Scientific Publications No. 45),* International Agency for Research on Cancer, Lyon

Volume 7 (1985)
Some Volatile Halogenated Hydrocarbons (IARC Scientific Publications No. 68), International Agency for Research on Cancer, Lyon

Volume 8 (1986)
Some Metals: As, Be, Cd, Cr, Ni, Pb, Se, Zn (IARC Scientific Publications No. 71), International Agency for Research on Cancer, Lyon

Volume 9 (in preparation)
Passive Smoking

Volume 10 (in preparation)
Benzene, Toluene and Xylene

CONTENTS

METHODS

Determination of metals and their compounds in work-place air

Determination of metals and their compounds in water

Determination of metals and their compounds in food

Biological monitoring

FOREWORD

International working groups, having evaluated the experimental and epidemiological literature, considered some forms of arsenic, beryllium, chromium and nickel to be human carcinogens. Evidence on cadmium and lead is less clear in this regard; however, there is a stronger indication of carcinogenicity for cadmium compounds. There is evidence of some protective nature of selenium and zinc, both of which are essential elements for humans as are also chromium and nickel. In order to be able to resolve these complexities and to control or assesses exposures, it is essential to use validated procedures that permit an estimation of exposures to all the elements of interest and distinguish the different combined forms of these elements where appropriate.

Food, water and air exposure routes are covered in this volume, and validated biological monitoring techniques are included where available. Thanks are due to the many workers in government and research laboratories who freely contributed chapters or rewrote and clarified their techniques for inclusion in these pages. It is with particular pleasure that I record the support given by the United Nations Environment Programme for this volume.

L. Tomatis, M.D.
Director, IARC

SCOPE OF MANUAL AND CRITERIA FOR THE SELECTION OF ANALYTICAL METHODS

Scope

1. The Manual consists of a number of individual volumes, each concerned a specific group of compounds, the purpose of which is to present selected (preferably validated) methods in systematic format, based on ISO Guide 78 (ISO/ R.78.1969[E]), to analysts and others interested in the field.

2. Each volume will normally comprise a general introduction to the field of analysis concerned, representing up to one-third of its length, and a description of the selected analytical and sampling methods, comprising not less than two-thirds of its length. The overall balance of each volume reflects the needs for analytical methods and the importance of the introductory material in relation to IARC and WHO requirements.

3. The chemicals (or groups of chemicals) considered have been evaluated in an *IARC Monograph on the Evaluation of the Carcinogenic Risk of Chemicals to Humans* and thus indicated to have, or to be likely to have, some carcinogenic effect in experimental animals and/or man, with evidence that a risk of human exposure exists. Chemicals for which carcinogenicity evaluations are still in progress and for which evidence of occurrence is needed, may also be included.

4. The methods of analysis and sampling selected are related primarily to the environmental substrates in which potential carcinogenic risks have been established or from which the major human exposures are known to occur.

Criteria for selection

1. Preference is given to methods of analysis and sampling for which the reliability (i.e., accuracy, precision and inter- and intra-laboratory variations) has been statistically established in collaborative or cooperative analytical studies.

2. Preference is also given to methods that have alredy been recommended or adopted by relevant international organizations or that have been adopted by a national organization and subsequently entered into wide use.

3. When an international organization has made separate provision for reference, routine screening or field test methods, these provisions are to be adopted.

4. If other methods have been shown to be equivalent to these methods, they may be accepted as alternatives. When inclusion of analytical procedures for additional substances is necessary in order to complete the description of a group of substances covered by the volume, a short review of available methods is provided, if no particular method is deemed suitable for selection.

5. When appropriate methods for analysis are uniformly applicable to substrates, these are selected in preference to those which apply only to individual substrates.
6. When no method that has been subjected to full international collaborative study is available, methods are selected from those in the published literature to guide those who need to make a choice from the large field of published methods.
7. In selecting methods, particular consideration is given to the requirements of epidemiologists, hygienists and others concerned with the evaluation of carcinogenic and other toxic effects. Particular consideration is given to biological test methods that establish individual past exposure to environmental carcinogens.
8. The need has frequently been expressed by governments of developing countries for simple, specific, low-cost methods for use in the field; and, while it is recognized that such methods are often desirable, it is unlikely, in view of the very low levels and complexity of the contaminants concerned, that these can be developed easily.

MEMBERS ATTENDING THE EDITORIAL BOARD MEETING ON ENVIRONMENTAL CARCINOGENS – SELECTED METHODS OF ANALYSIS, VOLUME 8

(Lyon, 28–30 October 1981)

MEMBERS ATTENDING THE REVIEW BOARD ON ENVIRONMENTAL CARCINOGENS – SELECTED METHODS OF ANALYSIS, VOLUME 8

(Lyon, 17 June 1981)

---

* Present address: Lancaster Laboratories, Lancaster, PA, USA
** Deceased in 1984

ACKNOWLEDGEMENTS

Dr Harold Egan, Chairman Editorial Board, 1975–1983

Dr Egan, who was at the time UK Government Chemist, assumed chairmanship of the Editorial Board at its inception in 1975. Under his chairmanship, the Editorial Board guided volumes 1 to 6 into print and also saw the commencement of volumes 7 and 8. The establishment of this series owes much to his organizational skills in recruiting eminent scientists to freely contribute or to participate in the Boards, and also to his expert chairmanship and knowledge of international analytical progress. Therefore, we were saddened to learn of his death, working for the international community even up to his last day, in June 1984. His contribution to this series will be greatly missed.

Preparation of Volume 8

We should like to thank the following persons whose considerable efforts have greatly expedited publication of this volume: Dr. A. Mackenzie Peers (technical editor), B. Dodet (compiling editor), E. Heseltine and her staff (publication). The detailed advice of the Review Board, during and subsequent to the Review Board meeting in London, UK, and of Dr E. King (The National Occupational Hygiene Service Ltd, Manchester, UK) Dr B. Goelzer (WHO, Geneva) and Dr P.J. Kalliokoski (University of Kuopio, Finland), has been most helpful. For secretarial assistance, we are grateful to M. Wrisez (IARC).

The Editors

GENERAL ASPECTS

CHAPTER 1

CONSIDERATIONS OF SAMPLING, INTERACTIONS AND IARC EVALUATIONS FOR THIS GROUP OF ELEMENTS

I.K. O'Neill & B. Dodet

International Agency for Research on Cancer, 150 cours Albert-Thomas, 69372 Lyon Cedex 8, France

INTRODUCTION

The eight elements (As, Be, Cd, Cr, Ni, Pb, Se and Zn) dealt with in this volume were chosen by the Review Board for coverage on the basis of either known or possible carcinogenic risk or of possible protective effects (Se, Shamberger, 1985; Zn, Nordberg & Andersen, 1981); carcinogenic effects have been observed almost entirely in association with high occupational exposures; however, analytical methods for food and water are included in this volume to assist determination of intake from the environment. Analytical methods, classified in Table 1, have been selected as having proved suitable for the trace-level determinations that are necessary for environmental and biological samples, and guidance is provided in setting up a trace-element laboratory (Chapter 12) and in taking biological specimens (Chapter 10).

The genetic activity of these and other elements is reviewed in Chapter 2. Detailed descriptions are given of As, Cr and Ni in Chapters 3, 4 and 5, since certain of their compounds are established human carcinogens and, owing to their technical importance, widespread possibilities for occupational exposure continue. Similarly, Cd and Pb are described in detail in Chapters 6 and 7; most environmental concern about these elements has arisen from their biological effects other than cancer, and more work is needed to establish whether or not they pose a carcinogenic risk in humans.

Some general references are given below for information on carcinogenicity evaluations, sampling, biological monitoring and element–element interactions, since limitations of space precluded detailed discussion of these aspects in this volume.

IARC MONOGRAPHS ON THE EVALUATION OF CARCINOGENIC RISK

Seven of the elements have been considered by IARC working groups. The evaluations listed in Table 2 are precisely defined in the *IARC Monographs* series,

Table 1.   Coverage of elements in this volume for principal matrices of interest[a]

Element	Matrix					
	Air	Food	Water	Human tissue	Blood/serum	Excreta
As[b]	1,2,3[c]	15	9	15	15	–
Be	1,8	–	–	–	–	–
Cd[b]	1	18	13	–	25	–
Cr	1,4[d]	16	10[c]	23	–	–
Ni	1,5[e],6[e]	17	11	11	11	11
Pb[b]	1	18	12	–	26	–
Se	1	20	14	27	27,28	27
Sb	7	–	–	–	–	–
Zn	–	21	–	–	–	–

[a] Numbers are those of methods in this volume
[b] Chapter 9 describes analysis of this element in cigarette smoke
[c] Method 3 describes speciation of arsenic in air
[d] Methods 4 and 10 describe speciation of chromium in air and water
[e] Methods 5 and 6 describe determination of nickel carbonyl in air

which should be consulted. In order to clarify them, the following excerpt is taken from *Supplement 4* of the *IARC Monographs* series (IARC, 1982):

Group 1 – The chemical is carcinogenic to humans. This category was used only when there was *sufficient* evidence from epidemiological studies to support a causal association between the exposure and cancer.

Group 2 – The chemical is probably carcinogenic to humans. This category includes exposures for which, at one extreme, the evidence of human carcinogenicity is almost '*sufficient*' as well as exposures for which, at the other extreme, it is inadequate. To reflect this range, the category was divided into higher (Group 2A) and lower (Group 2B) degrees of evidence. Usually, category 2A was reserved for exposures for which there was at least *limited* evidence of carcinogenicity to humans. The data from studies in experimental animals played an important role in assigning studies to category 2, and particularly those in group B; thus the combination of *sufficient evidence* in animals and *inadequate* data in humans usually resulted in a classification of 2B.

Group 3 – The chemical cannot be classified as to its carcinogenicity to humans.

INTERACTIONS BETWEEN THE ELEMENTS AND WITH NUTRITIONAL COMPONENTS

Most of these elements interact very strongly even at trace levels, both with other trace elements and with substances commonly present in the diet. Some of these interactions have been found to be very complex, with regard to both trace element chemistry and to their relevance to carcinogenesis. Several of the elements have been shown both to enhance and to inhibit experimental carcinogenesis or tumour growth (Nordberg & Andersen, 1981) depending on the type of tumour, tissue or carcinogenic

Table 2. Involvement of certain elements in carcinogenesis

Substance or industry	Evidence for carcinogenicity in animals[a]	Evidence for activity in short-term tests	Human exposure of main epidemiological interest	Evidence for involvement of carcinogenicity in humans	Summary evaluation of carcinogenic risk in humans[a]
Certain inorganic As compounds	Inadequate	Limited	Smelters pesticides drinking H_2O	Sufficient	1 (IARC, 1980)
Cr and certain Cr compounds	Some Cr[VI]- sufficient; Cr[III] and other Cr[VI] – inadequate	Cr[VI] – sufficient Cr[III] – inadequate	Chromium, Cr compounds, use and production	Sufficient	1 (IARC, 1980)
Ni refining	–	–	Certain processes[b]	Sufficient	1 (IARC, 1976)
Certain Ni compounds	Sufficient	Inadequate	Certain industrial processes[b]	Limited	2A (IARC, 1976)
Be and Be compounds	Sufficient	Inadequate	Beryllium production	Limited	2A (IARC, 1980)
Cd and certain Cd compounds	Sufficient	Inadequate	Industrial CD use, food, smoking	Limited	2A (IARC, 1976, 1982)
Pb and Pb compounds	Sufficient (some salts)	Inadequate	Industrial Pb use	Inadequate	2 (IARC, 1980)
Se compounds	[c]	–	Environmental Se levels	–	–
Zn compounds	–	–	Environmental Zn levels	–	–

[a] Evidence and summary evaluations are those given in the *IARC Monographs* series, with 1, 2A, 2B, 3 designating precise summary evaluations (see text)
[b] For extended recent discussion, see Sunderman, 1984
[c] Not evaluated

agents administered. Before embarking on any programme to measure particular elements in environmental or tissue samples, it is strongly recommended that the proceedings of three recent international meetings be consulted, in which many synergistic or inhibitory factors are described that can profoundly affect the biological significance of these elements:

Health Effects and Interactions of Essential and Toxic Elements (Abdulla et al., 1985);

International Conference on Heavy Metals in the Environment (CEP Consultants, 1983); and

Trace Elements in Health and Disease (Boström & Ljungstedt, 1985).

SAMPLING

The importance of appropriate sampling procedures cannot be overemphasized, as it is far from simple to obtain samples that truly represent concentrations in the work-place, the environment or the body, and then to derive a correct assessment of exposure. Some key features and useful references are given below which give information on sampling from the environmental sources described in this volume.

(a) *Work-place air*

The highest exposures to these elements have occurred in the work-place. Table 3 lists regulatory limits in several industrialized nations; the duration of sampling is related not only to a 15-min or 8-hour time-span, but also to the periodic nature of the process(es) believed to be the major emission sources. These elements can be present in gaseous (e.g., arsine, nickel carbonyl), droplet (e.g., chromate solutions) or particulate form. The size of particulates depends on their method of formation: e.g., the diameters of particles produced by condensation of vapours formed at high temperatures or by grinding are usually, respectively, < 0.05 μm and > 2 μm. The site and extent of deposition within the respiratory tract (Fig. 1) is critically dependent upon particulate size (International Committee on Radiological Protection, 1966). Appropriate sampling of airborne particulates is dependent on an adequate knowledge of the materials involved, so a thorough consideration of sampling strategy (Leidel et al., 1977; Eller, 1984) must always be undertaken. The fraction of airborne particulate that is indeed 'respirable' is the subject of some debate, but usually one of two slightly different profiles (Fig. 1) has been used in the design of sampling equipment (Medical Research Council of Great Britain, 1952; American Conference of Governmental Industrial Hygienists, 1982). Particle-size profiling (Allen, 1981) is usually performed with multistage impactors and should form part of the preliminary characterization of airborne material. The deposition and clearance of inhaled particles have recently been reviewed (Stuart, 1984).

Care must be taken in the choice of sampling equipment, since much equipment has been designed for use with airborne nuisance dust rather than for particulates with potential systemic effects (WHO, 1984a). Use of personal samplers with sampling heads within the workers' breathing zone is foreseen by the US National Institute for

Table 3. Some recently established exposure limits (mg/m³) [a]

Element	ACGIH 1984–1985		FRG 1984	Sweden 1981	Finland 1984	
	TWA	STEL			8h.	15 min.
As	0.2	–	0.2	0.05	0.1	–
AsH₃	0.2	–	–	0.05	0.15	0.45
Be	0.002	–	0.002	0.002	0.002	0.006
Cd	0.05	0.2	–	0.05	0.02	–
Cr metal	0.5	–	–	0.5	0.5	–
Cr[III]	0.5	–	–	0.02	0.5	–
Cr[VI]	0.05	–	–	0.02	0.05	–
Ni metal	1	–	0.5	0.5	1	–
Ni soluble	0.1	0.3	0.05	0.1	0.1	–
Ni(CO)₄	0.35	–	0.7	0.007	0.007	0.021
Ni sulfide	1	–	–	0.01	–	–
Pb	0.15	0.45	–	–	–	–
Se	0.2	–	0.1	0.1	0.1	0.3
ZnO	5	10	5	5	–	–

[a] Measured as content of element; A more extensive listing is available (International Labour Office, 1980)

Occupational Safety and Health (Eller, 1984) as a prerequisite for the methods presented in this volume. Taking into account possible fluctuations arising from process emissions, a statistically calculable minimum number of samples is necessary in order to estimate exposure (Bar-Shalom et al., 1975; Leidel & Busch, 1975; Ulfvarson, 1977).

(b) *Biological Monitoring*

In view of the difficulties in estimating exposures based on measurements of airborne material, concentrations of which vary from place to place and time to time, biological monitoring techniques for measuring exposures in the work-place have been developed for most of the elements of interest (Baselt, 1980; Lauwerys, 1983). These indicate past exposure of an individual but, apart from Pb, reflect only very recent exposures (Table 4). Urinary concentrations of some elements are expressed as a ratio with creatinine excretion, in order to offset dilution factors. Levels of As, Cd and Pb arising from non-occupational exposures can be significant relative to those arising from occupational exposure. The analytical methods given in this volume are for total concentrations of the elements in biological samples, and due account should be taken of the relative amounts (see Chapter 7) and bioavailabilities of elements from different sources, as well as the known or possible essential nature of As, Cr, Ni, Se and Zn (Davidson et al., 1979). Sampling and storage of tissue

Fig. 1. (a) Deposition as a function of particle size for 15 respirations/min, 1 450 cm³ tidal volume
(International Committee on Radiological Protection, 1966)
(b) Medical Research Council of Great Britain (MRC), Atomic Energy Commission (Los Alamos)
(AEC) and American Conference of Governmental Industrial Hygienists (ACGIH) acceptance
curves fur sampling airborne particulate materials.

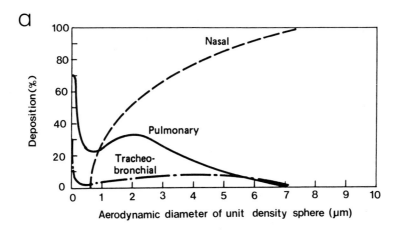

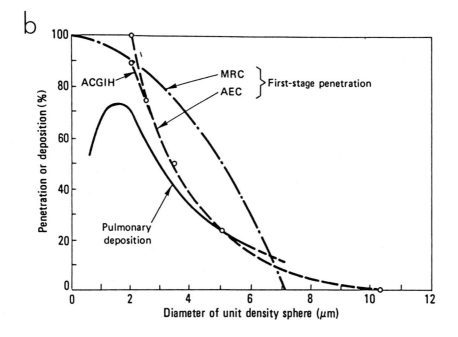

specimens is reviewed in Chapter 10, and further details for other elements may be
found in a publication of the International Atomic Energy Agency (1980).

Table 4. Biological Monitoring for Exposure to As, Be, Cd, Ni, Pb and Se [a]

Element	Biological sample	Utility [b]	Levels expected in non-occupationally exposed	Biological half-life found in this fluid	Increased concentration (μg/L) for each 1.0 μg/m³ of exposure	Main non-occupational source
As	Urine [c]	Quant.	<20μg/gC	1–2 days for As_2O_3	4.4 μg/gC	Seafood
Be	Urine	Qual.	0.9 μg/L	Unknown	–	Smoking
Cd	Urine [c]	Quant. [d]	<2 μg/gC	>30 years	–	Smoking
Cd	Whole body	Quant. [e]	–	>30 years	–	–
Cr[VI]	Urine [c]	Quant. [f]	5 μg/gC	15–41 h.	0.6 μg/gC	–
Ni	Plasma	Quant. [f]	2–4 μg/L	17–39 h	0.07 μg/L	?
Pb	Blood	Quant.	200 mλ/L common	35 days	10–20 μg/L	General environment
Pb	Urine ALAD [g]	Quant.	–	?	–[h]	General environment
Pb(alkyl)$_4$	Urine [c]	Qual.	<50 μg/gC	?	–	General environment
Se	Urine	Qual.	7–79 μg/L	Not known	–	Diet

[a] As adapted from Lauwerys (1983) (see also chapter I)
[b] Quantitative utility indicates suitability for routine biological monitoring; qualitative utility unsuitable for this purpose
[c] Creatinine (C) control used for these urinary samples
[d] Due to exceptionally long binding of Cd within tissue, this form of biological monitoring is of doubtful utility
[e] In-vivo neutron activation analysis of kidney and liver burden
[f] Although Cr[VI] and Ni monitoring is well developed, its utility for the relatively insoluble compounds that have been associated with carcinogenesis (IARC 1976, 1980) is doubtful, since biological monitoring relies on prior dissolution in body fluids
[g] δ-Aminolaevulinic acid
[h] Non-linear

Table 5.   Recommended intake minima and maxima and estimated bioavailability of the elements

Element	Recommended[a] minimum intake (mg/day)	WHO[b] guideline maximum values for drinking water (µg/L)	WHO estimated[b] proportion absorbed from	
			Food and water (%)	Air (%)
As	–	50	Unknown	Unknown
Be	–	None set	<1	Variable
Cd	–	5	6	64
Cr	0.05	50	10	50 overall
Ni	–	None set	<1	–
Pb	–	50	10	40 overall
Se	0.05	10	>90	–
Zn	15	5000[c]	Variable	Unknown

[a] Food and Nutrition Board (1980)
[b] WHO, 1984b
[c] Zinc limit set for aesthetic reasons alone

(c) *Food and water*

Prior to undertaking analyses of food or water samples, it is recommended that the literature on market-basket surveys (WHO, 1983), on procedures for studying dietary intake (WHO, 1985) and on water sampling (WHO, 1978; Wilson, 1982) be consulted. The preparation of representative samples of bulk food items has been described for only a few foods (Williams, 1984). The bioavailability of these elements from food and water is frequently very low (Table 5), as they may be tightly complexed by food components or adsorbed onto suspended particulates in the water (American Public Health Association, American Water Works Association, Water Pollution Association, 1976). Especially for Cr, where distinction of Cr[VI] from Cr[III] is important, it is necessary that the element be preserved in its naturally-occurring valency. The methods presented in this volume are based on the assumption that water samples are collected and suitably stored in plastic containers (Allen & Minear, 1982) to prevent irreversible adsorptive loss of the elements onto the container walls.

(d) *Geological background*

To ascertain differences in elemental concentrations between areas that differ in geology, urbanization, mining activity, etc., surveys of stream sediments have been performed. This technique indicated marked local differences for all the elements under consideration, e.g., in element-distribution maps for the United Kingdom (Webb *et al.*, 1978). Extensive multi-element surveys of stream water are used for mineral prospecting (e.g., for possible resources of uranium, Floyd *et al.*, 1985), and such data may also indicate geological sources of exposure to these elements.

(e) *Air pollution*

The literature on measurement of air pollutants has been reviewed, and equipment and methods have been described for collecting airborne particulates from external air (WHO, 1976). The factors of time and meteorological conditions and the necessity for appropriate data interpretation techniques have been discussed in detail in this regard (WHO, 1980). A world-wide air pollution monitoring system, operated by the WHO and the World Meterological Organization, has been in operation for some years (Koning & Köhler, 1978); this includes the monitoring of some of the elements under consideration.

OVERALL ENVIRONMENTAL SURVEYS OF TRACE ELEMENTS

Determination of human intake of trace elements from the general environment requires multi-media sampling; the WHO and the United Nations Environment Programme (UNEP) have undertaken this for Cd and Pb. Segments of this effort were described above with regard to food (WHO, 1983), water (WHO, 1978) air (WHO, 1976) and biological monitoring (Vahter, 1982) and are part of the Global Environment Monitoring System. These four components are brought together in the UNEP/WHO Human Exposure Assessment (HEAL) project.

Environmental Health Criteria documents of the International Programme on Chemical Safety have been published on Pb (WHO, 1977) and As (WHO, 1981) and are in preparation for all the other elements covered in this volume.

REFERENCES

Abdulla, M., Nair, B.M. & Chandra, R.K., eds (1985) *Health Effects and Interactions of Essential and Toxic Elements, Supplement 1, Nutr. Res.*

Allen, H.E. & Minear, R.A. (1982) *Metallic ions.* In: Suess, M.J., ed., *Examination of Water for Pollution Control,* Vol. 2, Oxford, Pergamon Press, pp. 43–168

Allen, T. (1981) *Particle Size Measurement,* 3rd ed., London, Chapman & Hall

American Conference of Governmental Industrial Hygienists (1982) *TLV's of Airborne Contaminants for 1982,* Threshold Limits Committee, Cincinatti, OH

American Public Health Association, American Water Works Association, Water Pollution Association (1976) *Standard Methods for the Examination of Water and Wastewater,* 14th ed., Washington DC, American Public Health Association, pp. 38–45

Bar-Shalom, Y., Budenaers, R., Schainker, R. & Segall, A. (1975) *Handbook of Statistical Tests for Evaluating Employee Exposure to Air Contaminants,* Cincinatti, OH, US Department of Health, Education and Welfare

Baselt, R.C. (1980) *Biological Monitoring Methods for Industrial Chemicals,* Davis, CA, Biomedical Publications

Boström, H. & Ljungstedt, N., eds (1985) *Trace Elements in Health and Disease,* Stockholm, Almgvist & Wiksell International

CEP Consultants (1983) *International Conference on Heavy Metals in the Environment,* Vols 1 and 2, Edinburgh

Davidson, S.S., Passmore, R., Brock, J.F. & Truswell, A.S. (1979) *Human Nutrition and Dietetics,* 7th ed., Edinburgh, Churchill Livingston, pp. 90–116

Eller, P.M., ed. (1984) *NIOSH Manual of Analytical Methods,* 3rd ed., Cincinatti, OH, National Institute for Occupational Safety and Health

Floyd, M.A., Halouma, A.A., Morrow, R.W. & Farrar, R.B. (1985) Rapid multi-element analysis of water samples by sequential ICEP-AES. *Int. Lab.,* 24–36

Food and Nutrition Board (1980) *Recommended Dietary Allowances,* Washington DC, National Academy of Sciences

International Atomic Energy Agency (1980) *Elemental Analysis of Biological Materials. Current Problems and Techniques with Special Reference to Trace Elements.* Technicap Rep. Series No. 197, Vienna

IARC (1976) *IARC Monographs on the Evaluation of Carcinogenic Risk of Chemicals to Man,* Vol. 11, *Cadmium, Nickel, Some Epoxides, Miscellaneous Industrial Chemicals and General Considerations on Volatile Anaesthetics,* Lyon

IARC (1980) *IARC Monographs on the Evaluation of the Carcinogenic Risk of Chemicals to Humans,* Vol. 23, *Some Metals and Metallic Compounds,* Lyon

IARC (1982) *IARC Monographs on the Evaluation of the Carcinogenic Risk of Chemicals to Humans,* Suppl. 4, *Chemicals, Industrial Processes and Industries Associated with Cancer in Humans, IARC Monographs, Volumes 1 to 29,* Lyon

International Committee on Radiological Protection (1966) Task Group on Lung Dynamics Committee. 2. Deposition and retention models for internal dosimetry of the human respiratory tract. *Health Phys., 12,* 173–207

International Labour Office (1980) *Occupational Exposure Limits for Airborne Toxic Substances (Occupational Safety and Health Series No. 3),* Geneva

Koning, H.W. & Köhler, A. (1978) Monitoring global air pollution. *Environ. Sci. Technol., 12,* 884–889

Lauwerys, R.R. (1983) *Industrial Chemical Exposure: Guidelines for Biological Monitoring,* Davis, CA, Biomedical Publishing Corporation

Leidel, N.A. & Busch, K.A. (1975) *Statistical Methods for the Determination of Non-compliance with Occupational Health Standards,* Cincinatti, OH, US Department of Health, Education and Welfare

Leidel, N.A., Busch, K.A. & Lynch, J.R. (1977) *Occupational Exposure Sampling Strategy Manual,* Cincinatti, OH, US Department of Health, Education, and Welfare

Medical Research Council of Great Britain (1952) *Dust Subcommittee, Industrial Pulmonary Disease Committee. Recommendations of the MRC Panels Relating to Selective Sampling. Minutes of a Joint Meeting, London, March 4, 1952.* London, Her Majesty's Stationery Office

Nordberg, G.F. & Andersen, O. (1981) Metal interactions in carcinogenesis: Enhancement, inhibition. *Environ. Health Perspect., 40,* 65–81

Shamberger, R.J. (1985) The genotoxicity of selenium. *Mutat Res., 154,* 29–48

Stuart, B.O. (1984) Deposition and clearance of inhaled particles. *Environ. Health Perspect., 55,* 369–390

Sunderman, F.W., Jr, ed.-in-chief (1984) *Nickel in the Human Environment (IARC Scientific Publications No. 53),* Lyon, International Agency for Research on Cancer

Ulfvarson, U. (1977) Statistical evaluation of the results of measurements of occupational exposure to air contaminants. *Scand. J. environ. Health, 3,* 109–115

Vahter, M., ed. (1982) *Assessment of Human Exposure to Lead and Cadmium through Biological Monitoring,* Stockholm, National Swedish Institute of Environmental Medicine and Karolinska Institute

Webb, J.S., Thornton, I., Howarth, R.J., Thompson, M. & Lewenstein, P.L. (1978) *The Wolfson Geochemical Atlas of England and Wales,* Oxford, Oxford University Press

Williams, S., ed. (1984) *Official Methods of Analysis of the Association of Official Analytical Chemists,* 14th ed., Arlington, VA, Association of Official Analytical Chemists

Wilson, A.L. (1982) Design of sampling programmes. In: Suess, M.J., ed., *Examination of Water for Pollution Control,* Vol. 1. Oxford, Pergamon Press, pp. 23–77

WHO (1976) *Selected Methods of Measuring Air Pollutants (WHO Offset Publication No. 24),* Geneva

WHO (1977) *Environmental Health Criteria. 3: Lead,* Geneva

WHO (1978) *Global Environmental Monitoring System – Water Operational Guide,* Geneva

WHO (1980) *Analysing and Interpreting Air Monitoring Data (WHO Offset Publication No. 51),* Geneva

WHO (1981) *Environmental Health Criteria 18: Arsenic,* Geneva

WHO (1983) *Joint FAO/WHO Food Contamination Monitoring Programme (WHO-EFP/83.53),* Geneva

WHO (1984a) *Evaluation of Exposure to Airborne Particles in the Work Environment (WHO Offset Publication No. 80),* Geneva

WHO (1984b) *Guidelines for Drinking Water Quality,* Vols 1, 2, Geneva

WHO (1985) *Guidelines for the Study of Dietary Intakes of Chemical Contaminants (WHO Offset Publication No. 87),* Geneva

BIOLOGICAL EFFECTS

CHAPTER 2

CARCINOGENICITY AND MUTAGENICITY OF SOME METALS AND THEIR COMPOUNDS

F.W. Sunderman Jr

Departments of Laboratory Medicine and Pharmacology,
University of Connecticut School of Medicine,
263 Farmington Avenue, Farmington, CT 06032, USA

INTRODUCTION, WITH PROVISIONAL STATUS OF ELEMENTS THAT ARE PROVEN OR SUSPECT CARCINOGENS FOR HUMANS

Scope

This chapter provides a review of the carcinogenic and mutagenic effects of selected elements and their compounds, emphasizing recent research on molecular mechanisms whereby carcinogenic metal compounds may elicit genotoxic effects. This discussion is intended to introduce the subsequent chapters and to supplement other reviews of metal carcinogenesis (Sunderman, 1977, 1978, 1979a,b; Kazantzis & Lilly, 1979; Belman & Nordberg, 1981; Kappus, 1982; Helmes *et al.*, 1983). Sections of this chapter are condensed from a recent review of progress in metal carcinogenesis (Sunderman, 1984b). Designating those elements that are proven or suspect carcinogens or mutagens is a controversial task. In the author's opinion, the most authoritative statements concerning the metals that are proven or suspect carcinogens for humans are set forth in the following verbatim conclusions of the relevant IARC Working Groups.

Arsenic

'There is inadequate evidence for the carcinogenicity of arsenic compounds in animals. There is *sufficient evidence* that inorganic arsenic compounds are skin and lung carcinogens in humans. The data suggesting an increased risk for cancer at other sites are inadequate for evaluation' (IARC, 1980).

Beryllium

'There is *sufficient evidence* that beryllium metal and several beryllium compounds are carcinogenic to three experimental animal species. The epidemiological evidence that occupational exposure to beryllium may lead to an increased lung cancer risk is limited. Taken together, the experimental and human data indicates that beryllium should be considered suspect of being carcinogenic to humans' (IARC, 1980).

a) *Evidence for carcinogenicity to humans* (limited) – 'Studies have suggested that human exposure to cadmium (primarily as the oxide) is associated with increased risks of prostatic, respiratory and genito-urinary cancers (IARC, 1980; Piscator, 1982), although in some cases the excess risk was not statistically significant. Three further studies have been reported. One is a follow-up of an investigation of 269 cadmium-nickel battery workers and 94 cadmium-copper alloy factory workers (Kjellström, 1980). Additional cases of nasopharyngeal, colorectal, prostatic and lung cancer increased the already elevated relative risks. A separate study (Holden, 1980) of 347 cadmium-copper allow workers exposed to cadmium fume has been reported, in which their mortality is compared with that of workers exposed indirectly to cadmium but also to arsenic. A third group of iron or brass founders was included, and the mortality rates were compared separately with statistics for the general population. The study shows a significant increase in deaths from prostatic, genito-urinary and lung cancers in people working in the vicinity, but not in the cadmium workers themselves. Insufficient information is given regarding the movement of men between or out of the three adjacent plants to assess the relative contribution of arsenic, cadmium or smoking to the results (which run counter to those of most other studies). A preliminary report has been published (Sorahan, 1981) of a mortality study of 3026 nickel-cadmium battery workers over the period 1923–1975, with an analysis of 659 deaths. The standardized mortality ratio for all cancers was 100, and no statistically significant excess was noted for cancer at any major site, including the prostate. The limitations and inconsistencies in the epidemiological studies persuaded the Group that it was still far from clear which were the target organs for the putative carcinogenic action of cadmium in humans.'

b) *Evidence for carcinogenicity to animals* (sufficient) – 'Cadmium chloride, oxide sulfate and sulfide are carcinogenic in rats, causing local sarcomas after their subcutaneous injection. Cadmium powder and cadmium sulfide produce local sarcomas in rats following their intramuscular administration. Cadmium chloride and cadmium sulfate produce testicular atrophy followed by testicular tumours in mice and rats after their subcutaneous administration (IARC, 1980; Reddy *et al.,* 1973). Administration of up to 50 mg/kg (ppm) cadmium chloride in the diet to rats did not produce tumours' (IARC, 1982).

Chromium

'There is *sufficient evidence* for the carcinogenicity of calcium chromate and some relatively insoluble chromium [VI] compounds (sintered calcium chromate, lead chromate, strontium chromate, sintered chromium trioxide, and zinc chromate) in rats. There is limited evidence for the carcinogenicity of lead chromate [VI] oxide and cobalt-chromium alloy in rats. The data were inadequate for the evaluation of the carcinogenicity of other chromium [VI] compounds, and of chromium [III] compounds. There is *sufficient evidence* of respiratory carcinogenicity in men occupationally exposed during chromate production. Data on lung cancer risk in other chromium-associated occupations and for cancer at other sites are insufficient. The epidemiological data do not allow an evaluation of the relative contributions to carcinogenic risk of metallic chromium, chromium III, and chromium [VI] or of soluble *versus* insoluble chromium compounds' (IARC, 1980).

Lead

'Experimental and epidemiological data on metallic lead and organic lead compounds were either unavailable or inadequate, and no evaluation of their carcinogenicity was possible. There is *sufficient evidence* that lead subacetate is carcinogenic to mice and rats and that lead acetate and lead phosphate are carcinogenic to rats. In the absence of adequate human data, it is reasonable for practical purposes, to regard these compounds as if they presented a carcinogenic risk to humans' (IARC, 1980).

Nickel

'Nickel subsulfide is carcinogenic in rats following its inhalation: it produced malignant lung tumours. Intramuscular injection and/or implantation of nickel subsulfide, nickel powder, nickelocene or nickel oxide, carbonate or hydroxide produce local rhabdomyosarcomas and/or fibrosarcomas in rats; nickel subsulfide and nickel oxide produced similar tumours in mice and nickel powder and nickelocene in hamsters. A dose-response relationship for local tumour induction after intramuscular injection of nickel subsulfide has been demonstrated in rats. Administration of nickel carbonyl to rats by repeated intravenous injection was associated with increased incidence of malignant tumours in various tissues. Inhalation exposure of rats to nickel carbonyl was associated with a few pulmonary malignancies. Epidemiological studies conclusively demonstrate an excess risk of cancer of the nasal cavity and lung in workers in nickel refineries. It is likely that nickel in some form(s) is carcinogenic to man' (IARC, 1976).

Citations and references to other elements

For citations of scientific articles that support the Working Groups' evaluations, readers should consult the respective IARC monographs (1976, 1980, 1982) and specific reviews on arsenic (Leonard & Lauwerys, 1980a; Pershagen, 1981; Furst, 1981), beryllium (Kuschner, 1981), cadmium (Degraeve, 1981; Piscator, 1981), chromium (Leonard & Lauwerys, 1980b; Hatherhill, 1981; Norseth, 1981; Hayes, 1982; Hertel, 1982; Levis & Bianchi, 1982), nickel (Furst & Radding, 1980; Norseth, 1980; Raithel & Schaller, 1981; Leonard *et al.*, 1981; Sunderman, 1981, 1983, 1984a), and lead (Moore & Meredith, 1979). For discussions of the possible carcinogenic or anticarcinogenic roles of Al, Co, Cu, Fe, Hg, Mn, Pt, Se, Sn, Ti and Zn, readers should consult reviews by Sunderman (1977, 1979b), Kazantzis and Lilly (1979), Kazantzis (1981) and Helmes *et al.* (1983). Scientific reports that have been published from 1979 to July 1983 are summarized in this chapter.

EPIDEMIOLOGICAL AND CLINICAL ASPECTS

Arsenic

Recent epidemiological studies have confirmed that the risk of lung cancer mortality is increased in copper smelters workers, who are exposed to inhalation of arsenic trioxide dust (Lubin *et al.*, 1981; Higgins *et al.*, 1981; Enterline & Marsh, 1980, 1982a). Certain epidemiological evidence suggests that arsenic may act as a cancer promotor rather than as an initiator: the lung cancers can develop within less than ten years after initial exposure to arsenic compounds, and the effects of arsenic exposure tend to disappear with time (Enterline & Marsh, 1980, 1982a); moreover, lung cancer mortality of arsenic-exposed workers increases with age at initial exposure, and the excess mortality is independent of age since last exposure (Brown & Chu, 1983). Comparison of histological types of 42 bronchogenic cancers in As-exposed smelter workers with those in 42 matched controls showed that 38% of the cancers in the As-exposed workers were adenocarcinomas *versus* 12% in the controls (Wicks *et al.*, 1981). Analysis of cancer incidence in 478 patients who ingested Fowler's solution (potassium arsenite) demonstrated an excess of skin cancers, but mortality from internal malignancies was not increased (Cuzik *et al.*, 1982). The IARC Working Group (1980) compiled seven cases of hepatic hemangio-sarcoma in individuals exposed to various arsenical compounds. Eight additional cases of hepatic angiosarcoma have subsequently been reported in subjects who ingested arsenic medications or arsenic-polluted water (Zaldivar *et al.*, 1981; Falk *et al.*, 1981a,b; Roat *et al.*, 1982). In view of the rarity of this tumour, it seems likely that arsenic plays an etiological role.

Cadmium

Epidemiological evidence that prostatic cancer risk may be increased in Cd-exposed workers continues to be equivocal and inconclusive. Kjellstrom *et al.* (1979) analysed cancer mortality in two groups of cadmium exposed-workers. Among 269 Cd-Ni battery workers there were two deaths from nasopharyngeal cancer (*versus* 0.20 expected, O/E = 10.0, p < 0.005) and two deaths from prostatic cancer (*versus* 1.2 expected, O/E = 1.67, not significant). Among 94 Cd-Cu allow workers there were four deaths from prostatic cancer (*versus* 2.7 expected, O/E = 1.49, not significant).

Chromium

Recent studies in England and Japan confirmed that workers who are exposed to chromate compounds have significantly increased risks of lung cancer mortality (Alderson *et al.*, 1981; Satoh *et al.*, 1981). Abe *et al.* (1982) found that the latent period between initial exposure to chromate dust and detection of lung cancer was shorter in cases of small cell carcinoma than in cases with squamous cell carcinoma. Sarto *et al.* (1982) detected statistically significant increases of chromosomal aberrations and sister chromatid exchanges in cultured lymphocytes from CrO_3-exposed workers in four electroplating factories; the clastogenic effects of CrO_3 exposure were positively correlated with chromium concentrations in urine specimens from these workers. Ohsaki (1980) described an early detection program for lung cancer in chromate workers, involving semiannual sputum cytology and chest X-ray examinations and annual fiber-optic bronchoscopy; the program identified four cases of bronchogenic carcinoma in a small group of exposed men.

Nickel

Epidemiological studies of cancer mortality in nickel refinery workers in Canada, Wales and the USA have confirmed increased risks of lung and/or sinonasal cancers (Chovil *et al.*, 1981; Magnus *et al.*, 1982; Enterline & Marsh, 1982b). On the other hand, risks of respiratory cancers were not increased in other workers who had various industrial exposures to nickel compounds (Godbold & Tompkins, 1979; Cuckle *et al.*, 1980; Burges, 1980; Cox *et al.*, 1981). Burges (1980) found four cases of gastric cancer in a small cohort of Ni-plating workers (*versus* 0.6 expected, $O/E = 6.23$, p < 0.005). Burges stressed that this finding should be interpreted cautiously; he urged further cancer mortality studies of workers in the nickel electroplating trade. According to Chovil *et al.* (1981), the histological classification of 43 bronchogenic carcinomas in nickel-refinery workers included 39 squamous cell carcinomas, two oat-cell carcinomas and two adenocarcinomas. Waksvik and Boysen (1982) reported cytogenetic analyses on blood lymphocytes of nickel refinery workers; they observed increased incidence of chromosomal gaps, but no increases in chromosomal breaks or sister-chromatid exchanges. Boysen and Reith (1980, 1982a,b) described a gradual, multi-step progression of dysplastic, metaplastic and neoplastic lesions in nasal epithelium of nickel refinery workers, based upon light microscopy, transmission electron microscopy and scanning electron microscopy of nasal mucosal biopsies. Kotlar *et al.* (1982) employed a leukocyte adherence inhibition test to assay serum from nickel refinery workers for immune responses to carcinoma antigens. The frequency of positive response against a lung carcinoma antigen was 41% in the nickel-exposed workers, compared to 18% in controls. In nickel workers with nasal dysplasia, 56% gave a positive reaction against the lung carcinoma antigen, compared to 25% in nickel workers without dysplasia. Similar trends were found for immune responses to a nasal carcinoma antigen. Kotlar *et al.* (1982) concluded that the leukocyte adherence inhibition assay may help to identify nickel workers with increased risk of respiratory cancer.

CARCINOGENESIS BIOASSAYS

Arsenic

Arsenic has been the only metal for which epidemiological evidence of human carcinogenicity was largely unsubstantiated by carcinogenesis bioassays in experimental animals (IARC, 1980). Three recent studies suggest that carcinogenicity of arsenic compounds in animals may eventually be documented. Rudnai and Borzsonyi (1981) exposed mice to AsO_3 on days 15–18 of intrauterine life and on days

1–3 post-partum. The lung tumour incidence one year later was 63% in the As-treated rats *versus* 18% in controls. Chung and Liu (1982) reported positive carcinogenesis tests in rats that were observed for three years following intratracheal instillations of As-containing ore dusts; lung cancers were found in 3 of 20 rats treated with ore that contained 2% As, 54% Fe and 0.1% Pb, and in three of 21 rats treated with ore that contained 16% As, 26% Fe and 16% Pb. No lung tumours were detected in 18 controls. The authors did not exclude Fe or Pb as factors that might contribute to the pulmonary neoplasia. Ishinishi and Yamamoto (1983) administered AsO_3 to female Syrian hamsters as 15 intratracheal instillations (once weekly for four months). During observations for the life span, pulmonary adenomas occurred in 5/30 hamsters in the treated groups, *versus* 0/35 in the control groups. The authors concluded that AsO_3 is weakly tumorigenic for hamster lung.

Cadmium

Loser (1980) reported a negative carcinogenesis bioassay of $CdCl_2$ in Wistar rats. Groups of male and female rats were fed diets containing 1, 3, 10 or 500 ppm of Cd [II] for 2 years. Cadmium treatment did not increase the total number of tumours or induce any specific types of neoplasms, although the highest level tested resulted in non-neoplastic adverse effects. Oldiges *et al.* (1983) exposed Wistar rats to continuous inhalation of $CdCl_2$ for 18 months, and continued observation for 13 months thereafter. Primary lung carcinomas were found in 70% of rats at the 50 µg/m^3 exposure level; 53% at 25 µg/m^3 and 15% at 12.5 µg/m^3. No primary lung tumours were found in control rats. These studies reveal a dose-dependent incidence of lung carcinomas after inhalation of $CdCl_2$ in rats.

Nickel

In order to bring up-to-date the 1976 IARC monograph on nickel and nickel compounds, Sunderman (1981) compiled the voluminous literature from 1976 to 1980 on carcinogenesis bioassays of nickel compounds. The following discussion summarizes additional studies that have been published from 1981 to mid-1983. Hildebrand and Tetaert (1981) analysed myosin light-chains in leiomyosarcomas induced in rabbits by i.m. injection of Ni_3S_2. The tumoral myosin light-chains were characteristic of fetal smooth muscle cells rather than smooth muscle cells of blood vessels, suggesting that the tumours arose from retro-differentiated muscle cells, rather than from pre-existing mesenchymal cells. Sunderman and McCully (1983b) found that Ni_3S_2-induction of sarcomas in rats was inhibited by combined administration of Mn dust at the same injection site, but was not affected when Ni_3S_2 was injected in one thigh and Mn dust was injected in the other thigh, indicating that inhibition of Ni_3S_2-carcinogenesis by Mn dust is a local rather than a systemic effect. Kasprzak *et al.* (1983) reported that i.m. administration of crystalline Ni_3S_2 or $Ni(OH)_2$ induced local sarcomas in Wistar rats, whereas colloidal $Ni(OH)_2$ and soluble $NiSO_4$ were not carcinogenic under comparable bioassay conditions; the tumour incidences were inversely related to the in-vitro dissolution rates of the nickel compounds. Yamashiro *et al.* (1983) described the ultrastructural features of 24 tumours induced in rats by i.m. injection of Ni_3S_2, including rhabdomyosarcomas, leiomyosarcomas, fibrosarcomas, lymphosarcomas and poorly-differentiated sarcomas. Sunderman (1984a) and Sunderman and McCully (1983a) reported marked differences in the incidences of sarcomas induced in rats by i.m. injection of 18 nickel compounds at equivalent dosages (14 mg Ni/rat). The nickel compounds fell into five categories: compounds in Class A (Ni_4FeS_4, αNi_3S_2, βNiS) induced sarcomas at the injection site in 100% of the rats; compounds in Class B (NiO, Ni_3Se_2, NiAsS, NiS_2, Ni_5As_2) induced sarcomas in 85 to 93% of the rats; compounds in Class C (Ni dust, NiSb, NiTe, NiSe, $Ni_{11}As_8$) induced sarcomas in 50 to 65% of the rats; compounds in Class D (amorphous NiS, $NiCrO_4$) induced local sarcomas in 6 to 12% of the rats and compounds in Class E (NiAs, $NiTiO_3$, NiFe alloy) did not induce any sarcomas. No sarcomas occurred at the injection site in control rats that received i.m. injections of the vehicles. Sarcoma incidences in rats that received i.m. injections of the 18 nickel compounds were significantly correlated ($P = 0.02$) with the massfractions of nickel in the respective compounds (Sunderman, 1984a). Sarcoma incidences were not significantly related to dissolution rates of the nickel compounds in rat serum or renal cytosol (Kuehn & Sunderman, 1981), or to the susceptibilities of the compounds to phagocytosis by rat peritoneal macrophages *in vitro* (Kuehn *et al.*, 1982). Striking rank correlation ($P < 0.0001$) was evident between the sarcoma incidences and the capacities of the Ni-compounds to induce erythrocytosis after intrarenal administration to rats (Sunderman & Hopfer, 1983), indicating that derepression of the gene that regulates renal production of erythropoietin can serve as an index of carcinogenic activity of nickel compounds in rats, and suggesting that Ni-stimulation of erythropoietin production and oncogenesis may, in some way, be related.

Platinum

Leopold *et al.* (1979) tested the carcinogenic activities of several cis-platinum compounds in rodents. Repeated i.p. doses of cis-dichlorodiammine-platinum, with concurrent and subsequent topical applications of croton oil, induced papillomas in 50% of female CD-1 mice, while mice treated only with the platinum complex or only with croton oil developed no papillomas. Sarcomas developed in 35% and 25%, respectively, of male Fischer rats that received multiple s.c. injections of cis-dichlorobis(cyclopentylamine)-platinum[II] and cis-dichlorobis(pyrrolidine)-platinum[II]. Based upon these findings, Leopold *et al.* (1979) cautioned that treatment of patients with platinum antitumour complexes may impose a risk of induction of second tumours in long-term survivors.

Tin

The National Toxicology Program (1982) performed a carcinogenesis bio-assay of Sn[II] in rodents; diets containing 1000 or 2000 ppm of $SnCl_2$ were fed to groups of Fischer rats and B6C3F1/N mice of each sex for two years. $SnCl_2$ was judged not to be carcinogenic for either rats or mice, although the incidence of C-cell tumours of the thyroid gland seemed to be increased in male rats.

BACTERIAL MUTAGENESIS ASSAYS

Arsenic

Contrary to a previous report by Nishioka (1975), recent studies by Rossman *et al.* (1980), Rossman (1981a,b) and Simmon (1981) indicate that As[III] does not induce mutations in tryptophan auxotrophic strains of *E. coli*. Rossman *et al.* (1980) observed, however, that As[III] enhances the susceptibility of *E. coli* to mutagenic effects of ultra-violet radiation. This comutagenic effect of As[III] occurs only in the excision-proficient strain, WP2, and is absent in strains deficient in excision-repair, indicating that As[III] interferes with excision repair. Consistent with earlier findings of Lofroth and Ames (1978), Tiedemann and Einbrodt (1982) reported negative results for As[III] and As[V] in Ames's Salmonella microsome test. Nishioka (1975) and Kanematsu *et al.* (1980) observed positive results for As[III] in the rec-assay in *B. subtilis,* but Simmon (1981) obtained negative results using the same tester strains and procedures.

Chromium

Flessel (1980) concluded that Cr[VI] is the most mutagenic metal ion in Ames's Salmonella microsome assay, while Cr[III] has little, if any, mutagenic activity in this system. The genotoxicity of Cr[VI] in *S. typhimurium* involves frame-shift and base-pair mutations. De Flora *et al.* (1980) and Venier *et al.* (1982) tested 28 industrial chromium compounds for mutagenicity in *S. typhimurium;* the mutagenic potencies of the Cr[VI] compounds were of comparable magnitude, excepting two water-insoluble compounds, chromium hexacarbonyl and chrome yellow; on the other hand, Cr[III] compounds were all inactive, unless they were contaminated with Cr[VI]. These results, indicating selective mutagenicity of Cr[VI] and Cr[III] compounds in *S. typhimurium,* are in agreement with those obtained with trp strains of *E. coli* (Vernier *et al.,* 1982). Witmer *et al.* (1982) showed that the sensitivity for detecting mutagenicity of Cr[VI] in Ames's Salmonella microsome test can be enhanced by lowering the salt concentrations, varying the histidine concentration and prolonging the incubation period.

Nickel

As reviewed by Sunderman (1981), nickel compounds are not mutagenic in the *S. typhimurium* or *E. coli* test systems. Pikalek and Necasek (1983) showed that Ni[II] is mutagenic for a homoserine-dependent strain of Corynebacterium (sp. 887 hom), using a simplified fluctuation test as well as the clone method.

Other metals

Kanematsu *et al.* (1980) performed rec-assays in *B. subtilis* on 127 metal compounds, in order to test their DNA-damaging capacities. Certain compounds of As, Be, Cd, Co, Cr, Cs, Hg, Ir, Mo, Os, Pt, Rh, Sb, Se, Te, Tl and V were positive, whereas the tested compounds of Ag, Al, Au, Ba, Bi, Ca, Cu, Fe, Ga, In, K, La, Mg, Mn, Nb, Ni, Pb, Rb, Ru, Si, Sn, Sr, Ti, Ta and Y were negative. Reverse mutation assays with *E. coli* and *S. typhimurium* strains demonstrated that certain compounds of Rh, Te and Pt are potent mutagens in bacteria (Kanematsu *et al.*, 1980).

MAMMALIAN CELL MUTAGENESIS ASSAYS

Miyaki *et al.* (1979) examined the mutagenicity of Be[II], Co[II], Mn[II] and Ni[II] in cultured V79 Chinese hamster cells at the hypoxanthine-guanine phosphoribosyl transferase (HGPRTase) locus, by selecting for resistance to 8-azaguanine. Treatment with beryllium caused a six-fold increase in resistance to 8-azaguanine; cobalt, manganese and nickel increased the resistance two to four-fold. Hsie *et al.* (1979) used a similar technique to test the mutagenicity of 14 metal compounds in cultured Chinese hamster ovary cells, using 6-thioguanine as the purine analogue. Preliminary results showed that cis-Pt(NH$_3$)$_2$Cl$_2$, Ag[I], Be[II], Cd[II], Cu[II], Fe[II], Mn[II], Ni[II], Pb[II] and Zn[II] are mutagenic, whereas Mg[II], Rb[I], Se[IV] and Ti[IV] are non-mutagenic. Hsie *et al.* (1979) cautioned that such results need confirmation, since mutagenesis assays are influenced by subtle variations in ionic composition of the medium and the physiological state of the cells during treatment. Amacher and Paillet (1980) tested eight metal compounds for induction of trifluorothymidine-resistant mutants at the thymidine kinase locus in mouse lymphoma cells. In cells exposed to varied concentrations of each compound for 3 h, Cd[II], Ni[II] and trans-Pt(NH$_3$)$_2$Cl$_2$ consistently produced dose-dependent increases in the absolute number of mutants; As[V], Co[II], Mg[II] and Zn[II] gave negative responses. Oberly *et al.* (1982) tested eleven metal compounds for mutagenic effects at the thymidine kinase locus in mouse lymphoma cells, including, in certain experiments, activation with rat liver microsomes and NADP as a cofactor. Strongly positive responses were obtained with Cd[II], Cr[VI] and Mn[II]; weakly positive responses (i.e., two- to three-fold increases in mutation frequency) were obtained with Hg[II], As[III], As[V] and Pb[II]; negative responses were obtained with Al[III], Mg[II] and Na[I].

CHROMOSOMAL DAMAGE INDUCED BY METALS

General review

The literature on clastogenic effects of metals has been summarized by Sunderman (1979a), Kazantzis and Lilly (1979) and Flessel (1980). Four groups of investigators have subsequently performed extensive investigations of chromosomal damage and sister chromatid exchanges induced by in-vitro exposures of mammalian cells to metal compounds. Umeda and Nishimura (1979) exposed FM3A cells from a C3H mouse mammary carcinoma to Cr[III], Cr[VI], Ni[II], Mn[II], Cd[II] and Hg[II] compounds at various concentrations for 24 or 48 h. Cr[VI] compounds induced numerous chromosomal breaks and exchanges, while Cr[III] was inactive; NiS caused a definite increase of aberrations, while the effects of NiCl$_2$ and Ni(C$_2$H$_3$O$_2$)$_2$ were equivocal;

Mn[II] and Mn[V] compounds induced a few aberrations; Cd[II] and Hg[II] compounds were not clastogenic. Larramendy *et al.* (1981) exposed Syrian hamster embryo cells and human lymphocyte cultures to various concentrations of five metal compounds for 24 h prior to examination for chromosomal damage and sister chromatid exchanges. As[III], As[V], Be[II] and Ni[II] caused chromosomal damage and increased the frequencies of sister chromatid exchanges in human and hamster cells; W[VI] was negative in both test systems. Ohno *et al.* (1982) exposed Don Chinese hamster cells to various metal compounds for 28 h prior to examination for sister chromatid exchanges; under these conditions, As[III], As[V], Ni[II] and Cr[VI] compounds caused significantly increased numbers of sister chromatid exchanges, while Cr[III], Ti[III], Fe[II], Fe[III], Cd[II], Sn[II] and Hg[II] did not. Andersen (1983) investigated the effects of metals on sister chromatid exchanges in human lymphocytes and in a macrophage cell line, $P388D_1$, which originated from a mouse lymphoma; in-vitro exposures to the test compounds ranged from 24 to 72 h. Increased incidences of sister chromatid exchanges were observed in human lymphocytes exposed to As[III], Cd[II], Co[II], Cr[VI], Hg[II], Mn[II], Ni[II] and Pb[II]. Similar results were observed in $P388D_1$ cells, except that Cr[III] was strongly positive and Be[II] was weakly positive. Since human lymphocytes exclude Cr[III], whereas $P388D_1$ cells take up Cr[III] by phagocytosis (Andersen, 1983), these observations are consistent with the concept, discussed subsequently, that Cr[III] may be the ultimate carcinogenic form of chromium.

Arsenic

Zanzoni and Jung (1980), Wen *et al.* (1981) and Crossen (1983) confirmed that in-vitro exposures to As[III] or As[V] compounds induce sister chromatid exchanges in human lymphocytes. Based upon tests with lymphocytes from 16 donors, Crossen (1983) concluded that individuals vary considerably in their sister chromatid responses to arsenic. Wen *et al.* (1981) noted higher frequency of baseline sister chromatid exchanges in cultured lymphocytes from patients with blackfoot disease, compared to healthy controls; lymphocytes from the patients and controls were equally susceptible to induction of sister chromatid exchanges following in-vitro exposure to As[III].

Chromium

Levis and Majone (1979, 1981), Majone and Levis (1979) and Majone *et al.* (1983) studied clastogenic effects of numerous Cr[VI] and Cr[III] compounds on cell cultures derived from Chinese hamster ovary (CHO), baby hamster kidney (BHK) or mouse spleen T-lymphocytes. Water-soluble compounds of Cr[VI] and Cr[III] induced mitotic delays and chromosomal aberrations; Cr[III] was incapable of inducing sister chromatid exchanges, only Cr[VI] being active. Levis and Majone (1981) concluded that the state of oxidation is the most important parameter that affects the mutagenic activity of chromium compounds; other properties, such as solubility in water, ability to penetrate cell membranes and intracellular stability of Cr[VI] ion may account for differences between the results of long-term carcinogenesis tests and short-term mutagenesis tests. Further evidence concerning this point was obtained by Elias *et al.* (1983), who studied the induction of sister chromatid exchanges in Chinese hamster V79 cells exposed to soluble $CrCl_3$ and insoluble Cr_2O_3. Both of these Cr[III] compounds induced dose-dependent increases in sister chromatid exchanges, up to two-fold ($CrCl_3$) and four-fold (Cr_2O_3) over control levels. Elias *et al.* (1983) attributed the pronounced effect of Cr_2O_3 to cellular uptake of particles by phagocytosis; the particles presumably dissolve gradually in the cytoplasm and release Cr^{3+}, which enters the nucleus and reacts with DNA or related macromolecules.

Nickel

Nishimura and Umeda (1979) compared the effects of four nickel compounds [$NiCl_2$, $Ni(CH_3COO)_2$, $K_2Ni(CN)_4$ and NiS] on induction of chromosomal aberrations in cultured FM3A cells. The four nickel compounds were similarly incorporated in the cells and elicited similar inhibitory effects on synthesis of protein, RNA and DNA. The maximum incidence of chromosomal aberrations, including breaks, exchanges and fragmentation, was observed after reincubation in control medium for one or two days, by which time the cells were entering their second or third division. Wulf (1980) found that in-vitro exposures to human lymphocytes to Ni[II] (as $NiSO_4$) at concentrations as low as 2×10^{-6} mol/L, or Pb[II] (as $PbSO_4$) at concentrations as low as 2×10^{-5} mol/L, cause significant increases in sister chromatid exchanges. Saxholm *et al.* (1981) noted a small but statistically significant increase of sister chromatid exchanges in human lymphocytes exposed *in vitro* to crystalline Ni_3S_2. Newman *et al.* (1982) observed increased sister chromatid exchanges in human lymphocytes exposed to $NiCl_2$ in the range from 10^{-4} to 10^{-6} mol/L.

Platinum

Popescu *et al.* (1981) reported dose-dependent induction of sister chromatid exchanges in Syrian hamster fetal cells exposed *in vitro* to cis-$Pt(NH_3)_2Cl_2$.

MAMMALIAN CELL TRANSFORMATION ASSAYS

Mammalian cell transformation assays of metal compounds have been reviewed by Heck and Costa (1982). Casto *et al.* (1979) and DiPaolo and Casto (1979) evaluated 45 metal salts for their capacities to induce morphological transformation of Syrian hamster fetal cells *in vitro*. Positive transformation assays were obtained with Ag[I], As[III], Be[II], Cd[II], Co[II], Cr[VI], Cu[II], Fe[II], Hg[II], Mn[II], Ni[II], Pb[II], Pt[II], Pt[IV], Sb[III], Tl[I] and Zn[II]; negative results were obtained with Al[III], Ba[II], Ca[II], Li[I], Mg[II], Na[I], Sr[II], Ti[IV] and W[VI]. The highest percentage of transformed cells was obtained with Ni_3S_2; under the same conditions amorphous NiS gave negative results in the transformation assay. When Ni[II], Be[II], Cd[II] or Cr[VI] were administered to pregnant Syrian hamsters on day 11 of gestation, morphological transformation was observed in cell cultures derived from progeny excised on day 13 of gestation. Costa *et al.* (1978, 1979) showed that morphological transformation of Syrian hamster embryo cells by Ni_3S_2 is dose-dependent and can be prevented by addition of Mn dust to the incubation medium; several clones of Ni_3S_2-transformed cells produced fibrosarcomas following s.c. implantation in nude mice. Costa and Mollenhauer (1980), Costa *et al.* (1981) and Costa and Heck (1982) studied particle uptake of six crystalline compounds (Ni_3S_2, NiS, Ni_3Se_2, CuS, CdS and CoS_2) and four amorphous compounds (NiS, CuS, CdS and CoS) by Chinese hamster ovary cells. The cells avidly phagocytized the crystalline particles, whereas they engulfed few amorphous particles, suggesting that the greater transforming activities of the crystalline compounds may be attributed to differences in their rates of cellular uptake. Abbrachio *et al.* (1982b) presented evidence that the phagocytosis and transforming activity of crystalline metal sulfide particles are related to their negative surface changes. By means of video time-lapse microscopy, Evans *et al.* (1982) described endocytosis and intracellular, translocation of crystalline NiS particles in Chinese hamster ovary cells. After 24 to 48 h, the NiS particles became fixed in the perinuclear region, often situated within cytoplasmic vacuoles. Abbrachio *et al.* (1982c) showed that crystalline ^{63}NiS particles are phagocytized by Chinese hamster ovary cells and gradually dissolve in the cytosol; a portion of the liberated ^{63}Ni becomes localized in nuclei. Costa *et al.* (1982) found that soluble $NiCl_2$ induces morphological transformation of Syrian hamster embryo cells; its potency averages two-fifths that of crystalline NiS, probably owing to higher cellular uptake of crystalline NiS by phagocytosis, compared to lower uptake of ionic nickel under the usual conditions of incubation. Abbrachio *et al.* (1982a) noted that cells incubated in a minimal medium accumulate 10-fold more ^{63}Ni[II] than when incubated in complete medium containing histidine, cysteine and fetal bovine serum. Saxholm *et al.* (1982) demonstrated that Ni_3S_2 induces morphological transformation of C3H/10T½ cells; scanning electron microscopy revealed an oncogenic marker, long microvilli, on the transformed cells. Hansen and Stern (1982) compared the activity of five nickel compounds [Ni dust, Ni_3S_2, Ni_2O_3, NiO and $Ni(C_2H_3O_2)_2$] for in-vitro transformation of BHK-21 cells. Although the nickel compounds varied substantially in their transforming potencies, the compounds produced the same number of transformed colonies at the same degree of toxicity (e.g., 50% survival). The authors concluded that the sole property that determines the transforming potency of nickel compounds is the intracellular bioavailability of Ni[II].

Costa and Mollenhauer (1980), Rivedal and Sanner (1980, 1981) and Uziel and Butler (1983) observed synergistic effects of nickel compounds and benzo[*a*]pyrene (BP) on morphological transformation of Syrian hamster embryo cells. Costa and Mollenhauer (1980) found that pretreatment of the cells with BP enhances cellular uptake of Ni_3S_2 particles. According to Rivedal and Sanner (1980), combined treatment of Syrian hamster embryo cells with $NiSO_4$ and BP results in a transformation frequency of 10.7%, compared to 0.5% and 0.6% for the individual substances. No synergistic effect could be detected between $NiSO_4$ and methylcholanthrene. Rivedal and Sanner (1981) found that Ni[II], Cd[II] and Cr[VI] exert synergistic effects on BP-transformation of Syrian hamster embryo cells, while Cr[III] and Zn[II] do not. These reports are consistent with an earlier observation of carcinogenic synergism between Ni_3S_2 and BP, following i.m. administration to Fischer rats (Maenza et al., 1971).

MICROSOMAL METABOLISM OF METALS AND THEIR COMPOUNDS

Chromium VI, as chromate or dichromate, is readily taken up by bacteria and eukaryotic cells, while Cr[III] is less capable of traversing cell membranes (Bianchi et al., 1980). Differences in cellular penetration of Cr[VI] and Cr[III] may, in part, account for the observed disparities in mutagenic and carcinogenic activities of chromium compounds. Jennette (1982) showed that incubation of chromate with rat liver microsomes and NADPH leads to formation of a stable reactive intermediate, Cr[V]; hence Cr[V], rather than Cr[III], may represent the ultimate electrophilic form of chromium that reacts with critical nucleophilic targets to initiate genotoxicity. Jennette (1979) and Garcia and Jennette (1981) demonstrated that microsomal reduction of Cr[VI] is an enzymatic process that requires NADPH or NADH; the process apparently involves cytochrome P-450 and NADPH-cytochrome P-450 reductase. These findings suggest that microsomal reduction of Cr[VI] to an electrophilic reactant may be a critical step in the initiation of chromium carcinogenesis. Microsomes may also play a role in the metabolism of nickel compounds, since Lee et al. (1982) observed release of Ni[II] during in-vitro incubation of Ni_3S_2 with rat liver microsomes, claf thymus DNA and NADPH. Under these experimental conditions, microsomes evidently mediate the binding of Ni[II] to DNA by formation of a ternary protein-Ni-DNA complex.

BINDING OF METALS TO DNA AND NUCLEAR PROTEINS

Bryan (1981) reviewed the literature on nuclear localization of toxic metals, emphasizing experimental problems from metal contamination or reassociation during nuclear isolation procedures. Sigee and Kearns (1982), using X-ray microanalysis, demonstrated Ni, Cu, Zn and Fe binding in dinoflagellate chromatin, associated with high molecular weight proteins and nucleic acids. Kovacs and Darvas (1982), using dimethylglyoxime staining, showed that Ni is localized in centrioles of HeLa cell cultures. Hui and Sunderman (1980) found 0.2 to 2.2 mol [63]Ni/mol of DNA nucleotides in DNA isolated from liver and kidney of rats treated with [63]$NiCl_2$ or [63]$Ni(CO)_4$. Lee et al. (1982) measured in-vitro binding of Ni to calf thymus DNA incubated in the presence of Ni_3S_2, rat liver microsomes and NADPH; the saturation binding value was 0.42 mol Ni/mol of DNA nucleotides. Ciccarelli and Wetterhahn (1982, 1983) demonstrated the presence of Ni[II]-nucleic acid-histone complexes in liver and kidney of $NiCO_3$-treated rats. They proposed that nickel may initiate DNA damage by forming a covalent Ni-DNA complex, which appears to be associated with histone proteins. Ono et al. (1981) analysed trace metal concentrations in nuclei and nucleoli of normal and regenerating rat liver. The contents of Ca, Cu, Mn and Zn in nuclei were less than 3% of those in whole cells, but the contents of Cr and Ni in nuclei were 20 to 30% of those in whole cells. The metal contents of nucleoli, expressed per mg of protein, ranged from 3-times (Zn) to 11-times (Cr) and 18-times (Ni) those in nuclei. The Cr and Ni that was bound to nucleoli was more resistant than the other metals to treatment with nucleases.

Parker and Stevens (1979) demonstrated that in-vitro exposures of rat liver nuclei to Be[II] results in binding of Be[II] to a highly phosphorylated constituent of non-histone proteins. Perry et al. (1982) showed that exposure of rat hepatoma cells in tissue culture to Be[II] (1×10^{-6} mol/L) reduces glucocorticoid induction of tyrosine transaminase activity by 50%, but does not affect inductions of the enzyme by insulin or cyclic-AMP. Growth of the hepatoma cells is not affected by Be[II] under the experimental conditions. Perry et al. (1982) speculated that impaired ability of Be[II]-treated cells to respond to a specific regulator of gene expression may point to a possible mechanism of beryllium carcinogenesis. Olson (1981) reviewed the effects of metal ions on phosphorylation of nuclear proteins, including his finding that in-vitro exposure to Zn[II] influences phosphorylation of H1-histone in tissue cultures of rat hepatoma cells. After incubation in medium containing $ZnCl_2$, 85 to 90% of H1-histone was phosphorylated, as opposed to 65% in untreated cells. Furthermore, five of the seven serine residues in H-1 histone were phosphorylated, compared to only two in untreated cells. Hyperphosphorylation of H1-histone was attended by increased susceptibility of the chromatin to digestion by micrococcal nuclease and by diminished stability of oligonucleosomal fragments to thermal denaturation and salt disassociation. These observations illustrate a molecular mechanism whereby metal ions can influence chromatin structure.

DNA STRAND-BREAKS AND CROSSLINKS INDUCED BY METALS

Zwelling et al. (1979a,b) demonstrated DNA-protein and DNA-interstrand crosslinks in L1210 mouse leukaemia cells and V79 Chinese hamster cells treated with cis- and trans-Pt[II]-dichlorodiammine (cis-Pt and trans-Pt). Fornace and Little (1980) showed that trans-Pt produces DNA-protein crosslinks in mouse C3H 10T ½ and 3T3 cells and induces morphological transformation in both cell types. Fornace et al. (1981) reported that in-vitro exposure to Cr[VI] compounds induces DNA-protein crosslinks in several types of mammalian cells, and that exposure to Cr[III] compounds induces DNA-protein crosslinks in isolated nuclei. These data are consistent with the hypothesis that Cr[VI] traverses the cell membrane into the cytoplasm, where it is reduced to Cr[III], and that Cr[III] enters the nucleus, where it forms stable DNA-protein linkages. Fornace et al. (1981) suggested that the linkage of DNA to protein may influence DNA polymerase activity during DNA replication and repair, with resultant mutagenic and carcinogenic consequences. Tsapakos et al. (1981) identified DNA-protein crosslinks in liver and kidney nuclei from rats treated with Cr[VI]. Ciccarelli et al. (1981) and Ciccarelli and Wetterhahn (1982) demonstrated DNA-protein crosslinks and DNA strand-breaks in kidney nuclei from rats treated with $NiCO_3$. These observations are consistent with findings of Robison and Costa (1982), Robison et al. (1982) and Costa et al. (1982) that exposure to crystalline NiS, CoS, CdS, AgS, CuS and Ni_3S_2 particles produces DNA strand-breaks in cultured Chinese hamster ovary cells. Additions of Ni[II], Hg[II], Cr[VI] or

Cd[II] to the culture medium also produced DNA strand-breaks, whereas Mn[II] Zn[II] and Fe[II] did not. McLean *et al.* (1982) used a fluorescence technique to measure DNA damage in human leukocytes exposed *in vitro* to various metal salts; Cr[II], Cr[VI] and Sn[II] gave positive results; Ni[II], Cd[II] and Zn[II] gave equivocal results, and As[III], V[II] and Mn[II] gave negative results. McLean *et al.* (1983) reported that exposure of CHO cells to Sn[II] caused extensive DNA damage, as detected by alkaline sucrose gradient analysis; treatment of CHO cells with Sn[IV] produced no DNA damage under the same conditions.

DNA POLYMERASE INFIDELITY INDUCED BY METALS

Zakour *et al.* (1981a,b) summarized DNA fidelity assays of 40 metal compounds, indicating that cations of Ag, Be, Cd, Co, Cr, Cu, Mn, Ni and Pb increase misincorporation of nucleotide bases in the daughter strand of DNA that is synthesized *in vitro* from polynucleotide templates by microbial DNA polymerases, while Al, As, Ba, Ca, Fe, K, Rb, Mg, Na, Se, Sr and Zn give negative responses. Pt compounds were not tested. Miyaki *et al.* (1980) confirmed that carcinogenic metal cations cause notable increases in the misincorporation of all four nucleotides by DNA polymerases *in vitro,* whereas noncarcinogenic metals do not change the fidelity. Tkeshelashvili *et al.* (1980) showed that Cr[III] and Cr[VI] diminish the fidelity by which *E. coli* DNA polymerase I copies synthetic polynucleotide templates, leading to single-base substitutions. Cr[VI] also decreases the fidelity by which *E. coli* DNA polymerase I copies $\Phi\chi 174$ DNA, a natural DNA template. Zakour *et al.* (1981a,b) proposed three possible explanations for metal-induced infidelity of DNA replication: (*a*) altered conformation at the substrate-binding site of DNA polymerase, (*b*) altered conformation at the catalytically active site of DNA polymerase, possibly involving allosteric transitions produced by interactions of metals with the enzyme at loci distant from the active site, and (*c*) altered template-base specificity, interfering directly with complementary base-pairing during DNA replication.

EFFECTS OF METALS ON RNA CHAIN INITIATION

Niyogi and Feldman (1981) and Niyogi *et al.* (1981) examined the effects of metal ions on transcription of calf thymus DNA and phage T4 DNA by RNA polymerase from *E. coli* B. These studies confirmed previous observations that, at metal ion concentrations that inhibit overall transcription, Be [II], Cd[II], Co[II], Mn[II], Ni[II] and Pb [II] increase RNA chain initiation, whereas Ca[II], Mg[II], Sr[II], Zn[II], Li[I], Na[I] and K[I] decrease RNA chain initiation (Hoffman & Niyogi, 1977). Interactions of metal ions with DNA result in multiple initiation of new RNA chains, either at the same or at different sites on DNA templates (Niyogi *et al.,* 1981). Loeb and Mildvan (1981) discussed the general concordance between the metal ions that decrease the fidelity of DNA polymerase and those that stimulate chain initiation with RNA polymerase; they inferred that a common underlying mechanism (e.g., metal interactions with the DNA template) could account for both phenomena.

EFFECTS OF METALS ON HELICAL TRANSITION OF B-DNA TO Z-DNA

DNA is normally found as a right-handed double-helix (B-DNA), but it can, under certain conditions, adopt a left-handed double-helical form (Z-DNA). Sande *et al.* (1982) showed that Ni[II], Co[II] or Mn[II] induce the transition of poly(dG-dC) DNA from B to Z helices. Removal of the divalent cation with EDTA produces instantaneous Z to B reversal. Bourtayre *et al.* (1984) studied B to Z conformational transition of double-stranded poly(dG-dC) DNA induced by $NiCl_2$, $NiSO_4$, $NiCO_3$ and Ni_3S_2. In all cases, the nickel compounds induced the B to Z transition at sub-millimolar concentrations; Bourtayre *et al.* (1983) proposed that stabilization of Z-DNA may be involved in the mechanism of nickel carcinogenesis. Eichhorn *et al.* (1983) and Shin *et al.* (1983) investigated the ability of metal compounds to induce interconversions among four conformers of poly(dG-dC) DNA; they showed that $Co(NH_3)_6Cl_3$ first brings about conversion of the B-DNA to Z-DNA, then to a structure that resembles A-DNA, and finally to the highly-compacted ψ-DNA. Moreover, they found that Z-DNA is less active than B-DNA as a template for *E. coli* RNA polymerase.

CONCLUSIONS, WITH HYPOTHESES CONCERNING MOLECULAR MECHANISMS OF GENOTOXICITY

Recent investigations on metal carcinogenesis have confirmed and extended the evaluations of the IARC Working Groups that are summarized in the introduction to this chapter. Elucidation of relationships between the physical, chemical and biological properties of metal compounds and their carcinogenic and mutagenic activities has become a major focus of current research on metal carcinogenesis. Experiments with nickel and/or chromium compounds suggest that differences in (a) mass-fraction of metal, (b) solubility in body fluids and (c) rate of cellular uptake, may contribute to the marked disparity in carcinogenic and mutagenic activities of these compounds. Further investigations are needed to confirm or refute the attractive hypothesis that intracellular bioavailability of specific metal cations is the crucial factor.

In-vitro experiments that may be related to metal carcinogenesis and mutagenesis are summarized in Table 1, based upon publications cited in this article and in previous reviews on this subject (Sunderman, 1977, 1978, 1979a,b). The following hypothetical mechanisms for metal induction of somatic mutations seem to provide the most promising avenues for research:

(1) metal cations may bind covalently to DNA, causing strand breakage and excision of specific nucleotide bases and leading to frame-shift mutations during subsequent repair of DNA damage;

(2) metal cations may form crosslinks between DNA and proteins or between adjacent DNA strands, causing aberrant DNA replication or repair and disturbing the orderly progression of mitosis;

Table 1. In-vitro experiments related to carcinogenesis

Experimental system	Metals whose compounds have yielded positive results																
	Ag	As	Be	Cd	Co	Cr	Cu	Fe	Hg	Mn	Ni	Pb	Pt	Sb	Sn	Tl	Zn
Mutagenesis and recassays in bacteria[a]	?	X	X	X	X		X	X	X	X		X	X			X	X
Mutagenesis in mammalian cells	X	X	X	X	X	X	X	X	X	X	X	X	X				X
Chromosomal damage and sister chromatid exchanges		X	X		X	X			X	X	X	X	X				X
Morphological transformation	X	X	X	X	X	X	X	X	X	X	X	X	X	X		X	X
DNA strand-breaks, DNA-protein crosslinks	X			X	X	X	X				X		X			X	
DNA polymerase infidelity	X		X	X	X	X	X			X	X	X					
RNA strand initiation			X	X	X					X	X	X					
Conversion of B-DNA to Z-DNA				X						X	X						

[a] Certain Cs, Ir, Mo, Os, Rh, Ru, Se and V compounds have also yielded positive results

(3) metal cations may cause helical transition from B-DNA to Z-DNA, affecting chromatin structure and expressing normally repressed segments of the genome (e.g., oncogenes);

(4) metal cations may impair the fidelity of DNA replication by altering the conformation of DNA polymerases at the substrate-binding or catalytically active sites, or by modifying template-base specificity by disturbing complementary base-pairing during DNA replication;

(5) metal cations may bind to histones, non-histone nuclear proteins, or nucleolar RNA, influencing chromatin structure and gene expression, perhaps by modifying the phosphorylation of regulatory proteins.

Current knowledge is insufficient to substantiate that one or more of these hypothetical mechanisms are specifically involved in the molecular pathogenesis of carcinogenesis by any particular metal compound. The major advance has been the emergence of such hypotheses, which may be amenable to experimental testing by existing techniques of molecular biology.

ACKNOWLEDGEMENTS

This work was supported by US Department of Energy Grant EV-03140 and National Institute of Environmental Health Sciences Grant ES-013377.

REFERENCES

Abbrachio, M.P., Evans, R.M., Heck, J.D., Cantoni, O. & Costa, M. (1982a) The regulation of ionic nickel uptake and cytotoxicity by specific amino acids and serum components. *Biol. Trace Element Res., 4,* 289–301

Abbrachio, M.P., Heck, J.D. & Costa, M. (1982b) The phagocytosis and transforming activity of crystalline metal sulfide particles are related to their negative surface charge. *Carcinogenesis, 3,* 175–180

Abbrachio, M.P., Simmons-Hansen, J. & Costa, M. (1982c) Cytoplasmic dissolution of phagocytized crystalline nickel suflide particles: A prerequisite for nuclear uptake of nickel. *Environ. Health, 9,* 663–676

Abe, S., Ohsaki, Y., Kimura, K., Tsuneta, Y., Mikami, H. & Murao, M. (1982) Chromate lung cancer with special reference to its cell type and relation to the manufacturing process. *Cancer, 49,* 783–787

Alderson, M.R., Rattan, N.S. & Bidstrup, L. (1981) Health of workmen in the chromate-producing industry in Britain. *Br. J. Ind. Med., 38,* 117–124

Amacher, D.E. & Paillet, S.C. (1980) Induction of trifluorothymidine-resistant mutants by metal ions in L5178/TK$^{+/-}$ cells. *Mutat. Res., 78,* 279–288

Andersen, O. (1983) Effects of coal combustion products and metal compounds on sister chromatid exchange in a macrophage cell line. *Environ. Health Perspect., 47,* 239–253

Belman, S. & Nordberg, G., eds (1981) Proceedings of workshop/conference on the role of metals in carcinogenesis. *Environ. Health Perspect., 40,* 1–254

Bianchi, V., Dal Torso, R., Debetto, P., Levis, A.G., Luciani, S., Majone, F. & Tamino, G. (1980) Mechanisms of chromium toxicity in mammalian cell cultures. *Toxicol., 17,* 219–224

Bourtayre, P., Liquier, J., Taboury, J., Pizzorni, L., Labarre, J.F. & Taillandier, E. (1984) *Z-form induction in DNA by carcinogenic nickel compounds: An optical spectroscopy study.* In: Sunderman, F.W., Jr, ed., *Nickel in the Human Environment, (IARC Scientific Publication No. 53),* Lyon, International Agency for Research on Cancer, pp. 227–234

Boysen, M. & Reith, A. (1980) A morphometric model for light microscopic analysis of metaplastic, dysplastic, and carcinomatous alterations in the nasal mucosa in nickel workers. *Pathol. Res. Pract., 166,* 362–371

Boysen, M. & Reith, A. (1982a) The surface structure of the human nasal mucosa. II. Metaplasia, dysplasia, and carcinoma in nickel workers. *Virchows Arch. Cell Pathol., 40,* 295–309

Boysen, M. & Reith, A. (1982b) Stereological analysis of nasal mucosa. III. Stepwise alterations in cellular and subcellular components of pseudostratified, metaplastic and dysplastic epithelium in nickel workers. *Virchows Arch. Cell Pathol., 40,* 311–325

Brown, C.C. & Chu, K.C. (1983) Implications of the multi-stage theory of carcinogenesis applied to occupational arsenic exposure. *J. natl. Cancer Inst., 70,* 455–463

Bryan, S.E. (1981) *Heavy metals in the cell's nucleus.* In: Eichorn, G.L. & Marzilli, L.G., eds, *Metal Ions in Genetic Information Transfer,* New York, Elsevier/North Holland, pp. 87–101

Burges, D.C.L. (1980) *Mortality study of nickel platers.* In: Brown, S.S. & Sunderman, F.W., Jr, eds, *Nickel Toxicology,* London, Academic Press, pp. 15–18

Casto, B.C; Meyers, J. & DiPaolo, J.A. (1979) Enhancement of viral transformation for evaluation of the carcinogenic or mutagenic potential of inorganic metal salts. *Cancer Res., 39,* 193–198

Chovil, A., Sutherland, R.B. & Halliday, M. (1981) Respiratory cancer in a cohort of nickel sinter plant workers. *Br. J. Ind. Med., 38,* 327–333

Chung, H.C. & Liu, C.T. (1982) Induction of lung cancer in rats by intratracheal instillation of arsenic-containing ore dust. *Zhonghua Zhongliu Zazhi, 4,* 14–16

Ciccarelli, R.B. & Wetterhahn, K.E. (1982) Nickel distribution and DNA lesions induced in rat tissues by the carcinogen nickel carbonate. *Cancer Res., 42,* 3544–3549

Ciccarelli, R.B. & Wetterhahn, K.E. (1983) Isolation of nickel-nucleic acidprotein complexes from rat tissues. *Proc. Am. Assoc. Cancer Res., 24,* 45 (Abstr. 177)

Ciccarelli, R.B., Hampton, T.H. & Jennette, K.W. (1981) Nickel carbonate induces DNA-protein crosslinks and DNA strandbreaks in rat kidney. *Cancer Lett., 12,* 349–354

Costa, M. & Heck, J.D. (1982) Specific nickel compounds as carcinogens. *Trends Pharmacol. Sci., 3,* 408–410

Costa, M. & Mollenhauer, H.H. (1980) Phagocytosis of nickel subsulfide particles during the early stage of neoplastic transformation in tissue culture. *Cancer Res., 40,* 2688–2694

Costa, M., Nye, J.S. & Sunderman, F.W., Jr (1978) Morphological transformation of Syrian hamster fetal cells induced by nickel compounds. *Ann. Clin. Lab. Sci., 8,* 502–503

Costa, M., Nye, J.S., Sunderman, F.W., Jr, Allpass, P.R. & Gondos, B. (1979) Induction of sarcomas in nude mice by implantation of Syrian hamster fetal cells exposed *in vitro* to nickel subsulfide. *Cancer Res., 19,* 3591–3596

Costa, M., Simmons-Hansen, J., Bedrossian, C.W.M., Bonura, J. & Caprioli, R.M. (1981) Phagocytosis, cellular distribution, and carcinogenic activity of particulate nickel compounds in tissue culture. *Cancer Res., 41,* 2868–2876

Costa, M., Heck, J.D. & Robison, S.H. (1982) Selective phagocytosis of crystalline metal sulfide particles and DNA strandbreaks as a mechanism for the induction of cellular transformation. *Cancer Res., 42,* 2757–2763

Cox, J.E., Doll, R., Scott, W.A. & Smith, S. (1981) Mortality of nickel workers: Experience of men working with metallic nickel. *Br. J. Ind. Med., 38,* 235–239

Crossen, P.E. (1983) Arsenic and SCE in human lymphocytes. *Mutat. Res., 119,* 415–419

Cuckle, H., Doll, R. & Morgan, L.G. (1980) *Mortality study of men working with soluble nickel compounds.* In: Brown, S.S. & Sunderman, F.W., Jr, eds, *Nickel Toxicology,* London, Academic Press, pp. 11–15

Cuzik, J., Evans, S., Gillman, M. & Price-Evans, D.A. (1982) Medicinal arsenic and internal malignancies. *Br. J. Cancer, 45,* 904–911

De Flora, S., Coppola, R., Camoirano, A., Battaglia, M.A. & Bennicelli, C. (1980) Mutagenicity and toxicity of chromyl chloride and its vapours. *Carcinogenesis, 1,* 583–587

Degraeve, N. (1981) Carcinogenic, teratogenic and mutagenic effects of cadmium. *Mutat. Res., 86,* 115–135

DiPaolo, J.A. & Casto, B.C. (1979) Quantitative studies of in-vitro morphological transformation of Syrian hamster cells by inorganic metal salts. *Cancer Res., 39,* 1008–1013

Eichhorn, G.L., Butzow, J.J., Shin, Y.A. & Karlik, S.J. (1983) Changes of biologic significance induced by metal ions in the structure of nucleic acids and nucleotides. *Inorg. Chim. Acta, 79*(B7), 307

Elias, Z., Schneider, O., Aubry, F., Daniere, M.C. & Poirot, O. (1983) Sister chromatic exchanges in Chinese hamster V79 cells treated with the trivalent chromium compounds, chromic chloride and chromic oxide. *Carcinogenesis, 4,* 605–611

Enterline, P.E. & Marsh, G.M. (1980) Mortality studies of smelter workers. *Am. J. Ind. Med., 1,* 251–259

Enterline, P.E. & Marsh, G.M. (1982a) Cancer among workers exposed to arsenic and other substances in a smelter. *Am. J. Epidemiol., 116,* 895–911

Enterline, P.E. & Marsh, G.M. (1982b) Mortality among workers in a nickel refinery and alloy manufacturing plant in West Virginia. *J. natl Cancer Inst. 68,* 925–933

Evans, R.M., Davies, P.J.A. & Costa, M. (1982) Video time-lapse microscopy of phagocytosis and intracellular fate of crystalline nickel sulfide particles in cultured mammalian cells. *Cancer Res., 42,* 2729–2735

Falk, H., Caldwell, G.G., Ishak, K.G., Thomas, L.B. & Popper, H. (1981a) Arsenic-related hepatic angiosarcoma. *Am. J. Ind. Med., 2,* 43–50

Falk, H., Herbert, J.T., Edmonds, L., Heath, C.W., Jr, Thomas, L.B. & Popper, H. (1981b) Review of four cases of childhood hepatic angiosarcoma–Elevated environmental arsenic exposure in one case. *Cancer, 47,* 382–391

Flessel, C.P. (1980) *Metals as mutagenic initiators of cancer.* In. Kharasch, N., ed., *Trace Metals in Health and Disease,* New York, Raven Press, pp. 109–122

Fornace, A.J., Jr & Little, J.B. (1980) Malignant transformation by the DNA-protein crosslinking agent trans-Pt(II)-diamminedichloride. *Carcinogenesis, 1,* 989–994

Fornace, A.J., Jr, Seres, D.S., Lechner, J.F. & Harris, C.C. (1981) DNA-protein crosslinking by chromium salts. *Chem.-biol. Interact., 36,* 345–354

Furst, A. (1981) *A new look at arsenic carcinogenesis.* In: Lederer, W.H. & Fensterheim, R.J., eds, *Arsenic: Industrial, Biomedical and Environmental Perspectives,* New York, Van Nostrand/Reinhold Co., pp. 151–165

Furst, A. & Radding, S.B. (1980) *An update on nickel carcinogenesis.* In: Nriagu, J.O., ed., *Nickel in the Environment,* New York, John Wiley and Sons, pp. 585–600

Garcia, J.D. & Jennette, K.W. (1981) Electron-transport cytochrome P-450 system is involved in the microsomal metabolism of the carcinogen chromate. *J. Inorg. Biochem., 14,* 281–295

Godbold, J.H., Jr & Tompkins, E.A. (1979) A long-term mortality study of workers occupationally exposed to metallic nickel at the Oak Ridge gasseous diffusion plant. *J. occup. Med., 21,* 799–806

Hansen, K. & Stern, R.M. (1982) *In Vitro and Transformation Potency of Nickel Compounds.* Copenhagen, Danish Welding Institute, Report No. 82/22, pp. 1–10

Hatherhill, J.R. (1981) A review of the mutagenicity of chromium. *Drug Chem. Toxicol., 4,* 185–195

Hayes, R.B. (1982) Carcinogenic effects of chromium. In: Langard, S., ed., *Biological and Environmental Aspects of Chromium,* Amsterdam, Elsevier Biomedical Press, pp. 221–247

Heck, J.D. & Costa, M. (1982) In vitro assessment of the toxicity of metal compounds. *Biol. Trace Element Res., 4,* 71–82

Helmes, C.T., Casey, S., Fung, V.A., Johnson, O.H., McCaleb, K.E., Miller, A., Miller, J., Papa, P., Sigman, C. & Strauss, E. (1983) A study of metals for the selection of candidates for carcinogen bioassay. *J. environ. Sci. Health, A18,* 203–295

Hertel, R.F. (1982) Chromium as a problem in physiology, epidemiology and biological monitoring. *Staub. Reinhalt. Luft., 42,* 135–137

Higgins, I., Welsh, K., Oh, M., Bond, G. & Hurwitz, P. (1981) Influence of arsenic exposure and smoking on lung cancer among smelter workers: A pilot study. *Am. J. Ind. Med., 2,* 33–41

Hildebrand, H.F. & Tetaert, D. (1981) Ni_3S_2-induced leiomyosarcomas in rabbit skeletal muscle: Analysis of the tumoral myosin and its significance in the retrodifferentiation concept. *Oncodevelop. Biol. Med., 2,* 101–108

Hoffman, D.J. & Niyogi, S.K. (1977) Metal mutagens and carcinogens affect RNA synthesis rates in a distinct manner. *Science, 198,* 513–514

Holden, H. (1980) *Further mortality studies on workers exposed to cadmium fume.* In: *Seminar on Occupational Exposure to Cadmium,* London, Cadmium Association

O'Neill, J.P., Hoeschele, J.D., Rahn, R.O. & Forbes, N.L. (1979) *Quantitative mammalian cell mutagenesis and a preliminary study of the mutagenic potential of metallic compounds.* In: Kharasch, N., ed., *Trace Metals in Health and Disease,* New York, Raven Press, pp. 55–69

Hui, G. & Sunderman, F.W., Jr (1980) Effects of nickel compounds on incorporation of thymidine-^{3}H into DNA in rat liver and kidney. *Carcinogenesis, 1,* 297–304

IARC (1976) *IARC Monographs on the Evaluation of the Carcinogenic Risk of Chemicals to Humans.* Volume 11, *Cadmium, Nickel, Some Epoxides, Miscellaneous Industrial Chemicals and General Considerations on Volatile Anaesthetics.* Lyon, International Agency for Research on Cancer, Vol. 11, pp. 39–112

IARC (1982) *IARC Monographs on the Evaluation of the Carcinogenic Risk of Chemicals to Humans,* Supplement 4, *Chemicals, Industrial Processes and Industries Associated with Cancer in Humans.* Lyon, International Agency for Research on Cancer, pp. 91–93

Ishinishi, N. & Yamamoto, A. (1983) Discrepancy between epidemiological evidence and animal experimental result. *J. Univ. occup. environ. Health Jpn., 5 (Suppl.),* 109–116

Jennette, K.W. (1979) Chromate metabolism in liver microsomes. *Biol. Trace Element Res., 1,* 55–62

Jennette, K.W. (1982) Microsomal reduction of the carcinogen chromate produces chromium[V]. *J. Am. Chem. Soc., 104,* 874

Kanematsu, N., Hara, M. & Kada, T. (1980) Rec assay and mutagenicity studies on metal compounds. *Mutat. Res., 77,* 109–116

Kappus, H. (1982) Carcinogenic effects of metal compounds. *Umwelthygiene, 14,* 83–95

Kasprzak, K.S., Gabryel, P. & Jarczewska, K. (1983) Carcinogenicity of nickel[II] hydroxides and nickel[II] sulfate in Wistar rats and its relation to the in-vitro dissolution of rates. *Carcinogenesis, 4,* 275–279

Kazantzis, G. (1981) Role of cobalt, iron, lead, manganese, mercury, platinum, selenium and titanium in carcinogenesis. *Environ. Health Perspect., 40,* 143–162

Kazantzis, G. & Lilly, L.J. (1979) *Mutagenic and carcinogenic effects of metals.* In: Friberg, L., Nordberg, G.F. & Vouk, V.B., eds, *Handbook on the Toxicology of Metals,* Amsterdam, Elsevier Biomedical Press, pp. 237–272

Kjellstrom, T. (1980) *Further evaluation of cancer morbidity in Swedish cadmium exposed workers.* In: *Edited Procedings. Second International Cadmium Conference, Cannes 1979,* Worcester Park, Surrey, Metal Bulletin Ltd

Kjellstrom, T., Friberg, L. & Rahnster, B. (1979) Mortality and cancer morbidity among cadmium-exposed workers. *Environ. Health Perspect., 28,* 199–204

Kotlar, H.K., Boysen, M. & Sanner, T. (1982) A serum immune factor in detection of an occupational group with increased risk for lung and nose cancer. *Eur. J. Cancer Clin. Oncol., 18,* 957–965

Kovacs, P. & Darvas, Z. (1982) Studies on the Ni-content of the centriole. *Acta Histochem., 71,* 169–173

Kuehn, K. & Sunderman, F.W., Jr (1981) Dissolution half-times of nickel compounds in water, rat serum and renal cytosol. *J. inorg. Biochem., 17,* 29–39

Kuehn, K., Fraser, C.B. & Sunderman, F.W., Jr (1982) Phagocytosis of particulate nickel compounds by rat peritoneal macrophages *in vitro. Carcinogenesis, 3,* 321–326

Kuschner, M. (1981) The carcinogenicity of beryllium. *Environ. Health Perspect., 40,* 101–106

Larramendy, M.L., Popescu, N.C. & DiPaolo, J.A. (1981) Induction by inorganic metal salts of sister chromatid exchanges and chromosome aberrations in human and Syrian hamster cell strains. *Environ. Mutagen., 3,* 597–606

Lee, J.E., Ciccarelli, R.B. & Jennette, K.W. (1982) Solubilization of the carcinogen nickel subsulfide and its interaction with deoxyribonucleic acid and protein. *Biochemistry, 21,* 771–778

Leonard, A. & Lauwerys, R.R. (1980a) Carcinogenicity, mutagenicity and teratogenicity of arsenic. *Mutat. Res., 75,* 49–62

Leonard, A. & Lauwerys, R.R. (1980b) Carcinogenicity and mutagenicity of chromium. *Mutat. Res., 76,* 227–239

Leonard, A., Gerber, G.B. & Jacquet, P. (1981) Carcinogenicity, mutagenicity and teratogenicity of nickel. *Mutat. Res., 87,* 1–15

Leopold, W.R., Miller, E.C. & Miller, J.A. (1979) Carcinogenicity of antitumor cis-platinum[II] coordination complexes in the mouse and rat. *Cancer Res., 39,* 913–918

Levis, A.G. & Bianchi, V. (1982) *Mutagenic and cytogenetic effects of chromium compounds.* In: Langard, S., ed., *Biological and Environmental Aspects of Chromium,* Amsterdam, Elsevier Biomedical Press, pp. 171–208

Levis, A.G. & Majone, F. (1979) Cytotoxic and clastogenic effects of soluble chromium compounds on mammalian cell cultures. *Br. J. Cancer.* **40,** 523–533

Levis, A.G. & Majone, F. (1981) Cytotoxic and clastogenic effects of soluble and insoluble compounds containing hexavalent and trivalent chromium. *Br. J. Cancer,* **44,** 219–235

Loeb, L.A. & Mildvan, A.S. (1981) *The role of metal ions in the fidelity of DNA and RNA synthesis.* In: Eichhorn, G.L. & Marzilli, E.G., eds, *Metal Ions in Genetic Information Transfer,* New York, Elsevier/North Holland Co., pp. 125–142

Lofroth, G. & Ames, B.N. (1978) Mutagenicity of inorganic compounds in *Salmonella typhimurium:* Arsenic, chromium and selenium. *Mutat. Res.,* **53,** 65–66

Loser, E. (1980) A two-year oral carcinogenicity study with cadmium on rats. *Cancer Lett.,* **9,** 191–198

Lubin, J.H., Pottern, L.M., Blot, W.J., Tokudome, S., Stone, B.J. & Fraumeni, J.F., Jr (1981) Respiratory cancer among copper smelter workers. Recent mortality statistics. *J. occup. Med.,* **23,** 779–784

Maenza, R.M., Pradhan, A.M. & Sunderman, F.W., Jr (1971) Rapid induction of sarcomas in rats by combination of nickel sulfide and 3,4-benzpyrene. *Cancer Res.,* **31,** 2067–2071

Magnus, K., Andersen, A. & Hogetveit, A.C. (1982) Cancer of the respiratory organs among workers at a nickel refinery in Norway. *Int. J. Cancer,* **3,** 681–685

Majone, F. & Levis, A.G. (1979) Chromosome aberrations and sister chromatid exchanges in Chinese hamster cells treated *in vivo* with hexavalent chromium compounds. *Mutat. Res.,* **67,** 231–238

Majone, F., Montaldi, A., Ronchese, F., DeRossi, A., Chieco-Bianchi, L. & Levis, A.G. (1983) Sister chromatid exchanges induced *in vivo* and *in vitro* by chemical carcinogens in mouse lymphocytes carrying endogenous Maloney leukemia virus. *Carcinogenesis,* **4,** 33–37

McLean, J.R., McWilliams, R.S., Kaplan, J.G. & Birnboim, H.C. (1982) Rapid detection of DNA strand breaks in human peripheral blood cells and animal organs following treatment with physical and chemical agents. *Prog. Mutat. Res.,* **3,** 137–141

McLean, J.R.N., Blakey, D.H., Douglas, G.R. & Kaplan, J.G. (1983) The effect of stannous and stannic (tin) chloride on DNA in Chinese hamster ovary cells. *Mutat. Res.,* **119,** 195–201

Miyaki, M., Akamatsu, N., Ono, T. & Koyama, H. (1979) Mutagenicity of metal cations in cultured cells from Chinese hamster rats. *Mutat. Res.,* **68,** 259–263

Miyaki, M., Akamatsu, N., Suzuki, K., Araki, M. & Ono, T. (1980) *Quantitative and qualitative changes induced in DNA polymerases by carcinogens.* In: Gelboin, H.V., ed., *Genetic and Environmental Factors in Environmental and Human Cancer,* Tokyo, Japan Sci. Soc. Press, pp. 201–213

Moore, M.R. & Meredith, P.A. (1979) The carcinogenicity of lead. *Arch. Toxicol.,* **42,** 87–94

National Toxicology Program (1982) *Carcinogenesis Bioassay of Stannous Chloride,* Bethesda, National Institutes of Health, Publication No. 82–1787, pp. 1–59

Newman, S.M., Summitt, R.L. & Nunez, L.J. (1982) Incidence of nickel-induced sister chromatid exchange. *Mutat. Res., 101,* 67–75

Nishimura, M. & Umeda, M. (1979) Induction of chromosomal aberrations in cultured mammalian cells by nickel compounds. *Mutat. Res., 68,* 337–349

Nishioka, H. (1975) Mutagenic activities of metal compounds in bacteria. *Mutat. Res., 31,* 185–190

Niyogi, S.K. & Feldman, R.P. (1981) Effect of several metal ions on misincorporation during transcription. *Nucleic Acid Res., 22,* 9–21

Niyogi, S.L., Feldman, R.P. & Hoffman, D.J. (1981) Selective effects of metal ions on RNA synthesis rates. *Toxicology, 22,* 9–21

Norseth, T. (1980) Cancer Hazards caused by nickel and chromium exposure. *J. Toxicol. Environ. Health, 6,* 1219–1227

Norseth, T. (1981) The carcinogenicity of chromium. *Environ. Health Perspect., 40,* 121–130

Oberly, T.J., Piper, C.E. & McDonald, D.S. (1982) Mutagenicity of metal salts in the L51784 mouse lymphoma assay. *J. Toxicol. Environ. Health, 9,* 367–376

Ohono, H., Hanaoka, F. & Yamada, M.A. (1982) Inducibility of sister chromatid exchanges by heavy metal ions. *Mutat. Res., 104,* 141–145

Ohsaki, Y. (1980) Occupational lung diseases: Chromate lung cancer. *Nippon Kyobu. Shikkan. Gakkai Zasshi, 18,* 886–889

Olson, M.O.J. (1981) *Metal ion effects on nuclear protein phosphorylation.* In: Eichhorn, G.L. & Marzilli, L.G., eds, *Metal Ions in Genetic Information Transfer,* New York, Elsevier/North Holland Press, pp. 167–191

Ono, H., Wada, O. & Ono, T. (1981) Distribution of trace metals in nuclei and nucleoli of normal and regenerating rat liver with special reference to the different behavior of nickel and chromium. *J. Toxicol. Environ. Health, 8,* 947–957

Parker, V.H. & Stevens, C. (1979) Binding of beryllium to nuclear acidic proteins. *Chem.-biol. Interact., 26,* 167–177

Perry, S.T., Kulkarni, S.B., Lee, K.-L. & Kenney, F.T. (1982) Selective effect of the metallocarcinogen beryllium on hormonal regulation of gene expression in cultured cells. *Cancer Res., 42,* 473–476

Pershagen, G. (1981) The carcinogenicity of arsenic. *Environ. Health Perspect., 40,* 93–100

Pikalek, P. & Necasek, J. (1983) The mutagenic activity of nickel in Corynebacterium sp. *Folia Microbiol., 28,* 17–21

Piscator, M. (1981) Role of cadmium in carcinogenesis with special reference to cancer of the prostate. *Environ. Health Perspect., 40,* 107–120

Popescu, N.C., Amsbaugh, S.C. & DiPaolo, J.A. (1981) Relationship of carcinogen-induced sister chromatid exchange and neoplastic cell transformation. *Int. J. Cancer, 28,* 71–77

Raithel, H.-J. & Schaller, K.H. (1981) Toxicity and carcinogenicity of nickel and its compounds. A review of the current status. *Zentralbl. Bakteriol. Hyg., Abt. I, (Orig. B), 173,* 63–91

Reddy, J., Svoboda, D., Azarnoff, D. & Dawar, R. (1973) Cadmium-induced Leydig cell tumors of rat testis: Morphologic and cytochemical study. *J. natl Cancer Inst.*, *51*, 891–903

Rivedal, E. & Sanner, T. (1980) Synergistic effect on morphological transformation of hamster embryo cells by nickel sulfate and benzo[*a*]pyrene. *Cancer Lett.*, *8*, 203–208

Rivedal, E. & Sanner, T. (1981) Metal salts as promotors of in-vitro morphological transformation of hamster embryo cells induced by benzo[*a*]pyrene. *Cancer Res.*, *41*, 2950–2953

Roat, J.W., Walt, A., Mendelow, H. & Pataki, K.I. (1982) Hepatic angiosarcoma associated with short-term arsenic ingestion. *Am. J. Med.*, *73*, 933–936

Robison, S.H. & Costa, M. (1982) The induction of DNA strand breakage by nickel compounds in cultured Chinese hamster ovary cells. *Cancer Lett.*, *15*, 35–40

Robison, S.H., Cantoni, O. & Costa, M. (1982) Strand breakage and decreased molecular weight of DNA induced by specific metal compounds. *Carcinogenesis*, *3*, 657–662

Rossman, T.G. (1981a) Effect of metals on mutagenesis and DNA repair. *Environ. Health Perspect.*, *40*, 189–195

Rossman, T.G. (1981b) Enhancement of UV-mutagenesis by low concentrations of arsenite in *E. coli*. *Mutat. Res.*, *91*, 207–211

Rossman, T.G., Stone, D., Molina, M. & Troll, W. (1980) Absence of arsenite mutagenicity in *E. coli* and Chinese hamster cells. *Environ. Mutagen.*, *2*, 371–379

Rudnai, P. & Borzsonyi, M. (1981) Tumor-inducing effect of arsenic trioxide treatment in CFLP mice. *Magy. Onkol.*, *25*, 73–77

van de Sande, J.H., McIntosh, L.P. & Jovin, T.M. (1982) Mn^{2+} and other transition metals at low concentration induce the right-to-left helical transformation of poly(d(G–C)). *EMBO*, *1*, 777–782

Sarto, F., Cominato, I., Bianchi, V. & Levis, A.G. (1982) Increased incidence of chromosomal aberrations and sister chromatid exchanges in workers exposed to chromic acid (CrO_3) in electroplating factories. *Carcinogenesis*, *3*, 1011–1016

Satoh, K., Fukuda, Y., Torii, K. & Katsumo, N. (1981) Epidemiological study of workers engaged in the manufacture of chromium compounds. *J. occup. Med.*, *23*, 835–838

Saxholm, H.J.K., Reith, A. & Brogger, A. (1981) Oncogenic transformation and cell lysis in C3H/10T ½ cells and increased sister chromatid exchange in human lymphocytes by nickel subsulfide. *Cancer Res.*, *41*, 4136–4139

Shin, Y.A., Butzow, J.J. & Eichhorn, G.L. (1983) Metal complex induced changes in DNA conformation and template activity. *Inorg. Chim. Acta*, *79(B7)*, 243

Sigee, D.C. & Kearns, L.P. (1982) Differential retention of proteins and bound divalent cations in dinoflagellate, chromatin fixed under varied conditions: An X-ray microanalytical study. *Cytobios*, *33*, 51–64

Simmon, V.F. (1981) *Is arsenic a mutagen?* In: Lederer, W.H. & Fensterheim, R.J., eds, *Arsenic: Industrial, Biomedical and Environmental Perspectives*, New York, Van Nostrand Reinhold Co., pp. 166–171

Sorahan, T. (1981) *A mortality study of nickel-cadmium battery workers.* In: Edited Proceedings. *Third International Cadmium Conference, Miami, 1980,* Worcester Park, Surrey, Metal Bulletin Ltd, pp. 138–141

Sunderman, F.W., Jr (1977) *Metal carcinogenesis.* In: Goyer, R.A. & Mehlman, M.A., eds, *Advances in Modern Toxicology,* Washington DC, Hemisphere Publishing Co., Vol. 1, pp. 257–295

Sunderman, F.W., Jr (1978) Carcinogenic effects of metals. *Fed. Proc., 37,* 40–46

Sunderman, F.W., Jr (1979a) Mechanisms of metal carcinogenesis. *Biol. Trace Element Res., 1,* 64–86

Sunderman, F.W., Jr (1979b) *Carcinogenicity and anticarcinogenicity of metal compounds.* In. Emmelot, P. & Kriek, E., eds, *Environmental Carcinogenesis,* Amsterdam, Elsevier Biomedical Press, pp. 65–192

Sunderman, F.W., Jr (1981) Recent research on nickel carcinogenesis. *Environ. Health Perspect., 40,* 131–141

Sunderman, F.W., Jr (1983) *Organ and species specificity in nickel subsulfide carcinogenesis.* In: Langenbach, R., Nenow, S. & Rice, J.M., eds, *Organ and Species Specificity in Chemical Carcinogenesis,* New York, Plenum Publishing Co., pp. 107–126

Sunderman, F.W., Jr (1984a) *Carcinogenicity of nickel compounds in animals.* In: Sunderman, F.W., Jr, ed., *Nickel in the Human Environment (IARC Scientific Publication No. 53),* Lyon, International Agency for Research on Cancer, pp. 127–142

Sunderman, F.W., Jr (1984b) Recent advances in metal carcinogenesis. *Ann. Clin. Lab. Sci., 14,* 93–122

Sunderman, F.W., Jr & Hopfer, S.M. (1983) *Correlation between the carcinogenic activities of nickel compounds and their potencies for stimulating erythropoiesis in rats.* In: Sarkar, B., ed., *Biological Aspects of Metals and Metal-Related Diseases,* New York, Raven Press, pp. 171–181

Sunderman, F.W., Jr & McCully, K.S. (1983a) Carcinogenesis tests of nickel arsenides, nickel antimonide and nickel telluride in rats. *Cancer Invest., 1,* 469–474

Sunderman, F.W., Jr & McCully, K.S. (1983b) Effects of manganese compounds on carcinogenicity of nickel subsulfide in rats. *Carcinogenesis, 4,* 461–465

Takenaka, S., Oldiges, H., König, H., Hochrainer, D. & Oberdörster, G. (1983) Carcinogenicity of cadmium chloride aerosols in W rats. *J. natl Cancer Inst., 70,* 367–373

Tiedemann, G. & Einbrodt, H.J. (1982) Mutagen reaction of inorganic arsenic compounds. *Wiss. Umwelt., 3,* 170–173

Tkeshelashvili, L.K., Shearman, C.W., Zakour, R.A., Koplitz, R.M. & Loeb, L.A. (1980) Effect of arsenic, selenium and chromium on the fidelity of DNA synthesis. *Cancer Res., 40,* 2455–2460

Tsapakos, M.J., Hampton, T.H. & Jennette, K.W. (1981) The carcinogen chromate induces DNA cross-links in rat liver and kidney. *J. Biol. Chem., 256,* 3623–3626

Umeda, M. & Nishimura, M. (1979) Inducibility of chromosomal aberrations by metal compounds in cultured mammalian cells. *Mutat. Res., 67,* 221–229

Uziel, M. & Butler, A. (1983) Adaptive toxic responses on exposure of HEC to Ni^{+2} and BAP. *Fed. Proc., 42,* 2109 (Abstract 2057)

Venier, P., Montaldi, A., Majone, F., Bianchi, V. & Levis, A.G. (1982) Cytotoxic, mutagenic and clastogenic effects of industrial chromium compounds. *Carcinogenesis, 3*, 1331–1338

Waksvik, H. & Boysen, M. (1982) Cytogenetic analyses of lymphocytes from workers in a nickel refinery. *Mutat. Res., 103*, 185–190

Wen, W.N., Leiu, T.L., Change, H.J., Wuu, S.W., Yan, M.L. & Jan, K.Y. (1981) Baseline and sodium arsenite-induced sister chromatid exchanges in cultured lymphocytes from patients with blackfoot disease and healthy persons. *Hum. Genet., 59*, 201–203

Wicks, M.J., Archer, V.E., Auerbach, O. & Kuschner, M. (1981) Arsenic exposure in a copper smelter as related to histological type of lung cancer. *Am. J. Ind. Med., 2*, 25–31

Witmer, C., Cooper, K. & Kelly, J. (1982) Effects of plating efficiency and lowered concentrations of salts on mutagenicity assays with Ames' Salmonella strains. *Adv. Exp. Med. Biol., 136B*, 1271–1284

Wulf, H.C. (1980) Sister chromatid exchanges in human lymphocytes exposed to nickel and lead. *Dan. Med. Bull., 27*, 40–42

Yamashiro, S., Basrur, P.K., Gilman, J.P.W., Hulland, T.J. & Fujimoto, Y. (1983) Ultrastructural study of Ni^3S_2-induced tumors in rats. *Acta Pathol. Jpn., 33*, 45–58

Zakour, R.A., Kunkel, I.A. & Loeb, L.A. (1981a) Metal-induced infidelity of DNA synthesis. *Environ. Health Perspect., 40*, 197–205

Zakour, R.A., Tkeshelashvili, L.K., Shearman, C.W., Koplitz, R.M. & Loeb, L.A. (1981b) Metal-induced infidelity of DNA synthesis. *J. Cancer Res. Clin. Oncol., 99*, 187–196

Zaldivar, R., Prunes, L. & Ghai, G.L. (1981) Arsenic dose in patients with cutaneous carcinomata and hepatic haemangeo-endothelioma after environmental and occupational exposure. *Arch. Toxicol., 47*, 145–154

Zanzoni, F. & Jung, E.G. (1980) Arsenic elevates the sister chromatid exchange rate in human lymphocytes *in vitro*. *Arch. Dermatol. Res., 267*, 91–95

Zwelling, L.A., Anderson, T. & Kohn, K.W. (1979a) DNA-protein and DNA interstrand cross-linking by cis- and trans-platinum[II] diammine-dichloride in L1210 mouse leukemia cells and relation to cytotoxicity. *Cancer Res., 39*, 365–369

Zwelling, L.A., Bradley, M.O., Sharkey, N.A., Anderson, T. & Kohn, K.W. (1979b) Mutagenicity, cytotoxicity and DNA crosslinking in V79 Chinese hamster cells treated with cis- and trans-Pt[II]-diamminedichloride. *Mutat. Res., 67*, 271–280

CHAPTER 3

SOURCES OF EXPOSURE AND BIOLOGICAL EFFECTS OF ARSENIC

G. Pershagen

*The National Institute of Environmental Medicine,
Box 60208, S-104 01 Stockholm, Sweden*

INTRODUCTION

Arsenic is a metalloid and occurs in both inorganic and organic compounds with major differences in metabolism and toxicity. It is thus of paramount importance to distinguish between various forms of arsenic in the environment. That this has often been neglected can be explained to a large extent by a lack of suitable analytical methods. The poor determination of dose (exposure) and form of arsenic in many epidemiological studies often makes it difficult to assess dose-response relationships for specific arsenic compounds.

A knowledge of the metabolism of various forms of arsenic is important for an understanding of their toxic effects. Recent studies have shown differences in metabolism between arsenite (trivalent arsenic) and arsenate (pentavalent arsenic), the two most common forms of inorganic arsenic in the environment, as well as between different animal species (Vahter, 1983). Although the metabolism of inorganic arsenic compounds generally will result in less toxic organic forms, an in-vivo reduction of arsenate to more toxic arsenite may also occur. The metabolism of organic arsenic compounds is less well understood; however, available data indicate that the common arsenic forms in seafood are stable and rapidly excreted *via* urine after ingestion (Creceluis, 1977a).

The sources of arsenic in the environment will be discussed, together with exposure levels in various media. An effort has been made to specify the types of arsenic compounds in each exposure situation. The present review is based primarily on studies concerning human subjects. Both carcinogenic and noncarcinogenic effects will be treated, as well as genotoxicity.

SOURCES

Arsenic is widely distributed in the biosphere and on the earth's crust. Sulfidic ores may contain high levels of arsenic, often associated with copper, lead, gold, silver or antimony. High concentrations are found in some coals; i.e., up to 1500 mg/kg (Cmarko, 1963). The average content in coal is usually below 10 mg/kg (NAS, 1977). On a global scale, emissions of arsenic to the atmosphere from anthropogenic sources have been estimated to be nearly 30 times higher than natural emissions (Lantzy & MacKenzie, 1979). Industrial and fossil fuel emissions are the dominant anthropogenic sources.

Arsenic emissions to air of several hundred tons per year have been reported from smelters (Creceluis, 1974; Lindau, 1977). This has led to substantial contamination of soils in their vicinity. Increased concentrations of arsenic in air may thus be found near smelters, as well as following the use of arsenic-containing defoliants (Nelson, 1977; Attrep & Anirudhan, 1977). In the USA, coal ranked third as a source of airborne arsenic (after copper smelting and pesticide use) in 1974 (Fishbein, 1981). Burning of wood treated with arsenic-containing preservatives is another source of arsenic in air.

Pollution of the aquatic environment can also result from industrial emissions. It has been estimated that more than 500 tons were emitted to water per year at a major Swedish copper smelter (Lindau, 1977). Within 8–15 km of a US copper smelter, the arsenic concentrations of bottom sediments were raised two-three times (Creceluis, 1974). Contamination of ground water has also been reported in the vicinity of arsenic-producing plants (Terada *et al.,* 1962; Gonzalez, 1963).

The world production of arsenic was about 50 000 tons per year in the 1970's (US Bureau of Mines 1975). Major producers include Sweden, France, Namibia and the Phillipines. Arsenic compounds are widely used as pesticides; i.e., as insecticides, herbicides, fungicides and wood preservatives (Fishbein, 1981). Some of the compounds used are lead arsenate, calcium arsenate, sodium arsenite, monosodium methane arsonate, disodium methane arsonate and cacodylic acid. Some organic arsenicals, e.g., arsanilic acid and 3-nitro-4-hydroxyphenylarsonic acid, have found an increased use as feed additives. Arsenic is also used in some alloys and in glass.

Various arsenic compounds have been important constituents of drugs; however, in recent years this use has diminished. Inorganic trivalent arsenic, often in the form of potassium arsenite (Fowler's solution), was used in the treatment of leukaemia, psoriasis, asthma and as a tonic (Goodman & Gilman, 1955). A few organic arsenicals are still used as antiparasitic drugs, e.g., carbarsone, glycobiarsol, melalsoprol and tryparsamide.

EXPOSURE

Air

The concentration of arsenic in ambient air of unpolluted areas is generally less than 10 ng/m^3 (NAS, 1977). In urban areas, airborne arsenic concentrations of several hundred nanograms per m^3 have been measured (Vondracek, 1963; NAS, 1977). Near smelter locations, levels of arsenic in air have exceeded 1000 ng/m^3 (Rozenshtein, 1970; Nelson, 1977).

Both inorganic and organic arsenic compounds may be present in ambient air particulates (Attrep & Anirudhan, 1977). Stack dust from smelters contains arsenic mainly in the trivalent inorganic form, the extent of subsequent oxidation remaining largely unknown (Rosehart & Chu, 1975). In rain from an urban area, only 35% was present in the inorganic trivalent form (Crecelius, 1974). Organic arsenic compounds in air have been reported to be present as methylarsines (Johnson & Braman, 1975).

Occupational exposure to inorganic arsenic compounds occurs primarily among smelter workers and workers engaged in the production and use of arsenic-containing pesticides. Concentrations in air exceeding 1 mg/m^3 were reported some decades ago (Perry *et al.,* 1948; Lundgren, 1954), but now the levels are generally considerably lower (Pinto *et al.,* 1976; Smith *et al.,* 1977). In smelters, the airborne arsenic particulates are considered to consist mainly of arsenic trioxide, but there is also evidence of arsenic sulfides (Smith *et al.,* 1976).

Food and beverages

Arsenic levels in most foodstuffs are below 1 mg/kg (Westöö & Rydälv, 1972). Marine organisms often have concentrations between 1 and 10 mg/kg and certain bottom-feeding fish, crustaceans and algae may have an even higher arsenic content (Crecelius, 1974; Walkiw & Douglas, 1975). About 5–10% of the arsenic in seafood is inorganic (Lunde, 1977). The remainder is present in lipid- and water-soluble organic compounds. Arsenobetaine appears to be the major water-soluble organoarsenic compound in lobster and shrimp (Edmonds *et al.,* 1977; Norin, 1983). This compound has a high chemical stability and its presence in human urine following ingestion of cooked lobster has been confirmed (Cannon *et al.,* 1981). The use of some organic arsenic compounds as feed additives for poultry and swine can lead to accumulation of arsenic in certain organs (Ledet *et al.,* 1973; Calvert, 1975).

Wine may contain appreciable amounts of arsenic as a result of the use of arsenic-containing pesticides. During the 1930's and 1940's, levels between 3 and 30 mg As/L were found in German wine from an area where such sprays were used (Grobe, 1976). This use of arsenic has been prohibited in most countries, which has led to a lowering of the arsenic concentrations. In US table wines produced between 1949 and 1974, Noble *et al.* (1976) found levels between 0.02 and 0.11 mg/L. In another sample of US wines, more than half had levels exceeding 0.05 mg/L, which is the tentative WHO drinking-water standard (Crecelius, 1977b). Most of the arsenic present was in the inorganic trivalent form.

Drinking water

In both ground and surface water, the arsenic concentration normally is less than 0.01 mg/L (McCabe *et al.,* 1970; Sagner, 1973). In certain areas the concentrations may be substantially higher. From regions in Argentina, Taiwan and the US, levels exceeding 1 mg/L have been reported (Arguello *et al.,* 1938; Goldblatt *et al.,* 1963;

Kuo, 1968). Increased arsenic concentrations in drinking water have also occurred in Northern Chile, where water was taken from a river originating in an area with volcanic activity (Borgono *et al.*, 1977). The discharge from geothermal power plants may contaminate adjacent water reservoirs and levels close to 10 mg/L have been reported (Crecelius *et al.*, 1976; Jernelöv *et al.*, 1976).

Only a few studies have been performed to elucidate the forms of arsenic in water. Both inorganic and organic compounds may be present in fresh water (Braman & Foreback, 1973). Where increased concentrations are found in well water, the inorganic forms seem to predominate, and often no organic compounds are found (Harrington *et al.*, 1978; Wagner *et al.*, 1979; Southwick *et al.*, 1980).

Tobacco

The use of arsenic-containing pesticides has resulted in increased arsenic concentrations in tobacco. In the 1950s, levels of up to 40 mg/kg were found in US cigarettes (Holland & Acevedo, 1966). The levels have decreased considerably since then because of restricted use of arsenicals. In tobacco not treated with arsenic-containing pesticides, the levels are usually below 3 mg/kg (Bailey *et al.*, 1957). It has been estimated that 10 to 20% of the arsenic in cigarettes is volatilized in smoking (Thomas & Collier, 1945; Bailey *et al.*, 1957). No data are available on the form of arsenic in tobacco smoke.

Drugs

Arsenical compounds have been widely used in medicine. A common preparation was Fowler's solution, containing 7.6 g As/L in inorganic trivalent form. The daily dose often reached several milligrams of arsenic (Goodman & Gilman, 1955). Even higher doses of organic arsenicals were given; e.g., tryparsamide.

Total daily intake

It can be estimated that the daily exposure from ambient air and water ordinarily will not exceed a few micrograms of arsenic. The intake *via* food is often much higher, and greatly influenced by the amount of seafood in the diet. Estimations of the daily intake *via* food have ranged from tens of micrograms to over one milligram (Nakao, 1960; Wester, 1974; Jelinek & Corneliussen, 1977). Data on the form of arsenic in most foodstuffs are limited. However, from data on the urinary excretion of various arsenic compounds, it can be estimated that the total daily absorption in individuals not excessively exposed to arsenic should not exceed 50 μg of inorganic arsenic (Braman & Foreback, 1973; Smith *et al.*, 1977). An ordinary smoker may inhale a few micrograms of arsenic daily. If arsenical pesticides have been used on the tobacco, the daily intake may exceed 100 μg for an average smoker. In some situations, the daily doses of inorganic arsenic may exceed 1 mg; e.g., in certain occupations or due to the use of drugs or drinking water with high arsenic concentrations.

NORMAL LEVELS OF ARSENIC IN MAN AND BIOLOGICAL INDICATORS OF EXPOSURE

Urine

Inorganic and organic arsenic compounds are excreted mainly *via* the kidneys. Both trivalent and pentavalent inorganic arsenic are to some extent methylated prior to excretion (Tam *et al.,* 1979; Yamauchi & Yamamura, 1979a,b; Buchet *et al.,* 1981). The major metabolites are monomethyl arsonic acid (MMA) and dimethylarsinic acid (DMA), which together make up more than half of the total urinary arsenic in humans not subject to excessive exposure.

The concentration of inorganic arsenic, together with MMA and DMA, in urine normally lies below 50 µg/L (Braman & Foreback, 1973; Smith *et al.,* 1977). Ingestion of arsenic-rich seafood may result in levels exceeding 1 mg/L (Pinto *et al.,* 1976; Norin & Vahter, 1981). The seafood arsenic is apparently not metabolized to inorganic arsenic or to MMA or DMA to any large extent. Thus, the urinary excretion of inorganic arsenic, together with MMA and DMA, primarily reflects the exposure to inorganic arsenic.

Workers exposed to high levels of inorganic arsenic in air have increased urinary concentrations of inorganic arsenic, as well as of MMA and DMA (Smith *et al.,* 1977). The total arsenic concentration in urine has often been used to assess occupational exposure to arsenic (Carlsson, 1976; Kodoma *et al.,* 1976; Pinto *et al.,* 1977). In some situations, the levels may exceed 1 mg As/L urine. If total urinary arsenic is used to monitor exposure to inorganic arsenic, seafood consumption should be avoided during two or three days prior to sampling.

Hair

Inorganic arsenic has a special affinity for hair and other keratin-rich tissues. Arsenic in hair can arise from incorporation into the hair root and from external contamination. The firm binding of arsenic to hair makes it virtually impossible to remove external arsenic contamination by washing techniques (Atalla *et al.,* 1965).

The level of arsenic in hair is usually below 1 mg/kg (Smith, 1964). A log-normal distribution of arsenic concentrations in hair has been reported from Scotland, where the median levels ranged from about 0.1–0.5 mg/kg (Liebscher & Smith, 1968).

If external contamination is negligible, the hair content of arsenic can be used as an indicator of absorbed arsenic. Furthermore, the concentration along the length of the hair show the exposure over a period of time (Pearson & Pounds, 1971). Arsenic levels in hair may reach several tens of milligrams per kg following medication with inorganic arsenic compounds or ingestion of arsenic-rich water (Pearson & Pounds, 1971; Harrington *et al.,* 1978).

Occupational exposure may give rise to arsenic concentrations in hair reaching several hundreds of milligrams per kg (Atalla *et al.,* 1965; Leslie & Smith, 1978). Because of the difficulties encountered in determining external contamination, hair is often of limited value as an indicator of absorbed arsenic in exposed workers.

Other tissues

As a rule, the arsenic levels in blood of subjects without excessive exposure lie below 0.01 mg/kg (Brune *et al.,* 1966; Bencko & Symon, 1977). Increased concentrations in blood may be found in smokers (Kagey *et al.,* 1977), in exposed workers (Yamamura & Yamauchi, 1976) and in patients with chronic renal failure (Bergström & Wester, 1966). The short biological half-life of arsenic in blood limits its usefulness as a biological indicator of exposure.

The concentration of arsenic in most tissues normally does not exceed 0.05 mg/kg (Larsen *et al.,* 1972; Brune *et al.,* 1980). Among deceased smelter workers, increased levels have been observed in the lung, but not in liver or kidney (Brune *et al.,* 1980). Uraemic patients have high arsenic levels in some tissues (Larsen *et al.,* 1972; Pershagen *et al.,* 1982), probably as a result of reduced renal clearance.

BIOLOGICAL AND GENOTOXIC EFFECTS

Non-carcinogenic effects

Inorganic arsenic compounds can cause acute toxic effects in a large number of organs. Some incidents of accidental mass poisonings have occurred, and give a good picture of the diversity of acute and sub-acute effects following exposure to comparatively high doses of arsenic. In 1900, several thousand people were intoxicated by arsenic-containing beer in Manchester, UK (Reynolds, 1901). The arsenic content of the beer was 1.5–3 mg/L (type of compound unknown). Two mass poisonings took place in Japan in the 1950's. In one instance, about 12 000 infants were fed dry milk containing 15–24 mg/kg of arsenic which was reported to be in a pentavalent inorganic form (Hamamoto, 1955; Nakagawa & Iibuchi, 1970). In the other instance, more than 400 people were poisoned by soy-sauce containing 100 mg As/L (Mizuta *et al.,* 1956). The form of the arsenic was not determined, but the original contaminant was probably calcium arsenate.

Gastrointestinal symptoms were common in the intoxicated subjects. Enlargement of the liver was often seen and, in cases of fatal poisoning among the infants, haemmorhagic necrosis sometimes occurred. Reversible changes in the electrocardiogram and in bone marrow function were also encountered. Peripheral neurological symptoms of both sensory and motor type developed some weeks after initial exposure. Hyperpigmentation of the skin occurred in some cases, as well as transverse white lines across the nails (Mees' lines).

Chronic effects after exposure to arsenic have also been reported in many different organ systems, often the same as those where acute effects are seen. Characteristic wart-like skin lesions of the palms and soles (palmoplantar hyperkeratosis) have been observed in workers exposed to pesticides containing inorganic arsenic, as well as in subjects exposed *via* drinking water or drugs (Perry *et al.,* 1948; Fierz, 1965; Tseng *et al.,* 1968; Wolf, 1974; Hamada & Horiguchi, 1976). As a rule, these lesions are first seen after about two years of exposure, indicating that a minimum total dose of about 0.5–1 g of arsenic is needed.

Occupational exposure to irritant arsenic compounds in air, e.g., arsenic trioxide, may give rise to lesions in the upper respiratory tract (Pinto & McGill, 1953; Lundgren, 1954; Mabuchi *et al.*, 1980). Rhinitis, pharyngitis and laryngitis have been observed in smelter workers and pesticide production workers, exposed primarily to inorganic arsenic compounds. If the exposure is high, nasal septum perforation may develop within two or three weeks.

Portal hypertension without liver cirrhosis has been reported in patients treated with potassium arsenite (Fowler's solution) over several years (Neale & Azzopardi, 1971; Morris *et al.*, 1974; Knolle *et al.*, 1974; Huet *et al.*, 1975; Szuler *et al.*, 1979; Cowlishaw *et al.*, 1979). Liver cirrhosis has also been attributed to medication with inorganic arsenic compounds (Franklin *et al.*, 1950), but the data are not conclusive (Zachariae *et al.*, 1974). An increased mortality from liver cirrhosis has been reported in arsenic-exposed smelter and vineyard workers (Roth, 1957; Lee & Fraumeni, 1969; Axelson *et al.*, 1978). This has not been verified in other occupational groups and a confounding effect of heavy alcohol consumption cannot be ruled out among the vineyard workers.

Disturbances of the peripheral vascular system, sometimes leading to gangrene, have been described in vineyard workers and in people exposed to arsenic in drinking water in Chile and Taiwan (Tseng *et al.*, 1968; Grobe, 1976; Borgono *et al.*, 1977). Similar effects have not been reported in US populations with increased levels of arsenic in drinking water (Harrington *et al.*, 1978; Southwick *et al.*, 1980). However, the average arsenic concentrations were lower than in Chile and Taiwan, and it is also probable that the US populations were less dependent on drinking water from local sources. An increased mortality from cardiovascular diseases has been observed in some epidemiological studies on smelter workers exposed to arsenic (Lee & Fraumeni, 1969; Axelson *et al.*, 1978), but this has not been confirmed in other studies.

Effects on the central nervous system, e.g., encephalopathy, may be induced by both inorganic and organic arsenic compounds. This has been reported following the mass poisoning of infants in Japan described above, as well as in patients treated with organic arsenicals, e.g., tryparsamide (Ohira & Aoyama, 1972; Sina *et al.*, 1977). Peripheral neurological disturbances have been noted after long term exposure to inorganic arsenic compounds in the workplace, *via* drugs or in drinking water (Tay & Seah, 1975; Hindmarsh *et al.*, 1977; Feldman *et al.*, 1979). The symptoms are often similar to those reported following short-term exposure.

Excessive exposure to inorganic arsenic compounds, e.g., in drinking water, may give rise to disturbed erythropoiesis, with anemia, as well as to granulocytopenia (Terada *et al.*, 1962; Kyle & Pease, 1965; Feussner *et al.*, 1979). As a rule, the bone marrow disturbance is reversible by adequate therapy or if exposure is terminated.

Carcinogenic effects

As early as 1888, Hutchinson associated inorganic arsenic medication with skin cancer. Ever since, numerous reports have linked arsenic exposure to the development of tumours of the lung and skin. An intriguing feature has been that most attempts to induce tumours in laboratory animals have failed. Some experimental data indicated that inorganic trivalent and pentavalent arsenic compounds could play a role in the induction of carcinomas of the respiratory tract (Ishinishi *et al.,* 1977; Ivankovic *et al.,* 1979; Ishinishi *et al.,* 1980) but strong evidence was not obtained until recently (Pershagen *et al.,* 1984). An animal model for arsenic-induced skin cancer has not yet been developed.

An increased lung cancer mortality has occurred among workers engaged in the production of pesticides containing inorganic arsenic compounds (Hill & Faning, 1948; Ott *et al.,* 1974; Mabuchi *et al.,* 1979). Both trivalent and pentavalent arsenic compounds have been used in the production processes, e.g., calcium arsenate, lead arsenate and sodium arsenite. The spraying of such compounds in vineyards has also been associated with lung cancer (Roth, 1958; Galy *et al.,* 1963), but negative findings for this type of exposure have been published as well (Nelson *et al.,* 1973).

Copper smelter workers exposed to arsenic have been shown to experience an increased risk of lung cancer (Lee & Fraumeni, 1969; Tokudome & Kuratsune, 1976; Pinto *et al.,* 1977; Rencher *et al.,* 1977; Wall, 1980). Positive dose-response relationships have often been obtained. A recent study showed that arsenic exposure and tobacco smoking had a multiplicative interaction in relation to lung cancer in workers at a Swedish copper smelter (Pershagen *et al.,* 1981).

Exposure to arsenic in ambient air has been considered to be a possible causative agent for lung cancer. Four epidemiological studies on populations living near point sources of emission of arsenic to air have revealed moderate increases in lung cancer mortalities (Blot & Fraumeni, 1975; Newman *et al.,* 1976; Matanoski *et al.,* 1976; Pershagen *et al.,* 1977). It is not possible to assess the role of arsenic in this excess mortality.

Skin tumours have been observed after long-term exposure to inorganic arsenic compounds, *via* both medication and drinking water (Fierz, 1965; Tseng *et al.,* 1968). There are also reports of skin cancer among workers engaged in the production of arsenical pesticides and among vineyard workers (Hill & Faning, 1948; Wolf, 1974). Both basal cell carcinomas (often multiple) and squamous cell carcinomas may develop. Neither of these tumours possesses any unique histological features when attributed to arsenic (Morton *et al.,* 1976; Sanderson, 1976). As a rule, the carcinomas appear only after ingestion of a total dose of several grams of arsenic, often with latency times of ten years or more.

Angiosarcoma (or haemangioendothelioma) of the liver has been associated with arsenic exposure *via* contaminated wine, drinking water or drugs (Roth, 1957; Rosset, 1958; Regelson *et al.,* 1968; Rennke *et al.,* 1971; Lander *et al.,* 1975; Popper *et al.,* 1978). Only case reports of this rare tumour exist; however, the evidence is highly suggestive of an etiological role for arsenic.

Two epidemiological studies of workers exposed to inorganic arsenic compounds have shown an increased mortality from cancer of the lymphatic and haematopoietic systems (Ott *et al.,* 1974; Axelson *et al.,* 1978). The numbers are small and there is no supporting evidence from other instances of exposure to inorganic arsenic compounds.

Genotoxic effects

The genotoxic effects of arsenic have been studied in several experimental systems. Inorganic arsenic is apparently not mutagenic in bacterial tests (Löfroth & Ames, 1978; Rossman *et al.*, 1980), although some conflicting evidence exists (Nishioka, 1975). There are indications, both in bacteria and in human cells, that arsenic may interfere with DNA repair mechanisms, raising the possibility of a cocarcinogenic effect (Jung, 1971; Rossman *et al.*, 1977).

An increased frequency of chromosomal aberrations has been observed in workers exposed to inorganic arsenic compounds, as well as in patients taking drugs containing arsenic (Petres *et al.*, 1977; Nordenson *et al.*, 1978, 1979). An elevated sister chromatid exchange (SCE) rate was observed in one study of patients treated with potassium arsenite (Burgdorf *et al.*, 1977), but not in another (Nordenson *et al.*, 1979). A higher frequency of SCE has been reported in patients with gangrene following ingestion of drinking water with high arsenic concentrations (Wen *et al.*, 1981). In-vitro experiments show that inorganic arsenic, especially in the trivalent state, can induce both chromosomal aberrations and SCE (Oppenheim & Fishbein, 1965; Paton & Allison, 1972; Petres *et al.*, 1977; Zanzoni & Jung, 1980; Nakamuro & Sayato, 1981; Nordenson *et al.*, 1981; Andersen *et al.*, 1982; Wan *et al.*, 1982). No data are available concerning this type of effect following treatment with organic arsenic compounds.

REFERENCES

Andersen, O., Wulf, H., Rönne, M. & Nordberg, G. (1982) Effects of metals on sister chromatid exchange in human lymphocytes and Chinese hamster V 79-E cells. *ILO Occuo. Saf. Health Ser.*, *46*, 491–501

Argüello, R.A., Cenget, D.D. & Tello, E.E. (1938) Cancer and endemic arsenism in the Cordoba Region. *Rev. Argent. Dermatosifilogr.*, *22*, 461–487

Atalla, L.T., Silva, C.M. & Lima, F.W. (1965) Activation analysis of arsenic in human hair–some observations on the problem of external contamination. *Ann. Acad. Bras. Cienc.*, *37*, 431–441

Attrep, M., Jr & Anirudhan, M. (1977) Atmospheric inorganic and organic arsenic. *Trace Subst. Environ. Health, 11*, 365–369

Axelson, O., Dahlgren, E., Jansson, C.-D. & Rehnlund, S.O. (1978) Arsenic exposure and mortality: A case-referent study from a Swedish copper smelter. *Br. J. Ind. Med., 35*, 8–15

Bailey, E.J., Kennaway, E.L. & Urquhart, M.E. (1957) Arsenic content of cigarettes. *Br. J. Cancer, 11*, 49–53

Bencko, V. & Symon, K. (1977) Health aspects of burning coal with a high arsenic content. *Environ. Res., 13*, 378–385

Bergström, J. & Wester, P.O. (1966) *The effects of dialysis on the arsenic content of blood ans muscle tissue from uraemic patients.* In: Kerr, D.D.S., Fraeger, J., Friends, D. & Elliott, R.W., eds, *Replacement of Renal Function,* Amsterdam, Excerpta Medica Foundation (International Congress Series No. 131), pp. 38–40

Blot, W.J. & Fraumeni, J.F., Jr (1975) Arsenical air pollution and lung cancer. *Lancet, ii,* 142–144

Borgono, J.M., Vincent, P., Venturino, H. & Infante, A. (1977) Arsenic in the drinking water of the city of Antofagasta: Epidemiological and clinical study before and after the installation of the treatment plant. *Environ. Health Perspect., 19,* 103–105

Braman, R.S. & Foreback, C.C. (1973) Methylated forms of arsenic in the environment. *Science, 182,* 1247–1249

Braman, R.S., Johnson, D.L., Foreback, C.C., Ammons, J.M. & Bricker, J.L. (1977) Separation and determination of nanogram amounts of inorganic arsenic and methylarsenic compounds. *Anal. Chem., 49,* 621–625

Brune, D., Samsahl, K. & Wester, P.O. (1966) A comparison between the amounts of As, Au, Br, Cu, Fe, Mo, Se and Zn in normal and uraemic human whole blood by means of neutron activation analysis. *Clin. Chim. Acta, 13,* 285–291

Brune, D., Nordberg, G. & Wester, P.O. (1980) Distribution of 23 elements in the kidney, liver and lungs of workers from a smeltery and refinery in North Sweden exposed to a number of elements and of a control group. *Sci. Total Environ., 16,* 13–35

Buchet, J.P., Lauwerys, R.R. & Roels, H. (1981) Comparison of the urinary excretion of arsenic metabolites after a single oral dose of sodium arsenite, monomethyl arsonate or dimethylarsinate in man. *Int. Arch. Occup. Environ. Health, 48,* 71–79

Burgdorf, W., Kurvink, K. & Cervenka, J. (1977) Elevated sister chromatid exchange rate in lymphocytes of subjects treated with arsenic. *Hum. Genet., 36,* 69–72

Calvert, C.C. (1975) *Arsenicals in animal feeds and wastez.* In: Woolson, E.A., ed., *Arsenical Pesticides,* Washington, DC, American Chemical Society, pp. 70–80

Cannon, J., Edmonds, J., Francesconi, K., Raston, C.L., Saunders, J., Skelton, B. & White, A. (1981) Isolation, chrystal structure and synthesis of arsenobetaine, a constituent of the western rock lobster, dusky shark and some samples of human urine. *Aust. J. Chem., 34,* 878

Carlsson, G. (1976) Correlation between industrial arsenic exposure and excretion in urine. Examination Report [in Swedish]. Stockholm, The National Board of Industrial Safety, Dept. of Occupational Health

Cmarko, V. (1963) Hygienic problems of arsenic exhalations of ENO plant. *Cesk. Hyg., 8,* 359–362

Cowlishaw, J.L., Pollard, E.J., Cowen, A.E. & Powell, L.W. (1979) Liver disease associated with chronic arsenic ingestion. *Aust. N.Z. J. Med., 9,* 310–313

Crecelius, E.A. (1974) *The Geochemistry of Arsenic and Antimony in Puget Sound and Lake Washington, Washington.* Thesis, University of Washington, Seattle, Washington, USA

Crecelius, E.A. (1977a) Changes in the chemical speciation of arsenic following ingestion by man. *Environ. Health Perspect., 19,* 147–150

Crecelius, E.A. (1977b) Arsenite and arenate levels in wine. *Bull. Environ. Contam. Toxicol., 18,* 227–230

Crecelius, E.A., Robertson, D.E., Fruchter, J.S. & Ludwick, J.D. (1976) *Chemical forms of mercury and arsenic emitted by a geothermal power plant.* In: Hemphill,

D.D., ed., *Trace Substances in Environmental Health,* University of Missouri Press, pp. 187–293

Edmonds, J.S., Francesconi, K.A., Cannon, J.R., Raston, C.L., Skelton, B.W. & White, A.H. (1977) Isolation, crystal structure and synthesis of arsenobetaine, the arsenical constituent of the western rock lobster Panulirus Longipes Cygnus George. *Tetrahedron Lett., 18,* 1543–1546

Feldman, R.G., Niles, C.A., Kelly-Hayes, M., Sax, D.S., Dixon, W.J., Thompson, D.J. & Landu, E. (1979) Peripheral neuropathy in arsenic smelter workers. *Neurology, 29,* 939–944

Feussner, J.R., Shelburne, J.D., Bredehoeft, S. & Cohen, H.J. (1979) Arsenic-induced bone marrow toxicity: Ultrastructural and electron probe analysis. *Blood, 53,* 820–827

Fierz, U. (1965) Catamnestic research into the side effects of inorganic arsenotherapy in skin diseases. *Dermatologica, 131,* 41–58

Fishbein, L. (1981) Sources, transport and alterations of metal compounds. An overview. *Environ. Health Perspect., 40,* 43–64

Franklin, M., Bean, W.B. & Hardin, R.C. (1950) Fowler's solution as an etiologic agent in cirrhosis. *Am. J. Med. Sci., 219,* 589–596

Galy, P., Touraine, R., Brune, J., Roudier, P. & Gallois, P. (1963) Le cancer pulmonaire d'origine arsenicale des vignerons du Beaujolais. *J. Fr. Med. Chir. Thorac., 17,* 3303–3311

Goldblatt, E.L., Vandenburgh, A.S. & Marsland, R.A. (1963) *The Usual and Widespread Occurrence of Arsenic in Well Waters of Lane County, Oregon.* Oregon Department of Health, USA

Gonzalez, E.E. (1963) Intoxication colectiva por arsenico en Torreon, Coah, Mexico. *Bol. Epidemiol., 27,* 213

Goodman, L. & Gilman, A. (1955) *The pharmacological basis of therapeutics.* New York, The MacMillan Company, pp. 948–969

Grobe, J.W. (1976) Peripheral circulatory disorders and acrocyanosis in Moselle valley vineyard workers with arsenic poisoning. *Berufsdermatosen, 24,* 78–84

Hamada, T. & Horiguchi, S. (1976) Occupational chronic arsenical poisoning. On the cutaneous manifestations. *Jpn. J. Ind. Health, 18,* 103–115

Hamamoto, E. (1955) Infant arsenic poisoning by powdered milk. *Nihon Iji Shimpo, 1649,* 3–12

Harrington, J.M., Middaugh, J.P., Morse, D.L. & Housworth, J. (1978) A survey of a population exposed to high concentrations of arsenic in well water in Fairbanks, Alaska. *Am. J. Epidemiol., 108,* 377–385

Hill, A.B. & Faning, E.L. (1948) Studies in the incidence of cancer in a factory handling inorganic compounds of arsenic. I. Mortality experience in the factory. *Br. J. Ind. Med., 5,* 1–6

Hindmarsh, J.T., McLetchie, O.R., Heffernan, L.P.M., Hayne, O.A., Ellenberger, H.A., McCurdy, R.F. & Thiebaux, H.J. (1977) Electromyographic abnormalities in chronic environmental arsenicalism. *J. Anal. Toxicol., 1,* 270–276

Holland, R.H. & Acevedo, A.R. (1966) Current status of arsenic in American cigarettes. *Cancer, 19,* 1248–1250

Huet, P.-M., Guillaume, E., Cote, J., Legare, A., Lavoie, P. & Viallet, A. (1975) Noncirrhotic presinusoidal portal hypertension associated with chronic arsenic intoxication. *Gastroenterology, 68,* 1270–1277

Ishinishi, N., Kodama, Y., Nobutomo, K. & Hisanaga, A. (1977) Preliminary experimental study on carcinogenicity of arsenic trioxide in rat lung. *Environ. Health Perspect., 19,* 191–196

Ishinishi, N., Mizunoe, M., Inamasu, T. & Hisanaga, A. (1980) Experimental study on carcinogenicity of beryllium oxide and arsenic trioxide to the lung of rats by an intratracheal instillation. *Fukuoka Acta Med., 71,* 19–26

Ivankovic, S., Eisenbrand, G. & Preussmann, R. (1979) Lung carcinoma induction in BD rats after single intratracheal instillation of an arsenic-containing pesticide mixture formerly used in vineyards. *Int. J. Cancer, 24,* 786–789

Jelinek, C.F. & Corneluissen, P.E. (1977) Levels of arsenic in the US food supply. *Environ. Health Perspect., 19,* 83–87

Jernelöv, A., Hultberg, H. & Rosenblum, I. (1976) The geothermal plant at Ahuachapan in El Salvador and its possible effects on the water quality on the border river Rio Paz between El Salvador and Guatemala. Institute for Water and Air Pollution, Stockholm

Johnson, D.L. & Braman, R.S. (1975) Alkyl- and inorganic arsenic in air samples. *Chemosphere, 6,* 333–338

Jung, E. (1971) Research in the molecular biology of arsenism. *Z. Haut. Geschlechtskr., 46,* 35–36

Kagey, B.T., Bumharner, J.E. & Creason, J.P. (1977) *Arsenic levels in maternal-fetal tissue sets.* In: Hemphill, D.D., ed., *Trace Substances in Environmental Health XI. A Symposium.* Columbia, University of Missouri Press, pp. 252–256

Knolle, J., Förster, E., Rössner, A., Themann, H., Höhn, P. & Meyer zum Buschenfelde, K.-H. (1974) Non-cirrhotic portal fibrosis (hepatoportal sclerosis) following arsenism. *Dtsch. Med. Wochenscr., 99,* 903–908

Kodama, Y., Ishinishi, N., Kunitake, E., Inamasu, T. & Nobutomo, K. (1976) *Subclinical signs of exposure to arsenic in a copper refinery.* In: Nordberg, G.F., ed., *Effects and Dose-response Relationships of Toxic Metals,* Amsterdam, Elsevier Scientific Publishing Company, pp. 464–470

Kuo, T. (1968) Arsenic content of artesian well water in endemic area of chronic arsenic poisoning. *Rep. Inst. Pathol. natl Taiwan Univ., 20,* 7–13

Kyle, R.A. & Pease, G.L. (1965) Hematologic aspects of arsenic intoxication. *New Engl. J. Med., 273,* 18–23

Lander, J.J., Stanely, R.J., Sumner, H.W., Boswell, D.C. & Aach, R.D. (1975) Angiosarcoma of the liver associated with Fowler's solution (potassium arsenite). *Gastroenterology, 68,* 1582–1586

Lantzy, K. & MacKenzie, F. (1979) Atmospheric trace metals. Global cycles and assessment of man's impact. *Geochim. Cosmochim. Acta, 43,* 511–525

Larsen, N.A., Nielsen, B., Pakkenberg, H., Christoffersen, P., Damsgaard, E. & Heydorn, K. (1972) *Neutron activation analysis of arsenic, manganese and selenium concentrations in organs of uraemic and normal persons.* In: Kripper, M., ed., *Proceedings of a Symposium (IAEA-SM-157/4),* Bled, Yugoslavia, pp. 561–568

Ledet, A.E., Duncan, J.R., Buck, W.B. & Ramsey, F.K. (1973) Clinical, toxicological and pathological aspects of arsanilic acid poisoning in swine. *Clin. Toxicol., 6,* 439–457

Lee, A.M. & Fraumeni, J.F., Jr (1969) Arsenic and respiratory cancer in man: An occupational study. *J. natl Cancer Inst., 42,* 1045–1052

Leslie, A.C.D. & Smith, H. (1978) Self-poisoning by the abuse of arsenic containing tonics. *Med. Sci. Law, 18,* 159–162

Liebscher, K. & Smith, H. (1968) Essential and non-essential trace elements. A method of determining whether an element is essential or non-essential in human tissue. *Arch. Environ. Health, 17,* 881–890

Lindau, L. (1977) Emissions of arsenic in Sweden and their reduction. *Environ. Health Perspect., 19,* 25–29

Lunde, G. (1977) Occurrence and transformation of arsenic in the marine environment. *Environ. Health Perspect., 19,* 47–52

Lundgren, J.D. (1954) Damages in the respiratory organs of workers at a smeltery. *Nord. Hyg. Tidskr., 3,* 66–82

Löfroth, G. & Ames, B.N. (1978) Mutagenicity of inorganic compounds in *Salmonella typhimurium:* Arsenic, chromium and selenium. *Mutat. Res., 54,* 65–66

Mabuchi, K., Lilienfeld, A.M. & Snell, L.M. (1979) Lung cancer among pesticide workers exposed to inorganic arsenicals. *Arch. Environ. Health, 34,* 312–319

Mabuchi, K., Lilienfeld, A.M. & Snell, L.M. (1980) Cancer and occupational exposure to arsenic: A study of pesticide workers. *Prev. Med., 9,* 51–77

Matanoski, G., Landau, E. & Elliott, E. (1976) *Epidemiology Studies. Task I. Pilot Study of Cancer Mortality near an Arsenical Pesticide Plant in Baltimore.* Washington, DC., Environmental Protection Agency

McCabe, L.J., Symons, J.M., Lee, R.D. & Robeck, G.G. (1970) Survey of community water supply systems. *J. Am. Water Works Assoc., 62,* 670–687

Mizuta, N., Mizuta, M., Ito, F., Ito, T., Uchida, H., Watanabe, Y., Akama, H., Murakami, T., Hayashi, F., Nakamura K., Yamaguchi, T., Mizuia, W., Oishi, S. & Matsumura, H. (1956) An outbreak of acute arsenic poisoning caused by arsenic contaminated soysauce (shoyu): A clinical report of 220 cases. *Bull. Yamaguchi Med. Sch., 4,* 131–150

Morris, J.S., Schmid, M., Newman, S., Scheuer, P.J. & Sherlock, S. (1974) Arsenic and noncirrhotic portal hypertension. *Gastroenterology, 6,* 86–94

Morton, W., Starr, G., Pohl, D., Stoner, J., Wagner, S. & Weswig, P. (1976) Skin cancer and water arsenic in Lane County, Oregon. *Cancer, 37,* 2523–2532

Nakagawa, Y. & Iibuchi, Y. (1970) On the follow-up investigation of Morinaga milk arsenic poisoning. *Igaku no Ayumi, 74,* 1–3

Nakamuro, K. & Sayato, Y. (1981) Comparative studies of chromosomal aberration induced by trivalent and pentavalent arsenic. *Mutat. Res., 88,* 73–80

Nakao, M. (1960) A study on the arsenic content in daily food consumption in Japan. *Osaka City Med. J., 9,* 541–571

National Academy of Sciences (NAS) (1977) *Medical and Biologic Effects of Environmental Pollutants: Arsenic.* Washington DC

Nelson, W.C., Lykins, M.H., MacKey, J., Newill, V.A., Finklea, J.F. & Hammer, D.I. (1973) Mortality among orchard workers exposed to lead arsenate spray: A cohort study. *J. chron. Dis., 26,* 105–118

Nelson, K.W. (1977) Industrial contributions of arsenic to the environment. *Environ. Health Perspect., 19,* 31–34

Newman, J.A., Archer, V.E., Saccomanno, G., Kuschner, M., Auerbach, O., Grondahl, R.D. & Wilson, J.C. (1976) Occupational carcinogenesis. Histologic types of bronchogenic carcinoma among members of coppermining and smelting communities. *Ann. N.Y. Acad. Sci., 271,* 260–268

Nishioka, H. (1975) Mutagenic activities of metal compounds in bacteria. *Mutat. Res., 31,* 185–189

Noble, A.C., Orr, B.H., Cook, W.B. & Campbell, J.L. (1976) Trace element analysis of wine by proton-induced X-ray fluorescence spectrometry. *J. Agric. Food Chem., 24,* 532–535

Nordenson, I., Beckman, G., Beckman, L. & Nordström, S. (1978) Occupational and environmental risks in and around a smelter in northern Sweden. II. Chromosomal aberrations in workers exposed to arsenic. *Hereditas, 88,* 47–50

Nordenson, I., Salmonsson, S., Brun, E. & Beckman, G. (1979) Chromosome aberrations in psoriatic patients treated with arsenic. *Hum. Genet., 48,* 1–6

Nordenson, I., Sweins, A. & Beckman, L. (1981) Chromosomal aberrations in cultured human lymphocytes exposed to trivalent and pentavalent arsenic. *Scand. J. Work environ. Health, 7,* 277–281

Norin, H. (1983) Analysis of organic and inorganic arsenicals in biological material. Thesis, Department of Analytical Chemistry, University of Stockholm, and Department of Toxicology, Karolinska Institute, Stockholm

Norin, H. & Vahter, M. (1981) A rapid method for the selective analysis of total urinary metabolites of inorganic arsenic. *Scand. J. Work environ. Health, 7,* 38–44

Ohira, M. & Aoyama, H. (1972) Epidemiological studies on the Morinaga powdered milk poisoning incident. *Jpn. J. Hyg., 27,* 500–531

Oppenheim, J.J. & Fishbein, W.N. (1965) Induction of chromosome breaks in cultured normal human leukocytes by potassium arsenite, hydroxyurea and related compounds. *Cancer Res., 25,* 980–985

Ott, M.G., Holder, B.B. & Gordon, H.L. (1974) Respiratory cancer and occupational exposure to arsenicals. *Arch. Environ. Health, 29,* 250–255

Paton, G.R. & Allison, A.C. (1972) Chromosome damage in human cell cultures induced by metal salts. *Mutat. Res., 16,* 332–336

Pearson, E.F. & Pounds, C.A. (1971) A case involving the administration of known amounts of arsenic and its analysis in hair. *J. Forensic Sci. Soc., 11,* 229–234

Perry, K., Bowler, R.G., Buckell, H.H., Druett, H.A. & Shilling, R.S.F. (1948) Studies in the incidence of cancer in a factory handling inorganic compounds of arsenic. II. Clinical and environmental investigations. *Br. J. Ind. Med., 5,* 6–15

Pershagen, G., Elinder, C.-G. & Bolander, A.M. (1977) Mortality in a region surrounding an arsenic emitting plant. *Environ. Health Perspect., 19,* 133–137

Pershagen, G., Wall, S., Taube, A. & Linnman, L. (1981) On the interaction between occupational arsenic exposure and smoking and its relationship to lung cancer. *Scand. J. Work environ. Health, 7,* 302–309

Pershagen, G., Hast, R., Lins, L.-E. & Pehrsson, K. (1982) Increased arsenic concentration in the bone marrow in chronic renal failure – a contributor to anaemia? *Nephron, 30,* 250–252

Pershagen, G., Nordberg, G. & Björklund, N.-E. (1984) Carcinomas of the respiratory tract in hamsters given arsenic trioxide and/or benzo[a]pyrene by the pulmonary route. *Environ. Res., 34,* 227–241

Petres, J., Baron, D. & Hagedorn, M. (1977) Effects of arsenic cell metabolism and cell proliferation: Cytogenic and biochemical studies. *Environ. Health Perspect., 19,* 223–227

Pinto, S.S. & McGill, C.M. (1953) Arsenic trioxide exposure in industry. *Ind. Med. Surg., 22,* 281–287

Pinto, S.S., Varner, M.O., Nelson, K.W., Labbe, A.L. & White, L.D. (1976) Arsenic trioxide absorption and excretion in industry. *J. occup. Med., 18,* 677–680

Pinto, S.S., Enterline, P.E., Henderson, V. & Varner, M.O. (1977) Mortality experience in relation to a measured arsenic trioxide exposure. *Environ. Health Perspect., 19,* 127–130

Popper, H., Thomas, L.B., Telles, N.C., Falk, H. & Selikoff, I.J. (1978) Development of hepatitic angiosarcoma in man induced by vinyl chloride, thorotrast and arsenic. *Am. J. Pathol., 92,* 349–369

Regelson, W., Kim, U., Ospina, J. & Holland, J.F. (1968) Hemangioendothelial sarcoma of liver from chronic arsenic intoxication by Fowler's solution. *Cancer, 12,* 514–522

Rencher, A.C., Carter, M.W. & McKee, D.W. (1977) A retrospective epidemiological study of mortality at a large western copper smelter. *J. occup. Med., 19,* 754–758

Rennke, H., Prat, G.A., Etcheverry, R.B., Katz, R.U. & Donoso, S. (1971) Malignant hemangioendothelioma of the liver and chronic arsenicism. *Rev. Med. Chil., 99,* 664–668

Reynolds, E.S. (1901) An account of the epidemic outbreak of arsenical poisoning occurring in beer-drinkers in the north of England and the Midland counties in 1900. *Lancet, i,* 166–170

Rosehart, R.G. & Chu, R. (1975) Methods for identification of arsenic compounds. *Water Air Soil Pollut., 4,* 395–398

Rosset, M. (1958) Arsenical keratoses associated with carcinomas of the internal organs. *Can. Med. Assoc. J., 78,* 416–419

Rossman, T., Meyn, S. & Troll, W. (1977) Effects of arsenite on DNA repair in E. coli. *Environ. Health Perspect., 19,* 229–233

Rossman, T., Stone, D., Molina, M. & Troll, W. (1980) Absence of arsenite mutagenicity in E. coli and Chinese hamster cells. *Environ. Mut., 2,* 371–379

Roth, F. (1957) Arsenic-induced liver tumours (haemangio-endothelioma). *Z. Krebsforsch., 61,* 468–503

Roth, F. (1958) Bronchial cancer in vineyard workers with arsenic poisoning. *Virchows Arch., 331,* 119–137

Rozenshtein, I.S. (1970) Sanitary toxicological assessment of low concentrations of arsenic trioxide in the atmosphere. *Hyg. Sanit., 35,* 16–22

Sagner, G. (1973) Zur Toxikologie des Arsens im Trinkwasser. *Schriftenr. Ver. Wasser Boden Lufthyg., 40,* 189

Sanderson, K.V. (1976) *Arsenic and skin cancer.* In: Andrade, R., Gumport, S.L., Popkin, G.L. & Rees, T.D., eds, *Cancer of the Skin,* Philadelphia, London, Toronto, W.B. Saunder Company, pp. 473–491

Sina, G., Triolo, N., Trova, P. & Clabaut, J.M. (1977) L'encephalopathie arsenicale lors du traitement de la trypanosomiase humaine africaine a T. Gambiense (à propos de 16 cas). *Ann. Soc. Belg. Med. Trop., 57,* 67–74

Smith, H. (1964) The interpretation of the arsenic content of human hair. *Forensic Sci. Soc. J., 4,* 192–199

Smith, T.J., Eatough, D.J., Hansen, L.D. & Mangelsen, N.F. (1976) The chemistry of sulfur and arsenic in airborne copper smelter particulates. *Bull. Environ. Contam. Toxicol., 15,* 651–658

Smith, T.J., Crecelius, E.A. & Reading, J.C. (1977) Airborne arsenic exposure and excretion of methylated arsenic compounds. *Environ. Health Perspect; 19,* 89–93

Southwick, J., Western, A., Beck, M., Whitley, T., Isaacs, R., Petajan, J. & Hansen, C. (1980) Community health associated with arsenic in drinking water in Millard County, Utah. Health Effects Research Laboratory, Office of Research and Development, US Environmental Protection Agency, Cincinatti, Ohio

Szuler, I.M., Williams, C.N., Hindmarsch, J.T. & Park-Dincsoy, H. (1979) Massive variceal hemorrhage secondary to presinusoidal portal hypertension due to arsenic poisoning. *Can. Med. Assoc. J., 120,* 168–171

Tam, G.K.H., Charbonneau, S.M., Bryce, F., Pomroy, C. & Sandi, E. (1979) Metabolism of inorganic arsenic (^{74}As) in humans following oral ingestion. *Toxicol. appl. Pharmacol., 50,* 319–322

Tay, C.-H. & Seah, C.-S. (1975) Arsenic poisoning from anti-asthmatic herbal preparations. *Med. J. Aust., 2,* 424–428

Terada, H., Sasagawa, T., Saito, H., Shirata, H. & Sekiya, T. (1962) Chronic arsenical poisoning and hematopoietic organs. *Acta Med. Biol., 9,* 279–292

Thomas, M.D. & Collier, T.R. (1945) The concentration of arsenic in tobacco smoke determined by a rapid titrimetric method. *J. Ind. Hyg. Toxicol., 27,* 201–206

Tokudome, S. & Kuratsune, M. (1976) A cohort study on mortality from cancer and other causes among workers at a metal refinery. *Int. J. Cancer, 17,* 310–317

Tseng, W.-P., Chu, H.M., How, S.W., Fong, J.M., Lin, C.S. & Yeh, S. (1968) Prevalence of skin cancer in an endemic area of chronic arsenicism in Taiwan. *J. natl Cancer Inst., 40,* 453–463

US Bureau of Mines (1975) *Metals, minerals and fuels.* In: *Minerals Year-Book,* Washington DC, US Department of the Interior

Vahter, M. (1983) Metabolism of inorganic arsenic in relation to chemical form and animal species. Thesis, Departments of Toxicology and Environmental Hygiene, Karolinska Institute, Stockholm

Vondracek, V. (1963) Concentration of 3.4-benzpyrene and arsenic compounds in the Prague atmosphere. *Cesk. Hyg., 8,* 333–339

Wagner, S.L., Maliner, S.J., Morton, W.E. & Braman, R.S. (1979) Skin cancer and arsenical intoxication from well water. *Arch. Dermatol., 115,* 1205–1207

Walkiw, O. & Douglas, D.E. (1975) Health food supplements prepared from kelp – a source of elevated urinary arsenic. *Clin. Toxicol., 8,* 325–331

Wall, S. (1980) Survival and mortality pattern among Swedish smelter workers. *Int. J. Epidemiol., 9,* 73–87

Wan, B., Christian, R.T. & Soukup, S.W. (1982) Studies of cytogenetic effects of sodium arsenicals on mammalian cells *in vitro. Environ. Mut., 4,* 493–498

Wen, W.-N., Lieu, T., Chang, H.-J., Wuu, S.W., Yau, M.-L. & Jan, K.Y. (1981) Baseline and sodium arsenite-induced sister chromatid exchanges in cultured lymphocytes from patients with blackfoot disease and healthy persons. *Hum. Genet., 59,* 201–203

Wester, P.O. (1974) Trace element balances in relation to variations in calcium intake. *Atherosclerosis, 20,* 207–215

Westöö, G. & Rydälv, M. (1972) Arsenic levels in foods. *Var Föda, 24,* 21–40

Wolf, R. (1974) On the question of occupational arsenic poisoning in vineyard workers. *Berufsdermatosen, 22,* 34–47

Yamauchi, H. & Yamamura, Y. (1979a) Dynamic change of inorganic arsenic and methylarsenic compounds in human urine after oral intake as arsenic trioxide. *Ind. Health, 17,* 79–83

Yamauchi, H. & Yamamura, Y. (1979b) Urinary inorganic arsenic and methylarsenic excretion following arsenate-rich seaweed ingestion. *Jpn. J. Ind. Health, 21,* 47–54

Yamamura, Y. & Yamauchi, H. (1976) Arsenic in biological samples of workers exposed to arsenic trioxide. *Jpn. J. Ind. Health, 18,* 530–531

Zachariae, H., Sogaard, H. & Nyfors, A. (1974) Liver biopsy in psoriatics previously treated with potassium arsenite. *Acta Derm. Venreol.* (Stockholm), **54,** 235–236

Zanzoni, F. & Jung, E.G. (1980) Arsenic elevates the sister chromatid exchange (SCE) rate in human lymphocytes *in vitro. Arch. Dermatol. Res., 267,* 91–95

CHAPTER 4

SOURCES OF EXPOSURE AND BIOLOGICAL EFFECTS OF CHROMIUM

R.F. Hertel

*Fraunhofer-Institute for Toxicology and Aerosol Research, Nikolai-Fuchs-Str. 1,
D-3000 Hannover 61, FRG*

INTRODUCTION

This chapter will describe the occurrence and the sources of exposure to chromium, and will briefly outline the penetration and metabolism of the different forms of Cr in the human organism, as well as their physiological and toxicological effects.

Chromium is ubiquitous in nature and can occur in a number of oxidation states from -2 to $+6$. The physiological action of Cr depends on the oxidation state, as well as on the chemical and physical form.

It is not proven that metallic Cr has adverse physiological effects. Cr[II] is unstable under physiological conditions, and easily oxidized to Cr[III]; Cr[IV], used as the dioxide in magnetic tapes, has sensitizing effects; Cr[V] intermediates have been shown to persist for over 1 h *in vitro* and it is therefore hypothesized that they may play a role in carcinogenicity (Wetterhahn, 1982).

Cr[III] and Cr[VI], however, are agreed to be the most important oxidation states with regard to human health: Cr[III] is considered to be an essential element in nutrition, while some forms of Cr[VI] are recognized to be carcinogenic.

OCCURRENCE

Natural sources

Chromium is widely distributed and is found in concentrations up to 0.1 μg/m³ in air and up to 0.4% in soils. In natural deposits, it is almost always present in the metallic or the trivalent oxidation state.

The concentration of Cr in rocks varies from an average of 5 mg/kg (granitic rocks) to 1 800 mg/kg (ultramafic and serpentine rocks). The major sources of the world's chromium supplies are the ultra basic rocks of Rhodesia, South Africa, Turkey and the USSR. The high Cr concentration in phosphorites in sedimentary rocks is of agricultural importance as phosphate fertilizer. Chromium can also be found in coal (5–20 mg/kg, Merian, 1984). Small occurrence of Cr [VI] deposits (crocoite $PbCrO_4$) in the Ural mountains were described by Lomonossow in 1793 (Hintze, 1930).

The weathering of rocks produces soluble Cr[III] complexes in soils. Only a fraction of the complexes are available to the plant, but the amount available is relatively independent of the total concentration. In most soils, Cr occurs in low concentrations (about 50 mg/kg) and several regions, e.g., in Europe, are considered to be Cr-deficient (Mertz, 1969), since crop yields and quality improve when Cr is added to the soil, but the effects may require interactions with other elements or agents. The geographical distribution of Cr levels in water suggests that, except for areas with substantial Cr deposits, higher Cr concentrations arise from industrial sources. Sea water contains less than 1 µg/L. The natural sources of chromium in air are forest fires and volcanic eruptions. In the air of non-industrialized areas, Cr concentrations are less than 0.1 µg/m^3. Man-made sources include many types of emissions (e.g., combustion of coal or oil, cement production, ferrochromium refining, etc.).

A significant source of Cr for animals and humans is food intake. All plants contain the element, which is taken up by roots or leaves. Plants growing in Cr-containing nutrient solutions retain most of the Cr in the roots. Only chelated Cr compounds, if any, seem to be translocated from the site of absorption. The Cr content of plants growing on normal soils ranges up to 0.2 mg/kg wet weight. In three different kinds of grasses, Kirchgessner *et al.* (1960) found strong seasonal variations in the Cr levels, the highest content being 590 µg/kg dry weight in hay. The Cr content of meat (beef, pork, chicken) ranges from 10–60 µg/kg wet weight (Koivistoinen, 1980).

Urban and industrial waste

In sewage-treatment plants, Cr is found in substantial amounts. For example, the total daily Cr burden for New York City is 676 kg (Klein *et al.,* 1974). In Los Angeles, USA, waste water, the final discharge from the plant (mixture of primary and secondary effluent with digested sludge) represents a significant source of contamination (200 µg Cr/L). Waste waters from Cr industries may contain Cr levels up to 50 g/L (Cr-plating industry, Cheremisinoff & Habib, 1972). After reduction of Cr[VI] to Cr[III] in acid solution, the waste is precipitated, collected in settling ponds and disposed of by landfill, incineration or dumping in the ocean (US-EPA, 1980). In the leachate from a simulated landfill, Pholand (1975) did not detect measurable concentrations of Cr. The solubility of Cr in sewage sludge depends on the properties of the soil and climatic conditions; thus very slow rates of disappearance are reported (7% within 8 years), as well as high values (75% within 3 years). The energy necessary to oxidize Cr[III] to Cr[VI] has not been demonstrated to be available in living matter, thus nearly all Cr[VI] in the environment is man-made. The industrial use of Cr did not begin until 1816 (US-EPA, 1978).

Occupational exposure

The US National Institute for Occupational Safety and Health estimated in 1975 that there were 175 000 workers in the US who were potentially exposed to hexavalent chromium and listed 104 occupations in which such exposure could occur. In 1973, it was estimated that 15 000 workers in the US were potentially exposed to Cr[VI] trioxide mist.

Chromium and its compounds are found in three main types of industrial activity: (i) most chromium derivatives are used in the metallurgical industry (about 76% of total consumption), particularly in relation to the production and use of ferrochromium alloys and stainless steel; (ii) chromium compounds are also an important component of refractory materials, such as bricks, glass, ceramics and certain ferrous metals; and (iii) many of the highly-coloured chromate salts of various metals are used in the pigment, paint, tanning and dyeing industries.

To indicate the occupational exposures in various industries, the average airborne Cr[VI] concentrations ($\mu g/m^3$) are given below (low: high) (after Stern, 1982).

Stainless steel welding (50:400), chromate production (100:500), chrome plating, old plants (50:1000) new plants (5:25), ferro-chrome (10:140), chrome pigment (60:600), tanning (10:50, as Cr[III] only).

The standards for industrial exposure to Cr[VI] in various countries range between 100 and 50 $\mu g/m^3$ air and depend on the compounds (see chapter 9, Table 1); a standard for domestic water supply is 50 μg Cr[VI]/L.

BIOLOGICAL AND TOXIC EFFECTS

Physiology

Trivalent Cr occurs in biological materials and is the only physiologically active form of the metal. It was found to be an essential component of the 'glucose tolerance factor' (GTF) (Schwarz & Mertz, 1959). Brewer's yeast, an excellent source of GTF, was used to correct impaired glucose tolerance in rats which had been fed a Cr-deficient (Torula yeast) diet (Mertz & Schwartz, 1959). These experiments and subsequent studies led to the acceptance of Cr as an essential trace element for human and animal nutrition. The biological availability of Cr in food is of great importance, but poorly understood. In several areas of the world, dietary chromium deficiency is believed to be a serious problem. The nutritional Cr requirement, exclusively Cr[III], is several orders of magnitude below chronic toxic levels, which are mainly caused by Cr[VI] compounds.

The normal route of entry for physiologically essential Cr is the gastrointestinal tract. Uptake through the skin occurs (mainly in several occupational groups) as a pathological chronic toxic effect. In the general population, contact with Cr or with Cr-treated objects can cause skin sensitization. The most important route of entry in occupational exposure is by inhalation.

Absorption from the gastrointestinal tract has been reviewed by Mertz (1969), Saner (1980) and Guthrie (1982). The daily Cr intake with food ranges between 30 and 200 μg. The absorption efficiency for ingested Cr compounds is influenced by variables such as oxidation state, physico-chemical form and water solubility, and by numerous biological factors (acidity and ionic milieu, passage time in the gastrointestinal tract, amount of entero-hepatic bile flow, etc.). Most Cr [III] compounds are so poorly absorbed (about 1%) that they have been used as faecal markers. The absorption of Cr[VI] does not exceed 5% of a given sub-acute toxic dose.

Skin penetration by chromium has been studied *in vivo* and *in vitro*, using various animal systems and human skin, with or without epidermis. This topic has been reviewed by Polak *et al.* (1973) and Bang-Pedersen (1982). Under ordinary conditions with undamaged skin, this route of entry has very limited importance, if any, for the total Cr uptake. In general, Cr[VI] compounds penetrate the skin more easily and faster than Cr[III] salts and are of greater importance as a cause of dermatitis. The absorption depends on the condition and acidity of the skin (higher penetration in alkaline milieu) and the physico-chemical properties of the compounds.

Under ordinary conditions, the absorption by inhalation is calculated to be less than 1 μg/day (NAS, 1974). In occupational groups, the absorption by inhalation has been reviewed by Stern (1982). It depends on aerosol characteristics (e.g., size and shape, hygroscopicity and electric charge), ambient temperature, humidity, solubility in body fluids and reaction with other airborne agents, as well as with respiratory mucosa cells. The first animal inhalation studies were performed by Baetjer *et al.* (1959). Large particles (>5 μm mass median aerodynamic diameter) are deposited on the mucosa of nasal membrane, trachea and bronchi. They are carried to the pharynx (cilia) and swallowed; smaller particles (<2 μm), if not exhaled, are cleared from the airways less efficiently, after having been taken up by macrophages in non-ciliated areas. Soluble particles and droplets (Cr[VI] compounds) are rapidly absorbed into the blood, from which Cr is taken up by red cells or excreted in the urine. In a recent study, it was shown that Cr[III], organically bound as Cr-lingosulfate, was excreted by exposed workers at rates corresponding to Cr[VI] exposure data (Langård, 1982), showing that this organic Cr compound is also taken up in the lungs.

The absorption of Cr depends on its oxidation state. Cr[III] is taken up by plasma protein fractions almost entirely by bonding to the iron-bonding protein, transferrin, and Cr[VI] is taken up by red blood cells. Thus, Cr is transported and distributed by the blood stream. The uptake by tissues depends on chemical state; soluble, chelated forms of Cr are cleared quite rapidly, colloidal or protein-binding forms, however, are cleared more slowly, having a great affinity for the reticuloendothelial system (liver, spleen, bone marrow). Cr, retained in tissues, is not immediately available for physiological functions, but needs to be organically bound, probably in the form of GTF.

To evaluate experimental studies, however, one must proceed with caution if no data are given concerning the purity of chemical compounds. Firstly, because industrial as well as reagent-grade Cr[III] compounds can be contaminated by Cr[VI] and, secondly, because Cr[VI] is reduced to Cr [III] in tissues after penetration of membranes (Gray & Sterling, 1950; NAS, 1974) as well as by acid gastric juice following the oral route (Donaldson & Barreras, 1966).

A four-compartment clearence from the blood stream was demonstrated by Sargent *et al.* (1979), with mean half-times of 13 min. 6.3 h, 1.9 days and 8.3 days, the whole-body disappearance was slower (a three-compartment model showed half times of 0.56 days, 12.7 days and 192 days). This study showed that blood does not reflect the tissue stores of Cr, but functions as a carrier for accumulation or excretion.

Human tissue Cr concentrations were determined by Schroeder *et al.* (1962). In all tissues except lung, a rapid decline of Cr concentrations was observed, following an initially high level at the time of birth. Since it is not in equilibrium with the general Cr pool in the body, it is suggested that Cr accumulation in lungs may be related to airborne Cr contamination of the environment. The Cr content of tissues and body fluids was determined in occupational exposure situations and in unexposed control groups. Using standard reference material for control, Seeling *et al.* (1979) found Cr levels ranging from 0.7 to 2.2 μg/L in serum and from 1 to 1.5 μg/L in plasma, but somewhat higher (Simonoff *et al.*, 1984) and somewhat lower (Kumpulainen *et al.*, 1983) values have also been proposed. Urinary Cr was determined in 24-h samples and collected from 12 male adults (Guthrie *et al.*, 1978). Daily excretion ranged between 0.4 and 1.9 μg, with a mean value of 0.8 ± 0.4 μg/d. Urine samples of 189 Japanese subjects were analysed by Nomiyama *et al.* (1980) using direct flameless AAS. Cr levels averaged 0.41 ± 0.37 μg/L. Schaller and Zober (1982) determined urinary Cr in smokers (median value 1.6 μg/L and non-smokers (1.4 μg/L). Commercially-available urine samples were used for quality control.

Concentrations of Cr in organs were determined by Brune *et al.* (1980) and ranged from below detection (0.003 mg/kg wet weight) to 0.72 mg/kg in lung. Hyodo *et al.* (1980) analysed various tissues and found concentration ranges up to 0.01 mg/kg in cerebrum, aorta and skin, up to 0.02 mg/kg in bone marrow and kidney, up to 0.03 mg/kg in pancreas and pharyngeal wall, up to 0.04 mg/kg in liver, up to 0.16 mg/kg in suprarenal gland and from 0.02 to 0.88 mg/kg in lung tissue. Zober *et al.* (1984) analysed lung and kidney from 45 autopsies and found a median value of 0.097 mg Cr/kg wet weight in lungs and 9.6 μg/kg in kidneys. The results were not influenced by age or sex.

Chromium excretion depends on the oxidation state and the particular compound; it is excreted in urine and faeces, with kidney and urine as the major routes, accounting for 80% of injected Cr (Mertz, 1969). Glomerular filtration is followed by tubular reabsorption. Decreasing reabsorption rate, probably caused by increased Cr load in renal tubular cells, is followed by increased Cr excretion in rats (Mutti *et al.*, 1979a). After i.v. administration of ^{51}Cr, about 2% to 20% was excreted with the faeces. It seems that most excretion takes place in the liver through the bile, thus causing hepatotoxicity after intoxication with high doses of chromates. It is uncertain whether sweat, nails, hairs and milk contribute to the daily Cr excretion.

As far as we know, the most prominent biological function of Cr concerns its role as an essential cofactor for the actions of insulin (Mertz, 1969), which is involved in carbohydrate and lipid metabolism, as well as protein metabolism (Hambidge, 1974). The observations of Schroeder *et al.* (1963), showing increased growth rates, mature weights and longevity in animals reared on a Cr-supplemented diet, are presumably accounted for by the importance of biologically-active Cr-containing compounds in many, if not all, insulin-dependent systems.

In human subjects, the necessity of small amounts of dietary Cr has been demonstrated in two cases of proved Cr deficiency in patients under long-term parenteral nutrition: Jeejeebhoy et al. (1977) found 20 µg Cr/day to be sufficient. Freund et al. (1979) supplemented with 150 µg Cr/day. Chromium supplementation has also been shown to improve impaired glucose tolerance in elderly subjects (Doisy et al., 1976) and in malnourished Jordanian and Turkish children. Furthermore, recent studies suggest a link between chromium deficiency and increasing risk of cardiovascular diseases (Newman et al., 1978; Simonoff, 1984).

Toxicology

The toxicology of Cr compounds has been reviewed by the US National Academy of Science (NAS, 1974), Langård and Norseth (1979) and the US Environmental Protection Agency (US-EPA, 1984). When orally administered, Cr[III] does not appear to have any harmful effect, even when given in large doses; cats were unaffected when fed with chromic phosphate or oxidicarbonate ($Cr_2O(CO_3)_2$, Akatsuka & Fairhall, 1934) at 50 to 1 000 mg/day for 80 days. Following parenteral administration, 800 mg/kg body weight is required to kill mice. Acute and chronic toxic effects of Cr are mainly caused by hexavalent compounds; the LD_{50} of Cr[VI], as potassium dichromate, administered orally by stomach tube to rats, was 177 mg/kg body weight in males and 149 mg/kg in females (Hertel, 1982). Low concentrations of Cr[VI] may be tolerated in feed or drinking water because of the small degree of absorption; rats tolerate 25 mg Cr[VI] in drinking water for a year (NAS, 1974). In human adults, the lethal oral dose of soluble chromates is considered to lie between 50 mg and 70 mg/kg body weight. Clinical features are vomiting, diarrhoea, haemorrhagic diathesis and blood loss into the gastrointestinal tract, causing cardiovascular shock. If the patient survives about 8 days, liver necrosis, tubular necrosis of kidneys and poisoning of blood-forming organs and cerebral oedema are observed.

Occupational exposure to Cr can result in a number of effects; irritative lesions of the skin and upper respiratory tract, allergic reactions and cancers of the respiratory tract. Other effects concerning gastrointestinal, circulatory and urogenital systems have been reported, but the data given are insufficient for evaluation.

Contact with chromates can give rise to ulcers which are called chrome holes or chrome sores. There is no evidence that the ulcers undergo malignant transformation, nor that they influence the development of allergic sensitization to chromates. Another effect is perforation of the nasal septum, described with loss of the sense of smell and taste. The most important aspect of prevention is personal hygiene, combined with the observance of threshold limit values at the working place.

Bearing in mind that allergy is a growing health problem, chromium's ability to act as sensitizer is of outstanding interest. This topic has been reviewed by Polak et al. (1973) and Fregert (1981). Cr[VI] penetrates the skin, where it is reduced to Cr[III] and acts as a hapten before it conjugates forming the antigen. Cr metal in alloys is not sensitizing (Fregert, 1981). When present in the raw material for the manufacture of cement, Cr[III] is partly oxidized to Cr[VI] in the kiln. Thus, in combination with the alkaline exposure conditions, Cr causes the very well-known cement dermatitis.

Tanner dermatitis is caused by a basic Cr[III] sulfate complex used as tanning agent. The same compound can also cause dermatitis as a result of wearing leather products which are affected by sweat. Patients suffering from Cr-induced allergic skin dermatoses were shown to have a tendency to develop cross-correlated hypersensitivity to other metals, such as cobalt and nickel (Kogan *et al.*, 1972). These dermatoses are not fatal and no case of cancer of the skin due to Cr exposure has been reported.

Occupational exposure to airborne chromium can cause corrosive reactions in the broncho-pulmonary tract; an obstructive respiratory syndrome is observed in Cr electroplaters and in electrofurnace workers in ferrochromium- and ferrosilicon-producing plants, but it may be questioned whether Cr is the only aetiological factor. The same is true for the suggestion that Cr induces pneumoconiosis. Bronchial irritation may occur, followed by sensitization, resulting in typical asthmatic attacks which recur later on, even at lower exposure levels (Langård & Norseth, 1979).

Bronchitis is observed in welders using Cr-containing electrodes. Depending on the type and conditions of the welding processes, Cr[VI] is present in welding fume particles as one of the most important sources of occupational exposure (Lautner *et al.*, 1978). These particles have been shown to constitute a carcinogenic risk for humans (Knudsen, 1980). Measuring urinary Cr excretion and Cr clearance of 22 welders, Mutti *et al.* (1979b) showed that the levels of exposure to hexavalent, airborne Cr are reflected in the urinary excretion rates (expressed by the Cr to creatinine ratio). This correlation, however, is confounded by the influence of increasing Cr clearance rates with increasing total Cr burden over the daily and weekly work periods. Thus the exposure history is measured, rather than the exposure, just prior to sampling. With atmospheric Cr concentrations of 50 $\mu g/m^3$, the Cr content of welder's urine was found to range between 10 $\mu g/L$ and 40 $\mu g/L$. These values may be affected by smoking habits, because of the generally delayed clearance rate of the airways found in smokers. Coughing or clearing one's throat and swallowing may contribute to the observation that faecal Cr excretion in welders is increased and parallels the clearance from the lungs.

Mutagenicity

The mutagenicity of Cr compounds was reviewed by IARC (1980, 1982), Léonard and Lauwerys (1980), Lewis and Bianchi (1982), Petrilli and De Flora (1982) and Baker (1984). De Flora (1981) has published studies of Cr compounds using the Ames test.

As reported by IARC (1980), 'hexavalent chromium caused DNA damage (IARC, 1980; Matsui, 1980; Warren *et al.*, 1981; Levis & Bianchi, 1982) and misincorporation of nucleotides in an in-vitro DNA transcription assay (IARC, 1980). It was mutagenic in bacteria in the absence of an exogenous metabolic activation system (IARC, 1980; Levis & Bianchi, 1982; Knudsen, 1980) and mutagenic in fungi (IARC, 1980; Levis & Bianchi, 1982) and in mammalian cells *in vitro* (IARC, 1980; Levis & Bianchi, 1982) and *in vivo* (IARC, 1980). Potassium dichromate induced dominant lethal mutations in mice treated *in vivo* (Paschin *et al.*, 1982). Hexavalent chromium caused chromosomal aberrations in mammalian cells *in vitro* (IARC, 1980; Levis & Bianchi,

1982; Leonard & Lauwerys, 1980), and micronuclei in mice *in vivo* (IARC, 1980). It produced cell transformation in a number of systems (IARC, 1980; Levis & Bianchi, 1982). Micronuclei were formed in peripheral lymphocytes from exposed workers (IARC, 1980)'.

Douglas *et al.* (1980) showed dose-dependent chromosome aberrations, sister chromatid exchanges and DNA damage in cultured lymphocytes ($PbCrO_4$, K_2CrO_4; concentration range: 10^{-4} to 10^{-6} mol/L), Sarto *et al.* (1980), also using lymphocytes, found a dose-dependent decrease of mitotic index and an increase of chromosome aberrations due to $Na_2Cr_2O_7$ (range: 0.1 to 50 µmol/L). $CrCl_3$ was devoid of clastogenic activity over the range 10 to 7 500 µmol/L. Inhibition of mitosis in embryonic fibroblast cultures and chromosomal aberrations of peripheral blood leukocytes were reported by Bigaliev *et al.* (1978), using $K_2Cr_2O_7$ at about 0.45 µg/mL.

'There is no good evidence that trivalent chromium causes mutations in bacteria, fungi or mammalian cells in culture ot that it transforms mammalial cells *in vitro* (IARC, 1980). The few positive results in assays for chromosomal aberrations were obtained only with very high doses and could be explained by non-specific toxic effects (Fornace *et al.*, 1981; Kubinski *et al.*, 1981). No data on humans were available' (IARC, 1982).

Cr[III], however, is bound to the genetic material and is therefore discussed as the ultimate mutagen after being produced in the cell by the reduction of Cr[VI] (Léonard & Lauwerys, 1980).

Teratogenicity

The teratogenicity of Cr[VI] has been shown in several animal studies. The teratogenic potency of Cr[III] is still being discussed.

Carcinogenicity

Early human case reports, followed by epidemiological studies of workers, and studies of mutagenic effects of chromium, together with long-term experimental animal studies, have led to the general agreement that chromium has carcinogenic potency. The carcinogenicity of Cr compounds was first reviewed by Baetjer (1950). Recent reviews are published by IARC (1980, 1982), Hayes (1980), Norseth (1981), Hertel (1982) and Langård (1983).

In 1932 chromium was considered to cause lung cancer. Since that time, a large number of animal experiments have been performed to differentiate between the carcinogenic, cocarcinogenic and promotoric potencies of various chromium compounds held responsible for the development of cancer in man, and to understand the mechanism involved.

Various types of animal models, methods of administration and different chromium compounds have been studied. Sarcomas restricted to the site of injection have been produced by subcutaneous, intramuscular or intrapleural injection. The most relevant exposure of workers, however, is by inhalation. The nasal filter in rodents is more effective than in humans, which is probably the main reason why animal inhalation experiments show no marked results. After inhalation of 13 mg/m³ calcium-chromate (5 h/d, 5 d/week for life span), Nettesheim *et al.* (1971) found 14 lung adenomas in 136 treated animals compared to 5/136 untreated controls. The only carcinoma of the lung in animals were found by Hueper (1958) after intrapleural implantation of roasted chromate [III] ore. Laskin *et al.* (1970), Levy and Venitt (1975) and Levy and Martin (1983) implanted stainless steel pellets loaded with cholesterol, mixed with various Cr[VI] compounds, in the bronchi of rats and observed bronchogenic carcinomas. Steinhoff *et al.* (1983) performed intratracheal instillations (1.25 mg/kg b.w. per week) of chromates in rats during 30 months. A weak carcinogenic effect (12/880) was found, all tumours developed at the end of the lifetime study and none was the cause of death.

Tumours of workers exposed in the chromate chemical industry were found to be of various histological types and occurred primarily in the main bronchi. These cancers are indistinguishable from cancers developed in the general population. Thus, it is not possible to estimate how many cases in the epidemiological studies presented on this topic have resulted from Cr exposure. In most studies, there is no information on tobacco smoking histories and periods of exposure to other chemical carcinogens or radiation. This may contribute to the reported variation of the time interval between initial exposure and the diagnosis of onset of cancer (average: 20 years, range 3 to 40 years).

The uncertain characterization of the level of exposure is another source of difficulty in the discussion of epidemiological studies aiming to show dose-dependent relationships. It is generally accepted that there were excessive concentrations of Cr in the air of old chromate chemical plants until the role of Cr in lung cancer was established. Among employees of that time an excess risk up to 29-fold was reported.

Some of the epidemiological studies of occupational exposure to Cr are partly inconsistent or incomplete with regard to the methods used, and Hayes (1980) has pointed out that conclusions drawn from such studies depend upon the methods applied (incomplete follow-up, identification of deaths, comparability of controls, statistical analyses, individual case reports). Summing up the various reports, a consistent relationship has been demonstrated between an increased risk for bronchial carcinoma and employment in the production of chromate salts (IARC, 1980, 1982; Alderson *et al.,* 1981; Korallus *et al.,* (1982), pigments and chromate (Davies, 1978; IARC, 1980, 1982, Sheffet *et al.* 1982; Langård & Vigander, 1983; Frentzel-Beyme, 1983) and, less pronounced, in the chromium plating industry (Royle, 1975; IARC, 1982). The multicentric European study (Frentzel-Beyme, 1983) does not show a clear dose-response effect of increased lung cancer risk with time of employment. A study of the incidence of cancer in the ferrochrome industry (Langård *et al.,* 1980) is inconsistent with the study of Axelsson *et al.* (1980), who did not observe a significant excess of respiratory cancer. Generally, in this industry, the presence of benzo[*a*]pyrene must be considered in evaluating the causes of carcinogenic effects. Among welders, a slight excess risk of respiratory tract cancer incidences is found in the world literature (Langård & Stern, 1984).

The epidemiological data do not permit an evaluation of the effects of Cr[III] *versus* Cr[VI] or the role of solubility, nor can the ultimate carcinogenic form of Cr or a dose-response relationship be determined from these studies. There is no definite evidence that Cr causes cancers other than in lung, although excesses of cancers of the oesophagus, stomach, pancreas, maxillary sinus and prostate have been reported in some studies (IARC, 1980; Sheffet *et al.,* 1982).

REFERENCES

Akatsuka, K. & Fairhall, L.T. (1934) The toxicology of chromium *J. Ind. Hyg., 16,* 1–24

Alderson, M.R., Rattan, N.S. & Bidstrup, L. (1981) Health of workmen in chromate-producing industry in Britain *Br. J. ind. Med.,38,* 117–124

Axelsson, G., Rylander, R. & Schmidt, A. (1980) Mortality and incidence of tumours among ferrochromium workers. *Br. J. ind. Med., 37,* 121–127

Baetjer, A.M. 1950) Pulmonary carcinoma in chromate workers. I. A review of the literature and report of cases. *Arch. ind. Hyg. occup. Med., 2,* 487–504

Baetjer, A.M., Lowney, J.F., Steffee, H. & Budacz, V. (1959) Effect of chromium on incidence of lung tumours in mice and rats. *Am. Med. Assoc. Arch. ind. Health, 20,* 124–135

Baker, R.S.V. (1984) Evaluation of metals in in-vitro assays interpretation of data and possible mechanisms of action. *Toxicol. Environ. Chem., 7,* 191–212

Bang-Pedersen, N. (1982) *The effects of chromium on the skin.* In: Langard, S., ed., *Biological and Environmental Aspects of Chromium,* Amsterdam, Elsevier Biomedical Press, pp. 249–270

Bigaliev, A.B., Elemesova, M.S., Turebaev, M.N. & Bigalieva, R.K. (1978) Cytogenetic study of the mutagenic activity of industrial substances [in Russian]. *Zdravookhr. Kaz., 8,* 48–50 (Chem. Abstr. *89,* 191930j)

Brune, D., Nordberg, G. & Wester, P.O. (1980) Distribution of 23 elements in the kidney, liver and lungs of workers from a smeltery and refinery in North Sweden exposed to a number of elements and of a control group. *Sci. total Environ; 16,* 13–35

Cheremisinoff, P.N. & Habib, Y.H. (1972) Cadmium, chromium, lead, mercury: A plenary account for water pollution. Part I. Occurrence, toxicity and detection. *Water Sewage Works, 119,* 73–86

Davies, J.M. (1978) Lung cancer mortality of workers making chrome pigments. *Lancet, i,* 384

De Flora, S. (1981) Study of 106 organic and inorganic compounds in the Salmonella microsome test. *Carcinogenesis, 2,* 283–298

Doisy, R.J., Streeten, D.H.P., Freiberg, J.M. & Schneider, A.J. (1976) *Chromium metabolism in man and biochemical effects.* In: Prasad, A.S., ed., *Trace Elements in Human Health and Disease,* Vol. II, New York, Academic Press, pp. 79–104

Donaldson, R.M., Jr & Barreras, R.F. (1966) Intestinal absorption of trace quantities of chromium. *J. lab. clin. Med., 68,* 484–493

Douglas, G.R., Bell, R.D.L., Grant, C.E., Wytsma, J.M. & Bora, K.C. (1980) Effect of lead chromate on chromosome aberration, sister chromatid exchange and DNA damage in mammalian cells *in vitro. Mutat. Res., 77,* 157–163

Fornace, A.J., Jr, Seres, D.S., Lechner, J.F. & Harris, C.C. (1981) DNA-protein cross-linking by chromium salts. *Chem.-biol. Interact., 36,* 345–354

Fregert, S. (1981) Manual of Contact Dermatitis. *Munksgaard Copenhagen,* 2nd edition, 139 pp.

Frentzel-Beyme, R. (1983) Lung cancer mortality of workers employed in chromate pigment factories. *J. Cancer Res. Clin. Oncol., 105,* 183–188

Freund, H., Atamian, S. & Fischer, J.E. (1979) Chromium deficiency during total parenteral nutrition. *J. Am. med. Assoc., 241,* 496–498

Gray, S.J. & Sterling, K. (1950) The tagging of red cells and plasma proteins with radioactive chromium. *J. clin. Invest., 29,* 1604–1613

Guthrie, B.E. (1982) *The nutritional role of chromium.* In: Langård, S., ed., *Biological and Environmental Aspects of Chromium,* Amsterdam, Elsevier Biomedical Press, pp. 117–140

Guthrie, B.E., Wolf, W.R. & Veillon, C. (1978) Background correction and related problems in the determination of chromium in urine by graphite furnace atomic absorption spectrometry. *Anal. Chem., 50,* 1900–1902

Hambidge, K.M. (1974) Chromium nutrition in man. *Am. J. clin. Nutr., 27,* 505–514

Hayes, R.B. (1980) *Cancer and occupational exposure to chromium chemicals.* In: Lilienfeld, A.M., ed., *Reviews in Cancer Epidemiology,* Vol. 1, New York, Elsevier/North-Holland, pp. 293–333

Hertel, R.F. (1982) Chromium as a problem in physiology, epidemiology and biological monitoring [in German]. *Staub.-Reinhalt. Luft, 42,* 135–137

Hintze, C. (1930) *Handbuch der Mineralogie,* Bd 1. III/2, Berlin, Leipzig, de Gruyter, pp. 4012–4030

Hueper, W.C. (1958) Experimental studies in metal cancerogenesis. X. Cancerogenic effects of chromite ore roast deposited in muscle tissue and pleural cavity of rats. *Arch. ind. Health, 18,* 284–291

Hyodo, K., Suzuki, S., Furuya, N. & Meshizuka, K. (1980) An analysis of chromium, copper and zinc in organs of a chromate worker. *Int. Arch. occup. environ. Health, 46,* 141–150

IARC (1980) *IARC Monographs on the Evaluation of the Carcinogenic Risk of Chemicals to Humans,* Volume 23, *Some Metals and Metallic Compounds,* Lyon, International Agency for Research on Cancer, pp. 205–323

IARC (1982) *IARC Monographs on the Evaluation of the Carcinogenic risk of Chemicals to Humans,* Supplement 4, *Chemicals, Industrial Processes and Industries Associated with Cancer in Humans,* Lyon, International Agency for Research on Cancer, pp. 91–93

Jeejeebhoy, K.N., Chu, R.G., Marliss, E.B., Greenberg, G.R. & Bruce-Robertson, A. (1977) Chromium deficiency, glucose intolerance and neuropathy reversed by chromium supplementation in a patient receiving long-term total parenteral nutrition. *Am. J. clin. Nutr., 30,* 531–538

Kirchgessner, M., Merz, G. & Oelschlaeger, W. (1960) Effect of vegetation state on content of macro and micro elements of three species of grass [in German]. *Arch. Tierern., 10,* 414–427

Klein, L.A., Lang, M., Nash, N. & Kirschner, S.L. (1974) Sources of metals in New York City wastewater. *J. Water Pollut. Control Fed., 46,* 2653–2662

Knudsen, I. (1980) The mammalian spot test and its use for the testing of potential carcinogenicity of welding fume particles and hexavalent chromium. *Acta Pharmacol. Toxicol., 47,* 66–70

Kogan, V.Y., Arutyunyan, K.E. & Kochinyan, Y.E. (1972) *A comparative characteristic of chromium, nickel and cobalt salts as a causative factor in allergic contact dermatosis [in Russian].* In: *Clinical Pathology of Chemical Aetiology* [in Russian]. *Materials of the I, All-Union Conference, Kiev, USSR, 24–25 October 1972,* USSR, Kiev, pp. 144 and 146

Koivistoinen, P., ed. (1980) Mineral element composition of Finnish foods. *Acta agric. Scand. (Stockholm),* Suppl. 22, 171 pp.

Korallus, U., Lange, H.J., Neiss, A., Wuestefeld, E. & Zwinger, T. (1982) Correlations between reorganisation measures and bronchial carcinoma mortality in the chromate-manufacturing industry [in German]. *Arbeitsmed. Sozialmed. Präventivmed., 17,* 159–167

Kubinski, H., Gutzke, G.E. & Kubinski, Z.O. (1981) DNA-cell-binding (DCB) assay for suspected carcinogens and mutagens. *Mutat. Res., 89,* 95–136

Kumpulainen, J. Lehto, J., Koivistoinen, P., Uusitupa, M. & Vuori, E. (1983) Determination of chromium in human milk serum and urine by electrothermal atomic absorption spectrometry without preliminary ashing. *Sci. Total Environ., 31,* 71–80

Langård, S. (1982) *Absorption, transport and excretion of chromium in man and animals.* In: Langård, S., ed., *Biological and Environmental Aspects of Chromium,* Amsterdam, New Elsevier Biomedical Press, pp. 149–169

Langård, S. (1983) *The carcinogenicity of chromium compounds in man and animals.* In: Burrows, D., ed., *Chromium: Metabolism and Toxicity,* Boca Raton, Florida, USA, CRC Press, pp. 13–30

Langård, S. & Norseth, T. (1979) *Chromium.* In: Friberg, L., Nordberg, G.F. & Vouk, V.B., eds, *Handbook on the Toxicology of Metals,* Amsterdam, Elsevier/North-Holland Biomedical Press, pp. 383–397

Langård, S., Andersen, A. & Gylseth, B. (1980) Incidence of cancer among ferrochromium and ferrosilicon workers. *Br. J. ind. Med., 37,* 114–120

Langård, S. & Vigander, T. (1983) Occurrence of lung cancer in workers producing chromium pigments. *Br. J. Ind. Med., 40,* 71–74

Langård, S. & Stern, R.M. (1984) Nickel in welding fumes – a cancer hazard to welders? In: Sunderman, F.W. Jr. Editor-in-chief, eds, *Nickel in the human environment. (IARC Scientific Publications* No. 53), Lyon, International Agency for Research on Cancer, pp. 95–103

Laskin, S., Kuschner, M. & Drew, R.T. (1970) *Studies in pulmonary carcinogenesis.* In: Hanna, E.G., Nettesheim, P. & Gilbert, J.R., eds, *Inhalation Carcinogenesis,* US Atomic Energy Commission, pp. 321–351

Lautner, G.M., Carver, J.C. & Konzen, R.B. (1978) Measurement of chromium VI and chromium III in stainless steel welding fumes with electron spectroscopy for chemical analysis and neutron activation analysis. *Am. ind. hyg. Assoc. J., 39,* pp. 651–660

Leonard, A. & Lauwerys, R.R. (1980) Carcinogenicity and mutagenicity of chromium. *Mutat. Res., 76,* 227–239

Levis, A.G. & Bianchi, V. (1982) *Mutagenic and cytogenetic effects of chromium compounds.* In: Langård, S., ed., *Biological and Environmental Aspects of Chromium,* Amsterdam, Elsevier/North-Holland Biomedical Press, pp. 171–208

Levy, L.S. & Martin, P.A. (1983) *The effect of a range of chromium-containing materials on rat lung.* Aston/Birmingham. Department of Environmental and Occupational Health, 224 pp.

Levy, L.S. & Venitt, S. (1975) Carcinogenic and mutagenic activity of chromium containing materials. *Br. J. Cancer, 32,* 254–255

Matsui, S. (1980) Evaluation of a *Bacillus subtilis rec*-assay for the detection of mutagens which may occur in water environments. *Water Res., 14,* 1613–1619

Merian, E. (1984) Introduction on environmental chemistry and global cycles of arsenic, beryllium, cadmium, chromium, cobalt, nickel, selenium and their derivatives. *Toxicol. Environ. Chem., 8,* 9–38

Mertz, W. (1969) Chromium occurrence and function in biological systems. *Physiol. Rev., 49,* 163–239

Mertz, W. & Schwarz, K. (1959) Relation of glucose tolerance factor to impaired glucose tolerance in rats on stock diets. *Am. J. Physiol., 196,* 614–618

Mutti, A., Cavatorta, A., Borghi, L., Canali, M., Giaroli, C. & Franchini, I. (1979a) Distribution and urinary excretion of chromium. Studies on rats after administration of single and repeated doses of potassium dichromate. *Med. Lavoro, 70,* 171–179

Mutti, A., Cavatorta, A., Pedroni, C., Borghi, A., Giaroli, C. & Franchini, I. (1979b) The role of chromium accumulation in the relationship between airborne and urinary chromium in welders. *Int. Arch. occup. environ. Health, 43,* 123–133

National Academy of Sciences (NAS) (1974) *Chromium.* Washington DC, 155 pp.

Nettesheim, P., Hanna, M.G., Doherty, D.S., Newell, R.F. & Hellmann, A. (1971) Effect of chromium chromate dust, influenza virus and 100 R-whole-body X radiation on lung tumor incidence in mice. *J. natl Cancer Inst., 47* 1129–1144

Newman, H.A.I., Leighton, R.F., Lanese, R.R. & Freeland, N.A. (1978) Serum chromium and angiographically determined coronary artery disease. *Clin. Chem., 24,* 541–544

Nomiyama, H., Yotoriyama, M. & Nomiyama, K. (1980) Normal chromium levels in urine and blood of Japanese subjects determined by direct flameless AAS, and valency of chromium in urine after exposure to hexavalent chromium. *Am. Ind. Hyg. Assoc. J., 41,* 98–102

Norseth, T. (1981) The carcinogenicity of chromium. *Environ. Health Perspect., 40,* 121–130

Paschin, Y.V., Zacepilova, T.A. & Kozachenko, V.I. (1982) Induction of dominant lethal mutations in male mice by potassium dichromate. *Mutat. Res., 103,* 345–347

Petrilli, F.L. & De Flora, S. (1982) *Interpretations on chromium mutagenicity and carcinogenicity.* In: Sorsa, E. & Vainio, H., eds, *Mutagens in our Environment,* New York, Alan R. Liss, pp. 453–464

Pohland, F.G. (1975) *Sanitary Landfill Stabilization with leachate recycle and residual treatment.* EPA-600/2-75-043. Cincinnati, OH, US Environmental Protection Agency, 106 pp.

Polak, L., Turk, J.L. & Frey, J.R. (1973) *Studies on contact hypersensitivity to chromium compounds.* In: Kallos, P., Waksman, B.H. & DeWeck, A., eds, *Progress in Allergy,* Vol. 17, Basel, Karger, pp. 145–226

Royle, H. (1975) Toxicity of chromic acid in the chromium plating industry. *Environ. Res., 10,* 39–53

Saner, G. (1980) *Chromium in nutrition and disease.* In: (eds?) *Current Topics in Nutrition and Disease,* Vol. 2, New York, Alan R. Liss, Inc, 135 pp.

Sargent III, T., Lim, T.H. & Jenson, R.L. (1979) Reduced chromium retention in patients with hemochromatosis, a possible basis of hemochromatotic diabetes. *Metabolism, 28,* 70–79

Sarto, F., Levis, A.G. & Paulon, C. (1980) Clastogenic activity of hexavalent and trivalent chromium in cultured human lymphocytes. *Caryologia, 33,* 239–250

Schaller, K.H. & Zober, A. (1982) Renal excretion of toxicologically relevant metals in occupationally non-exposed individuals. *Ärztl. Lab., 28,* 209–214

Schroeder, H.A., Balassa, J.J. & Tipton, I.H. (1962) Abnormal trace metals in man – chromium. *J. chron. Dis., 15,* 941–964

Schroeder, H.A., Vinton, W.H., Jr & Balassa, J.J. (1963) Effects of chromium, cadmium and other trace metals on the growth and survival of mice. *J. Nutr., 80,* 39–47

Schwarz, K. & Mertz, W. (1959) Chromium [III] and the glucose tolerance factor. *Arch. biochem. Biophys., 85,* 292–295

Seeling, W., Grünert, A., Kienle, K.H., Opferkuch, R. & Swobodnik, M. (1979) Determination of chromium in human serum and plasma by flameless atomic absorption spectrometry [in German]. *Z. Anal. Chem., 299,* 368–374

Sheffet, A., Thind, J., Miller, A.M. & Louria, D.B. (1982) Cancer mortality in a pigment plant utilizing lead and zinc chromates. *Arch. Environ. Health, 37,* 44–52

Simonoff, M. (1984) Chromium deficiency and cardiovascular risk. *Cardiovasc. Res., 18,* 591–596

Simonoff, M., Llabador, Y., Hamon, C., MacKenzie Peers, A. & Simonoff, G.N. (1984) Low plasma chromium in patients with coronary artery and heart disease. *Biol. Trace Element Res., 6.,* 431–439

Steinhoff, D., Gad, S.C., Hatfield, G.K. & Mohr, U. (1983) *Testing sodium dichromate and soluble calcium chromate for carcinogenicity in rats.* Report to the Industrial Health Foundation, Wuppertal, FRG., Bayer, A.G. Inst. Toxicol., 126 pp.

Stern, R.M. (1982) *Chromium compounds: Production and occupational exposure.* In: Langård, S., ed., *Biological and Environmental Aspects of Chromium,* Amsterdam, Elsevier Biomedical Press, pp. 5–44

US-EPA (1978) *Reviews of the Environmental Effects of Pollutants: III Chromium.* ORNL/EIS-80, PEA-600/1-78-023. Washington DC, US Environmental Protection Agency, 285 pp.

US-EPA (1980) *Ambient Water Quality Criteria for Chromium.* Washington DC, US Environmental Protection Agency, pp. A1–C48

US-EPA (1984) *Health Assessment Document for Chromium,* EPA-600/8-83-014F. Research Triangle Park NC 27711, U.S. Environmental Protection Agency, pp. 1–9/65

Warren, G., Schultz, P., Bancroft, D., Bennett, K., Abbott, E.H. & Rogers, S. (1981) Mutagenicity of a series of hexacoordinate chromium [III] compounds. *Mutat. Res., 90,* 111–118

Wetterhahn, J. (1982) Microsomal reduction of the carcinogen chromate produces chromium[V]. *J. Am. chem. Soc., 104,* 874–875

Zober, A., Kick, K., Schaller, K.H., Schellmann, B. & Valentin, H. (1984) "Normal values" of chromium and nickel in human lung, kidney, blood and urine samples. *Zentralbl. Bakteriol. Hyg., Abt. I (Orig. B), 179,* 80–95

CHAPTER 5

SOURCES OF EXPOSURE AND BIOLOGICAL EFFECTS OF NICKEL[1]

F.W. Sunderman Jr

Departments of Laboratory Medicine and Pharmacology,
University of Connecticut School of Medicine,
263 Farmington Avenue, Farmington, CT 06032, USA

INTRODUCTION

This chapter briefly summarizes the biological effects of nickel and discusses the sources of exposure. For additional information, readers may consult several recent books and reviews (Nriagu, 1980; Brown & Sunderman, 1980, 1984; Sunderman, 1981a, 1984; Bencko, 1983; Mushak, 1984; IARC, 1984).

BIOLOGICAL EFFECTS

Nutritional essentiality

Nickel has been shown to be an essential trace nutrient for animals (Kirchgessner & Schnegg, 1980; Anke *et al.,* 1983, 1984). In rats, goats, swine and fowl, nickel deficiency is associated with stunted growth, skeletal malformations, anaemia and biochemical disorders, including abnormal carbohydrate, lipid and/or iron metabolism, and diminished activities of various enzymes in liver and pancreas. Nickel is an essential constituent of certain enzymes and metabolic cofactors in plants and bacteria, including ureases, hydrogenases, dehydrogenases and factor F_{430} (Diekert *et al.,* 1979, 1980; Dixon *et al.,* 1980; Graf & Thauer, 1981; Friedrick *et al.,* 1982). Nickel has not been identified as an essential constituent of any mammalian enzyme and the biological roles of nickel in humans and animals remain to be established (Thauer *et al.,* 1980). The nutritional requirement of nickel for growing cattle is < 500 µg/kg (dry weight) of ration; the nutritional requirement of nickel for

[1] Supported by US Department of Energy Grant EV-03140 and National Institute of Environmental Health Sciences Grant ES-01337

man has not been established, but is probably $> 200 \, \mu g/kg$ (dry weight) of food (Anke et al., 1983, 1984).

Nickel metabolism in animals

Following oral administration of $^{63}NiCl_2$ to animals, most ^{63}Ni remains unabsorbed and is excreted in the faeces (Spears et al., 1978). A fraction ($< 10\%$) of the ^{63}Ni is absorbed from the intestine, enters the plasma and is eliminated *via* the urine. Following parenteral administration of $^{63}NiCl_2$ to animals, ^{63}Ni transiently accumulates in kidney, pituitary, cartilage, bone, lung, skin, adrenals and gonads (Smith & Hackley, 1968; Parker & Sunderman, 1974; Oskarsson & Tjalve, 1979). During three days after an injection of $^{63}NiCl_2$, the ^{63}Ni is excreted primarily in the urine, and, to a lesser degree, in the bile (Soestbergen & Sunderman, 1972; Sunderman et al., 1976a). $^{63}Ni[III]$ is transported in blood by binding to serum albumin and several ultrafiltrable ligands, including L-histidine (Sarkar, 1980). A non-exchangeable fraction of serum nickel is tightly bound to nickeloplasmin, an α-macroglobulin (Nomoto et al., 1971; Decsy & Sunderman, 1974). Renal cytosol from $^{63}NiCl_2$-treated rats contains ^{63}Ni that is bound to five distinct macromolecular components, as well as to ultrafiltrable constituents (Sarkar, 1980; Sunderman et al., 1981, 1983b). The kinetics of $^{63}Ni[III]$ metabolism in rodents has been described by two-compartment and three-compartment models (Onkelinx & Sunderman, 1980; Machado-Carvalho & Ziemer, 1982).

Nickel metabolism in healthy humans

Based upon a comprehensive assessment of the available data, Bennett (1981) estimated that the body burden of nickel in healthy adults averages 0.5 mg (7.3 µg/kg body weight for a 70-kg person). Oral intake of nickel averages 170 µg/day, of which approximately 5% is absorbed (8.5 µg/day). Inhalation of nickel averages 0.4 µg/day for urban dwellers and 0.2 µg/day for rural dwellers, of which 35% is retained (0.007 to 0.014 µg/day). This assessment of nickel metabolism involves the assumption that 70% of absorbed nickel is promptly excreted by the kidneys and the remaining 30% is deposited in the tissues, with a mean retention time of 200 days (Bennett, 1981).

Pathophysiology of nickel in humans

Serum nickel concentrations usually increase in patients during the first four days after myocardial infarction, severe angina pectoris, acute stroke or extensive thermal burns; the pathophysiological mechanisms of hypernickelemia in these patients have not been elucidated (McNeely et al., 1971; Leach et al., 1984). Concentrations of serum nickel are decreased in patients with hepatic cirrhosis, presumably as a consequence of marked hypoalbuminemia (McNeely et al., 1971). Rubanyi et al. (1982) noted increased nickel concentrations in serum obtained from women immediately after obstetrical delivery, but Nomoto et al. (1983) did not confirm the occurrence of postpartum hypernickelemia.

Non-carcinogenic effects of nickel compounds in humans

Nickel alloys and nickel compounds are among the most common causes of allergic contact dermatitis. This problem is not limited to those subjected to industrial exposure; nickel sensitization occurs in the general population from exposure to nickel-containing coins, jewelry, watch cases, clothing fasteners and other objects. Nickel dermatitis often begins as a papular erythema of the hands; the skin gradually becomes eczematous and, in the chronic stage, lichenification may develop. Nickel sensitization may also cause conjunctivitis, eosinophilic pneumonitis, asthma and local or systemic reactions to nickel-containing prostheses, such as intraosseous pins, cardiac valve replacements and dental inlays. Kaaber *et al.* (1979) and Cronin *et al.* (1980) showed that oral ingestion of nickel can exacerbate hand eczema in nickel-sensitive patients. The lymphocyte transformation test and the leukocyte migration inhibition test can serve as in-vitro procedures for diagnosis of nickel sensitivity (Swoboda *et al.*, 1977; Svejgaard *et al.*, 1978).

Hypertrophic rhinitis and nasal sinusitis frequently occur in workers in nickel refineries and nickel electroplating shops. Associated findings are anosmia, nasal polyposis and perforation of the nasal septum; chronic pulmonary irritation has also been encountered (NIOSH, 1977).

Webster *et al.* (1980) reported nickel intoxication in 23 patients during extracorporeal haemodialysis, owing to leaching of nickel from a nickel-plated heating tank for the dialysate fluid. The patients' symptoms included nausea, vomiting, weakness, headache and palpitations; remission of symptoms occurred within a few hours after cessation of haemodialysis. Hopfer *et al.* (1984a) and Savory *et al.* (1984) documented hypernickelemia in patients with end-stage renal disease undergoing extracorporeal haemodialysis, leading to the speculation that hypernickelemia may contribute to dialysis-associated hypersensitivity, encephalopathy and arteriosclerosis. Sunderman (1983) noted the potential clinical hazards from nickel contamination of intravenous fluids; he recommended that the maximum permissible level of nickel be set at 5 µg/L for common intravenous fluids and 10 µg/L for solutions that contain albumin or amino acids.

Inhalation of nickel carbonyl, $Ni(CO)_4$, results in acute poisoning. $Ni(CO)_4$ is a volatile, colorless liquid and is an intermediate product in the Mond process for nickel refining; it is also used as a catalyst in the petroleum, plastics and rubber industries. Inadvertent formation of $Ni(CO)_4$ may occur in chemical processes that use nickel catalysts, such as coal gasification, petroleum refining and hydrogenation of fats. Exposure to $Ni(CO)_4$ causes coughing, dyspnea, tachycardia, cyanosis and profound weakness. Diffuse interstitial pneumonitis and cerebral haemorrhage or edema are the usual causes of death in these cases. Pathological lesions have been reported in lungs, brain, liver, kidneys, adrenals and spleen of deceased workers (NAS, 1975). Chelation with sodium diethyldithiocarbamate is the preferred treatment (Sunderman, 1971). The clinical manifestations, pathogenesis and therapy of acute $Ni(CO)_4$ poisoning have been summarized by Sunderman (1981a).

Carcinogenic effects of nickel compounds in humans

Epidemiological studies of nickel refinery workers in Canada, Wales, Germany, Norway and the USSR have demonstrated increased mortality rates from cancers of the lung and nasal cavities (IARC, 1976, 1984; NIOSH, 1977; NAS, 1978). Certain groups of nickel refinery workers have also been reported to have increased incidences of other malignant tumours, including carcinomas of the larynx, kidney, prostate or stomach, and sarcomas of soft tissues, but the statistical significance of these observations is questionable (NAS, 1975; IARC, 1976, 1984; NIOSH, 1977). Recent epidemiological studies of cancer mortality in nickel refinery workers indicate that increased risks of cancers of the nasal cavities and lungs have occurred primarily among workers in refinery operations that entail high nickel exposures, such as grinding, calcining, sintering and leaching (IARC, 1984). It appears that the cancer risks have been associated with exposures to insoluble nickel compounds, such as nickel subsulfide (Ni_3S_2) and nickel oxide (NiO). In one refinery, enhanced cancer risks were noted in electrolysis workers; the nature of the nickel compounds giving rise to concern in the electrolysis department is a subject of controversy (IARC, 1984).

Epidemiological studies of cancer risks among workers in nickel-using industries have generally been negative, although a recent population-based study suggests increased lung cancer risk for welders, grinders and electroplaters; it must be emphasized, however, that such workers are exposed to mixed dusts and fumes that often contain both nickel and chromium (IARC, 1984).

Acute effects of nickel compounds in animals

Administration of $NiCl_2$ to rodents by parenteral routes induces a broad spectrum of toxic responses, including the following:

(a) *Lipid peroxidation* is enhanced in kidney, liver and lung of $NiCl_2$-treated rats, as demonstrated by increased in-vivo production of malondialdehyde precursors (Sunderman *et al.*, 1984b). These findings implicate lipid peroxidation as a molecular mechanism that may contribute to cell injury and death in acute nickel poisoning.

(b) *Hyperglycemia* occurs in rats following intraperitoneal or intratracheal injections of $NiCl_2$ (Clary, 1975; Horak & Sunderman, 1975a, b). Horak *et al.* (1978) showed that the marked hyperglycemic response to Ni[II] upon the central nervous system, which may induce pancreatic secretion of glucagon by stimulating the vagal and splanchnic nerves.

(c) *Induction of heme oxygenase activity* occurs in renal microsomes following parenteral administration of $NiCl_2$ to rats (Maines & Kappas, 1977). The induction of heme oxygenase activity begins 6 hours after an injection of $NiCl_2$ (0.25 mmol/kg, s.c.), reaches a maximum of five-to-six times the baseline activity at 17 hours and diminishes thereafter, with threefold increase persisting at 72 hours (Sunderman *et al.*, 1983c). The stimulatory effect of $NiCl_2$ on renal heme oxygenase activity is abrogated by actinomycin D, an inhibitor of RNA synthesis (Sunderman *et al.*, 1983a).

(d) *Induction of metallothionein* occurs in livers and kidneys of $NiCl_2$-treated rodents (Maitani & Suzuki, 1983; Sunderman & Fraser, 1983).

(e) *Nephrotoxicity,* manifested by glomcrular and tubular lesions, proteinuria, enzymuria and aminoaciduria, occurs in rats during one to four days after parenteral administration of NiCl$_2$ (Gitlitz *et al.,* 1975; Sunderman & Horak, 1981).

(f) *Inhibition of natural killer (NK) cell activity* occurs in spleens of NiCl$_2$-treated mice (Rogers *et al.,* 1983). Smialowciz *et al.* (1984) found that administration of NiCl$_2$ to mice predominantly suppresses NK cell activity and, to a lesser degree, T-cell mediated immune responses, whereas NiCl$_2$ treatment does not affect B-cell mediated immune responses.

Chronic, non-carcinogenic effects of nickel compounds in animals

Chronic exposure of rabbits to inhalation of metallic nickel dust causes nodular accumulation of macrophages in the lungs and marked proliferation of granular pneumocytes, associated with increased pulmonary content of phospholipids (Camner *et al.,* 1978; Curstedt *et al.,* 1984).

Administration of nickel subsulfide (Ni$_3$S$_2$) and certain other nickel compounds to rats by intrarenal injection produces marked erythrocytosis from one week to six months post-injection, attended by intesne erythroid hyperplasia in bone marrow and spleen (Jasmin & Solymoss, 1975; Morse *et al.,* 1977; Sunderman *et al.,* 1982, 1984a). The induction of erythrocytosis is mediated by increased renal production of erythropoietin (Solymoss & Jasmin, 1978; Hopfer *et al.,* 1979, 1984a). McCully *et al.* 1982a,b) observed arteriosclerotic lesions in the major arteries of rats at 8 to 18 weeks after intrarenal injection of Ni$_3$S$_2$. Studies by Hopfer *et al.* (1984b) excluded hypertension and hyperlipidemia as pathogenic factors in Ni$_3$S$_2$-induced arteriosclerosis.

Embryotoxicity and teratogenicity of nickel compounds in animals

The literature on embryotoxicity and teratogenicity of nickel compounds in experimental animals has been summarized by Sunderman *et al.* (1983d). Evidence of nickel embryotoxicity has been obtained in a dozen investigations, involving a variety of nickel compounds, in four test species (chick, mouse, hamster and rat). Fetal malformations have been observed in chicken, mice and hamsters following exposures to soluble nickel compounds, such as NiCl$_2$, NiSO$_4$ and NICO$_3$, during organogenesis. Nickel carbonyl, Ni(CO)$_4$, is the most potent teratogen among the nickel compounds that have been studied; exposure of pregnant rats and hamsters to inhalation or injection of Ni(CO)$_4$ causes frequent fetal malformations. The propensity of Ni(CO)$_4$, to induce fetal anomalies probably reflects its lipid solubility, which may facilitate transport of Ni(CO)$_4$ across placental and fetal membranes. Nickel compounds, including NiCl$_2$ and Ni(CO)$_4$, also induce internal bleeding in fetuses, with subcutaneous haematomas and extravasations of blood into peritoneal, pleural, pericardial and subdural spaces (Sunderman *et al.,* 1983d).

Carcinogenic effects of nickel compounds in animals

Cancers have been induced in experimental animals by administration of numerous nickel compounds by various routes, excepting oral (IARC, 1976; Sunderman, 1981b,

1984). Pulmonary carcinomas have developed in rats following inhalation of Ni_3S_2 and $Ni(CO)_4$ (Sunderman & Donnelly, 1965; Ottolenghi et al., 1975). Ni_3S_2 has been shown to induce carcinomas in tracheal epithelium of rats, using heterotopic tracheal transplants (Yarita & Nettesheim, 1978). In most experimental studies of nickel carcinogenesis, the malignant neoplasms have developed locally at the sites of exposure, injection or implantation. However, pulmonary carcinomas were observed in mice that received repeated intraperitoneal injections of nickel acetate (Shimkin et al., 1978), suggesting that certain nickel compounds may induce tumours at sites that are distant from the point of primary contact. Nickel subsulfide (Ni_3S_2) and the crystalline monosulfide (NiS) appear to be the most highly carcinogenic of the nickel compounds that have been tested in experimental animals. Sunderman et al. (1984a) reported association between the incidence of erythrocytosis and renal cancers in rats that received intrarenal injections of 17 nickel compounds. Manganese suppresses the carcinogenicity of Ni_3S_2 in rats (Sunderman et al., 1974, 1976b, 1979; Sunderman & McCully, 1983). Experimental evidence that pertains to the molecular mechanisms of nickel carcinogenesis and pertinent studies of the genotoxicity and mutagenicity of nickel compounds in microorganisms and cultured mammalian cells are summarized in Chapter 2 and are reviewed in recent publications (Raithel & Schaller, 1981; Sunderman, 1981b, 1984; Leonard et al., 1983; IARC, 1984).

SOURCES AND EXPOSURES

Environmental sources and human exposure to nickel have been reviewed by Nriagu (1980), Bennett (1981), Bencko (1983) and Grandjean (1984). Nickel is the 24th element in order of natural abundance in the earth's crust. Nickel compounds are relatively soluble and the element is widely distributed in the environment. Nickel concentrations in soils depend on the composition of sedimentary and igneous rocks; farm soils contain nickel concentrations from 3 to 1 000 mg/kg. The natural sources of nickel in the atmosphere are wind-blown dusts and volcanic emissions. Estimates of the global environmental input of nickel are given in Table 1 and estimates of global production and use of nickel are given in Table 2. Atmospheric nickel concentrations average 6 ng/m^3 in non-urban areas of the USA. In urban areas of the USA, atmospheric nickel concentrations average 17 ng/m^3 in summer and 25 ng/m^3 in winter (NAS, 1975). In industrialized areas and large cities, atmospheric nickel concentrations as high as 120 to 170 ng/m^3 have been recorded (NAS, 1975; Bennett, 1981). Sea water contains 0.1 to 0.5 µg Ni/L. Surface waters average 15 to 20 µg Ni/L and drinking water usually contains less than 10 µ Ni/L (NAS, 1975; Bennett, 1981; Bencko, 1983; Grandjean, 1984). Drinking water samples occasionally contain much higher nickel concentrations, owing to nickel pollution of the water supply or leaching from nickel-containing pipes or nickel-plated faucets.

Nickel contents of human foodstuffs are illustrated by the following data selected from Bennett (1981), NAS (1975) and Nriagu (1980): grains, vegetables and fruits, 0.02 to 2.7 µg/g; meats, 0.06 to 0.4 µg/g; seafoods, 0.02 to 20 µg/g. Estimates of daily human dietary intake of nickel range from 100 to 500 µg/day (Bennett, 1981; Grandjean, 1984). Nickel is present in tobacco, with nickel contents of cigarettes

Table 1. Estimated global input of nickel into the environment[a, b]

Category	Source	Metric tonnes per year	Percentage of total
Natural	Biological cycles	100 000	30
	Weathering of rocks and soils	50 000	15
	Volcanoes	?	<1
Anthropogenic	Emissions from metal use	100 000	30
	Emissions from combustion	75 000	23
	Emissions from ore and metal production	5 000	2
Total		330 000	100

[a] Personal communication from E. Merian, 1983
[b] The eventual input of Ni into the sea is estimated to be 100 000 tonnes/year. The balance is immobilized or recycled

Table 2. Estimated global production and use of nickel[a]

Category		Metric tonnes per year	Percentage of total
Ni production (primarily by refining oxide and sulfide ores)		700 000	100
Ni uses	Steel making	420 000	60
	Pure Ni and alloys	140 000	20
	Ni plating	100 000	14
	Balance (includes coinage, batteries, catalysts, enamels, glass, pigments and electronic components	40 000	6

[a] Personal communication from E. Merian, 1983

ranging from 1 to 3 μg/cigarette; approximately 10 to 20% of the nickel is released into the main-stream smoke (Bennett, 1981).

Human exposure to nickel is ubiquitous from man-made materials and substances. Nickel is present in stainless steels and nickel-plated materials, including coins and jewelry, nickel-cadmium batteries and certain paint pigments (such as yellow nickel titanate). Residual nickel is present in soaps, fats and oils that are manufactured by hydrogenation using nickel catalysts. Human exposure to nickel also derives from disposal or incineration of wastes and from the burning of fossil fuels (Grandjean, 1984).

Iatrogenic exposures to nickel derive from (a) nickel-containing prostheses (joint replacements, intraosseous pins, cardiac valve replacements, cardiac pacemaker wires and dental prostheses). (b) intravenous fluids and medications that are contaminated with nickel, and (c) extracorporeal haemodialysis, owing to nickel contamination of the dialysate fluid (Sunderman, 1983; Hopfer *et al.*, 1984a). Tjalve & Stahl (1984) have suggested that increased intestinal absorption of nickel and other metals may be responsible for the subacute myelo-optic neuropathy syndrome, associated with use of chloroiodohydroxyquinoline (Clioquinol) for treatment of enteric infections. Clioquinol forms a lipohilic nickel chelate that increases the intestinal absorption and tissue concentrations of nickel in rodents (Tjalve & Stahl, 1984).

Reference values for nickel concentrations in biological materials from humans without occupational exposures to nickel are summarized on page 333. For illustrative data on nickel concentrations in body fluids and excreta of nickel-exposed workers, readers may consult articles by Bernacki *et al.* (1978, 1980), Hogetveit *et al.* (1978, 1980), Morgan & Rouge (1979), Tola *et al.* (1979), Torjussen & Andersen (1979) and Grandjean *et al.* (1980).

REFERENCES

Anke, M., Grün, M., Groppel, B. & Kronemann, H. (1983) *Nutritional requirements of nickel.* In: Sarkar, B., ed., *Biological Aspects of Metals and Metal Related Diseases,* New York, Raven Press, pp. 89–105

Anke, M., Groppel, B., Kronemann, H. & Grün, M. (1984) *Nickel – an essential element.* In: Sunderman, F.W., Jr, ed., *Nickel in the Human Environment (IARC Scientific Publication No. 53),* Lyon, International Agency for Research on Cancer, pp. 339–365

Bencko, V. (1983) Nickel: A review of its occupational and environmental toxicology. *J. Hyg. Epidemiol. Microbiol. Immunol., 27,* 237–247

Bennett, B.G. (1981) *Summary exposure assessment for nickel.* In: *MARC Reports on Exposure Committment Assessments of Environmental Pollutants,* Vol. 1, Monitoring and Assessment Research Centre, Chelsea College, University of London, pp. 17–30

Bernacki, E.J., Parsons, G.E., Roy, B.R., Mikac-Devic, M., Kennedy, C.D. & Sunderman, F.W., Jr (1978) Urine nickel concentrations in nickel-exposed workers. *Ann. Clin. Lab. Sci., 8,* 184–189

Bernacki, E.J., Zygowicz, E. & Sunderman, F.W., Jr (1980) Fluctuations of nickel concentrations in urine of electroplating workers. *Ann. Clin. Lab. Sci., 10,* 33–39

Brown, S.S. & Sunderman, F.W., Jr, eds (1980) *Nickel Toxicology,* London, Academic Press

Brown, S.S. & Sunderman, F.W., Jr, eds (1984) *Progress in Nickel Toxicology,* Oxford, Blackwell

Camner, P., Johansson, A. & Lundborg, M. (1978) Alveolar macrophages in rabbits exposed to metallic nickel dust. Ultastructural changes and effect on phagocytosis. *Environ. Res., 16,* 226–235

Clary, J.J. (1975) Nickel chloride-induced metabolic changes in the rat and guinea pig. *Toxicol. Appl. Pharmacol., 31,* 55–56

Cronin, E., DiMichiel, A.D. & Brown, S.S. (1980) *Oral challenge in nickel-sensitive women with hand eczema.* In: Brown, S.S. & Sunderman, F.W., Jr, eds, *Nickel Toxicology,* London, Academic Press, pp. 149–152

Curstedt, T., Casarett-Bruce, M. & Camner, P. (1984) Changes in glycerophosphatides and their ether analogs in lung lavage of rabbits exposed to nickel dust. *Exp. Mol. Pathol., 41,* 26–34

Decsy, M.I. & Sunderman, F.W., Jr (1974) Binding of ^{63}Ni to rabbit serum α_1-macroglobulin *in vivo* and *in vitro. Bioinorg. Chem., 3,* 95–105

Diekert, G.B., Graf, E.F. & Thauer, R.K. (1979) Nickel requirement for carbon monoxide dehydrogenase formation in Clostridium pasteurianum. *Arch. Microbiol., 122,* 117–120

Diekert, G., Gilles, H.H., Jaenchen, R. & Thauer, R.K. (1980) Incorporation of 8 succinate per mol nickel into factor F_{430} by Methanobacterium thermoautotrophicum. *Arch. Microbiol., 128,* 256–262

Dixon, N.E., Gazzola, C., Asher, C.J., Lee, D.S.W., Blakely, R.L. & Zerner, B. (1980) Jack bean urease (EC 3.5.1.5). II. The relationship between nickel, enzymatic activity and the 'abnormal' ultraviolet spectrum. The nickel content of jack beans. *Can. J. Biochem., 58,* 474–480

Friedrich, C.G., Schneider, K. & Friedrich, B. (1982) Nickel in the catalytically active hydroxygenase of Alkaligenes eutrophus. *J. Bacteriol., 152,* 42–48

Gitlitz, P.H., Sunderman, F.W., Jr & Goldblatt, P.J. (1975) Aminoaciduria and proteinuria in rats after a single intraperitoneal injection of Ni[II]. *Toxicol. Appl. Pharmacol., 34,* 430–440

Graf, E.G. & Thauer, R.K. (1981) Hydrogenase from Methanobacterium thermoautotrophicum, a nickel-containing enzyme. *FEBS Lett., 136,* 165–169

Grandjean, P. (1984) *Human exposure to nickel.* In: Sunderman, F.W., Jr, ed., *Nickel in the Human Environment, (IARC Scientific Publication No. 53),* Lyon, International Agency for Research on Cancer, pp. 469–485

Grandjean, P., Selikoff, I.J., Shen, S.K. & Sunderman, F.W., Jr (1980) Nickel concentrations in plasma and urine of shipyard workers. *Am. J. Ind. Med., 1,* 181–189

Hogetveit, A.C., Barton, R.T. & Kostol, C.O. (1978) Plasma nickel as a primary index of exposure in nickel refining. *Ann. occup. Hyg., 21,* 113–120

Hogetveit, A.C., Barton, R.T. & Andersen, I. (1980) Variations of nickel in plasma and urine during the work period. *J. occup. Med., 22,* 597–600

Hopfer, S.M., Sunderman, F.W., Jr, Fredrickson, T.N. & Morse, E.E. (1979) Increased serum erythropoietin activity in rats following intrarenal injection of nickel subsulfide. *Res. Commun. Chem. Pathol. Pharmacol., 23,* 155–170

Hopfer, S.M., Linden, J.V., Crisostomo, C., Catalanotto, F., Galen, M. & Sunderman, F.W., Jr (1984a) Hypernickelemia in hemodialysis patients. *Ann. Clin. Lab. Sci., 14,* 412–413

Hopfer, S.M., Sunderman, F.W., Jr, McCully, K.S., Reid, M.C., Liber, C., Spears, J.R & Serur, J. (1984b) Studies of the pathogenesis of arteriosclerosis induced in rats by intrarenal injection of a carcinogen, nickel subsulfide. *Ann. Clin. Lab. Sci.*, *14*, 355–365

Hopfer, S.M., Sunderman, F.W., Jr, Reid, M.C. & Goldwasser, E. (1984c) Increased immunoreactive erythropoietin in serum and kidney extracts of rats with Ni_3S_2-induced erythrocytosis. *Res. Commun. Chem. Pathol. Pharmacol.*, *43*, 299–305

Horak, E. & Sunderman, F.W., Jr (1975a) Effects of Ni[II], other divalent metal ions and glucagon upon plasma glucose concentrations in normal, adrenalectomized and hypophysectomized rats. *Toxicol. appl. Pharmacol.*, *32*, 316–329

Horak, E. & Sunderman, F.W., Jr (1975b) Effects of Ni[II] upon plasma glucagon and glucose in rats. *Toxicol. appl. Pharmacol.*, *33*, 388–395

Horak, E., Zygowicz, E.R., Tarabishi, R., Mitchell, J.M. & Sunderman, F.W., Jr (1978) Effects of nickel chloride and nickel carbonyl upon glucose metabolism in rats. *Ann. Clin. Lab. Sci., 8*, 476–482

IARC (1976) *IARC Monographs on the Evaluation of Carcinogenic Risk of Chemicals to Man,* Volume 11, *Cadmium, Nickel, Some Epoxides, Miscellaneous Industrial Chemicals and General Considerations on Volatile Anaesthetics,* Lyon, International Agency for Research on Cancer, pp. 75–121

IARC (1984) *Nickel in the Human Environment,* Sunderman, F.W., Jr, ed., *(IARC Scientific Publication No. 53),* Lyon International Agency for Research on Cancer

Jasmin, G. & Solymoss, B. (1975) Polycythemia induced in rats by intrarenal injection of nickel subsulfide, αNi_3S_2. *Proc. Soc. Exp. Biol. Med., 148*, 774–776

Kaaber, K., Menne, T., Tjell, J.C. & Veien, N. (1979) Antabuse treatment of nickel dermatitis. Chelation – a new principle in the treatment of nickel dermatitis. *Contact Dermatitis, 5*, 221–228

Kirchgessner, M. & Schnegg, A. (1980) *Biochemical and physiological effects of nickel deficiency.* In: Nriagu, J.O., ed., *Nickel in the Environment,* New York, John Wiley and Sons, pp. 635–652

Leach, C.N., Jr, Linden, J., Hopfer, S.M., Chrisostomo, C. & Sunderman, F.W., Jr (1984) Serum nickel concentrations in patients with unstable angina and myocardial infarction. *Ann. Clin. Lab. Sci., 14*, 414–415

Leonard, A., Gerber, G.B., Jacquet, P. & Lauwerys, R.R. (1983) *Carcinogenicity, mutagenicity and teratogenicity of industrially used metals.* In: Kirsch-Volders, M., ed., *Mutagenicity, Carcinogenicity and Teratogenicity of Industrial Pollutants,* New York, Plenum Press, pp. 59–126

Machado-Carvalho, S.M. & Ziemer, P.L. (1982) Distribution and clearance of [63]Ni administered as [63]$NiCl_2$ in the rat. Intratracheal study. *Arch. Environ. Contam. Toxicol., 11*, 245–248

Maines, M.D. & Kappas, A. (1977) Metals as regulators of heme metabolism. *Science, 198*, 1215–1221

Maitani, T. & Suzuki, K.T. (1983) Dose-dependent induction of metallothionein in kidneys of mice injected with indium and nickel ions. *Chem. Pharm. Bull., 31*, 979–984

McCully, K.S., Rinehimer, L.A., Gillies, C.G., Hopfer, S.M. & Sunderman, F.W., Jr (1982a) Erythrocytosis, glomerulomegaly, mesangial hyperplasia, sialyl hyperplasia and arteriosclerosis induced in rats by nickel subsulfide. *Virchows Arch. Pathol. Anat.*, *394*, 207–220

McCully, K.S., Sunderman, F.W., Jr, Hopfer, S.M., Kevorkian, C.B. & Reid, M.C. (1982b) Effects of unilateral nephrectomy on erythrocytosis and arteriosclerosis induced in rats by intrarenal injection of nickel subsulfide. *Virchows Arch. Pathol. Anat.*, *397*, 251–259

McNeely, M.D., Sunderman, F.W., Jr, Nechay, M.W. & Levine, H. (1971) Abnormal concentrations of nickel in serum in cases of myocardial infarction, stroke, burns, hepatic cirrhosis and uremia. *Clin. Chem.*, *17*, 1123–1128

Morgan, L.G. & Rouge, P.J.C. (1979) A Study into the correlation between atmospheric and biological monitoring of nickel in nickel refinery workers. *Ann. occup. Hyg.*, *22*, 311–317

Morse, E.E., Lee, T.-Y., Reiss, R.F. & Sunderman, F.W., Jr (1977) Dose-response and time-response study of erythrocytosis in rats after intrarenal injection of nickel subsulfide. *Ann. Clin. Lab. Sci.*, *7*, 17–24

Mushak, P. (1984) *Nickel metabolism in health and disease.* In: Homburger, H.A. & Batsakis, J.G., eds, *Clinical Laboratory Annual – 1984*, Vol. 4, Norwalk, Connecticut, Appleton-Century-Crofts Inc., pp. 249–269

National Academy of Sciences (NAS) (1975) *Medical and Biological Effects of Environmental Pollutants: Nickel.* Washington DC

National Institute for Occupational Safety and Health (NIOSH) (1977) *Criteria for a Recommended Standard: Occupational Exposure to Inorganic Nickel.* Washington DC, US Government Printing Office

Nomoto, S., Hirabayashu, T. & Fukuda, T. (1983) *Serum nickel concentrations in women during pregnancy, parturition and post-partum.* In: Brown, S.S. & Savory, J.S., eds, *Chemical Toxicology and Clinical Chemistry of Metals*, London, Academic Press, pp. 351–352

Nomoto, S., McNeely, M.D. & Sunderman, F.W., Jr (1971) Isolation of a nickel α_2-macroglobulin from rabbit serum. *Biochemistry*, *10*, 1647–1651

Nriagu, J.O., ed. (1980) *Nickel in the Environment.* New York, John Wiley and Sons

Onkelinx, C. & Sunderman, F.W., Jr (1980) *Modeling of nickel metabolism.* In: Nriagu, J.O., ed., *Nickel in the Environment*, New York, John Wiley and Sons, pp. 525–545

Oskarsson, A. & Tjalve, H. (1979) An autoradiographic study on the distribution of $^{63}NiCl_2$ in mice. *Ann. Clin. Lab. Sci.*, *9*, 47–59

Ottolenghi, A.D., Haseman, J.K., Payne, W.W., Falk, H.L. & MacFarland, H.N. (1975) Inhalation studies of nickel sulfide in pulmonary carcinogenesis of rats. *J. natl Cancer Inst.*, *54*, 1165–1172

Parker, K. & Sunderman, F.W., Jr (1974) Distribution of ^{63}Ni in rabbit tissues following intravenous injection of $^{63}NiCl_2$. *Res. Commun. Chem. Pathol. Pharmacol.*, *7*, 755–762

Raithel, H.-J. & Schaller, K.H. (1981) About the toxicity and carcinogenicity of nickel and its compounds. A review of the current knowledge. *Zentralbl. Bakteriol. Hyg. Abt. I, (Orig. B)*, *173*, 63–91

Rogers, R.R., Garner, R.J., Riddle, M.M., Luebke, R.W. & Smialowicz, R.J. (1983) Augmentation of murine natural killer cell activity by manganese chloride. *Toxicol. appl. Pharmacol., 70,* 7–17

Rubanyi, G., Birtalan, I., Girgely, A. & Kovach, A.G.B. (1982) Serum nickel concentration in women during pregnancy, during parturition and post-partum. *Am. J. Obstet. Gynecol., 143,* 167–169

Sarkar, B. (1980) *Nickel in blood and kidney.* In: Brown, S.S. & Sunderman, F.W., Jr, eds, *Nickel Toxicology,* London, Academic Press, pp. 81–84

Savory, J., Brown, S., Bertholf, R., Ross, R., Savory, M.G. & Wells, M.R. (1984) Serum and lymphocyte nickel and aluminium concentrations in patients with extracorporeal hemodialysis. *Ann. Clin. Lab. Sci., 14,* 413–414

Shimkin, M.B., Stoner, G.D. & Theiss, J.C. (1978) *Lung tumor response in mice to metals and metal salts.* In: Schrauzer, G.N., ed., *Inorganic and Nutritional Aspects of Cancer,* New York, Plenum Press, pp. 85–91

Smialowicz, R.J., Rogers, R.R., Riddle, M.M. & Scott, G.A. (1984) Immunologic effects of nickel. I. Suppression of cellular and humoral immunity. *Environ. Res., 33,* 413–427

Smith, J.C. & Hackley, B. (1968) Distribution and excretion of nickel-63 administered intravenously to rats. *J. Nutr., 95,* 541–546

Soestbergen, M.V. & Sunderman, F.W., Jr (1972) ^{63}Ni complexes in rabbit serum and urine after injection of ^{63}NiCl$_2$. *Clin. Chem., 18,* 1478–1484

Solymoss, B. & Jasmin, G. (1978) Studies on the mechanism of polycythemia induced in rats by Ni$_3$S$_2$. *Exp. Hematol., 6,* 43–47

Spears, J.W., Hatfield, E.E., Forbes, R.M. & Koenig, S.E. (1978) Studies on the role of nickel in the ruminant. *J. Nutr., 108,* 313–320

Sunderman, F.W. (1971) The treatment of acute nickel carbonyl poisoning with sodium diethyldithiocarbamate. *Ann. Clin. Res., 3,* 182–185

Sunderman, F.W., Jr (1981a) *Nickel.* In: Bronner, F. & Coburn, J.W., eds, *Disorders of Mineral Metabolism,* Vol. 1, New York, Academic Press, pp. 201–232

Sunderman, F.W., Jr (1981b) Recent research on nickel carcinogenesis. *Environ. Health Persp., 40,* 131–141

Sunderman, F.W., Jr (1983) Potential toxicity from nickel contamination of intravenous fluids. *Ann. Clin. Lab. Sci., 13,* 1–4

Sunderman, F.W., Jr (1984) Recent progress in nickel carcinogenesis. *Toxicol. Environ. Chem., 8,* 235–252

Sunderman, F.W. & Donnelly, A.J. (1965) Studies of nickel carcinogenesis: Metastasizing pulmonary tumors in rats induced by the inhalation of nickel carbonyl. *Am. J. Pathol., 46,* 1027–1042

Sunderman, F.W., Jr & Fraser, C.B. (1983) Effects of nickel chloride and diethyldithiocarbamate on metallothionein in rat liver and kidney. *Ann., Clin. Lab. Sci., 13,* 489–495

Sunderman, F.W., Jr & Horak, E. (1981) *Biochemical indices of nephrotoxicity, exemplified by studies of nickel nephropathy.* In: Brown, S.S. & Davies, D.S., eds, *Organ-Directed Toxicity, Chemical Indices and Mechanisms,* Oxford, Pergamon Press, pp. 55–67

Sunderman, F.W., Jr & McCully, K.S. (1983) Effects of manganese compounds on carcinogenicity of nickel subsulfide in rats. *Carcinogenesis, 4,* 461–465

Sunderman, F.W., Jr, Lau, T.J. & Cralley, L.F. (1974) Inhibitory effect of manganese upon muscle tumorigenesis by nickel sulfide. *Cancer Res., 34,* 92–95

Sunderman, F.W., Jr, Kasprzak, K., Horak, E., Gitlitz, P. & Onkelinx, C. (1976a) Effects of triethylenetetramine upon the metabolism and toxicity of ^{63}NiCl$_2$ in rats. *Toxicol. appl. Pharmacol., 38,* 177–188

Sunderman, F.W., Jr, Kasprzak, K.S., Lau, T.J., Minghetti, P.P., Maenza, R.M., Becker, N., Onkelinx, C. & Goldblatt, P.J. (1976b) Effects of manganese on carcinogenicity and metabolism of nickel subsulfide. *Cancer Res., 36,* 1790–1800

Sunderman, F.W., Jr, Maenza, R.M., Hopfer, S.M., Mitchell, J.M., Allpass, P.R. & Damjanov, I. (1979) Induction of renal cancers in rats by intrarenal injection of nickel subsulfide. *J. environ. Pathol. Toxicol., 2,* 1511–1527

Sunderman, F.W., Jr, Costa, E.R., Fraser, C., Hui, G., Levine, J.L. & Tse, T.P.H. (1981) ^{63}Ni-constituents in renal cytosol of rats after injection of ^{63}NiCl$_2$. *Ann. Clin. Lab. Sci., 11,* 488–496

Sunderman, F.W., Jr, Hopfer, S.M., Reid, M.C., Shen, S.K. & Kevorkian, C.B. (1982) Erythropoietin-mediated erythrocytosis in rodents after intrarenal injection of nickel subsulfide. *Yale J. Biol. Med., 55,* 123–136

Sunderman, F.W., Jr, Bibeau, L.M. & Reid, M.C. (1983a) Synergistic induction of microsomal heme oxygenase activity in rat liver and kidney by diethyldithiocarbamate and nickel chloride. *Toxicol. appl. Pharmacol., 71,* 436–446

Sunderman, F.W., Jr, Mangold, B.L.K., Wong, S.H.Y., Shen, S.K., Reid, M.C. & Jansson, I. (1983b) High-performance size-exclusion chromatography of ^{63}-Ni-constituents in renal cytosol and microsomes from ^{63}NiCl$_2$-treated rats. *Res. Commun. Chem. Pathol. Pharmacol., 39,* 477–492

Sunderman, F.W., Jr, Reid, M.C., Bibeau, L.M. & Linden, J.V. (1983c) Nickel induction of microsomal heme oxygenase activity in rodents. *Toxicol. appl. Pharmacol., 68,* 87–95

Sunderman, F.W., Jr, Reid, M.C., Shen, S.K. & Kevorkian, C.B. (1983d) *Embryotoxicity and teratogenicity of nickel compounds.* In: Clarkson, T.W., Nordberg, G.F. & Sager, P.R., eds, *Reproductive and Developmental Toxicity of Metals,* New York, Plenum Press, pp. 399–416

Sunderman, F.W., Jr, McCully, K.S. & Hopfer, S.M. (1984a) Association between erythrocytosis and renal cancers in rats following intrarenal injection of nickel compounds. *Carcinogenesis, 5,* 1511–1517

Sunderman, F.W., Jr, Zaharia, O. & Reid, M.C. (1984b) Lipid peroxidation induced by nickel chloride in rat liver and kidney. *Ann. Clin. Lab. Sci., 14,* 405–406

Svejgaard, E., Morling, N., Svejgaard, A. & Veien, N.K. (1978) Lymphocyte transformation induced by nickel sulfate. *Acta Derm. Venereol., 58,* 245–250

Swoboda, B., Fritz, J. & Ludvan, M. (1977) Nickel allergy and leukocyte migration inhibition. *Dermatol. Monatsschr., 163,* 208–212

Thauer, R.K., Diekert, G. & Schonheit, P. (1980) Biological role of nickel. *Trends Biochem. Sci., 5,* 304–306

Tjalve, H. & Stahl, K. (1984) Effect of 5-chloro-7-iodo-8-hydroxy-quinoline (Clioquinol) on the uptake and distribution of nickel, zinc and mercury in mice. *Acta Pharmacol. Toxicol., 55,* 65–72

Tola, S., Kilpio, J. & Virtamo, M. (1979) Urinary and plasma concentrations of nickel as indicators of exposure to nickel in an electroplating shop. *J. occup. Med., 21,* 184–188

Torjussen, W. & Andersen, I. (1979) Nickel concentrations in nasal mucosa, plasma and urine in active and retired nickel workers. *Ann. Clin. Lab. Sci., 9,* 289–298

Webster, J.D., Parker, T.F., Alfrey, A.C., Smythe, W.R., Kubo, H., Neal, G. & Hull, A.R. (1980) Acute nickel intoxication by dialysis. *Ann. intern. Med., 92,* 931–933

Yarita, T. & Nettesheim, P. (1978) Carcinogenicity of nickel subsulfide for respiratory tract epithelium. *Cancer Res., 38,* 3140–3145

CHAPTER 6

CADMIUM: SOURCES, EXPOSURE AND POSSIBLE CARCINOGENICITY

G. Kazantzis

Department of Occupational Health,
London School of Hygiene and Tropical Medicine,
Keppel Street, London WC1E 7HT, UK

SOURCES

Cadmium is widely but sparsely distributed over the earth's surface, being found most commonly as the sulfide, in association more often with zinc, but also with lead or copper. Crustal weathering releases cadmium in soils and aquatic systems, although this natural release is surpassed by the mining of zinc/cadmium deposits. Volcanic action is probably the major natural source of cadmium in the atmosphere. However, atmospheric emissions from man-made sources exceed those from natural sources by about one order of magnitude.

Cadmium release to the environment resulting from human activity has been considered by Nriagu (1979) and Fishbein (1981). Flow patterns in the United States have been analysed by Yost (1979), emissions in Japan by Yamagata (1979) and sources of environmental concentrations in the European Community by Hutton (1982). Total cadmium usage in the western world in 1980 has been estimated to be of the order of 13 000 metric tons, with electroplating and nickel-cadmium battery manufacture each accounting for 29% of total consumption, cadmium-based pigments for 24% of this total, and stabilizers, alloys, solar cells, electronic components and fungicides accounting for the remainder. Currently, the use of cadmium in batteries is increasing, although environmental restrictions, particularly in Sweden and Japan, may alter the pattern of usage in the future. Cadmium-containing products tend to be disposed of with minimal recycling after use, probably not more than 5% in Europe and 15–20% in the USA.

Cadmium emissions into the atmosphere from human activity result principally from iron and steel production, followed by waste incineration and non-ferrous metal production. Fossil fuel combustion accounts for only a small proportion of total atmospheric emissions. Waste disposal accounts for the largest single source of cadmium emission to land in the European Community, and is greater than the combined total of coal combustion, iron and steel production, phosphate fertilizer manufacture and use and zinc production (Hutton, 1982). These five sources account for 90% of the total emissions to land. Sewage sludge has been found to contain 2–1 500 mg Cd/kg, and its regular application to crop land results in a steady accumulation of cadmium in soil.

The cadmium content of phosphate fertilizers varies widely, depending on the cadmium content in the rock phosphate of the country of origin (mainly between 2 and 20 mg/kg). However, the regular application of phosphate fertilizer again progressively increases the cadmium content of surface soil. There is less information available on cadmium release to water, the most significant sources being the manufacture of cadmium-containing articles and phosphate fertilizer.

ENVIRONMENTAL LEVELS

Atmospheric cadmium concentrations have ranged from 1–6 ng/m^3 in rural areas, 4–20 ng/m^3 in urban areas, 18–54 ng/m^3 in industrial Liège, Belgium (Kretzschmar et al., 1980) and 200–11 000 ng/m^3 in the vicinity of a lead recovery plant (Muskett et al., 1979). With regard to occupational exposure, the threshold limit value for cadmium fume and dust is currently 50 $\mu g/m^3$. In the past, very high atmospheric concentrations of cadmium fume and cadmium oxide dust were recorded, frequently exceeding 1 mg/m^3 in the 1950's.

Municipal waters in industrialised countries generally contain less than 1 μg Cd/L, the upper limit set in the International Standards for Drinking Water being 10 μg/L (WHO, 1971). Cadmium concentrations in soil can vary widely. In the majority of soils, cadmium is found in concentrations of 1 mg/kg, or less. A geochemical atlas of England and Wales based on stream sediment samples showed 83% of the land with a level below 1 mg/kg and 0.33% of the total area examined with a level above 4 mg/kg. However, in the vicinity of Shipham, Somerset, where mining operations for zinc carbonate or calamine had been carried out in the past, cadmium concentrations have been found ranging up to 800 mg/kg (Marples & Thornton, 1980). These levels are far in excess of those found in the cadmium-polluted region of Toyama, Japan, where itai-itai disease has been endemic. The transfer of cadmium from soil to pasture and crop plants is not directly related to soil cadmium levels, but is more dependent on the trace element composition of the soil (zinc, in particular), soil pH, plant species and other factors.

HUMAN EXPOSURE

Diet and cigarette smoking represent the principal sources of cadmium intake in the non-industrially exposed population. Examples of foods which may have high cadmium levels are liver and kidney, shellfish and certain vegetables grown on contaminated soil. Estimates of average daily intake of cadmium vary with the method used. In general, duplicate diet studies have given higher levels than estimates from faecal analysis. Average dietary intakes of cadmium in the European

Community have been estimated at 10–20 µg/day (Walters & Sherlock, 1981), to 48 µg/day in the Federal Republic of Germany (Essing *et al.,* 1969). In the USA, levels of 26–61 µg/day have been quoted, (FDA, 1977), while in unpolluted areas in Japan a range of 59–113 µg/day has been given (Japan Public Health Association, 1970). A Provisional Tolerable Weekly Intake of 400–500 µg has been proposed by the Joint FAO/WHO Expert Committee on Food Additives (WHO, 1972).

With an average daily intake of 10–25 µg cadmium, assuming a 5% absorption rate from the gastrointestinal tract, the total amount of cadmium absorbed from food and water would be 0.5–1.5 µg. Assuming a 50% absorption rate from the respiratory tract, a smoker of 20 cigarettes a day would absorb an additional 1–2 µg cadmium, thus exceeding absorption from dietary sources.

Cadmium intake and absorption is greater following occupational exposure and exceeds that from all other sources. With atmospheric concentrations of cadmium within the Threshold Limit Value at 10–50 µg/m^3 and total respired air of 10 m^3 per work shift, inhaled cadmium would be 100–500 µg/day. Assuming an absorption rate of 25% for cadmium-containing particulates, 25–125 µg cadmium/day would be absorbed from the respiratory tract and additional absorption would occur following translocation to the gastrointestinal compartment. A cadmium-exposed worker who is a smoker would absorb a further amount of cadmium by ingestion as a result of contamination (Hassler *et al.,* 1983).

While the newborn infant is free of cadmium, the body burden increases with age to a maximum in the range of 5–20 mg at about 50 years in unexposed subjects. Smoking increases the body burden significantly. Using in-vivo neutron activation analysis, the total body burden in unexposed subjects in the USA was estimated to be 19.3 mg in non-smokers and 35.5 mg in smokers (Ellis *et al.,* 1979). The highest concentration of cadmium is found in the kidneys, with about a third of the body burden, whilst liver and kidneys together account for about half the body burden. Cadmium concentrations in kidney cortex, expressed as geometric means, have varied from 9.0–30.5 mg Cd/kg (wet weight), depending on the country, with 56.2 mg/kg reported from Japan (Vahter, 1982).

Cadmium excretion in the urine of unexposed subjects if generally below 2 µg/L, with higher values again in smokers. Cadmium levels in blood of unexposed males from different countries have varied between median values of 0.7–3.9 µg/L (90th percentiles 1.2 and 9.0 µg/L) in smokers and 0.2–1.1 µg/L (90th percentiles 0.8 and 1.7 µg/L) in non- and former smokers (Vahter, 1982). Further data on cadmium levels in kidney and blood, together with the sampling and quality-control procedures employed, are given by Vahter (1982).

Quantitative determination of trace amounts of cadmium in biological samples is a difficult and painstaking process. Special care must be taken to avoid contamination in the collection and storage of samples. The initial step of sample preparation by wet or dry ashing is followed by separation of cadmium from interfering compounds and concentration by means of chelation, solvent extraction or ion-exchange techniques. Analytical procedures determine cadmium as the element. Isotope-dilution mass spectrometry (Everson & Patterson, 1980) probably gives the nearest approximation to a true value, but is extremely expensive. Atomic absorption spectrometry, colorimetry, polarography, anodic-stripping voltammetry, atomic emission and fluorescence spectrometry, neutron activation analysis and proton-induced X-ray emission (PIXE) have been used, and some of these methods have been reviewed by Stoeppler (1982). Atomic absorption spectrometry is the most widely used method, but careful correction for interference is required. Flameless atomic absorption using a graphite furnace can detect cadmium in blood and urine down to 0.1–0.3 µg/L (Delves, 1982). Interference from sodium chloride gave erroneously high values for cadmium in biological samples before background correction was applied in the 1970's. Activation analysis is of particular value for the determination of cadmium in tissue samples and PIXE, in particular, is useful for estimation in very small samples. In-vivo neutron activation analysis has been developed for the determination of cadmium in liver and kidney. Problems relating to the localisation of the kidney have now been overcome, but the detection limit remains too high for accuracte measurement of tissue levels in unexposed subjects (Ellis *et al.,* 1981). Strict quality-control and quality-assurance procedures are essential for cadmium estimation in biological samples. Inter-laboratory comparisons in the past have shown wide variations in results. Blood and urinary cadmium levels using atomic absorption, in particular, were erroneously high in many laboratories until the mid 1970's and sample contamination and method bias are still responsible for poor performance in inter-laboratory comparison studies.

EVIDENCE FOR CARCINOGENICITY IN HUMANS

Cadmium has been a suspect human carcinogen as a result of epidemiological studies in workers with heavy past exposure to cadmium oxide fume and dust. Four deaths from prostatic cancer were observed, compared to an expected number of 0.58, in a group of 248 nickel-cadmium battery workers in Britain (Kipling & Waterhouse, 1967). These findings were supported in a second study of smelter workers with heavy past exposure to cadmium oxide dust and fume. A significant excess mortality from lung cancer was also noted, but there was concomitant exposure to arsenic (Lemen *et al.,* 1976). A follow-up study from this plant has confirmed a significant excess mortality from lung cancer in workers employed for two years or more and has shown a significant dose-response relationship between lung cancer mortality and cumulative exposure to cadmium (Thon *et al.,* 1985). However the effects of past exposure to arsenic, may have been underestimated. No further death from prostatic cancer was observed. A Swedish study examined mortality in two cohorts of workers, one from a cadmium-nickel battery plant (where exposure levels were above 1 µg/m^3) the other from a copper-cadmium alloy plant. A small non-significant excess of prostatic cancer was found (Kjellstrom *et al.,* 1979). A further follow-up of the Swedish nickel-cadmium battery plant showed, in those exposed for more than 15 years, small non-significant increases in deaths from cancer of the prostate, bladder and lung (Andersson *et al.,* 1983). In copper-cadmium alloy workers in Britain, a small excess of lung cancer was found in workers with more than 10 years exposure, again to concentrations of cadmium fume exceeding 1 mg/m^3 in the early 1950's (Holden, 1980). The mortality from both lung and prostatic cancer was significantly raised in vicinity workers from the same plant, in whom no evidence of a dose-response

Table 1. Observed and expected cases of prostatic and lung cancer in principal epidemiological studies of cadmium workers

	Observed	Expected	Reference
Prostate	4	0.58[a]	Kipling & Waterhouse, 1967
	4	0.88[a]	Lemen et al., 1976
	4	2.69	Kjellstrom et al., 1979
	2	1.2	Kjellstrom et al., 1979
	3	1.6	Andersson et al., 1973
	8	6.6	Sorahan & Waterhouse, 1983
	23	23.3	Armstrong & Kazantzis, 1983
Lung	12	5.1[a]	Lemen et al., 1976
	7	3.9	Holden, 1980
	3	2.5	Andersson et al., 1983
	89	70.2[a]	Sorahan & Waterhouse, 1983
	199	185.6	Armstrong & Kazantzis, 1983
	20	11.43[a]	Thon et al., 1985

[a] $p < 0.05$

relationship could be elicited. The British nickel-cadmium battery plant originally investigated by Kipling and Waterhouse in 1967 has been further studied by Sorahan and Waterhouse (1983). No new evidence of any association between occupational exposure to cadmium and cancer of the prostate was found in 3025 employees who started work between 1923 and 1975, although there was an excess mortality from cancer of the respiratory system significant at the 5% level. However, as in other studies, smoking histories were not available and confounding factors were present here in the form of nickel hydroxide and oxyacetylene welding fumes.

A WHO study group (1980) considered the existing epidemiological studies to be inconclusive because of the small numbers of workers involved. To investigate mortality in a larger sample than previously available, a cohort mortality study has been performed in England in 17 plants with processes using cadmium (Kazantzis & Armstrong, 1982; Armstrong & Kazantzis, 1983). The cohort comprised 6 995 cadmium-exposed male workers born before 1940 and first employed before 1970 for a minimum period of one year. Jobs were assessed as involving high, medium or low exposure to cadmium. With an overall trace rate of over 96%, the mean duration of exposure was 11 years and the mean interval from first exposure to the end of follow-up was 27 years. However, only 17% were in the medium and only 3% were in the high-exposure categories, 80% being classified as having had 'always low' exposure. No excess of prostatic cancer was found, with a small but non-significant excess of lung cancer in all exposure categories. However, in men with more than 10 years exposure, this excess was significant at the 5% level, but only in the 'always low' exposure category. The observed and expected cases of prostatic and lung cancer in the principal epidemiological studies are shown in Table 1.

Cadmium workers are generally exposed to other carcinogens in the working environment, which act as confounding factors in epidemiological studies. Examples of such confounding factors are nickel, arsenic and polycyclic hydrocarbons. Furthermore, many cadmium-exposed workers belong to semi-skilled or unskilled social classes and are likely to be heavier cigarette smokers than members of 'higher' social class. Smoking histories are difficult to obtain retrospectively in cohort studies. Again, accurate information about the intensity of past exposure to cadmium is lacking, in particular before the introduction of reliable environmental and biological monitoring procedures. Prostatic cancer is a common condition in elderly males, with a complex etiology and multiple predisposing factors (Piscator, 1981). It frequently occurs *in situ* without giving rise to clinical effects and its incidence in epidemiological studies may relate to the frequency of histological examination of the prostate gland. Bias may be introduced by performing such examinations more frequently in subjects known to have been cadmium workers. Careful differentiation should be made between prostatic cancer incidence and mortality. The recent epidemiological studies provide no new evidence of an association between cadmium exposure and prostatic cancer. However, the findings cannot be taken as evidence against an association of prostatic cancer with high levels of past exposure to cadmium. In general, recent epidemiological studies have weakened the case of cadmium as a prostatic carcinogen and strengthened suspicion with regard to the lung.

EVIDENCE FOR CARCINOGENICITY IN ANIMALS

IARC (1976, 1982) has accepted the evidence for cadmium powder, cadmium chloride, sulfate, sulfide and oxide giving rise to injection-site sarcoma in rats and for the first two compounds inducing interstitial cell tumours, following testicular atrophy, in rats and mice after intramuscular injection. They found oral studies inadequate for evaluation. However, the interstitial-cell tumours are not now considered to be neoplasms but instead to represent a hyperplastic response to the necrotizing effect of cadmium on the testis. More recently, the inhalation by Wistar rats of a cadmium chloride aerosol at concentrations of 12.5, 25 and 50 mg/m^3 has been shown to give rise to a high incidence of primary lung cancer, with clear evidence to a dose-response relationship (Takenaka *et al.*, 1983). The animals were exposed continuously for 18 months and followed for a further period of 13 months. The relevance of these animal studies to human exposure situations is unknown.

Evidence for the mutagenic activity of cadmium is conflicting, and is summarized by IARC (1982) and by Kazantzis (1983). Cadmium acetate was shown to be as potent as sodium chromate in producing transformation of Syrian hamster embryo cells. Transformation was also observed after transplacental exposure, the cadmium salt having been injected into pregnant hamsters (DiPaolo & Casto, 1979).

REFERENCES

Andersson, K., Elinder, C.G., Hogstedt, C., Kjellström, T. & Spang, G. (1984) Mortality among cadmium and nickel exposed workers in a Swedish battery factory. *Toxicol. environ. Chem., 9,* 53–62

Armstrong, B.G. & Kazantzis, G. (1983) The mortality of cadmium workers. *Lancet, i,* 1425–1427

Delves, H.T. (1982) *Analytical Techniques for Measuring Cadmium in Blood.* Proc. Int. Workshop on Biological Indicators of Cadmium Exposure, Diagnostic and Analytical Reliability. Luxembourg, 7–9 July 1982, Commission of the European Communities, and International Union of Pure and Applied Chemistry

DiPaolo, J.A. & Casto, B.C. (1979) Quantitative studies of in-vitro morphological transformation of Syrian hamster cells by inorganic metal salts. *Cancer Res., 39,* 1008–1013

Ellis, K.J., Vartsky, D., Zanzi, I. & Cohn, S.H. (1979) Cadmium: In-vivo measurement in smokers and non-smokers. *Science, 205,* 323–325

Ellis, K.J., Morgan, W.D., Zanzi, I., Yasumura, S., Vartsky, D.D. & Cohn, S.H. (1981) Critical concentrations of cadmium in human renal cortex: Dose effect studies in cadmium smelter workers. *J. Toxicol. environ. Health, 7,* 691–703

Essing, H.G., Schaller, K.H., Szadowski, D. & Lehnert, G. (1969) Usuelle cadmium belastung durch Nahrungs mettel und Getranke. *Arch. Hyg. Bakteriol., 153,* 490–494

Everson, J. & Patterson, C.C. (1980) 'Ultraclean' isotope dilution/mass spectrometric analyses for lead and cadmium in human blood plasma indicate that most reported values are artificially high. *Clin. Chem., 26,* 1603–1607

FDA (1977) Compliance Program Evaluation FY 1974 Total Diet Studies (7320.08) Washington DC, FDA Bureau of Foods

Fishbein, L. (1981) Sources, transport and alterations of metal compounds: An overview. 1. Arsenic, beryllium, cadmium, chromium and nickel. *Environ. Health Perspect., 40,* 43–64

Hassler, E., Lind, B. & Piscator, M. (1983) Cadmium in blood and urine related to present and past exposure. A study of workers in an alkaline battery factory. *Br. J. ind. Med., 40,* 420–425

Holden, H. (1980) *Further mortality studies in workers exposed to cadmium fume.* In: *Occupational Exposure to Cadmium,* Report on a Seminar, London, 20 March 1980, Cadmium Association, pp. 23–24

Hutton, M. (1982) *Cadmium in the European Community: A prospective assessment of sources, human exposure and environmental impact.* MARC Technical Report No. 26, London, Monitoring and Assessment Research Centre

IARC (1976) *IARC Monographs on the Evaluation of Carcinogenic Risk of Chemicals to Man,* Volume 11, *Cadmium, Nickel, Some Epoxides, Miscellaneous Industrial Chemicals and General Considerations on Volatile Anaesthetics,* Lyon, International Agency for Research on Cancer

IARC (1982) *IARC Monographs on the Evaluation of the Carcinogenic Risk of Chemicals to Humans,* Supplement 4, *Chemicals, Industrial Processes and Industries Associated with Cancer in Humans,* Lyon, International Agency for Research on Cancer

Japan Public Health Association (1970) *Study on Cadmium Intake and Accumulation in Areas Requiring Official Observation* [in Japanese], Tokyo, pp. 1–49

Kazantzis, G. (1984) Mutagenic and carcinogenic effects of cadmium. *Toxicol. environ. Chem., 8,* 267–278

Kazantzis, G. & Armstrong, B.G. (1982) A mortality study of cadmium workers in the United Kingdom. *Scand. J. Work environ. Health, 8* (Suppl. 1), 157–160

Kipling, M.D. & Waterhouse, J.A.H. (1967) Cadmium and prostatic carcinoma (Letter to the Editor). *Lancet, i,* 730–731

Kjellström, T., Friberg, L. & Rahnster, B. (1979) Mortality and cancer morbidity among cadmium exposed workers. *Environ. Health Perspect., 28,* 199–204

Kretzschmar, J.G., Delespaul, I. & De Rijck, T.H. (1980) Heavy metal levels in Belgium: A five-year survey. *Sci. total Environ., 14,* 85–97

Lemen, R.A., Lee, J.S., Wagoner, J.K. & Blejer, H.P. (1976) Cancer mortality among cadmium production workers. *Ann. N.Y. Acad. Sci., 271,* 273–279

Marples, A.E. & Thornton, I. (1980) *The distribution of cadmium derived from geochemical and industrial sources in agricultural soils and pasture herbage in parts of Britain.* In: *Cadmium 79* (Edited Proceedings Second International Cadmium Conference, Cannes) *Metal Bulletin,* London, Cadmium Association, pp. 74–79

Muskett, C.J., Roberts, L.H. & Page, B.J. (1979) Cadmium and lead pollution from secondary metal refinery operations. *Sci. total Environ., 11,* 73–87

Nriagu, J.O. (1979) Global inventory of natural and anthropogenic emissions of trace metals to the atmosphere. *Nature, 279,* 409–411

Piscator, M. (1981) Role of cadmium in carcinogenesis with special reference to cancer of the prostate. *Environ. Health Perspect., 40,* 107–120

Sorahan, T. & Waterhouse, J.A.H. (1983) Mortality study of nickel cadmium battery workers by the method of regression models in life tables. *Br. J. ind. Med., 40,* 293–300

Stoeppler, M. (1982) *Analysis of cadmium in biological materials.* In: Wilson, D. & Volpe, R.A., eds, *Cadmium 81* (Edited Proceedings Third International Cadmium Conference, Miami), London, Cadmium Association, pp. 95–102

Takenaka, S., Oldiges, H., König, H., Hochrainer, D. & Oberdörster, G. (1983) Carcinogenicity of cadmium chloride aerosols in W rats. *J. natl Cancer Inst., 70,* 367–373

Thun, M., Schnorr, T.M., Smith, A.B., Halperin, W.E. & Lemen, R.A. (1985) Mortality among a cohort of US cadmium production workers – an update. *J. natl Cancer Inst., 74,* 325–333

Vahter, M. (1982) *Assessment of human exposure to lead and cadmium through biological monitoring.* National Swedish Institute of Environmental Medicine and Department of Environmental Hygiene, Stockholm, Karolinska Institute

Walters, B. & Sherlock, J. (1981) *Studies on the dietary intake of heavy metals.* In: *Heavy Metals in the Environment* (International Conference, Amsterdam, September 1981), Edinburgh, CEP Consultants Ltd, pp. 506–512

WHO (1971) *International Standards for Drinking Water,* 3rd Edition. Geneva, World Health Organization

WHO (1972) *Evaluation of Certain Food Additives and the Contaminants Mercury, Lead and Cadmium.* Sixteenth Report of the Joint FAO/WHO Expert Committee on Food Additives, Geneva, World Health Organization

WHO (1980) *Recommended Health Based Limits in Occupational Exposure to Heavy Metals.* Geneva, World Health Organization, pp. 21–35

Yamagata, N. (1979) Industrial emission of cadmium in Japan. *Environ. Health Perspect., 28,* 17–22

Yost, K.J. (1979) Some aspects of cadmium flow in the US. *Environ. Health Perspect., 28,* 5–16

CHAPTER 7

LEAD: SOURCES, EXPOSURE AND POSSIBLE CARCINOGENICITY

G. Kazantzis

Department of Occupational Health,
London School of Hygiene and Tropical Medicine,
Keppel Street, London WC1E 7HT, UK

SOURCES

Lead is a relatively abundant element in the earth's crust. The erosion of lead-containing rocks and volcanic activity are responsible for average soil concentrations of the order of 5–25 mg/kg and fresh-water concentrations, remote from human activity, often below 1 µg/L. Lead, which has been mined more often as the sulfide, galena, has been widely used for about 4 000 years, so that the natural human body burden can only be surmised. Atmospheric lead emissions from human activity have been estimated to total 450 000 t/year, compared with 25 000 t/year from natural sources (Nriagu, 1979).

World production of lead over the past decade has been of the order of 2.5 million t/year, with battery production accounting for about one half of the lead consumed. About half the lead used in battery manufacture is recycled. The second largest usage of lead is accounted for by alkyl lead fuel additive, none of which is recoverable. Considerable amounts of lead are also used in the manufacture of cable sheathings, lead sheet, pipes and tubes, solders, alloys, type metal, paints and glazes. Red lead is used as a protective paint for structural steel work and lead chromate as a yellow pigment.

Lead is released into the environment not only from lead recovery processes, but also in the processing of other non-ferrous metal ores, such as zinc and cadmium. Thermal processes, such as iron and steel production, coal combustion and refuse incineration, provide additional sources of environmental lead. However, the combustion of alkyl lead in petrol probably accounts for over one half of the total emission from man-made sources (Nriagu, 1979).

ENVIRONMENTAL LEVELS

Atmospheric lead concentrations range from less than 0.2 $\mu g/m^3$ in rural areas (Cawse, 1977) to average concentrations of about 1 $\mu g/m^3$ in urban environments. In the latter, however, atmospheric concentrations can vary widely, depending on traffic density, distance from main roads, meteorological conditions and the configuration of buildings. On the central reservation of motorways, levels as high as 20 $\mu g/m^3$ have been recorded (Stocks, *et al.,* 1961; Waldron, 1980). In a London borough, mean atmospheric concentrations of 28 $\mu g/m^3$ over 24 hours and 3 $\mu g/m^3$ over a six-month period were observed (Department of the Environment, 1974). The American Conference of Governmental Industrial Hygienists have set a Threshold Limit Value (TLV) of 0.15 mg/m^3 for occupational exposure to lead. The Maximum Allowable Concentration in the USSR is 0.01 mg/m^3. In the past, many lead workers were exposed to atmospheric concentrations well above the current TLV (in particular in lead smelting and refining and in battery manufacture) and lead poisoning was one of the more common industrial intoxications.

Lead particulates emitted from motor vehicle exhausts, although highly aggregated, have a maximum dimension less than 1 μm and may be widely dispersed. In urban environments, their deposition gives rise to lead levels in street dust of around 1–2 mg/g, with lower values in homes and schools (Duggan & Williams, 1977; Culbard *et al.,* 1983). While contamination of food plants occurs by direct deposition of particulates, uptake through the root system is influenced by other factors in addition to the lead content of the soil.

The concentration of lead in drinking water is generally below 10 $\mu g/L$, but 'first draw' samples are often higher. Soft water, which may be slightly acidulated, is plumbosolvent and levels above the WHO (1971) limit of 100 $\mu g/L$ are frequently found in old housing estates with lead piping.

HUMAN EXPOSURE AND ABSORPTION

As the above discussion suggests, lead intake by inhalation can be extremely variable, but in urban environments could be of the order of 20–100 μg or more per day. A further 1–5 μg would be contributed by the smoking of 20 cigarettes per day. Assuming a consumption of 2.5 litres of water/day, lead intake at a mean level of 10 $\mu g/L$ would contribute 25 μg. Total diet studies in industrialised countries indicate an intake of lead of the order of 200–300 $\mu g/day$ and do not suggest any upward trend over the past forty years. On the assumption that about 10% of lead ingested from food and from water is absorbed, a Provisional Tolerable Weekly Intake of 3 mg lead per person, equivalent to 0.05 mg/kg body weight, was proposed by WHO (1972). Such an intake, however, is not considered tolerable for infants and children. It was further stated that any increase in the amount of lead derived from drinking water or inhaled from the atmosphere should reduce the amount that can be tolerated in food. With regard to individual foodstuffs, shellfish may contain relatively large quantities of lead because of their propensity to concentrate heavy metals. Canned foods may contain higher amounts of lead than those normally found in fresh foods if lead is a constituent of the solder used to weld the seams of the cans, and levels up to 10 mg/kg have been reported. Lead contamination of canned foods has lessened over recent years, due to restrictions placed on the use of lead in the food industry. Contamination with lead will also occur following the storage of food and drink in lead-glazed pots, and lead poisoning has resulted from the use of poorly glazed earthenware. Other important sources of lead intake, particularly in children, are lead-containing paints, lead-containing cosmetics and household and playground dust (DHHS, 1980). Contamination of food by particulate fall-out from the combustion of leaded petrol may also be a major source of lead intake in children (Russel Jones & Stephens, 1983).

Lead absorption following ingestion is dependent on a number of factors, in particular the composition of the diet. Calcium, iron, phosphate and protein deficiency affect the uptake of lead from the gastrointestinal tract. While the absorption rate in the adult is likely to be of the order of 10%, in children this may be as high as 50% (Alexander et al., 1973). There is uncertainty about the relative contribution of inhaled and ingested lead on the body burden in the general population, absorption following inhalation accounting for between 15 and 45% of total uptake in different studies (Royal Commission on Environmental Pollution, 1983). Studies using radioactive-labelled lead have shown a much greater absorption efficiency from the gastrointestinal tract in the fasting compared with the fed state (Blake, 1976; Chamberlain et al., 1978). A study of airborne particulates in a smelter concluded that lead absorption for the more soluble forms of airborne lead can be reduced by more than one half if the workers consume a full meal just before exposure (O'Neill et al., 1982).

Following absorption, lead is stored in bone rather than in soft tissues, which accounts for the increase of total body burden with age to a total of about 200 mg in the sixth decade. The blood lead concentration is the best available indicator of recent exposure. A biological monitoring programme in ten countries, initiated by UNEP/WHO, showed median levels of lead in blood in the general population to range from 60 µg/L to 220 µg/L, with 90th percentile values ranging from 89 µg/L to 345 µg/L (Vahter, 1982). Higher blood levels were found in males, compared with females. Blood levels tend to be higher in city dwellers than in those living in rural areas, the highest values being found in those living in areas with the greatest traffic density or close to local emission sources (WHO, 1977). The concentration of lead in urine does not normally exceed 65 µg/L in the general population. The level of lead in urine is also a reliable indicator of exposure, if taken on a group basis.

The early effects of lead are observed on the haemopoietic system, on peripheral nerve conduction and possibly on higher nervous function in children. The effects on the haemopoietic system are summarized in Table 1. The earliest measurable effect on the haemopoietic system is a decrease in the activity of δ-aminolaevulinic acid dehydratase. A rise in the level of erythrocyte protoporphyrin is also an early, readily-measurable effect, and the estimation of zinc erythrocyte protoporphyrin has been recommended as a screening test in the health surveillance of lead-exposed workers (CEC, 1983).

Table 1.   Effects of lead on the haemopoietic system

Decreased activity of δ-ALA dehydratase
Increased δ-ALA in serum and urine
Increased protoporphyrin in erythrocytes
Increased ether-extractable coproporphyrin III in urine
Decreased haemoglobin concentration
Decreased red cell life span
Increased reticulocyte count
Increased punctate basophil count
Increased serum iron concentration

ANALYTICAL CONSIDERATIONS

Special care has to be taken in the collection and storage of samples for blood lead estimation. Because of the problem of external contamination where trace levels are involved, venous rather than capillary blood samples should be collected. This introduces an additional difficulty in population studies on infants and young children. Quality control and quality assurance are considered in detail in the UNEP/ WHO biological monitoring programme involving sample collection and analysis in ten countries (Vahter, 1982). Alternative analytical methods can be used for blood lead estimation, provided adequate quality control is observed. The collaborating centres in the UNEP/WHO programme used atomic absorption spectrophotometry with background correction. Three laboratories used the modified Delves cup method (Delves, 1970). Seven laboratories used electrothermal atomisation; three by the method of Fernandez (1975), involving dilution with Triton X-100, and four by the method of Stoeppler et al. (1978), involving deproteinization with nitric acid. One laboratory used differential pulse anodic stripping voltammetry (Stoeppler et al., 1979) for quality control runs. Technical problems encountered in this cooperative study are discussed by Vahter (1982). Because of the low concentrations of blood lead in population studies, conventional atomic absorption spectrophotometric techniques are inadequate.

EVIDENCE FOR CARCINOGENICITY IN HUMANS

In their original evaluation in 1972, IARC concluded there was no evidence to suggest that exposure to lead salts causes cancer in man. However, only one epidemiological study, that by Dingwall-Fordyce and Lane (1963), was available. A later cohort study (Cooper & Gaffey, 1975; Cooper, 1976) in over 7 000 smelter and battery workers exposed for a minimum period of one year and followed up over a 23-year interval showed a significant excess mortality from all malignant neoplasms in smelter workers (69 observed, 55 expected), but not in battery plant workers (186 observed, 180 expected). This was largely accounted for by a non-statistically significant excess mortality from cancer of the respiratory system and of the digestive organs. The statistical significance of the SMRs obtained for respiratory and digestive tract cancer was questioned by Kang *et al.* (1980), who considered the magnitude of the risk to have been underestimated. These authors referred also to the preamble to the IARC Monograph Programme (IARC, 1977), which advocated an analysis by latency and considered latency periods of twenty years or longer to be relatively more sensitive in the identification of a carcinogenic risk.

In a five-year follow-up study of over 5 000 workers from the above cohort (Cooper, 1981), the initial mortality pattern was not maintained, a small deficit of malignant neoplasms in smelter workers and a small, but significant, excess in battery plant workers being largely accounted for by a non-significant excess of cancer of the respiratory system (24 observed, 21 expected) and cancer of unknown primary site. One renal cancer was also recorded. No consistent relationships were found between early initial exposure, high exposure or length of employment and mortality from cancer. Since there were no internal trends with exposure and smoking histories were not investigated (an excess of heavy smokers in the lead-exposed group could account for the relatively small increased mortality from lung cancer), a carcinogenic role for lead could not be supported. In a further update of this cohort (Cooper, 1984), mortality was examined for the 34-year period 1947–1980. Elevated standardized mortality ratios for malignant neoplasms were found for both battery and smelter workers, the excesses being predominantly for stomach and lung cancer. In interpreting these findings, account should be taken of the complex etiology of both stomach and lung cancer and the difficulty of taking into account confounding factors.

IARC (1980) commented that further follow-up of Cooper's original cohort was warranted in order to determine the presence of an excess risk with greater reliability. IARC considered that no evaluation of the carcinogenicity of metallic lead and organic lead compounds was possible due to the inadequacy of experimental and epidemiological data. However, on the basis of animal experiments and in the absence of data for humans, IARC (1980) concluded that it would be reasonable, for practical purposes, to regard lead acetate, lead subacetate and lead phosphate as presenting a carcinogenic risk to humans.

The long history of exposure to lead and the lack of clinical observations which suggest a carcinogenic effect, together with the epidemiological observations cited above, make the existence of a high cancer risk rather unlikely. However, further epidemiological studies are needed. A follow-up of cases of childhood and occupational lead poisoning could allow assessment of the long-term effects of heavy, although possibly short-term, exposure. One case of a smelter worker with a renal carcinoma similar in appearance to lead-induced tumours in animals has been reported recently (Baker *et al.,* 1980). As the kidney is the only organ clearly implicated in experimental cancer with lead compounds, studies assessing lead exposures in cases of renal cancer would be indicated.

EVIDENCE FOR CARCINOGENICITY TO ANIMALS

IARC (1980) reviewed the experimental data concerning animals and concluded that there is sufficient evidence to indicate that lead subacetate is carcinogenic to mice and rats and that lead acetate and lead phosphate are carcinogenic to rats. These compounds produced both benign and malignant tumours of the kidney, following oral as well as parenteral administration. Lead subacetate also produced an increased incidence of lung adenomas in mice following intraperitoneal administration. The significance of these observations for a human cancer risk from lead and lead compounds is uncertain. An IARC working group (1982) commented that although soluble lead salts have been shown to be carcinogenic to experimental animals, human beings are exposed primarily to metallic lead and lead oxide. Furthermore, large doses of lead were used in these experiments and gave rise to cystic nephritis, tubular cell damage, eosinophilic inclusion bodies and foci of regenerating tubular epithelium before the development of cancer. In the interpretation of these findings with regard to humans, it should be borne in mind that the renal tumours were observed in animal species that are relatively insensitive to the toxic effects of lead, as compared with humans, and could therefore tolerate the large doses required to produce these tumours (Kazantzis, 1981).

EVIDENCE FOR ACTIVITY IN SHORT-TERM TESTS

Lead compounds have not given rise to mutagenic effects in bacterial test systems. Lead acetate has induced dose-related transformations in hamster embryo cells (DiPaolo & Casto, 1979), lead oxide has enhanced transformation by Simian adenovirus (Casto et al., 1979) and lead chloride has been shown to decrease the fidelity of DNA synthesis (Sirover & Loeb, 1976). The IARC working group (1982) commented on the conflicting observations of chromosomal aberrations and sister chromatid exchanges in cultured mammalian cell systems and in in-vivo studies, both in animals and in humans, following exposure to lead. With regard to human exposure, the IARC working group referred to seven studies with negative and nine with positive results. A single study of sister chromatid exchange in cultured peripheral lymphocytes from people exposed to lead was negative (Maki-Paakkanen et al., 1981). Multiple exposures in occupationally-exposed groups give rise to difficulties with the interpretation of positive results, for lead workers may also be exposed to other compounds, arsenic and cadmium in particular.

REFERENCES

Alexander, F.W., Delves, H.T. & Clayton, B.E. (1973) In: *International Symposium on Environmental Health Aspects of Lead,* Luxembourg, Commission of the European Communities, pp. 319–330

Baker, E.L., Goyer, R.A., Fowler, B.A., Khettry, U., Bernard, D.B., Adler, S., White, R. de V., Babayan, R. & Feldman, R.G. (1980) Occupational lead exposure, nephropathy and renal cancer. *Am. J. Ind. Med., 1,* 139–148

Blake, K.C.H. (1976) Absorption of ^{203}Pb from gastrointestinal tract of man. *Environ. Res., 11,* 1–4

Casto, B.C., Meyers, J.D. & DiPaolo, J.A. (1979) Enhancement of viral transformation for evaluation of the carcinogenic or mutagenic potential of inorganic metal salts. *Cancer Res., 39,* 193–198

Cawse, P.A. (1977) *A Survey of Atmospheric Trace Elements in the UK: Results for 1976 (Report R-8869),* Harwell, Atomic Energy Research Establishment

CEC (1983) *Human biological monitoring of industrial chemical series. Lead.* Luxembourg, Commission of the European Communities, pp. 107–132

Chamberlain, A.C., Heard, M.S., Little, P., Newton, D., Wells, A.C. & Wiffen, R.D. (1978) *Investigations into Lead from Motor Vehicles (Report 9198),* Harwell, Atomic Energy Research Establishment, pp. 152

Cooper, W.C. & Gaffey, W.R. (1975) Mortality of lead workers. *J. occup. Med., 7,* 100–107

Cooper, W.C. (1976) Cancer mortality patterns in the lead industry. *Ann. N.Y. Acad. Sci., 271,* 250–259

Cooper, W.C. (1981) *Mortality in employees of lead production facilities and lead battery plants, 1971–1975.* In: Lynam, D.R. & Piantanida, L., eds, *Environmental Lead,* New York, Academic Press, pp. 111–143

Cooper, W.C. (1984) *Final Report Prepared for the International head Zinc Research Organization, New York*

Culbard, E., Thornton, I., Watt, J., Moorcroft, S. & Brooks, K. (1983) *Sources and distribution of lead and cadmium in United Kingdom dusts and soils.* In: *International Conference on Heavy Metals in the Environment,* Volume 1, Edinburgh, CEP Consultants Ltd, pp. 426–429

Delves, H.T. (1970) A microsampling method for rapid determination of lead in blood by atomic absorption spectrophotometry. *Analyst, 95,* 431–438

Department of the Environment (1974) Lead in the environment and its significance to man. London, Her Majesty's Stationery Office

DHSS (1980) Lead and health: The report of a Department of Health and Social Security Working Party on lead in the environment. London, Her Majesty's Stationery Office

Dingwall-Fordyce, I. & Lane, R.E. (1963) A follow-up study of lead workers. *Br. J. ind. Med., 20,* 313–315

DiPaolo, J.A. & Casto, B.C. (1979) Quantitative studies of in-vitro morphological transformation of Syrian hamster cells by inorganic metal salts. *Cancer Res., 39,* 1008–1013

Duggan, M.J. & Williams, S. (1977) Lead in dust in city streets. *Sci. total Environ., 7,* 91–97

Fernandez, F.J. (1975) Micromethod for lead determination in whole blood by atomic absorption with use of the graphite furnace. *Clin. Chem., 21,* 558–561

IARC (1972) *IARC Monographs on the Evaluation of Carcinogenic Risk of Chemicals to Man.* Volume 1, *Lead Salts,* Lyon, International Agency for Research on Cancer, pp. 40–50

IARC (1977) *IARC Monograph Programme on the Evaluation of the Carcinogenic Risk of Chemicals to Humans. Preamble (IARC intern. tech, Rep. No. 75/002),* Lyon, International Agency for Research on Cancer

IARC (1980) *IARC Monographs on the Evaluation of the Carcinogenic Risk of Chemicals to Humans.* Volume 23, *Lead and Lead Compounds,* Lyon, International Agency for Research on Cancer, pp. 325–415

IARC (1982) *IARC Monographs on the Evaluation of Carcinogenic Risk of Chemicals to Humans,* Supplement 4, *Chemicals, Industrial Processes and Industries Associated with Cancer in Humans,* Lyon, International Agency for Research on Cancer, pp. 149–150

Kang, H.K., Infante, P.F. & Carra, J.S. (1980) Occupational lead exposure and cancer. *Science, 207,* 935–936

Kazantzis, G. (1981) Role of cobalt, iron, lead, manganese, mercury, platinum, selenium and titanium in carcinogenesis. *Environ. Health Perspect., 40,* 143–161

Maki-Paakkanen, J., Sorsa, M. & Vainio, H. (1981) Chromosome aberrations and sister chromatid exchanges in lead-exposed workers. *Hereditas, 94,* 269–275

Nriagu, J.O. (1979) Global inventory of natural and anthropogenic emissions of trace metals to the atmosphere. *Nature, 279,* 409–411

O'Neill, I.K., Harrison, R.M. & Williams, C.R. (1982) Characterization of airborne particulates in a zinc-lead smelter: Potential importance of gastrointestinal absorption. *Trans. Inst. Min. Metall., 91,* C84–C90

Royal Commission on Environmental Pollution (1983) *Lead in the Environment.* Ninth Report, Commnd 8852, London, Her Majesty's Stationery Office

Russell Jones, R. & Stephens, R. (1983) *The contribution of lead in petrol to human lead intake.* In: Rutter, M. & Russell Jones, R., eds, *Lead* versus *Health: Sources and Effects of Low Level Lead Exposure.* Chichester, Wiley, pp. 141–177

Sirover, M.A. & Loeb, L.A. (1976) Infidelity of DNA synthesis *in vitro:* Screening for potential metal mutagens or carcinogens. *Science, 194,* 1434–1436

Stocks, R., Commins, B.T. & Aubrey, K.V. (1961) A study of polycyclic hydrocarbons and trace elements in smoke in Merseyside and other northern localities. *Int. J. Air Water Pollut., 4,* 141–153

Stoeppler, M., Brandt, K. & Rains, T.C. (1978) Contributions to automated trace analysis. Part II. Rapid method for the automated determination of lead in whole blood by electrothermal atomic absorption spectrophotometry. *Analyst, 103,* 714–722

Stoeppler, M., Valenta, P. & Nurnberg, H.W. (1979) Application of independent methods and standard materials: An effective approach to reliable trace and ultratrace analysis of metals and metalloids in environmental and biological matrices. *Fresenius Z. Anal. Chem., 297,* 22–34

Vahter, M. (1982) Assessment of human exposure to lead and cadmium through biological monitoring. *National Swedish Institute of Environmental Medicine and Department of Environmental Hygiene,* Stockholm, Karolinska Institute

Waldron, H.A. (1980) *Lead.* In: Waldron, H.A., ed., *Metals in the Environment.* London, Academic Press, pp. 155–197

WHO (1971) *International Standards for Drinking Water.* Geneva, World Health Organization

WHO (1972) Evaluation of certain food additives and the contaminants mercury, lead and cadmium. *Sixteenth Report of the Joint FAO/WHO Expert Committee on Food Additives.* Geneva, World Health Organization

WHO (1977) *Environmental Health Criteria. III. Lead.* Geneva, World Health Organization

OCCURRENCE

CHAPTER 8

EXPOSURE ASSESSMENT FOR METALS INVOLVED IN CARCINOGENESIS

B.G. Bennett

Monitoring and Assessment Research Centre,
The Octogon Building,
459A Fulham Road,
London SW10 OQX, UK

INTRODUCTION

There are numerous factors to be considered in evaluating exposures of individuals to metals. The major routes of exposure are inhalation and ingestion, and the main factors are the concentrations of the metals in environmental media (air, water, diet), the intake or contact with such media and the absorption and retention within the body. The general features of these processes are well-enough known and are presented in textbooks and reviews (e.g., NAS, 1975; WHO, 1978; Friberg *et al.,* 1979). Representative data used for estimating average exposure to various metals are shown in a number of Tables throughout this chapter. However, exposure assessments are also needed for specific metal compounds, since the behaviour and toxicity of the various chemical forms may be quite different. This is broadly true for the organic and inorganic forms, but even further speciation is required. Mass balances and transfer evaluations for total metals may provide useful starting points, but health evaluations require more detailed information.

It should be particularly noted that exposures to metals or other trace contaminants do not occur in isolation and under fixed conditions. Metals occur in mixtures in the environment, and transfer rates and amounts are determined by the various associations and interactions, as well as chemical form, route of intake, age of individual, etc. Each situation thus requires careful consideration and assessment.

THE CONCEPT OF EXPOSURE

The terms 'exposure' and 'dose' (closely related and often interchangeable) are variously used in toxicology and environmental science. Classically, 'exposure' may simply refer to the presentation of a substance or physical agent to a receptor and 'dose' to the amount administered or taken in *via* inhalation, ingestion, injection or absorption through the skin. 'Dose' has been further defined as the amount reaching the site of effect (Nordberg, 1976), but 'exposure' is also used in this context (Butler, 1978). The terms 'intake' and 'uptake' overlap these usages, intake referring to the amount entering and uptake the amount absorbed.

In their customary usage, exposure and dose are simply alternative expressions of concentrations, the former in environmental media and the latter within the organism. It seems hardly satisfactory that such possibilities for confusion should exist. Concentrations should be called concentrations, with specification of the terms of reference (amount of substance per unit mass or volume of the environmental medium, per unit body mass or per unit mass of the specific tissue or organ).

Concentration is the parameter most frequently available, whether in the external environment or following intake or absorption. To give exposure (or dose) some biological meaning, the concentration should, if possible, be expressed at the level of the target biological structure.

A more specific definition of exposure, other than concentration, for relating chemicals to health effects would require more detailed knowledge of the interactions and uncertain mechanisms which produce the effects. It has been proposed to define exposure as the number of primary chemical events leading to the final effect (Ehrenberg *et al.,* 1974). It is only in rare cases, however, that the nature of such primary events is known and their quantification possible.

Exposure may best be defined in terms of a combined measure of the concentration and the time during which a contaminant is present at the point of interest. In addition to the concentration, the duration of the interaction is an important factor in the manifestation of effects. This reflects the time required for the accumulation of the contaminant (or metabolites) to sufficient levels to induce damage, or the accumulation of damaged elements that eventually inhibit proper functioning.

The most direct combination of concentration and duration is the time integral of the concentration,

$$E = \int_{0}^{T} C(t)\, dt$$

This formulation of exposure is particularly useful in describing the movement of chemical substances in the environment. The transfer between environmental reservoirs is described by linear, first-order kinetics. The integrated concentrations and fluxes maintain constant relationships in this case.

In terms of effects, this definition of exposure must be used with some caution. The various combinations of concentration and time giving equal exposure, for example, may not be associated with equal occurrence of adverse effects. Some metals are harmless or even essential in trace amounts, but toxic at higher levels. Only within a mid-range between specified lower and upper limits may it be correct to assume a linear relationship between exposure and effect.

Other functional forms of the exposure relationship may be required for the evaluation of specific effects in particular biological systems. Some of these forms, involving exponential or power functions of time, have been discussed by Piotrowski and Buchanan (1982). It will be necessary for toxicologists to give further consideration to the concentration-time relationship, i.e., the expression of exposure which is most closely associated with the occurrence of effects.

In using estimates of exposure, it must be recognized that there are differences in the chemical forms of the substance concerned. Integrated concentrations or intakes of specific compounds will be absorbed and retained in the body in different fashions. Exposure evaluations are specific to the particular substance and cannot be generalized to widely varying exposure conditions. If possible, it is necessary to account for altered behaviour due to the presence of other chemical forms of the metal or to exposures to other substances. How substances might interact and how exposures can be combined to relate to subsequent effects are questions concerning which no general guidance can yet be given.

EXPOSURE ROUTES

Inhalation

The most direct route of entry of an airborne contaminant is by inhalation. This route is particularly important in occupational settings. Metal fumes are released in mining and refining operations and in various other activities, such as welding.

Metals are released to the environment from numerous industrial, agricultural and natural sources, such as volcances and windblown dusts. Many metals are released in combustion of fossil fuels, particularly coal. The use of lead additives in petrol results in a significant source of release of lead to the environment. Vapours and small particles from combustion sources become attached to the ambient aerosol. Respirable particles are those less than about 10 μm in diameter.

Smoking is another source of inhaled contaminants. Significant intakes of some metals, such as cadmium, can result.

Transfer of metals to the body following inhalation depends on deposition in the lungs and absorption into blood. Deposition is governed by the physical characteristics of the contaminant and absorption primarily by the chemical properties.

A model for the respiratory tract and clearance pathways has been formulated and is widely used (Table 1) (ICRP, 1966, 1979). Three compartments are specified in the lung model – the nasopharyngeal, tracheobronchial and pulmonary regions. The deposition pattern as a function of particle size is given in Table 2. For the general case, a respiration rate of 15/min is assumed, representing moderate physical activity. The tidal volume is 1 450 mL. For ambient aerosols of the order of 0.5 μm in size, deposition of 14% in the nasopharyngeal region, 8% in the tracheobronchial region and 30% in the pulmonary region would be expected. The remainder of the amount inhaled is exhaled without deposition.

Table 1.   Parameters for pathways and clearance rates of the ICRP lung model [a]

Region [b]	Pathway	Compound class [c]		
		D	W	Y
N-P	(a)	0.01 d/0.5	0.01 d/0.1	0.01 d/0.01
	(b)	0.01 d/0.5	0.4 d/0.9	0.4 d/0.01
T-B	(c)	0.01 d/0.95	0.01 d/0.5	0.01 d/0.01
	(d)	0.2 d/0.05	0.2 d/0.5	0.2 d/0.99
P	(e)	0.5 d/0.8	50 d/0.15	500 d/0.05
	(f)	– –	1 d/0.4	1 d/0.4
	(g)	– –	50 d/0.4	500 d/0.4
	(h)	0.5 d/0.2	50 d/0.05	500 d/0.15
L	(i)	0.5 d/1.0	50 d/1.0	1 000 d/0.9

Fig. 1.

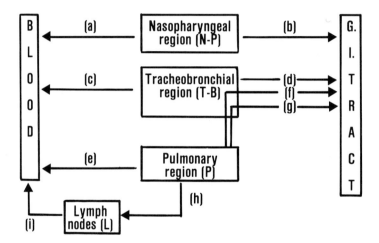

[a] The first value listed in the Table is the biological half-time; the second is the fractional transfer along pathways leaving the particular lung region (ICRP, 1979)
[b] Lung regions: N-P, nasopharyngeal; T-B, tracheobronchial; P, pulmonary; L, lymph nodes
[c] Compound classes: retention times of the order of days (D), weeks (W) or years (Y)

    The parameters specified for the lung model are intended to apply to the 'standard' (or 'reference') man in the occupational setting. Respiration patterns are not identical, however, from one person to the next and are not even constant for an individual. Deposition is affected by nose or mouth breathing. Respiratory rates may change by a factor of three or more from resting to strenuous activity. Estimates of average inhalation rates as a function of age and sex are given in Table 3.

Table 2. Fractional region deposition of particles in the lung[a]

Particle size (μm)	Naso-pharyngeal region	Tracheo-bronchial region	Pulmonary region
0.05	0.002	0.08	0.59
0.10	0.01	0.08	0.50
0.30	0.07	0.08	0.36
0.50	0.14	0.08	0.30
0.70	0.21	0.08	0.26
1.0	0.30	0.08	0.23
3.0	0.64	0.08	0.13
5.0	0.77	0.08	0.10
7.0	0.84	0.08	0.08

[a] ICRP (1966)

Table 3. Average inhalation rates for adults and children (m³/d)[a]

	Adult		Child	
	Male	Female	10 years	1 year
Resting	7.5	6.0	4.8	1.5
Light activity	20	19	13	4.2
Daily average[b]	15.8	14.7	10.3	2.6

[a] ICRP (1975)
[b] Assumes 8 h resting and 16 h light activity, except for the 1-year-old-child (14 h resting and 10 h light activity)

Ingestion

Ingestion is the exposure route of greatest significance for the general population, which is subject to the chronic intake of low-level metal contaminants, residues or additives in food and water. Adventitious intake can occur as well, from contaminants in dirt or dust on foods or hands or which arise from contact of foods with processing or preparation equipment.

It is difficult to make accurate estimates of ingestion intakes of metals, due to the variability of concentrations in foods and the uncertain consumption patterns of individuals. The concentrations of metals in individual food items or in composite diet samples may be measured. The composite or duplicate diet samples are most suited to smaller individual surveys or to institutional studies. The total amounts of contaminants actually consumed may be accurately determined in these cases, but the contributions of individual foods to total dietary intake are not measured. Analysis

Table 4.   Regional food consumption for the adult individual (g/d)[a]

Food group	Africa	Europe	Far East	Latin America	North America
Milk	96	484	51	240	850
Vegetables, fruits	215	316	128	313	516
Cereals, flour, rice	330	375	404	281	185
Roots, pulses, nuts	510	392	212	293	155
Meat	40	111	24	102	248
Eggs	4	23	3	11	55
Fish	16	38	27	18	26
Fats, oils	19	44	9	24	56
Sugar	29	79	22	85	113

[a] ICRP (1975)

of separate foods, on the other hand, provides detailed information which can be combined with consumption estimates for individuals or sub-groups of the population for evaluating intakes of the contaminant.

It is possible that a large number of foods must be considered in determining intake by ingestion. For example, in the United States it has been estimated that 240 different food items are needed to represent the dietary habits of most of the population. The list can be shortened by considering only the most commonly consumed foods or by investigating food groups, such as fresh vegetables, canned fruit, meat, fish, etc. Some metal contaminants may be particularly concentrated in certain foods which may require special attention, e.g., mercury in fish and cadmium in kidneys, liver and some shellfish.

There are large variations in food consumption patterns in regional areas, as well as local differences due to age, occupation, ethnic background, etc. Some very broad average consumption estimates are presented in Table 4.

Drinking water is usually a secondary source of ingestion of metals, but this is not always the case. Water flowing through mineralized areas or receiving effluents from mining or other industrial or agricultural activities may have greatly elevated levels of metals. Metals may be transferred to the water from pipes and fixtures. This is particularly so when lead piping is used with soft water. Reviews of the levels of metals and other substances in drinking water and guidelines for safe levels have recently been published (WHO, 1984).

Metals on dust and dirt may constitute an important source of exposure, especially for lead intake by children. The pica habit of young children results in greater exposures to metals in dirt and paint chips. It is generally most satisfactory to measure the environmental conditions and estimate intake on the basis of assumed or observed behaviour patterns. Reviewing the assumptions made in various investigations, daily intakes of about 20 mg dirt on fingers and 40 mg dust on foods may be taken as very approximate representative estimates to be used for children (Duggan & Williams, 1977; Stephens, 1981).

Absorption through the skin may occur with specific metal compounds, e.g., in jewellery or cosmetics. This is not usually a significant route of exposure, but it should not be disregarded in individual cases. Dermatitis or allergic reactions may be caused by contact with metals, such as nickel in coins or other objects and in orthopaedic implants (Grandjean, 1984).

METABOLISM

Absorption

The absorption of metals following intake depends on their physical and chemical forms and on the physiological condition of the subject. Following inhalation, absorption depends on the location of deposition in the respiratory tract. Absorption is greatest from the pulmonary region. Particles deposited in the upper regions of the respiratory tract are more likely to be cleared relatively rapidly by mucociliary action, with translocation by swallowing to the gastro-intestinal tract. For the ICRP lung model, pathways and clearance rates are given for several classes of particle solubilities (Table 1). There is insufficient experimental information concerning the fractions of specific chemical compounds absorbed and any effects due to age.

Metals may also be inhaled in gaseous or vaporous forms. Highly-soluble gases and vapours are dissolved in the mucous membranes of the upper respiratory tract. Less-soluble gases and vapours will reach the pulmonary region, where absorption will depend on the ease of penetration of the alveolar membrane. Mercury vapour is not dissolved in the mucous membranes, but is transferred to the pulmonary region, where it is absorbed to an extent of about 30% of the inhaled amount.

Absorption of metals following ingestion depends primarily on chemical form; however, particle size or the matrix of attachment may also be a factor. Organic or complexed forms are usually absorbed more than inorganic forms. Shifts in pH along the gastro-intestinal tract may change the valence form of the metal and alter its absorption. Metal interactions affect absorption; for example, lead absorption is increased if there are calcium or iron deficiencies in diet. Absorption fractions are greater following fasting and may also be greater in pregnant and lactating women and in young children.

Distribution and retention

Metals absorbed into blood are available for distribution to organs and tissues throughout the body. Both plasma and blood cells take part in the transport, but cell-bound metals do not exchange with other tissues as readily as metals bound to plasma constituents. The distribution between blood cells and plasma varies with the metal and also depends on the chemical form of the metal (TGMA, 1973). The low molecular weight, diffusible fraction of metal in plasma, is of fundamental interest for the transfer of the metal to and from various organs and for excretory mechanisms.

The organ distributions vary from one metal to another and depend on similarities to essential elements and filtration or storage locations. Thus cadmium is found primarily in kidneys and lead in bone. Other metals are more widely distributed throughout the body.

Many of the published concentrations of metals in tissues have been of uncertain validity, due to insensitive analytical methods and contamination of the samples with tools, containers and chemical reagents. More recently determined levels of mercury in tissues or lead in blood, for example, are lower than those previously reported, due partly to lower levels in the environment, but also reflecting increased care in sampling and analysis.

The retention characteristics of metals may be expressed by the biological half-time ($t\frac{1}{2}$) or the mean retention time ($T = 1.44\,t\frac{1}{2}$). Several components of retention may be recognized, reflecting various distribution or binding conditions, or a single 'effective' retention time may be specified. Some specific retention functions are quoted or estimated by ICRP (1979), and these have been used in evaluations of exposures to metals (Bennett, 1981a,b, 1982).

It is most useful to know the distribution fractions and retention characteristics for specific organs and tissues, but in many cases only estimates for the total body are available. When data are available, more or less comprehensive metabolic models may be formulated, such as the sevencompartment model for cadmium (Kjellström & Nordberg, 1978). Further developments of this sort are needed for other metals and for specific metal compounds.

It is important that the metabolism of metals in the body be fully understood in order to select more readily-available tissues and fluids as indicators of wider concentrations in the body and of earlier, as well as recent, exposures. It is also necessary to know how metabolism changes with the physiological state of the individual and with interactions with other metals, chemicals or environmental conditions. Consideration of biological monitoring to determine exposures is given by Berlin *et al.,* (1979) and in the WHO Environmental Health Criteria Reports for individual metals.

REPRESENTATIVE EXPOSURE ASSESSMENT

It may be useful to examine the values of parameters which seem pertinent to representative, background exposures to metals in the environment. Tables 2 to 9 are related to the expected behaviour of broad, average age groups of the general population. Specific values for particular individuals may be widely different. Exposure conditions, such as environmental concentrations and selection of items in diet, can easily vary by a factor of three between the mean and the more extreme individuals in the population distribution. Biological variability can add at least another factor of three, so that background tissue concentrations of metals may range over an order of magnitude.

The representative values, however, give at least the general behaviour patterns. More specific environmental conditions can then be examined. Exposures from occupations, smoking and other sources would be additional considerations. The metals and metalloids considered in the Tables are only some of those involved in carcinogenesis and other health effects.

Table 5.   Representative inhalation and consumption rates[a]

		Adult	Child (2 y old)
Inhalation	Air	20 m³/d	6 m³/d
Consumption	Foods	1 200 g/d	750 g/d
	Fish	25 g/d	
	Milk	0.3 L/d	0.5 L/d
	Water	1.2 L/d	1.3 L/d
	Dirt		20 mg/d

[a] ICRP (1975)

Table 6.   Approximate mean concentrations of metals in environmental media[a]

Metal	Air (ng/m³)	Water (µg/L)	Food (µg/g)	
			Fish	Other Foods
Arsenic	20	1.2	3.6	0.03
Cadmium	30	–	–	0.025
Chromium	7	0.2	–	0.05
Lead	2 000	10	–	0.09
Mercury	7	–	0.4	0.004
Nickel	20	8	–	0.13
Selenium	3	0.2	–	0.06
Tin	30	0.04	–	0.2
Zinc	300	40	–	10

[a] Bennett (1981a,b, 1982)

Some background discussion of environmental and metabolic behaviour of metals, which has led to the selection of the parameters of Tables 5–9, has been published (Bennett, 1981a,b, 1982). The estimates of fractional absorption following inhalation and the mean retention times in the body are particularly uncertain. The assessments concern the total amounts of each metal, except for arsenic and mercury, for which a distinction is made between intakes of inorganic and organic forms, due to differences in absorption and retention. Results are given for the adult, except in the case of lead, where the two-year-old child is also considered. For some metals, such as cadmium, for which long-term accumulation occurs, the adult is most at risk. However, absorption and toxicity in the child can often be important, as it is for lead. Efforts must be made to improve information concerning the metabolism of metals in children.

Table 7. Intake rates of metals *via* ingestion and inhalation (μg/d)[a]

Metal	Fish	Other foods	Water	Total ingestion	Inhalation
Arsenic	90	40	1.4	130	0.4
Cadmium	–	30	–	30	0.6
Chromium	–	60	0.2	60	0.1
Lead (adult)	–	110	12	180[b]	40
Lead (child)	–	70	13	170[c]	6
Mercury	10	5	–	15	0.14
Nickel	–	160	10	170	0.4
Selenium	–	70	0.2	70	0.06
Tin	–	200	–	200	0.6
Zinc	–	10 000	50	10 000	6

[a] Bennett (1981a,b, 1982)
[b] Includes 60 μg/d from surface contamination of food
[c] Includes 40 μg/d from surface contamination of food and 48 μg/d from dirt on hands

Table 8. Fractional absorption of ingested and inhaled metals by blood[a]

Metals	Absorption	
	Following ingestion	Following inhalation
Arsenic	0.9	0.3
Cadmium	0.05	0.25
Chromium	0.01	0.2
Lead (adult)	0.1	0.2
Lead (child)	0.25	0.4
Mercury (organic)	1.0	–
Mercury (inorganic)	0.05	0.7
Nickel	0.05	0.3
Selenium	0.8	0.2
Tin	0.2	0.2
Zinc	0.3	0.2

[a] Bennett (1918a,b, 1982)

Rates of uptake by blood (Table 9) are determined from the product of intake rate and the fractional absorption, which includes retention in the lungs and absorption to blood following inhalation, and absorption through the gastro-intestinal tract following ingestion. The concentrations in tissue are determined by multiplying the uptake rate by the mean retention time, dividing by the organ mass and accounting

Table 9.   Distribution and retention of metals in man[a]

Metals	Uptake rate (μg/d)	Distribution		Mass (kg)	Retention time (d)	Concentration (μg/g)
Arsenic	81*	1.0	(body)	70	4	
	37**	1.0	(body)	70	8	0.009***
Cadmium	1.7	0.3	(kidneys)	0.31	10 950	18
Chromium	0.6	0.05	(bone)	5	1 400	0.008
		0.65	(body)	65	50	0.0003
Lead (adult)	26	1.0	(blood)	5.2	23	0.12
(child)	45	1.0	(blood)	2	?	?
Mercury	10*	1.0	(body)	70	100	
	0.4**	1.0	(body)	70	60	0.015***
Nickel	8.6	0.3	(body)	70	200	0.007
Selenium	56	0.9	(body)	70	140	0.1
Tin	4.1	0.35	(bone)	5	350	0.1
		0.15	(body)	65	350	0.003
Zinc	3 000	1.0	(body)	70	380	16

[a] Bennett (1981a,b, 1982)
*   From intake of organic forms
**   From intake of inorganic forms
***   From combined intake of organic and inorganic forms.

for the distribution fraction if the metal is partially retained by specific organs. In most cases, the metal is assumed to be uniformly distributed in the body. The distribution of lead beyond blood has not been included.

For the general case considered here, ingestion intake of metals is more significant than inhalation intake. The metals are assumed to be incorporated into foods, but some surface contamination may also be present. An estimate of this source of lead intake is included in Table 7. An additional contribution to intake of lead by children is from dirt on hands contacting food or mouth. This is obviously quite variable. The lead concentrations in dust particles in urban areas range from 0.5 to 1.0 mg/g, with generally somewhat higher levels indoors and in smaller particles adhering to hands (Duggan & Williams, 1977).

Lead in blood is partially retained before distribution to other tissues. The concentrations in blood are most often measured. These may be used with analyses of lead in shed teeth, but further estimates of the transfers to bone and teeth are required. The estimated concentration (Table 9) of lead in adult blood ($\pm$ 50%) is typically observed. The associations between uptake and blood lead levels in the child are uncertain, as estimates of the residence time of lead in blood are unavailable.

Cadmium is retained primarily in the kidneys, which receive an estimated 30% of the amount which reaches the blood. As a first-order approximation, the mean residence time of cadmium in the kidneys is taken to be 30 years. The estimated uptake rate of cadmium then results in an eventual concentration in the kidneys of 10 μg/g. The concentration would be 50% higher if cadmium is considered to be localized in the kidney cortex. Consideration of age-dependent renal changes can improve the estimated results; in articular, to show declining cadmium concentrations after about the age of 50 years (Travis & Haddock, 1980).

The estimated concentrations of other metals in the body (Table 9) are in reasonable agreement with more recent measurements. The parameters can be adjusted to account for different concentrations in environmental media, other estimates of intake or improved determinations of absorption, retention or tissue concentrations.

REFERENCES

Bennett, B.G. (1981a) Exposure commitment assessments of environmental pollutants. Summary exposure assessments for lead, cadmium, arsenic. *Vol. 1, No. 1, MARC Report No. 23,* London, Monitoring and Assessment Research Centre

Bennett, B.G. (1981b) Exposure commitment assessments of environmental pollutants. Summary exposure assessments for mercury, nickel, tin. *Vol. 1, No. 2, MARC Report No. 25,* London, Monitoring and Assessment Research Centre

Bennett, B.G. (1982) Exposure commitment assessments of environmental pollutants. Summary exposure assessments for PCBs, selenium, chromium. *Vol. 2, MARC Report No. 28,* London, Monitoring and Assessment Research Centre

Berlin, Wolff & Hasegawa, eds (1979) *The use of biological specimens for the assessment of human exposure to environmental pollutants.* Commission of the European Communities, The Hague, M. Nijhoff, Publisher

Butler, G.C., ed. (1978) *Principles of Ecotoxicology, Scope 12,* Chichester, John Wiley and Sons

Duggan, M.J. & Williams, S. (1977) Lead in dust in city streets. *Sci. total Environ.,* **7,** 91–97

Ehrenberg, L., Hiesche, K.D., Osterman-Golkar, S.& Wennberg, I. (1974) Evaluation of genetic risks of alkylating agents: Tissue doses in the mouse from air contaminated with ethylene oxide. *Mutat. Res., 24,* 83–103

Friberg, L., Nordberg, G.F. & Vouk, V.B., eds (1979) *Handbook on the Toxicology of Metals,* Amsterdam, Elsevier/North Holland Biomedical Press

Grandjean, P. (1984) *Human exposure to nickel.* In: Sunderman, F.W., Jr, ed., *Nickel in the Environment (IARC Scientific Publication No. 53),* Lyon, International Agency for Research on Cancer

ICRP (1966) International Commission on Radiological Protection. Task Group of the ICRP on lung dynamics, deposition and retention models for internal dosimetry of the human respiratory tract. *Health Phys., 12,* 173–207

ICRP (1975) International Commission on Radiological Protection. *Report on the Task Group on Reference Man, ICRP Publication 23,* Oxford, Pergamon Press

ICRP (1979) International Commission of Radiological Protection. *Limits for Intakes of Radionuclides by Workers. ICRP Publication 30, Part 1,* Oxford, Pergamon Press

Kjellström, T. & Nordberg, G.F. (1978) A kinetic model of cadmium metabolism in the human being. *Environ. Res., 16,* 248–269

National Academy of Sciences (NAS) (1975) *Principles for Evaluating Chemicals in the Environment.* Washington DC

Nordberg, G.F., ed. (1976) *Effects and Dose-response Relationships of Toxic Metals.* Task Group on Metal Toxicity, Amsterdam, Elsevier Scientific Publishing Co.

Piotrowski, J.K. & Buchanan, J.M. (1982) Dose-time response functions for toxic chemicals. *Environ. monit. Assess., 2,* 139–156

Stephens, R. (1981) Human exposure to lead from motor vehicle emissions. *Int. J. environ. Stud., 17,* 73–83

TGMA (1973) Task Group on Metal Accumulation. Accumulation of toxic metals with special reference to their absorption, excretion and biological half-times. *Environ. Physiol. Biochem., 3,* 65–107

Travis, C.C. & Haddock, A.G. (1980) Interpretation of the observed age dependency of cadmium body burdens in man. *Environ. Res., 22,* 46–60

WHO (1978) Principles and methods for evaluating the toxicity of chemicals, Part 1. *Environmental Health Criteria, 6,* Geneva, World Health Organization

WHO (1984) Guidelines for drinking-water quality, *Vol. 1, Recommendations.* Geneva, World Health Organization

CHAPTER 9

OCCURRENCE OF SELECTED METALS IN CIGARETTE TOBACCOS AND SMOKE

R.A. Jenkins

Analytical Chemistry Division,
Oak Ridge National Laboratory,
PO Box X, Oak Ridge, TN 37831, USA

INTRODUCTION

Metallic elements (hereafter referred to as metals) can be incorporated into a growing tobacco plant from many sources. The metals may occur naturally in the growing soil, or can be added thereto in fertilizers, soil mulchers, pesticides or polluted rainfall. Airborne particles can be deposited directly onto the plant surface and the metals can be incorporated into the tobacco on a local or systemic basis.

During the smoking process, metals in the cigarette tobacco transfer into the smoke by several mechanisms. First, ultra-fine (< 0.1 μ diameter) particles of ash, which contain much of the metallic constituents, can be entrained into the stream of hot, super-saturated vapours. These particles serve as nucleation centres, upon which the vapours can condense as they cool. In this manner, the relatively insoluble metals become part of the main-stream smoke particulate matter. Secondly, the more volatile metals may react with volatile gases to form gaseous species, such as arsine or nickel carbonyl. Others may react with, or be chelated by, more complex organic species and condense with other organic vapours to become dissolved in the liquid smoke droplets.

The predominant route of exposure of humans to metals in cigarette smoke is inhalation. The smoker will likely inhale both the main-stream gas and particle phase of the smoke, plus some of the smoke that is generated while the cigarette is smouldering between puffs (side-stream smoke). The non-smoker may also be exposed to metals in cigarette smoke, through 'passive' inhalation of environmental tobacco smoke (ETS). The purposes of this document are to review briefly the procedures required to determine the amounts of certain metals in cigarette smoke, including chromium (Cr), arsenic (As), lead (Pb), zinc (Zn), selenium (Se), cadmium (Cd) and nickel (Ni), and to describe the amounts of these metals to which the smoker is likely to be directly exposed *via* the inhalation of main-stream smoke. Exposure of non-smokers to metals in environmental tobacco smoke is an exceedingly complex issue, and is beyond the scope of this article.

SAMPLING AND ANALYTICAL METHODS

For analytical studies, cigarette smoke is usually generated on analytical smoking machines, designed to smoke the cigarette under standard conditions. In the United States, these are one puff per minute (2.0 second duration, 35 mL volume) to a butt length of 23 mm for non-filter cigarettes, or to within 3 mm of the filter overwrap for filtered varieties (Pillsbury et al., 1969). The conditions may be somewhat different in other countries (Brunnemann et al., 1976). Note that these conditions do not strictly simulate the smoking habits of humans but rather provide a standard set of conditions under which all cigarettes may be compared.

Typically, cigarette smoke is collected for analysis using one of two methods. In the first case, the particle phase of the smoke is trapped separately from the gas phase. This is accomplished by drawing the smoke through a filter, such as a standard 44-mm Cambridge filter pad (Wartman et al., 1959). These filters have high collection efficiencies for particles with diameters corresponding to those in cigarette smoke. The vapour phase passes through the filter and is trapped in a bubbler or cold trap, immediately down-stream of the filter (Szadkowski, et al., 1969). Such a system needs only a relatively simple analytical smoking machine (Pillsbury et al., 1969; Horton & Guerin, 1974), and the smoke particulate matter can be generated and collected with great quantitative reproducibility (Jenkins et al., 1983). However, the glass fibres of the Cambridge filter have a relatively high metal content which, if not accounted for in careful blank determinations, can seriously affect the experimental results. In addition, the filters have a maximum capacity of approximately 200 mg. If analytical sensitivity requirements demand larger amounts, then multiple-filter samples must be generated and extracted. Lower-background Teflon membrane filters may offer an alternative, but their use with cigarette smoke remains to be validated.

The second procedure involves the collection of both particle and vapour phases together, producing a material referred to as cigarette smoke condensate (CSC). The chief advantage of this approach lies in the use of an analytical smoking machine that smokes many cigarettes through one collection channel (Snook & Fortson, 1979; Patel, 1980), allowing much larger quantities (up to 1 kg) of CSC to be collected. However, the smoking machines are somewhat more sophisticated, the trapping much less quantitatively reproducible, and the sample work-up considerable.

The two most popular analytical methods for the determination of the metals in question in a cigarette smoke matrix are probably atomic absorption (AA), both conventional (Morie & Morrisett, 1974; Westcott & Spincer, 1974) and graphite-furnace (Perinelli & Carugno, 1978), and neutron activation analysis (Nadkarni & Ehmann, 1970; Wyttenbach et al., 1976; Ahmad et al., 1979) (NAA). Of the seven metals discussed in this review, all but Se and As have been determined by AA in cigarette tobacco or smoke. However, both selenium and arsenic can be very accurately determined by hydride generation, with subsequent AA determination of their concentration in the vapours.

Neutron activation analysis requires access to a neutron flux source and gamma-ray counting facilities, so that the more conventional analytical laboratories are less likely to pursue this approach. In addition, Pb and Ni are not determinable by NAA under most circumstances, because of either very low sensitivity or strong interference from other metals found with Pb and Ni.

METAL CONTENT OF CIGARETTE TOBACCO AND SMOKE

Tables 1 to 7 present the levels of cadmium, lead, zinc, chromium, arsenic and selenium determined in cigarette tobaccos and main-stream smoke in selected studies. The variation in the levels observed is at least partly due to the wide variety of tobacco types, soil conditions, smoke collection and analytical methods involved. For many of the tobaccos surveyed, the levels of Cd, Cr, As, Ni and Se fall into the 1–10 μg per gram of tobacco (ppm) range. The levels of Zn and Pb are somewhat higher, ranging up to 70 ppm. Overall, between one and ten per cent of the surveyed metals transfer into the main-stream smoke when the cigarette is smoked under standard conditions. Zn had the lowest transfer efficiency; about 1%. This can be compared with nicotine, of which about 10–15% transfers into the main-stream smoke (Guerin, 1976). That most of the metals are not in a particularly volatile form is supported by the finding that in only one case were any of the deliveries of metals to the gas phase of the smoke higher than to the particle phase.

Estimation of the amounts of metals inhaled and retained by smokers is a complex matter. There is a great deal of evidence to indicate that smokers generate smoke (especially from low-'tar' cigarettes) under more severe puffing conditions (higher puff volumes) than those employed in these studies (Creighton & Lewis, 1978; Herning et al., 1981; Benowitz et al., 1983). However, most of the cigarettes included in this survey appeared not to be low-tar cigarettes, so that drastic compensational smoking behaviour for cigarettes in these studies would not be expected. On balance, the absolute levels of metals found in the main-stream smoke in the reports surveyed probably represent a middle range of exposure. Maximal exposures may be greater by factors of 2–5.

RADIOACTIVE SPECIES IN TOBACCO AND SMOKE

The role of radioactive metals, namely polonium-210 (Po^{210}) and lead-210 (Pb^{210}) in tobacco smoke-related carcinogenesis has been the subject of controversy for a number of years (Martell, 1982). However, there seems to be general agreement that these species arise from the decay of airborne radon daughters incorporated into the growing tobacco plant. Several reports (Radford & Hunt, 1964; Kelley, 1965; Ferri & Christiansen, 1967; Harley et al., 1980) place the level of Po^{210} in cigarette tobacco in the range of 0.2–0.5 pico curies (pCi) per gram tobacco. About 0.03–0.12 pCi/cigarette is present in the main-stream smoke, suggesting that Po^{210} has a somewhat higher transfer efficiency than most of the other metals mentioned in this report. The longer-lived Pb^{210}, the likely source of much of the Po^{210} found in the bodies of

Table 1. Levels of cadmium in cigarette tobacco and smoke

Type of cigarettes	Tobacco content (µg/g)	Smoke delivery (µg/cigarette)	Smoke matrix analysed	Reference
Experimental – Virginia tobaccos	3.2	0.21 0.03	Particle phase Gas phase	Gutenmann et al., 1982
Commercial – Germany	1.5 – 2.2[a]	0.007 – 0.275 0.1 – 0.6	Particle phase Gas phase	Szadkowski et al., 1969
Commercial – Poland	1.3 – 3.8	0.2 0.14	Particle phase Gas phase	Bronisz et al., 1983
Unspecified	1.1 – 2.0	–	–	Wyttenbach et al., 1976
Commercial – five countries	1.2 – 2.2	0.07 – 0.19 0.007 – 0.05	Particle phase Gas phase	Westcott & Spincer, 1974
Commercial – Germany	0.20 – 1.94	0.03 – 0.1	Particle phase	Scherer & Barkmeyer, 1983
Commercial – Italy	1.3 – 1.60	0.04 – 0.06 $2 \times 10^{-6} - 3 \times 10^{-6}$	Particle phase Gas phase	Perinelli & Carugno, 1978
Experimental – USA	–	0.04 – 0.35[b]	Condensate	Guerin, 1976
Kentucky Reference – USA	1.39	0.12	Particle phase	Menden et al., 1972

[a]Reported in terms of µg per cigarette. Converted to present units assuming 800 mg tobacco per cigarette
[b]Reported in terms of ng per milligram of condensate. Converted to present units assuming 1 mg condensate equivalent to 1 mg 'tar'

Table 2. Levels of lead in cigarette tobacco and smoke

Type of cigarettes	Tobacco content (µg/g)	Smoke delivery (µg/cigarette)	Smoke matrix analysed	Reference
Experimental – Virginia tobaccos	4.1	Not detected	–	Gutenmann et al., 1982
Commercial – Germany	2.4 – 5.0[a]	0.065 – 0.447 0.09 – 0.61	Particle phase Gas phase	Szadkowski et al., 1969
Commercial – five countries	14.7 – 22.8	0.37 – 0.98 0.14 – 0.18	Particle phase Gas phase	Westcott & Spincer, 1974
Experimental – USA	–	0.017 – 0.29[b]	Condensate	Guerin, 1976
Commercial – Italy	8.2 – 10.1	0.034 – 0.085 $6 \times 10^{-6} - 60 \times 10^{-6}$	Particle phase Gas phase	Perinelli & Carugno, 1978

[a]Reported in terms of µg per cigarette. Converted to present units assuming 800 mg tobacco per cigarette
[b]Reported in terms of ng per milligram of condensate. Converted to present units assuming 1 mg condensate equivalent to 1 mg 'tar'

Table 3. Levels of zinc in cigarette tobacco and smoke

Type of cigarettes	Tobacco content (μg/g)	Smoke delivery (μg/cigarette)	Smoke matrix analysed	Reference
Experimental – Virginia tobaccos	28	–	–	Gutenmann et al., 1982
Unspecified	30 – 79	–	–	Wyttenbach et al., 1976
Commercial – USA	–	0.6 – 1.2	Condensate	Morie & Morrisett, 1974
Experimental – USA	–	0.34 – 1.21[b]	Condensate	Guerin, 1976
Commercial – Jordan	28 – 33[a]	0.12 – 0.26	Particle phase	Hallack, 1981
Commercial – Iran	12.6	0.21[b]	Condensate	Abedinzadeh et al., 1977
Commercial – Turkey	15 – 54	–	–	Gülovali & Gündüz, 1983
Commercial – Italy	29 – 40	0.25 – 0.35	Particle phase	Perinelli & Carugno, 1978
		0.26 – 0.030	Gas phase	
Commercial – Pakistan	8.1 – 21.5	–	–	Ahmad et al., 1979
Kentucky reference – USA	33 – 69	0.35[b]	Condensate	Nadkarni & Ehmann, 1970
Kentucky reference – USA	29.8	0.36	Particle phase	Menden et al., 1972

[a] Reported in terms of μg per cigarette. Converted to present units assuming 800 mg tobacco per cigarette
[b] Reported in terms of ng per milligram of condensate. Converted to present units assuming 1 mg condensate equivalent to 1 mg 'tar'

Table 4. Levels of chromium in cigarette tobacco and smoke

Type of cigarettes	Tobacco content (μg/g)	Smoke delivery (μg/cigarette)	Smoke matrix analysed	Reference
Experimental – USA	–	0.004 – 0.069	Condensate	Guerin, 1976
Commercial – Jordan	Not detected	0.018 – 0.049	Particle phase	Hallack, 1981
Commercial – Turkey	4.4 – 13.5	–	–	Gülovali & Gündüz, 1983
Commercial – Pakistan	2.9 – 6.2	–	–	Ahmad et al., 1979
Kentucky reference – USA	0.39 – 2.05[a]	0.021	Condensate	Nadkarni & Ehmann, 1970

[a] Reported in terms of μg per cigarette. Converted to present units assuming 800 mg tobacco per cigarette

Table 5. Levels of arsenic in cigarette tobacco and smoke

Type of cigarettes	Tobacco content (µg/g)	Smoke delivery (µg/cigarette)	Smoke matrix analysed	Reference
Unspecified	0.26 – 0.66	–	–	Wyttenbach et al., 1976
Commercial – Jordan	Not detected	0.015 – 0.022	Particle phase	Hallack, 1981
Commercial – Turkey	0.7 – 1.6	–	–	Gülovali & Gündüz, 1983
Commercial – Pakistan	0.25 – 2.7	–	–	Ahmad et al., 1979
Kentucky reference – USA	1.79 – 3.52	0.100	Condensate	Nadkarni & Ehmann, 1970

Table 6. Levels of nickel in cigarette tobacco and smoke

Type of cigarettes	Tobacco content (µg/g)	Smoke delivery (µg/cigarette)	Smoke matrix analysed	Reference
Experimental – Virginia tobaccos	1.29	0.07	Particle phase	Gutenmann et al., 1982
		0.01	Gas phase	
Commercial – Germany	1.4 – 3.95 [a]	0.0051 – 0.0675	Particle phase	Szadkowski et al., 1969
		0.03 – 0.51	Gas phase	
Commercial – seven countries	3.28 – 9.41	0 – 0.19	Particle phase	Westcott & Spincer, 1974
		0.04 – 0.08	Gas phase	
Experimental – USA	–	0.006 – 0.074 [b]	Condensate	Guerin, 1976
Commercial – Italy	0.336 – 0.354	0.004 – 0.005	Particle phase	Perinelli & Carugno, 1978
		<0.00005	Gas phase	
Kentucky reference – USA	3.79	0.08	Particle phase	Menden et al., 1972

[a] Reported in terms of µg per cigarette. Converted to present units assuming 800 mg tobacco per cigarette
[b] Reported in terms of ng per milligram of condensate. Converted to present units assuming 1 mg condensate equivalent to 1 mg 'tar'

Table 7. Levels of selenium in cigarette tobacco and smoke

Type of cigarettes	Tobacco content (µg/g)	Smoke delivery (µg/cigarette)	Smoke matrix analysed	Reference
Commercial – Iran	2.28	0.063[a]	Condensate	Abedinzadeh et al., 1977
Commercial – Turkey	0.14 – 0.29	–	–	Gülovali & Gündüz, 1983
Commercial – Pakistan	0.11 – 3.15	–	–	Ahmad et al., 1979
Kentucky reference – USA	0.1 – 1.25	0.0077[a]	Conensate	Nadkarni & Ehmann, 1970
Experimental – Virginia tobaccos	0.03	0.0086	Particle phase	Gutenmann et al., 1983
		0.012	Gas phase	

[a]Reported in terms of ng per milligram of condensate. Converted to present units assuming 1 mg condensate equivalent to 1 mg 'tar'

smokers, is present in the tobacco at 0.4 pCi/gram, while about 0.024–0.052 pCi per cigarette transfers into the main-stream smoke (Martell, 1974; Ferri & Christiansen, 1967).

REFERENCES

Abedinzadeh, Z., Razeghi, M. & Parsa, B. (1977) Neutron activation analysis of an Iranian cigarette and its smoke. *J. radioanal. Chem., 35,* 373–376

Ahmad, S., Chaudhry, M. & Qureshi, I.H. (1979) Determination of toxic elements in tobacco products by instrumental neutron activation analysis. *J. radioanal. Chem., 54,* 331–341

Benowitz, N.L., Hall, S.M., Herning, R.I., Jacob, P., III, Jones, R.T. & Osman, A.L. (1983) Smokers of low yield cigarettes do not consume less nicotine. *New Engl. J. Med., 309,* 139–142

Bronisz, H., Szost, T., Lipska, M. & Zawada, M. (1983) Cadmium content in cigarettes. *Bromatol. Chem. Toksykol., 16,* 121–127

Brunnemann, K.D., Hoffmann, D., Wynder, E.L. & Gori, G.B. (1976) *Determination of tar, nicotine and carbon monoxide in cigarette smoke. A comparison of international smoking conditions.* In: Wynder, E.L., Hoffmann, D. & Gori, G.B., eds, *Smoking and Health; Modifying the Risk for the Smoker. Proceedings of Third World Conference on Smoking and Health,* New York City, 2–5 June 1975, DHEW Publications No. (NIH) 76–1221, pp. 441–449

Creighton, D.E. & Lewis, P.H. (1978) *The effect of smoking pattern on smoke deliveries.* In: Thornton, R.E., ed., *Smoking Behaviour: Physioligical Influences,* Edinburgh, Scotland, Churchill Livingstone, pp. 289–300

Ferri, E.S. & Christiansen, H. (1967) Lead-210 in tobacco and cigarette smoke. *Public Health Rep., 82,* 828–832

Guerin, M.R. (1976) *Chemical characterization of experiment cigarettes and cigarette smoke condensate.* In: Gori, G.B., ed., *Report No. 1 Toward Less Hazardous Cigarettes, The First Set of Experimental Cigarettes,* DHEW Publication No. (NIH) 76–905, pp. 59–84

Gülovali, M.C. & Gündüz, G. (1983) Trace elements in Turkish tobacco determined by instrumental neutron activation analysis. *J. radioanal. Chem., 78,* 189–198

Gutenmann, W.H., Bachem C.A., Lisk, D.J., Hoffmann, D., Adams, J.D. & Elfving, D.C. (1982) Cadmium and nickel in smoke of cigarettes prepared from tobacco cultured on municipal sludge-amended soil. *J. Toxicol. environ. Health, 10,* 423–431

Gutenmann, W.H., Lisk, D.J., Hoffmann, D. & Adams, J.D. (1983) Selenium in particulates and gaseous fractions of smoke from cigarettes prepared from tobacco grown in fly-ash-amended soil. *J. Toxicol. environ. Health, 12,* 385–393

Hallack, A.B. (1981) Proton-induced X-ray emission analysis of Jordanian cigarettes. *J. radioanal. Chem., 67,* 459–465

Harley, N.H., Cohen, B.S. & Tso, T.C. (1980) *Polonium-210: A questionable risk factor in smoking related carcinogenesis.* In: Gori, G.B. & Bock, F.G., eds, *Banbury Report No. 3: A Safe Cigarette?,* Cold Spring Harbor, NY, Cold Spring Harbor Laboratory, pp. 93–101

Herning, R.I., Jones, R.T., Bachman, J. & Mines, A.H. (1981) Puff volume increases when low nicotine cigarettes are smoked. *Br. med. J., 283,* 187–189

Horton, A.D. & Guerin, M.R. (1974) Gas-solid chromatographic determination of carbon monoxide and carbon dioxide in cigarette smoke. *J. Assoc. off. anal. Chem., 57,* 1–7

Jenkins, R.A., White, S.K., Griest, W.H. & Guerin, M.R. (1983) *Chemical Characterization of the Smokes of Selected US Commercial Cigarettes: Tar, Nicotine, Carbon Monoxide, Oxides and Nitrogen, Hydrogen Cyanide and Arolein.* ORNL/TM-8749, Available through the National Technical Information Service, Springfield, VA 22161

Kelley, T.F. (1965) Polonium-210 content of mainstream cigarette smoke. *Science, 149,* 537–538

Martell, E.A. (1974) Radioactivity of tobacco trichomes and insoluble cigarette smoke particles. *Nature, 249,* 215–217

Martell, E.A. (1982) Radioactivity in cigarette smoke. *New. Engl. J. Med., 307,* 309–310

Menden, E.E., Elia, V.J., Michael, L.W. & Petering, H.G. (1972) Distribution of cadmium and nickel of tobacco during cigarette smoking. *Environ. Sci. Tech., 6,* 830–832

Morie, G.P. & Morrisett, P.E. (1974) Determination of transition metals in cigarette smoke condensate by solvent extraction and atomic absorption spectroscopy. *Beitr. Tabakforsch., 7,* 302–304

Nadkarni, R.A. & Ehmann, W.D. (1970) Further analyses of University of Kentucky reference and alkaloid series cigarettes by instrumental neutron activation analysis. *Radiochem. radioanal. Lett., 4,* 325–335

Patel, A.R. (1980) *Preparation and monitoring of cigarette smoke condensate samples.* In: Gori, G.B., ed., *Report No. 4 Toward Less Hazardous Cigarettes. The Fourth Set of Experimental Cigarettes.* US Department of Health, Education & Welfare, pp. 99–114

Perinelli, M.A. & Carugno, N. (1978) Determination of trace metals in cigarette smoke by flameless atomic absorption spectrometry. *Beitr. Tabakforsch., 9,* 214–217

Pillsbury, H.C., Bright, C.C., O'Connor, K.J. & Irish, F.W. (1969) Tar and nicotine in cigarette smoke. *J. Assoc. off. anal. Chem., 52,* 458–462

Radford, E.P., Jr & Hunt, V.R. (1964) Polonium-210: A volatile element in cigarettes. *Science, 143,* 247–249

Scherer, G. & Barkemeyer, H. (1983) Cadmium concentrations in tobacco and tobacco smoke. *Ecotoxicol. environ. Saf., 7,* 71–78

Snook, M.E. & Fortson, P.J. (1979) Gel chromatographic isolation of catechols and hydroquinones. *Anal. Chem., 51,* 1814–1819

Szadkowski, D., Schultze, H., Schaller, K.-H. & Lehnert, G. (1969) Zur ökologischen Bedeutung des Schwermetallgehaltes von Zigaretten, Blei-, Cadmium- und Nickelanalysen des Tabaks sowie der Gas- und Partikelphase. (On the ecological significance of the heavy metal content of cigarettes: lead, cadmium and nickel analyses of tobacco, as well as gas and particle phase). *Arch. Hyg. Bakteriol., 153,* 1–8

Wartman, W.B., Jr, Cogbill, E.C. & Harlow, E.S. (1959) Determination of particulate matter in concentrated aerosols. Application to tar and nicotine in cigarette smoke. *Anal. Chem., 31,* 1705–1709

Westcott, D.T. & Spincer, D. (1974) The cadmium, nickel and lead content of tobacco and cigarette smoke. *Beitr. Tabakforsch., 7,* 217–221

Wyttenbach, A., Bajo, S. & Haekkinen, A. (1976) Determination of 16 elements in tobacco by neutron activation analysis. *Beitr. Tabakforsch., 8,* 247–249

SAMPLING AND ANALYSIS OVERVIEW

CHAPTER 10

SAMPLING, STORAGE AND PRETREATMENT OF BIOLOGICAL MATERIAL

G.V. Iyengar

Principal Investigator,
Joint FDA-IAEA-NBS-USDA Project
on Dietary Intakes of Trace Elements,
NBS, Gaithersburg, MD 20899, USA

INTRODUCTION

In trace element analysis of biological systems, sampling and pretreatment operations are not exciting steps, yet they are crucial ones. Many factors may invalidate the results of an analysis and it cannot be emphasized too strongly that, in spite of recent improvements in the sensitivity and specificity of the analytical methods, the reliability of an analytical result still depends strongly on the quality of the sample. Stringent precautions and strict adherence to a variety of requirements are therefore mandatory if the results are to be reliable. For successful work, close collaboration between the analytical and biomedical community is essential, or the investigator must combine both functions, since assays of arbitrarily chosen materials without due consideration of their potential biomedical relevance can only lead to an accumulation of largely useless data (Iyengar, 1982).

THE BIOLOGICAL MATRIX

The matrix bulk element composition of a biological sample is an important factor in the choice of an analytical procedure, because of possible interference. The biological matrix is made up of the basic structural elements C, H, N, O, P, S and Ca (in the case of hard tissues). Ca, Cl, K, Mg and Na constitute the group of major elements required for electrolyte balance, along with HCO_3^- and, to a small extent, SO_4^{2-} and HPO_4^{2-}. The rest of the elements occur as traces. A few matrices can be characterized by relatively high amounts of certain trace elements, such as Al, Ba, Cd, Cu, F, Fe, I, Si, Sn, Sr and Zn, which are found at concentration levels of approximately 0.001 to 0.01 percent.

A typical distribution pattern for metals in biological systems is shown in Table 1. This Table shows the metal composition of Reference Man, proposed by the ICRP (1975) assuming a body weight of 70 kg. Bone is a target tissue in the sense that it shows exceptional preference for the accumulation of some elements, including Pb. Mg, Na, Rb, Al, Mn, Co and Be are also present in the skeleton at relatively higher proportions, compared with soft tissues (Iyengar *et al.*, 1978a). Other target structures in the body are blood, spleen and liver for Fe, kidney for Cd, thyroid for I, lymph nodes and connective tissues for Si, hair for S, semen and prostate for Zn and liver for Cu. The high concentration of Al and Fe seen in lung is mostly due to accumulation from dust, probably because these two elements are not cleared from the lung by the circulating blood. Based on individual matrix composition, there are a few other tissues and body fluids which contain certain elements at high levels, e.g., Zn in hair and nail.

THE SAMPLE

Procurement of medical samples for trace element analysis is basically governed by two conventions: single samples are taken from living subjects and multiple samples (if necessary) from autopsy cases. The sampling problems which arise in these two situations are therefore different. For example, drawing a blood specimen or excising a piece of muscle by biopsy would require procedures which are both sterile and free of analyte contamination. In the case of autopsy, however, only the latter factor is of primary importance.

The number of primary samples and their location within a given organ depend, of course, on the objectives of the study and the characteristics (anatomical structure, physiological function) of the material selected for analysis. As a rule, in the biomedical field, it is considerably more difficult to meet analytical requirements concerning the number (e.g., duplicates) and size of samples than in most other areas of trace element research.

Finally, trace element analysis in biological systems is also faced with some unusual and complex problems unlike those encountered in inorganic systems. Several pre-sampling factors, such as biological variations, postmortem changes, preferrential accumulation of certain elements in some organs (or segments of an organ) and some intrinsic errors associated with certain types of matrices complicate the situation and pose difficulties in obtaining 'valid' samples for analysis (Iyengar, 1982).

SAMPLING

When planning the analytical work it is advisable to visualize clearly the requirements to be met at the sampling stage. These requirements include (a) background information concerning the sample, e.g., nature of the sample, probable

Table 1.   Metal concentrations in Reference Man

Element	Total quantity	Average body concentration (mg/kg)	Distribution in the body components[a]
Iron	4.2	60	RBC (60), muscle (26), lung (8), liver (7), skeleton (2.5)
Zinc	2.3 g	33	Muscle (65), skeleton (22), liver (4)
Rubidium	630 mg	10	Skeleton (31), muscle (25), liver (8), brain (5), blood (2)
Strontium	320 mg	4.6	Skeleton (ca 98)
Lead	120 mg	1.7	Skeleton (92), liver (1.5), muscle (1), blood (0.7), hair (0.5)
Copper	72 mg	1.0	Muscle (32), liver (17), brain (11), skeleton (10), blood (7), skin (3)
Aluminium	61 mg	0.9	Skeleton (35), lung (20), muscle (9), skin (8), lymph nodes (5), blood (3)
Cadmium	50 mg	0.7	Muscle ($<$30), skeleton ($<$25), kidney (20), liver (8)
Barium	22 mg	0.3	Skeleton (91), blood ($<$5)
Tin	$<$17 mg	$<$0.2	No particular target tissue
Manganese	12 mg	0.2	Skeleton (44), liver (21), muscle (13)
Nickel	10 mg	0.1	No particular target tissue
Gold	$<$10 mg	$<$0.1	No particular target tissue
Molybdenum	$<$9.3 mg	$<$0.1	Liver (20)
Chromium	$<$6.8 mg	$<$0.1	Bone, liver, muscle, skin (highly variable data)
Caesium	1.5 mg	0.02	Muscle (38), skeleton (11)
Cobalt	$<$1.5 mg	$<$0.02	Hair (22?), skeleton (18), muscle (13), liver (7)
Uranium	90 µg	0.001	Skeleton (65), muscle (6), blood (5)
Beryllium	36 µg	0.0005	Skeleton (24), muscle (12), lung (20), brain (4)

[a] Figures in parentheses are percentages
[b] Assuming a mean Fe concentration of 10 mg/kg
[c] Relates to 20 g in Reference Man

bulk elemental composition of the matrix and topographical details, (b), clear perception of the sampling tools required and the associated sample contamination hazards, (c) consideration of collection of timed samples and samples under dietary control, and (d) sample pre-treatment and storage precautions prior to the measurement of the analytical signals.

As a general rule, the analyst should be directly involved in the sampling procedure, in order to ensure that the samples are representative and that no significant changes in composition occur during sampling, transport and storage. When medical restrictions prevent the analyst from applying special sampling procedures, the medical staff should be familiar with the requirements of valid sampling.

There are a few basic hazards faced in all the steps of sampling, storage, pre-treatment and analysis. These are contamination, loss of elements and changes in the mean composition of the sample. These are discussed briefly under sample preparation, below, and in more detail elsewhere (Iyengar & Sansoni, 1980; Sansoni & Iyengar, 1980). Contamination is by far the most serious threat, especially at the ultra-trace level. A striking, but by no means atypical, illustration of this problem is provided by observations on inadequately collected and processed serum samples for the determination of Mn (Versieck & Speecke, 1972). In nine samples transferred with an automatic dispenser (inadequate procedure), the following figures were obtained: 4.83 $\pm$ 5.17 µg/L, with a range of 0.61 to 16.81 µg/L. On the other hand, in nine adequately handled samples from the same serum pool, using exactly the same analytical procedure, the values obtained were 0.72 $\pm$ 0.1 µg/L, with a range of 0.56 to 0.89 µg/L; i.e., a factor of almost 7 lower.[1]

Sampling procedures for solids

Sampling of solids is often more complex than that of liquids. As a general rule, the homogeneity of the total sample and of subsamples should never be assumed to be satisfactory until proved to be so. Because of the lower reactivity of solids, however, the dangers of contamination, losses of trace elements (due to absorption and other effects) and changes in mean composition are generally less than with liquids.

The site or topographical situation for sampling and subsampling has to be selected carefully. Attention should be paid to the different regions of kidney (cortex/medulla), bone (marrow/hard parts), skin (dermis/epidermis), tooth (enamel/dentin) and hair (distance from the scalp).

Removal of surface contamination may be accomplished by washing, trimming or freeze-drying, followed by scraping off of the surface layer.

Sampling procedures for liquids

The problems of heterogeneity and sampling statistics are generally less difficult for liquids than for solids, because of the relatively high degree of homogeneity. In the case of suspensions or emulsions, it has to be decided whether these should be sampled whole or whether the phases should be sampled separately. If necessary, the two phases can be separated and weighed before analysis, and data for the whole sample can be obtained by calculation.

Timed collection is necessary for several body fluids; for example, a 24-h collection period for urine samples.

Transport to the laboratory

When the time taken for transport is only a few hours, it may be sufficient if the samples are kept cool (4 °C) during this period; otherwise, they should be deep-frozen. Suitable containers for this purpose are now available commercially. Because of the

---

[1] J. Versieck, 1983, personal communication.

Table 2. Metallic impurities in EDTA[a,b]

Element	Mass fraction (ng/g, dry)
Cr	50
Se	15
Zn	300

[a] Merck, p.a., quality
[b] D. Behne, 1983 (personal communication)

problem of losses and contamination, most workers use clean polyethylene or Teflon containers, which are non-wettable and therefore reduce liquid-container interactions. Special care must be taken to exclude dust. It is also advisable to avoid exposing the samples to extremes of humidity.

If segregation of solids cannot be avoided, the samples should be thoroughly re-mixed after transport.

Whenever possible, whole organs should be transported with their capsules. Sensitive liquids, such as whole blood, should be transported with a minimum of turbulence to avoid breakdown of cells. Blood cells from serum preparation should be transported within a few hours. Preferably, they should be centrifuged within one hour of collection in order to minimize haemolysis.

Post-mortem samples

When normal metabolic processes stop and active transport through membranes ends, passive diffusion may cause profound changes in the distribution of elements. In addition, cell swelling, imbibition and autolysis may cause detrimental changes. These problems cannot be completely avoided, but their effects can be minimized by standardizing autopsy sampling conditions (Iyengar, 1980).

PRESERVATION AND STORAGE

Preservation of a sampled specimen depends largely on the matrix properties, the time interval between collection and arrival at the laboratory and the subsequent handling for analysis. The preservation of bone, hair or nail, for example, is relatively simple, compared with that of brain, liver, lung or kidney. The conventional method of treating the latter group of samples with formaldehyde is generally unacceptable, due to contamination and leaching problems, so that preservation by freezing should be preferred. For short-term preservation, temperatures of 2–4 °C (normal refrigeration) are low enough, but long-term preservation should generally involve deep freezing (< -15 °C). Where possible (autopsy cases, animal experiments), whole organs or large pieces of tissues (e. g., muscle) should be preserved with their capsules. Samples can be sealed in clean polyethylene bags and packed in plastic containers with tight caps.

Preservation by freezing, however, also gives rise to some minor problems. For example, the yield of dry weight diminishes with freezing time (Adrian & Stevans, 1979; Iyengar, 1981) and further studies of this observation are needed. Moreover, not all the fluids can be subjected to this method of preservation; e.g., whole blood samples become invalid because of lysis of erythrocytes. It is possible to preserve whole blood (also serum and plasma) for several days at refrigeration temperatures, but it is necessary to add an anticoagulant, such as citrate or EDTA, which are potential sources of contamination (Table 2).

Storage of specimens directly after sampling or from primary preserved material may become necessary for several reasons. In such cases, freeze-drying is well suited. Even oven-drying at relatively low temperatures (e.g., 80 °C) may be employed. In all cases, certain precautions are necessary and exceptions have to be made with respect to some elements. Storage containers should have non-porous, smooth and non-wettable (e.g., Teflon) walls. The total surface area and the free space within the container should be kept to a minimum. The exclusion of humidity and dust from the storage compartment is mandatory.

Contamination and modification of samples may depend strongly on container material, humidity, pH, temperature and duration of storage because of adsorption, leaching and chemical and biochemical interactions. In a study involving Cu, Zn, K, Na, Mg and Ca in serum, for example, several types of containers have been found to be suitable, provided that conditions tending to increase pH are avoided and that samples are quickly frozen in tightly-capped containers with a minimum of air space above the serum (Fisher *et al.,* 1976). Recommended storage conditions for a commercial lyophilized seronorm protein (dry substance = 1 mL of serum, Nyegaard & Co, Oslo) are as follows:

in lyophilized form:

    at least 3 years   at < -20 °C
    6 months   at 2–8 °C

after reconstitution:

    1 month   at < -20 °C
    4 days   at 2–8 °C
    8 hours   at 20 °C.

For the problem elements, such as Mn and Cr, the use of polyethylene tubes to freeze the serum below -10 °C has been shown to be safe (Anand & Ducharme, 1973; Damsgaard *et al.,* 1973), whereas polycarbonate tubes were otherwise found to be adequate for storage of serum and plasma for up to 2 weeks at refrigeration temperature. Acceptable procedures for cleaning containers are described under sample preparation, below; the subject is treated in greater detail by Sansoni and Iyengar (1978).

SAMPLE PREPARATION

In many cases, unfortunately, the analyst becomes acquainted with a sample for the first time when it arrives at the laboratory. It is thus essential that the complete history of the sample be communicated to the analyst before the material is prepared for analysis.

The sample which reaches the laboratory must generally be reduced in amount by subsampling, to provide the test portion to be analysed. With solid samples, subsampling involves washing, drying, ashing, powdering, homogenization and perhaps homogeneity tests. Body fluids are generally suspensions or emulsions. For these, separation into pure liquid and solid phases or stabilization and homogenization, followed by homogeneity tests, have to be considered. The reader may refer to the generalized sample preparation scheme outlined by Iyengar and Sansoni (1980).

All the above-mentioned manipulations may give rise to contamination, loss of elements and change in mean composition of the sample and call for careful selection of methods of treatment, including a clean handling environment and tools that are compatible with the aim of the analysis. Contamination or loss of the analyte is seldom corrigible and in extreme circumstances, the analytical result may be irretrievably compromised. This has been the case until now with the majority of the results reported for elements at extremely low concentrations. It is therefore good practice on the part of the analyst, firstly, to assess the potential sources of error within his working environment, secondly, to take measures to minimize such errors and, thirdly, to maintain appropriate monitoring of surface and other contaminations at regular intervals. For example, introduction (leaching) or loss (adsorption) of analyte can be studied by preparing a particular type of sample in containers of different materials, as illustrated by Damsgaard et al. (1973) for Mn in serum. The recognition of errors in an analytical procedure can be facilitated by repeated analysis of a certified reference material (CRM). When a laboratory is involved in the analysis of materials for which no CRM is yet available, periodic analysis of a carefully prepared 'in-house' standard can greatly contribute to the good performance of the laboratory.

The analytical laboratory

Contamination is a relative concept, the danger of which is related to the concentration of the analyte. For example, Cr and Pb analyses are more susceptible to airborne contamination than are certain other elements. Table 3 compares the metal contents of particulates in the air of an ordinary laboratory, a clean room and a class-100 hood (Murphy, 1976). Both the air of the clean room and the class-100 hood showed a dramatic reduction of contamination. The concentrations of Pb were reduced by a factor of 200 and the levels of other elements, which were already low, were reduced by a factor of 10. It is interesting, in this context, to examine the results of a questionnaire circulated by IUPAC (Mitzuike & Pinta, 1978) to assess the experience of 96 laboratories concerning the stages of analysis where contamination

Table 3. Metal concentrations in laboratory air particulates ($\mu g/m^3$)

Air source	Iron	Copper	Lead	Cadmium
Ordinary laboratory	0.2	0.02	0.4	0.002
Clean room	0.001	0.002	0.0002	N.D.[a]
Clean hood (class-100)	0.0009	0.007	0.0003	0.0002

[a] N.D., not detected

Table 4. Stages where contamination occurred

Stages	No. of laboratories (total = 96)	%
Collection of sample	44	44
Storage of sample	44	46
Comminution (pulverization)	17	18
Sieving	10	10
Filtration	17	18
Desiccation	11	11
Decomposition of sample	62	65
Separation	53	55
Instrumental measurement	31	32

occurred (Table 4). It was found that 46% of the laboratories observed contamination at the collection and storage stages, whereas 65% and 55% incriminated the decomposition and separation stages, respectively. Hamilton (1980) has described various aspects of setting up a trace-element laboratory, e.g., air supply, clean benches, walls, floors, clothing and footwear, fume cupboards, glove boxes and water supply (see also Boyer and Horwitz, this volume, chap. 12). The impact of operating personnel, through sweat, cosmetics, tobacco ash and smoke, has been discussed as well (Hamilton *et al.,* 1973; Murphy, 1976). Strict adherence to good laboratory practices, such as using separate sets of glass and plastic ware for standards, cleaning them separately, not preparing the standards in the same room as the sample, and keeping the work table free of loose contamination, needs to be emphasized.

Table 5. Some impurity levels (ng/g) in quartz containers made from Heraeus Suprasil AN[a]

Element	HF etched	Not etched	Heraeus certified
Cr	0.173 ± 0.019	1	5
Ni	0.64	2.8	–
Zn	0.15	3.0	10
Se	0.04	–	–

[a] Michel et al., 1980

Materials

The primary concern for sample handling is to obtain tools and containers with very low concentrations of the trace elements of interest. At the moment, there seem to be no good alternatives to plastic, quartz and some high-purity metals such as Ti, which has been slowly gaining in popularity. The use of stainless-steel knives continues to be controversial (Heit & Klusek, 1982; J. Versieck, 1983, personal communication). Heit and Klusek (1982), comparing the effects of dissecting tools made of stainless steel, Lexan plastic, titanium and Teflon-coated stainless steel, report that no significant differences were observed for the analysis of Al, Cd, Cr, Cu, Hg, Ni, Pb, Se, Sn, Te and V in fish or mussel samples. However, it should be recognized that the purpose of the analysis (i.e., the elements determined and the concentrations involved) is the deciding factor in the handling of samples, and the concept of controlled contamination can be advantageously used (Behne, 1980). The use of a Ti knife or a Ni needle, for example, should not present a problem as long as these elements are not to be determined. In all cases, disposable plastic gloves, Teflon forceps, polyethylene and Teflon foils and way paper are very handy aids. Concerning impurity levels, Murphy (1976) lists six different materials in order of increasing impurity content: Teflon, synthetic quartz, polyethylene (high pressure, conventional), natural quartz, platinum and borosilicate. Some trace-element impurities have been determined in a number of laboratory-ware materials (IAEA, 1980). Very high-purity quartz (Michel et al., 1980) is now available (Table 5).

With regard to contamination from reagents, the addition of an anticoagulant to blood to obtain plasma presents a typical example. Considering that about 4 mg of EDTA is required per mL of blood, and assuming that all the EDTA remains in the plasma, it can be seen (Table 2) that the 1.2 ng of Zn introduced does not affect the determination of Zn, whereas the quantity of Cr introduced (0.2 ng) may be unacceptable, although the Cr level in plasma is a subject of controversy (Simonoff et al., 1984).

Cleaning procedures

Since the sample container is one of the more important sources of contamination, much of the analytical accuracy will depend not only on the choice of the container materials, but also on the method of cleaning them. For example, Maziere et al. (1976)

have convincingly demonstrated the need for etching the inner surface of quartz tubes to a depth of 20 micrometers with HF, in order to remove surface contamination by Cr, Zn and other elements. Several laboratories have developed standard washing procedures for laboratory ware and a few examples are cited below.

Levi and Purdy (1980) used the following procedure for cleaning glassware. The vessels are soaked for 6 h in a 1:1 (v/v) mixture of 6 mol/L HCl and 7.5 mol/L HNO_3, then rinsed three times with distilled water and once with deionized water. They are subsequently soaked for 12 h in deionized water, then rinsed three times with conductivity water. Finally, the vessels are dried in a clean oven, or at room temperature in a clean area, inverted on fresh paper towels.

Moody and Lindström (1975) suggest the following procedure for cleaning plastic containers: (1) fill with (1+1) HCL (AR grade); (2) allow to stand for one week at room temperature (80 °C for Teflon); (3) empty and rinse with distilled water; (4) fill with (1+1) HNO_3 (AR grade); (5) allow to stand for one week at room temperature (80 °C for Teflon); (6) empty and rinse with distilled water; (7) fill with purest available distilled water; (8) allow to stand for several weeks or until needed, changing water periodically to ensure continued cleaning; (9) rinse with purest water and allow to dry in a particle- and fume-free environment.

Cornelis *et al.* (1979) followed a very strict procedure for cleaning quartz vials and pipettes used for V analysis. The vials and related accessories are boiled in 6 mol/L HNO_3 p.a. and H_2SO_4 p.a. for 8 h, then rinsed three times with deionized water and another times with double-distilled water. The acid treatment is repeated for 8 h with 'suprapure' HNO_3 and 'suprapure' H_2SO_4, followed by two rinses with double-distilled water and a 3-h steaming treatment, using vapour from double-distilled water.

Harrison (Harrison, S.H., 1981, personal communication) recommends the following method for cleaning a titanium knife. Place the knife in a clean glass container and cover with reagent-grade chloroform for one hour or longer. Pour off the chloroform and cover with reagent-grade ethanol and rinse with high-purity water. Cover the knife with dilute HCl (1:3), using high-purity water for dilution. After 2 h, pour off the acid and rinse with high-purity water, once with ethanol, then twice with high-purity water. Place the knife on a clean surface (only the handle should touch the surface) and air-dry, preferably in a laminar-flow hood. Store the dry knife in bags made of clean Teflon sheets.

Practical handling steps

Biological fluids are more susceptible to bacterial growth in the unfrozen state and sample preparation should be finished preferably within 24 h. Since most biological fluids are suspensions or emulsions, care should be taken to select the phase of interest or, in the case of the whole sample, to ensure that the phases are properly mixed.

When processing blood to obtain serum, it is important to minimize haemolysis by gentle handling, using dry syringes, transferring slowly to dry test tubes and leaving sufficient time for clotting. Blood clotting takes about 15 min at room temperature, but is delayed if siliconized glassware, Teflon or polyethylene containers are used. Fractionation is carried out at $2000 \times g$ for 5 to 10 min. The centrifuge tube should be kept closed to avoid contamination and evaporation. To obtain plasma, blood containing an anticoagulant is handled in the same way as for serum. Depending upon the degree of haemolysis, serum levels of elements such as Zn may be affected. Kasperek *et al.* (1981) have investigated the influence of haemolysis on serum concentrations of elements, including Se and Zn. Fe, Rb and Zn showed significantly higher concentrations in serum than in plasma; the average differences were 320, 12 and 20 ng/mL, respectively. Procedures for handling other body fluids, such as urine, milk, cerebrospinal fluid and sweat, are discussed elsewhere (Iyengar & Sansoni, 1980).

Sample washing

Some solid samples, such as hair, nail and autopsy specimens, are washed prior to analysis to remove non-intrinsic contamination of the first two and to eliminate the influence of residual blood on the third. In the case of hair, pre-washing helps to eliminate most of the Na, and thereby facilitates neutron activation analysis. The problem is complex, however, and there is no consensus of opinion concerning the type and extent of washing to be undertaken in the case of hair and nail, and the excised tissue from autopsy. For example, a mild and highly-reproducible pre-irradiation washing procedure for hair (Ryabukin, 1980), using acetone and water, has been found to be unsuitable for Cr analysis (Kumpulainen *et al.,* 1982) because the Cr content continued to fall on lengthy washing. According to Kumpulainen *et al.,* sodium lauryl sulfate and hexane/ethanol are the most reliable washing agents for hair intended for Cr analysis. Salmela *et al.* (1981) also expressed doubt concerning washing methods for Cd determination. Further evidence of the unsuitability of the acetone wash is provided by Das *et al.* (1981), who found that levels of As, Co, Cr, Fe and Hg in hair dropped sharply as a result of the first wash, then remained approximately constant. Bank *et al.* (1981) have re-examined the washing problem with regard to nail, making use of nine different washing media previously tested by other investigators. They reached the conclusion that aqueous acids caused the greatest loss and organic solvents readily extracted Fe and Mg, while Ca, Cu and Zn were relatively less affected. Virtually all of the Mg was extracted by distilled water or aqueous detergents.

The problem of washing autopsy and placenta samples to free them from residual blood and its components has, until now, received very little attention. It has been shown that rinsing rat liver with distilled water depletes the electrolytes by about 30%, whereas protein-bound trace elements (e.g., Se and Zn) remain relatively unaffected (Iyengar, 1980; Iyengar *et al.,* 1982a). Ehman *et al.* (1980) have used ashless filter paper to wipe the sample surface. On the whole, the effects of washing on concentration profiles in biological specimens is still an open question.

Drying

It is important to control temperature while oven-drying biological samples. Temperatures exceeding 100 °C lead to matrix decomposition. In an oven-drying experiment measuring dehydration rates in a number of samples of human and rodent origin, the loss of dry residue was found to be more pronounced in serum and urine

(Table 6). Hg (Iyengar *et al.,* 1978b) and Sn (Iyengar *et al.,* 1980) were lost to a small extent at 80 °C from liver and muscle. In another experiment using radioactive Cr, a loss of up to 10% (mostly Cr[III]) was observed in rat tissues at 120 °C. The loss may be due to slow volatilization because of the extended heat-treatment period of 72 h (Iyengar *et al.,* 1982b). Rook and Wolf (1977) showed that a small fraction of Cr in Brewer's yeast volatilized between 150 and 300 °C, indicating that a small fraction of Cr in the sample is chemically different from the rest. Recoveries of Cr from rat tissues following freeze-drying were satisfactory (Iyengar *et al.,* 1982b). De Goeij *et al.* (1979) have recovered Cr satisfactorily from wet and lyophilized liver. Lyophilization, also known as freeze-drying or vacuum-drying, is well suited for drying biological materials. It involves three stages, pre-freezing, primary drying and secondary drying. Ensuring adequate vacuum and pre-freezing of the samples before lyophilization are important for good retention yields and for preventing contamination. Failure of the vacuum may lead to thawing of the frozen material, promoting sample-container interactions. For this reason, it is better to control the sample cooling separately by means of an additional pump which is not part of the freeze-drier system. Metallic contamination from the housing of the freeze drier should be prevented by using non-metallic components (e.g., perspex) for sample housing. One disadvantage of freeze-drying is that fluids such as urine leave a hygroscopic residue (Cornelis *et al.,* 1975) and care is necessary to avoid errors from this source; if the analytical technique permits, analysis of whole urine is recommended. Freeze-drying has been used satisfactorily for several elements in a variety of samples, with occasional exceptions for Hg (Iyengar & Sansoni, 1980).

Ashing

Removal of the organic matrix is usually accomplished either by dry ashing with air in an open muffle furnace, or in oxygen plasma at temperatures below 150 °C, or by 'wet ashing' (digestion) with various acid mixtures. Dry ashing around 500 °C is effective even for large samples, but has the disadvantage of volatilizing a number of elements. On the positive side, dry ashing does not require the addition of chemicals. In low-temperature ashing, the decomposition is brought about by nascent oxygen and is essentially a surface phenomenon, so that agitation of the sample is required to accelerate the rate of ashing. It is effective for small samples only. It is not totally safe for volatile elements, but yields fairly reproducible losses under uniform methods of operation. Wet ashing, where applicable, is recommended, since it is faster, efficient and results in lower analyte losses. More details concerning the relative merits of various ashing techniques, with special reference to select metals, are given in Chapter 12 of this volume. A literature survey concerning the loss of elements from various matrices following dry ashing and a discussion of the various ashing techniques has also been published by Iyengar & Sansoni (1980).

Homogenization

Where possible, normally liquid samples should be dispensed in the fluid state, since it is relatively simple to retain homogeneity in that form. With adequate care, even body fluids such as whole blood can be dispensed satisfactorily, provided that caution

Table 6. Comparison of the dry residues (%) from various biological samples following freeze-drying and oven-drying at different temperatures [a]

| Sample | Freeze-drying (108 h) | | Oven-drying | | | |
| | Approx. sample size (g) | Residue % | Approx. sample size (g) | Residue (%) | | |
				80°C (108 h)	105°C (36 h)	120°C (36 h)
Human						
Whole blood	1	22.54 ± 0.50	3	21.90 ± 0.22	21.34 ± 0.12	20.80 ± 0.10
Blood serum	1	9.52 ± 0.35	3	9.70 ± 0.20	9.37 ± 0.20	9.06 ± 0.20
Erythrocytes	1	32.38 ± 0.64	3	33.26 ± 0.57	32.67 ± 0.57	32.05 ± 0.53
Urine	2	4.04 ± 0.25	3	3.82 ± 0.01	3.26 ± 0.03	2.62 ± 0.05
Rat						
Brain	1.5	22.00 ± 0.51	2	21.40 ± 0.42	20.95 ± 0.44	20.80 ± 0.54
Kidney	2	25.60 ± 0.58	2.5	26.20 ± 0.70	25.40 ± 0.60	25.20 ± 0.60
Liver	2	30.25 ± 0.61	2	29.58 ± 0.45	29.03 ± 0.42	28.34 ± 0.41
Lung	1	21.30 ± 0.54	1.5	20.30 ± 0.65	20.05 ± 0.50	20.00 ± 0.62
Muscle	2	28.32 ± 0.58	2	27.36 ± 1.33	27.14 ± 1.32	26.17 ± 1.68
Ovary	0.1	43.40 ± 0.72	–	–	–	–
Spleen	0.4	27.30 ± 0.66	–	–	–	–
Testis	1.5	14.50 ± 0.42	2	14.30 ± 0.65	13.80 ± 0.55	13.43 ± 0.60
Uterus	0.2	24.30 ± 0.36	0.2	23.40 ± 0.72	22.75 ± 0.66	22.15 ± 0.72

[a] Iyengar et al., 1980

is exercised to recover the entire sample aliquot during the analysis. Frozen samples should be allowed to thaw completely and stirred well before dispensing.

With the exception of a few solids, such as hair and nail, most biological samples are intricately mixed with other body components, such as connective tissue, capsule, layers of skin, fat, blood vessels, nerve pieces, hair (during skin sampling), glandular parts, gastro-intestinal tract contents, etc. Some of these interfering components are very difficult to remove without severely damaging the integrity of the parent tissue. Since the interfering components have differing composition profiles (Iyengar *et al.,* 1978a) and their total exclusion from a given sample is not always possible, some degree of heterogeneity among aliquots of a sample analysed without prior homogenization should always be anticipated. Even at the cellular level, the distribution may be expected to be non-homogeneous because of the structure of the cell itself. Strictly speaking, therefore, lack of homogeneity is inherent in biological tissue samples.

In assessing the degree of homogeneity, a first indication is given by the particle size distribution. The finer the particle size of the powdered material, the better are the chances of good results, even with relatively small aliquots. It should be recognized, however, that the concentration of an element in the sample and the analytical difficulties associated with that element are two crucial parameters, with regard to conclusions concerning overall homogeneity. This is amply illustrated in the case of Zn, which presents no analytical difficulties at the level at which occurs in most biological samples, so that the degree of homogeneity observed for Zn is usually superior to that of an element which is found at lower concentrations and/or presents analytical problems. A second example is provided by the NBS bovine liver standard. Although the recommended weight of an aliquot for analysis of this material is 250 mg, accurate and reproducible determination of Zn, Ag, Br, Co, Cs, Fe, Rb and Se are possible with aliquots of only 25 mg, because all these elements can be measured efficiently using instrumental neutron activation analysis (Behne & Jürgensen, 1978). Very little can be said about the true homogeneity of a biological sample with respect to elements at lower concentrations if the measurements are not dependable. In general, the problem of homogenization of biological materials may be summarized as follows:

As the amount of the sample material increases, the need for homogenization also increases.

For samples such as composite meal and faeces, however, homogenization is inevitable.

For muscle and liver, on the other hand, if the interfering components are sorted carefully during the sample handling stage, the problem of heterogeneity does not appear to be serious (Iyengar & Kasperek, 1977; Livens *et al.,* 1977). By analysing multiple aliquots from such samples, reasonably good results can be obtained.

Brain and lung present an intermediate situation. By proper segregation of anatomical regions, inhomogeneity can be minimized. In the case of lung, special treatment may be necessary if there is visible deposition of particles. However, when information is needed for whole brain or lung, homogenization is mandatory. The case of kidney provides a good example where even small sections of anatomically segregated parts, such as cortex and medulla, require homogenization prior to analysis. Metal sequestration within the kidney is site-dependent (Livingstone, 1971).

Sample homogenization may be achieved for both wet and dry tissues. Cryogenic techniques are generally well suited for this purpose. The brittle fracture technique (BFT) is a handy aid for dealing with small samples, up to 5 or 10 g (Iyengar & Kasperek, 1977). For samples of the order of a few hundred grams, the disc mill (a vast improvement of the BFT) is recommended (R. Zeisler, 1983, personal communication).

REFERENCES

Adrian, W.J. & Stevans, M.L. (1979) Wet versus dry weights for heavy metal toxicity determinations in duck liver. *J. Wildl. Dis., 15,* 125–126

Anand, V.D. & Ducharme, D.M. (1976) *Stability of Cr ions at low concentrations in aqueous and biological matrices stored in glass, polyethylene and polycarbonate.* In: LaFleur, P.D., ed. *Accuracy in Trace Analysis. Sampling, Sample Handling, Analysis,* Vols I and II. Washington DC, National Bureau of Standards, pp. 611–619

Bank, H.L., Robson, J., Bigelow, J.B., Morrison, J., Spell, L.H. & Kantor, R. (1981) Preparation of fingernails for trace element analysis. *Clin. Chim. Acta, 116,* 179–190

Behne, D. (1980) *Problems of sampling and sample preparation for trace element analysis in the health sciences.* In: Bräter, P. & Schramel, P., eds, *Trace Element Analytical Chemistry in Medicine and Biology,* Berlin, de Gruyter, pp. 769–782

Behne, D. & Jürgensen, H. (1978) Determination of trace elements in human blood serum and in SRM bovine liver by INAA. *J. radioanal. Chem., 42,* 447–453

Cornelis, R., Speecke, A. & Hoste, J. (1975) NAA for bulk and trace elements in urine. *Anal. Chim. Acta, 78,* 317–327

Cornelis, R., Mees, L., Hoste, J., Ryckenbusch, J., Versieck, J. & Barbier, F. (1979) Determination of V in human blood serum and liver. Proc. Int. Symp. Nucl. Act. Tech. Life Sci., Vienna, IAEA-SM-227/115, pp. 165–177

Damsgaard, E., Heydorn, K., Larsen, N.A. & Nielsen, B. (1975) Simultaneous determination of As, Mn and Se in human serum by NAA. *RISO Report-271,* Rosekilde, June 1973

Das, H.A., Dejkumhang, M., Herber, R.F.M., Hoede, D. & van der Sloot, H.A. (1981) Instrumental neutron activation analysis of human hair and related radiotracer experiments on washing and leaching. *ECN Report 107,* Petten, November 1981

De Goeij, J.J.M., Volkers, K.J. & Tijoe, P.S. (1979) A search for losses of Cr and other trace elements during lyophilization of human liver tissue. *Anal. Chim. Acta, 109,* 139–143

Ehman, W.D., Markebery, W.R., Alauddin, M., Goodin, D.T. & Hossain, T.I.M. (1980) INAA study of normal and diseased human brain. *Proc. 4th Int. Nat. Conf.*

in Nuclear Methods in Environmental and Energy Research, University of Missouri, Columbia, pp. 459–469

Fisher, G.L., Davies, L.G. & Rosenblatt, L.S. (1976) *The effect of container composition on serum minerals.* In: LaFleur, P.D., ed., *Accuracy in Trace Analysis: Sampling, Sample Handling, Analysis,* Volumes I and II, Washington DC, National Bureau of Standards, pp. 575–591

Hamilton, E.I. (1980) The chemical laboratory and trace element analysis. *IAEA Technical Report 197,* Vienna, International Atomic Energy Agency, pp. 303–315

Hamilton, E.I., Minski, M.J. & Cleary, J.J. (1973) Problems concerning multielement assay in biological materials. *Sci. total Environ., 1,* 1–14

Heit, M. & Klusek, C.S. (1982) The effect of dissecting tools on the trace element concentrations of fish and mussel tissues. *Sci. total Environ., 24,* 129–134

IAEA (1980) Elemental Analysis of Biological Materials. *IAEA Technical Report 197,* Vienna, International Atomic Energy Agency

ICRP (1975) Report of the Task Group on Reference Man. *ICRP-23,* New York, Pergamon Press

Iyengar, G.V. (1980) Post mortem changes of the elemental composition of autopsy specimens: Variations of K, Na, Mg, Ca, Cl, Fe, Zn, Cu, Mn and Rb in rat liver. *Sci. total Environ., 15,* 217–236

Iyengar, G.V. (1981) Autopsy sampling and elemental analysis: Errors arising from post mortem changes. *J. Path., 134,* 173–180

Iyengar, G.V. (1982) Presampling factors in trace element analysis of biological systems. *Anal. Chem., 54,* 554A–558A

Iyengar, G.V. & Kasperek, K. (1977) Application of brittle fracture technique to homogenize biological samples and some observations regarding the distribution behaviour of the trace elements at different concentration levels in a biological matrix. *J. radioanal. Chem., 39,* 301–316

Iyengar, G.V. & Sansoni, B. (1980) Sample preparation of biological materials for trace element analysis. *IAEA Technical Report 197,* Vienna, International Atomic Energy Agency, pp. 73–101

Iyengar, G.V., Kollmer, W.E. & Bowen, H.J.M. (1978A) *The Elemental Composition of Human Tissues and Body Fluids,* Weinheim, New York, Verlag Chemie

Iyengar, V.G., Kasperek, K. & Feinendegen, L.E. (1978b) Retention of metabolized trace elements in biological tissues following different drying procedures (I). *Sci. total Environ., 10,* 1–16

Iyengar, V.G., Kasperek, K. & Feinendegen, L.E. (1980) Retention of metabolized trace elements in biological tissues following different drying procedures (II). *Analyst, 105,* 794–801

Iyengar, V.G., Kasperek, K. & Feinendegen, L.E. (1982a) Post-mortal changes of the elemental composition of autopsy specimens: Variations of Cs, Co and Se in rat liver studied by instrumental neutron activation analysis. *J. radioanal. Chem., 69,* 463–472

Iyengar, G.V., Kasperek, K. & Feinendegen, L.E. (1982b) Retention of Cr-III and Cr-VI in rat tissues after different drying procedures. *Anal. Chim. Acta, 138,* 355–360

Kasperek, K., Kiem, J., Iyengar, G.V. & Feinendegen, L.E. (1981) Concentration difference between serum and plasma of the elements Co, Fe, Hg, Rb, Se and Zn determined by NAA. *Sci. total Environ.,* **17,** 133–143

Kumpulainen, J., Salmela, S., Vuori, E. & Lehto, J. (1982) Effects of various washing procedures on the Cr content of human scalp hair. *Anal. Chim. Acta,* **138,** 361–364

Levi, S. & Purdy, C. (1980) Continuous sampling of dialysate for the atomic absorption spectrometric determination of Cu and Zn from hemodialysis patients. *Anal. Chim. Acta,* **116,** 375–381

Livens, P., Versieck, J., Cornelis, R. & Hoste, J. (1977) The distribution of trace elements in normal human liver determined by semiautomated radiochemical NAA. *J. radioanal. Chem.,* **37,** 483–496

Livingstone, H.D. (1971) *Distribution of Zn, Cd and Hg in human kidneys.* In: Hemphill, D.D., ed., *Trace Substances in Environmental Health,* Vol. V, Columbia MO, University of Missouri, pp. 399–411

Maziere, B., Gaudry, A., Gross, J. & Comar, D. (1976) *Biological sample contamination due to quartz container in NAA.* In: LaFleur, P.D., ed., *Accuracy in Trace Analysis: Sampling, Sample Handling, Analysis,* Volumes I and II, Washington DC, National Bureau of Standards, pp. 593–604

Michel, R., Hofman, J. & Zilkens, J. (1980) *Trace element behaviour of human and mammalian tissues during excessive supply of metals.* In: Bräter, P. & Schramel, P., eds, *Trace Element Analytical Chemistry in Medicine and Biology,* Berlin, de Gruyter, pp. 769–782

Mizuike, A. & Pinta, M. (1978) General aspects of trace analytical methods. III. Contamination in trace analysis. *Pure appl. Chem.,* **50,** 1521–1529

Moody, J.R. & Lindström, P. (1975) Selection and cleaning of plastic containers for storage of trace element samples. *Anal. Chem.,* **47,** 2264–2267

Murphy, T.J. (1976) *The role of analytical blank in accurate trace analysis.* In: LaFleur, P.D., ed., *Accuracy in Trace Analysis: Sampling, Sample Handling, Analysis,* Volumes I and II, Washington DC, National Bureau of Standards, pp. 509–539

Rook, H.L. & Wolf, W. (1977) *The quantitative determination of volatile trace elements in NBS biological standard reference material 1569, Brewer's yeast.* In: Hemphill, D.D., ed., *Trace Substances in Environmental Health,* Vol. XI, Columbia MO, University of Missouri, pp. 324–333

Ryabukin, S. (1980) Nuclear based methods for the analysis of trace element pollutants in human hair. *J. radioanal. Chem.,* **60,** 7–30

Salmela, S., Vuori, E. & Kilpio, J.O. (1981) The effect of washing procedures on the trace element content of human hair. *Anal. Chim. Acta,* **125,** 131–137

Sansoni, B. & Iyengar, G.V. (1978) Sampling and sample preparation methods for the analysis of trace elements in biological materials for trace element analysis. Jül-Spez-Report 13, Juelich.

Sansoni, B. & Iyengar, G.V. (1980) Sampling of biological materials for trace element analysis. IAEA Technical Report 197, Vienna, International Atomic Energy Agency, pp. 57–71.

Simonoff, M., Llabador, Y., Hamon, C., Mackenzie Peers, A. & Simonoff, G.N. (1984) Low plasma chromium in patients with coronary artery and heart diseases. *Biol. Trace Elem. Res., 6,* 431–439

Versieck, J. & Speecke, A. (1972) Study of contamination induced by collection of liver biopsies and human blood. *Proc. IAEA Symp. Nucl. Act. Tech. Life Sci.,* Bled, pp. 39–49

CHAPTER 11

GENERAL REVIEW OF ANALYTICAL METHODS

S.R. Koirtyohann & J.S. Morris

*Department of Chemistry, College of Arts and Science,
123 Chemistry Building, Columbia, MI 65211, USA*

INTRODUCTION

In this chapter, we will review the analytical methods that are commonly used to measure arsenic, chromium, nickel, beryllium, cadmium, lead, antimony, selenium and zinc in biological and related materials. Suitable methods, recommendations and performance characteristics will be outlined for each element. Comparatively new methods for distinguishing the chemical form of the elements are also discussed. No attempt is made to provide detailed procedures which the non-specialist could follow. Rather, the objective is to identify methods which may be applicable in certain cases, to provide an introduction to the basic concepts, to give a realistic assessment of capabilities and limitations and to indicate areas where collaboration with workers in specialized analytical areas might be the most productive approach.

Many factors determine the best analytical method to be used in a given situation. Obvious ones include availability of equipment, sample size, analyte concentrations, numbers of analyses required and whether single or multi-element determinations are sought. Most of the methods discussed below are capable of giving good results within their range of applicability: all are capable of producing bad data. The difference depends on the analyst. Obvious factors, such as skill and familiarity with the methods, come into play, as well as less obvious ones, such as confidence and prejudice regarding individual methods. High-quality analytical work, especially at the trace level, requires a certain state of mind on the part of the analyst. He must have great confidence in the method being used, while being skeptical of every result it produces, always looking for ways in which it can generate erroneous values. In spite of recent advances in instrumentation, automation, etc, the most important component of any analytical scheme remains the analyst.

GENERAL DESCRIPTION OF METHODS

Atomic spectroscopic methods

A. *Fundamental theory* – Emission or absorption of light by gas phase atoms is accompanied by transitions in energy levels of the outer electrons of the atom. When all electrons are at their lowest permitted energy, an atom is said to be in its ground state. If one of the electrons gains energy, an excited state results. Only certain discrete, well-defined energy states are permitted for atoms of a given element and transitions between states must be accompanied by a definite energy change. Emission or absorption of electromagnetic radiation (a photon) is one means by which the energy may be lost or gained. Since, for a given element, the difference between energy levels (and therefore the energy change) is fixed, the characteristic photon energy is given by the following equation:

$$\triangle E_{atom} = E_{photon} = h\nu = hc/\lambda \tag{1}$$

where h is Plank's constant (6.63×10^{-34} J.s), ν is the frequency of the radiation in s^{-1}, c is the speed of light (3.00×10^8 m/s) and λ the wavelength. Thus each element exhibits its own characteristic spectrum of atomic emission and absorption. Qualitative information comes from the wavelength of emission or absorption and quantitative information from the amount of absorption or emission at that wavelength.

A simple case is illustrated in Fig. 1, where only the ground and a single excited state are considered. Energy gain, excitation, can occur by collision, especially at elevated temperatures, or by photon absorption. Deexcitation takes place by collision or photon emission. Atomic emission methods are based on collisional excitation and radiational de-excitation. Atomic absorption occurs by radiational excitation; the path for energy loss by the atom is immaterial. When both excitation and de-excitation occur by radiation, atomic fluorescence can be observed. In the simple case considered here, the same two states are involved for all three modes. Their energy difference is the same, so that the atoms emit, absorb and fluoresce at the same wavelength.

Figure 1 shows the simplest possible case for atomic energy lvels. All elements have numerous excited states, and the spectra resulting from permitted transitions between the states can be quite complex, ranging from a few to thousands of wavelengths. Specificity is retained because a 'line' covers a very narrow wavelength region (~0.003 nm) and coincidences in wavelength from two or more elements, while known, are comparatively rare. Fortunately, the analytical spectroscopist needs to be concerned with only a few lines for each element, those which have proved useful analytically.

Fig. 1. Simplified diagram of atomic energy levels

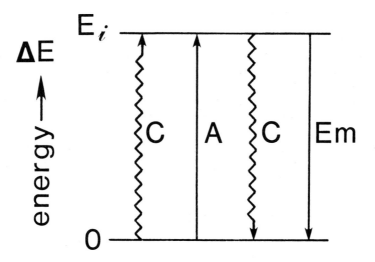

C = collisional activation or deactivation
A = absorption
Em = emission
ΔE = energy change

The fundamental equations which describe atomic absorption and emission are, respectively,

$$\ln \frac{I_{o\lambda}}{I_\lambda} = \frac{2\lambda^2}{D_\lambda} \frac{\ln 2}{\pi} \frac{\pi e^2}{mc^2} Nlf \tag{2}$$

$$I_{em} = h\nu \, A_{ij} \frac{g_i}{g_j} Nle - E_i/kT \tag{3}$$

where
$I_{o\lambda}$ = incident intensity at λ
I_λ = transmitted intensity at λ
l = length of the absorbing or emitting path

D_λ = Doppler half-width of the line
e = charge on the electron
m = mass of the electron
c = velocity of light
N = number of atoms/cc of atomic vapour
f = oscillator strength
I_{em} = intensity (energy) emitted for transition i, j
h = Plank's constant
ν = frequency of emitted radiation
A_{ij} = Einstein transition probability
g_i, g_j = statistical weights of states i and j
E_i = energy of the i *th* state above the atomic ground state
k = Boltzmann's constant
T = absolute temperature.

Similarities between the absorption and emission equations include direct dependence on various well-known constants, in addition to N, l and a transition probability. The absorption process depends on neither the excitation energy nor the temperature (except as temperature affects N and D_λ), while emission depends exponentially on both.

Equations (2) and (3) are seldom used analytically because several terms, especially N, are not easily known. Instead, conditions are chosen such that N is proportional to the analyte concentration in the sample solution. Under constant atomizer conditions:

$$\log \frac{I_{o\lambda}}{I_\lambda} = \text{absorbance} = KC \qquad (4)$$

and

$$I_{em\lambda} = KC \qquad (5)$$

where K is a proportionality constant and C is the concentration in the sample or standard solution. K is normally established by calibrating with standards just prior to measuring samples and is valid only for the specific transitions and atomizer conditions used.

These simple equations do not accurately describe instrumental response in all cases. Deviations are seen at high concentrations when instrument parameters are not properly optimized and when species other than the analyte emit or absorb at the wavelength in question. However, equations (4) and (5) apply quite well in a large number of practical situations and readily-applied corrections extend their utility to many more.

Fig. 2. The essential components of an atomic absorption spectrophotometer

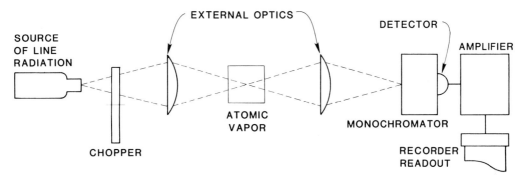

B. *Atomic absorption (AA)*

(a) Instrumentation – Figure 2 shows a schematic diagram of an atomic absorption spectrophotometer. The light source is either a hollow cathode lamp or an electrodeless discharge lamp which contains the analyte element. Emission from the lamp is at precisely the correct wavelength for absorption by analyte atoms in the atomic vapour (see Fig. 1). The monochromator separates the wavelength of interest from other source radiation. For most elements, this can be accomplished by a small, inexpensive unit.

The electronics respond to the source radiation and the output is normally in absorbance units, as required by equation (4). Many modern instruments also have provision for automation and computer data handling.

(b) Atomization methods

(i) Flames – Few elements form gaseous atoms at room temperature. Therefore, the sample atomic vapour indicated in Fig. 2 must be contained in a heated environment. Classically, a flame is placed just below the optical path, sample solution is aspirated through a nebulizer and a portion of the mist passes into the flame where atoms are formed. Flame AA will not be described further here because its capabilities are widely known and because, of the elements of interest, only zinc can be measured by flame AA at normal levels in biological and related samples.

(ii) Furnace atomic absorption (FAA) – The principles of FAA are quite simple. An electrically-heated tubular furnace, shown schematically in Figure 3, is placed on the optical axis of an AA unit. The tube, usually pyrolytically-coated graphite, is resistively heated through water-cooled contacts. It is protected from atmospheric oxidation by an inert gas, usually argon, flowing over the surface of through an enclosing chamber. Typical tubes are 3–8 mm i.d. and 10–30 mm long. The electrical resistance of the tubes is low, which necessitates a power supply capable of delivering several hundred amperes at 10–12 volts. During operation, 5–50 µL of sample solution are placed on the inner tube wall, which is then heated in three or more stages. The 'dry' conditions are chosen to evaporate the solvent as quickly as is practical without spattering (110 °C for 30 s). The second, 'char', stage (350–1200 °C

Fig. 3. Schematic drawing of a graphite furnace for atomic absorption

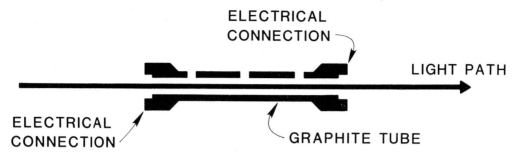

for 45 s) removes volatile sample components at a temperature as high as practical without loss of analyte, which is then quickly vaporized and atomized in the third stage (2000–3000 °C for 5 s). The atoms rapidly diffuse out of the observation zone and the result is a brief absorption peak, the height or area of which is used for quantification.

FAA requires very little sample and many elements are detectable in the sub-ng/mL range. Background absorption from sample matrix components can be a problem, but correction based on the use of the well-known continuum source method or on Zeeman splitting of the absorption line (Koizumi & Yasuda, 1977) is usually adequate, if cautiously applied. The other common interference, that of rather severe matrix-dependent changes in the slope of the working curve, has been more troublesome until recently. L'vov (1978) suggested placing the sample aliquot on a small graphite platform within the furnace tube. The temperature of this platform, which is heated primarily by radiation, lags behind that of the tube wall. Hence, the sample vaporization is delayed until the furnace atmosphere reaches a high and nearly constant temperature.

Koirtyohann and Kaiser (1982) have used the platform technique quite extensively in combination with matrix modification. In this approach, reagents are added which form relatively non-volatile compounds with the analyte and provide nearly constant chemical compositions for samples and standards. Ammonium phosphate has been one of the more effective matrix-modifying reagents for metal analysis. Excess nickel is added to solutions for As and Se determination. The combination of platform use, matrix modification and the use of the absorption peak area (Slavin *et al.*, 1981) has virtually eliminated matrix problems for a large number of analyte/matrix combinations, including Cd, As, Cr and Ni in fresh waters, NBS materials, clinical samples (blood, liver, urine), sewage sludge and stream sediment samples. The use of peak areas is greatly facilitated by modern computerized instruments. Many people who have been disappointed by FAA in the past may wish to reconsider its use with the above modifications.

The advantages of FAA are good sensitivity, small sample requirements (10–20 μL), relatively inexpensive instrumentation and applicability to a large number of elements, including all those of interest in this chapter. Typical sensitivity data for this and all other methods discussed are given in section C, which deals with preferred methods for each element. Among the disadvantages of FAA is the careful work sometimes required to avoid errors due to background absorption and matrix problems; in addition, the method is slower than flame AA or plasma emission (2–3 min/sample) and, as commonly used, it is not a multi-element technique.

(iii) Hydride generation AA – Many group 5a and 6a elements can be reduced to a volatile hydride if treated with active hydrogen in acid solution. The active hydrogen is generated either from zinc metal or sodium borohydride. The resulting hydrides of the analyte element(s) can be efficiently purged from the sample solution by bubbling gas through it, and are usually passed directly to an atomization cell. Alternatively, the hydrides may be caught in a cold trap for later atomization. (The possibility of obtaining chemical species differentiation based on differing hydride volatilities is discussed later in this chapter under 'Speciation'.)

The evolved hydrides are thermally decomposed and atomized in the sample beam of an AA spectrophotometer. The atomization cell may be an electrically heated quartz tube ($\sim 1000\,°C$), a quartz tube heated in an air-acetylene flame or a flame formed with argon, hydrogen and entrained air. This rather cool flame atomizes the hydride-forming elements quite effectively and is transparent at the short wavelengths where their resonance lines lie. Alternatively, the hydrides may be passed into a plasma emission source, discussed later. The hydride-forming elements of interest here are As, Se, Sb, and possibly Pb.

Advantages of hydride evolution, in addition to chemical species information mentioned earlier, include high sensitivity due to the use of a large sample volume, reduced interference due to the chemical separation step, and the fact that little additional equipment is required if a laboratory has a good AA spectrophotometer. Disadvantages include the need for oxidation-state adjustment prior to hydride formation, the requirement for critical control of the acid concentration in which the reaction is carried out and the fact that large amounts of other easily-reduced elements may prevent quantitative hydride formation.

C. *Inductively-coupled plasma emission (ICP)* – Emission spectroscopic methods based on flames, arcs and sparks have long been popular in many analytical areas. ICP, in particular, shows a particularly desirable combination of capabilities which has led to a rapid recent increase in its popularity.

The ICP technique was developed largely by Greenfield and co-workers, with Albright and Wilson in the United Kingdom, and by Fassel's group at Iowa State University in the United States (Fassel & Kniseley, 1974a,b). The plasma, shown schematically in Fig. 4, is formed in a quartz torch by interaction of a radio-frequency field with electrons and argon ions. Plasma operating conditions vary, but the popular commercial units operate at a frequency of 20–50 MHz and 1–2 kW power. The feature which distinguishes the ICP from other plasmas is its toroidal shape. Most of the power transfer is to the body of the toroid, where temperatures may reach 10 000°K, while the sample is introduced into a somewhat cooler central channel where it experiences 5000–7000°K temperatures. The central channel serves to confine the sample and ensure relatively long exposure to the high-temperature environment.

Samples are usually introduced as an aerosol, formed by nebulization of the sample solution, and are carried into the central channel with a stream of argon (about 1 L/

Fig. 4. Schematic drawing of an inductively-coupled plasma

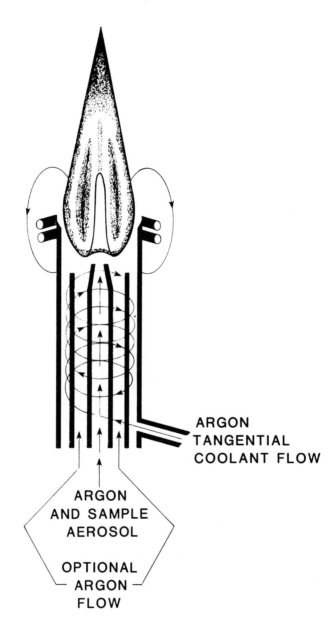

ARGON
TANGENTIAL
COOLANT FLOW

ARGON
AND SAMPLE
AEROSOL

OPTIONAL
ARGON
FLOW

min). The hydrides of group 5a and 6a elements, on the other hand, are directly introduced into the ICP. Multi-element anàlysis by a combination of conventional

Fig. 5. Schematic drawing of a multi-channel spectrometer for simultaneous multi-element determinations by the inductively coupled plasma

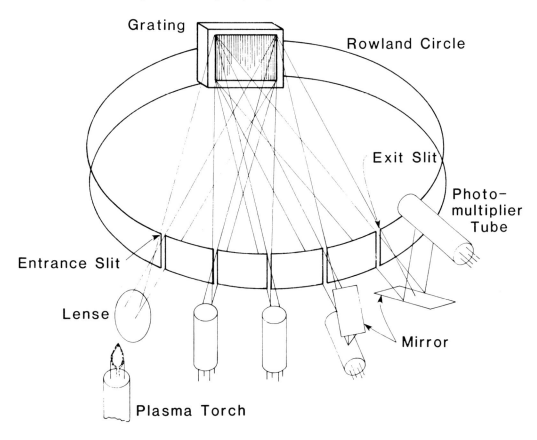

nebulization and hydride formation has also been reported (Wolnik *et al.*, 1981). The high temperature of the central channel is quite effective in converting the sample constituents into atoms and ions, and in exciting the species formed to emit light at their characteristic wavelengths. Optimum plasma conditions vary somewhat from one element to another, but compromise conditions are readily established which allow 30 or more elements to be measured either simultaneously or in rapid sequence.

Simultaneous measurements are made on a multi-channel spectrometer, shown schematically in Figure 5, which has a separate detector set to receive each wavelength (element) of interest. Sequential measurements are made using a computer-controlled monochromator, which rapidly scans to the vicinity of a wavelength of interest, slowly scans across the line (gathering the analytical data), then scans rapidly to the next line. A measurement each ten seconds after an initial 30 s equilibration period is readily attained with sequential units.

Advantages of the ICP include freedom from most types of chemical interference, high sensitivity, a linear range of about 10^5 for many elements, multi-element capability and the large number of elements fo which it is suitable. Relatively high instrument costs (\$ 50 000–\$ 200 000) and the presence of spectral interference of several types are the main disadvantages. Spectral problems are caused by the high plasma temperature, which excites most elements to emit complex spectra, leading to overlap between analytical lines of analyte elements and extraneous emissions from sample matrix components.

Although they will not be discussed in detail here, methods exist for detection of, and correction for, these interferences. Such corrections are normally the work of a highly-trained individual with a thorough understanding of the technique. This is true for most analytical methods, especially if one is operating near the limit of their capability. It is less true for atomic absorption methods than for most others, and many potential ICP users are experienced in AA. They should not assume, however, that their knowledge of the spectrum and interference correction methods which were adequate for spectral problems in AA will suffice for the ICP.

D. *The direct-current plasma (DCP)* – The direct-current plasma consists of a specially-shaped d.c. arc into which sample aerosol is directed. The shape of the DCP is not toroidal and, while sensitivity figures are comparable with those of the ICP, it shows greater matrix effects. Proponents will undoubtedly dispute our conclusion that its current popularity in applications to biological and related systems does not justify a detailed description here.

Neutron activation analysis (NAA)

Neutron activation analysis is a qualitative and quantitative method of analysis which is based on interaction of the nuclei of individual atoms with a neutron. This interaction can result in either excitation of, or neutron capture by, the nucleus; with the latter being more important in most analysis applications. When neutron capture occurs, a compound nucleus forms which, for a nuclear reaction, is analogous to the activated complex associated with chemical reactions. Like the activated complex, the compound nucleus is unstable and very quickly rearranges (10^{-10} to 10^{-15} s) *via* emission of photons (gamma-rays) or elementary particles (i.e., protons, electrons, neutrons and alphas), or through fission. In many cases, the resulting nuclide is radioactive and will decay in a manner characteristic of that radionuclide (i.e., beta emission, positron emission, alpha emission, electron capture, internal conversion). The type of nuclear reaction which occurs is dependent on the nuclear structure of the target atom and the energy of the incident neutron.

In principle, any of these nuclear reactions and decay modes could be used in either of the two fundamental NAA experiments. In practice, the neutron capture reaction, which results in photon emission, the so-called n,γ reaction, has the widest application in NAA, particularly for the elements of interest in this manual.

The two fundamental NAA experiments can be represented by the following example:

$$\underset{33}{^{75}}\text{As} + \underset{0}{^{1}}\text{n} \rightarrow \underset{33}{^{76}}\text{As} + \gamma\text{'s}_{\text{p}} \tag{6}$$

$$\underset{33}{^{76}}\text{As} \rightarrow \underset{-1}{^{0}}\beta + \underset{34}{^{76}}\text{Se} + \gamma\text{'s}_{\text{d}} \ (t^{\frac{1}{2}} = 26.37 \text{ h}) \tag{7}$$

During the capture process [equation (6)], gamma-rays are emitted immediately subsequent to the formation of the compound nucleus (10^{-14}–10^{-15} s.) These are the so-called prompt gammas (γ_p) and must be measured during the irradiation process. If the target atom produces a radioactive product [equation (7)] and if that product has gamma-rays associated with its decay (as almost all do), then these delayed gammas (γ_d) can be measured at some time following the irradiation. Most applications of NAA use the delayed gammas, because of advantages in both sensitivity and selectivity for most, but not all, elements. For the remainder of the NAA discussion in this chapter, we refer to the conventional, delayed gamma, approach.

The mathematical expressions governing conventional NAA are shown in equations (8)–(10).

$$A_o = nf\sigma(1 - e^{-\lambda t_i}) \tag{8}$$

$$A_{td} = A_o e^{-\lambda t_d} \tag{9}$$

$$A_{td} = nf\sigma(1 - e^{-\lambda t_i})e^{-\lambda t_d} \tag{10}$$

where

A_o	=	activity (nuclear transitions per second) at the end of the irradiation
A_{td}	=	activity at some time t_d
n	=	number of target atoms
f	=	neutron flux in neutrons per cm^2 per second
σ	=	neutron capture cross section (1 barn = 1×10^{-24} cm^2)
λ	=	decay constant ($\ln 2 / t^{\frac{1}{2}}$)
$t^{\frac{1}{2}}$	=	half-life
t_i	=	irradiation time
t_d	=	decay time.

The counting rate (counts per second, cps) observed at some time, t_d, subsequent to the irradiation, dictates the sensitivity at which the element of interest in a particular matrix can be determined. The counting rate for a particular gamma-ray is related to A_{td} by equation (11).

$$cps = A_{td}\varepsilon b \tag{11}$$

where

cps = counts per second
ε = detection efficiency of the gamma-ray being measured
b = branching ratio of the gamma-ray being measured.

The detector efficiency, ε, depends on intrinsic properties of the detector material, the size of the detector, the solid angle between sample and detector and the gamma-ray energy. Typically, efficiency curves are determined for different counting geometries and detectors, using calibrated sources having gamma-rays spanning the widest practical energy range. The branching ratio, b, is the fraction of the total number of disintegrations which produce the gamma ray in question. Considering equation (7) as an example, the principal gamma-ray associated with the decay of ^{76}As has an energy of 559 keV and is produced by $45 \pm 2\%$ of the nuclear transitions, which in this case are exclusively *via* beta emission. Therefore, for ^{76}As, the branching ratio of the 559 keV gamma-ray is 0.45.

In equations (8) and (10), n is the number of target atoms, which is defined in equation (12).

$$n = \frac{m_s \omega a N^\circ}{10^6 W} \tag{12}$$

where

m_s = weight of the sample
ω = mass fraction (concentration) of the target element in the sample (μg/g)
a = abundance of the target nuclide
N° = Avogrado's number
W = atomic weight of the element.

Rearranging equations (10), (11) and (12) gives

$$cps = \frac{P}{t_c} = \frac{m_s \omega a N^\circ \varepsilon b f \sigma (1 - e^{-\lambda t_i})(e^\lambda t_d)}{10^6 W} \tag{13}$$

where

P = net gamma-ray peak (counts)
t_c = count time (seconds).

From (13), it can be seen that the observed signal is directly proportional to the mass fraction ('concentration') of the element of interest. In addition, several other factors, such as sample size, counting position, flux, irradiation time, decay time and count time, are at least partially, if not totally, under the control of the analyst. For a given trace element, these factors can be optimized to produce the best possible sensitivity and selectivity.

Two factors which can be controlled by the analyst and deserve special consideration are the irradiation and decay times, t_i and t_d, respectively. As a sample is being irradiated, activity is being produced for each type of nuclide (most elements in the sample) that captures a neutron and produces a radionuclidic product [see equations (6) and (7)]. As soon as a radioactive species forms, it begins to decay, and this production-decay process is defined by the $(1-e^{-\lambda t_i})$ term in equation (13). This is often referred to as the 'saturation factor'. Remembering that $\lambda = \ln 2/t^{1/2}$, we can see that, if t_i is short compared to $t^{1/2}(1-e^{-\lambda t_i})$ is approximated by (λt_i); when t_i is long compared to $t^{1/2}$, $(1-e^{-\lambda t_i})$ approaches unity. Consequently, the analyst can increase activity, hence sensitivity, up to a point beyond which the decay during irradiation approximates the build-up. Irradiation time should be considered in terms of numbers of half-lives of the product nuclide of interest, realizing that 50% of saturation is reached after irradiation during one half-life, 75% after two half-lives and so on. Extended irradiation times, i.e., $> 4 \times t^{1/2}$, produce very small increases of activity and, in fact, often result in reduced sensitivity due to build-up of radioactive products from matrix elements. Decay time, which is the period between the end of the irradiation and approximately the midpoint of the count, should also be thought of in terms of half-life. The analyst has the opportunity to select a decay time or times that optimize sensitivity for an element or group of elements. Thus interference from a matrix element with a short half-life relative to that of the analyte can be reduced by delaying the count until most matrix activity has decayed.

As previously mentioned [equation (13)], the observed signal (cps) is directly proportional to the mass fraction of the element. All other parameters in equation (13) are constants or can be computed. Therefore, it would seem that direct determinations could be made by collecting data on a calibrated detector and solving equation (13) for ω. In principle, this can be done; however, the result in many cases is semi-quantitative, due primarily to the uncertainty in the neutron capture cross section (σ). In equation (13), σ is shown as a constant and the analyst would use the capture cross section given for thermal neutrons (0.025 eV). However, this fails to take into account epithermal, resonance, intermediate and fast neutron contributions, which in certain cases can be substantial. In fact, σ is not a constant, but rather a function of neutron energy. The neutron spectrum, in turn, can be affected by many events not typically under the control of the analyst. Therefore, NAA is most often accomplished *via* standard comparison, which eliminates the need to know accurately the capture cross section-neutron energy relationship. The standard comparator approach is described by equation (14):

$$\omega_s = \frac{m_{st} \left[\dfrac{Pe^{-\lambda t d}}{t_c \varepsilon f(1-e^{-\lambda t_i})} \right]_s}{m_s \left[\dfrac{Pe^{-\lambda t d}}{t_c \varepsilon f(1-e^{-\lambda t_i})} \right]_{st}} \tag{14}$$

where all terms have the same meaning as in equations (12) and (13); subscripts 's' and 'st' refer to sample and standard, respectively, and m_{st} is expressed in μg.

If irradiation time, decay time, count time, flux and counting geometry are held constant for sample and standard, then equation (14) becomes:

$$\omega_s \; (\mu g/g) = \frac{P_s m_{st}}{P_{st} m_s} \tag{15}$$

In general, the sensitivity of NAA is quite good for those elements with $Z > 10$. Interference-free detection limits can be estimated from equation (13) for different irradiation, decay and counting conditions. However, in the case of biological samples, the existence of a truly interference-free matrix rarely, if ever, occurs.

There are three types of interferences which can occur in NAA experiments: matrix, competing nuclear reactions, and spectral.

In a sense, all interference arises in some way from the matrix; however, in this context we are referring to the gross background due to Compton, Bremsstrahlung and scattering. These can all be thought of as secondary interactions of radiation with matter, which result in an increased noise level from which the signal must be extracted.

The secondary category of NAA interference is due to competing nuclear reactions, i.e., different reactions which produce the same product. In order to illustrate the problem, consider the following neutron-capture reactions. If one were analysing a serum sample for aluminium (Al)

$$^{27}_{13}\text{Al} + {}^{1}_{0}\text{n} \rightarrow {}^{28}_{13}\text{Al} + \gamma's \tag{r_1}$$

$$^{31}_{15}\text{p} + {}^{1}_{0}\text{n} \rightarrow {}^{28}_{13}\text{Al} + {}^{4}_{2}\alpha \tag{r_2}$$

via NNA, (r_1) would be used to produce the measured signal and, because it involves thermal neutrons which are dominant in most irradiation positions, it would be favoured. Reaction 2 occurs with fast neutrons, for which both flux and capture cross section are normally a factor of 10 or more lower, and could thus be ignored. However, in the case of serum, the phosphorus (P) concentration is approximately 10^5 to 10^6 times that of Al; therefore, the fast-neutron capture by ^{31}P to produce ^{28}Al would be a serious interference with respect to the determination of Al.

Fig. 6. Schematic diagram of a computer-controlled gamma-ray spectrometer

Component Diagram for a Gamma–ray Spectrometer

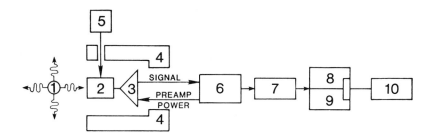

1. irradiated sample
2. detector
3. preamplifier
4. detector shielding
5. detector power supply
6. amplifier
7. analog–to–digital converter
8. memory
9. computer
10. output devices (CRT, printers, plotters, magnetic tapes, disk, etc.)

The third category of NAA interferences is spectral interference. NAA is almost always done *via* high-resolution, gamma-ray spectroscopy. The gamma-ray peaks are generated using a solid state detector coupled to a multichannel pulse-height analyser. These components are normally computer-controlled and make up a gamma-ray spectrometer. A schematic diagram is given in Figure 6. The most important characteristic of the spectrometer system is its resolution. Resolution is a measurement, expressed in keV, of the energy width of a gamma-ray peak. Typical values are 1 to 3 keV, full width at one half of the peak maximum (FWHM) (see Fig. 7). Therefore, if gamma-rays are separated by more than 3 keV in energy, they will be resolved from each other in the gamma-ray spectrum. An interference situation arises when this is not the case.

Any one of the types of interference discussed, or some combination of them acting in concert, can render the analysis of some samples impossible for certain elements using a purely instrumental NAA approach. When this occurs, the analyst must turn to some type of chemical separation scheme designed to isolate the element or elements of interest, or remove the interferences. This procedure is referred to as

Fig. 7. Gamma-ray peak obtained using a high-resolution detector

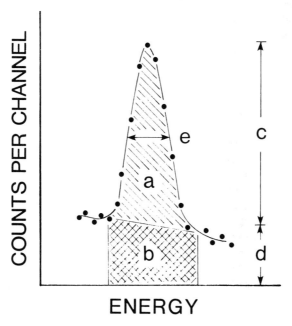

Features of a Gamma–ray Peak
MEASURED USING A HIGH RESOLUTION
DETECTOR (expanded scale)

a – net peak area
b – background
c – peak height
d – average background
     c/d – signal–to–noise
e – resolution, full width at one half
    maximum (FWHM)

radiochemical neutron activation analysis (RNAA). RNAA techniques are particularly useful for the analysis of biological samples, and will be specifically discussed with respect to some of the elements dealt with in this manual. In certain cases, the RNAA can improve sensitivity by several orders of magnitude over that otherwise attainable. A distinct advantage of RNAA, when compared to separation steps applied to other methods, is that the chemical operations are carried out on the sample after irradiation, hence the signal has already been induced. This advantage has three components. First, the analyst need not be concerned about post-irradiation contamination, because the measurement to be made is sensitive only to those nuclides of the element(s) of interest that are radioactive. Second, the separation chemistry is conducted on the macro-scale by the use of carriers of the element(s) of interest that have been purposefully added. Again, this can be done because the signal has already been generated. Third, the separation does not have to be quantitative. If a known amount of carrier is added and a separation carried out, the carrier yield can easily be measured by a variety of methods. The observed peak(s) is corrected using the carrier yield.

Reference has been made throughout this description of NAA to counting the sample and the method has been described as both qualitative and quantitative. A schematic diagram of a gamma-ray spectrometer is given in Figure 6 and some features of a typical peak from a high-resolution detector are illustrated in Figure 7. A gamma-ray spectrum from a high-resolution, Ge(Li) detector is shown in Figure 8. The sample is the protein fraction of a 3 mL aliquot of whole cow's milk. The irradiation, decay and counting parameters have been optimized for iodine. The iodine in the sample is qualitatively identified by its gamma-ray energy (442 keV) and its half-time (25 min), if necessary. It is quantitatively determined by comparing its peak area (see Fig. 8) to that of a standard treated similarly. Other elements also present in the sample can be identified and quantified in a similar manner. By changing the analytical parameters, a different suite of elements can be determined.

Comparing NAA with other analytical methods in the context of biological sample analysis is difficult on anything but a case-by-case basis. In most situations, multi-element capability and sensitivity are among the NAA advantages (especially if radiochemical separations are used). Costs are generally higher and sample through-put lower than for methods such as the ICP or AA. Radiochemical separations increase the cost, but probably no more than for other methods where a chemical separation is required. NAA, furthermore, enjoys an advantage with respect to chemical separation procedure through a lower risk of sample and reagent blank contamination and the fact that the chemistry steps may be executed on a macro scale. These advantages are unique to NAA, since it is the only technique that does not require immediate detection of the induced signal. On the other hand, the scarcity of NAA facilities must be considered a distinct disadvantage to the researcher who wants or needs to become actively involved with the analysis. Comparatively, there are but a handful of reactors throughout the world at which NAA expertise and facilities exist. This problem is well known to those in the field; therefore, we would advise a potential NAA user to seek out a practitioner and discuss the analysis requirements. Quite often, fruitful collaborative arrangements will result.

Of the nine elements with which this manual is concerned (As, Cr, Ni, Be, Cd, Pb, Sb, Se and Zn), Be and Pb cannot be reasonably analysed by NAA.

Fig. 8. High-resolution gamma-ray spectrum from the NAA of milk protein. Analysis parameters optimized for the determination of iodine

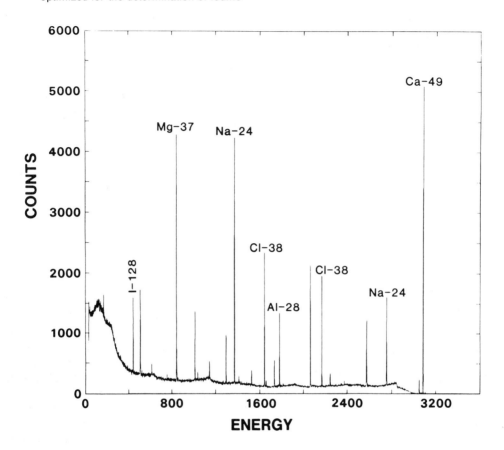

Electrochemical methods

Electrochemical methods are in the rather unusual position of having undergone an improvement in capability while waning in popularity over the last 15 years. The principal reason is the wide acceptance of atomic absorption and, more recently, ICP methods. Numerous techniques can be used to obtain analytical information electrochemically, but only anodic stripping voltammetry (ASV) will be discussed here, because it is most applicable to the elements of interest at trace levels.

In ASV, an electrode consisting of a small mercury drop, or a thin film of mercury on graphite, is immersed in the stirred sample solution. The electrode is held at a potential sufficiently negative to reduce the metals of interest, forming an amalgam according to the reaction:

$$M^{+n} + ne \rightarrow M_{(Hg)}$$

After this plating reaction has proceeded for several minutes, the stirring is stopped and the potential of the electrode swept toward more positive (anodic) values. The sweep may be linear or, preferably, a linear ramp upon which voltage pulses are superimposed [differential pulse ASV (DPASV)]. In the linear sweep mode, the plating reaction is reversed (stripping) at a potential characteristic for each metal and a measurable current is caused by the electrons generated in the reaction. In DPASV, the *difference* in current measured before and after application of a voltage pulse (typically ~ 20 mv) is measured and presented.

Advantages of the method include quite simple equipment, extremely good sensitivity, multi-element capability and good specificity, if some care is exercised. Sensitivity is enhanced because the analyte(s) is concentrated in the mercury during the several-minute deposition. In DPASV, one has the added advantage that capacitive currents which limit many voltammetric methods can be discriminated against by appropriate electronic gating of the measurement circuitry. It is also possible to gain some chemical species information. Stable compounds shift the potential at which metals plate and strip. Irreversible compound formation may prevent plating completely.

The primary disadvantages of ASV are the need for a highly-purified supporting electrolyte, the potential for error due to intermetallic compound formation in the amalgam, overlapping stripping potentials (especially if one of the components is present in large excess), low through-put relative to AA or ICP methods and applicability to a limited number of elements. Three of the elements of interest here, Cd, Pb and Zn, would be readily measured in a single solution so long as the concentrations of Pb and Cd are within an order of magnitude of each other. If one is present in large excess, the wave from the other may be obscured. Numerous studies have been carried out on electrochemical methods for additional elements. Arsenic is noteworthy in this regard, with literally dozens of papers describing its determination in various ways. Such methods have evidently not withstood the test of practical sample analysis, since none have become popular and one sees few reports of their applications.

Spectrophotometric methods

Spectrophotometry is such a common laboratory practice that no detailed description of the technique is required here. Most, if not all, of the elements of interest in this chapter will react with appropriate reagents to yield light-absorbing species which can be measured. Historically, spectrophotometry played an important role in early trace-element work and the methods are still capable of producing high-quality results in many cases. Advantages include low equipment cost, moderate sensitivity and, except for labour, low operating costs. Disadvantages include limited selectivity, high contamination risk due to the numerous manipulations usually required, and the need for a skilled and patient analyst. In places where more modern (and expensive) instruments are available, they offer many advantages and should be used. However, in parts of the world where the expensive instruments cannot be obtained, spectrophotometry can still make important contributions.

Miscellaneous methods

Atomic fluorescence spectroscopy (AFS) – Although described nearly 20 years ago, atomic fluorescence spectroscopy methods have never become popular, in spite of very good sensitivity for certain elements, including Cd and Zn. Part of the problem has been a lack of commercial instruments. Also, the elements for which AFS worked well were also easily determined by AA. Recently, an ICP instrument for multi-element AFS using plasma atomization was introduced by a major US manufacturer (Baird Atomic Corp., Bedford, MA). The impact of this instrument remains to be established, and AFS still must be regarded as an interesting analytical concept that is more useful for basic diagnostic studies of atomizers than for practical analysis.

X-ray fluorescence (XRF) – The good energy resolution of the lithium-drifted silicon detector makes X-ray fluorescence spectroscopy an attractive method for many analytical problems. The major and many minor constituents in biological samples are readily measured and, in principle, the method is applicable to all of the elements of interest here. However, for most of them in the majority of biological samples, the concentrations of interest are below the levels of XRF quantification. Chemical preconcentration methods have been described, but these greatly increase analysis costs and introduce severe contamination control problems. X-ray methods would be quite attractive for substances with elevated levels of analytes, such as ores or relatively highly-polluted media.

Mass spectrometry – Inorganic mass spectrometry involves the formation of ions of the elements in a sample by a spark discharge, by vaporization from a filament or by a plasma. The ions are then separated according to their mass/charge ratio by either a magnetic field or in a quadrupole mass spectrometer. In principle, the method is applicable to all elements. Isotopic abundance information is obtained, which makes possible the technique of isotope-dilution mass spectrometry (IDMS). In IDMS, the sample is spiked with a known amount of a specific isotope of the analyte, usually one of low natural abundance. After the isotope is equilibrated with the analyte in the sample, the analyte is separated and isotope ratios measured. The amount of analyte originally present is calculated from the change in isotope ratios caused by the spike. Done carefully, isotope-dilution mass spectrometry is the closest approach available to an absolute trace-element method. Unfortunately, analyses by this method are quite costly. The services of a skilled specialist are usually required and a very expensive instrument is usually occupied for several hours to obtain results. For these reasons, mass spectrometry is of more value as a reference method than as a routine tool. It is easy to justify the high cost for reference materials and for other samples where it is of extreme importance to obtain high accuracy. For routine or semi-routine work, the methods described earlier are usually adequate.

Recently, inductively-coupled plasmas have been used as an ionization source for elemental analysis with a mass spectrometer (Houk *et al.,* 1980). It is much too early to judge the impact that ICP-MS may have, but it is an area worthy of careful scrutiny for the next few years by those interested in trace-element analysis.

Spectrofluorimetry

Molecular fluorescence is observed by illuminating the sample solution with intense light of a specific wavelength and viewing light emitted by fluorescing compounds at a somewhat longer wavelength. Many elements form fluorescing compounds when treated with appropriate reagents. A popular method for selenium will illustrate the procedure. Diaminonaphthalene forms a fluorescing piazselenol with selenium [IV], which is extractable into cyclohexane and similar solvents. The compound gives intense fluorescence at 520 nm when excited by 377 nm radiation.

Advantages of the method are that it uses only relatively low cost equipment and simple reagents, sensitivity is good (< 1 ng), response is linear and the results are quite reliable in the hands of a well-trained analyst. Limitations include the need to recrystalize the reagent carefully, the necessity of monitoring the excitation and fluorescence spectra to ensure the absence of extraneous fluorescent compounds, and relatively high unit labour cost.

PREFERRED METHODS BY ELEMENT

Arsenic

Furnace atomic absorption and AA methods based on hydride generation are the most popular methods for this element. However, if the analyst has access to a nuclear reactor and is interested primarily in total arsenic content, NAA is probably to be preferred.

For arsenic, the target abundance, capture cross section, product half life and gamma-ray branching ratio are 100%, 4.4 b, 26.3 h and 45% respectively. Taken together, those parameters result in a good sensitivity for this element *via* NAA. However, in biological matrices the expected As level is normally quite low (ng/g range) unless unusual exposure conditions existed. Consequently, if the As level is below 0.1 µg/g, a post-irradiation, radiochemical separation is necessary. The availability of solid state detectors having both high resolution and efficiency can normally be assumed. Therefore, it is not necessary to produce a highly radio-pure ^{76}As sample for counting. The separation needs only to remove the bulk of the interfering elements normally found in biological samples (i.e., ^{24}Na and ^{32}P). The irradiated sample is mineralized, normally by wet acid digestion, and a small amount of arsenic carrier (~ 10 mg) is then added and reduced to the elemental state. The As precipitate can then be collected on a filter, washed and weighed to determine the chemical yield. The sample can then be counted directly on the face of the detector for an appropriate period, depending on the concentration and desired sensitivity. Data reduction is performed by standard comparison [see equations (14) and (15)], using the 559 keV gamma-ray associated with the decay of ^{76}As. If a biological sample (~ 0.25 g) is irradiated to a fluence of $\sim 10^{17}$ n cm^{-2}, subjected to the radiochemical separation and counted for 30 min, a sensitivity of ~ 1 ng/g can be obtained. There is no serious spectral interference, especially if a chemical separation has been carried out. If an instrumental approach is used, possible interference could arise if the sample contained large amounts of bromine or antimony, which produce ^{82}Br and ^{122}Sb, respectively, when irradiated. ^{82}Br has a gamma-ray at 554 keV and ^{122}Sb has one at 564 keV. Normally, these peaks would be completely resolved from the 559 keV gamma-ray of ^{76}As by a good detector. However, if either the ^{82}Br or ^{122}Sb activities are high compared to the ^{76}As (i.e., 10 or more times higher), then there may be a source of significant error in quantitatively resolving the multiplet.

Arsenic is readily measured by furnace AA in most samples, after partial or complete digestion by appropriate acid mixtures. Nickel is normally added as a matrix modifier at about 500 µg/mL in the solution injected into the furnace. The exact heating cycle will depend on the furnace used and the manufacturers' recommendations should be the starting point for optimization. Measurements are made at either the 193.6 or 197.2 nm resonance lines. Arsenic hollow-cathode lamps are not very satisfactory and an electrodeless discharge lamp and power supply are normally required. Matrix-dependent changes in working-curve slope are reduced by the use of a L'vov platform. The arsenic detection limit is about 0.5 ng/mL, or slightly less, in the sample solution.

With all FAA methods, the analyst must proceed cautiously with each new sample type to assess the degree of change of the working-curve slope due to the matrix. Spike recoveries and the method of standard additions usually reveal any problems. Biological matrices often show evidence of structured background in the vicinity of the arsenic lines, probably due to phosphorus. In severe cases, continuum source background correction may not be adequate. Better background compensation is obtained with Zeeman systems, which should be used if available.

Most manufacturers of AA instruments offer hydride generation equipment which is quite satisfactory for As. The AsH$_3$ is formed by adding NaBH$_4$ in the form of a pellet, or as a basic solution, into an acidic sample solution. A stream of hydrogen or argon sweeps the arsenic into an atomization cell or flame. Few spectral problems are encountered because the arsenic is separated from the matrix. As[V] must be reduced to As[III] by iodide for efficient hydride formation. Easily-reduced matrix elements can interfere, but these are low in most biological and related samples. Detection limits of 0.2–0.3 ng/mL can be obtained using 10-mL samples. The method is usually somewhat slower than FAA and requires more sample, but in other respects is probably to be preferred. If a less sensitive method will suffice, the ICP has a detection limit of about 50 ng/mL and other elements can be measured simultaneously. Wolnik et al. (1981) used a tandem nebulizer system and hydride generation to increase As sensitivity of the ICP about 10-fold, without loss of multi-element capability.

Arsine generation is also used in the most popular colorimetric procedure for As. The arsine is bubbled through silver diethyldithiocarbamate in pyridine. The detection limit based on absorption at 560 nm is about 0.5 µg of As, which gives a concentration limit of about 20 ng/mL in the sample solution.

Antimony

Antimony is a hydride-forming element which can be measured using procedures similar to those described for arsenic. The detection limit is about 0.1 ng/mL in the sample solution. Reduction to Sb[III] is required prior to borohydride solution. Elevated levels of copper and other hydride-forming elements interfere, but response is restored by adding KSCN (Cu) or more $NaBH_4$. Furnace atomic absorption also provides good sensitivity for this element with a detection limit of about 0.3 ng/mL. Background absorption problems are significant at the 217.6 nm resonance wavelength, but not as serious as for the shorter wavelengths used for As and Se. In most cases, the deuterium arc background correction works well. The method of choice for Sb would appear to be one of the hydride methods, with final detection by AA (flame or heated-cell atomizer) or the ICP. If the amount of sample is limited, FAA would have a net advantage.

Antimony can also be determined spectrophotometrically using the complex of Sb[V] with Rhodamine B (0.1 µg detection limit) and fluorometrically using 3.4.7-trihydroxyflavone (0.04 µg detection limit). Detection limits for ICP (with conventional sample introduction) and ordinary flame AA are about 50 and 300 ng/mL, respectively, which will be inadequate except for elevated levels.

The determination of antimony *via* NAA can be performed using either Sb-122 (half-life = 2.68 d) or Sb-124 (half-life = 60.2 d), with a sensitivity of ~1 ng/g for either procedure. In practice, the shorter-lived Sb-122 radionuclide is normally used, unless a multi-element analysis including an element requiring long irradiation is to be done.

The principal gamma-ray for the detection of Sb-122 occurs at an energy of 564 keV. If arsenic levels are high with respect to the antimony, interference can arise from the 559 keV gamma-ray from As-76.

In biological samples, antimony sensitivity normally must be enhanced *via* a post-irradiation chemical separation, due to the large amount of Na-24 (half-life = 15 h) also produced. Since high-resolution detectors are normally used, the separation need only remove the majority of the Na-24 from the Sb-122 fraction. This can be easily done by digesting the tissue and depositing the Na-24 on a hydrated antimony pentoxide (HAP) column, letting the Sb-122 be eluted. This chemical separation is nearly quantitative with respect to the recovery of antimony; however, yields can be conveniently determined by employing Sb-124 as a tracer which can be added subsequent to the irradiation, but prior to the digestion step.

Beryllium

All of the atomic spectroscopic methods show quite good sensitivity for beryllium, using the atomic resonance line at 234.9 nm. Detection limits for FAA are about 0.01 ng/mL with vaporization from the furnace tube wall and 0.1 ng/mL when using the L'vov platform. Stiefel *et al.* (1980) used both direct injection of sample solutions into a furnace and a chemical preconcentration based on extraction of beryllium acetylacetonate into benzene prior to FAA determination. They report a normal concentration of about 1 ng/g in guinea pig blood. Fractionation of the blood components revealed that most (60–73%) of the beryllium was associated with serum proteins.

Flame atomic absorption and the ICP give detection limits of about 2 and 1 ng/mL, respectively. Some preconcentration would be necessary for measurement at normal levels, but elevated levels could be measured and the ICP certainly has the potential to screen for high Be levels while monitoring for other elements.

Beryllium can also be determined fluorometrically using the complex formed with 2-hydroxy-3-naphthoic acid. A complete procedure, which includes a preliminary separation by acetylacetonate extraction, is given by Wicke and Burke (1977).

Cadmium

Cadmium and lead present many similar analytical problems, except that cadmium concentrations are considerably lower in most sample types. FAA is quite sensitive (detection limit 0.01 ng/mL) and is probably the method of choice in most cases. Good quality control is required to ensure that matrix effects are adequately controlled, although the L'vov platform discussed earlier is quite helpful. Background absorption is usually significant at the 228.8 nm wavelength, but there appears to be little fine structure and the popular continuum source correction systems are trustworthy up to background absorbances of about 0.5. Zeeman systems will handle higher background.

ASV is probably the most sensitive cadmium method available. Detection limits can vary widely, depending on analytical variables and blank control, but detection in the 10^{-11} mol/L range is possible. Most biological samples contain much more lead than cadmium and the large Pb peak can sometimes obscure the Cd signal.

Flame AA and ICP methods, with detection limits of about 2 and 10 ng/mL, respectively, are quite convenient for elevated levels or for normal levels in certain tissues, such as adult human kidney.

The determination of cadmium by NAA is carried out using Cd-111 (half-life = 48.6 min) or Cd-115 (half-life = 53.4 h), with the latter having the better sensitivity ($\sim$1 ng/g) if a chemical separation is used. There are no particular problems with spectral interference; however, to obtain the best sensitivity the analyst must process the irradiated sample after only a few days decay, which can increase the personnel exposure levels to some extent.

In our laboratories, NAA has been conveniently used to study cadmium levels in human nails, using the automated methods described later for zinc. This experiment can be done instrumentally *via* standard comparison and has the advantage of not requiring a sample dissolution step.

Chromium and nickel

These elements are treated together because they show similar analytical problems. Stated bluntly, no really satisfactory methods exist for their routine determination at physiological levels. Versieck *et al.* (1982) have documented the challenge of obtaining uncontaminated samples and have shown that normal values are lower than those accepted only a few years ago. Parr (1977) has shown the extreme spread in analytical results from chromium on samples carefully prepared in large lots.

FAA is probably the only common method with sufficient sensitivity to measure these elements without chemical separation. Great care must be exercised to avoid contamination during sample collection and digestion and to ensure that background absorption is accurately subtracted. Detection limits are about 0.2 ng/mL for both elements under carefully optimized furnace conditions.

Other methods, the ICP for example, can be used after at least 10-fold chemical enrichment. (Detection limits are about 5 ng/mL for both elements.) The problem then becomes one of contamination control, because Cr and Ni are ubiquitous in most laboratory environments. Special laboratory facilities and specially-purified reagents are needed for trustworthy work. Contamination is a less severe problem with NAA.

The determination of chromium in biological samples by NAA has a sensitivity of approximately 1 ng/g, unless extreme analytical conditions are used, i.e., very long irradiation time (> 1000 h) or counting time (> 24 h) or both. The analysis is based on the capture of a neutron by Cr-50 to produce Cr-51, which decays with a 27.7 d half-life. The capture cross-section for this reaction is quite good (15.9 b); however, both the abundance of the target (Cr-50) and the branching ratio for the 320 keV gamma-ray are relatively low, 4.35% and 10%, respectively.

In the case of biological samples, with few exceptions, a post-irradiation chemical separation must be employed due to baseline interference generated by the Bremsstrahlung caused by the beta decay of the ^{32}P characteristic of most biological samples. Hair and nails can be listed among the exceptions and have been analysed for chromium in our laboratories via INNA.

Chemical separations that have been used range from those with large decontamination factors, such as distillation, when sensitivity is to be increased via NaI counting; to those with much smaller factors, such as precipitation, when high-resolution counting is to be employed.

The determination of nickel in biological samples is rarely performed by NAA. In principle, there are two possible nuclear reactions, but neither provides sufficient sensitivity for the routine determination of Ni in typical biological samples.

Regardless of the method used, careful documentation of quality control procedures must accompany reported results for these two elements. The scarcity of certified reference materials in the normal range increases the challenge of establishing the accuracy of results. Most reference materials are also contaminated during preparation and little assurance of accuracy is gained by analysing a reference material that is 10-fold higher in analyte concentration than the sample. Hoepfully, more reference standards will be developed soon.

Flame AA and ICP are useful for the determination of higher levels of chromium and nickel. They have detection limits of about 5 ng/mL in the sample solution and interference is not particularly severe in biological matrices. A nitrous acetylene flame should be used for chromium. Numerous spectrophotometric procedures are also avilable.

Lead

Furnace atomic absorption is probably the method of choice for lead in most biological samples. Platform and matrix modification methods give excellent control of matrix interference problems formerly encountered. A matrix modifier of 0.5% $NH_4H_2PO_4$, purified by extraction with ammonium pyrrolidinecarbodithioate and methylisobutyl ketone, works quite well (Koirtyohann & Kaiser, 1982). Urine samples are often run without digestion, but most tissues require digestion to homogenize the sample and destroy the bulk of the organic material. Blood can be analysed directly, unless the sample contains clots. Even a small amount of clotting seriously affects sampling when 10–20 μL samples are used and the clots are not easily broken up. Digestion is probably the simplest way to handle a blood sample with known or suspected clots.

The detection limit for FAA is about 0.1 ng/mL and precision of 2–3% (RSD) is readily attained with automatic pipetting into the furnace. The 283.3 nm lead line is usually preferable to the 217.0, because of less severe background at the longer wavelength. There are disadvantages, however; FAA is a single element method and careful work is needed to ensure that spectral background and matrix problems are overcome.

Anodic stripping voltametry works well for lead, with a detection limit well below 1 ng/mL. Most biological samples will require complete digestion to ensure that lead plating is not inhibited by binding on organic matter. In many samples, lead and cadmium can be determined simultaneously. Disadvantages of ASV include relatively long analysis times, because nitrogen gas must be bubbled through the solution for ~10 min to remove dissolved oxygen. Great care in purifying the supporting electrolyte is required and a large excess of cadmium (seldom encountered in biological materials) can cause interference with the lead peak.

The ICP may be useful for screening for high lead levels while other elements are being determined. However, the detection limit is about 50 ng/mL in solution, which is inadequate for normal levels in most biological and related samples.

Lead can also be measured spectrophotometrically using dithizone, with a detection limit somewhat below 1 μg. Excellent results can be obtained by a skilled and patient analyst.

Selenium

Selenium can be accurately determined in biological samples by several different methods, provided the analyst is very well acquainted with the specific problems associated with the method chosen. The method if choice is probably NAA. In a recent IUPAC inter-laboratory comparison study on human sera, Se was measured in 21 different laboratories by six different methods (M. Ihnat, 1983, personal communication). These were fluorescence (F), furnace atomic absorption (FAA), furnace atomic absorption with a chemical separation (CSFAA), instrumental neutron activation analysis (INAA), X-ray fluorescence (XRF) and isotope-dilution mass spectrometry (IDMS). The results of the study (listed in the following order: method used, number of laboratories reporting that method, number of laboratories having acceptable results, percentage acceptable results for that method) were: F, 7,

4, 57%; FAA, 6, 2, 33%; CSFAA, 5, 1, 20%; INAA, 4, 4, 100%; XRF, 1, 1, 100%; IDMS, 1, 1, 100%. For any given method, there was at least one laboratory which reported an acceptable result; however, in the case of INAA, all four laboratories produced acceptable results, suggesting a possible superiority of that method in the case of Se.

Selenium can be determined *via* NAA using either ^{77m}Se or ^{75}Se. Target abundances, capture cross sections, product half-lives and gamma-ray branching ratios for the two isotopes are 9.0%, 0.87%, 21 b, 52 b; 17.4 s, 119 d and 52%, 58%, for ^{77m}Se and ^{75}Se, respectively.

The conventional NAA experiment for Se is to produce the long-lived (t ½ = 119 d) ^{75}Se radionuclide and count the samples following relatively long irradiation and cooling periods, i.e., 50–100 h and 2–10 weeks, respectively. In doing so, Se can normally be determined in biological samples without a chemical separation. There are several usable gamma-rays associated with the electron-capture decay of ^{75}Se, but interference is possible for each line. For example, the 121 keV line of ^{75}Se could be obscured by the 122 keV line of ^{152}Eu, the 136 keV line by the 136 keV line of ^{181}W, the 265 keV line by the 264 line of ^{182}Ta and the 279 keV line by the 279 line pf ^{203}Hg. By judiciously examining the entire gamma-ray spectrum, the analyst should be able to find at least one gamma-ray from ^{75}Se which is either not interfered with, or can be accurately corrected *via* existing spectrum stripping codes.

A second, and much faster, NAA method for determination of Se in biological samples utilizes ^{77m}Se. The principal advantage is shorter analysis time. Since the half-life of ^{77m}Se is quite short (17.4 s), the irradiation, decay and counting periods are also relatively short; i.e., 5, 15 and 25 s, respectively, are the times used at our laboratories. Consequently, a Se determination can be made on a prepared sample in approximately one minute. Sample preparation of biological samples normally consists of freeze-drying and weighing into the small polyethylene containers in which the sample is irradiated and counted. Primarily because of the short irradiation, there is no serious spectral interference with the 162 keV gamma-ray associated with the decay of ^{77m}Se.

Much of the description of the determination of arsenic by atomic spectroscopy (see this Chapter, 'Preferred Methods') applies equally well to selenium. Furnace AA, using a nickel matrix modifier, or hydride-generation AA, are both satisfactory using the 196.0 nm resonance line. The sensitivity, as well, is similar to that for As (0.5 ng/mL by furnace, 0.2 ng/mL in 10-mL sample by hydride generation). The ICP shows unacceptably low sensitivity (50 ng/mL), except for screening purposes, with the potential for enhanced sensitivity through hydride generation (Volnik *et al.*, 1981).

The fluorescence method for Se using diaminonaphthalene was described earlier, to illustrate fluorescence analysis.

Zinc

Flame atomic absorption using the 213.8 nm resonance line is quite satisfactory for zinc in most biological materials. Fluids can generally be analysed after dilution (at least 10-fold) and solutions from wet-ashed tissues cause relatively few problems. Dry ashing is sometimes recommended, but must be used cautiously because of risk of loss of zinc due to vaporization. The detection limit for zinc in the air-acetylene flame is 2–5 ng/mL in the sample solution. Even when one considers the inevitable dilution during preparation of the sample solution, the sensitivity is usually adequate. Little interference is encountered, other than a small background signal when samples are high in total solids. Continuum source background correction readily solves this problem. Only with samples which are difficult to dissolve are more serious problems likely to arise.

Furnace AA can also be used for zinc determination, but is recommended only for special cases because flames are usually satisfactory and because contamination problems become quite severe when working at furnace levels (< 1 ng/mL) for such a common element. FAA is attractive if the amount of sample available is severely limited.

If zinc is to be measured along with other elements, the ICP may be the method of choice. About 5 ng/mL in solution can be detected on most commercial units. One must ensure that the line used is free from spectral interference from common matrix elements and that background radiation is properly subtracted or otherwise corrected for. The 202.55 or 213.86 nm Zn emission lines are usually used.

Anodic stripping voltammetry can also be used for zinc determination, although other methods will usually be preferred unless additional elements (Pb, Cd) are being measured by ASV. The analyses are usually run in neutral or basic solution to prevent reduction of H^+ at the rather negative ($- \sim 1.3$ V *versus* saturated calomel electrode) potential required to plate Zn. Sensitivity will normally not be a problem; sub-ng/mL levels are readily measured on most equipment. Limitations include the need to purge the solutions to remove dissolved O_2 (greatly slows analyses), rather severe contamination problems and the possibility of interference due to intermetallic compound formation.

Zinc can be analysed by NAA with a sensitivity which is adequate for most biological samples using either ^{69m}Zn or ^{65}Zn. The target abundances, capture cross sections, product half-lives and gamma-ray branching ratios are 18.8%, 48.6%; 0.07 b, 0.78 b; 13.8 h, 244 d and 95%, 51% for ^{69m}Zn and ^{65}Zn, respectively.

The principal disadvantages of determining Zn *via* NAA is the long irradiation and cooling periods required if the longer-lived ^{65}Zn radionuclide is used, or the necessity of using a radiochemical separation if the short-lived ^{69m}Zn is used.

In cases where time is not a major problem, or a multi-element procedure is desirable, or sample dissolution is risky or impractical, NAA may become more attractive. In our laboratories, we analyse biological samples for Zn by NAA by counting the samples on an automatic sample changer, with storage of the data on disk or magnetic tape. When all samples and standards have been counted, data reduction can easily be carried out by computer using the 1115 keV gamma-ray from the decay of ^{65}Zn. Spectral interferences from ^{152}Eu ($E\gamma = 1113$ keV) and ^{46}Sc ($E\gamma = 1120$ keV) can occur in geological samples, but are not normally a problem in biological media.

Spectrophotometric methods based on dithizone or other colour-forming reagents are also satisfactory for the determination of zinc in most samples of biological origin.

SPECIATION

Introduction

In recent years, great interest has been aroused by methods which give information about the chemical form of trace elements, rather than just the total concentration. Unfortunately, the term 'speciation' has become a catch-all word, applied in too many distinctly different situations. In the first of these, the metal of interest is associated with a specific component of the sample. In this case, the sample is fractionated by appropriate methods and the total metal is measured in the fraction of interest. Measurement of zinc in serum protein fractions is an example. The second distinct case arises when the metal can exist in several oxidation states and the primary question concerns the amounts of As[III] and As[V], for example. A third situation arises when metal-carbon covalent bonds are formed with one or more organic groups as, for example, in tetraethyl lead. In the fourth and most difficult case, the metal may be loosely coordinated with one or more sample components, without formation of stable, identifiable compounds. The form of lead in a soil sample is an example. The metal may be associated with clay particles, organic matter, hydrated iron or manganese oxides, or exist as a separate solid phase, such as $PbCO_3$.

The second and third cases are of most interest here. Methods applicable to case four are currently being studied, especially by environmental chemists, but are not yet mature enough for a general discussion. Selective extraction procedures are most often used to yield information about the chemical behaviour of an element in a given sample type. However, at the current stage of development, definitive species information is seldom obtained in cases where several types of non-specific interaction with sample components is possible.

Oxidation state

Arsenic, selenium, antimony and chromium are likely to be found in multiple oxidation states, although As and Se, with lead, may be covalently bound to organic, usually alkyl, groups as well.

A challenge for all speciation work with complex samples lies in sample preparation. In most cases, the compound of interest will have to be separated from the bulk of the sample without alteration of its form. The usual vigorous digestions employed in trace element work obviously do not apply. A concern for species preservation must be maintained throughout the procedure.

Methods for differentiating Cr[III] and Cr[VI] are routinely applied in water and waste water analysis (Rand et al., 1976). However, as discussed earlier in 'Preferred Methods', the measurement of total chromium in tissue samples remains an analytical challenge and we are unlikely to see good methods for oxidation-state determination for such low levels in the near future.

Arsenic species

Numerous methods have been described for arsenic species. The fact that As[III] is more readily reduced to the hydride can be used to measure As[III] under gentle reduction conditions, then total As can be determined after reduction of As[V]. Selective extraction was used by Yasui *et al.* (1978) for As[III], As[V] and organic arsenic. The biological samples were treated with 6 mol/L hydrochloric acid to solubilize the As compounds. As[III] was extracted into toluene from 8 mol/L hydrochloric acid. As[V] was reduced by potassium iodide and also extracted into toluene, while organic forms of As remained in the aqueous phase. The As[III] and As[V] were back-extracted into water and the organic As compounds wet-ashed. The final determination was made by atomic absorption in each case. Bramon and Foreback (1973) treated organic arsenic compounds to form the corresponding arsines, which were caught in a cold trap and separated by selective volatilization, prior to excitation in a d.c. plasma. Morita *et al.* (1981) separated various organic As forms, as well as inorganic As[III] and [V], by ion-exchange chromatography, prior to detection by the ICP. A phosphate buffer was used to solubilize the As compounds. The danger inherent in all speciation work, noted earlier, was encountered by this group. As[III] in dilute standards was oxidized, presumably by air, to As[V]. More concentrated standards were stable, however, and the problem was solved by preparing dilute standards just prior to HPLC analysis. A rather similar separation was used by Aggett and Kadwani (1983) for methylated As species, as well as the oxidation-state determination. They extracted the As compound from aquatic weeds with water, then with methanol and ethanol in separate procedures. Hydride AA was used for the final measurement, though furnace AA or ICP were suggested as more convenient for routine detection.

Antimony and selenium

Selective methods for Sb and Se have not been investigated as extensively as those for As, but generally similar methods seem to apply. The fact that Se[VI] and Sb[V] do not readily form hydrides without reduction is used to differentiate between oxidation states. Separation of the corresponding hydride chromatographically, followed by AA detection, has been reported for methylated forms (Andreae *et al.*, 1981).

Lead

Most of the effort for specific compounds of lead has been directed toward tetraalkyl lead species, because of their common use as motor fuel additives. The methods for measuring organic lead compounds in air were recently reviewed by De Jonghe and Adams (1982). For most of the methods, the sample is filtered prior to collection and the volatile lead compounds which pass through the filter are measured. Total organic lead can be measured by adsorbing volatile species on activated carbon or reacting them with iodine to produce inorganic lead. Any appropriate method may then be used to determine the total lead collected (dithizone, furnace AA, X-ray fluorescence). Methods for measuring specific volatile lead compounds usually employ a chromatographic separation, followed by lead-specific detection. The procedure described by Chau *et al.* (1976) is typical of such methods. Air was passed through a short section of GLC column held at $-70\,^{\circ}$C. The collection tube was then heated to $\sim 100\,°C$ and the lead compounds swept into a GLC column for separation. Effluents were passed through a heated quartz cell ($980\,°C$) aligned on the optical path of an AA unit. Separation and analysis of tetraalkyl lead compounds (Me_4Pb, Me_3EtPb, Me_2Et_2Pb, $Me\ Et_3Pb$ and Et_4Pb) was achieved with a detection limit of 0.1 ng of Pb. The detection was highly specific for lead and the various compounds were identified by their chromatographic behaviour. Later workers have used similar collection and separation procedures with graphite furnace atomic absorption detection (Sirota & Uthe, 1977). Tetraalkyl lead compounds were extracted from biological samples with a benzene/aqueous EDTA solution. The benzene portion was digested and the resulting lead measured by furnace AA. About 10 ng/g of R_4Pb could be measured. Less alkylated leads, R_3PbX, R_2Ph_2, etc, were not extracted. Trialkyl lead compounds may be extracted into benzene from an aqueous solution saturated with sodium chloride. The n-butyltrialkyl-lead compounds were then formed prior to gas chromatographic separation.

Other methods can be used to obtain chemical species information in special cases. For example, electron spectroscopy (ESCA) provides species information for major constituents at the surface of samples. Most such methods require specialized equipment and are beyond the scope of the present chapter.

REFERENCES

Aggett, J. & Kadwani, R. (1983) Anion-exchange method for speciation of arsenic and its application to some environmental analyses. *Analyst, 108,* 1495–1499

Andreae, M.O., Asmode, J.F., Foster, P. & Van't dack, L. (1981) Determination of antimony[III], antimony[V] and methylantimony species in natural waters by atomic absorption spectrometry with hydride generation. *Anal. Chem., 53,* 1766–1771

Braman, R.S. & Foreback, C.C. (1973) Methylated forms of arsenic in the environment. *Science, 182,* 1247–1249

Chau, Y.K., Wong, P.T.S. & Saitoh, H. (1976) Determination of tetraalkyl lead compounds in the atmosphere. *J. Chromatogr. Sci., 14,* 162–164

De Jonghe, W.R.A. & Adams, F.C. (1982) Measurements of organic lead in air – a review. *Talanta, 29,* 1057–1068

Estes, S.A., Uden, P.C. & Barnes, R.M. (1982) Determination of n-butylated trialkyllead compounds by gas chromatography with microwave plasma emission detection. *Anal. Chem., 54,* 2402–2405

Fassel, V.A. & Kniseley, R.N. (1974a) Inductively coupled plasma – optical emission spectroscopy. *Anal. Chem., 46,* 1110A–1120A

Fassel, V.A. & Kniseley, R.N. (1974b) Inductively coupled plasmas. *Anal. Chem., 46,* 1155A–1164A

Houk, R.S., Fassel, V.A., Flesch, G.D., Svec, H.J., Gray, A.L. & Taylor, C.E. (1980) Inductively coupled argon plasma as an ion source for mass spectrometric determination of trace elements. *Anal. Chem., 52,* 2283–2289

Koirtyohann, S.R. & Kaiser, M.L. (1982) furnace atomic absorption – A method approaching maturity. *Anal. Chem., 54,* 1515A–1524A

Koizumi, H. & Yasuda, K. (1977) A novel method for atomic absorption spectroscopy based on the analyte-Zeeman effect. *Spectrochim. Acta,* Part B, *31B,* 523–535

L'vov, B.V. (1978) Electrothermal atomization – the way toward absolute methods of atomic absorption analysis. *Spectrochim. Acta, Part B, 33B,* 153–193

Morita, M., Uehiro, T. & Fuwa, K. (1981) Determination of arsenic compounds in biological samples by liquid chromatography with inductively coupled argon plasma-atomic emission spectrometric detection. *Anal. Chem., 53,* 1806–1808

Parr, R.M. (1977) Problems of chromium analysis in biological materials: An international perspective with special reference to results for analytical quality control samples. *J. radioanal. Chem., 39,* 421–433

Rand, M.C., Greenberg, A.E. & Taras, M.J., eds (1976) Method 307B in: *Standard Methods for the Examination of Water and Wastewater,* 14th Ed., Washington DC, American Public Health Association

Sirota, G.R. & Uthe, J.F. (1977) Determination of tetraalkyllead compounds in biological materials. *Anal. Chem., 49,* 823–825

Slavin, W., Manning, D.C. & Carnrick, G.R. (1981) The stabilized temperature platform furnace. *At. Spectrosc., 2,* 137–145

Stiefel, T., Schulze, K. & Tolg, G. (1980) Analysis of trace elements distributed in blood. Determination of beryllium concentrations. gt$_0$req. 0.01 ng/g in human and animal blood components by preparative electrophoresis and flameless atomic absorption spectrometry. *Fresenius Z. Anal. Chem., 300,* 189–196

Versieck, J., Barbier, F., Cornelis, R. & Hoste, J. (1982) Sample contamination as a source of error in trace-element analysis of biological samples. *Talanta, 29,* 973–984

Wicke, S.A. & Burke, R.W. (1977) Determination of beryllium by fluorescence spectrometry. *NBS Spec. Publ. (US), 492,* 85–89

Wolnik, K.A., Fricke, F.L., Hahn, M.H. & Caruso, J.A. (1981) Sample introduction system for simultaneous determination of volatile elemental hydrides and other elements in foods by inductively coupled argon plasma emission spectrometry. *Anal. Chem., 53,* 1030–1035

Yasui, A., Tsutsumi, C. & Toda, I. (1978) Selective determination of inorganic arsenic[III], [V] and organic arsenic in biological materials by solvent extraction-atomic absorption spectrophotometry. *Agric. Biol. Chem., 42,* 2139–2145

CHAPTER 12

SPECIAL CONSIDERATIONS IN TRACE ELEMENT ANALYSIS OF FOODS AND BIOLOGICAL MATERIALS

K.W. Boyer[1] & W. Horwitz

Divison of Chemical Technology, Bureau of Foods, Department of Health and Human Services, Food and Drug Administration, Washington, CD 20204, USA

INTRODUCTION

Analytical results from trace element analysis will often be employed to draw conclusions which will have an important bearing on the health and well-being of the citizens of many countries, the degree of contamination of the environment or the economic value of goods in commerce. Such obligations place a severe demand on the reliability of the reported values. But all analytical measurements are subject to variability, which is a feature of the measurement process that can affect both the accuracy and precision of the final results. Variability is contributed at every stage of the operation, from sample collection and preparation, through the manipulations involved in analytical procedures and, finally, from the interpretation of the finished product, i.e., the analytical result. Because of the unavoidable uncertainty in the final values, an estimate of the degree of confidence that can be placed in the reported quantities is an essential component of the final record.

The process of monitoring the analytical operations (and related steps) to maintain variability at a level acceptable for the purpose of the analysis is called quality assurance (QA). Some of the sources of variability are common to all analytical processes and can probably be suppressed only to a limited extent, while others are unique to elemental analyses and may be controlled by close attention to detail. Indeed, an examination by Horwitz *et al.* (1090) of the results of over 200 inter-laboratory collaborative studies of various analytes, including trace metals in a wide range of matrices, strongly suggested that the expected coefficient of variation of analytical results increases by a factor of 2 for each 100-fold decrease in analyte concentration, independent of the measurement technique, analyte and matrix.

Using the computer program 'FDACHEMIST', recently developed by Horwitz and Albert (1984), Boyer *et al.* (1985) statistically analysed the data from 18

---

[1] New address: Lancaster Laboratories, 2425 New Holland Pike, Lancaster, PA 17601, USA

collaborative studies conducted by the Association of Official Analytical Chemists (AOAC) between 1973 and 1983, which apecifically involved trace elements. Figure 1 is a plot of the data from 11 of these studies after removal of influential outliers at the 95% (or greater) confidence interval, using the Dixon and Grubbs tests for extreme values and the Cochran test for excessive range within a laboratory. Figure 1 shows that the mean inter-laboratory coefficients of variation for these studies were distributed about a curve defined by equation 1,

$$CV = 2^{(1-0.5 \, \text{Log} \, \omega)}$$ Equation 1

where ω is the mass fraction of the analyte in the sample. This gives example CV's of 8% at the 100 mg/kg analyte level, 11% at 10 mg/kg, 16% at 1 mg/kg, 22% at 0.1 mg/kg, and 32% at 0.01 mg/kg, regardless of the analyte, matrix or measurement technique. Thus, Fig. 1 indicates the 'normal' inter-laboratory precision that would be expected from an analytical method for trace elements in this concentration range. The intra-laboratory precision is usually ½ to ⅔ of these values. Much poorer precision than twice the value given by equation 1, such as that displayed by the other 7 methods studied by Boyer et al. (1985), would indicate that the method is not applicable at eht analyte level involved.

However, Fig. 1 says nothing about the accuracy of analytical methods. The accuracy of a method can be established only by using it to analyse well-characterized reference materials, as discussed below in 'Data treatment'. Finally, whether a method is sufficiently accurate or precise depends on the intended use of the data obtained by the method.

Sources of variability and inaccuracy that require special attention in trace element analyses include sample heterogeneity, sample contamination by ubiquitous contaminants, loss or gain of analytes during sample preparation and positive or negative interferences during the determinative step of the analyses. Tschopel and Tolg (1982) have recently published an excellent review concerning the sources and control of contaminants and of systematic errors in trace and ultratrace element analysis.

In this chapter we discuss the quality assurance of the total analytical process, from sample collection to reporting of data, to help ensure that the accuracy and confidence accorded to the final results serve the purpose of the analyses.

CONTAMINATION CONTROL

The ability to perform analyses at trace (mg/kg) and ultratrace (µg/kg) levels depends on the identification and elimination of contaminants. For many analytical methods for trace elements, the lower limit of reliable quantification is not set by the capabilities of the instrument used in the determinative step, but rather by variable contamination, as exhibited by the analytical blank. Contamination can arise from many sources, including the laboratory air, apparatus and equipment, sample and reagent containers, glassware, reagents and even the analyst. Improvement of laboratory facilities can reduce the general level of contamination from the laboratory environment. Adherence to specific procedures during sample collection, preparation

Fig. 1. Inter-laboratory coefficient of variation (CV) as a function of analyte concentration (mass fraction)

$- - -$, CV $= 2^{(2-0.5 \, \text{Log} \, \omega)}$
——, CV $= 2^{(1-0.5 \, \text{Log} \, \omega)}$

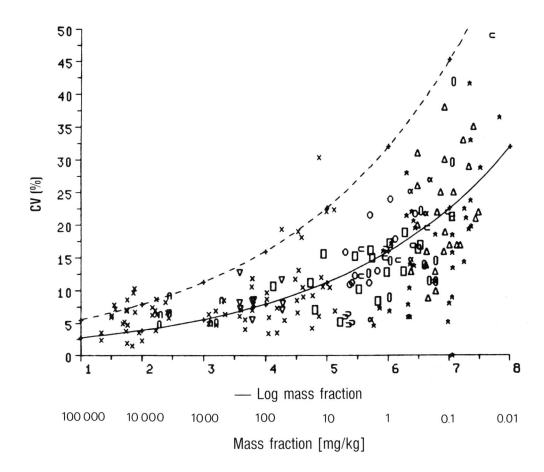

and analysis can minimize contamination sources that are unrelated to the laboratory environment. The present section will deal with contamination control in the analytical laboratory.

In setting priorities for implementing an effective contamination control programme, it is logical to begin with improvements and procedural changes that will provide the largest reduction in contamination for the smallest expenditure. As progressively more stringent contamination control measures are taken, the time and cost involved usually increase. An excellent book on this subject has been written by Zief and Mitchell (1976).

Facilities improvement

The following check-list cites, in approximate priority order, steps for progressively upgrading a conventional laborabory to make it more suitable for trace element analyses. For more detail, see chapter 3 of Zief and Mitchell (1976).

Check-list for laboratory facilities improvement

Status	Item
————	Replace all rusted and corroded hot plates, heating units, ashing ovens, etc. with ceramic-top hot plates and ceramic-lined ovens. Replace rusting ring stands, clamps, racks, hood and window panels, metal cabinets, etc. or strip and paint with epoxy paint.
————	Remove all unnecessary shelving, partitions, furniture and other dust-collecting items from the laboratory.
————	Install filters on all incoming air sources (air conditioning, heating, ventilation, make-up air, etc). Filters should be 85% efficient for 0.5–5.0 μm particles and 95% efficient for particles greater than 5.0 μm.
————	Install a high-purity ion-exchange water purification system, capable of producing water with 18 megohm cm^{-1} resistance. Use distilled water as the water source for the ion-exchange system. All trace element analyses should use water for which the final purification step is ion-exchange, rather than distillation.
————	Install an exhausting laminar-flow, high-efficiency, particulate air (HEPA) filter hood to be used for operations in which the analyst would be exposed to acid fumes and other noxious gases.
————	Install non-exhausting HEPA filter modules approximately 1 m above bench tops where critical (low-level or regulatory) work will be done.
————	Coat all bench tops with epoxy paint, then cover them with adhesive-backed Teflon or polyethylene sheeting.
————	Coat all metal drawer handles, metal valve handles, metal fixtures, name-plates, etc, with epoxy paint or replace with plastic wherever possible.
————	If possible, remove all metal gas cylinders from the laboratory to an adjacent laboratory or separate gas cylinder room. Run a Teflon or polyethylene distribution line from each gas source to each laboratory requiring that gas.
————	Paint walls in analysis area with two-component epoxy paint (one component being bisphenol A epoxy ether in a solvent, cured by addition

of an amine or amide curing agent in a second solvent).

——————— Cover floors with one-piece vinyl flooring coved at floor and wall intersections.

Of course the highest degree of elimination of contamination from the laboratory environment is achieved in specially designed 'clean laboratories', such as the trace element clean laboratory at the US National Bureau of Standards Center for analytical Chemistry (Moody, 1982). Whether specially designed 'clean' laboratories are necessary will be dictated by the degree to which contamination-free analyses are required.

Contamination control during sample collection

It is important that contamination control be exercised during collection, shipping, handling and storage of samples, especially when ubiquitous contaminants, such as Pb and Fe, are involved. Whenever possible, the analyst should be involved in specifying the sample collection and handling procedures. This will minimize the possibility that the material collected will become contaminated with the analyte of interest, or with an interfering analyte, before it reaches the laboratory.

Contamination control during sample preparation and analysis

Most samples are not amenable to direct analysis and must therefore be treated chemically and/or physically to convert them to a form suitable for analysis. Physical methods of treatment are necessary to ensure a homogeneous composite, since generally only a fraction of the total sample is taken for analysis. Routine procedures commonly used in sample homogenization of biological materials may include washing, chopping, freeze-drying, blending and grinding. These procedures must be closely monitored to avoid introduction of contaminants. Chemical methods of treatment include conventional digestion and extraction procedures for separating interfering matrix elements and concentrating the species of interest. Performance of all sample pretreatment with meticulous care will reduce random contamination from the laboratory environment. Systematic contamination is controlled by careful choice of equipment, reagents and cleaning procedures. Procedures should be designed to prevent contamination and provide an acceptable blank level.

The following check-list provides steps that should be taken in order to minimize contamination, wheter or not extensive improvement of laboratory facilities has been possible.

Check-list for analysis contamination control

Status	Item

——————— Design or modify equipment which comes in contact with the samples so that it is free from the species to be measured. Use no spatulas or other metal utensils unless they have been coated with Teflon or other suitable polymeric material (e.g., Kynar, a difluoroethylene polymer).

————— Remove all metal stopcock leashes from volumetric glassware. Dedicate this glassware entirely to a particular analysis. Polypropylene or Teflon volumetric ware is proferable to glass because of reduced memory effects.

————— In sample preparation, use only equipment made of glass (Pyrex or quartz) or plasticware (knives, strainers, wash tubs, vegetable drainers, sample bags, etc) of possible).

————— Perform all sample handling with polyethylene or polyvinylchloride gloves. Pre-powdered gloves are *not* acceptable.

————— Where feasible, use sample-processing equipment which is entirely of plastic, including cutting blades, or which has been coated with an acceptable polymeric material (e.g., food cutter coated with Kynar). If homogenization requires the use of metal, use equipment incorporating hardened stainless steel blades. Incorporate checks (analysis of blanks and reference materials) into any homogenization procedure to determine the levels of systematic contaminants that may have been introduced.

————— Wherever possible, carry out all sample preparation and analysis steps under clean air modules or in clean air hoods.

————— Acid-wash all inert equipment used in sample preparation, storage or analysis, with 10% HNO, (72% HNO_3 diluted $1 \rightarrow 10$) prior to use. The extent to which equipment must be washed is determined by the level of elements of interest in comparison to the blank level.

————— Soak plasticware and sample bottles (linear polyethylene or polypropylene) in dilute $(1 \rightarrow 10)$ HNO_3 for 15 min; soak for 15 min in distilled deionized water (DDW) and rinse 3 times with DDW. In each case, the analyst must determine the cleaning procedure most applicable to the analysis to be performed. For example, laboratory ware used for trace Pb and Fe analyses requires more stringent cleaning procedures than ware used for analyses of other elements, as discussed by Zief and Mitchell (1976).

————— Determine and control the level of trace elements in the water, acids, solvents, buffers, chelating agents and supporting electrolytes used in the analytical determination. Zief and Mitchell (1976, chapter 5) provide an excellent discussion of the purification of these reagents.

Regardless of the validity of the analytical method or the capability of the analyst, reliable data cannot be obtained without proper contamination control during sample preparation and analysis.

ANALYTICAL STANDARDS AND REFERENCE MATERIALS

In any analysis, the quality of the resulting data can be only as good as that of the standards used in the analysis. The preparation and preservation ot essential, pure and highly accurate standard solutions for trace element analyses requires that many variables be taken into account. Well-characterized starting materials and suitable storage containers must be selected, and strict contamination control and quality assurance procedures must be followed during preparation and use of standard solutions. Finally, good quality-assurance practice requires the analysis of reference materials with each bath of samples, as an independent check of the analytical procedure and contamination control. For this purpose, Standard Reference Materials (SRM) such as those produced by the US National Bureau of Standards (NBS), or well-characterized 'in-house standard materials', are suitable.

Standard solution preparation: general procedures

Accurately weigh the standard material into a previously tared and acid-washed plastic weighing dish so that the final concentration of the standard will give 1000 µg of analyte/mL of solution. Record the weight to four decimal places in a standards log book. Recheck the recorded weight against the scale reading or weights used, as many errors are caused by unintentional transposition of a pair of digits. Carefully transfer the material to a previously acid-washed 1-L volumetric flask, using some of the 100 mL of recommended solvent (see Table 1), then add the remaining solvent directly to the volumetric flask. If necessary, gently heat the flask in a water bath to effect complete dissolution. Cool to room temperature, then bring the solution to volume with deionized water. Transfer the standard solution to the recommended acid-washed container (see Table 1 for recommended weights and containers). The references consulted in preparing Table 1 included Moody & Lindstrom, 1977; NBS, 1977; Ward, 1978; Miller & DeManna, 1980.

Stock solutions: special considerations

The use of 'spec pure' materials, three-nines (99.9%) or better, or solutions made from material of this purity is recommended. Purchase of stock solutions from commercial sources is permissible, provided the purity of the starting material used in the preparation was 99.9% or better. Hydrates are generally a poor choice of starting material for the preparation of standard solutions, since the water content may vary from one lot to another, and most are hygroscopic. Electronic grade or ultra-high purity acids should be used in the solubilization of the standard when acid is required. In all cases, deionized water of resistivity approaching 18 megohm cm^{-1} should be used. Systems that can supply water of this purity are commercially available.

Check the purity of new standard solutions by one or more of the following procedures:

(a) Compare the calibration curve prepared with the new standard solution with the calibration curve prepared with the old standard solution, using independently

Table 1.   Stock standard solution preparation. Dilute to one (1) liter.

Element	Recommended form	Weight (g)	Solvents[a]	Container[b]
Antimony	Sb°	1.0000	Aqua-Regia	Glass
Arsenic	As$_2$O$_3$[f]	1.3203	[c]	TFE, CPE
Beryllium	Be°	1.0000	0.5 mol/L HCl	TFE, CPE
Bismuth[d]	Bi°	1.0000	4 mol/L HNO$_3$	TFE, CPE
Cadmium	Cd°	1.0000	4 mol/L HNO$_3$	TFE, CPE
Cadmium	CdSO$_4$	1.9546	0.3mol/L HCl	TFE, CPE
Chromium	Cr°	1.0000	4 mol/L HCL	TFE, CPE
Cobalt	Co°	1.0000	4 mol/L HCl	TFE, CPE
Copper	Cu°	1.0000	4 mol/L HNO$_3$	TFE, CPE
Lead	Pb°	1.0000	4 mol/L HNO$_3$	TFE, CPE
Lead	Pb(NO$_3$)$_2$	1.5985	0.5 mol/L HNO$_3$	TFE, CPE
Manganese	MnO$_2$	1.5825	Conc. HCl	Glass
Mercury	Hg°	1.0000	5mol/L HNO$_3$	TFE, CPE
Mercury	HgCl$_2$	1.3540	0.5 mol/HNO$_3$	TFE, CPE
Molybdenum	MoO$_3$	1.5003	Aqua-Regia	Glass
Nickel	Ni°	1.0000	4 mol/L HCl	TFE, CPE
Selenium	Se	1.0000	0.5 mol/L HNO$_3$	TFE, CPE
Selenium	SeO$_2$	1.4053	Water	TFE, CPE
Silver[e]	Ag°	1.0000	4 mol/L HNO$_3$	TFE, CPE
Zinc	Zn°[f]	1.0000	4 mol/L HNO$_3$	TFE, CPE

[a] Use 100 mL of solvent to dissolve, then bring to volume with deionized water
[b] TEF, preleached, tretrafluorethylene (Teflon); CPE, preleached conventional polyethylene; Glass, preleached borosilicate glass
[c] Dissolve in 20 mL of 10% NaOH. After dissolution, dilute to 200 mL with deionized water, then neutralize with HCl and bring to volume with deionized water
[d] Boil gently to expel brown fumes then bring to volume
[e] Store in brown CPE and keep in the dark
[f] Available from US National Bureau of Standards

diluted solutions for each point on the curves.

(b)   Compare standards from two different sources.

(c)   Analyse an NBS-SRM or other laboratory reference material for the element of interest, using the new standard solution to prepare the calibration curve.

(d)   Assay by coulometric deposition, if deposition of the element in question is known to be 100% efficient.

(e)   Assay using a proven, definitive, fundamental method, such as a gravimetric or titrimetric method.

Analysis of the new standard or standard solution should be within 0.5% of the expected value before it is accepted for use. Stock solutions should be replaced yearly. Analysts checking methods or results should always make a fresh stock solution.

Working standard solutions

All working standard solutions should be prepared fresh on the day of use with a concentration range encompassing the concentration of the sample solution. If a single working standard solution is to be employed, its concentration should be as close as possible to that of the solution to be analysed. Usually, working standard solutions will be prepared by serial dilution of intermediate standard solutions, which are in turn prepared by serial dilution of stock standard solutions. Since the errors associated with each step may be additive, the volumetric ware used for the serial dilutions should be chosen to give a maximum cumulative uncertainty of $< 0.5\%$ in the working standard solution. Working standard solutions should be acidic enough (2%) to ensure stability (for exceptions, see Table 1).

Containers for standard solutions

The best choice for containers is either Teflon or polyethylene bottles, with caps made of the same material. Containers specially cleaned for storage of stock solutions may be used for the same stock standard solution when the latter is replaced.

Cleaning procedure for standard solution containers:

(a) Fill with $1 + 1$ HNO_3 (72% HNO_3, reagent grade, diluted 1:1 with deionized water).
(b) Allow to stand one week at room temperature (80°F for Teflon).
(c) Empty and rinse with purest available deionized water.
(d) Fill with purest available deionized water.
(e) Allow to stand several weeks, changing water periodically to ensure continued cleaning.
(f) Rinse with purest water available and allow to dry in a particle-free and fume-free environment.

Always acid-wash any working standard container, after cleaning, with diluted $(1 \rightarrow 10)$ HNO, (reagent grade) and rinse with purest water available; allow to dry in particle-free and fume-free environment.

Record keeping

Good laboratory quality assurance dictates that histories of stock solutions be maintained in one permanent register. All significant data concerning the freshly-prepared solution should be entered into this Laboratory Record Book for Metal Stock Standards. This information includes:

(a) Source, material, lot number and manufacturer's purity.
(b) Assayed purity, if applicable.
(c) Standard weight and final dilution volume.
(d) Final element concentration in appropriate units, e.g., g/L.
(d) Final acid content, if applicable.
(f) Comparison data for old stock standard and new stock standard, as well as results of any other concentration or purity analyses.
(g) Name of preparer and date of preparation.
(h) Name of person doing calculation check.

Use of reference materials

Analytical samples should be analysed together with SRM's and/or reference materials selected to match as closely as possible the sample matrix and the anticipated concentrations of the elements of interest. Table 2 gives the levels of elements in some of the NBS-SRM's. Insofar as possible, the reference material(s) should be carried through the entire analysis simultaneously with the unknown samples. This practice will subject the reference material(s) to the same potential for contamination or losses of the element of interest as the sample being analysed. If the analytical results from the reference material do not agree with the expected results within a predetermined error range, the source of the error should be determined and eliminated, and the analyses of both sample and reference material repeated. When using NBS-SRM's, it is essential to follow the drying procedures and other instructions provided in the Certificates of Analysis. Analytical results for samples should not be corrected for differences between the reference material values found and the certified values; instead, both of the latter values should be reported in addition to the sample results.

SAMPLING AND SAMPLE PREPARATION

The first step in conducting an analysis is the collection of a sample that takes into account the purpose of the analysis and is representative of the material being sampled. Thus, it is important to know why the analysis is being conducted. More often than not, the person seeking the analytical results and the analyst producing these results are not the same. Too frequently the analyst is given a sample to analyse with no opportunity to influence the collection procedure. Even with the greatest analytical expertise and care, meaningful results cannot be achieved if the test material is improperly sampled or, worse yet, the wrong material is sampled.

When the bulk or size of the material being sampled is too great to allow analysis of the entire material, a sampling plan to achieve representative sampling should be followed. Representative sampling requires that the number and size of subsamples be large enough to overcome the variability of the analyte in the parent material. The error associated with sampling decreases as the number of sample units and their size increases. Optimum sampling is achieved when the mean and standard deviation calculated from analyses of individual subsamples are no longer appreciably affected by the incorporation of data from additional subsamples (Horwitz *et al.*, 1978).

Once samples are collected, they must be preserved and protected from degradation and contamination until they are analysed. Samples collected for trace element analysis should normally be kept in acid-cleaned (see 'Contamination control') non-metal containers such as glass, Teflon or polyethylene jars, or polyethylene bags. If the sample is subject to microbial growth or enzymatic changes, shipment and storage of the frozen sample (or just above freezing for samples that should not be frozen) will help to slow degradation. If long-term storage of the sample is required, freeze-drying may be desirable. However, the analyst must verify that the elements of interest are not lost due to volatilization during the freeze-drying.

Table 2. Element contents of standard reference materials, U.S. National Bureau of Standards [Content in mg/kg (or, where noted, WT. %)][a, b]

Element	Oyster/1566	Wheat flour/1567	Rice flour/1568	Yest/1569	Spinach/1570	Orchard leaves/1571	Tomato leaves/1573	Pine needles/1575	Bovine[c] liver/1577	Albacore tuna/RM60	Water/1643a (ng/g)
Antimony					(0.04)	2.9 ± 0.3		(0.2)			
Arsenic	13.4 ± 1.9	(0.006)	0.41 ± 0.05		0.15 ± 0.05	10 ± 2	0.27 ± 0.05	0.21 ± 0.04	(0.055)	(3.3 ± 0.4)	76 ± 7
Beryllium						0.027 ± 0.010					
Bismuth						(0.1)					
Cadmium	3.5 ± 0.4	0.032 ± 0.007	0.029 ± 0.004		(1.5)	0.11 ± 0.01	(3)	(<0.5)	0.27 ± 0.04		10 ± 1
Chromium	0.69 ± 0.27			2.12 ± 0.05	4.6 ± 0.3	2.6 ± 0.3	4.5 ± 0.5	2.6 ± 0.2	(0.18)		17 ± 2
Cobalt	(0.4)				(1.5)	(0.2)	(0.6)	(0.1)			19 ± 2
Copper	63.0 ± 3.5	2.0 ± 0.3	2.2 ± 0.3		12 ± 2	12 ± 1	11 ± 1	3.0 ± 0.3	193 ± 10		18 ± 2
Lead	0.48 ± 0.04				1.2 ± 0.2	45 ± 3	6.3 ± 0.3	10.8 ± 0.5	0.34 ± 0.08		27 ± 1
Manganese	17.5 ± 1.2	8.5 ± 0.5	20.1 ± 0.4		165 ± 6	91 ± 4	238 ± 7	675 ± 15	10.3 ± 1.0		
	31 ± 2										
Mercury	0.057 ± 0.15				0.030 ± 0.005	0.155 ± 0.015	(0.1)	0.15 ± 0.05	0.016 ± 0.002	0.95 ± 0.1[d]	(<0.2)
Molybdenum	(<0.2)	(0.4)	(1.6)		(6)	0.3 ± 0.1			(3.2)		95 ± 6
Nickel	1.03 ± 0.19	(0.18)	(0.16)			1.3 ± 0.2		(3.5)			55 ± 3
Selenium	2.1 ± 0.5	1.1 ± 0.2	0.4 ± 0.1				0.17 ± 0.03		1.1 ± 0.1	(3.6 ± 0.4)	11 ± 1
Silver	0.89 ± 0.09				(0.03)			(0.05)	(0.06)		
Thallium	(<0.005)							0.020 ± 0.004	(0.05)		
Uranium	0.116 ± 0.006				0.046 ± 0.009	0.029 ± 0.005			(0.0008)		2.8 ± 0
Zinc	852 ± 14	10.6 ± 1.0	19.4 ± 1.0		50 ± 2	25 ± 3	62 ± 6		130 ± 10	(13.6 ± 1)	72 ± 4

[a] Values in parentheses are non-certified values
[b] All values are based on dry weight, except the tuna and water
[c] "Old" Bovine liver, "new" liver, 1577a, has different values.
[d] As methyl mercury, 0.93 ± 0.1

In some cases, the heterogeneous nature of the material being analysed may require special sampling and sample preparation procedures prior to trace element analysis. For example, lead distribution has been found to be sufficiently heterogeneous in foods packed in lead-soldered cans (Jones & Boyer, 1979) and in fortified laboratory rat diets (Boyer & Capar, 1977) to require special homogenization procedures.

Useful equipment and materials for sample preparation

(a) Clean air laminar flow hoods – class 100 (capable of producing air containing no more than 100 particles/ft^3($\sim 3\,500$ particles/m^3) between 0.5 and 5.0 µm and zero particles larger than 5.0 µm).

(b) Distilled, deionized water system (18 megohm cm^{-1}).

(c) Food cutter (Kynar coated).

(d) Homogenizer – capable of both shear and sonic action, with Teflon bearings and hardened stainless steel or vanadium steel cutting probe (e.g., Polytron or Dupont).

(e) Food processor with short plastic blades (e.g., Cuisin-art).

(f) Blender – glass bowl with stainless steed blaces (e.g., Waring or Sears).

(g) Freeze-dryer, flasks, lids.

(h) Glove box – plastic.

(i) Can opener – stainless steel.

(j) Knives, spatulas, potato peeler, etc. – stainless steel or epoxy-coated stainless steel.

(k) Sample storage bottles – linear polyethylene or polypropylene.

(l) Gloves – polyethylene or polyvinylchloride, not powdered.

(m) Plasticware – knives, spoons, spatulas, strainers, wash tubs, drainers, vegetable brush, sample bags, vegetable spinner.

(n) 40-mesh polypropylene sieve.

During preparation of the sample or sample composite for analysis, it is important to follow the contamination control procedure given below.

Sample preparation procedures for foods and biological materials

(a) Use only distilled, deionized water (DDW), specific resistance = 18 megohm cm^{-1} unless otherwise stated.

(b) Always wear plastic powder-free gloves when handling samples.

(c) Carry out all sample preparation steps under clean air hoods.

(d) Allow samples to contact only acid-washed plastic or glass (Pyrex, quartz), unless otherwise stated.

(e) Washing sample preparation equipment:

    (i)   Glass-ware (including blender jars and freeze-dry jars) – wash glassware with DDW and a high quality laboratory detergent (e.g., Alconox), rinse with DDW, soak for 15 min in DDW, soak for 15 min in $(1 \rightarrow 3)$ HNO$_3$ + H$_2$O, rinse with DDW, and place in drainer in hood to dry. Note: Omit acid step when washing blender cutting unit.

    (ii) Plastic-ware (including sample storage bottles) – rinse with DDW, soak for

15 min in 1:9 (v/v) $HNO_3:H_2O$, soak for 15 min in DDW, rinse with DDW and place in drainer in hood to dry.

(f) Sample cleaning and preparation: some samples, such as raw agricultural products, may require washing or other cleaning to remove unwanted surface contamination.

(g) Compositing:

  (i)   If knowing the degree of variability within the lot or bulk material is not important, it may be desirable to composite subsamples to decrease the number of analyses necessary. If a reserve portion of the sample is required for later analyses or other purposes, it should be taken in the preparation procedure at the point where representative portions may be obtained with the least amount of sample preparation (in order to minimize subsequent contamination). The reserve sample should then be properly labelled for future identification and stored in a refrigerator or freezer to minimize decomposition.

  (ii) Freeze-drier composite – if sample is to be freeze-dried before compositing, place it in weighed, freeze-dry jars and record sample weight before and after freeze-drying. Place the freeze-dried sample in blender and grind to pass a 40-mesh polypropylene (not metal) sieve. Transfer the sample to plastic storage bottle.

  Note: When freezen-drying a sample with < 10% moisture, water must be added (which is absorbed by the sample) before freeze-drying. This reduces the density of the sample after freeze-drying, which facilitates grinding.

  (iii) Wet composite – homogenization of samples based on % water:

  < 25% water – Weigh sample for homogenization into a blender; add an equal weight of DDW and blend to a particle size small enough for final homogenization with a homogenizer. Transfer this slurry to a homogenizer and grind to a homogeneous state. Additional equal weights of DDW may be necessary. It is preferable to add equal weights to DDW to maintain proportionate ratios, i.e., 1:1, 1:2, etc. Record this ratio to account for sample dilution. Transfer sample to plastic storage bottle.

  > 25% water – DDW is added at the analyst's discretion. If water content is > 50%, addition of DDW is usually unnecessary. Obtain a homogeneous slurry by first using a conventional blender and finishing with a homogenizer. Transfer sample to plastic storage bottle.

Sample storage

(a) Store freeze-dried samples or composites in laboratory cabinets until analysis is complete. These cabinets should be cool, dry and not exposed to direct sunlight or other bright light.

(b) Refrigerate or freeze wet composites until analysis is complete. Samples that are homogenized and stored in this manner will separate physically; restore homogeneous state before sampling for analysis.

SAMPLE MINERALIZATION

Ideally, one would prefer to analyse for an element in an organic matrix without having to destroy the matrix. This would eliminate contamination from the reagents and apparatus used to destroy the matrix. Although there are a number of techniques for performing non-destructive analyses, such as neutron activation or X-ray fluorescence, the accessibility, detection limits and ease of quantification of these techniques in many cases may not be adquate for the elements of interest. For more commonly used analytical techniques, most materials require some sort of treatment to prepare them for the determinative step.

Some materials can be prepared for analysis by simply diluting them with water or another reagent. In other cases, partial desctuction of the organic matrix may be adequate. For example, acid hydrolysis, using either HNO_3 or HCl, produces partial digestion of many materials. Although carbohydrate and fat are not destroyed by acid hydrolysis, most trace elements can be completely extracted into the aqueous phase.

The most common method for the complete destriction of organic material is by ashing, either wet or dry. Gorsuch (1970) has made a thorough study of this subject.

Problems encountered in the mineralization of organic matrices

(a) *Contamination:* Digestion vessels may introduce contamination if they are not clean, or from etching of the vessel itself. External contamination from dirty vessels can be removed by acid cleaning. See 'Contamination control' for further details. To overcome the problem of contamination by etching of the vessel, consideration should be given to its composition and to the possible reaction of the reagents being used in the digestion. The use of quartz vessels (pure silica) is recommended for dry ashing at temperatures up to 600 °C. Below these temperatures, HNO_3, H_2SO_4 and HCl have no action on quartz. However, alkali hydroxides and carbonates will etch quartz. If Si is not one of the elements of interest and does not interfere with the analysis reactions, etching of the container usually is not of great importance.

(b) *Absorption:* In trace and ultra-trace analysis there is always the possibility that the element being determined may combine with the wall of the vessel and may not be removed by the acids used to dissolve the ash. If the total amount of the element in the sample is very small to start with, the small amount that binds with the wall could introduce a significant error. If the sample digest solution contains a small amount of acid-insoluble material such as silica, this material should not be filtered out (because the filtration process may introduce contamination), but should be allowed to settle out before the supernatant liquid is analysed.

(c) *Coprecipitation:* In a strongly acidic or strongly basic solution, the formation of a heavy precipitate can occlude ions of low concentration. For example, samples with a high Ca concent (e.g., milk, bone, etc.) in the presence of sulfate ion can form insoluble calcium sulfate, causing the loss of Pb by coprecipitation. The presence of precipitates in the digest solution should be viewed with suspicion as a possible source of loss of analyte. If necessary, the precipitate should be analysed separately for the analyte to determine if it is necessary to avoid its formation or if it may be ignored in similar materials.

(d) *Volatilization losses:* If the element is in a volatile form or can be converted to a volatile form, it may be lost during the oxidation process when the temperature exceeds the vaporization temperature. Because mercury is quite volatile in almost any of its forms, special refluxing conditions are necessary to avoid its loss. Chlorine in the sample, in either the ionic or covalent form, can cause losses of metals such as Pb, Ge and As. For example, $PbCl_2$ can be lost through sublimation well below its melting point of 501 °C (Boyer & Laitinen, 1974). Care should be taken when ashing compounds, such as polyvinyl chloride (PVC), which contain covalent chlorine. At the high temperature required to ash PVC, chloride ion is released and may combine with and volatilize metals of interest.

(e) *Physical losses:* Excessive foaming can be a problem during ashing of high-carbohydrate materials, such as sugar. Spattering can result when high watercontent samples are dried too rapidly prior to ashing.

Primary ashing technique

Table 3 compares the advantages and disadvantages of wet and dry ashing.

(a) 'Wet ashing' refers to destruction of the organic matrix by reaction with oxygen produced by one or more reagents, such as HNO_3, H_2SO_4, $HClO_4$ or H_2O_2, in solution. While each of the oxidizing agents hat its own particular advantages, in many cases a combination of reagents is used to resolve a particular problem.

Nitric acid has a low boiling point (120 °C) and thus will tend to boil off before wet ashing is complete. This can be an advantage in that the excess acid can be boiled off before the determinative step. Nitric acid is often added to samples containing chlorides. The HNO_3 prevents the loss of the volatile metal chlorides by driving off the chlorides as NOCl.

Sulfuric acid, which has a considerably higher boiling point (338 °C), is often added to HNO_3 to raise the boiling point of the wet ashing liquid. It also acts as an oxidizing and dehydrating agent. When used by itself, it has a tendency to char organic samples and produce reducing conditions, which can cause loss of volatile compounds of As and Se. The high boiling point of H_2SO_4 makes removal of the excess acid difficult at the end of the wet ashing. For samples having a large amount of Ca (e.g., milk, cheese, etc.), precipitation of insoluble $CaSO_4$ may also coprecipitate Pb.

Perchloric acid is often used in combination with other acids and is a very strong oxidizing agent. Mixtures of HNO_3, H_2SO_4 and $HClO_4$ are used for wet ashing of difficult samples containing fat. Wet ashing with $HClO_4$ alone and in mixtures has been discussed extensively by Smith (1965). The hazards of using $HClO_4$ are dealt with by Smith (1965) and by the Analytical Methods Committee (1959).

Hydrogen peroxide is another strong oxidizing agent now available in high purity at strengths of 50% or more. An advantage of its use is that the only decomposition product other than O_2 is water.

An excellent and comprehensive review of mineralization procedures for the determination of trace metals in foods has been presented by Crosby (1977).

(b) 'Dry ashing' refers to oxidation of organic matter through the action of atmospheric O_2 at high temperatures. The objective of dry ashing is to oxidize and volatilize the organic matter while quantitatively retaining the elements of interest in

Table 3.   Comparison of wet and dry ashing

Wet ashing – advantages	Dry ashing – disadvantages
Low temperature minimizes volatilization losses	High temperatures promote volatilization losses
Liquid medium minimizes retention onto vessels	Dry conditions promote retention losses
Methods generally adaptable to wide variety of sample matrices for many different elements	Methods must be tailored to specific sample matrix for specific elements
Short ashing time required	Long ashing time required
Simple apparatus	Specialized and expensive equipment for ultra-trace analysis

Dry ashing – advantages	Wet ashing – disadvantages
Large sample size	Smaller sample size
Small amounts or no reagents required	Large amounts of reagents required
Very low blanks possible	Higher blanks
Minimal supervision required	Constant supervision required
Large number of samples handled easily	Few number of samples possible at a time
	Coprecipitation losses
	Some elements tend to volatilize (As, Hg and Se)

recoverable form and without contamination. In the trace element analysis of foods and other biological materials, the organic matter itself constitutes the principal source of interference.

Dry ashing involves four main steps:

(i) The first step, dehydration, is usually done in an oven at 60 to 120 °C to drive off moisture. Care must be taken to avoid losses through spattering and volatilization. If all moisture is not driven off, spattering losses may occur during elevation to the higher temperatures of the next step. Most samples can be dehydrated at 100 to 120 °C. Although volatilization is rarely a problem at these temperatures, some samples contain elements in a volatile form (e.g., $ZnCl_2$) that may be partially lost. If so, a 60 to 70 °C drying temperature with the addition of an ashing aid, as discussed later, may be appropriate. The first step is completed when the sample is dry.

(ii) The second step, volatilization and partial oxidation, is usually carried out under an infrared lamp or in a muffle furnace at less than 350 °C. In this step, fats, oils and other volatile and easily-oxidized organic compounds are driven off, so they will not ignite in a later step at higher temperatures. Care must be taken to avoid analyte loss through particle ejection, ignition and volatilization. If this step proceeds too vigorously, sample particles may be blown out, carried out with heavy smoke or foam out of the ashing vessel. Also, the sample may ignite, causing the temperature to rise uncontrollably with accompanying losses. Ashing aids that increase the ash bulk help to reduce particle loss and the hazard of ignition, as discussed later. The second step is completed when smoke is evolved from the charred sample at only a small rate.

(iii) The third step, complete oxidation, is usually carried out in a muffle furnace at 450 to 650 °C. Because it is practically impossible to maintain a uniform temperature within the furnace, sample dishes should always be placed in the muffle furnace in a random fashion to avoid introducing any systematic error due to hot or cold spots in the furnace. This step is completed when no carbonaceous material (black particles) remains. The main problems with the oxidation step are losses through incomplete oxidation, volatilization and absorption or retention, and formation of highly-insoluble refractory compounds. Below 450 °C, many organic materials are not completely oxidized. Above 650 °C, some compounds that are otherwise considered non-volatile may be lost. Incomplete oxidation can cause losses by failure to free an organically-bound element or by absorption of trace elements by carbon particles. Most volatilization losses occur during this step. Retention losses are due to the element of interest being unavailable for dissolution because it remains fixed to the vessel or the ash. Use of an ashing aid can both speed oxidation and reduce retention losses. Keeping the ashing temperature in the 450 to 500 °C range greatly reduces both volatilization and retention losses, at the sacrifice of some ashing speed. It is essential to keep the furnace temperature at the lowest level consistent with complete oxidation of the sample in a reasonable time.

(iv) The fourth step, dissolution, is usually accomplished by dissolving the ash in a dilute acid, which is frequently heated to assist dissolution. This step is finished when the sample ash is completely in solution. If the entire ash does not go into solution, it is important to ensure that the element of interest is not being retained by the insoluble material.

Although retained elements can be solubilized by extreme measures (e.g., hydrofluoric acid treatment), the object is to prevent retention in the first place. Elements with a positive oxidation potential (e.g., Cd, Pb) can react with silica to form stable insoluble silicates. Elements with a negative oxidation potential (e.g., Cu, Ag, Au) are reduced and diffuse into the silica. These reduced elements can also alloy with Pt vessels. Retention losses increase with increasing temperature, especially beyond 550 °C. Ionic chlorides (e.g., NaCl) promote retention losses in silica by weakening the silica bonds. These chlorides can be eliminated by using sulfating or nitrating ashing aids.

Ashing aids

An ashing aid is added to the sample to assist the oxidation process or to enhance the recovery of a particular element. Il can be added before or during the ashing process, but generally is added early in the process and should be mixed to make contact with all parts of the sample. The most serious problem with an ashing aid is possible contamination from the ashing aid itself.

The majority of the metals volatilize as chlorides. If the metal is in the chloride form in the sample matrix, treatment with sulfating or nitrating ash aids will usually produce nonvolatile forms. Metal chlorides can also be produced during the ashing process, however, due to breakdown of covalent chlorides (e.g., polyvinylchloride) and some ionic chlorides (e.g., NH_4Cl) with heat to produce HCl. The HCl can then react with many metals to form metal chlorides (e.g., $PbCl_2$ or $ZnCl_2$), which are volatile. The sulfating and nitrating aids do not work as well with covalent chlorides.

(a) *Wet ashing aids:* A number of reagents are used with wet ashing procedures as catalysts and/or oxidizing agents. Some of the more common reagents used are V_2O_5, NH_4VO_3, $KMnO_4$ and Na_2MoO_4. They tend to shorten the time required for the sample to be completely oxidized and minimize analyte losses by completing the oxidation under milder conditions. This is especially advantageous for As, Se and Hg.

(b) *Dry ashing aids:* Sulfuric acid dehydrates the organic matrix and sulfates volatile elements (e.g., Pb, Cd, Zn), making them more heat stable and thereby reducing volatility. It also eliminates ionic chlorides through the release of HCl (e.g., $2\,NaCl + H_2SO_4 \rightarrow 2\,HCL + Na_2SO_4$) at low temperature, reducing both retention and volatility losses. However, covalent chlorides are not eliminated as efficiently. The H_2SO_4 will slow down the rate of oxidation, but in doing so, it reduces the risk of ignition.

Nitric acid helps to oxidize the sample and nitrates the volatile elements, making them more heat-stable, while eliminating ionic chlorides. Most nitrates are heat-stable, but some $Cd(NO_3)_2$ is lost through volatilization, even at 550 °C. If HNO_3 is added too early in the ashing process, deflagration may occur with accompanying losses. Nitric acid should be added when only small amounts of organic matter remain.

Sodium, potassium or magnesium nitrate helps to oxidize and nitrate the sample much as HNO_3 does. These three nitrates add bulk to the final ash and help dilute the ash and reduce its contact with reactive surfaces, thereby lowering retention losses. An equimolar mixture of KNO_3 and $NaNO_3$ has been used for the dual purpose of completely destroying organic matter and serving as the supporting electrolyte for anodic stripping voltammetry (Holak, 1975).

Potassium sulfate produces sulfates of volatile elements much as H_2SO_4 does, but, unlike H_2SO_4, it does not volatilize chlorides. Il also adds bulk to the final ash, as does $Mg(NO_3)_2$.

Phosphoric acid promotes retention through formation of phosphosilicate glass with silica; thus its use as an ashing aid generally should be avoided. Alkaline carbonates and hydroxides are sometimes used as ashing aids in specific applications, usually to aid in retention of volatile elements, or to make interfering elements less available.

Ashing vessels

Wet ashing is usually carried out in small Kjeldahl flasks (e.g., 100 mL) or round-bottom flasks constructed of borosilicate glass. Quartz vessels are also used when borosilicate glass produces unacceptable levels of contamination (e.g., Al, Ti).

Dry ashings are usually carried out in beakers, dishes or crucibles constructed of quartz or Pt. Borosilicate glass, Vycor and glazed porcelain are less often used because of temperature limitations or contamination problems. A discussion of the types of construction materials follows.

Vitreous silica vessels are $> 99.9\%$ SiO_2. Common impurities in silica are Na, Al, Fe, Mg and Ti, at or below trace levels. High-purity quartz may contain less than 1 ppm of total metal contaminants. Silica resists HNO_3, H_2SO_4 and HCL up to 1000 °C. Phosphoric acid, hydrofluoric acid and alkali hydroxides and carbonates attack silica at elevated temperatures. Silica is not suitable for dry ashing samples containing high levels of K, Ca or Mg. It forms stable silicates with the oxide of many elements (e.g., Pb, Cd, Zn). Chlorides (e.g., NaCl) at high temperatures weaken the silica structure by replacing some of its oxygen with chlorine, thereby increasing its reactivity with metal oxides. The previous history of a silica vessel has an effect on its retention of metals; new vessels seem to be the worst offenders.

Platinum is usually alloyed with Ir and contains Cu and Fe as impurities. It can alloy with readily-reducible metals (e.g., Cu, Ag, Au) in the sample. Platinum resists HCl, HF, molten halides and sulfates. It has a working temperature of up to 1400 °C. The fused nitrates, nitrites, cyanides, oxides and hydroxides of Na and K attack Pt, as will mixtures of HNO_3 and HCl. Platinum dishes prevent retention of positive oxidation-potential elements (e.g., Cd, Pb) onto the ashing vessel, although these elements may still react with silica in the sample.

Vycor vessels are 95 to 96% SiO_2 and about 3% B_2O_3. The main impurities are Na, K and Al. Vycor, which has fewer impurities than Pyrex glass, but more than quartz, has about the same properties as quartz.

Borosilicate glass (Pyrex) has a low continuous-use working temperature of 500 °C. Its major components are Si, Al, Na, K, Ca, B and Ba, as well as relatively high trace levels of Mg, Fe, Ti, As and Sb. Any of its components can be leached out, but the main contaminant is Na. Metals (e.g., Pb) can be adsorbed onto the glass and at a later time be desorbed into solution.

Glazed porcelain has a fused glaze coating on a much more refractory body. Its working temperature is 1100 °C. The glaze determines the resistance to etching by the sample and nature of potential contamination of the sample. It is usually too contaminated for trace and ultra-trace analysis. Lead and copper are important impurities.

Other techniques

(a) *Low-temperature ashing (LTA):* Low-temperature ashing is a process whereby a gas plasma is generated by a high-frequency electromagnetic field in oxygen, air, or other gas to produce reactive atoms and radicals which react with organic material. Ideally, the reaction products are gaseous and these are purped away during the ashing, leaving a residual dry ash which contains most of the inorganic material in the sample. With LTA, complete destruction of organic material generally occurs below 100 °C. Because of the relatively low temperature, loss of trace elements by volatilization or by reaction with the vessel is decreased or eliminated.

Low-temperature ashing is not widely used at the present time because the instrumentation is expensive and the technique is time-consuming and limited to small quantities. However, since LTA is essentially a contamination-free technique, it can be used in special circumstances for analyses at very low levels.

(b) *Fusion:* Conventional fusions involve the treatment of the sample material with acidic, basic or nitrate fluxes at fairly high temperatures before determination of the element. However, if crucibles are used, the blank value is seldom sufficiently low or reproducible to permit reliable determination at submicrogram levels.

(c) *Teflon decomposition vessel:* Many of the drawbacks of conventional wet ashings can be eliminated by heating a small amount of an oxidizing acid, such as HNO_3, and a small sample in a closed-system Teflon decomposition vessel. This vessel typically consists of a metal jacket containing a Teflon cup, which is closed by a Teflon disk retained in a metal screw-cap. Several designs of Teflon vessels are commercially available, ranging in size from 25 to 125 mL and capable of withstanding pressures of about 1200 psi ($\sim$ 8 300 kPa).

The procedure for digesting food samples in a 70-mL Teflon vessel is as follows: the sample (not exceeding 0.3 g on a dry basis) is placed in the vessel, 5 mL HN), is added and the vessel is closed and placed in an oven at 150 °C for 1–2 hours. After cooling, the contents can be transferred to a volumetric flask and diluted to volume for the required determinations.

Some of the advantages of this procedure are: (a) volatilization losses are eliminated, (b) only a small volume of acid is required, (c) close analyst attention is not required, and (d) contamination problems are minimized. For safety reasons, it is important not to overload the vessel. Numerous published applications for Teflon vessels have been summarized by Uniseal Decomposition Vessels, Ltd (1982).

Special considerations for various elements (Gorsuch, 1979, and references cited below)

(a) *Arsenic:* Wet ashing with $HNO_3:HClO_4:H_2SO_4$ (4:1:1, v/v) mixture has been used successfully to digest materials before the determination of As by atomic absorption spectrophotometry, using the hydride-generation technique (Fiorino *et al.*, 1976). It is important not to allow the mixture to char, because losses of volatile As may occur, especially in the presence of covalent chlorine. Dry ashing oxidation can generally be carried out successfully in the presence of an ashing-aid, particularly $Mg(NO_3)_2$.

(b) *Beryllium:* Both wet ashing and dry ashing procedures have been used with mixed results. If low recoveries occur due to the formation of very insoluble BeO, the Be can be taken into solution by treatment of the ashed residue with HF.

(c) *Cadmium:* Wet ashing procedures have been widely used for the decomposition of a variety of samples for the determination of Cd, with no difficulty. In general, dry ashing procedures have not worked as well. Even at a temperature as low as 500 °C, Cd losses have been found to occur. The addition of HNO_3 to speed up the oxidation has, in some cases, made the losses even greater.

(d) *Chromium:* The destruction of organic matter prior to the determination of Cr is generally a straightforward procedure. Weg or dry ashing procedures can be used. However, losses of Cr by its retention on silica during dry ashing have been reported, as well as losses of Cr during wet ashing, presumably due to the formation of volatile CrO_2Cl_2. The presence of chromium in a food sample often indicates previous contact with stainless steel.

(d) *Lead:* Wet ashing procedures for Pb give uniformly good results with any of the common acid mixtures if the following precautions are observed: In the presence of high levels of the alkaline earth elements, H_2SO_4 forms insoluble compounds which may coprecipitate Pb. Thus, in the presence of large amounts of Ca, it is best to avoid H_2SO_4 if possible. Lead contamination in reagents, as well as glassware, can contribute significant errors in trace analysis. Dry ashing procedures, with and without ashing aids, at temperatures from 450 to 550 °C have been used successfully. Potential problems include losses of Pb due to valatilization and retention. The presence of covalent, as well as ionic, chlorine makes Pb losses even greater. Lead losses can also occur due to reaction of lead oxide with silica. The use of ashing aids at a temperature not exceeding 500 °C generally gives good results.

(f) *Nickel:* Either wet ashing or dry ashing in the presence of H_2SO_4 acid to sulfate the Ni is usually satisfactory for the determination of Ni in foods and tissues.

(g) *Selenium:* Wet ashing procedures are normally used for Se determinations, because losses occur during dry ashing. Losses due to Se volatilization have been reported for samples dried at 100 °C. Wet ashing using a $HNO_3:HClO_4:H_2SO_4$ (4:1:1, v/v) mixture gives good results if the reaction is carefully controlled and oxidizing conditions are maintained throughout the digestion (Fiorino *et al.*, 1976).

(h) *Zinc:* Wet or dry ashing procedures may be used for Zn determination. Acid hydrolytic methods have also given good results. Dry ashing procedures, with and without ashing aids, at temperatures from 450 to 900 °C have been used successfully. Potential problems include losses of Zn due to volatilization, and retention in the presence of high chloride. In the absence of a large amount of chlorides, good results can be obtained by ashing at or below 500 °C. If a large amount of chloride is present, wet ashing procedures should be used.

ANALYTE CONCENTRATION AND INTERFERENCE ELIMINATION

The ability to determine the level of any analyte is often complicated by the presence of interfering substances in the sample matrix. In addition to matrix problems, the analyte concentration in many samples may be at, or below, the quantification limit. Organic interfering substances are generally removed by the mineralization techniques described in the previous section. Following mineralization, further removal of inorganic interfering compounds and concentration of analyte may be required. The most frequently used techniques for this purpose are chelation alone, chelation followed by solvent extraction, adsorption by ion-exchange resins or chelation-adsorption by chelating ion-exchange resins.

Chelation-extraction

The most commonly used technique to eliminate interference is the formation of a metal chelate which may be subsequently concentrated by extraction into a non-polar solvent (Morrison & Freiser, 1957; Stary, 1964; Zolotov, 1970; Komarek & Sommer, 1982), Commonly used chelating agents include dithiocarbamates, β-diketones, diphenylthiocarbazone and quinolin-8-ol. Acetyl acetone is an example of a chelating agent which can also be the organic phase. When a smaller volume of organic solvent than aqueous solvent is used, a concentration increase can be achieved.

Ion-exchange resins

Ion-exchange resins can be used for the removal of interfering cations and anions and for the concentration of trace amounts of analyte from large volumes of sample (Samuelson, 1963; Komarek & Sommer, 1982). A strongly basic anion exchanger is used to separate anions of acidic, basic and neutral salts. A strongly acidic cation exchanger is used to concentrate and separate cationic solutes for determination.

Chelating ion-exchange resins

Chelating ion-exchange resins have increased specificity and decreased capacity compared to conventional ion-exchangers. The former consist of chelating ligands, such as dithiocarbamate or iminodiacetate (Chelex 100), attached to a solid support (Biechler, 1965; Baetz & Kenner, 1973). Polydithiocarbamate resins have been used to separate transition elements of interest from alkali earth elements (Barnes & Genna, 1979; Jones *et al.*, 1982). Chelating ion-exchange resins might also play a role in speciation (Miyazaki & Barnes, 1981).

DATA TREATMENT

One of the most commonly overlooked sources of error or variation in reported data is non-standardized data reduction and reporting procedures. The purpose of this section is to summarize the standard data reduction and reporting procedures most frequently used in those trace element analytical methods which destroy the sample matrix and present a portion of the sample to the measuring instrument as a solution containing the analyte. These data treatment procedures are not directly applicable to methods using non-destructive techniques, such as neutron activation analysis or X-ray fluorescence, which require little or no sample preparation. More extensive treatments are available in the publications of Natrella (1963), Ostle (1963), Youden and Steiner (1975) and Mendenhall and Ott (1976).

Definition of terms

(a) 'Standard solution reagent blank': the concentration of analyte in a solution containing the same reagents used to prepare calibration standard solutions (before the analyte is added).

(b) 'Sample solution reagent blank': the concentration of analyte acquired by a solution which was obtained by carrying out the entire analytical procedure employed with the sample being analysed, but did not include the sample.

(c) 'Replicate analyses': separate analyte determinations made by analysis of independent portions of the laboratory sample, which are carried through the

entire analytical method separately, but under identical conditions.
(d) 'Replicate measurements': separate determinative step measurements made on a single sample solution.
(e) 'Standard solution calibration curve': a linear regression plot of the response of the measuring instrument to the analyte *versus* the concentration of the analyte in the standard solution. Standard solution calibration curves should have at least five concentration levels (including zero, the standard solution reagent blank), with at least three measurements at each concentration, and must encompass the range that will include the concentrations of the samples. The three or more measurements at each concentration level should not be carried out consecutively, but should be randomly interspersed with measurements at different concentration levels.
(f) 'Standard additions analytical curve': a linear regression plot of the response of the measuring instrument to the analyte *versus* the concentration of analyte added to the sample solution being measured. Standard additions analytical curves should have at least three concentration levels (including zero added analyte). The added analyte levels should result in solutions with at least 2-times and 3-times the concentration for zero added analyte, or 5-times and 10-times the lowest concentration that can be quantified, whichever is greater.

Note: If there are no sample matrix effects, or no inherent bias in the measurement step, the slopes of the standard solution calibration curve and the standard additions analytical curve will be equal, and the slopes of standard additions analytical curves for dissimilar samples will also be equal. The standard additions analytical curve is normally used if either a sample matrix effect and/or an inherent bias in the measurement step is suspected.

Useful statistics

(a) *Mean,* $\bar{y}$: the sum of a set of measurements (or analyses) divided by the number (n) of measurements (y_i) (or analyses) in the set.

$$\bar{y} = \frac{\Sigma y_i}{n} = \frac{y_1 + y_2 \ldots + y_n}{n} \qquad \text{Equation 2}$$

(b) *Median* – (i) Odd number of measurements: the middle value when the measurements are arranged in order of magnitude; (ii) Even number of measurements: the mean of the two middle values when the measurements are arranged in order of magnitude.
(c) *Range:* the difference between the largest and smallest measurements.
(d) *Variance,* S^2: the sum of the squared deviations of the measurements from their

mean, divided ty (n – 1), where n is the number of measurements.

$$S^2 = \frac{\Sigma(y_i - \bar{y})^2}{n-1}$$ Equation 3

(e) *Standard deviation,* s: the positive square root of the variance.

$$s = \sqrt{S^2}$$ Equation 4

(f) *Relative standard deviation (RSD):* the standard deviation of a set of measurements divided by the average value, usually expressed as a percent (also called the coefficient of variation).

$$RSD(\%) = 100s/\bar{y}$$ Equation 5

(g) *95% Confidence interval (CI) of a set of n measurements:* the limits around the measured mean within which the mean value for an infinite number of measurements can be expected to be found with a probability of 0.95.

$$95\% \text{ C.I.} = \bar{y} \pm t\left(\frac{s}{\sqrt{n}}\right)$$ Equation 6

where t can be obtained from Table 4. One can say that 95% of all similarly constructed confidence bands would encompass the true answer. It does not mean that 95% of each set of readings will be in that confidence band. It can also be said that there is a 95% probability that the true answer lies between those limits. Other values, e.g., 90% or 99% CI, can also be used, which result in narrower or broader confidence bands.

(h) *Recovery (R) analyte from a fortified sample by a method of analysis:* the fraction of an analyte added to a sample (fortified sample), prior to analysis, which is measured (recovered) by the method. When the same analytical method is used to analyse both the unfortified and fortified sample, calculate %R as follows:

$$\%R = 100(C_f - C_u)/C_a$$ Equation 7

where C_f = concentration of analyte measured in fortified sample;
C_u = concentration of analyte measured in unfortified sample;
C_a = concentration of analyte added to fortified sample.
Note: C_a is a *calculated* value, not a value measured by the method being used.

The concentration of added analyte should be about the same (not less) than the concentration of analyte in the unfortified sample. The addition of analyte must not cause response of the measuring instrument to fall outside the linear portion of the standard curve. Both fortified and unfortified samples must be treated identically during analysis to minimize experimental bias.

Table 4.   The t-statistic for 95% confidence interval[a]

n	t	n	t
2	12.706	19	2.101
3	4.303	20	2.093
4	3.182	21	2.086
5	2.776	22	2.080
6	2.571	23	2.074
7	2.447	24	2.069
8	2.365	25	2.064
9	2.306	26	2.060
10	2.262	27	2.056
11	2.228	28	2.052
12	2.201	29	2.048
13	2.179	30	2.045
14	2.160	31	2.042
15	2.145	41	2.021
16	2.131	61	2.000
17	2.120	120	1.980
18	2.110		1.960

[a] Two-sided interval, $t_{1-\alpha/2} = t_{1-0.05/2} = t_{0.975}$

Linear regression

Linear regression computer programmes are readily available on both large computer systems and hand-held calculators. However, not all linear regression programmes are identical, particularly with regard to treatment of the sample reagent blank and multiple measurements. It is recommended that only programmes having the characteristics outlined below be used to calculate the slope and intercept of linear analytical curves. If suitable computer programmes are not available, the calculation procedure in Figure 2 may be used. For our present purposes it is necessary to calculate only through step 13 of Figure 2. In this approach, b_1 is the slope and b_0 is the intercept. When performing the linear regression calculation, the following rules are to be applied:

(a) The linear regression slope and intercept (i.e., regression coefficients) are computed by using the standard concentrations for the X values and their respective responses for the Y values.

(b) It is assumed that only the Y values contain measurement error.

(c) It is not assumed that the regression line has intercept = zero, that is, a value of zero is not to be entered for a blank solution unless it is actually the measured value. Also, computer programmes must not 'force' the intercept to be zero.

(d) If multiple measurements are made on a particular standard solution (or standard addition), then all the measurements are used for the linear regression calculation and not their mean.

Fig. 2. Basic worksheet for all types of linear relationships[a]

[a] Taken from Natrella (1963) pp. 5–10

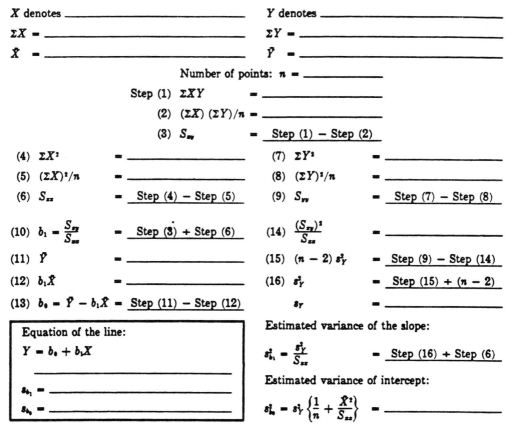

X denotes _____ Y denotes _____

ΣX = _____ ΣY = _____

$\bar{X}$ = _____ $\bar{Y}$ = _____

Number of points: n = _____

Step (1) ΣXY = _____

(2) $(\Sigma X)(\Sigma Y)/n$ = _____

(3) S_{xy} = Step (1) − Step (2)

(4) ΣX^2 = _____   (7) ΣY^2 = _____

(5) $(\Sigma X)^2/n$ = _____   (8) $(\Sigma Y)^2/n$ = _____

(6) S_{xx} = Step (4) − Step (5)   (9) S_{yy} = Step (7) − Step (8)

(10) $b_1 = \dfrac{S_{xy}}{S_{xx}}$ = Step (3) + Step (6)   (14) $\dfrac{(S_{xy})^2}{S_{xx}}$ = _____

(11) $\bar{Y}$ = _____   (15) $(n-2)s_Y^2$ = Step (9) − Step (14)

(12) $b_1\bar{X}$ = _____   (16) s_Y^2 = Step (15) + $(n-2)$

(13) $b_0 = \bar{Y} - b_1\bar{X}$ = Step (11) − Step (12) s_Y = _____

Equation of the line:

$Y = b_0 + b_1X$

_____

s_{b_1} = _____

s_{b_0} = _____

Estimated variance of the slope:

$s_{b_1}^2 = \dfrac{s_Y^2}{S_{xx}}$ = Step (16) + Step (6)

Estimated variance of intercept:

$s_{b_0}^2 = s_Y^2\left\{\dfrac{1}{n} + \dfrac{\bar{X}^2}{S_{xx}}\right\}$ = _____

If a linear regression computer programme is used, it may be checked for possession of the above attributes by comparison of the results it provides with those calculated using the procedure outlined in Figure 2.

Sample quantification using standard solution calibration curve

(NOTE: Use of this procedure does not correct for any sample matrix effects, or for inherent bias in a method. It should be used only if the absence of matrix effects and bias are verified by recovery measurements on matrices containing negligible amounts of analyte.)

Measure the instrument response to each of the working standard solutions being used to prepare the standard solution calibration curve.

Compute the slope and intercept from the resulting standard solution data, using linear regression. Construct the standard solutions calibration curve by plotting concentrations relative to the X-axis and the corresponding instrument responses relative to the Y-axis. Assign the standard reagent blank response(s) (Y-value) a corresponding X-value of O. Check the curve for acceptable linearity over the desired response range. Measure the instrument response for each sample solution and for the sample reagent blank solution(s).

Finally, determine the concentration of analyte in a sample as follows:

(a) Calculate each sample reagent blank concentration by dividing its measuring instrument response by the slope of the linear regression line of the calibration curve for the standard solution. Compute the mean sample reagent blank concentration.

(b) Calculate each sample concentration result by dividing its response to the measuring instrument by the slope of the linear regression line of the calibration curve for the standard solution.

(c) Calculate each net sample concentration result by subtracting the mean of the sample reagent blank concentration result(s) from the sample concentration result.

(d) Calculate final sample concentration result by multiplying the net sample concentration result by the 'dilution factor'.

Thus, the mass fraction, ω, of analyte in a sample is given by

$$\omega = (\rho_s - \rho_b)V/m \qquad \qquad \text{Equation 8}$$

where

ρ_s = mass concentration of analyte in sample solution
ρ_b = mass concentration of analyte in sample reagent blank
V = final volume of sample solution (should be same for both sample and sample reagent blank)
m = mass of original sample represented by V.

Example:

ρ_s = 9.8 mg/L
ρ_b = 0.1 mg/L
V = 50 mL
m = 10 g

$\overline{\omega}$ = 48.5 mg/kg

Sample quantification by standard addition analytical curve

(Use this procedure when sample matrix effects and/or biases in the measurement step are suspected.)

Measure the instrument response to the sample and reagent blank solutions. For each sample and reagent blank solution, fortify portions of the solution (or progressively fortify the solution itself) with a standard solution of the analyte to give concentrations approximately 2-times and 3-times the level present in the unfortified solution (or 5-times and 10-times the lowest level that can be quantified, whichever is greater). Measure the responses of the fortified solutions. Construct a standard addition analytical curve by plotting the concentration of added analyte relative to the X-axis *versus* the instrument response relative to the Y-axis for each sample and reagent blank solution. The unfortified response(s) (Y-value) is included with a corresponding X-value of zero (NOTE: Be sure to correct for volume change due to standard solution added if volume change is significant, i.e., taking the accuracy requirements for the data into consideration. Treat the negative X-axis intercept as having positive values.) Calculate the linear regression slope and X-axis intercept for each sample and sample reagent blank from the standard additions date.

Finally, determine the concentration of analyte present in the sample as follows:

(a) Calculate the concentration of each sample reagent blank solution by dividing its X-axis intercept by the slope of the standard additions analytical curve for the sample reagent blank.

(b) Calculate the concentration of each sample solution by dividing its X-axis intercept by the slope of the standard additions analytical curve for the sample solution.

(c) Calculate the mean sample and reagent blank concentrations independently.

(d) Calculate net sample concentration by subtracting the mean of the sample reagent blank concentration from each sample concentration.

(e) Calculate final sample concentration using Equation 8.

NOTE: If the blank value is greater than the sample value, the individual sample concentration may be reported as zero. However, if the sample value is to be averaged with other values, the negative result should be retained.

ACKNOWLEDGEMENTS

The authors gratefully acknowledge the contributions of Richard Albert, Paul Beavin, Stephen Capar, Curtis Edwards, Fred Fricke, Walter Holak, Michael Loges, Ronald Marts, Jerry McNerny, Kenneth Panaro, Helen Reynolds, Duane Satzger and Karen Wolnik of the US Food and Drug Administration.

REFERENCES

Analytical Methods Committee (1959) Notes on perchloric acid and its handling in analytical work. *Analyst, 84,* 214–215

Baetz, R.A. & Kenner, C.T (1973) Determination of heavy metals in foods. *J. Agric. Food Chem., 21,* 436–440

Barnes, R.M. & Genna, J.S. (1979) Concentration and spectrochemical determination of trace metals in urine with a poly (dithiocarbamate) resin and inductively coupled plasma – Atomic emission spectroscopy. *Anal. Chem., 51,* 1065–1070

Biechler, D.G. (1965) Determination of trace copper, lead, zinc, cadmium, nickel and iron in industrial waste waters by atomic absorption spectrometry after ion exchange concentration on Dowex A-1. *Anal. Chem., 37,* 1054–1055

Boyer, K.W. & Capar, S.G. (1977) Fortofication variability in rate diets fortified with arsenic, cadmium and lead. *J. Toxicol. environ. Health, 3,* 745–753

Boyer, K.W. & Laitinen, H.A. (1974) Lead halide aerosols: Some properties of environmental significance. *Environ. Sci. Technol., 13,* 1093–1096

Boyer, K.W., Horwitz, W. & Albert, R. (1985) Interlaboratory variability in trace element analysis. *Anal. Chem., 57,* 454–459

Crosby, N.T. (1977) Determination of metals in foods – A review. *Analyst, 102,* 225–268

Fiorino, J.A., Jones, J.W. & Capar, S.G. (1976) Sequential determination of arsenic, selenium, antimony and tellurium in foods *via* rapid hydride evolution and atomic absorption spectrometry. *Anal. Chem., 48,* 120–126

Gorsuch, T.T. (1970) *The Destruction of Organic Matter,* Oxford Pergamon Press

Holak, W. (1975) Determination of heavy metals in foods by anodic stripping voltammetry after sample decomposition with sodium and potassium nitrate fusion. *J. Assoc. off. anal. Chem., 58,* 777–780

Horwitz, W. & Albert, R. (1984) Performance of methods of analysis used for regulatory purposes. I. Drug dosage forms. A. Chromatographic separation/spectrophotometric measurement. *J. Assoc. off. anal. Chem., 67,* 81–90

Horwitz, W., Kamps, L.R. & Boyer, K.W. (1980) Quality assurance in the analysis of foods for trace constituents. *J. Assoc. off. anal. Chem., 63,* 1344–1354

Horwitz, W., Cohen, S., Haulein, L., Krett, J., Perrin, C.H. & Thornburg, W. (1978) *Analytical food chemistry.* In: S.L. Inhom, ed., *Quality Assurance Practices in Public Health Laboratories.* Washington DC, American Public Health Association, pp. 545–646

Jones, J.W. & Boyer, K.W. (1979) Sample homogenization procedure for determination of lead in canned foods. *J. Assoc. off. anal.Chem., 62,* 122–128

Jones, J.W., Capar, S.G. & O'Haver, T.C. (1982) Critical evaluation of a multi-element scheme using plasma emission and hydride evolution-atomic absorption spectrometry for the analysis of plant and animal tissues. *Analyst, 107,* 353–377

Komarek, J. & Sommer, L. (1982) Organic complexing agents in atomic absorption spectrometry – a review. *Talanta, 29,* 159–166

Mendenhall, W. & Ott, L. (1976) *Understanding Statistics,* 2nd Ed., Belmont, CA, Doxburg Press

Miller, W. & DeManna, G. (1980) Preparation of standards for plasma emission spectroscopy. *The Spex Speaker,* Year 25, Issue 3, 1–4

Miyazaki, A. & Barnes, R.M. (1981) Complexation of some transition metals, rare earth elements and thorium with a poly (dithiocarbamate) chelating resin. *Anal. Chem., 53,* 299–304

Moody, J.R. (1982) NBS clean laboratories for trace element analysis. *Anal. Chem., 54,* 1358A–1376A

Moody, J.R. & Lindstrom, R.M. (1977) Selection and cleaning of plastic containers for storage of trace element samples. *Anal. Chem., 49,* 2264

Morrison, G.H. & Freiser, H. (1957) *Solvent Extractions in Analytical Chemistry,* New York, NY, John Wiley & Sons, Inc.

National Bureau of Standards Special Publications 492 (1977) *Procedures used at the National Bureau of Standards to determine selected trace elements in biological and botanical materials.* R. Mavrodineanu, ed., Appendix XIV, p. 247

Natrella, M.G. (1963) *Experimental Statistics Handbook 91,* Reprinted, US Department of Commerce

Ostle, B. (1963) *Statistics in Research,* 2nd E. Ames, IA, The Iowa State University Press

Samuelson, O. (1963) *Ion Exchange Separations in Analytical Chemistry.* New York, NY, John Wiley & Sons, Inc.

Smith, G.F. (1965) *The Wet Chemical Oxidation of Organic Compositions Employing Perchlorid Acid.* Columbus, OH, The G. Frederick Smith Chemical Co. Inc.

Stary, J. (1964) *The Solvent Extraction of Metal Chelates.* New York, NY, Macmillan

Tschopel, P. & Tolg, G. (1982) Comments on the accuracy of analytical results in ng – and pg – trace analysis of the elements. *J. Trace Microprobe Tech., 1,* 1–77

Uniseal Decomposition Vessels Ltd (1982) *A Literature Study on Applications of Uniseal Decomposition Vessels in Chemical Analysis and Research 1968–1982.* Uniseal Decomposition Vessels Ltd. PO Box 9463, Haifa, Israel, IFU 7602

Ward, A. (1978) Stock standard preparation. *Jarrell-Ash Plasma Newsletter, 1,2,* 13–15

Youden, W.J. & Steiner, E.H. (1975) *Statistical Manual of the AOAC.* Arlington, VA, Association of Official Analytical Chemists

Zief, M. & Mitchell, J.W. (1976) *Contamination Control in Trace Element Analysis.* New York, NY, John Wiley & Sons, Inc.

Zolotov, Y.A. (1970) *Extraction of Chelate Compounds.* Ann Arbor, MI, Ann Arbor-Humphrey Science Publishers

METHODS

Determination of metals and their compounds in work-place air

METHOD 1 – DETERMINATION OF ARSENIC, CHROMIUM, NICKEL, CADMIUM, LEAD, BERYLLIUM AND SELENIUM IN AIR AND AIRBORNE PARTICULATES BY INDUCTIVELY-COUPLED ARGON PLASMA ATOMIC EMISSION SPECTROSCOPY

Adapted from Method 7300, NIOSH 'Manual of Analytical Methods',
3rd Ed., Vol. 1 (1984)

1. SCOPE AND FIELD OF APPLICATION

This method is suitable for the simultaneous determination of the title elements in air over the range $5\,\mu g$ to $2\,mg/m^3$, with an estimated limit of detection of $1\,\mu g$/sample. (The method may also be used for Ag, Al, Ca, Co, Cu, Fe, Li, Mg, Mn, Mo, Na, P, Pt, Sn, Te, Ti, TI, V, W, Y, Zn and Zr. See Eller, P.M., ed., 1984).

2. REFERENCE

Eller, P.M., ed. (1984) *NIOSH Manual of Analytical Methods,* 3rd Ed., Vol. 1, Cincinnati OH, U.S. Department of Health and Human Services, Method 7300

3. DEFINITIONS

Not applicable.

4. PRINCIPLE

A known volume of air is drawn through a cellulose ester membrane filter by means of a personal sampling pump. The filters are treated with a mixture of concentrated nitric and perchloric acids and the clear solution evaporated to dryness. The residue is dissolved in a dilute acid mixture and the analytes determined by inductively-coupled argon plasma atomic emission spectroscopy (ICP-AES).

5. HAZARDS

Perchloric acid (70%) will explode in contact with organic materials, or by shock or heat, and is a strong irritant. All digestions should be performed in a perchloric acid hood.

6. REAGENTS[1]

Argon	Grade suitable for argon plasma
Nitric acid, concentrated	68–71%, specific gravity 1.42
Perchloric acid, concentrated	70%
Distilled, deionized water	
Ashing acid	4:1 (v/v) nitric acid:perchloric acid (mix 4 volumes concentrated nitric acid with 1 volume concentrated perchloric acid)
Dilution acid	4% nitric acid:1% perchloric acid (add 50 mL ashing acid to 600 mL distilled water and dilute to 1 L)
Calibration stock solutions	1.00 g/L solutions of each of the elements of interest. Obtain commercially or prepare according to instrument manufacturers instructions
Calibration standard solutions	10 mg/L (add 1.0 mL of stock solution to 5 mL of dilution acid and dilute to 100 mL with distilled water). Prepare separate solutions for Pb and As. Ni, Be and Cd may be combined in one standard, and Cr and Se in another. Prepare fresh weekly.

7. APPARATUS[1]

Sampler unit	Cellulose ester membrane filter, 0.8-μm pore size, 37-mm diam., in cassette filter-holder (Millipore Filter Corp., Bedford, Mass., or equivalent)

---

[1] Reference to a company and/or product is for the purpose of information and identification only and does not imply approval or recommendation of the company and/or product by the International Agency for Research on Cancer, to the exclusion of others which may also be suitable.

Personal sampling pump	1 to 4 L/min, with flexible connecting tubing. Calibrate pump with a representative sampler in line (accuracy, $\pm 5\%$), using a bubble-meter or equivalent device. Record air temperature and pressure during calibration
Inductively-coupled plasma atomic emission spectrometer	Equipped as specified by the manufacturer for the analysis of the elements of interest
Regulator	Two-stage, for argon cylinder
Beakers	Phillips, 125-mL, or Griffin, 50-mL, with watch-glass covers
Volumetric flasks	10-mL and 100-mL
Volumetric pipettes	Various sizes
Hotplate	Surface temperature, 150 °C.

NOTE: Clean all glassware with concentrated nitric acid and rinse thoroughly before use.

8. SAMPLING

8.1 Assemble filter in the cassette filter-holder. Support filter by a stainless-steel screen or cellulose back-up pad. Close firmly to prevent sample leakage around the filter and seal the holder with plastic tape or shrinkable cellulose band.

8.2 Remove filter-holder plugs and attach holder to sampling pump tubing. Fix holder to workers' lapel and sample at an accurately-known flow rate between 1 and 4 L/min for total sample size of 5–1 000 L (Cr, Ni), 50–2 000 L (Pb, As), 13–2 000 L (Cd, Se) or 1 250–2 000 (Be). Do not exceed filter loading of $\simeq 2$ mg total dust. Record ambient temperature and pressure.

8.3 Take two to four replicate samples (for quality control) for each set of ten field samples.

8.4 Prepare at least two field blanks (maximum of ten) for each set of ten samples. The field blanks consist of sampler units from the same lot used for sample collection. They must be handled in all respects like the units used for air sampling, but no air should be drawn through them.

9. PROCEDURE

9.1 *Blank tests*

9.1.1 Field blanks: see 8,4, follow procedures 9.4 and 9.5.

9.1.2   Media blanks: approximately 5 media blanks should be analysed with every set of ten samples. Media blanks are unused sampling units taken from the same lot as those used for sample collection, but not sent to the field. Follow procedures 9.4, 9.5.

9.1.3   Reagent blanks: follow the analytical procedure beginning with step 9.4.2. Analyse one reagent blank per ten samples, and whenever reagents are renewed.

9.2 *Check test*

Not applicable.

9.3 *Test portion*

Not applicable.

9.4 *Sample extraction and preparation for ICP-AES*

9.4.1   Open the cassette filter-holders and transfer the filters to clean beakers (discard back-up pad).

9.4.2   Add 5 mL ashing acid to each beaker and cover with a watchglass. Let stand 30 min at room temperature.

9.4.3   Heat on hotplate (120 °C) until ± 0.5 mL remains.

9.4.4   Add 2 mL ashing acid and repeat 9.4.3.

9.4.5   Repeat 9.4.4 until solution is clear, then rinse watchglass into beaker with distilled water.

9.4.6   Heat to 150 °C and evaporate to dryness.

9.4.7   Dissolve residue in 2 to 3 mL of dilution acid (6) and transfer quantitatively to 10-mL volumetric flask. Dilute to volume with dilution acid and retain for ICP-AES.

9.5 *Analyte determination by ICP-AES*

9.5.1   Set the instrument conditions as specified by the manufacturer. The wavelengths for the title analytes are as follow:

chromium:	205.6 nm	arsenic:	193.7 nm
nickel:	231.6 nm	selenium:	190.6 nm
lead:	220.4 nm	beryllium:	313.0 nm
cadmium:	226.5 nm		

9.5.2   Analyse the extracts (9.4.7) and calibration standards (6) for each analyte (analyse a standard for every ten samples). Typically, a two-point standardization (dilution acid and 10 mg/L standard) is used. Obtain instrument output in the concentration mode, corrected for background and spectral line overlap.

10. METHOD OF CALCULATION

Obtain the mass concentrations of the analyte in the sample and media-blank extracts from the instrument.

The mass concentration, ρ_a (mg/m^3), of the analyte in the air sample is given by

$$\rho_a = (\rho_s - \rho_b)\, v/V$$

where

ρ_s = mass concentration of analyte in sample extract (μg/mL)

ρ_b = average mass concentration of analyte in media-blank extracts (μg/mL)

v   = final volume of extracts (9.4.7) (mL)

V   = volume of air sample (L)

NOTE: For personal sampling pumps with rotameters only, the correct air volume, V, is given by

$$V = \frac{Ft}{1\,000}\, (P_1 T_2 / P_2 T_1)^{0.5}$$

where

F   = indicated flow rate (L/min)

t   = sampling time (min)

P_1 = pressure during calibration

P_2 = pressure during sampling (same units as P_1)

T_1 = temperature during calibration (°K)

T_2 = temperature during sampling (°K).

11. REPEATABILITY AND REPRODUCIBILITY

Precision and recovery data have been determined at 2.5 μg and 1 mg of each element per sample on spiked filters, using a Jarrell-Ash Model 1160 ICP-AES.

Element	Recovery (%)		Coefficient of variation (%)[a]	
	2.5 µg per filter	1 mg per filter	2.5 µg per filter	1 mg per filter
Cadmium	107	99	3.2	2.0
Chromium	98	106	5.3	1.6
Nickel	105	97	2.7	2.0
Lead	105	95	6.0	1.1
Arsenic	103	99	6.2	2.6
Selenium	105	97	6.8	4.9
Beryllium	107	90	4.0	3.4

[a] N = 3.

12. NOTES ON PROCEDURE

Not applicable.

13. SCHEMATIC REPRESENTATION OF PROCEDURE

Sample air with cellulose ester filter
↓
Digest filter in 5 mL 4:1 (v/v)
conc. nitric acid:conc. perchloric acid
↓
Evaporate to $\simeq 0.5$ mL (120 °C)
↓
Repeat digestion with 2 mL 4:1 acids until solution clear
↓
Evaporate to dryness (150 °C)
↓
Dissolve residue in 4% nitric acid:1% perchloric acid
and make up to 10 mL
↓
Analyse by ICP-AES

14. ORIGIN OF THE METHOD

Method 7300, NIOSH Manual of Analytical Methods, 3rd Ed., Vol. 1 (1984)

Contact point: P.M. Eller
National Institute for Occupational Safety and Health
Division of Physical Sciences and Engineering
4676 Columbia Parkway
Cincinnati, OH 45226
USA

METHOD 2 – DETERMINATION OF ARSENIC IN AIR AND AIRBORNE PARTICULATES BY ATOMIC ABSORPTION SPECTROPHOTOMETRY

Adapted from Method 7901, NIOSH 'Manual of Analytical Methods',
3rd Ed., Vol. 1 (1984)

1. SCOPE AND FIELD OF APPLICATION

This method employs a small portable filter and a personal sampling pump and is suitable for the determination of vaporous and particulate arsenic in air. Arsine is not collected by the sampling method described.

The method has been evaluated over the range of 0.670–32.2 $\mu g/m^3$ for a 400-L air sample using an instrument with a sensitivity of 0.066 ng arsenic/0.0044 absorbance units. The lower limit of detection (2 S.D.) was 0.15 $\mu g/m^3$, for a 400-L air sample, and the upper limit may be extended by dilution. The working range is 1–60 $\mu g/m^3$ for a 200-L sample.

Copper (II) nitrate, chloride and sulfate have been shown not to interfere at concentrations up to 50 times the arsenic concentration.

Approximately 40 samples can be analysed in an 8-hour day.

2. REFERENCE

Carlin, L.M., Colovos, G., Garland, D., Jamin, M.E., Klenck, M., Long, T.J. & Nealy, C.L. *Analytical Methods Evaluation and Validation - As, Ni, W, V, Talc, and Wood Dust,* Rockwell International, Final Report on NIOSH Contract No. 210-79-0060, available as Order No. PB 83-155325 from NTIS, Springfield, VA 22161

Criteria for a Recommended Standard ... Occupational Exposure to Inorganic Arsenic (1975) U.S. Department of Health, Education and Welfare, Publ. (NIOSH) 75–149

Eller, P.M., ed. (1984) *NIOSH Manual of Analytical Methods,* 3rd Ed., Vol. 1, Cincinnati OH, U.S. Department of Health and Human Services, Method 7901.

3. DEFINITIONS

Not applicable.

4. PRINCIPLE

Air is drawn through a sodium carbonate-impregnated cellulose ester filter, to collect vaporous and particulate arsenic. The filter and back-up pad are digested with nitric acid, followed by hydrogen peroxide, and the residue taken up in 1% nitric acid. Nickel nitrate is added for matrix modification and arsenic is determined by graphite-furnace atomic absorption spectrophotometry.

5. HAZARDS

Cleaning of glassware with hot, concentrated nitric acid and sample digestion should be carried out under a fume hood (see 12. NOTES ON PROCEDURE).

6. REAGENTS[1]

All reagents should be ACS reagent grade, or better.

Argon	High purity, in a compressed gas cylinder
Water	Distilled or deionized
Glycerol	
Nitric acid	70% (w/w), redistilled in glass
Nitric acid, 1%	Dilute 10 mL 70% acid to 1 L with distilled water
Hydrogen peroxide	30% (w/w)
Nickel nitrate	
Sodium carbonate	
Sodium carbonate: glycerol solution	1 mol/L sodium carbonate: glycerol (20:1, (v/v) (Dissolve 9.5 g sodium carbonate in 100 mL distilled water and add 5 mL pure glycerol)
Nickel standard solution	Contains 1 000 mg Ni^+/L in 1% nitric acid (Take 4.95 g nickel nitrate and make up to 1.00 L with 1% nitric acid)

---

[1] Reference to a company and/or product is for the purpose of information and identification only and does not imply approval or recommendation of the company and/or product by the International Agency for Research on Cancer, to the exclusion of others which may also be suitable.

Arsenic stock standard solution

Use a commercially-prepared standard, containing 1 000 mg As/L. (J.T. Baker Chem. Co., Phillipsville, NJ, or equivalent) or dissolve 1.320 g primary standard As_2O_3 in 25 mL 200 g/L KOH. Neutralize with 20% (v/v) HNO_3 to phenolphthalein end point and dilute to 1 L with 1% HNO_3.

Arsenic working standard solutions

A. Dilute arsenic stock standard solution 1→100 with nickel standard solution to obtain 10 mg/L arsenic solution. Prepare fresh daily.
B. Prepare working standards to cover the range 0 to 1.25 μg/mL by adding aliquots of solution A to 10-mL volumetric flasks and diluting to volume with nickel standard solution.

7. APPARATUS[1]

Air filter units

Cassette assembly containing cellulose ester membrane filter (37-mm diam., 0.8-μm pore size) and cellulose back-up pad. (Millipore Corporation, Bedford, Mass., or equivalent) Prepare before use as follows: remove inlet plug from loaded cassette and add 250 μL of sodium carbonate:glycerol solution directly onto filter (wet entire surface). Draw 30–60 L of clean air through the filter, then allow to dry overnight. Replace inlet plug. Use within one week.

Personal sampling pump

Capable of sampling through impregnated filter unit at 1 to 3 L/min.
The pump must be calibrated to within ±5% with a representative filter unit in line and must be capable of maintaining a pressure drop of 51 cm of water across the impregnated filter unit over a period of 4 h. Record ambient temperature and pressure during calibration if pump is fitted with a rotameter.

---

[1] Reference to a company and/or product is for the purpose of information and identification only and does not imply approval or recommendation of the company and/or product by the International Agency for Research on Cancer, to the exclusion of others which may also be suitable.

Atomic absorption spectro-photometer (AAS)	Equipped with graphite furnace atomizer, electrodeless discharge lamp (+ power supply) for arsenic, readout device (recorder or digital peak-height analyser), gas control system for argon, pipetting system and simultaneous deuterium background corrector. Reproducible control of times and temperatures during drying, charring and atomatization cycles is essential.

Glassware (borosilicate)
  Volumetric pipettes
  Volumetric flasks
  Beakers
  Watchglasses
	See 12. NOTES ON PROCEDURE
	1.0, 2.0, 4.0, 6.0, 8.0, 10.0 and 100.0-mL
	10.0, 100.0 and 1000.0-mL
	50-mL, Griffin; or 125-mL, Phillips
	To cover beakers

Steam bath	
Ultrasonic bath	
Micropipette	250-µL
Regulator	Two-stage, for argon

8. SAMPLING

8.1 Remove plugs from cassette and attach to personal sampling pump by means of flexible tubing. Clip the cassette to the workers' lapel. (Air should enter the cassette directly, without passing through any tubing).

8.2 Adjust the flow rate to an accurately-known value between 1 and 3 L/min. A sample volume of 400 L is recommended. Check sampling rate frequently to ensure it has not changed. Record sampling time, air flow-rate, ambient temperature and pressure.

8.3 Replace plugs and ship, if necessary, without subjecting cassette to excessive vibration or shocks.

9. PROCEDURE

9.1 *Blank test*

9.1.1 Field blanks: with each batch of ten (or less) samples, take two impregnated filter units from the same lot. Ship, store and determine arsenic as for the batch of samples.

9.1.2   Media blanks: analyse about 5 media blanks with every set of 10 samples. Media blanks are unused, impregnated filter units taken from the same lot as those used for sampling, but not sent to the field.

9.2 *Check test*

Not applicable.

9.3 *Test portion*

Not applicable.

9.4 *Digestion of samples*

9.4.1   Open the cassette and carefully remove filter and back-up pad with clean tweezers. Transfer filter and pad to a beaker.

9.4.2   Add 15 mL of 70% nitric acid to each beaker, cover with a watchglass and reduce volume to about 1 mL on a hotplate at 150 °C.

9.4.3   With deionized water, rinse each watchglass and the sides of the beaker into the sample solution and add 6 mL of 30% hydrogen peroxide.

9.4.4   Place each beaker on a steam bath and evaporate just to dryness.

9.4.5   Cool each beaker, add 10.0 mL of nickel standard solution (section 6) and sonicate for 30 min in ultrasonic bath. Record final volume of solution.

9.5 *Determination of arsenic by AAS*

9.5.1   AAS operating conditions

Wavelength:	193.7 nm
Drying cycle:	100 °C, 70 s.
Charring cycle:	1 300 °C, 30 s.
Atomization cycle:	2 700 °C, 10 s.
Graphite atomizer:	non-pyrolytic tube
Readout mode:	peak-height in absorbance mode is most precise
Background correction:	simultaneous deuterium background correction is recommended.

9.5.2   AAS procedure

Inject 25-μL aliquots of working standard solutions and solution from

9.4.5 into the graphite furnace, in accordance with instrument manufacturers' instructions. (Inject a standard for every 2 samples to check instrument drift.)

9.6 *Calibration curve*

Construct a calibration curve of absorbance peak-height *versus* arsenic concentration (µg/mL), using the working standard solutions and the instrumental conditions employed in 9.5.1.

9.7 *Recovery*

For every 10 samples, prepare 2 spiked media blanks (add stock standard solution containing a known amount of As to an impregnated filter unit – use an amount of As roughly equal to that expected in samples). Dry overnight, then digest and determine As as in 9.4 and 9.5. Correct final result for recovery if recoveries of <90% are obtained.

10. METHOD OF CALCULATION

The mass concentration, ρ_a (mg/m^3), of arsenic in an air sample is given by

$$\rho_a = \frac{\rho_s V_s - \rho_b V_b}{V}$$

where

ρ_s = mass concentration or arsenic found in sample solution (9.4.5), calculated from absorbance peak-height and calibration curve (µg/mL)

V_s = final volume of sample solution in 9.4.5 (mL)

ρ_b = average mass concentration of arsenic found in media blank solution (9.4.5) (µg/mL)

V_b = final volume of blank solution in 9.4.5 (mL)

V = volume of air sample (L)

NOTE: For sampling pumps with rotameters only, the volume, V, is given by

$$V = \frac{Ft}{1\,000} \left(\frac{P_1 T_2}{P_2 T_1}\right)^{1/2}$$

where

F = sampling flow-rate (L/min)

t   = sampling time (min)

P_1 = ambient pressure during pump calibration (atm)

T_1 = ambient temperature during pump calibration (°K)

P_2 = ambient pressure during sampling (atm)

T_2 = ambient temperature during sampling (°K)

11. REPEATABILITY AND REPRODUCIBILITY

The coefficient of variation for the total sampling and analytical procedure was found to be 7.5% for the range 0.67–32.2-μg/m^3 (the detailed statistical treatment may be found in the first reference cited in section 2).

The recovery of arsenic from spiked filters was determined to be 100.5% ($\pm 2\%$) at the 6.5-μg/m^3 level.

The collection efficiency for arsenic trioxide vapour was 93%.

Stability studies of 'generated' samples showed that the mean analytical result after 14 days storage was the same as that after 1 day, at the 95% confidence level.

12. NOTES ON PROCEDURE

New glassware must be cleaned by soaking 2 to 8 h in hot, concentrated nitric acid, followed by rinsing with distilled or deionized water.

After each use, the glassware should be washed with detergent solution, deionized water, dilute nitric acid (soak 4 h or longer) and distilled water, in that order.

13. SCHEMATIC REPRESENTATION OF PROCEDURE

Pump 400 mL air sample through sodium carbonate-impregnated
membrane filter and back-up pad
↓
Digest filter and pad in 15 mL, 70% nitric acid
↓
Reduce volume to $\simeq 1$ mL and add 6 mL, 30% hydrogen peroxide
↓
Evaporate to dryness
↓
Dissolve residue in 10.0 mL of 1 g/mL nickel in 1% nitric acid
↓
Inject aliquot into graphite furnace AAS
↓

Calculate arsenic concentration from absorbance peak-height,
calibration curve and air sample volume.

14. ORIGIN OF THE METHOD

Method 7901, NIOSH Manual of Analytical Methods, 3rd Ed., Vol. 1 (1984)

Contact point: P.M. Eller
National Institute for Occupational Safety and Health
Division of Physical Sciences and Engineering
4676 Columbia Parkway
Cincinnati, OH 4526
USA

METHOD 3 – SPECIATION OF PARTICULATE ARSENICALS IN AIR BY ION-EXCHANGE CHROMATOGRAPHY WITH ATOMIC ABSORPTION PHOTOSPECTROMETRIC DETECTION

Adapted from Method P & CAM 320, NIOSH 'Manual of Analytical Methods',
2nd Edition, Vol. 6 (1980)
and from Method 5022, NIOSH 'Manual of Analytical Methods',
3rd Edition, Vol. 1 (1984)

1. SCOPE AND FIELD OF APPLICATION

This method employs a portable filter and sampling pump and has been found to be suitable for the separation and quantification of the particulate organoarsenic compounds, monomethylarsonic acid, dimethylarsenic acid and p-aminophenylarsonic acid, as well as inorganic arsenic [III] and arsenic [V]. The detection limits for these compounds (as As) are 0.72, 0.62, 0.64, 0.71 and 0.46 $\mu g/m^3$, respectively, using a 300-L air sample. The optimum working range for all these particulates is 1.7–6.7 $\mu g/m^3$, but the upper limit can be raised by using more concentrated standards and a smaller injection loop. The method is not suitable for the collection of As_2O_3 (see Method 1). About 15 samples can be analysed in an 8-hour day.

2. REFERENCE

Eller, P.M., ed. (1984) *NIOSH Manual of Analytical Methods,* 3rd Ed., Vol. 1, Cincinnati OH, U.S. Department of Health and Human Services, Method 5022

Ricci, G., Shepard, S., Hester, N. & Colovos, G. (1981) *Suitability of various filtering media for the collection and determination of organoarsenicals in air.* In: Choudhary, G., ed., *Chemical Hazards in the Workplace,* ACS Symp. Ser. 149, Washington, DC, American Chemical Society, pp. 383–399

Taylor, D.G., ed. (1980) *NIOSH Manual of Analytical Methods,* 2nd Ed., Vol. 6, P & CAM 320, Cincinnati, OH, U.S. Department of Health and Human Services

3. DEFINITIONS

Not applicable.

4. PRINCIPLE

Particulate arsenicals are collected on a 37-mm, 1-μm pore-size polytetrafluoro-ethylene (PTFE), polyethylene-backed, membrane filter and are extracted by ultrasonic agitation in aqueous carbonate:bicarbonate:borate buffer. The buffer extract is passed through an anion-exchange chromatographic column and the separated arsenical species are converted to gaseous arsines. These pass through a quartz furnace at 800 °C and are detected by atomic absorption spectrophotometry.

5. HAZARDS

Potassium persulfate is moderately toxic, a strong irritant, and constitutes a fire risk in contact with organic materials. Arsine gas is extremely toxic and can be fatal. The arsenic compounds used in the stock standards are poisonous.

6. REAGENTS[1]

All reagents should be ACS reagent grade, or better.

Argon   High purity, in compressed-gas cylinder

Deionized water

Sodium carbonate
(Na_2CO_3)

Sodium bicarbonate
($NaHCO_3$)

Sodium tetraborate
($Na_2B_4O_7 \cdot 10H_2O$)

Potassium persulfate   Saturated in 15% (v/v) HCl
($K_2S_2O_8$)

Sodium borohydride
($NaBH_4$)

Potassium hydroxide   Pellets
(KOH)

---

[1] Reference to a company and/or product is for the purpose of information and identification only and does not imply approval or recommendation of the company and/or product by the International Agency for Research on Cancer, to the exclusion of others which may also be suitable.

Monomethylarsonic acid	Reference purity available from the Ansul Co., Weslaco, Texas, USA.
Dimethylarsenic acid	Reference purity available from the Ansul Co., Weslaco, Texas, USA.
p-Aminophenylarsonic acid	Reference purity available from Matheson, Coleman & Bell, Norwood, Ohio, USA
Arsenic trioxide (As_2O_3)	
Arsenic pentoxide (As_2O_5)	
Hydrochloric acid (HCl)	15% (v/v)
Sodium hydroxide solution	1 mol/L, in deionized water
Potassium persulfate solution	Saturated, in 15% HCl
Sodium borohydride in potassium hydroxide solution	Add 5 g $NaBH_4$ and 1 g KOH to deionized water and dilute to 500 mL. Prepare fresh weekly.
Monomethylarsonic acid stock standard solution (1000 mg As/L)	Dissolve 0.9341 g $CH_3AsO_3H_2$ in deionized water and dilute to 500 mL.
Dimethylarsenic acid stock standard solution (1 000 mg As/L)	Dissolve 0.9210 g $(CH_3)_2AsO_2$ in deionized water and dilute to 500 mL.
p-Aminophenylarsonic acid stock standard solution (1 000 mg As/L)	Dissolve 1.4485 g p-$H_2NC_6H_4$-AsO_3H_2 in 5 ml of 1 mol/L NaOH and dilute to 500 mL with deionized water. Protect from light.
Arsenic trioxide stock standard solution (1 000 mg As/L)	Dissolve 0.6602 g As_2O_3 in 5 ml of 1 mol/L NaOH and dilute to 500 mL with deionized water.
Arsenic pentoxide stock standard solution (1 000 mg As/L)	Dissolve 0.7669 g As_2O_5 in 5 mL of 1 mol/L NaOH and dilute to 500 mL with deionized water.
Eluent A (0.0024 mol/L $NaHCO_3$: 0.0019 mol/L Na_2CO_3: 0.001 mol/L $Na_2B_4O_7$)	Dissolve 0.8067 g $NaHCO_3$, 0.8055 g Na_2CO_3 and 1.5257 g $Na_2B_4O_7 \cdot 10H_2O$ in 4 L deionized water.

Eluent B (0.005 mol/L $Na_2B_4O_7$)	Dissolve 7.6284 g $Na_2B_4O_7 \cdot 10H_2O$ in 4 L deion-ized water.
Mixed-analyte intermediate standard solution (5.0 mg As/L)	Mix equal portions of each of the five stock stan-dard solutions and dilute with eluent A so as to obtain a mixed solution containing 1.0 mg As/L from each analyte. Prepare fresh daily.
Mixed-analyte working standard solutions	Prepare working standards containing 10, 20, 40, 60 and 80 µg/L of each analyte (as As) by diluting 1, 2, 4, 6 and 8 mL of the mixed intermediate standard to 100 mL with eluent A. Prepare fresh daily.

7.   APPARATUS[1]

7.1 *Personal air sample collection*

Filter holder	3-piece polystyrene cassette, for 37 mm diam. fil-ters. (Millipore Corp., Bedford, Mass., USA, or equivalent).
PTFE membrane filters	Polyethylene-backed, 37-mm diam., 1.0 µm pore size (Millipore, type FA, or equivalent), with cel-lulose back-up pad.
Personal sampling pump	Calibrated with a representative filter assembly to an accuracy of ± 5% at the recommended flow rate of 1.5 L/min. Note ambient temperature and pres-sure during calibration.
Timer	
Forceps	
Beaker covering	e.g., watch glass, Parafilm, etc., to prevent sample loss during ultrasonic agitation.

7.2 *Ion-exchange chromatography (IC) system*

Ion-exchange chromato-graph	Pre-column, 3 mm i.d. × 150 mm (anion); separa-tor column, 3 mm i.d. × 150 mm (anion) (Dionex Corp., Sunnyvale, CA, USA). Modify chromato-graph so that effluent from separator column pass-es directly (*via* microbore Teflon tubing) into the arsine generation system (see Fig. 1).

---

[1] Reference to a company and/or product is for the purpose of information and identification only and does not imply approval or recommendation of the company and/or product by the International Agency for Research on Cancer, to the exclusion of others which may also be suitable.

| Microbore Teflon tubing | Dionex (0.3 mm i.d. × 0.6-mm o.d.), not more than 45 cm in length. |
| Plastic syringe | 10-mL (graduated), with male Luer fitting. |

7.3 *Arsine generation system*

Proportioning pump	Technicon (Technicon Instrument Corp., Tarrytown, NY, USA), or equivalent
Flow-rated pump tubes	2.00 mL/min and 0.80 mL/min, Technicon, or equivalent
Glass manifold mixing coils	5-turn and 20-turn (1.5 mm i.d. × 3 mm o.d.), Technicon, or equivalent
Gas-liquid separator	See Fig. 2 for specifications
Expansion chamber	See Fig. 2 for specifications
PTFE tubing	Approximately 75 cm long, 0.25 in (6.35 mm) o.d.
PTFE swagelok fittings	Three, 0.25 in (6.35 mm i.d.)
Rotameter	Range, 100–900 mL/min.

7.4 *Atomic absorption spectrophotometer (AAS) detection system*

Atomic absorption spectrophotometer	Monochromator must have reciprocal linear dispersion of about 0.65 nm/mm in UV region, and a direct readout in absorbance units.
Arsenic electrodeless lamp (EDL) for AAS	With EDL power supply
Quartz furnace atomization cell	16 cm long, 13 mm i.d. quartz tube, with inlet tube (4 mm i.d.) fused 8 cm from either end (see Fig. 3). The cell is wound with Nichrome wire (14 Ω/m), with a spacing of 2–3 mm between turns, and wrapped with several layers of asbestos tape. The terminals are connected to a Variac transformer and a thermocouple within the cell is used to measure the temperature (800 °C). The cell is mounted on the flat surface of a single-slot AAS burner-head assembly. Alignment of the cell in the optical path is accomplished by means of the burner alignment controls.

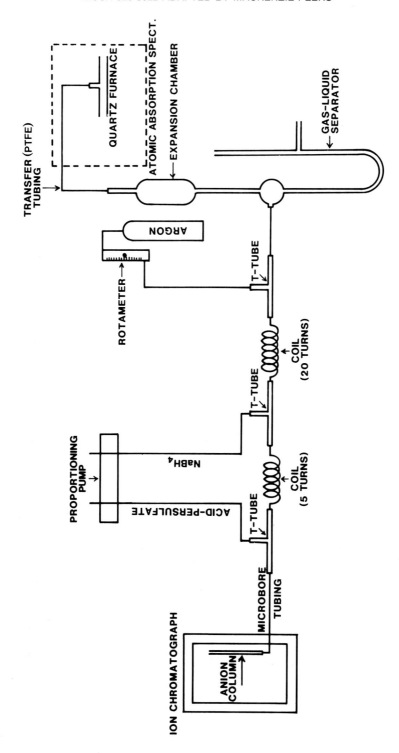

Fig. 1. IC/AAS analytical system

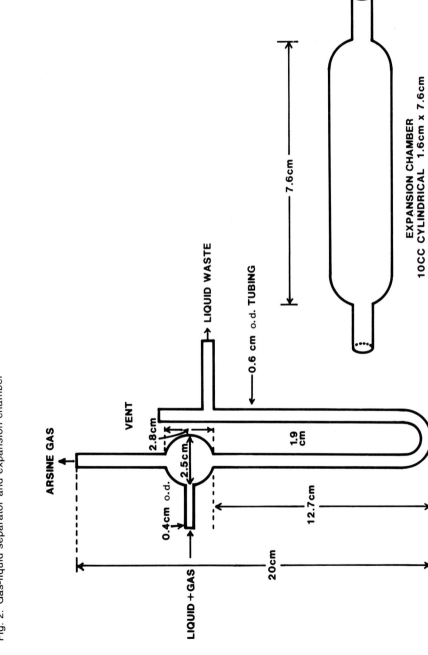

Fig. 2. Gas-liquid separator and expansion chamber

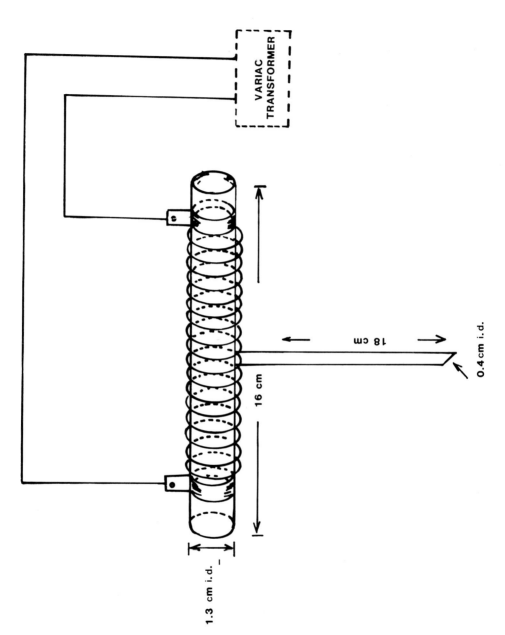

Fig. 3. Quartz furnace atomization cell

7.5 *Glassware*

Beakers	50-mL
Volumetric flasks	Various sizes
Pipettes	Delivery, various sizes

NOTE: For cleaning of glassware, see Method 1, section 12.

8. SAMPLING

8.1 Place a cellulose back-up pad in the rear section of the filter holder. On top of this, place a PTFE filter, then add the center retaining ring and the front section of the cassette. Close firmly to ensure that the center ring seals the edge of the filter.

8.2 Remove the cassette plugs and attach the sampling pump tubing. Clip the cassette to the workers' lapel.

8.3 Collect the sample at 1.5 L/min. A sample volume of 300 L is recommended.

8.4 Replace cassette plugs after sampling and record air flow-rate, sampling time and ambient temperature and pressure.

NOTE: Since a filter may become plugged by heavy particulate loading, the pump rotameter should be observed frequently. Discard sample if pump flow-rate does not remain constant ($\pm 5\%$).

9. PROCEDURE

9.1 *Blank test*

9.1.1 Field blanks: with each batch of ten samples, take two PTFE filters from the same lot and assemble a cassettes, as in 8.1. Ship and store with ten samples and analyse samples and blank at the same time for the presence of arsenicals.

9.1.2 Media blanks: approximately 5 media blanks should be analysed with every set of 10 samples. Media blanks are unused sampling units taken from the same lot as those used for sampling, but not sent to the field.

9.2 *Check test*

Not applicable.

9.3 *Test portion*

Not applicable.

9.4 *Sample extraction*

　9.4.1　For each of the ten samples, plus the blanks, pipette 25.0 mL of eluent A (section 6) into a clean, 50-mL beaker.

　9.4.2　Open the filter holders and transfer the PTFE filters into the beakers by means of clean forceps, placing the exposed side of the filter face-down in contact with the solution. Cover the beakers with watch glass or plastic film.

　9.4.3　Agitate contents of beakers for 30 min in an ultrasonic water bath. Store extracts in the sealed beakers at $\simeq 4\,°C$ until analysis.

9.5 *Analytical system operating conditions* (see Fig. 1)

　(a)　Ion-exchange chromatograph

Column temperature:	ambient
Flow rate:	2.6 mL/min
Pressure:	41 atm ($\simeq 41 \times 10^5$ Pa)
Injection volume:	0.8 mL

　(b)　Arsine generator

$K_2S_2O_8$-HCl solution flow rate:	0.8 mL/min
$NaBH_4$-KOH solution flow rate:	2.0 mL/min
Argon carrier gas flow rate:	300 mL/min

　(c)　Atomic absorption spectrophotometer
　　　(see Notes on Procedure, 12.1, 12.2)

Quartz furnace temperature:	800 °C
EDL power supply:	8 watts (or as recommended by manufacturer)
Wavelength:	193.7 nm
Slit width:	0.7 nm (or as recommended by manufacturer)
D_2 background correction:	none
Readout mode:	absorbance.

9.6 *Determination of monomethylarsonic acid,* p-*aminophenylarsonic acid and arsenic V* (see Notes on Procedure, 12.3)

　9.6.1　Before connecting separator column effluent to arsine generator, allow the column to equilibrate by pumping eluent A for at least one hour.

Connect effluent to arsine generator and, with full system in operation, allow to equilibrate until steady base-line is obtained on recorder.

9.6.2   Inject 0.8 mL of one of the mixed-analyte working solutions, using the 10-mL plastic syringe (see Notes on Procedure, 12.4).

9.6.3   Identify the peaks and record peak-heights, or areas, and concentration of standard solution. Typical retention times with eluent A are as follow:

dimethylarsenic acid + arsenic III: 1 min
monomethylarsonic acid: 2 min
p-aminophenylarsonic acid: 4 min
arsenic V: 7.5 min

If the resolution needs to be improved, adjust the eluent concentration accordingly.

9.6.4   Repeat 9.6.2 and 9.6.3 for the remainder of the mixed-analyte working standards and each of the ten sample extracts and the blank extracts (9.4.3).

9.6.5   *Calibration curve*

For each set of ten samples, construct a calibration curve (peak-height or area *versus* concentration) for monomethylarsonic acid, p-amino-phenylarsonic acid and arsenic V, using the results obtained in 9.6 with the mixed-analyte working standards.

9.7 *Determination of dimethylarsenic acid and arsenic III*

9.7.1   Following the procedure of 9.6.1, equilibrate the IC column with eluent B and wait for steady recorder base-line.

9.7.2   Inject 0.8 mL of one of the mixed analyte working standards, using the 10-mL plastic syringe.

9.7.3   Identify the peaks and record peak-heights, or areas, and concentration of standard solution. Typical retention times with eluent B are as follows:

dimethylarsenic acid: 1.5 min
arsenic III: 2.0 min

(the other three compounds have very long retention times with eluent B)

9.7.4   Repeat 9.7.2 and 9.7.3 for the remainder of the mixed-analyte working standards and each of the ten sample extracts and the blank extract (9.4.3).

9.7.5   *Calibration curve*

> For each set of 10 samples, construct a calibration curve (peak-height or area *versus* concentration) for dimethylarsenic acid and arsenic III, using the results obtained in 9.7 with the mixed analyte working standards.

9.8 *Regeneration of IC column*

After analysing each set of ten samples (plus standards) with eluent B, the compounds not eluted (9.7.3) must be flushed from the column with eluent A before another set of samples can be analysed.

10. METHOD OF CALCULATION

The mass concentration, ρ ($\mu g/m^3$), of a given arsenical in the air sample is given by:

$$\rho = \frac{m_s - m_b}{V}$$

where

m_s = mass of arsenical in sample extract, calculated from absorbance and calibration curve (μg)

m_b = average mass of arsenical in media blank extract (μg)

V = volume of air sample (m^3)

NOTE: For sampling pumps with rotameters only, the measured volume must be corrected for temperature and pressure (see Method 1, section 10)

11. REPEATABILITY AND REPRODUCIBILITY

The combined sampling and analytical method was tested using filters loaded with particulates of the three organoarsenical compounds in a dynamic aerosol generation-sampling system. The concentration levels tested for each species were 5, 10 and 20 μg As/m^3. Depending on concentration and species, the coefficients of variation were found to range from 14.4% at the lowest concentration to 4.7% at the highest.

The collection efficiency for the organoarsenicals in the range 5–20 μg As/m^3, using a 300 L sample, was found to be >99%. That for inorganic arsenic was not determined.

12. NOTES ON PROCEDURE

12.1 The instrumental parameters of the AAS must be optimized. Align the quartz cell in the optical path to maximize the amount of light passing through it.

12.2 Gradually increase the temperature of the quartz cell to 800 °C by means of the Variac transformer power supply.

12.3 Arsenic III and dimethylarsenic acid coelute with eluent A. They are determined by elution of a second injection of the extract with eluent B (see 9.7).

12.4 To rinse the injection loop of previous-sample contamination, it is preferable to push through it a sample volume of three times the injection loop volume, before injecting the sample. In addition, the plastic syringe should be rinsed with deionized water between samples.

13. SCHEMATIC REPRESENTATION OF PROCEDURE

Pump 300 L air sample through PTFE filter
↓
Place filter in 25 mL aqueous carbonate:bicarbonate:borate buffer
and agitate 30 min in ultrasonic bath
↓
Inject 0.8 mL buffer extract into ion-exchange column
(equilibrated with same buffer), connected to arsine generator
and quartz-furnace atomic absorption spectrophotometer
↓
Elute monomethylarsonic acid, p-aminophenylarsonic acid
and arsenic V with the same buffer
↓
Identify and quantify absorbance peaks by comparison
with those obtained with standard solutions
↓
Equilibrate IC column with dilute aqueous sodium
tetraborate and inject 0.8 mL of buffer extract
↓
Elute dimethylarsenic acid and arsenic III
with the tetraborate buffer solution
↓
Identify and quantify absorbance peaks by comparison
with those obtained with standard solutions

14. ORIGIN OF THE METHOD

Method P & CAM 320, NIOSH Manual of Analytical Methods, Vol.6

Contact point: P.M. Eller
National Institute for Occupational Safety and Health
Division of Physical Sciences and Engineering
4676 Columbia Parkway
Cincinnati, OH 4526
USA

METHOD 4 – DETERMINATION OF HEXAVALENT CHROMIUM IN AIR BY VISIBLE ABSORPTION SPECTROPHOTOMETRY

Adapted from Method 7600, NIOSH 'Manual of Analytical Methods',
3rd Ed., Vol. 1 (1984)

1. SCOPE AND FIELD OF APPLICATION

This method is suitable for the determination of soluble or insoluble chromium [VI] in air, over the range of 1–50 µg/m³ for a 200-L air sample. Interference may be observed from iron, copper, nickel and vanadium; 10 µg of any of these produces an absorbance equivalent to $\simeq 0.02$ µg Cr(VI). The estimated limit of detection is 0.05 µg/sample.

2. REFERENCE

Eller, P.M., ed. (1984) *NIOSH Manual of Analytical Methods,* 3rd Ed., Vol. 1., Cincinnati OH, U.S. Department of Health and Human Services, Method 7600

3. DEFINITIONS

VAS = visible absorption spectrophotometry.

4. PRINCIPLE

A known volume of air is drawn through a PVC filter which retains particulate matter (5-µm pore size). Soluble chromates and/or chromic acid are taken up in 0.25 mol/L sulfuric acid and a coloured complex is formed by addition of diphenylcarbazide. In presence of insoluble chromates, and chromium [VI] in presence of reducing agents, the sample is digested in hot 2% sodium hydroxide: 3% sodium carbonate. The digest is diluted and acidified with sulfuric acid and diphenylcarbazide is added. The alkaline carbonate procedure performs a more complete extraction. Absorbance is measured at 540-nm and quantification is effected by comparison with standard solutions.

5. HAZARDS

Insoluble chromates are suspected human carcinogens. Samples should be processed in a ventilated hood.

6. REAGENTS[1]

All reagents should be of Analytical Reagent grade.

Acetone

Nitrogen   Compressed, oxygen-free

Sodium carbonate, anhy-
drous

Sodium hydroxide

Potassium chromate

Deionized water

Sulfuric acid, concentrated (98%, w/w)

Sulfuric acid, 3 mol/L   Add 167 mL concentrated acid to deionized water
                             in a 1-L flask and dilute to the mark

Sulfuric acid, 0.25 mol/L   Add 14.0 mL concentrated acid to deionized water
                             in a 1-L flask and dilute to the mark

Chromium (VI) standard   1.00 g/L
solution

Chromium (VI) calibration   10 mg/L (dilute standard solution 1→100 with
solution   deionized water)

Chromium (VI) working   Transfer 6 or 7 mL of 0.25 mol/L sulfuric acid into
standard solutions   each of a series of 25-mL volumetric flasks. Pipette
                             0 to 100 µL of 10 ml/L stock solution into the
                             flasks, add 0.5-mL diphenylcarbazide solution to
                             each and make up to the mark with 0.25 mol/L
                             sulfuric acid. The flasks thus contain 0–1.0 µg
                             Cr(VI)

---

[1] Reference to a company and/or product is for the purpose of information and identification only and does not imply approval or recommendation of the company and/or product by the International Agency for Research on Cancer, to the exclusion of others which may also be suitable.

Filter extraction solution 2% sodium hydroxide:3% sodium carbonate (dissolve 20 g NaOH + 30 g Na_2CO_3 in deionized water and dilute to 1.0-L)

Diphenylcarbazide solution Dissolve 500 mg sym-diphenylcarbazide in 100 mL acetone plus 100 mL water.

7. APPARATUS[1]

Air sampler PVC filter, 5.0-μm pore size, 37 mm diam., in polystyrene filter holder (FWSB[MSA] or VM-1[Gelman] or equivalent).
NOTE: BSWP PVC filters (Millipore) are not acceptable for sampling Cr(VI), since they have been found to reduce a significant amount of a 5 μg Na_2CrO_4 spike within 24 h.

Personal sampling pump 1 to 4-L/min, with flexible connecting tubing. Pump must be calibrated with representative sampler in line (accuracy, $\pm 5\%$), using a bubble meter or equivalent device. Record air temperature and pressure during calibration if pump is fitted with a rotameter.

Spectrophotometer UV-visible, with cuvettes, 5-cm path length

Filtration apparatus, vacuum

Buchner funnel

Bottles 20-mL, glass, PTFE-lined screw caps

Beakers 50-mL, borosilicate

Volumetric flasks 25-, 100-, and 1000-mL

Watchglasses

Micropipettes 20-μL and other sizes

Centrifuge tubes 40-mL, graduated, with plastic stoppers

---

[1] Reference to a company and/or product is for the purpose of information and identification only and does not imply approval or recommendation of the company and/or product by the International Agency for Research on Cancer, to the exclusion of others which may also be suitable.

Forceps   Plastic

Hotplate   120 to 400 °C

NOTE: All glassware should be cleaned with 1:1 nitric acid and rinsed thoroughly with deionized water before use.

8. SAMPLING

8.1 Assemble filter and cassette filter-holder. Support filter by a stainless-steel or
cellulose back-up pad. Close firmly to prevent sample leakage around the filter
and seal the holder with plastic tape or shrinkable cellulose band. Remove
filter-holder plugs and attach holder to sampling pump tubing.

8.2 Fix holder to workers' lapel and sample at an accurately-known rate in the range
1–4-L/min for a sampling volume of 8–400 L. Do not exceed 1 mg particulate
loading on filter.

8.3 Remove the PVC filter from the cassette not later than one hour after completion
of sampling (handle with forceps only) and place it in a 20-mL bottle. Discard the
back-up pad.

8.4 Prepare at least two field blanks (maximum of ten) for each set of ten samples.
The field blanks consist of air samples from the same lot used for sample
collection. They must be handled in all respects like the samples used for sample
collection, but no air should be drawn through them. Ship and store with samples.
The latter are stable for about two weeks.

9. PROCEDURE

9.1 *Blank tests*

    9.1.1   Field blanks: see 8.4. Determine Cr(VI) content as described in 9.4
and 9.5.

    9.1.2   Reagent blanks

        9.1.2.1   For procedure 9.4.1, take a volume of 0.25 mol/L sulfuric acid
equal to that employed in steps 9.4.1.2 to 9.4.1.4, inclusive, then
filter as in step 9.4.1.5, using a moistened PVC filter in a Buchner
funnel and a clean centrifuge tube. Proceed as in 9.4.1.6, then
determine Cr(VI) as described in 9.5.

        9.1.2.2   For procedure 9.4.2, add 5.0 mL of filter extraction solution (6)
to a 50-mL beaker and carry out steps 9.4.2.2 to 9.4.2.6, in-

clusive, except for degassing and purging with nitrogen. Determine Cr(VI) as described in 9.5.

9.2 *Check tests*

Not applicable.

9.3 *Test portion*

Not applicable.

9.4 *Sample extraction and preparation for VAS*

9.4.1   Procedure for sample of soluble chromates and chromic acid

9.4.1.1 Remove blank and sample filters from bottles with forceps. Fold each filter and place it in a separate 40-mL graduated centrifuge tube.

9.4.1.2 Add 5 or 7 mL of 0.25 mol/L sulfuric acid to each tube and shake to wash all surfaces of filter.

9.4.1.3 Remove filter from tube with plastic forceps and carefully wash all surfaces into the tube with an additional 1 to 2-mL of 0.25 mol/L sulfuric acid. Discard the filters.

9.4.1.4 Rinse the bottle which contained the filter with 2 to 3 mL of 0.25 mol/L sulfuric acid and pour through a moistened PVC filter in a Buchner funnel, collecting the dust-free solution in a 40-mL centrifuge tube.

9.4.1.5 Filter sample solution (9.4.1.3) through a Buchner funnel into the centrifuge tube (9.4.1.4) and rinse the funnel and PVC filter with 5 to 8 mL of 0.25 mol/L sulfuric acid.

9.4.1.6 Add 0.5 mL diphenylcarbazide solution to each centrifuge tube and bring total volume in each tube to 25 mL with 0.25 mol/L sulfuric acid. Stopper and shake to mix, allowing a few minutes for colour to develop. Retain for VAS determination.

9.4.2   Procedure for insoluble chromates and Cr(VI) in presence of iron or other reducing agents

9.4.2.1 Remove PVC filter from the bottle (plastic forceps), place it in a 50-mL beaker and add 5.0 mL of filter extraction solution (6). If significant amounts of Cr(III) are expected to be present, degas the solution with nitrogen.

9.4.2.2   To avoid Cr(III) oxidation, purge head-space above the solution with nitrogen throughout the extraction process (9.4.2.3–9.4.2.4, until solution is cooled).

9.4.2.3   Cover beaker with a watchglass and heat to near boiling point for 30–45 min (do not boil solution or heat longer than 45 min). Do not allow solution to evaporate to dryness, as hexavalent chromium may react with PVC filter. A brown-coloured filter is an indication that hexavalent chromium has been lost in this manner.

9.4.2.4   Cool solution and transfer quantitatively to a 25-mL volumetric flask with distilled water rinses, keeping total volume to about 20 mL.
NOTE: If solution is cloudy, filter it through a PVC filter in a vacuum filtration apparatus, using distilled water rinses.

9.4.2.5   Add 1.90 mL of 3 mol/L sulfuric acid to the volumetric flask and swirl to mix (CAUTION: allow solution to stand several minutes until vigorous gas evolution ceases).

9.4.2.6   Add 0.5 mL diphenylcarbazide solution, dilute to the mark with distilled water, stopper and invert flask several times to mix thoroughly. Pour out (discard) about one-half the contents of the flask, stopper and shake vigorously several times, removing stopper each time to relieve pressure (this removes gas bubbles, which could cause high and erratic VAS readings). Retain for VAS determination.

9.5 *Chromium (VI) determination by VAS*

9.5.1   Set wavelength on spectrophotometer to 540 nm and set absorbance to zero using a 0.25 mol/L sulfuric acid blank.

9.5.2   Transfer extract (9.4.1.6 or 9.4.2.6) to a 5-cm cuvette and record absorbance.

9.6 *Calibration curve*

9.6.1   Analyse the chromium (VI) working standard solutions (6) as described in 9.5.

9.6.2   Prepare a graph of absorbance *versus* mass (µg) of Cr(VI) per 25 mL working standard solution.

10. METHOD OF CALCULATION

The mass concentration, ρ ($\mu g/m^3$), of Cr(VI) in the air sample is given by

$$\rho = (m_s - m_b)/V$$

where

m_s = mass of Cr(VI) found in sample filter calculated from sample absorbance and calibration curve (μg)

m_b = average mass of Cr(VI) found in field blanks (μg)

V = volume of air samples (m^3).

11. REPEATABILITY AND REPRODUCIBILITY

The coefficient of variation for the total sampling and analytical procedure has been determined to be 8.4% over the range 0.5–10 $\mu g/m^3$, with a sampling rate of 1.5 to 2.5 L/min (collection efficiency, 94.5%).

12. NOTES ON PROCEDURE

Not applicable.

13. SCHEMATIC REPRESENTATION OF PROCEDURE

Draw air sample through PVC filter
↓
Sample containing only soluble chromates and/or chromic acid
Place filter in 40-mL centrifuge tube and extract with
0.25 mol/L sulfuric acid (rinse and discard PVC filter)
↓
Filter extract through PVC filter
(rinse funnel and filter with acid)
↓
Add 0.5 mL diphenylcarbazide solution and make up to
25 mL with 0.25 mol/L sulfuric acid;
stopper tube and shake
↓
Determine absorbance at 540 nm
and convert to μg Cr(VI) using calibration curve
↓
Sample containing insoluble chromates and Cr(VI)
in presence of reducing agents
Place filter in 50-mL beaker and add 5.0 mL 2% sodium hydroxide:

3% sodium carbonate [in presence of Cr(III), degas and
purge with nitrogen during digestion]
↓
Heat to near boiling for 30–45 min, cool and transfer to
25-mL volumetric flask with distilled water rinses
↓
Add 1.90 mL 3mol/L sulfuric acid, mix and allow gas evolution
to reach near-completion; add 0.5 mL diphenylcarbazide solution
and dilute to mark with distilled water
↓
Discard about one-half of extract,
stopper and shake vigorously several times,
removing stopper to allow escape of gas
↓
Determine absorbance at 540 nm
and convert to Cr(VI) using calibration curve.

14. ORIGIN OF METHOD

Method 7600, NIOSH Manual of Analytical Methods, 3rd Ed., Vol. 1. (1984).
See Reference, section 2.

Contact point: P.M. Eller
           National Institute for Occupational Safety and Health
           Division of Physical Sciences and Engineering
           4676 Columbia Parkway
           Cincinnati, OH 45226
           USA

METHOD 5 – DETERMINATION OF NICKEL CARBONYL IN AIR BY COLORIMETRY

D.H. Stedman

1. SCOPE AND FIELD OF APPLICATION

This method can be used to determine nickel carbonyl ($Ni(CO)_4$) concentration in air as low as 1 µg/m^3. Any gaseous nickel compound will interfere, however, and high nickel levels from glassware and reagents will raise the detection limit. The method can be calibrated approximately using standard nickel solutions, but more accurate results are obtained using known concentrations of $Ni(CO)_4$ in air.

2. REFERENCES

Brief, R.S., Venable, F.S. & Ajemian, R.S. (1965) Nickel carbonyl, its detection and potential for formation. *Am. Ind. Hyg. Assoc. J., 26,* 72–76

Brown, S.S., Nomoto, S., Steppler, M. & Sunderman, F.W. (1981) IUPAC reference method for analysis of nickel in serum and urine by electrothermal atomic absorption spectrometry. *Pure Appl. Chem., 53,* 773–781

Lee, D.S. (1982) Determination of nickel in seawater by carbonyl generation. *Anal. Chem., 54,* 1182–1184

Nelson, G.O. (1981) *Controlled test atmospheres, principles and techniques,* Ann Arbor, Ann Arbor Scientific Publishers, Inc.

3. DEFINITIONS

Not applicable

4. PRINCIPLE

Nickel carbonyl is absorbed as Ni(II) in an alcoholic iodine solution, transferred to chloroform and determined at 425 nm as a coloured complex with α-furildioxime (Brief *et al.*, 1965).

5. HAZARDS

Ni(CO)$_4$ is highly toxic by inhalation, a dangerous fire risk and a possible carcinogenic agent. Handle only in an adequately-ventilated hood. If desired, a less hazardous calibration method leading directly to low concentrations of Ni(CO)$_4$ may be employed (Lee, 1982).

6. REAGENTS[1]

Water	Double-distilled or deionized
Octane	
Ethanol	
Isopropanol	
Chloroform	
Carbon monoxide	Technical grade
Nickel carbonyl	Liquid, in CO-pressurized steel cylinder
Iodine	Analytical reagent grade
Ammonium hydroxide	Sp. gr. 0.88
Sodium hydroxide	20% (w/w), aqueous
Nitric acid (1:1)	Dilute concentrated acid 1:1 with water
Hydrochloric acid	3% (dilute 83 mL concentrated acid to 1 L with water)
Activated charcoal	
Alcoholic iodine	1% (w/w), dissolve 10 g iodine in 990 g isopropanol
Alpha-furildioxime solution	1% (w/w), dissolve 1 g α-furildioxime in 99 g of 11:1 (w/w) ethanol:water
Phenolphthalein solution	1% in ethanol

---

[1] Reference to a company and/or product is for the purpose of information and identification only and does not imply approval or recommendation of the company and/or product by the International Agency for Research on Cancer, to the exclusion of others which may also be suitable.

Stock standard Ni solution	50 mg/L, dissolve 50 mg of pure, powdered Ni in 10 mL of 1:1 nitric acid and make up to volume with 3% hydrochloric acid in a 1-L volumetric flask.
Working standard Ni solutions	Prepare at least 3 working standard solutions, of Ni in 3% hydrochloric acid to cover the expected range (e.g., 1 to 3 µg per sample. In thise case, dilute 1, 2 and 3 mL aliquots of stock standard solution to 500 mL in volumetric flasks, to obtain concentrations of 1, 2 and 3 µg/10 mL).

7. APPARATUS[1]

Colorimeter	With 1-cm cuvettes
Air sampling pump	With flow meter (2–10 L/min)
Gas-washing bottle	125-mL, with extra-course, fritted glass bubbler tube
Separatory funnels	50-mL
Conical flasks	500-mL
Volumetric flasks	500-mL, 1000-mL
Serum bottle	50-mL, with septum caps
Syringe	1-mL, graduated
Micro-syringes	10-µL
Gas sampling bags	100-L, or larger
Millipore filter	0.8 micron
Hot plate	
Iodine-charcoal trap	Place a loosely-packed plug of glass wool in a glass tube (10 cm × 1.5 cm i.d.), followed by 5 g of activated charcoal, then ∼0.1 g of crystalline iodine and a second glass wool plug. The iodine layer is at the inlet end of the trap.

---

[1] Reference to a company and/or product is for the purpose of information and identification only and does not imply approval or recommendation of the company and/or product by the International Agency for Research on Cancer, to the exclusion of others which may also be suitable.

NOTE: Clean new glassware by soaking 24 h in 5% nitric acid. Rinse thoroughly with warm tap water, then with double-distilled water. Wash used glassware in detergent solution and rinse with tap water, then soak in 5% nitric acid for 1h, rinse thoroughly with double-distilled water and allow to dry. Use plastic containers for washing and handle the glassware with gloves which are impervious to perspiration.

8. SAMPLING

8.1 Draw 10^3–10^4 L of air (5 L/min) through the Millipore filter and the bubbler tube into 100 mL of alcoholic iodine in the gas washing bottle. For long collection times, the scrubbing liquid volume may be replenished with isopropanol.

8.2 Measure the sampling rate at the beginning and the end of the sampling period, using pre-calibrated flow meter. Use average of the two rates to calculate volume of air sampled. Measure the average atmospheric pressure and temperature over the sampling period.

9. PROCEDURE

9.1 *Blank tests*

9.1.1 Follow instructions 8.1 and 8.2, but with an iodine-charcoal trap in-line between the Millipore filter and the bubbler tube. Analyse the alcoholic iodine solution as described in 9.4.

9.1.2 Obtain a reagent blank by following procedure 9.4 with 100 mL of alcoholic iodine through which no air has been passed.

9.2 *Check test*

Not applicable

9.3 *Test portion*

Not applicable

9.4 *Colorimetric determination of Ni(CO)$_4$*

9.4.1 Quantitatively transfer the 100 mL of alcoholic iodine from the collector (8.1) to a 500-mL conical flask.

9.4.2 Place the samples and the blanks on a hot plate in a fume hood and heat to dryness and expulsion of all iodine vapour (typically, 10 min at 120 °C).

9.4.3   Cool and dissolve each residue in 10 mL of 3% hydrochloric acid.

9.4.4   Quantitatively transfer the acid solutions to 50-mL separatory funnels, using 3 rinses of 5 mL of 3% HCl.

9.4.5   Place 10 mL of each working standard Ni solution in individual separatory funnels (see 12, NOTES ON PROCEDURE).

9.4.6   To each funnel (samples, blanks and standards), add 2 drops of phenolphthalein solution and 6 drops of ammonium hydroxide.

9.4.7   Titrate the contents of each funnel to the phenolphthalein end-point with 20% sodium hydroxide and add three drops in excess.

9.4.8   Add 3 mL of α-furildioxime solution and 10 mL of chloroform to each separatory funnel.

9.4.9   Shake each funnel for 1 min, then allow chloroform layer to separate. Draw off the chloroform layer and immediately cover the container.

9.4.10   Measure the absorbance of the chloroform solution at 425 nm. Subtract the reagent blank absorbance from each sample and standard absorbance to obtain corrected values.

9.5 *Calibration curve using standard solutions*

Draw a calibration curve by plotting the corrected absorbance *versus* the amount of Ni(μg) in each standard (9.4.5).

9.6 *Calibration curve using (Ni(CO)₄ in air[1]*

9.6.1   Attach a short stainless-steel tube, terminated by a syringe needle, to the $Ni(CO)_4$ cylinder.

9.6.2   Invert the cylinder.

9.6.3   Flush a dry 50-mL serum bottle with carbon monoxide and close with septum cap.

9.6.4   Insert the syringe needle (9.6.1) into the bottle and inject less than 1 mL of liquid $Ni(CO)_4$. Aliquots (9.6.5) may be taken from this bottle with a micro-syringe.

9.6.5   Prepare a fresh solution of 10 μL $Ni(CO)_4$ in 10 μL octane.

---

[1] For a more detailed procedure than that described here, see Nelson (1971).

9.6.6   Inject 1, 2 and 4 μL of solution 9.6.5 into 3 identical gas sampling bags and fill with laboratory air pumped through a Millipore filter, followed by an iodine-charcoal trap.

9.6.7   Analyze the contents of the three bags, following procedures 8.1–8.2 and 9.4.

9.6.8   Draw a calibration curve by plotting the corrected absorbance against the amount of Ni in each standard (9.6.6). This calibration is, in principle, more accurate than that obtained in 9.5.

10. METHOD OF CALCULATION

The mass concentration, ρ ($\mu g/m^3$), of nickel carbonyl in the air sample at standard temperature (273°K) and pressure (1 atm) is given by

ρ = 10.78 mT/PV

where,

m   = mass of nickel determined from corrected absorbance (9.4.10) and calibration curve (μg)

T   = average temperature during sample collection (°K)

P   = average atmospheric pressure during sample collection (atm)

V   = volume of air sampled (L)

11. REPEATABILITY AND REPRODUCIBILITY

No data are available.

12. NOTES ON PROCEDURE

If atomic absorption procedures or the carbonyl generation technique are to be used for Ni determination, the solutions from step 9.4.4 should be subjected to the analytical procedure described by Brown et al. (1981) or by Lee (1982) respectively.

13. SCHEMATIC REPRESENTATION OF PROCEDURE

Bubble air sample through 1% iodine in isopropanol
↓
Evaporate isopropanol solution to dryness and expulsion of iodine
↓

Dissolve residue in 10 mL of 3% HCl, transfer to separatory funnels
and add 2 drops phenolphthalein and 6 drops ammonium hydroxide

↓

Titrate with 20% sodium hydroxide and add 3 drops in excess

↓

Add 3-mL α-furildioxime solution + 10 mL chloroform and shake

↓

Measure absorbance (425 mm) of chloroform layer, subtract reagent blank
absorbance and read Ni content from calibration curve

↓

Calculate $Ni(CO)_4$ concentration of air sample

14. ORIGIN OF THE METHOD

Brief *et al.* (1965) (Section 2)

Contact point: Professor D.H. Stedman
Chemistry Department
University of Denver
Denver CO, 8028
USA

METHOD 6 – DETERMINATION OF NICKEL CARBONYL IN AIR BY CHEMILUMINESCENCE

D.H. Stedman

1. SCOPE AND FIELD OF APPLICATION

This method responds continuously to nickel carbonyl ($Ni(CO)_4$) with a 10s delay time and a detection limit of about 0.2 μg/m³. The response is linear up to 2 mg/m³. The method can be made specific for $Ni(CO)_4$ with some loss of sensitivity, but is often used with greater sensitivity for combined Ni and Fe carbonyls.

2. REFERENCES

Hikade, D.A., Stedman, D.H. & Walega, J.G. (1984) An improved, portable $Ni(CO)_4$ detector. *Anal. Chem., 56,* 1629–1632

Lee, D.S. (1982) Determination of nickel in seawater by carbonyl generation. *Anal. Chem., 54,* 1182–1184

Nelson, G.O. (1971) *Controlled test atmospheres, principles and techniques.* Ann Arbor, Ann Arbor Science Publishers, Inc.

Stedman, D.H. (1980) Nickel carbonyl analyzer. U.S. Patent No. PC-1189/USA, June, 1980

Stedman, D.H. & Tammaro, D.A. (1976) Chemiluminescent measurements of parts-per-billion levels of nickel carbonyl in air. *Anal. Lett., 9,* 81–89

Stedman, D.H., Tammaro, D.A., Branch, D.K. & Pearson, R.Jr (1971) Chemiluminescence detector for the measurements of nickel carbonyl in air. *Anal. Chem., 51,* 2340–2342

3. DEFINITIONS

Not applicable

4. PRINCIPLE

The method depends on the carbon monoxide-enhanced chemiluminescence of metal carbonyls with ozone. The air sample is mixed with carbonyl-free CO, then reacted with ozone-enriched oxygen (or air) in a light-shielded reactor and viewed through an optical filter by an electronic photometer.

5. HAZARDS

$Ni(CO)_4$ is highly toxic by inhalation, a dangerous fire risk and a possible carcinogenic agent. Handle only in an adequately-ventilated hood. If desired, a less hazardous calibration method, leading directly to low concentrations of $Ni(CO)_4$ may be employed (Lee, 1982).

6. REAGENTS

Water	Double-distilled
Ethanol	
Octane	
Carbon monoxide	Technical grade
Nickel carbonyl	Liquid, in CO-pressurized steel cylinder
Nitric acid	Concentrated
Iodine	
Activated charcoal	

7. APPARATUS[1]

Serum bottle	50-mL, with septum caps
Syringe	1-mL, graduated
Micro-syringes	10-μL
Gas sampling bags	100-L, or larger
Millipore filter	0.8 micron
Iodine-charcoal trap	Prepare by placing a loosely-packed plug of glass wool in a glass tube (10 cm × 1.5 cm i.d.), followed by 5 g of activated charcoal, then about 0.1 g of crystalline iodine and a second glass-wool plug. The iodine layer is at the inlet end of the trap.

---

[1] Reference to a company and/or product is for the purpose of information and identification only and does not imply approval or recommendation of the company and/or product by the International Agency for Research on Cancer, to the exclusion of others which may also be suitable.

Nickel carbonyl detector   Construct according to description of Hikade *et al.*
                                  (1984), or modify a commercial nitric oxide detec-
                                  tor (Stedman & Tammaro, 1976). A complete
                                  nickel carbonyl detector can also be obtained
                                  from Thermo-Electron Corporation, Environ-
                                  mental Instruments Division, Hopkinton, MA,
                                  USA

NOTE: Clean new glassware by soaking for 24 h in 5% nitric acid. Rinse
      thoroughly with warm tap water, then with double-distilled water. Wash
      used glassware in detergent solution, then soak in 5% nitric acid for 1 h,
      rinse thoroughly with double-distilled water and allow to dry. Use plastic
      containers for washing and handle the glassware with gloves which are
      impervious to perspiration.

8. SAMPLING

Draw air sample through Millipore filter directly into the chemiluminescence
detector (see Hikade *et al.*, 1984).

9. PROCEDURE

9.1 *Blank test*

See step 9.4.6, below

9.2 *Check test*

Not applicable

9.3 *Test portion*

Not applicable

9.4 *Calibration of chemiluminescence detector*[1]

9.4.1   Attach a short stainless-steel tube, terminated by a syringe needle, to the
         $Ni(CO)_4$ cylinder.

9.4.2   Invert the cylinder.

9.4.3   Flush a dry 50-mL serum bottle with carbon monoxide, then close with
         septum cap.

---

[1] For a more detailed procedure than that described here, see Nelson (1971).

9.4.4   Insert the syringe needle (9.4.1) into the bottle and inject less than 1 mL of liquid (Ni(CO)$_4$. Aliquots (9.4.5) may be taken from this bottle with a micro-syringe.

9.4.5   Prepare a fresh solution of 10 μL of Ni(CO)$_4$ in 10 mL of octane

9.4.6   Inject 0, 1, 2 and 4 μL of Ni(CO)$_4$ solution (9.4.5) into four identical gas sampling bags and fill with laboratory air pumped through a Millipore filter, followed by an iodine-charcoal trap. The bag containing no Ni(CO)$_4$ solution is the blank.

9.4.7   Calibrate the chemiluminescence detector using the known mass concentrations (μg/m^3) of Ni(CO)$_4$ in the gas sampling bags.

9.5 *Determination of Ni(CO)$_4$ in air*

Once calibrated in terms of Ni(CO)$_4$ mass concentration, the detector can be used on any air sample and the Ni(CO)$_4$ concentration determined directly.

10. METHOD OF CALCULATION

Not applicable

11. REPEATABILITY AND REPRODUCIBILITY

No data are available.

12. NOTES ON PROCEDURE

Not applicable

13. SCHEMATIC REPRESENTATION OF PROCEDURE

Not applicable

14. ORIGIN OF THE METHOD

D.H. Stedman

Contact point: Professor D.H. Stedman
Chemistry Department
University of Denver
Denver CO, 80208
USA

METHOD 7 – DETERMINATION OF ANTIMONY IN AIR AND AIRBORNE PARTICULATES BY ANODIC STRIPPING VOLTAMMETRY

Adapted from Method P & CAM 189, NIOSH 'Manual of Analytical Methods' 2nd Edition, Vol. 1 (1977)

1. SCOPE AND FIELD OF APPLICATION

This method of air sampling and analysis is suitable for the determination of antimony in air and airborne particulates over the concentration range 0.15–5 µg/m^3 in a 100-L air sample. The corresponding limit of detection is $\simeq$ 15 ng for typical industrial air containing copper and/or bismuth, which interfere with the determination of antimony. In the absence of interference, the detection limit is $\simeq$ 0.5 to 1 ng.

2. REFERENCES

Taylor, D.G., ed. (1977) NIOSH Manual of Analytical Methods, 2nd Ed., Vol. 1, Cincinnati OH, U.S. Department of Health and Human Services, Method P & CAM 189

3. DEFINITIONS

Not applicable

4. PRINCIPLE

Airborne antimony is collected on a membrane filter by means of a personal sampling pump. The filter and particulates trapped from a known volume of air are digested with a mixture of nitric, perchloric and sulfuric acids. The Sb [V] is reduced to Sb [III] with hydrazine dihydrochloride in hydrochloric acid (the high chloride concentration minimizes possible interference by copper). The reduced antimony is determined by anodic stripping voltammetry (ASV) with a composite mercury-graphite electrode (CMGE). In principle, a hanging mercury drop can also be used, but the optimum analytical conditions may differ considerably from those described here.

5. HAZARDS

Concentrated hydrochloric, nitric and sulfuric acids are toxic by inhalation. Concentrated nitric acid represents a fire risk in contact with organic materials. Concentrated perchloric acid will explode in contact with organic materials or by shock or heat. These acids should be handled in a ventilated hood and protective clothing should be worn.

6. REAGENTS[1]

All reagents must be Analytical Grade or better, particularly the digestion acids, which must have an exceptionally low antimony content.

Hydrochloric acid (HCl)	Concentrated
Nitric acid (HNO$_3$)	Concentrated, double-distilled
Perchloric acid (HCl)$_4$)	70%, double-distilled
Sulfuric acid (H$_2$SO$_4$)	Concentrated, double-distilled from Vycor glass (Corning Glass Works)
Water	Distilled-deionized, or double-distilled
Hydrazine dihydrochloride	
Sodium hypochlorite	
Acid digestion solution	Add 24 volumes of concentrated HNO$_3$ to 24 volumes of 70% HClO$_4$ and 1 volume of concentrated H$_2$SO$_4$
Hydrazine dihydro-chloride-acid solution	0.001 mol/L hydrazine dihydrochloride in 5 mol/L HCl. Add 105 mg hydrazine dihydrochloride to a 1-L volumetric flask. Add $\simeq$ 400 mL water and swirl to dissolve the salt. Add 417 mL concentrated HCl, swirl and dilute to the mark with water. Store in polyethylene bottle, with screw cap.
Antimony reference standard solution	1 000 mg/L (Fisher Scientific Co., or equivalent)

---

[1] Reference to a company and/or product is for the purpose of information and identification only and does not imply approval or recommendation of the company and/or product by the International Agency for Research on Cancer, to the exclusion of others which may also be suitable.

Sb[III] standard solution B   100 mg/L. Pipette 10 mL of the reference standard solution into a 100-mL volumetric flask and dilute to the mark with water. Prepare fresh daily.

Sb[III] standard solution C   1 mg/L. Pipette 1 mL of standard solution B into at 100-mL volumetric flask and dilute to the mark with water. Prepare fresh daily.

Sodium hypochlorite solution   4 to 6% (w/w)

7. APPARATUS[1]

Air filter unit   Mixed cellulose ester filter, 0.8-μm pore size, 37-mm diameter (Millipore, type AA) and plastic cassette filter-holder with adaptor allowing flexible tubing to be attached.

Personal sampling pump   Capable of maintaining a flow rate of 1.5 to 2 L/min ($\pm$ 5%) through filter unit. Must be calibrated using bubble meter or equivalent device, with representative sampler in line. If pump is fitted with rotameter, record air temperature and pressure during calibration.

Digestion tubes (analysis cells)   Pyrex, 20 × 100 mm, for digesting filter samples and subsequent use as analysis cells. For cleaning instructions, see NOTES ON PROCEDURE, 12.1.

Digestion racks   to hold digestion tubes on hot plate.

Micro-pipettes   10-, 50-, 100- and 500-μL (Eppendorf, or equivalent)

Volumetric pipettes   1-, 5- and 10-mL, with bulbs.

Volumetric flasks   100- and 1000-mL

Bottle   1-L, polyethylene, with screw cap.

Assorted glassware   (beakers, graduated cylinders)

---

[1] Reference to a company and/or product is for the purpose of information and identification only and does not imply approval or recommendation of the company and/or product by the International Agency for Research on Cancer, to the exclusion of others which may also be suitable.

Single-cell anodic- stripping voltammeter	With composite mercury-graphite electrode (Model SA 2011, Environmental Science Associates, Inc., Burlington, Mass., or equivalent)
Potentiometric recorder	0–100 mV range.

Note: All glassware should be acid-washed and copiously rinsed with distilled water.

8. SAMPLING

8.1 Place the filter in the cassette filter-holder: the filter should be supported by a stainless-steel screen or cellulose back-up pad. Seal the filter-holder with plastic tape or shrinkable cellulose band.

8.2 Connect exit end of filter unit to the calibrated sampling pump with a short length of flexible tubing and sample air at a flow rate of 1.5 to 2 L/min. Sample a minimum volume of 100 L (see NOTES ON PROCEDURE, 12.2, 12.3).

8.3 For every ten samples, set aside two unexposed filters in filter-holders (from the same lot used for sampling). Mark them "field blanks" and ship with samples.

8.4 Disconnect filter unit from pump and cap inlet and outlet of filter holder. Ship in suitable containers to minimize contamination and prevent damage in transit. Loss of sample from heavy deposits on filter may be avoided by placing a clean filter in the holder, on top of the sample filter.

9. PROCEDURE

9.1 *Blank tests*

9.1.1 Field blanks (see 8.3): digest according to procedure 9.4.1 to 9.4.6, inclusive, and analyse with samples as described in 9.7.1 and 9.7.3.

9.1.2 Media blanks: from the same lot used for sampling, set aside one unexposed filter unit (not sent to the field) for every five samples. Digest according to procedure 9.4.1 to 9.4.6, inclusive, and analyse with samples as described in 9.7.1 and 9.7.3.

9.2 *Check test*

Not applicable

9.3 *Test portion*

Not applicable

9.4 *Sample digestion*

9.4.1   Carefully remove filter from holder by means of stainless-steel or plastic forceps. Fold filter in half, then into quarters and finally into eighths, without creasing or cracking filter material. Insert folded filter into digestion tube (analysis cell) and push well down with a glass rod.

9.4.2   Pipette 500 μL of acid digestion solution slowly onto filter in digestion tube. Place tube in rack on a hot plate with surface temperature of 220 °C to 240 °C. (The solution will become clear in $\simeq$ 10 min and a reflux line will be established about half-way up the tube.)

9.4.3   Continue digestion for 40 to 50 min, until the acid is almost completely evaporated (not to dryness).

9.4.4   Remove tube from hot plate and allow to cool.

9.4.5   Add 5 mL of the hydrazine dihydrochloride-acid solution, allowing it to run down the sides of the tube to wash down any spattered material.

9.4.6   Heat tube contents to about 90 °C for 15 min, then remove from hot plate and allow to cool. If necessary, readjust the volume to 5 mL with the hydrazine dihydrochloride-acid solution. [Using a 5-mL pipette, with bulb, carefully withdraw all the remaining solution from the tube into the pipette, stopping when a tiny air-bubble forms in the tip of the pipette. Then, from a suitable small volume in a small beaker, draw in hydrazine dihydrochloride-acid solution until the 5-mL mark is reached. Replace the 5-mL of solution in the original digestion tube, allowing pipette to drain thoroughly.]

9.4.7   If the sample digest (9.4.6) is estimated to contain more than 500 ng of antimony, transfer a suitable aliquot to a clean digestion tube and dilute to 5 mL with the hydrazine dihydrochloride-acid solution. Record the dilution factor and retain for ASV analysis.

9.5 *Preparation of calibration standards for response factor determination*

Add 50 μL of standard solution C (50 mg Sb) to 5 mL of the hydrazine dihydrochloride-acide solution in each of two digestion tubes. (If a 4-cell ASV unit is employed, prepare 8 of the 50 ng standards, two for each CMGE.) These standards will be used to obtain two peak-height values for 50 ng Sb for each electrode.

9.6 *Preparation of filter standards for recovery determination*

9.6.1   For every 30 samples, remove unexposed filters from 3 filter units (from batch used for sampling) and place each one on the center ring of a cassette so that only the edge of the filter is touching the rim of its holder.

9.6.2   Dilute standard solution B to provide 50, 100 and 500 ng of antimony in 10 μL volumes. Place each solution on the center of a filter (9.6.1) and allow to evaporate for $\simeq$ 30 min, then replace filter in holder until required for analysis.

9.6.3   Digest as described in 9.4.1 to 9.4.6, inclusive, and retain for ASV analysis.

9.7 *Antimony determination by ASV*

9.7.1   According to the manufacturers' instructions, operate the ASV unit under the following conditions (all voltages are given with respect to the Ag/AgCl reference electrode):

Plating potential $-$ 400 mV

Auto-hold cutoff potential $+$ 220 mV

Plating time   15–30 min (must be identical for all samples, blanks and standards)

Sweep rate $+$ 30 mV/s

Current range   0.1 to 2 mA (full scale)

Stirring flow-rate $\geq$ 170 mL/min

9.7.2   Using the above conditions, analyse a number of 50 ng calibration standards (9.5) equal to the number of cells (electrodes) on the ASV unit. Draw a base-line through the flat portions of the curve before and after the antimony peak (at $-$ 180 mV) and record the peak height in μA (perpendicularly from apex to base-line).

9.7.3   Analyse the sample solutions (9.4.6 or 9.4.7) along with the blanks (9.1) and the filter standards (9.6), interspersing 1 field blank for every 5 samples, 1 media blank for every 5 samples and 1 filter standard for every 10 samples. Measure and record the peak heights, as described in 9.7.2 (see NOTES ON PROCEDURE, 12.4).

9.7.4   Repeat step 9.7.2 with the remaining calibration standards.

NOTE: Steps 9.7.2–9.7.4 must be carried out in the order given.

10. METHOD OF CALCULATION

10.1 *Response factor*

For a given mercury electrode, the response factor, F (ng/μA), equals the amount of antimony in the standard (50 ng) divided by the average of the two peak-height values (9.7.2 and 9.7.4).

10.2 *Antimony concentration in air sample*

The mass concentration, ρ ($\mu g/m^3$), of antimony in the air sample is given by,

$$\rho \quad = \quad 100\ F\ (h_s - h_b)/RV$$

where

h_s = antimony peak height in sample solution (μA)

h_b = antimony peak height in media blank solution (μA)

R = average percent recovery of antimony from filter standards

V = volume of air sampled (L)

and F is defined in 10.1.

> NOTE: The result obtained with the above equation must be multiplied by the dilution factor employed in 9.4.7, if applicable. The results for field blanks should be reported separately.

11. REPEATABILITY AND REPRODUCIBILITY

For the analysis step alone (9.7), the coefficient of variation (CV) was found to be 4%. For the digestion and analysis steps combined, the CV was 10% over the range 0.2–2.5 $\mu g/m^3$. The variation introduced by sampling and stripping has not been evaluated.

12. NOTES ON PROCEDURE

12.1 All unused digestion tubes should be cleaned by the following procedure. Pipette 300 to 500 μL of the acid digestion solution into each of the tubes. Place the tubes in digestion racks on the hot plate, with surface temperature of 220° to 240 °C so that acid refluxes about half-way up the side of each tube. After 60 to 90 min, remove tubes from hot plate and allow to cool. Rinse tubes four times with distilled-deionized water and invert them in plastic rack with clean toweling on the bottom. After use for analysis, it is sufficient to repeat the rinsing procedure.

12.2 A larger air sample volume is desirable, provided the filter does not become coated with loose particulates which could fall off during handling or shipment. Terminate sampling at first evidence of excessive filter loading or change in sampling flow rate.

12.3 If sampling pump is fitted with rotameter, record initial and final air temperature and pressure during sampling. The volume of air sampled is given by $V = Ft (P_cT_s/P_sT_c)^{0.5}$, where F = indicated flow rate (L/min), t = sampling time (min), P_c = pressure during calibration, P_s = pressure during sampling (same units as P_c), T_c = temperature during calibration (°K), T_s = temperature during sampling (°K).

12.4 Bismuth is stripped at the same potential as antimony. If interference is suspected, the sample should be reanalysed after the addition of 20 μL of 5% sodium hypochlorite solution (to oxidize Sb(III) to Sb(V)). A reduction of the peak height by 80% or more signifies that the peak was due to antimony only.

13. SCHEMATIC REPRESENTATION OF PROCEDURE

Draw 100-L air sample through cellulose ester filter
↓
Add 500 μL of nitric, perchloric, sulfuric acid solution to filter
in digestion tube-analysis cell
↓
Heat at 220°–240 °C until acid evaporates to near-dryness
↓
Cool and add 5 mL of hydrazine dihydrochloride-acid solution
↓
Heat at 90 °C for 15 min and readjust volume to 5 mL if necessary
↓
Analyse by ASV and record antimony peak height (μA)
↓
Determine ASV response factor (ng/μA) using standard solutions
and calculate antimony content of sample solution,
corrected for media blank and recovery from filter.
Convert to concentration in air sample

14. ORIGIN OF METHOD

Method P & CAM 189, *NIOSH Manual of Analytical Methods*, 2nd Ed., Vol. 1 (1977)

Contact point: P.M. Eller
National Institute for Occupational Safety & Health
Division of Physical Sciences and Engineering
4676 Columbia Parkway
Cincinnati OH, 45226
USA

METHOD 8 – DETERMINATION OF BERYLLIUM IN AIR BY GRAPHITE FURNACE ATOMIC ABSORPTION SPECTROPHOTOMETRY

Adapted from Method 7102, In: Eller, P.M., ed. (1984)
NIOSH 'Manual of Analytical Methods', 3rd Ed., Vol. 1

1. SCOPE AND FIELD OF APPLICATION

This method is suitable for the determination of beryllium (Be) and its compounds (as Be) over the working range 0.5 to 10 $\mu g/m^3$ for a 90-L air sample. The estimated limit of detection is 5 ng/sample.

2. REFERENCES

Eller, P.M., ed. (1984) *NIOSH Manual of Analytical Methods,* 3rd Ed., Vol. 1, Cincinnati OH, U.S. Department of Health and Human Services, Method 7102

Taylor, D.G., ed. (1979) *NIOSH Manual of Analytical Methods,* 2nd Ed., Vol. 5, Cincinnati, OH, U.S. Department of Health, Education and Welfare, Method P & CAM 288

3. DEFINITIONS

Not applicable

4. PRINCIPLE

A known volume of air is drawn through a mixed cellulose ester membrane filter by means of a personal sampling pump. The filters are digested in a mixture of nitric and sulfuric acids and the solution evaporated to dryness. The residue is dissolved in 2% sodium sulfate/3% sulfuric acid (which eliminates possible interference from Ca, Na, K and Al) and Be is determined by graphite-furnace atomic absorption spectrophotometry (AAS).

5. HAZARDS

Concentrated sulfuric and nitric acids are toxic and the latter is a fire risk with organic materials.

Beryllium is very toxic and a suspected human carcinogen. Perform all acid digestions in a fume hood. Operator should wear protective clothing, gloves and safety glasses.

6. REAGENTS[1]

Argon	Pre-purified
Water	Distilled or deionized
Nitric acid	Concentrated
Sulfuric acid	Concentrated
Sodium sulfate	Reagent grade
Sodium sulfate, 2%/ 3% sulfuric acid	Add 10 g sodium sulfate and 15 mL concentrated sulfuric acid to deionized water and dilute to 500 mL in a volumetric flask.
Calibration stock solution	100 mg/L. Commercially available, or dissolve 100 mg Be metal in a minimum volume of 50% (v/v) hydrochloric acid and dilute to 1-L with 1% (v/v) hydrochloric acid. Dilute to 1 mg/L and use as intermediate stock solution.
Working standard solution	Prepare at least 5 working standard solutions over the range 0.005 to 1 µg Be per sample. Add known amounts of calibration stock solution to 2% sodium sulfate 3% sulfuric acid in 10-mL volumetric flasks. Dilute to the mark with 2% Na_2SO_4/3%/ H_2SO_4 and store in polyethylene bottles. Solution is stable at least 4 weeks.

7. APPARATUS[1]

Air sampler units	Mixed cellulose ester membrane filter, 0.8-µm pore size, 37-mm diameter in three-piece cassette filter holder (Millipore, or equivalent)
Personal sampling pump	1–4 L/min, with flexible connecting tubing. Calibrate with representative sampler in line.

[1] Reference to a company and/or product is for the purpose of information and identification only and does not imply approval or recommendation of the company and/or product by the International Agency for Research on Cancer, to the exclusion of others which may also be suitable.

Atomic absorption spectrophotometer	With graphite furnace, Be hollow-cathode lamp and background corrector.
Pressure regulator	Two-stage, for argon
Beakers	Phillips, 125-mL
Watch-glasses	
Volumetric flasks	10-mL, 500-mL and 1-L
Pipettes	10-mL, delivery, with bulb
Automatic pipettor	With tips, 10-μL and assorted sizes for standards
Hot-plate	150–400 °C
Water-bath	60–70 °C
Bottles	Polyethylene, 25-mL

NOTE: Clean all glassware with concentrated nitric acid and rinse thoroughly with distilled water before use.

8. SAMPLING

8.1 Assemble filter in the cassette filter holder. Support filter by a stainless-steel screen or back-up pad. Close firmly to prevent sample leakage around the filter and seal the holder with plastic tape or shrinkable cellulose band.

8.2 Remove filter holder plugs and attach holder to sampling pump tubing. Sample at an accurately-known flow rate between 1 and 4 L/min for a sample size of 25 to 1 000 L. Do not exceed 2 mg total dust loading on the filter.

8.3 Prepare 2 to 10 field blanks per set of 10 samples. The field blanks consist of complete sampler units from the same lot used for sample collection. They must be handled in all respects like the units used for air sampling, but no air should be drawn through them.

9. PROCEDURE

9.1 *Blank tests*

9.1.1   Field blanks: see 8.3 above. Follow procedures 9.4 and 9.5.

9.1.2 Media blanks: Approximately 5 media blanks should be analysed with every set of 10 samples. Media blanks are complete, unused sampling units taken from the same lot as those used for sampling, but not sent to the field. Follow procedures 9.4 and 9.5.

9.1.3 Reagent blanks: Analyse one reagent blank per 10 samples, or whenever reagents are renewed. Begin the analytical procedure at step 9.4.2, with no filter in the beaker.

9.2 *Check tests*

With each set of samples, analyse 3 quality-control blind spikes and 3 analyst spikes. Prepare the spiked membrane filters using membranes from the same lot used for sampling and spike with known amounts of the working standard solutions. The blind spikes should contain amounts of Be not known to the analyst.

9.3 *Test portion*

Not applicable

9.4 *Sample digestion and preparation for AAS*

9.4.1 Open cassettes and transfer filters to clean Phillips beakers. Discard back-up pads.

9.4.2 Add 10 mL concentrated HNO_3 and 1 mL concentrated H_2SO_4. Cover with a watch-glass.

9.4.3 Heat on hot-plate (150 °C) in fume hood until brown fumes of HNO_3 disappear, then at 400 °C until dense white fumes appear.
NOTE: Verify that all the compounds in the samples are soluble with this ashing procedure; e.g., ore or mining samples will require HF in the digestion. If additional ashing acids are used (HF, $HClO_4$ or H_3PO_4), evaporate to complete dryness at this point.

9.4.4 Cool and rinse watch-glass and sides of beaker with distilled water and evaporate just to dryness. Remove beaker immediately from hot-plate and cool in air.

9.4.5 Pipette 10.0 mL of 2% Na_2SO_4/3% H_2SO_4 solution into beaker and cover.

9.4.6 Heat in water-bath (60–70 °C) for 10 min. Allow to stand overnight before AAS analysis, to ensure complete dissolution of $BeSO_4$.

9.5 *AAS measurements*

9.5.1 Set the spectrophotometer and graphite furnace according to manufacturers; instructions, using the following conditions:

Wavelength: 234.9 nm
Graphite furnace: dry 20s at 110 °C
                                   char 10 s at 900 °C
                                   atomize 18 s at 2 800 °C
Background correction: D$_2$ or H$_2$ arc
Injection volume: 10 μL

9.5.2   Analyse samples, blanks and working standards and record absorbances (peak-heights). Analyse samples and working standards alternately, to compensate for increasing Be signal as graphite tube ages.

10. METHOD OF CALCULATION

The mass concentration, ρ_a (μg/m^3), of Be in the air sample is given by,

$$\rho_a = 10^4 \rho_s (A - A_m)/(A_s - A_o)V$$

where

ρ_s = mass concentration of the working standard analysed just after the sample of interest (μg/mL)

A = absorbance peak height obtained for sample

A_m = absorbance peak height obtained for media blank

A_s = absorbance peak height obtained with working standard analysed just after sample of interest

A_o = absorbance peak height obtained for 2% Na$_2$SO$_4$/3% H$_2$SO$_4$ solution alone

V = volume of air sampled (L)

11. REPEATABILITY AND REPRODUCIBILITY

This method was evaluated using NBS standard reference material No. 2675 over the range of 0.1 to 0.4 μg Be/filter. Be recovery was 98.2%, with a coefficient of variation of 0.8% [Taylor, D.G., ed. (1979)].

12. NOTES ON PROCEDURE

Not applicable

13. SCHEMATIC REPRESENTATION OF PROCEDURE

Sample air with cellulose ester filter
↓
Digest filter in 10 mL conc. HNO_3 + 1 mL conc. H_2SO_4
↓
Heat at 150 °C until HNO_3 fumes disappear, then
at 400 °C until H_2SO_4 fumes appear
↓
Cool, rinse watch-glass cover and sides of beaker with water,
then evaporate just to dryness
↓
Add 10.0 mL 2% Na_2SO_4/3% H_2SO_4 and cover
↓
Heat to 60–70 °C for 10 min. Stand overnight
↓
Determine Be content by AAS, correcting for blanks
and quantifying by comparison with standard solutions

14. ORIGIN OF THE METHOD

Method 7102, In: Eller, P.M., ed. (1984) *NIOSH Manual of Analytical Methods,* 3rd Ed., Vol. 1.

Contact point: P.M. Eller
National Institute for Occupational Safety and Health
Division of Physical Sciences and Engineering
4676 Columbia Parkway
Cincinnati, OH 45226
USA

Determination of metals and their compounds in water

METHOD 9 – DETERMINATION OF ARSENIC IN POTABLE AND SEA WATER BY SPECTROPHOTOMETRY

Adapted from *Methods for the Examination of Waters and Associated Materials,* The Standing Committee of Analysts, Department of the Environment, London, UK, with permission of the Controller of Her Majesty's Stationery Office.

1. SCOPE AND FIELD OF APPLICATION

This method is suitable for the determination of total arsenic in potable and sea water. The limits of detection are 0.67 µg/L and 0.19 µg/L respectively. Interfering cations are removed by an ion-exchange procedure, although only copper, silver and selenium interfere at the 0.5 mg/L level.

Excluding the time required for pre-treatment, six samples can be analysed in ~ 100 min, of which ~ 30 min is operator time.

2. REFERENCE

Heywood, M.G. & Riley, J.P. (1976) The determination of arsenic in sea water and other natural waters. *Anal. Chim. Acta,* **85,** 219–230

3. DEFINITIONS

Not applicable

4. PRINCIPLE

Inorganic arsenic is converted to arsine using sodium borohydride ($NaBH_4$), which is added slowly to the acidified samples by means of a peristaltic pump. The evolved hydrogen and entrained arsine are bubbled through an iodine/potassium iodide solution and the resultant arsenate is determined spectrophotometrically as an arseno-molybdenum blue complex at 866 nm. Some samples may contain organo-arsenic derivatives which may not be determined by this procedure; however, the total As content can be determined after pre-treatment of the sample with sulfuric and nitric acids. The application of this technique to representative samples will indicate whether pre-treatment is necessary.

5. HAZARDS

Particular care must be taken to avoid exposure to the intense UV radiation produced by the mercury lamp, which can cause permanent eye and skin damage. The photolysis process produces copious amounts of ozone, which is toxic, and the cooling air from the apparatus must be vented to a fume hood.

Addition of sulphuric acid (d_{20} 1.84) to water must be carried out slowly, with gentle swirling of the contents of the flask. The flask should be cooled by standing in a large beaker of cold water.

Sodium borohydride ($NaBH_4$) is caustic and can react violently with water. Care should be taken to avoid contact with eyes, skin and clothing (gloves and goggles should be worn). In the event of accidental spillage or contact, immediate copious washing with water is the simplest and most effective remedy. Subsequently, treat the affected areas as a caustic burn. If the compound gets into the eyes, irrigate with water immediately and obtain medical attention as quickly as possible.

Solutions containing As or potassium antimonyl tartrate are toxic. If any of these compounds have been ingested, immediately carry out gastric aspiration and lavage and obtain medical attention.

Very small quantities of toxic arsine are produced in step 9.6.4, which must be carried out in a fume cupboard.

6. REAGENTS[1]

All reagents and standard solutions should be kept in either glass or polyethylene bottles. Except where otherwise stated, analytical grade chemicals are suitable.

Distilled water	Water distilled from an all-glass apparatus has been found to be satisfactory.
Arsenic-free sea water	Pass sea water at approximately 2 mL/min through a 5 cm × 1.5 cm² bed of hydrous zirconium oxide, previously prepared by heating zirconyl chloride octahydrate in a muffle furnace at 260 ± 20 °C for 12 h, followed by sieving to 80–100 mesh. The bed should be sufficient to produce 20 L of As-free sea water. It is recommended that each batch of sea water be checked by carrying out a blank determination.
Sulfuric acid (H_2SO_4)	$d_{20} = 1.84$

---

[1] Reference to a company and/or product is for the purpose of information and identification only and does not imply approval or recommendation of the company and/or product by the International Agency for Research on Cancer, to the exclusion of others which may also be suitable.

Sulfuric acid	~ 2.5 mol/L
Hydrochloric acid (HCl)	$d_{20} = 1.18$
Hydrochloric acid	~ 6 mol/L, 1 mol/L, ~ 0.1 mol/L
Nitric acid (HNO_3)	$d_{20} = 1.42$
Ammonia (NH_4OH)	$d_{20} = 0.91$
Ammonia solution	~ 2 mol/L. Carry out dilution in a fume cupboard.
Aqueous sodium chloride (NaCl)	~ 1 mol/L
Aqueous sodium hydrogen carbonate ($NaHCO_3$) solution	42 g/L
Aqueous ethylenediaminetetraacetic acid, disodium (EDTA) solution	20 g/L
Aqueous ammonium molybdate (AM) solution	48 g/L. Store in a polyethylene bottle and reject if it becomes discoloured, or if a precipitate forms
Aqueous L-ascorbic acid (AA) solution	17.6 g/L. Store at 0 to 5 °C and reject the solution if it becomes discoloured.
Potassium antimonyl tartrate (PAT) solution	2.74 g/L. Dissolve 0.274 ± 0.01 g of PAT in water and make up to 100 mL
Mixed reagent solution	Mix 10.0 ± 0.1 mL of 2.5 mol/L H_2SO_4, 3.00 ± 0.05 mL AM solution, 1.00 ± 0.01 mL of PAT solution and 6.00 ± 0.05 mL of AA solution in a 25-mL stoppered flask. This reagent is NOT stable and should be used within 1 h of preparation.
Iodine	
Aqueous potassium iodide (KI) solution	80 g/L
Iodine/postassium iodide (I/KI) solution (absorption solution)	Dissolve 0.25 g ± 0.02 g of iodine in 5.00 ± 0.1 mL of 80 g/L KI solution and dilute with water to 100 mL.

Calcium hydroxide $(Ca(OH)_2)$	
Aqueous sodium borohydride ($NaBH_4$) solution	100 g/L Dissolve 25 ± 1 g of powdered $NaBH_4$ in 100 ± 5 mL water and filter the solution through a qualitative analytical-grade paper, capable of retaining 5 μm particles, into a 150-mL flask. To purify the solution, add 2.0 ± 0.1 g of $Ca(OH)_2$, loosely stopper the flask and place in a water-bath in a fume cupboard at 75 ± 3 °C for 20 min; under these conditions a small proportion of the borohydride decomposes rapidly, thus removing traces of As as arsine (this operation is hazardous). Cool the solution to room temperature, filter through a qualitative analytical grade filter paper capable of retaining 5 μm particles and dilute to 250 ± 5 mL with water. This solution decomposes slowly and should therefore be discarded after two days.
Aqueous sodium hydroxide solution	50 g/L. Prepare and store 100 mL in polyethylene vessels.
Cation-exchange resin	Treat a strongly-acidic cation-exchange resin of 50–100 mesh in a beaker at 80 °C (water bath) with approximately 20 times its own volume of 6 mol/L HCl. After 1 h, decant the acid and wash the resin several times with water until free from acid. Store as a slurry in water in a polyethylene bottle (pH greater than 5.0).
Standard As solution A	1 mg As/mL. Dissolve 1.321 ± 0.001 g of arsenic trioxide in 100 mL of 40 g/L NaOH solution in a 1-L volumetric flask. When dissolution is complete, dilute to the mark with water and mix well.
Standard As solution B	10 μg As/mL. Dilute 10.00 ± 0.02 mL of solution A to 600 mL with water in a 1-L volumetric flask, add 3.0 ± 0.1 mL of 6 mol/L HCl, dilute to the mark with water and mix well. This solution should be freshly prepared before use.
Standard As solution C	1 μg As/mL. Dilute 10.00 ± 0.02 mL of solution B to 60 mL with water in a 100-mL volumetric flask, add 2.0 ± 0.1 mL of 1 mol/L HCl, dilute to the mark with water and mix well. This solution should be freshly prepared before use.

Standard As solution D | 0.1 µg As/mL. Dilute 10.00 ± 0.02 mL of solution B to 600 mL with water in a 1-L volumetric flask, add 3.00 ± 0.1 mL of 6 mol/L HCl, dilute to the mark with water and mix well. This solution should be freshly prepared before use.

7. APPARATUS[1]

Spectrophotometer | Prism or grating type, or using narrow band pass optical filters, and fitted with 40-mm micro-cuvettes with a capacity of not greater than 1.5 mL.

Ultraviolet photolysis apparatus (Fig. 1) | For pretreatment of sea water samples. The apparatus consists of a cylindrical aluminium box containing an axially-mounted 1 kW medium-pressure mercury lamp, around which are arranged ten fused-silica photolysis tubes. Cooling to the optimum temperature of 60 ± 3 °C is accomplished by an externally-mounted fan and the expelled air containing toxic ozone is vented to a fume cupboard. The lid of the photolysis apparatus is fitted with an interlocked micro-switch, so that the mercury lamp cannot be operated when the lid is open.

Cation-exchange column | For removal of heavy metals.
Place a wad of silica wool (glass wool should not be used, since it tends to retain arsenic) at the bottom of a 5 cm × 5 mm i.d. ion-exchange column and fill with a slurry of approximately 5 mL of cation-exchange resin in the hydrogen form (section 6), taking care to avoid air bubbles and channelling. Convert the resin to the sodium form by passing 50 ± 1 mL of 1 mol/L NaCl at approximately 2 mL/min. Finally, wash the resin column with 50 ± 1 mL of water. After use, the column can be regenerated by washing it with 50 ± 1 mL of 6 mol/L HCl, then reconverting to the sodium form as described above.

---

[1] Reference to a company and/or product is for the purpose of information and identification only and does not imply approval or recommendation of the company and/or product by the International Agency for Research on Cancer, to the exclusion of others which may also be suitable.

Fig. 1. Ultraviolet photolysis apparatus.

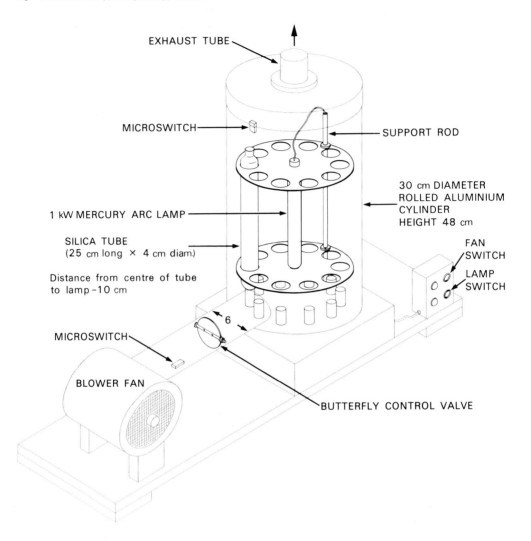

Apparatus for the evolution and collection of arsine (Fig. 2)	Sodium borohydride solution (100 g/L) is delivered from the reservoir *via* a manifold to a multichannel peristaltic pump fitted with acid-resistant tubing which serves to inject the reagent at a controlled rate (10 $\pm$ 1 and 15 $\pm$ 1 mL/h for potable water and sea water samples, respectively) into the 250-mL evolution flask mounted at an angle of approximately 35 °C on a stand. The evolved hydrogen, along with the entrained arsine, passes through the delivery tube jet into the absorption tube (Fig. 3) which has been calibrated to a volume of 2.50 $\pm$ 0.02 mL and which contains the absorption solution.
Ultrasonic bath	
Flasks	25-mL, stoppered; 150-mL, stoppered
Volumetric flasks	50-, 100-, 500- and 1000-mL
Measuring cylinders	Glass, polyethylene, 100-mL
Beakers	Borosilicate, 200-mL
Bottles	Polyethylene, 100-mL
Pipettes	5-, 10-, 15- and 20-mL, with bulb
Filter paper	Qualitative, analytical grade, capable of retaining 5-μm particles

NOTE: Clean all new glass and plastic ware by soaking in 10% (v/v) NHO_3 for 2 days. Rinse thoroughly with water. Thereafter, a thorough rinse in 10% (v/v) HNO_3, followed by a thorough rinse with water, should suffice.

8. SAMPLING

Sea water samples can be stored in either glass or polyethylene containers, with or without acidification (pH 1–8), for up to at least seven days without significant change. Potable water samples also appear to be stable under similar conditions. To a clean glass or polyethylene bottle, add 2.00 $\pm$ 0.1 mL of 6 mol/L HCl per litre of sample to be collected, then collect the sample.

Fig. 3. Absorption tube

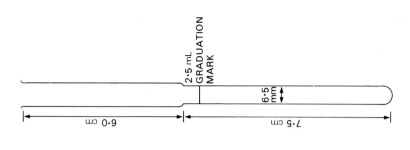

Fig. 2. Apparatus for the evolution and collection of arsine

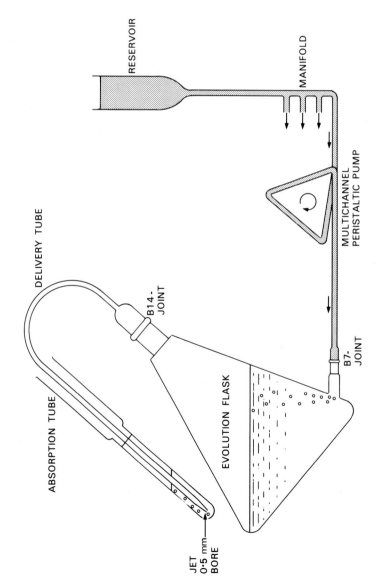

9. PROCEDURE

9.1 *Blank test*

9.1.1 Potable water – A blank must be run with each batch of determinations. To 50.00 ± 0.01 mL of distilled water, add 0.10 ± 0.02 mL of 6 mol/L HCl. If pre-treatment is used with samples, carry out procedures 9.4 to 9.6; otherwise carry out procedure 9.6 only.

9.1.2 Sea water – A blank must be run with each batch of determinations. To 150 ± 1 mL of As-free sea water, add 0.30 ± 0.02 mL of 6 mol/L HCl. If pre-treatment is used with samples, carry out procedures 9.9 and 9.10; otherwise, carry out procedure 9.10 only.

9.2 *Check test*

Analyse a standard solution of As of suitable concentration at the same time and in exactly the same way as the normal samples.

9.3 *Test portions*

Potable water 50 ± 0.05 mL of the sample

Sea water 150 ± 1 mL of the sample

9.4 *Pre-treatment of potable waters containing organic As compounds*[1]

NOTE: Some volatile As compounds may be lost by this procedure. If pre-treatment is not required, begin at step 9.6.

9.4.1 Add 50.00 ± 0.05 mL of the sample to a borosilicate glass beaker and evaporate to ~ 10 mL on a hot plate in a fume cupboard.

9.4.2 Cool to ambient temperature and add cautiously 2.0 ± 0.1 mL of HNO_3 (d_{20} 1.42) and 1.0 ± 0.1 mL of H_2SO_4 (d_{20} 1.84). Evaporate until dense white fumes begin to be evolved. Cool to ambient temperature.

9.4.3 Dissolve the residue cautiously in approximately 25 mL of water. When the concentration of certain heavy metals in the original sample exceeds 0.1 mg/L, they must now be removed. The removal procedure, 9.5, can be used for total heavy metal concentrations of up to 2 g/L. Application of procedure 9.5 to representative samples will show whether it is necessary. If it is, proceed directly to 9.5. If heavy metals removal is not necessary, proceed to 9.4.4.

---

[1] The procedure for sea water begins at section 9.9.

9.4.4   Transfer the solution of the residue to a 50-mL volumetric flask and dilute to the mark with water. Proceed to 9.6.

9.5 *Removal of heavy metals*

9.5.1   Using a pH meter, adjust the solution of the residue from 9.4.3 to pH 3.00 ± 0.5 by careful addition of 2 mol/L NH_4OH solution.

9.5.2   Pass the solution through a column of cation-exchange resin in the sodium form (section 7) at a rate of ~ 2 mL/min and wash the column with 4 × 5-mL aliquots of water.

9.5.3   Combine the percolate and washings, dilute with water to 50 ± 1 mL, transfer to an evolution flask and proceed to 9.6.2.

9.6 *Determination of inorganic As in potable water*

9.6.1   Place 50 ± 0.05 mL of the sample in the evolution flask (Fig. 2).

9.6.2   Add 5.00 ± 0.1 mL of 2.5 mol/L H_2SO_4 and 5.0 ± 0.1 mL of 20 g/L EDTA solution. Place the flask on the stand and fit the delivery tube.

9.6.3   To the absorption tube add 1.2 ± 0.1 mL of the absorption solution and 0.20 ± 0.02 mL of 42 g/L $NaHCO_3$ solution. Insert the delivery tube into the absorption tube until the jet is close to the bottom.

9.6.4   Using a peristaltic pump, add 100/L $NaBH_4$ solution to the evolution flask at a rate of 10 ± 1 mL/h. After 1 h, lower the absorption tube and rinse the tip of the delivery tube into it with not more than 0.3 mL water.

9.6.5   Add 0.5 ± 0.1 mL of the mixed reagent solution to the absorption tube and dilute with water to 2.50 ± 0.02 mL. Mix thoroughly (an ultrasonic bath is suitable) to release carbon dioxide. Allow to stand for 30 min (see NOTES ON PROCEDURE 12.1).

9.6.6   Set up the spectrophotometer according to the manufacturer's instructions and measure the absorbance of the solution at 866 nm in a 40-mm micro-cuvette against a reference cuvette containing water (see NOTES ON PROCEDURE, 12.2). Quantification is carried out by comparison with the absorbance of a calibration standard (9.7), assuming the calibration curve (9.8) to be linear.

9.7 *Calibration standard for potable water*

9.7.1   Add 20.00 ± 0.02 mL of standard As solution D and 0.10 ± 0.02 mL of 6 mol/L HCl to each of two 50-mL volumetric flasks and dilute to the mark with water. These duplicate standards contain 40 µg As/L.

9.7.2   Follow the entire procedure (9.4–9.6) employed with the samples and record the absorbance of each standard.

9.8 Calibration curve for potable water

NOTE: This procedure must be carried out regularly, and on at least two independent occasions before the method is applied to any samples.

9.8.1   To each of five 500-mL volumetric flasks, add 1.00 ± 0.01 mL of 6 mol/L HCl and, respectively, (by pipette) 0.0, 5.0, 10.0, 15.0 and 20.0 mL of standard As solution C. Dilute to the mark with water. These solutions contain, respectively, 0, 10, 20, 30 and 40 µg As/L.

9.8.2   Analyse each solution according to procedure 9.6. Plot the absorbance of each solution against the As concentration (µg/L). The calibration curve for As in potable water is normally linear between 0 and 60 µg/L.

9.9 Pre-treatment of sea water

NOTE: Experience has shown that organic As constitutes less than 0.5% of the total As in sea water. Some estuarine waters may contain a greater proportion of organic As. Application of procedure 9.9 to representative samples will indicate whether the pre-treatment is necessary. If pre-treatment is not necessary, proceed directly to section 9.10.

9.9.1   Using a pH meter, adjust the pH of 200 ± 1 mL of sample to pH 6.00 ± 0.3 by cautious addition of 40 g/L NaOH solution.

9.9.2   Transfer 150 ± 1 mL of the solution to a 25 cm × 4 cm fused silica tube and stopper loosely.

9.9.3   Irradiate the silica tube for 2 h in the photolysis apparatus, adjusting the flow of air from the fan by means of the butterfly valve (Fig. 1) so that an optimum solution temperature of $60 \pm 3\,^\circ$C is achieved.

9.9.4   Cool to ambient temperature and quantitatively transfer the solution to an evolution flask, using 2 mL portions of water to rinse the tube. Proceed to 9.10.2.

9.10 Determination of inorganic As in sea water

9.10.1   Place 150 ± 1 mL of sample in the evolution flask (Fig. 2).

9.10.2   Follow instructions 9.6.2 to 9.6.6, inclusive, except that the $NaBH_4$ solution is added at a rate of 15 ± 1 mL/h in step 9.6.4 (see NOTES ON PROCEDURE, 12.3).

9.11 *Calibration standard for sea water*

9.11.1   Add 4.00 ± 0.02 mL of standard As solution D, 0.40 ± 0.02 mL of 6 mol/L HCl and 196 ± 1 mL of As-free sea water to each of two beakers. These duplicate standards contain 2 µg As/L.

9.11.2   Follow the entire procedure employed with the sea water samples and record the absorbance of each standard.

9.12 *Calibration curve for sea water*

The NOTE at the beginning of section 9.8 applies equally here.

9.12.1   To each of a series of 500-mL volumetric flasks, add 1.00 ± 0.01 mL of 6 mol/L HCl and respectively (by pipette), 0.0, 5.0, 10.0, 15.0 and 20.0 mL of standard As solution D. Dilute to the mark with As-free sea water. These solutions contain, respectively, 0, 1, 2, 3 and 4 µg As/L.

9.12.2   Using 150-mL aliquots of these solutions, carry out procedure 9.10. Plot the absorbance of each solution against the As concentration (µg/L). The calibration curve for As in sea water is normally linear between 0 and 15 µg/L.

10. METHOD OF CALCULATION

10.1 *Potable water*

The mass concentration, ρ (µg/L), of As is given by

$$\rho = \frac{16V(S-B)}{C-B},$$

where,

V   = final volume of solution in step 9.6.5 (mL)
S   = absorbance of sample solution (step 9.6.6)
B   = absorbance of blank solution (9.1)[1]
C   = average absorbance of calibration standards (9.7)

10.2 *Sea water*

The mass concentration, ρ (µg/L), of As is given by,

$$\rho = \frac{0.8V\ (S-B)}{C-B},$$

---

[1] See NOTES ON PROCEDURE, 12.4

where the symbols, defined in 10.1, apply to the sea water samples, blanks and calibration standards.

11. REPEATABILITY AND REPRODUCIBILITY

The following results have been obtained for repeatability, using potable water spiked with the stated concentration of As (no pre-treatment) and with as-received sea water (no pre-treatment).

	Arsenic concentration (µg/L)	Standard deviation (µg/L)	Degrees of freedom
Potable water	0.0	0.18	7
	4.0	0.05	7
	20.0	0.12	7
	40.0	0.24	7
Sea water	0.00	0.048	9
	2.49	0.050	9
	2.63	0.050	9

12. NOTES ON PROCEDURE

12.1 The procedure given can be used to determine As in potable waters in the concentration range 0–40 µg/L. When the As concentration in the sample exceeds 40 µg/L, the final solution (9.6.5) must be further diluted with water. The upper concentration limit for the method is 800 µg/L.

12.2 The procedure used for measuring absorbance should be rigorously controlled to ensure satisfactory precision of measurement. The same cells should always be used for the reference and sample solutions, and they should always be placed in the same position in the cell holder with the same face towards the light source.

It is difficult to ensure reproducible alignment of cells with chipped corners, which should therefore be discarded. Similarly, the movement of the cell carrier should be kept scrupulously clean. Before every set of measurements, the sample cell should be measured against the reference cell when both are filled with water. This will help indicate when the cells need cleaning and it will also enable the true absorbance of the blank to be determined.

12.3 The procedure given can be used to determine As in sea water in the concentration range 0–2 µg/L. When the As concentration in the sample exceeds 2 µg/L, the final solution (step 9.6.5) must be diluted further with water. The upper concentration limit for the method is 800 µg As/L.

12.4 If arsenic is present in the water used for the blank, the results will be erroneously low. The following procedure for the determination of As in the water used for blanks has not been evaluated, but is thought likely to be satisfactory.

Carry out the As determinations, using the procedure described in 9.6, with 50-mL and 150-mL test portions of the water used for blanks. The As content of the blank water is equivalent to an absorbance, Y, where

$$Y = (B_{150} - B_{50})/2,$$

where B_{150} = absorbance obtained with 150 mL test portion
B_{50} = absorbance obtained with 50 mL test portion

The mass concentration, ρ_B ($\mu g/L$), of As in the blank water is given by

$$\rho_B = \frac{16VY}{C-B},$$

where V, C and B are defined in 10.1. The concentration ρ_B must be added to that calculated in 10.1.

13. SCHEMATIC REPRESENTATION OF PROCEDURE

13.1 *Potable waters*

Samples requiring pre-treatment   *Samples not requiring pre-treatment*

(Treat standard solutions and blanks as samples)   (Treat standard solutions and blanks as samples)

Place 50 mL sample in beaker   Place 50 mL sample in evolution flask

heat

Evaporate to 10 mL. Cool, add 2 mL HNO_3 + 1 mL H_2SO_4

heat

Evaporate to white fumes. Cool, dissolve residue in 25 mL H_2O

If necessary to remove heavy metals   If unnecessary to remove heavy metals

Adjust to pH 3.0 using 2 mol/L NH_4OH and pH meter

$\downarrow$

Pass solution through
ion exchange column,
and wash column with
4×5 mL H_2O

$\downarrow$

Combine percolate and   Make solution up to
washings, make up to   50 mL with H_2O
50 mL with H_2O

$\downarrow$

Transfer solution to evolution flask

$\downarrow$

Add 5 mL 2.5 mol/L H_2SO_4 + 5 mL 2% EDTA solution

$\downarrow$

Place flask on stand, fit delivery tube

$\downarrow$

Add 1.2 mL I/KI solution + 0.2 mL 4.2% $NaHCO_3$ solution to
absorption tube. Insert delivery tube in absorption tube

$\downarrow$

To evolution flask, add 10% $NaBH_4$ solution at 10 mL/h for 1 h

$\downarrow$

Add 0.5 mL of mixed reagent to absorption tube and dilute with H_2O
to 2.5 mL. Mix thoroughly, allow to stand for 30 min

$\downarrow$

Transfer portion of blue solution to micro-cuvette
and measure absorbance at 866 nm

$\downarrow$

Quantify by comparison with absorbance of calibration standards

13.2 *Sea water*

Samples requiring pre-treatment   *Samples not requiring pre-treatment*

(Treat standard solutions and blanks   (Treat standard solutions and blanks
as samples)   as samples)

Place 200 mL sample in beaker flask   Place 150 mL sample in evolution
                                           flask

$\downarrow$

Adjust to pH 6 using 4% NaOH
solution and pH meter

$\downarrow$

Transfer 150 mL to fused silica tube
and irradiate with UV for 2 h

$\downarrow$

Cool, transfer irradiated solution to
evolution flask

$\downarrow$

Add 5 mL 2.5 mol/L H_2SO_4 + 5 mL 2% EDTA solution

$\downarrow$

Place flask on stand, fit delivery tube

↓

Add 1.2 mL I/KI solution + 0.2 mL 4.2% $NaHCO_3$ solution to absorption tube
Insert delivery tube in absorption tube

↓

To evolution flask, add 10% $NaBH_4$ solution at 15 mL/h for 1 h

↓

Add 0.5 mL of mixed reagent to absorption tube
and dilute with water to 2.5 mL.
Mix thoroughly, allow to stand for 30 min

↓

Transfer portion of blue solution to micro-cuvette
and measure absorbance at 866 nm

↓

Quantify by comparison with absorbance of calibration standards

14. ORIGIN OF THE METHOD

The Standing Committee of Analysts
The Department of the Environment
2, Marsham Street
London, SW1P 3EB, UK

Contact point: The Secretary
                   The Standing Committee of Analysts

METHOD 10 – DETERMINATION OF HEXAVALENT CHROMIUM IN POTABLE WATERS AND TOTAL CHROMIUM IN WATER AND WASTE-WATER BY COLORIMETRY

Adapted from Method 307B, *Standard Method, for the Examination of Water and Wastewater,* 14th Ed. (1976), Washington DC, Am. Publ. Health Assoc., pp. 192–195

1. SCOPE AND FIELD OF APPLICATION

This method is suitable for the determination of hexavalent chromium in potable water and total chromium in water and waste-water, after oxidation of trivalent chromium. Large amounts of molybdenum and mercury salts will interfere, but concentrations up to 200 mg/L can be tolerated. Vanadium interferes strongly only at concentrations more than ten times that of chromium. An optional procedure is specified for the removal of interfering metals.

The method requires test portions containing 10–100 µg of chromium, so that sample volumes of several litres may have to be taken and subsequently evaporated to about 10 mL for the total chromium determination. The hexavalent chromium procedure is much less time-consuming.

2. REFERENCE

Allen, T.L. (1958) Microdetermination of chromium with 1,5-diphenylcarbohydrazide. *Anal. Chem., 30,* 447

3. DEFINITIONS

Not applicable

4. PRINCIPLE

Dissolved hexavalent chromium is determined colorimetrically by reaction with diphenylcarbazide in acid solution. If dissolved trivalent plus hexavalent chromium is to be determined, the trivalent form is first oxidized with potassium permanganate. If total chromium is to be determined in the presence of organic matter, the sample must be digested with a sulfuric acid/nitric acid mixture before oxidizing the trivalent chromium. Excess permanganate is reduced with sodium azide. The absorbance of the reaction product with diphenylcarbazide is measured photometrically at 540 nm.

5. HAZARDS

Concentrated HNO_3 and H_2O_2 are toxic by inhalation and a fire risk with organic materials. Concentrated H_2SO_4 and H_3PO_4 are toxic and irritant. Sodium azide is highly toxic and constitutes a severe explosion risk when shocked or heated. The acid digestion procedure should be carried out in a ventilated hood and protective gloves and glasses should be worn.

6. REAGENTS[1]

All chemicals employed should be Analytical Reagent grade, or better.

Redistilled water	Double-distilled in all-glass apparatus
Chloroform	
Nitric acid	$\sim$ 70% (w/w)
Sulfuric acid	98% (w/w), 50% (v/v)
Phosphoric acid	85% (w/w)
Hydrogen peroxide	30% (w/w)
Ammonium hydroxide	29% (w/w)
Potassium permanganate solution	Dissolve 4 g $KMnO_4$ in 100 mL of redistilled water
Sodium azide solution	Dissolve 0.5 g NaN_3 in 100 mL of redistilled water
Cupferron solution	Dissolve 5 g $C_6H_5N(NO)ONH_4$ in 95 mL of redistilled water
Diphenylcarbazide solution	Dissolve 250 mg 1,5-diphenylcarbazide in 50 mL of acetone. Store in a brown bottle. Discard when solution becomes discoloured.

---

[1] Reference to a company and/or product is for the purpose of information and identification only and does not imply approval or recommendation of the company and/or product by the International Agency for Research on Cancer, to the exclusion of others which may also be suitable.

Stock chromium solution	50 μg/mL. Dissolve 141.4 mg $K_2Cr_2O_7$ in redistilled water and dilute to 1 000 mL in volumetric flask.
Standard chromium solution	5 μg/mL. Dilute 10.00 mL of stock chromium solution to 100 mL in a volumetric flask.
Methyl orange indicator solution	Dissolve 500 mg methyl orange powder in redistilled water and dilute to 1 L.

7. APPARATUS[1]

Evaporating dish	250-mL capacity, with watch-glass cover
Conical flasks	125-mL, 250-mL
Glass beads	
Filter crucibles	Sintered-glass or porcelain, with holder (preferably adapted to filtration directly into a 50-mL volumetric flask)
Filter flasks	100-mL
Volumetric flasks	50-mL, 100-mL, 1 000-mL
Separatory funnels	125-mL, Squibb form, with glass or Teflon stopcock and stopper.
Pipettes	2-mL to 40-mL
Hot-plate	
Spectrophotometer	For use at 540 nm, with 1-cm absorption cells.

NOTE: Clean all glass-ware thoroughly, then rinse with 50% (v/v) HNO_3, followed by redistilled water.

8. SAMPLING

8.1 Acidify samples at time of collection by adding sufficient 70% HNO_3 to lower pH to 2.0 (with relatively clean water containing no particulate matter, 1.5 mL

---

[1] Reference to a company and/or product is for the purpose of information and identification only and does not imply approval or recommendation of the company and/or product by the International Agency for Research on Cancer, to the exclusion of others which may also be suitable.

of 70% HNO_3 per litre of sample will be sufficient). The sample should contain 10–100 µg Cr (VI) or 12–130 µg total Cr.

8.2   If sample contains particulate matter and only dissolved chromium content is desired, filter the sample through a 0.45-µm pore-size membrane filter, then acidify with 70% HNO_3.

9.   PROCEDURE

9.1   *Blank tests*

   9.1.1   Dissolved hexavalent Cr: acidify at least 100 mL of redistilled water to pH 2.0 with 70% HNO_3. Fill a 100-mL volumetric flask to the mark, then follow instructions 9.4.4 and 9.4.5. Record absorbance.

   9.1.2   Total chromium: add 5 mL 70% HNO_3 and 2 mL 30% H_2O_2 to 10 mL redistilled water. Beginning with step 9.5.1.2, follow the entire procedure employed with the samples to be analysed. Record absorbance.

9.2   *Check test*

   Not applicable

9.3   *Test portions*

   See 9.4.1 and 9.5.1.1

9.4   *Determination of hexavalent Cr in potable water*[1]

   9.4.1   If necessary, filter sample (8.2) and concentrate by evaporation to obtain 10 to 100 µg Cr in a test portion of less than 100 mL. Record volume of test portion before evaporation.

   9.4.2   Transfer cooled test portion to 100-mL volumetric flask, dilute to the mark with redistilled water and mix. If solution is clear, proceed to step 9.4.4.

   9.4.3   If solution is turbid transfer an appropriate portion to a 1-cm absorption cell and record absorbance at 540 nm, using redistilled water as reference.

   9.4.4   Add 2.0 mL diphenylcarbazide solution to solution in the volumetric flask (9.4.2), mix and let stand 5 to 10 min for full colour development.

---

[1] Hexavalent chromium can be determined only in the absence of appreciable organic matter. If presence of trivalent Cr is suspected, see section 12 (NOTES ON PROCEDURE).

9.4.5   Transfer appropriate amount to a 1-cm absorption cell and measure absorbance at 540 nm, using distilled water as reference. Correct the reading by subtracting absorbance measured in 9.4.3, if applicable.

9.4.6   Calculate hexavalent Cr content using calibration curve (9.5) and blank correction (9.1.1), as described in section 10.1.

9.5 *Calibration curve for hexavalent Cr*

9.5.1   Pipette measured volumes of standard chromium solution (5 μg/mL) from 2.00 to 20.0 mL (10–100 μg Cr) into 250-mL conical flasks. With these calibration solutions, carry out the entire procedure employed with the samples analysed, beginning by acidification to pH 2.0 (8.1) and continuing to 9.4.5, inclusive.

9.5.2   Correct the absorbance readings by substracting the absorbance of the reagent blank (9.1.1). Plot corrected absorbance *versus* μg Cr in the calibration solutions.

9.6 *Determination of total Cr in water and waste-water*

9.6.1   Digestion of organic matter

9.6.1.1   Agitate the acidified sample (8.1) and take a test portion containing 12–130 μg Cr. Record the volume and add 5 mL 70% HNO_3 and 2 mL 30% H_2O_2 to reduce chromate.

9.6.1.2   Transfer to an evaporating dish and reduce the volume to 8–10 mL on a hot-plate, covering the dish with a watch-glass if necessary to avoid loss by spattering.

NOTE: If the initial volume exceeds 250 mL, transfer to the evaporating dish in portions as the sample evaporates.

9.6.1.3   Transfer the concentrated solution, and any solids remaining in the dish, to a 125-mL conical flask and add 3 mL 70% HNO_3, used to rinse the evaporating disk.

9.6.1.4   Add 5 mL 98% H_2SO_4 and a few glass beads, then evaporate solution on a hot-plate (in a hood) until dense white fumes of SO_3 just appear in flask (do not continue heating beyond this point).
If solution is not clear, add 5 mL 70% HNO_3 and repeat evaporation until appearance of SO_3 fumes. All HNO_3 must be removed, as indicated by clarity of solution and absence of brown fumes in flask.

9.6.1.5   Cool to room temperature and dilute carefully to about 25 mL with distilled water.

9.6.1.6 Heat nearly to boiling, then filter through sintered-glass or porcelain filter crucible into a filter flask[1]. Rinse the sample flask with two 5-mL portions of redistilled water and pass them through the crucible into the filter flask.

9.6.1.7 Transfer filtrate to a 50-mL volumetric flask, rinse filter flask with two 5-mL portions of redistilled water and add rinsings to volumetric flask. Dilute to the mark with redistilled water and mix. The resulting solution is $\sim$ 1.5 mol/L with respect to H_2SO_4. If interfering amounts of Mo, V, Cu or Fe are present, carry out procedure 9.6.2. If not, proceed directly to 9.6.3.

9.6.2   Removal of Mo, V, Cu and Fe with cupferron

9.6.2.1 Pipette 40.0 mL of digested sample (9.6.1.7) into a 125-mL separatory funnel and chill in an ice bath.

9.6.2.2 Add 5 mL ice-cold cupferron solution, shake well and allow to stand for 1 min.

9.6.2.3 Extract solution 9.6.2.2 with three successive 5-mL portions of chloroform; shake each portion thoroughly with the aqueous solution and discard the chloroform layers.

9.6.2.4 Transfer the aqueous solution to a 125-mL conical flask, rinse separatory funnel with small amount of redistilled water and add rinsing to the flask. Boil for about 5 min to eliminate chloroform, then cool.

9.6.2.5 Add 5 mL 70% HNO_3 and boil to appearance of SO_3 fumes.

9.6.2.6 Cool slightly and repeat 9.6.2.5.

9.6.2.7 Cool, wash sides of flask with redistilled water and boil again to appearance of SO_3 fumes to eliminate all HNO_3. Cool and add 25 mL redistilled water. Proceed to 9.6.3.2.

9.6.3   Oxidation of trivalent Cr

9.6.3.1 Pipette 40.0 mL of digested sample (9.6.1.7) into a 125-mL conical flask.

9.6.3.2 Using methyl orange as indicator, add concentrated NH_4OH until the solution is just basic, than add 50% (v/v) H_2SO_4 dropwise until it is acidic, plus 1 mL (20 drops) in excess.

---

[1] Collection of the filtrate directly into a 50-mL volumetric flask is preferable, in which case the transfer step, 9.6.1.7, can be avoided.

9.6.3.3 Add a glass bead and heat to boiling.

9.6.3.4 Add 2 drops KMnO$_4$ solution to give dark-red colour. If fading occurs, add KMnO$_4$ dropwise to maintain an excess of about 2 drops.

9.6.3.5 Boil the solution for 2 min longer, add 1 mL of sodium azide solution and continue boiling gently. If red colour does not fade completely after about 30 s, add another 1 mL sodium azide solution.

9.6.3.6 Continue boiling for 1 min after colour has faded completely, then cool. Add 0.25 mL (5 drops) H$_3$PO$_4$.

9.6.4 Colour development and absorption measurement

9.6.4.1 With solution from 9.6.3.6, follow instructions 9.4.2 to 9.4.5, inclusive.

9.6.4.2 Calculate the total Cr content using calibration curve (9.7) and blank correction (9.1.2), as described in section 10.2.

9.7 *Calibration curve for total Cr*

9.7.1 Pipette measured volumes of standard chromium solution (5 μg/mL) from 2.50 to 25.0 mL into 250-mL conical flasks.

9.7.2 Add 5 mL 70% HNO$_3$ and 2 mL 30% H$_2$O$_2$ to each flask and carry out digestion procedure, beginning with step 9.6.1.2.

9.7.3 If procedure 9.6.2 was carried out with the water samples, chill 40.0 mL of each of the digested calibration solutions (i.e., 10–100 μg Cr) in a 125-mL separatory funnel and begin procedure 9.6.2 at step 9.6.2.2. Follow remainder of procedure to step 9.6.4.1, inclusive, as with water samples, then correct absorbance readings by subtracting absorbance of reagent blank (9.1.2). Plot corrected absorbance *versus* μg Cr in 40.0 mL of digest of each calibration solution.

9.7.4 If procedure 9.6.2 was omitted with the water samples, add 40.0 mL of each digested calibration solution to a 125-mL conical flask and proceed to step 9.6.3.2. Follow remainder of procedure to step 9.6.4.1, inclusive, then correct absorbance readings by subtracting absorbance of reagent blank (9.1.2). Plot corrected absorbance *versus* μg Cr in 40.0 mL of digest of each calibration solution.

10. METHOD OF CALCULATION

10.1 *Hexavalent Cr in potable water*

The mass concentration, ρ (μg/L), of hexavalent Cr in the water sample is given by,

$$\rho \quad = \quad m/V$$

where,

   m   =   mass of Cr obtained from calibration curve (9.5) and sample absorbance (9.4.5), corrected for blank (µg)

   V   =   initial volume of test portion in 9.4.1 (L)

10.2 *Total Cr in water and waste-water*

The mass concentration, ρ (µg/L), of total Cr in the sample is given by

$$\rho \quad = \quad 1.25 \ m/V$$

where,

   m   =   mass of Cr obtained from calibration curve (9.7) and sample absorbance, corrected for blank (µg)

   V   =   volume of test portion in 9.6.1.1 (L)

   1.25 =   ratio of volume of digest (9.6.1.7) to volume taken in 9.6.2.1 or 9.6.3.1.

11. REPEATABILITY AND REPRODUCIBILITY

11.1 *Repeatability*

   No data available

11.2 *Reproducibility*

   The following synthetic sample has been analysed for total dissolved (trivalent plus hexavalent) chromium in 31 laboratories (the figures in parentheses are concentrations in µg/L):

   Cr (110), Al (500), Cd (50), Ca (470), Fe (300), Pb (70), Mn (120), Ag (150), Zn (650).

   The coefficient of variation (relative standard deviation) obtained was 47.8%.

12. NOTES ON PROCEDURE

   The trivalent form of Cr rarely occurs in potable water. If its presence is suspected a total Cr determination may be carried out as follows, omitting the digestion and heavy-metal extraction procedures. Take a volume of acidified sample equal to that employed in 9.4.1 and evaporate to about 40 mL. Transfer to a 125-mL conical flask and follow instructions 9.6.3.2 to 9.6.4.1, inclusive. Determine total Cr from absorbance of sample, using a calibration curve prepared as described in 9.5, but following the procedure described immediately above (9.6.3.2–9.6.4.1) with the calibration solutions.

13. SCHEMATIC REPRESENTATION OF PROCEDURE

Total Cr in water and waste-water
Add 5 mL 70% HNO_3 + 2 mL 30% H_2O_2
to sample containing 12–130 μg Cr
↓
Evaporate to 8–10 mL and transfer
to 125-mL conical flask with 3 mL HNO_3
↓
Add 5 mL 98% H_2SO_4 and glass beads,
evaporate on hot-plate until white
SO_3 fumes observed.
↓
Cool and dilute to ∼ 25 mL with water
↓
Heat and filter through sintered-
glass into 50-mL volumetric flask.
Add water rinsings and make up to
50 mL

Extraction of interfering metals
Chill 40.0 mL of digest in 125-mL
separating funnel. Add ice-cold
cupferron solution. Shake well,
stand 1 min.
↓
Extract with 3 × 5 mL chloroform.
Discard organic layers.
↓
Transfer to 125 mL conical flask
with water rinse and boil 5 min.
↓
Cool, add 5 mL HNO_3 and boil to
appearance of SO_3 fumes. Repeat.
↓
Cool, wash down sides of flask, boil
again, then cool and add 25 mL water
↓
Pipette 40.0 mL digest into 125-mL
flask
↓

$\downarrow$

Add conc. NH_4OH until solution just
basic to methyl orange. Add 50% H_2SO_4
dropwise until acidic, plus 1 mL in
excess

$\downarrow$

Add glass beads and heat to boiling.
Add 2 drops $KMnO_4$ solution. If fading
occurs, add $KMnO_4$ dropwise to maintain
excess of 2 drops

$\downarrow$

Boil 2 min longer, add 1 mL NaN_3
solution and continue boiling. If
colour does not fade after 30 s, add
another 1 mL NaN_3

$\downarrow$

Continue boiling 1 min. Cool, add
5 drops H_3PO_4

Hexavalent Cr in potable water
Evaporate acidified (pH 2.0)
sample containing 10–100 μg Cr
to < 100 mL

Transfer to 100-mL volumetric flask and
make up to volume with water

$\downarrow$

Add 2.0 mL diphenylcarbazide solution
and let stand 5–10 min.

$\downarrow$

Measure absorbance at 540 nm and
calculate Cr content using calibration
curve and blank correction.

14. ORIGIN OF THE METHOD

Method 307B, *Standard Methods for the Examination of Water and Wastewater*,
16th Ed. (1985), Washington DC, American Public Health Association,
pp. 201–204

Contact point: P.M. Eller
National Institute for Occupational Safety and Health
Division of Physical Sciences and Engineering
4676 Columbia Parkway
Cincinnati, OH 45226
USA

METHOD 11 – DETERMINATION OF NICKEL IN WATER, BODY FLUIDS, TISSUES AND EXCRETA

F. Sunderman Jr

1. SCOPE AND FIELD OF APPLICATION

This method of nickel determination by electrothermal atomic absorbtion spectrophotometry (AAS) is suitable for measurements of nickel concentrations in human body fluids (e.g., serum, plasma, whole blood, urine, saliva, perspiration), solid excreta (e.g., faeces, hair) and tissues (e.g., lung, liver, kidney, heart). The method is also applicable to nickel determination in water. When 2 mL samples of body fluids are analysed, the linear working range of the method is 0.5 to 20 µg Ni/L. The limits of detection are 0.2 µg Ni/L of body fluid and 0.4 µg Ni/kg of tissue. Approximately 36 to 42 analyses can be carried out in a single run, comprising duplicate sets of blanks and standards, quality-control and recovery tests, and 9 to 12 samples. For analysis of nickel in serum, plasma, or urine, such a run requires approximately 12 hours; for analysis of faeces, whole blood or tissues, the required time is approximately 18 hours.

2. REFERENCES

Brown, S.S., Nomoto, S., Stoeppler, M. & Sunderman, F.W., Jr (1981) IUPAC reference method for analysis of nickel in serum and urine by electrothermal atomic absorption spectrometry. *Clin. Biochem., 14,* 295–299

Sunderman, F.W., Jr (1984) *Nickel.* In: Vercruysse, A., ed., *Techniques and Instrumentation in Analytical Chemistry,* Vol. 4B, Amsterdam, Elsevier, pp. 279–306

3. DEFINITIONS

Not applicable

4. PRINCIPLE

Organic constituents of the sample are digested with a mixture of nitric, sulfuric and perchloric acids. If substantial quantities of iron are present (e.g., whole blood, tissues), hydrochloric acid is added and ferric chloride is extracted into 4-methyl-2-pentanone (methyl isobutyl ketone, MIBK). The solution is then adjusted to pH 7 with ammonium hydroxide and ammonium tetramethylenedithiocarbamate (ammonium pyrrolidine dithiocarbamate, APDC) solution is added. The bis(1-

pyrrolidinecarbodithiato)nickel [II] complex is extracted into MIBK. The concentration of nickel in the MIBK extract is measured by electrothermal atomic absorption spectrophotometry (AAS).

5. HAZARDS

Concentrated perchloric acid will explode in contact with organic materials, or from shock or heat. Concentrated nitric and sulfuric acids are also hazards and should be handled with care under a fume hood.

6. REAGENTS[1]

All reagents should be of the best analytical quality, with particularly low nickel contents.

6.1 *General (all samples)*

Hydrochloric acid	Concentrated, 'ultra-pure'
Nitric acid	Concentrated, 'ultra-pure' (910 g/L, relative density 1.40)
Perchloric acid	Concentrated, 'ultra-pure' (1 169 g/L, relative density 1.67)
Sulfuric acid	Concentrated, 'ultra-pure' (1 766 g/L, relative density 1.84) 'Ultra pure' acids can be obtained from E. Merck Co., Darmstadt, FRG, or J.T. Baker Chemical Co., Phillipsburg, NJ, USA
Ammonium hydroxide	Concentrated, 'ultra-pure' (228 g/L, relative density 0.91). Place 150 mL in a 250 mL polyethylene wash bottle, with a screw cap fitted with a fine-tipped delivery tube.
Ultra-pure water	< 0.1 μg Ni/L, prepared by deionization, followed by double-distillation from a quartz still. Collect in a 1-L, polyethylene bottle, with a screw-cap, piston-type dispenser (3 mL).

---

[1] Reference to a company and/or product is for the purpose of information and identification only and does not imply approval or recommendation of the company and/or product by the International Agency for Research on Cancer, to the exclusion of others which may also be suitable.

4-Methyl-2-pentanone (MIBK)	Ultra-pure (Burdick & Jackson Inc., Muskegan MI, USA). Place in a 250 mL, borosilicate glass bottle with piston-type dispenser set to deliver 0.7 mL volumes.
Ammonium tetramethyl-enedithiocarbamate (APDC)	(1-Pyrrolidinecarbodithioic acid, ammonium salt, Eastman Chemicals Inc., Rochester NY, USA)
Chloroform	Ultra-pure
Bromothymol blue	'Certified reagent'
Potassium phosphate, dibasic	Anhydrous
Potassium phosphate, monobasic	Anhydrous
Nickel powder	99.99% pure (Ventrox Corp., Beverly MA, USA)
Argon	99.99% pure
Acid digestion mixture	In a 250-mL, glass-stoppered borosilicate glass bottle, place successively 120 mL of concentrated nitric acid, 40 mL of concentrated sulfuric acid and 40 mL of concentrated perchloric acid. Mix thoroughly. When the concentrated reagent is diluted $1 \rightarrow 5$ with ultra-pure water and pipetted directly into the the graphite cuvette of the electrothermal atomizer, no nickel should be detectable with routine operating parameters.
Dilute ammonium hydroxide solution	In a 250-mL screw-cap polyethylene wash bottle, place 50 mL of ultra-pure concentrated ammonium hydroxide solution and 80 mL of ultra-pure water. Fit a screw-cap with fine-tipped polyethylene delivery tube onto the bottle.
Dilute nitric acid solution	In a 250-mL, polypropylene volumetric flask, place 1 mL of concentrated, ultra-pure nitric acid. Dilute to volume with ultra-pure water and transfer to a polyethylene bottle. This solution is used for preparation of nickel working standard solutions.
Bromothymol blue indicator solution	In a 60-mL, screw-cap polyethylene drop-dispenser bottle, place 20 mg of bromothymol blue and 1 mL of dilute ammonium hydroxide solution. Dilute to 50 mL with ultra-pure water. Fit a screw-cap with fine-tipped polyethylene delivery tube onto the bottle.

Ammonium tetramethyl-enedithiocarbamate solution	In a 25-mL, screw-capped polypropylene graduated tube, place 0.5 g of APDC. Dissolve in 25 mL of ultra-pure water and extracted the solution at least three times with 1.4 mL portions of MIBK. Aspirate and discard the first 2 washings. Analyse the last washing by electrothermal atomic absorption spectrometry to verify that it contains no detectable nickel. The final aqueous solution of APDC should be colorless and free from precipitate. Prepare this solution immediately before use.
Potassium phosphate buffer (1.0 mol/L, pH 7)	Transfer 17.0 g of anhydrous KH_2PO_4 and 21.8 g of anhydrous K_2HPO_4 into a 250-mL volumetric flask. Dissolve and dilute to volume with ultra-pure water. Transfer the solution to a 250-mL separatory funnel, add 5 mL APDC solution and extract the mixture at least 3 times with 10-mL portions of ultra-pure chloroform. Analyse the last $CHCl_3$ washing by electrothermal atomic absorption spectrometry to verify that it contains no detectable nickel. Transfer the buffer solution to a polyethylene bottle, fitted with a fine-tipped polyethylene delivery tube.
Nickel stock standard solution (100 mg Ni/L)	Weigh 50 mg of nickel powder into a tared, 25-mL, borosilicate glass beaker. Add 5 mL ultra-pure water and 5 mL ultra-pure concentrated nitric acid and dissolve the nickel by cautiously warming the beaker. Transfer the cooled solution quantitatively to a 500-mL polypropylene volumetric flask and dilute to volume with ultra-pure water. This solution, stored in a screw-capped polyethylene bottle, is stable for at least 1 year.
Nickel standard solution (400 µg Ni/L)	Pipette 2 mL of nickel stock standard solution and 2 mL of concentrated ultra-pure nitric acid into a 500-mL polypropylene volumetric flask. Dilute to volume with ultra-pure water and transfer to a screw-capped polyethylene bottle. Prepare this solution every 3 months.
Nickel working standard solutions	Into six, 100-mL, polypropylene volumetric flasks. Pipette 0 (blank), 0.5, 1, 2, 3 and 4 mL of nickel standard solution and, respectively, 4, 3.5, 3, 2, 1 and 0 mL of the dilute nitric acid solution. Dilute to volume with ultra-pure water. These solutions contain 0, 2, 4, 8, 12 and 16 µg Ni/L.

6.2 *Blood samples*

Sodium heparin solution	10 000 USP units/mL (Eli Lilly Co., Indianapolis IN, USA)

6.3 *Urine and faeces samples*

Hydrochloric acid solution	6 mol/L. Dilute ultra-pure, concentrated acid with ultra-pure water and store in a screw-capped polyethylene bottle.

6.4 *Hair samples*

Detergent solution, non-ionic	("7-X Detergent", Limbro Chemical Co., New Haven CT, USA) 1% (v/v) in ultra-pure water

NOTE: All reagent bottles and attached dispensers must be shielded from dust by a polyethylene cover.

7. APPARATUS[1]

7.1 *General (all samples)*

Glass bottles	250-mL, borosilicate, glass-stoppered. 250-mL, borosilicate, with screw-cap, piston-type dispenser to deliver 0.7-mL volumes of MIBK.
Polyethylene bottles	1-L, with screw-cap, piston-type dispenser to deliver 3-mL volumes (Scientific Industries Inc., Berkeley CA, USA) 250-mL, screw-cap. 60-mL, screw-cap, with fine-tipped delivery tube.
Polyethylene wash bottles	250-mL, screw-cap, with fine-tipped delivery tubes.
Volumetric flasks	500-, 250- and 100-mL, polypropylene
Graduated tube	25-mL, polypropylene, screw-cap
Beaker	25-mL, borosilicate glass
Polypropylene tubes	10-mL, screw-capped

---

[1] Reference to a company and/or product is for the purpose of information and identification only and does not imply approval or recommendation of the company and/or product by the International Agency for Research on Cancer, to the exclusion of others which may also be suitable.

Digestion tubes	25-mL (150 mm × 18 mm o.d.) ("Pyrex" tubes from Corning Glass Works, Corning NY, are suitable) (See NOTES ON PROCEDURE, 12.2)
Pipettors, piston-type	0.5-mL, 2-mL, with only plastic surfaces exposed to reagents ("Finn-Pipets", Vanguard International, Neptune NJ, USA, or "Eppendorf Pipets", Brinkman Instruments Inc., Westbury NY)
Polyethylene microtubes	0.75-mL, with polyethylene stoppers
Centrifuge	900 × g
Digestion apparatus	The digestion apparatus consists of an electrically-heated aluminium block containing 42 holes (20-mm diameter; 100-mm depth) to accommodate digestion tubes, with a continuously-variable temperature regulator (to 300 °C). Pack aluminium foil in the bottom of each hole to facilitate heat transfer to the hemispherical base of the digestion tube. A suitable digestion apparatus may be obtained from Scientific Products, Inc., Evanston IL, USA. The digestion apparatus, placed in a fume hood, is shielded with a 'Pyrex' or 'Lucite' canopy. The temperature during digestion is monitored by a thermometer suspended in a digestion tube containing 5 mL of concentrated sulfuric acid.
Atomic absorption spectrophotometer with graphite-furnace atomizer	Desirable accessories for the electrothermal atomic absorption spectrophotometer include automatic sampling system, Zeeman background correction system, temperature-programming system with "ramp" modes, optical pyrometer to regulate the atomization temperature and strip-chart recorder. Ultra-pure argon (99.99%) is used to flush the electrothermal atomizer.

7.2 Blood samples

Intravenous cannulae	Teflon-polyethylene ("IV-Cath", Becton-Dickinson Co., Rutherford NJ, USA)
Syringes	10-mL, polypropylene ("Monovet" type, Walter Sarsted Inc., Princeton NJ, USA)
Test tubes	10-mL, polyethylene, with polyethylene stoppers

Dropper	Polyethylene, acid-washed
Vortex mixer	

7.3 *Urine samples*

Bottles	Screw-capped, polyethylene, acid-washed (for 24-h collection)

7.4 *Faecal samples*

Portable commode	
Polyethylene bags	Acid-washed, for portable commode
Polyethylene jars	2-L, screw-capped
Mechanical shaker	(designed for 2-L paint cans)

7.5 *Hair samples*

Centrifuge tubes	60-mL, polypropylene, screw-capped
Mechanical shaker	(for 60-mL centrifuge tubes)

7.6 *Perspiration*

Shoulder-length gloves	Polyethylene (Bolab Inc., Derry NH, USA)
Pasteur pipette	

7.7 *Tissue samples*

Knives	Plastic
Scissors	Teflon-coated
Vortex mixer	

NOTE: All glassware and plasticware should be cleaned as described in NOTES ON PROCEDURE, 12.3.

8. SAMPLING

8.1 *Whole blood, serum or plasma*

To obtain blood by venipuncture, cleanse the antecubital fossa of the arm with ethanol and allow to dry by evaporation. Apply a tourniquet and insert a polyethylene intravenous catheter into an antecubital vein. Remove the stylus of the catheter and flush with 3 mL of blood, which is discarded. Use a polypropylene syringe to collect 10 mL of blood, transfer to a polyethylene test tube and cap with a polyethylene stopper. If measurement of nickel in whole blood or plasma is desired, add 50 µL of sodium heparin solution (10 000 USP units/mL) to the tube and mix. If serum samples are required, allow the blood to clot for 45 min at room temperature. To separate plasma or serum, centrifuge the test tube at 900 × g for 15 min. By means of an acid-washed polyethylene dropper, transfer serum or plasma to a polyethylene test tube and stopper. Reject the serum or plasma specimen if there is visible hemolysis, lipemia, or turbidity. Store samples of whole blood, serum, or plasma at 4 °C until required. Take duplicate, 2 mL samples for nickel analysis.

8.2 *Urine*

Void urine directly into an acid-washed polyethylene bottle, with care to avoid contamination from faeces or dust on the clothing. When a 24-hour urine collection has been completed, add ultra-pure hydrochloric acid (6 mol/L) in the proportion of 10 mL of acid per litre of urine and store in the polyethylene bottle at 4 °C (or −20 °C) until required. Take duplicate, 2 mL samples for nickel analysis.

8.3 *Faeces*

Deposit faeces directly into acid-washed polyethylene bags for 3 days, using a portable commode. Pool the samples, weigh and transfer to a 2-L polyethylene jar containing 1 L of ultra-pure water. Homogenize the faeces by shaking the jar violently for 3 h with an apparatus designed for shaking paint cans. Adjust the sample volume to 2 L in an acid-washed cylinder. Place 10 mL of the faecal homogenate and 10 mL of ultra-pure hydrochloric acid (6 mol/L) in a 1-L volumetric flask and dilute to volume with ultra-pure water. Store at −20 °C until required. Take duplicate, 2 mL samples for nickel analysis.

8.4 *Hair*

Cut the hair (1 to 2 g) from the sub-occipital region of the scalp with scissors and mince to lengths of less than 3 mm. Place the sample in a 60-mL, polypropylene, screw-capped centrifuge tube containing 50 mL of non-ionic detergent solution. Agitate the tube for 15 min, using a mechanical shaking apparatus, then centrifuge for 5 min at 900 × g. Decant and discard the detergent solution. Using the above procedure, wash the hair sample two more times for 15 min with 50 mL volumes of detergent solution, then rinse with a total of one litre of ultra-pure water. Finally, dry the sample at 110 °C for 18 h. Weigh duplicate 20 mg samples of hair into digestion tube for nickel analysis.

8.5 *Perspiration*

Carefully clean and trim the fingernails and scrub each arm for 5 min with soap, then rinse copiously with ultra-pure water and dry by evaporation. Encase both arms in polyethylene shoulder-length gloves, which are secured beneath the axillae with rubber bands. Collect perspiration during 15-min exposure to "dry" heat in a sauna bath at 93 °C (< 5% relative humidity). Recover the samples from the gloves by puncturing each finger sheath with the tip of an acid-washed Pasteur pipette. Pool the perspiration from both arms and centrifuge at 900 × g for 15 min. Decant the supernatant into screw-capped, polypropylene tubes and store at 4 °C. Take duplicate, 0.5 mL samples for nickel analysis.

8.6 *Tissue*

Excise representative specimens (approximately 10 g) with plastic knives and store at − 20 °C until required. Mince duplicate samples (1 g, wet weight) with acid-washed, teflon-coated scissors and transfer to digestion tubes for nickel analysis.

8.7 *Water*

Collect ∼ 50-mL samples in acid-washed polyethylene bottles and store at 4 °C. Place duplicate 15-mL samples in digestion tubes and evaporate to dryness for nickel analysis.

9. PROCEDURE

9.1 *Blank test*

With each set of samples, analyse duplicate reagent blanks by carrying out procedures 9.4, 9.6 and 9.7, with no sample in the digestion tubes. Note that the concentration observed with 2 mL samples of the 0 µg Ni/L working standard solution may exceed (by 0.1 to 0.2 µg/L) the nickel concentration obtained for the reagent blanks.

9.2 *Check test*

Acidify a 24-hour urine specimen (containing 4 to 6 µg Ni/L) by addition of 10 mL of concentrated nitric acid per litre of urine. Divide the acidified specimen into 5 mL aliquots in screw-capped polypropylene tubes and store at − 20 °C. Include one tube of this "quality control" specimen in each set of nickel analyses. (The same 24-hour specimen of urine is also used to determine the recovery of nickel (see 9.9).

9.3 *Test portions*

The volumes or masses of the various types of sample for nickel analysis are specified in Section 8. Measure the samples of whole blood, plasma, serum, urine, perspiration and water with a coefficient of variation of approximately 1%, and the samples of faeces, tissues and hair with a coefficient of variation of approximately 5%.

9.4 *Digestion of serum, plasma, urine, faeces, perspiration, hair and water samples*

9.4.1   Transfer the specified quantity of sample (section 8) into duplicate digestion tubes.

9.4.2   Into pairs of digestion tubes, transfer 2 mL of each working standard solution (0, 2, 4, 8, 12 and 16 µg Ni/L) for determination of calibration curve (see also sections 9.2 and 9.9).

9.4.3   Dispense 2 mL of acid digestion mixture into all the above-mentioned tubes and into a pair of empty tubes (reagent blanks, 9.1), then place the tubes in the digestion apparatus at ambient temperature.

9.4.4   Heat the tubes at 110 °C for 1 h (this is the most critical stage of the digestion, because of the possibility of sample loss by foaming).

9.4.5   Continue heating as follows: 2 h at 140 °C, 30 min at 190 °C and, finally, 1 h at 300 °C. At the conclusion of the 4.5 hour digestion period, all nitric acid and perchloric acid should have evaporated. The contents of the tubes should be perfectly clear and colorless and the sample volume should be approximately 0.2 mL (corresponding to the volume of the residual sulfuric acid).

9.5 *Digestion of whole blood and tissue samples*

9.5.1   Proceed as in 9.4.1 to 9.4.4, inclusive.

9.5.2   Raise digestion temperature to 140 °C for 2 h, then add 2 mL acid digestion mixture and continue heating at 140 °C for a further 2 h.

9.5.3   Raise temperature to 190 °C for 30 min, then to 300 °C for 1 h.

9.5.4   Cool the tubes to ambient temperature and add 0.5 mL concentrated hydrochloric acid and 1 mL ultra-pure water, then heat to boiling in the digestion apparatus.

9.5.5   Cool, add 3 mL of MIBK and mix with a Vortex mixer to extract the iron into the MIBK layer.

9.6.5   Aspirate the MIBK layer and discard.

9.5.7   Repeat the extraction (9.5.5–9.5.6) at least twice (i.e., until black particles of $FeCl_3$ are completely extracted with MIBK).

9.6 *Extraction of nickel*

9.6.1 When the tubes from 9.4.5 and/or 9.5.7 are at ambient temperature, add 3 drops bromothymol blue indicator solution and 3 mL ultra-pure water to each tube, taking care to rinse down the wall.

9.6.2 Add concentrated ammonium hydroxide solution dropwise with constant swirling until the colour begins to change to blue.

9.6.3 Add 2 drops phosphate buffer followed by dilute ammonium hydroxide solution, dropwise, until the colour is light blue-green.

> NOTE: The end-point of the pH adjustment (pH 7) should be checked with a pH meter, so that the analyst is familiar with the specific shade of blue-green colour that is sought. A pH meter cannot be used directly to monitor the standard or unknown samples, however, owing to contamination by the pH electrode.

9.6.4 Add 0.5 mL APDC solution to each tube and mix the contents for 10 s with a Vortex mixer. Allow the samples to stand for 5 min.

9.6.5 Add 0.7 mL MIBK to each tube and mix for 40 s with a Vortex mixer. (The aqueous and MIBK phases separate without centrifugation. The MIBK extracts of biological samples are yellow, owing to extraction of copper as well as nickel).

9.6.6 Transfer approximately 0.5 mL of each MIBK extract to a polyethylene microtube, being careful to avoid transfer of aqueous phase. (If desired, the analysis can be interrupted at this point. Seal the microtube with a polyethylene stopper and store overnight at 4 °C).

9.7 *Nickel determination by AAS*

9.7.1 Instrumental conditions. For analysis with a Perkin-Elmer model 5000 electrothermal atomic absorption spectrophotometer, equipped with automatic sampler, temperature programmer, pyrolytic graphite tube and Zeeman background corrector, the following conditions are applicable; sample extract volume, 20 μL; wavelength, 232.0 nm; spectral band-width, 0.2 nm; Ni lamp current, 25 mA; time-constant, 0.3 s; chart speed, 100 mm/min; recorder range, 1A full-scale. For analysis with another type of electrothermal AAS, the analyst must determine the instrumental conditions for optimal sensitivity.

9.7.2 Analytical program. For analysis with a Perkin-Elmer model 5000 instrument, set the following temperature program:

(a) 30 s ramp from 25 °C to 120 °C, hold at 120 °C for 30 s;
(b) 20 s ramp from 120 °C to 140 °C, hold at 140 °C for 30 s;

(c) 20 s ramp from 140 °C to 250 °C, hold at 250 °C for 10 s;
(d) 20 s ramp from 250 °C to 700 °C, hold at 700 °C for 10 s;
(e) 10 s ramp from 700 °C to 1 100 °C, hold at 1 100 °C for 20 s;
(f) atomize at 2 700 °C for 5 s;
(g) 1 s ramp from 2 700 °C to 2 750 °C, hold at 2 750 °C for 3 s.

Set the argon flow-rate at 300 mL/min throughout the temperature program, excepting the last 5 s of step (e) and the 5 s of step (f). During this 10 s interval, reduce the argon flow to 10 mL/min. Program the instrument to record absorbance at 232.0 nm (with Zeeman background correction) during the last 5 s of step (e) and the 5 s of step (f). For analysis with another type of electrothermal atomizer, the analyst must determine the optimal analytical program.

9.8 *Calibration curve*

9.8.1   Measure the absorbance peak heights obtained with the six working standard solutions (9.4.2) and correct by subtracting the average value obtained with the 0 μg Ni/L solution from the average values with the other 5 working standard solutions.

9.8.2   Plot the corrected average peak heights *versus* the concentration (μg Ni/L) of the standard solutions.

9.9 *Recovery*

9.9.1   Transfer 5 mL of nickel standard solution (400 μg/L) to a 250 mL volumetric flask and dilute to volume with the acidified, quality-control urine specimen (9.2).

9.9.2   Divide foregoing spiked sample into 5-mL aliquots and store at −20 °C in screw-capped polypropylene tubes. Include one of these tubes in every set of sample analyses.

9.9.3   Subtract the peak height obtained with the quality-control sample (9.2) from that obtained with the spiked sample (9.9.2).

9.9.4   Convert the corrected peak-height to Ni concentration (μg/L) using the calibration curve (9.8). Divide the result by the concentration of added Ni (8 mg/L) and multiply by 100 to obtain the percent recovery.

NOTE: Recoveries outside the range 90–110% indicate that the results are doubtful and that the analysis should be repeated.

10   METHOD OF CALCULATION

10.1 Nickel concentrations in water and body fluids are reported as μg Ni/L; nickel concentrations in excreta (urine, faeces) are reported as μg Ni/day; nickel concentrations in tissues are reported as µg Ni/kg (wet weight) and nickel concentrations in hair are reported as µg Ni/kg (dry weight). Subtract the mean reagent-blank absorbance peak height from the mean sample peak height. Use the resulting value and the calibration curve to obtain the sample extract (9.6.6) concentrations, p_e, in µg Ni/L.

10.2 The mass concentrations, ρ_s (µg/L), in water and body-fluid samples are given by

$$\rho_s = \rho_e V_e/V_s$$

where

V_e = volume of MIBK added in 9.6.5 (mL)

V_s = volume of sample in 9.4.1 (mL)

10.3 The daily excretion of Ni in urine is given by

$\rho_s V_d$ (µg/day)

where

ρ_s is defined in 10.2 and

V_d = volume of 24-h urine sample (L/day).

10.4 For the sampling procedure described in 8.3, the daily excretion of Ni in faeces is given by

$2 \times 10^4 \rho_s/3$ (µg/day), where ρ_s is defined in 10.2

10.5 The mass fraction, ω (µg/kg), of Ni in tissue samples is given by

$$\omega = \rho_e V_e/m$$

where

m = wet weight of tissue sample taken in 9.5.1 (g) and

ρ_e and V_e are defined in 10.2.

10.6 The mass fraction of Ni in hair samples is given by the equation of 10.5, where m = dry weight of hair sample taken in 9.4.1 (g).

11. REPEATABILITY, REPRODUCIBILITY AND RECOVERY

The following data were obtained by evaluators of the IUPAC Reference Method (Brown *et al.*, 1981). One evaluator reported that the coefficient of variation was 7.8%, based upon 21 analyses on consecutive working days of a single urine specimen with a mean nickel concentration of 4.2 µg/L; the range of observed values was 3.6 to 5.8 µg/L. A second evaluator reported that the coefficient of variation within a single run was 4.1%, based upon 10 analyses of a single urine specimen on the same day, and that the coefficient of variation from run-to-run was 8.7%, based upon analyses of the same urine specimen on 10 successive working days (the average nickel concentration obtained was 10.5 µg/L). A third evaluator reported that the average recovery of nickel was 98% (CV = 3.4%, range = 94 to 107%), based upon additions of nickel (5 µg/L) to 12 specimens of urine (mean nickel concentration = 3.9 µg/L). A fourth evaluator reported that the average recovery of nickel was 97% (CV = 7.0%), based upon additions of nickel (8 µg/L) to 9 specimens of urine (mean nickel concentration = 2.2 µg/L).

12. NOTES ON PROCEDURE

12.1 *Precautions*

The major difficulty with this method is control of nickel contamination. Specimen containers and analytical utensils should be acid-washed and handled with plastic gloves to prevent nickel contamination from sweat on the analyst's fingers. The laboratory should be scrupulously clean and well-ventilated;cigarette smoking should be prohibited. In the vicinity of nickel refineries, special precautions are necessary to overcome nickel contamination, such as use of a laminar-flow hood and surgical attire.

12.2 When digestion tubes are used for the first time, they must be cleaned by adding 1 mL of acid digestion mixture to each tube and heating the tubes in the digestion apparatus at 300 °C for 1 hour. The tubes are then cooled, residual sulfuric acid is rinsed out with water, and the tubes are washed as described in 12.3, below. The tubes are discarded as soon as they become etched (e.g., after 50 to 75 analyses).

12.3 *Washing of glass-ware and plasticware*

Before each use, the digestion tubes, polypropylene syringes, polyethylene tubes and pipettor tips should be scrubbed in hot detergent solution (such as "7-X Detergent", section 6.4). The concentrated detergent solution is diluted 30-fold with hot deionized water before use. After washing in hot detergent, the utensils are rinsed in deionized water, then placed in 2-L polyethylene canisters and washed in batch fashion by filling with deionized water and decanting, without contact of the utensils with the hands. After 6 rinses with deionized water (which is completely drained), 50 mL of concentrated HCl is poured into the canister and the canister is capped tightly. The contents are mixed so that HCl fumes percolate over the surfaces of the utensils. The canister is allowed to stand at room temperature for 1 hour and is then filled with deionized water, shaken, and allowed to stand for 20 min. The utensils are allowed to drain, and are then rinsed 5 times with deionized water and twice with ultra-pure water. The canister is placed with the lid ajar in an oven at 110 °C until the utensils are dry.

12.4 *Matrix solution*

The IUPAC Reference Method (Brown *et al., 1981*) specified addition of a Fe[II]-Cu[II] matrix solution to the nickel intermediate calibration solution, in order to increase the recovery of nickel added to serum from 95% to 100%. Using the Zeeman background correction system for the Perkin-Elmer model 5000 electrothermal atomic absorption spectrophotometer, the author has found that the matrix solution is unnecessary for quantitative recovery of added nickel.

12.5 *Reference values*

Table 1 lists reference values for nickel concentrations in specimens from adults without occupational exposure to nickel compounds. These nickel analyses were performed by the present method or one of its antecedents, using atomic absorption spectrophotometry with flame or electrothermal atomization (Sunderman, 1983).

Table 1. Reference values for nickel concentrations in biological materials from humans without occupational exposure to nickel

Specimen	No. of subjects	Nickel concentrations		Units
		Mean ± SD	Range	
Whole blood	17	4.8 ± 1.3	2.9 − 7.0	µg/L
Serum	80	2.6 ± 0.9	0.8 − 5.2	µg/L
Urine	50	2.2 ± 1.2	0.7 − 5.2	µg/L
		2.6 ± 1.4	0.5 − 6.4	µg/day
Faeces	10	14.2 ± 2.7	10.8 − 18.7	µg/g (dry)
		258 ± 126	80 − 540	µg/day
Hair	20	220 ± 80	130 − 150	µg/kg (dry)
Sweat	33	52 ± 36	7 − 180	µg/L
Lung	12	85 ± 65	8 − 221	µg/kg (wet)
Kidney	8	10.5 ± 4.1	6.8 − 18.2	µg/kg (wet)
Liver	12	8.2 ± 2.3	5.2 − 13.2	µg/kg (wet)
Heart	12	6.4 ± 1.6	4.3 − 9.3	µg/kg (wet)

13. SCHEMATIC REPRESENTATION OF PROCEDURE

Digestion of sample in hot, nitric, sulfuric, perchloric acid mixture
↓
Whole blood and tissue samples only; add HCl, boil, cool and extract iron with MIBK (discard)
↓
Adjust pH to 7 with concentrated NH_4OH, phosphate buffer and dilute NH_4OH (bromothymol blue indicator)
↓
Add APDC solution and mix (Ni-chelation)
↓

Extract Ni-PDC complex into MIBK
↓
Determine Ni in extract using electrothermal AAS
and calibration curve (Ni standard solutions)

14. ORIGIN OF THE METHOD

Departments of Laboratory Medicine and Pharmacology
University of Connecticut School of Medicine
263 Farmington Avenue
Farmington, Connecticut 06032, USA

Contact point: F. William Sunderman Jr

METHOD 12 – DETERMINATION OF LEAD IN POTABLE WATERS BY ATOMIC ABSORPTION SPECTROPHOTOMETRY

Adapted from *Methods for the Examination of Waters and Associated materials,*
The Standing Committee of Analysts, Department of the Environment, London, UK,
with permission of the Controller of Her Majesty's Stationery Office.

1. SCOPE AND FIELD OF APPLICATION

This method is suitable for the determination of all forms of lead in potable waters. The limit of detection is 1–6 µg/L. The calibration curve is normally linear up to 100 µg/L, but higher concentrations can be measured using smaller test portions. No substances normally present in potable waters have been found to cause interference.

The total analysis (and operator) time, excluding eventual pre-treatment, is typically about 3 h for 10 samples, analysed together with blanks and calibration standards.

2. REFERENCES

Water Research Association (1972) *Technical Enquiry Report* TIR No. 254, Medmenham, UK

Water Research Centre (1976) *Technical Report 28,* Medmenham, UK

3. DEFINITIONS

Not applicable

4. PRINCIPLE

The lead chelate formed by reaction with ammonium pyrrolidine dithiocarbamate (APDC) is extracted into 4-methyl-2-pentanone (methyl isobutyl Ketone, MIBK) and the amount of Pb in the extract is determined by atomic absorption spectrophotometry (AAS).

Some samples may require preliminary boiling with nitric acid (see section 8.2) to convert Pb compounds to forms capable of reacting with APDC.

Since cadmium and Pb are quantitatively extracted together, both elements may be determined, if desired, in a somewhat larger volume of the same extract, but with loss of sensitivity (see Method 13, Determination of Cadmium).

5. HAZARDS

Concentrated nitric and hydrochloric acids are toxic by inhalation. The former is also a fire risk in contact with organic materials.

4-Methyl-2-pentanone is flammable, irritating to the eyes and mucous membranes and is narcotic in high concentrations. It must not be pipetted by mouth.

The exhaust fumes from the atomic absorption spectrophotometer are toxic and must be ducted away.

6. REAGENTS

NOTE: Keep all reagents and standard solutions in polyethylene bottles, unless otherwise stated. 'Analytical Reagent' grade chemicals are suitable, except for MIBK (see below).

Water	Deionized or distilled from an all-glass apparatus
Hydrochloric acid (HCl)	Concentrated ($d_{20} = 1.18$). 50% (v/v). Dilute 500 mL HCl (d_{20} 1.18) to 1 L with water 3% (v/v). Dilute 6.0 $\pm$ 0.1 mL 50% (v/v) HCl to 100 mL with water.
Nitric acid (HNO$_3$)	Concentrated ($d_{20} = 1.42$). 10% (v/v). Dilute 100 $\pm$ 1 mL HNO$_3$ (d_{20} 1.42) to 1 L with water.
Sodium hydroxide (NaOH) solution	100 g/L. Dissolve 10 $\pm$ 0.1 g NaOH in water in a polyethylene beaker. Cool and dilute to 100 mL in polyethylene cylinder.
Ammonium pyrrolidine dithiocarbamate (APDC)	10 g/L. Dissolve 1.0 $\pm$ 0.1 g APDC in water and dilute to 100 mL. This solution should be freshly prepared and thoroughly mixed before use.
4-Methyl-2-pentanone (MIBK)	A special grade for AAS is preferable. Store in a glass bottle.

Standard lead solution A   1 g/L. Weigh 1.000 ± 0.005 g of Pb wire ($> 99.9\%$ purity) and dissolve with gentle heating in a mixture of 7.0 ± 0.5 mL HNO_3 (d_{20} 1.42) and approximately 20 mL of water.
Quantitatively transfer solution to a 1-L volumetric flask, dilute to the mark with water and mix well. This solution is stable for several months (store in polyethylene bottle).

Standard lead solution, B   2mg/L. Dilute 2.00 ± 0.01 mL of solution A to 1 L with water in a volumetric flask. This solution should be freshly prepared before use.

Bromophenol blue solution   1 g/L. Dissolve 0.1 ± 0.01 g of bromophenol blue in 100 mL of 50% (v/v) aqueous ethanol.

7. APPARATUS

Beakers   400-mL, borosilicate glass, graduated 250-mL, polyethylene

Measuring cylinders   100-mL, glass, polyethylene

Volumetric flasks   500-mL, 1-L, glass

Separating funnels   250-mL, glass, with ground-glass stoppers and taps

Pipettes   2.0, 4.0, 5.0, 10.0, 15.0, 20.0 and 25.0-mL, with bulb

Glass tubes 20×50 mm, with snap-on polyethylene caps

Atomic absorption spectrophotometer   Air-acetylene flame, lead hollow-cathode lamp. A chart recorder is the most desirable form of readout

NOTE: If possible, apparatus should be reserved solely for Pb determinations. Clean all new glass- and polyethylene-ware by soaking in 10% (v/v) HNO_3 for 2 days. Rinse thoroughly with water. After each determination, a thorough rinse in 10% (v/v) HNO_3, followed by water, should suffice.

8. SAMPLING

8.1 To a clean polyethylene bottle, add 2.00 ± 0.05 mL of 50% (v/v) HCl per litre of sample to be collected, then collect the sample. (The acidification minimizes the adsorption of Pb onto the walls of the bottle).

8.2 Samples containing suspended and/or colloidal material may require pre-treatment (9.4) to convert Pb compounds to an extractable form (a few organic compounds may not be converted by this procedure). When it is known that pre-treatment will not be necessary, it is satisfactory to add to the empty bottle sufficient 50% (v/v) HCl to bring the sample pH to 2.5 $\pm$ 0.3. In that case, place 200 $\pm$ 1 mL of the sample in a separating funnel and begin the procedure at 9.5. Alternatively, place 200 mL of sample in a 400-mL, graduated borosilicate beaker and begin at step 9.4.3. Omit 9.4.4 and proceed to 9.5.

9. PROCEDURE

9.1 *Blank test*

A blank must be run with each set (e.g., up to 10) of samples, using the same batch of reagents as for the samples. To a 400-mL, graduated borosilicate beaker, add 0.40 $\pm$ 0.05 mL of 50% (v/v) HCl and 200 $\pm$ 1 mL of water (see NOTES ON PROCEDURE, 12.1). If the pre-treatment is employed for the samples, carry out procedures 9.4 and 9.5. If not, carry out step 9.4.3 and procedure 9.5.

9.2 *Check test*

Not applicable

9.3 *Test portion*

200 $\pm$ 1 mL of acidified sample (section 8, see also 12.2)

9.4 *Sample pre-treatment*

NOTE: If pre-treatment is not required, see 8.2.

9.4.1   Add 200 $\pm$ 1 mL of the sample to a 400-mL, graduated borosilicate beaker. (If the Pb concentration is likely to exceed 100 µg/L, a smaller test portion should be taken. See NOTES ON PROCEDURE, 12.2) Add 1.0 $\pm$ 0.1 mL HNO$_3$ (d$_{20}$ 1.42), cover beaker with a watch-glass and boil gently on a hot-plate until the volume is reduced to 20 $\pm$ 5 mL.

9.4.2   Cautiously wash down the watch-glass and the sides of the beaker with water until total volume in beaker reaches 150 $\pm$ 5 mL. Replace watch-glass and allow solution to cool to room temperature.

9.4.3   Add 3 drops of bromophenol blue solution and, while swirling, slowly add 100 g/L NaOH until blue colour persists. While swirling, add 3% (v/v) HCl dropwise until the blue colour just disappears, then add 2.0 $\pm$ 0.1 mL of 3% (v/v) HCl. (The pH at the end of this step should be

2.5 ± 0.3. Very occasionally, the pH may require readjustment to this value.)

9.4.4   Transfer the solution to a measuring cylinder and dilute with water to 200 ± 1 mL.

9.5 *Chelate formation and extraction*

9.5.1   Transfer the solution to a separating funnel. Add 4.00 ± 0.05 mL of APDC solution and shake to mix.

9.5.2   Add 10.00 ± 0.05 mL of MIBK, stopper the funnel and shake vigorously for 2 min. Allow to stand for 5 min, then discard the aqueous phase.

9.5.3   Run the organic phase into a sample tube and fit the cap.

Complete the atomic absorption measurement (9.7) during the same working day.

NOTE: All samples, blanks and calibration standards (9.6) should be processed to this stage before any atomic absorption measurements are made.

9.6 *Calibration standards*

Run duplicate calibration standards with each set of samples (e.g., up to 10) as follows:

9.6.1   Add 1.00 ± 0.05 mL of 50% (v/v) HCl to a 500-mL volumetric flask, then add 25.0 mL of standard Pb solution B, dilute to the mark with water and mix well.

9.6.2   Place duplicate 200 ± 1 mL portions of this solution in 400-mL graduated borosilicate beakers.

9.6.3   If the pre-treatment stage was used for the samples, carry out steps 9.4.1 to 9.5.3 inclusive. If not, carry out step 9.4.3 and procedure 9.5.

NOTE: Quantification by means of calibration standards assumes the calibration curve to be linear. See section 9.8.

9.7 *Atomic absorption measurement*

9.7.1   Set up the instrument according to the manufacturer's instructions for aspirating organic solvents into an air/acetylene flame. Set the wavelength at 283.3 nm.

9.7.2   Aspirate pure MIBK and adjust the zero. Aspirate one of the calibration standards (9.6)[1] and adjust the instrument to give a suitable response (e.g., 80% of full-scale deflection).

---

[1] Do not aspirate more than one-third of the organic phase at this step, as two further measurements are to be made (9.7.3 and 9.7.6).

NOTE: Keep the aspiration tube above the bottom of the sample tube to avoid aspiration of water, which may have collected in the bottom of the tube.

9.7.3   Aspirate pure MIBK and readjust zero if necessary. Aspirate both of the calibration standards, with an aspiration of pure MIBK after each, and measure the absorption peak heights (i.e., maximum instrument responses. See NOTES ON PROCEDURE, 12.3).

9.7.4   Aspirate the blank, then pure MIBK, and measure the absorption peak height.

9.7.5   Aspirate the samples, with an aspiration of pure MIBK after each and measure the absorption peak heights.

9.7.6   To check for instrument drift, aspirate both calibration standards and the blank, with an aspiration of pure MIBK after each, and measure the peak heights. If these are in satisfactory agreement with the first set (9.7.3 and 9.7.4), calculate the average absorption peak heights for calibration standards and blank.

9.8 *Calibration curve*

The procedure outlined in this section must be carried out on at least two independent occasions before application of the method to any samples, and thereafter repeated regularly.

9.8.1   To each of six 500-mL volumetric flasks, add 1.00 ± 0.05 mL of 50% (v/v) HCl. Prepare 6 standard solutions by pipetting 0.0, 5.0, 10.0, 15.0, 20.0 and 25.0 mL of standard Pb solution B into the flasks and dilute to the mark with water. The final concentrations are 0, 20, 40, 60, 80 and 100 µg/L, respectively.

9.8.2   Place 200 ± 1 mL of each of the solutions in 400-mL, graduated borosilicate beakers and carry out step 9.4.3 and procedures 9.5 and 9.7. Plot the absorption peak height *versus* the mass concentration (µg/L) of Pb. See NOTES ON PROCEDURE, 12.4.

10. METHOD OF CALCULATION

The mass concentration, ρ_s (µg/L), of Pb in the sample is given by

$$\rho_s = \rho_c (S - B)/(C - B)$$

where,

ρ_c = mass absorption of calibration standard prepared in 9.6.1 (µg/L)

S   = absorption peak height obtained with sample

B   = average absorption peak height obtained with blanks

C   = average absorption peak height obtained with calibration standards

NOTE: If the test portion was less than 200 mL (see 12.2), the equation for ρ_s must be multiplied by 200/V, where V (mL) is the volume of the test portion.

11. REPEATABILITY AND REPRODUCIBILITY

The repeatability has been determined in 11 laboratories with the following results:

Pb concentration (µg/L)	Standard deviation range (µg/L)[a]
0.0	0.3–2.1
50.0	0.9–3.2
100	3.0[b]

[a] Each estimate has approximately 8 degrees of freedom
[b] Measured in one laboratory only

12. NOTES ON PROCEDURE

12.1 If the water used for blank determinations contains Pb, the results will bee too low. The peak height obtained with the blank should be negligible compared with that obtained with the sample. If it is not, the following procedure may be used to determine the lead content of the water.

    12.1.1   To each of two 500-mL borosilicate beakers, add 200 ± 5 mL of water and 0.4 ± 0.05 mL of 50% (v/v) HCl.

    12.1.2   To each of two 500-mL borosilicate beakers, add 400 ± 10 mL of water and 0.40 ± 0.05 mL of 50% (v/v) HCl.

    12.1.3   Cover all beakers with watch-glasses and heat those from 12.1.2 on a hot plate until the volumes are reduced to about 200 mL, then add a further 200 ± 5 mL of water to both. Continue heating until the volumes are again reduced to 200 ± 5 mL, then allow to cool.

    12.1.4   Analyse the contents of the four beakers as described in sections 9.5 and 9.7 (the beakers from 12.1.1 contain the "blanks" and the heated beakers the "samples").

12.1.5   Let the average peak height for the water from the unheated beakers (12.1.1) be W_1 and from the heated beakers (12.1.3) be W_2. The Pb content of the blank water is equivalent to an absorption peak height of $W = (W_2 - W_1)/2$. The concentration of Pb in the blank water, ρ_b ($\mu g/L$), is then given by $\rho_b = \rho_c W/(C - W_1)$, where ρ_c and C are defined in section 10.

12.2 If the Pb concentration of the sample is likely to exceed 100 $\mu g/L$, a smaller test portion must be taken for analysis. Record the volume and add the amount of 50% (v/v) HCl that would have been added to a 200-mL test portion (section 8). Dilute with water to 200 mL and proceed to 9.4 or 9.5 (see 8.2).

12.3 The absorption peak height, or maximum instrument response, for a sample (or standard, or blank) is the difference between the equilibrium response with the sample and the equilibrium responses for pure MIBK, aspirated just before and just after aspiration of the sample.

12.4 The calibration curve is normally linear up to 100 $\mu g/L$. However, this may depend on the type of instrument used and must be checked. If the calibration curve departs from linearity at a lower concentration, that of the calibration standard cited in section 9.6 is not appropriate. In that case, the calibration standard chosen in 9.6 should be the highest concentration on the linear portion of the curve, which also determines the concentration range of the method.

13. SCHEMATIC REPRESENTATION OF PROCEDURE

Samples requiring pre-treatment   *Samples not requiring pre-treatment*

Add 1 mL HNO_3 to 200-mL test
portion and evaporate to $\sim$ 20 mL
↓
Dilute to $\sim$ 150 mL and cool   Take 200-mL test portion

Add 0.1% bromophenol blue and 100 g/L NaOH until
blue colour persists, then add 2 mL 3% HCl
↓
Transfer to graduated cylinder and dilute to 200 mL
↓
Transfer to separating funnel, add 4 mL APDC solution
and 10.0 mL MIBK, then shake funnel 2 min
↓
Allow to stand 5 min, then discard aqueous phase
↓
Aspirate organic phase into AAS flame and measure absorption peak
height at 283.3 nm
↓

$$\downarrow$$

Correct for blank absorption and quantify by comparison
with calibration solution

14. ORIGIN OF THE METHOD

The Standing Committee of Analysts
The Department of the Environment
43 Marsham Street
London SW1P 3PY, UK

Contact point: The Secretary
The Standing Committee of Analysts

METHOD 13 – DETERMINATION OF CADMIUM IN POTABLE WATERS BY ATOMIC ABSORPTION SPECTROPHOTOMETRY

Adapted from *Methods for the Examination of Water and Associated materials,*
The Standing Committee of Analysts, Department of the Environment,
London, UK, with permission of the Controller of Her Majesty's Stationery Office.

1. SCOPE AND FIELD OF APPLICATION

This method is suitable for the determination of all forms of cadmium (Cd) in potable waters. The limit of detection is 0.3 µg/L. The calibration curve is normally linear up to 10 µg/L, but hither concentrations can be measured using smaller test portions.

Substances usually present in potable waters at their normal concentrations do not cause interference, but Zn has been reported to interfere at concentrations >5mg/L. This can be overcome by dilution of the sample, but with some loss of sensitivity.

The total analytical (and operator) time, excluding eventual pre-treatment, is typically about 3 h for 10 samples, analysed together with blanks and calibration standards.

2. REFERENCE

Water Research Association (1972) *Technical Inquiry Report* TIR No. 254, Medmenham, UK

3. DEFINITIONS

Not applicable

4. PRINCIPLE

The cadmium chelate formed by reaction with ammonium pyrrolidine dithiocarbamate (APDC) is extracted into 4-methyl-2-pentanone (methyl isobutyl ketone, MIBK) and the amount of Cd in the extract is determined by atomic absorption spectrophotometry (AAS).

Some samples may require preliminary boiling with nitric acid to convert Cd compounds to forms capable of reacting with APDC.

Since Cd and Pb are quantitatively extracted together, both elements may be determined, if desired, in a somewhat larger volume of the same extract, buth with loss of sensitivity (see step 9.5.2).

5. HAZARDS

Concentrated nitric and hydrochloric acids are toxic by inhalation. The former is also a fire risk in contact with organic materials.

4-Methyl-2-pentanone is flammable, irritating to the eyes and mucous membranes and is narcotic in high concentrations. It must not be pipetted by mouth.

The exhaust fumes from the atomic absorption spectrophotometer are toxic and must be ducted away.

6. REAGENTS

NOTE: Keep all reagents and standard solutions in polyethylene bottles, unless otherwise stated. 'Analytical Reagent' grade chemicals are suitable, except for MIBK (see below).

Water	Deionized or distilled from an all-glass apparatus
Hydrochloric acid (HCl)	Concentrated. $d_{20} = 1.18$. 50% (v/v). Dilute 500 mL HCl (d_{20} 1.18) to 1 L with water. 3% (v/v). Dilute 6.0 ± 0.1 mL 50% (v/v) HCl to 100 mL with water
Nitric acid (HNO$_3$)	Concentrated ($d_{20} = 1.42$) 10% (v/v). Dilute 100 ± 1 mL HNO$_3$ (d_{20} 1.42) to 1 L with water.
Sodium hydroxide (NaOH) solution	100 g/L. Dissolve 10 ± 0.1 g NaOH in water in a polyethylene beaker. Cool and dilute to 100 mL in polyethylene cylinder.
Ammonium pyrrolidine dithiocarbamate (APDC)	10 g/L. Dissolve 1.0 ± 0.1 g APDC in water and dilute to 100 mL. This solution should be freshly prepared and thoroughly mixed before use.
4-Methyl-2-pentanone (MIBK)	A special grade for AAS is preferable. Store in a glass bottle.

Bromophenol blue solution	1 g/L. Dissolve 0.1 $\pm$ 0.01 g of bromophenol blue in 100 mL of 50% (v/v) aqueous ethanol.
Standard cadmium solution A	100 mg/L. Weigh 100.0 $\pm$ 0.5 mg of Cd wire ($>99.9\%$ purity) and dissolve with gentle heating in a mixture of 7.0 $\pm$ 0.5 mL of HNO_3 (d_{20} 1.42) and about 20 mL of water. Quantitatively transfer solution to a 1-L volumetric flask, dilute to the mark with water and mix well. This solution is stable for several months. (Store in a polyethylene bottle).
Standard cadmium solution B	0.2 mg/L. Dilute 2.00 $\pm$ 0.01 mL of solution A to 1 L with water in a volumetric flask. This solution should be freshly prepared before use.

7.   APPARATUS

Beakers	400-mL, borosilicate glass, graduated 250-mL, polyethylene
Measuring cylinders	100-mL, glass, polyethylene
Volumetric flasks	500-mL, 1-L, glass
Pipettes	1.0, 4.0, 5.0, 10.0, 15.0, 20.0 and 25.0-mL, with bulb
Glass tubes	20 $\times$ 50 mm, with snap-on polyethylene caps.
Atomic absorption spectrophotometer	Air/acetylene flame, cadmium hollow cathode lamp. A chart recorder is the most desirable form of read-out.

NOTE: If possible, apparatus should be reserved solely for Cd determinations. Clean all new glass- and polyethylene-ware by soaking in 10% (v/v) HNO_3 for 2 days. Rinse thoroughly with water. After each determination, a thorough rinse in 10% (v/v) HNO_3, followed by water, should suffice.

8.   SAMPLING

8.1 To a clean polyethylene bottle, add 2.00 $\pm$ 0.05 mL of 50% (v/v) HCl per litre of sample to be collected, then collect the sample. (The acidification minimizes the adsorption of Cd onto the walls of the bottle).

8.2 Samples containing suspended and/or colloidal material may require pre-treatment (9.4) to convert Cd compounds to an extractable form (a few organic
compounds may not be converted by this procedure). When it is known that
pre-treatment will not be necessary, it is satisfactory to add to the empty bottle
sufficient 50% (v/v) HCl to bring the sample pH to 2.5 ± 0.3. In that case, place
200 ± 1 mL of the sample in a separating funnel and begin the procedure at 9.5.
Alternatively, place 200 mL of sample in a 400-mL, graduated borosilicate beaker
and begin at step 9.4.3. Omit 9.4.4 and proceed to 9.5.

9. PROCEDURE

9.1 *Blank test*

A blank must be run with each set (e.g., up to 10) of samples, using the same batch
of reagents as for the samples. To a 400-mL, graduated borosilicate beaker, add
0.40 ± 0.05 mL of 50% (v/v) HCl and 200 ± 1 mL of water (see NOTES ON
PROCEDURE, 12.1). If the pre-treatment is employed for the samples, carry out
procedures 9.4 and 9.5. If not, carry out step 9.4.3 and procedure 9.5.

9.2 *Check test*

Not applicable

9.3 *Test portion*

200 ± 1 mL of acidified sample (section 8, see also 12.2)

9.4 *Sample pre-treatment*

NOTE: If pre-treatment is not required, see 8.2.

9.4.1   Add 200 ± 1 mL of the sample to a 400-mL, graduated borosilicate
beaker. (If the Cd concentration is likely to exceed 100 µg/L, a smaller
test portion should be taken. See NOTES ON PROCEDURE, 12.2.)
Add 1.0 ± 0.1 mL HNO_3 (d^o_2 1.42), cover beaker with a watch-glass and
boil gently on a hot-plate until the volume is reduced to 20 ± 5 mL.

9.4.2   Cautiously wash down the watch-glass and the sides of the beaker with
water until total volume in beaker reaches 150 ± 5 mL. Replace watch-
glass and allow solution to cool to room temperature.

9.4.3   Add 3 drops of bromophenol blue solution and, while swirling, slowly
add 100 g/L NaOH until blue colour persists. While swirling, add 3%
(v/v) HCl dropwise until the blue colour just disappears, then add 2.0
± 0.1 mL of 3% (v/v) HCl. (The pH at the end of this step should be

2.5 ± 0.3. Very occasionally, the pH may require readjustment to this value.)

9.4.4   Transfer the solution to a measuring cylinder and dilute with water to 200 ± 1 mL.

9.5 *Chelate formation and extraction*

9.5.1   Transfer the solution to a separating funnel. Add 4.00 ± 0.05 mL of APDC solution and shake to mix.

9.5.2   Add 10.00 ± 0.05 mL of MIBK (up to 25 mL may be used if Pb is to determined in the same aliquot), stopper the funnel and shake vigorously for 2 min. Allow to stand for 5 min, then discard the aqueous phase.

9.5.3   Run the organic phase into a sample tube and fit the cap. Complete the atomic absorption measurement (9.7) during the same working day.

NOTE: All samples, blanks and calibration standards (9.6) should be processed to this stage before any atomic absorption measurements are made.

9.6 *Calibration standards*

Run duplicate calibration standards with each set of samples (e.g., up to 10) as follows.

9.6.1   Add 1.00 ± 0.05 mL of 50% (v/v) HCl to a 500-mL volumetric flask, then add 25.0 mL of standard Cd solution B, dilute to the mark with water and mix well.

9.6.2   Place duplicate 200 ± 1 mL portions of this solution in 400-mL graduated borosilicate beakers.

9.6.3   If the pre-treatment stage was used for the samples, carry out steps 9.4.1 to 9.5.3 inclusive. If not, carry out step 9.4.3 and procedure 9.5.

NOTE: Quantification by means of calibration standards assumes the calibration curve to be linear. See section 9.8.

9.7 *Atomic absorption measurement*

9.7.1   Set up the instrument according to manufacturer's instructions for aspirating organic solvents into an air/acetylene flame. Set the wavelength at 228.8 nm.

9.7.2   Aspirate pure MIBK and adjust the zero. Aspirate one of the calibration standards (9.6)[1] and adjust the instrument to give a suitable response (e.g., 80% of full-scale deflection).

---

[1] Do not aspirate more than one-third of the organic phase at this step, as two further measurements are to be made (9.7.3 and 9.7.6).

NOTE: Keep the aspiration tube above the bottom of the sample tube to avoid aspiration of water, which may have collected in the bottom of the tube.

9.7.3 Aspirate pure MIBK and readjust zero if necessary. Aspirate both of the calibration standards, with an aspiration of pure MIBK after each, and measure the absorption peak heights (i.e., maximum instrument responses. See NOTES ON PROCEDURE, 12.3).

9.7.4 Aspirate the blank, then pure MIBK, and measure the absorption peak height.

9.7.5 Aspirate the samples, with an aspiration of pure MIBK after each, and measure the absorption peak heights.

9.7.6 To check for instrument drift, aspirate both calibration standards and the blank, with an aspiration of pure MIBK after each, and measure the peak heights. If these are in satisfactory agreement with the first set (9.7.3 and 9.7.4), calculate the average absorption peak heights for calibration standards and blank.

9.8 Calibration curve

The procedure outlined in this section must be carried out on at least two independent occasions before application of the method to any samples, and thereafter repeated regularly.

9.8.1 To each of six 500-mL volumetric flasks, add 1.00 ± 0.05 mL of 50% (v/v) HCl. Prepare 6 standard solutions by pipetting 0.0, 5.0, 10.0, 15.0, 20.0 and 25.0 mL of standard Cd solution B into the flasks and dilute to the mark with water. The final concentrations are 0, 2, 4, 6, 8 and 10 µg/L, respectively.

9.8.2 Place 200 ± 1 mL of each of the solutions in 400-mL, graduated borosilicate beakers and carry out step 9.4.3 and procedures 9.5 and 9.7. Plot the absorption peak height *versus* the mass concentration (µg/L) of Cd. See NOTES ON PROCEDURE, 12.4.

10. METHOD OF CALCULATION

The mass concentration, ρ_s (µg/L), of Cd in the sample is given by

$$\rho_s = \rho_c (S - B)/(C - B)$$

where,

ρ_c = mass concentration of calibration standard prepared in 9.6.1 (µg/L)

S = absorption peak height obtained with sample

B = average absorption peak height obtained with blanks

C = average absorption peak height obtained with calibration standards.

NOTE: If the test portion was less than 200 mL (see 12.2), the equation for ρ_s must be multiplied by 200/V, where V (mL) is the volume of the test portion.

11. REPEATABILITY AND REPRODUCIBILITY

Without using the nitric acid pre-treatment (9.4.1–9.4.2), the repeatability has been determined using deionized water and tap water spiked with 10 µg Cd/L, with the following results:

Cd concentration (µg/L)	Standard deviation (µg/L)[a]
0.0	0.07
10.0	0.30

[a] Each estimate has approximately 8 degrees of freedom

12. NOTES ON PROCEDURE

12.1 If the water used for blank determinations contains Cd, the results will be too low. The peak height obtained with the blank should be negligible compared with that obtained with the sample. If it is not, the following procedure may be used to determine the cadmium content of the water.

12.1.1 To each of two 500-mL borosilicate beakers, add 200 ± 5 mL of water and 0.4 ± 0.05 mL of 50% (v/v) HCl.

12.1.2 To each of two 500-mL borosilicate beakers, add 400 ± 10 mL of water and 0.40 ± 0.05 mL of 50% (v/v) HCl.

12.1.3 Cover all beakers with watch glasses and heat those from 12.1.2 on a hot plate until the volumes are reduced to about 200 mL, then add a further 200 ± 5 mL of water to both. Continue heating until the volumes are again reduced to 200 ± 5 mL, then allow to cool.

12.1.4 Analyse the contents of the four beakers as described in sections 9.5 and 9.7 (the beakers from 12.1.1 contain the "blanks" and the heated beakers the "samples").

12.1.5   Let the average peak height for the water from the unheated beakers
          (12.1.1) be W_1 and from the heated beakers (12.1.3) be W_2. The Cd
          content of the blank water is equivalent to an absorption peak height of
          $W = (W_2 - W_1)/2$. The concentration of Cd in the blank water, ρ_b
          (μg/L), is then given by $\rho_b = \rho_c W/(C - W_1)$, when ρ_c and C are defined
          in section 10.

12.2 If the Cd concentration of the sample is likely to exceed 10 μg/L, a smaller test
      portion must be taken for analysis. Record the volume and add the amount of
      50% (v/v) HCl that would have been added to a 200-mL test portion (section 8).
      Dilute with water to 200 mL and proceed to 9.4 or 9.5 (see 8.2).

12.3 The absorption peak height, or maximum instrument response, for a sample (or
      standard, or blank) is the difference between the equilibrium response with the
      sample and the equilibrium responses for pure MIBK, aspirated just before and
      just after aspiration of the sample.

12.4 The calibration curve is normally linear up to 10 μg/L. However, this may
      depend on the type of instrument and must be checked. If the calibration curve
      departs from linearity at a lower concentration, that of the calibration standard
      cited in 9.6 is not appropriate. In that case, the calibration standard in 9.6 should
      be the highest concentration on the linear portion of the curve, which also
      determines the concentration range of the method.

13. SCHEMATIC REPRESENTATION OF PROCEDURE

Samples requiring pre-treatment   *Samples not requiring pre-treatment*

Add 1 mL HNO_3 to 200-mL test
portion and evaporate to $\sim$ 20 mL
                    $\downarrow$
Dilute to $\sim$ 150 mL and cool   Take 200 mL test portion
                                        $\downarrow$
            Add 0.1% bromophenol blue and 100 g/L NaOH until
                blue colour persists, then add 2 mL 3% HCl
                                    $\downarrow$
            Transfer to graduated cylinder and dilute to 200 mL
                                    $\downarrow$
            Transfer to separating funnel, add 4 mL APDC solution
                and 10.0 mL MIBK, then shake funnel 2 min
                                    $\downarrow$
            Allow to stand 5 min, then discard aqueous phase
                                    $\downarrow$
        Aspirate organic phase into AAS flame and measure absorption peak

height at 228.8 nm
↓
Correct for blank absorption and quantify by comparison
with calibration solution

14. ORIGIN OF THE METHOD

The Standing Committee of Analysts
The Department of the Environment
43 Marsham Street
London SW1P 3PY, UK

Contact point: The Secretary
The Standing Committee of Analysts

METHOD 14 – DETERMINATION OF SELENIUM IN POTABLE WATERS BY SPECTROFLUORIMETRY

R.J. Hall & P.J. Peterson

1. SCOPE AND FIELD OF APPLICATION

This method is suitable for the determination of dissolved selenium in drinking water with a detection limit of 1 µg/L, without the use of pre-concentration techniques (see NOTES ON PROCEDURE, 12.1). The selenium concentrations usually found in water range from 0.05–1 µg/L, but may reach 300 µg/L or higher in seleniferous areas (Tsongas & Ferguson, 1977). Well water has been reported to contain up to 9 mg Se/L. The World Health Organization (1972) and the U.S. Environmental Protection Agency (1976) have established interim drinking water limits of 10 µg Se/L.

As sample preparation time is short, 20 samples can be analysed within a normal laboratory day.

2. REFERENCES

Cutter, G.A. (1982) Selenium in reducing waters. *Science, 217,* 829–831

Measures, C.I. & Burton, J.D. (1978) Behaviour and speciation of dissolved selenium in estuarine waters. *Nature* (Lond.), *273,* 293–295

Rankin, J.M. (1973) Fluorimetric determination of selenium in water with 2,3-di-aminonaphthalene. *Environ. Sci. Technol., 7,* 823–824

Shendrikar, A.D. & West, P.W. (1975) Rate of loss of selenium from aqueous solutions stored in various containers. *Anal. Chim. Acta, 74,* 189–191

Suzuki, Y., Sugimura, Y. & Miyake, Y. (1981) The content of selenium and its chemical form in rainwater and aerosol in Tokyo. *J. Meteorol. Soc. Jpn, 59,* 405–409

Tsongas, T.A. & Ferguson, S.W. (1977) *Human health effects of selenium in a rural Colorado drinking water supply.* In: Hemphill, D.D., ed., *Trace Substances in Environmental Health,* Vol. 11, pp. 30–34

U.S. Environmental Protection Agency (1976) *National interim primary drinking water regulations.* EPA-570/9-76-003, Washington DC, Office of Water Supply, pp. 113–117

Wilson, A.L. (1982) *Design of sampling programmes.* In: Suess, M.J., ed., *Examination of Water for Pollution Control,* Vol. 1, WHO Regional Office for Europe, Oxford, Pergamon Press, pp. 23–77

World Health Organization (1972) *Health Hazards of the Human Environment,* Geneva, WHO

3. DEFINITIONS

Not applicable.

4. PRINCIPLE

As the concentration of organic matter is low in drinking waters, oxidation with hydrogen peroxide is sufficient. The selenate produced by oxidation is reduced to selenite by hydrochloric acid and is reacted with 2,3-diaminonaphthalene to form the piazselenol, which is extracted with an organic solvent and determined fluorimetrically (Rankin, 1973).

5. HAZARDS

The procedures employing hydrogen peroxide and hydrochloric acid should be undertaken in a fume chamber and the operator is advised to wear safety spectacles and acid-resistant gloves.

6. REAGENTS[1]

The reagents used are the same as those listed in Method 20, except that nitric and perchloric acids are not required.

7. APPARATUS[1]

Filtration assembly	Using Nucleopore (0.4-μm pore size) or Millipore (0.45-μm pore size) filters
Freeze-drying equipment	Preferably of multi-flask capability (may be required to concentrate waters containing low levels of selenium)
Rotary thin-film evaporator	For concentrating acidified samples

The apparatus used is the same as that listed in Method 20, except that digestion flasks and reflux tubes are not required.

---

[1] Reference to a company and/or product is for the purpose of information and identification only and does not imply approval or recommendation of the company and/or product by the International Agency for Research on Cancer, to the exclusion of others which may also be suitable.

8. SAMPLING

8.1 *Sample collection*

A useful review of sampling programmes has been published by the WHO Regional Office for Europe (Wilson, 1982). If necessary, filter sample using 0.4–0.45-μm pore size filters.

8.2 *Sample storage*

Samples should be collected in polyethylene containers. Since selenium can be adsorbed on such containers, as well as on Pyrex-type glass (Shendrikar & West, 1975), samples should be analysed as soon as possible and within 24 h of collection. Samples for storage should be acidified (1.5 mL conc. nitric acid/L of sample) or frozen.

8.3 *Sample concentration*

Samples containing <1 μg Se/L will require pre-concentration by freeze-drying before analysis. To avoid possible damage to equipment, acidified samples should not be subjected to freeze-drying, but can be concentrated on a rotary thin-film evaporator.

9. PROCEDURE

9.1 *Blank test*

Analyse 50 mL of distilled water (if possible, from a much-used glass still) as described in section 9.6. The calibration curve (9.6) thus provides an automatic reagent blank correction.

9.2 *Check test*

Not applicable.

9.3 *Test portion*

50 mL of water sample with a Se content of 0.05 to 1 μg. The original sample may need to be pre-concentrated (8.3) or diluted with distilled water to obtain a Se content within the required range.

9.4 *Conversion of all Se species to Se[IV]*

9.4.1   To a 50-mL test portion (9.3) in a 250-mL heat-resistant, conical glass flask, add 2 mL of 30% hydrogen peroxide. Boil gently for 10 min on a hot-plate.

9.4.2   Remove from the hot-plate, add 25 mL of concentrated hydrochloric acid and several anti-bumping granules. Boil for 5 min.

9.4.3   Remove from the hot-plate, adjust the volume to approximately 75 mL with distilled water and slowly add 20 mL of 7 mol/L ammonia solution. Allow the flask to cool to room temperature.

9.5 *Formation and extraction of Se-DAN complex*

NOTE: All operations should be undertaken in diffuse light.

9.5.1   Add 5 mL of stabilizing solution to the solution in the conical flask (9.4.3) and adjust pH to 2.0 with dilute ammonia, using narrow-range pH papers.

9.5.2   Transfer the flask to a water bath maintained at 50 °C and, after 5 min, add 5 mL of the DAN reagent; mix and leave at 50 °C for 30 min.

9.5.3   Remove the flask from the water bath, cool to room temperature and transfer the contents to a 125-mL separating funnel.

9.5.4   Add 10 mL of cyclohexane and extract the piazselenol by shaking for 5 min. Drain the aqueous phase into a beaker and retain. Remove the organic layer with a Pasteur pipette and transfer to a 15-mL, graduated, stoppered, glass centrifuge tube.

9.5.5   Return the aqueous phase to the separating funnel, add 5 mL of cyclohexane and repeat the extraction. Discard the aqueous layer.

9.5.6   Pool the organic extracts in the 15-mL centrifuge tube and dilute to 15 mL. Centrifuge at $500 \times g$ for 5 min to clarify the organic phase. Retain for Se determination (9.7).

9.6 *Calibration graph (See Notes on Procedure, 12.2)*

9.6.1   Add 0, 0.05, 0.1, 0.25 and 0.5 mL of standard solution B (i.e., 0, 0.1, 0.2, 0.5 and 1 µg Se, respectively) to five 50-mL volumetric flasks and make up to volume with distilled water. The flask containing no added Se provides the blank (see 9.1).

9.6.2   Treat the five calibration solutions as described for samples in sections 9.4 and 9.5.

9.6.3   Zero the spectrofluorimeter using the pure organic solvent and set the sensitivity to give 100% deflection using the final extract (9.5.6) containing 1 µg Se (or less, depending on the concentrations found in the water samples).

9.6.4 Using a 10-mm cell and excitation wavelength of 366 nm, measure the intensity of emission at 520 nm for the five calibration solution extracts.

9.6.5 Prepare the calibration graph by plotting the emission intensity *versus* the amount of Se in each of the five calibration solutions. Prepare a fresh calibration graph for each set of samples analysed.

9.7 *Selenium determination*

Under the conditions described in 9.6.3, measure the green fluorescence of the piazselenol solutions (9.5.6) in a 10-mm cell, using excitation and emission wavelengths of 366 and 520 nm, respectively.

10. METHOD OF CALCULATION

The mass concentration, $\rho(\mu g/L)$, of Se in the water sample is given by

$$\rho = 10^3 m/V$$

where

m = mass of Se in sample extract (9.5.6), obtained from emission intensity, 9.7, and calibration graph, 9.6.5 (μg)

V = volume of sample test portion in 9.4.1 (mL).

11. REPEATABILITY AND REPRODUCIBILITY

Fifteen London potable water samples spiked with 10 μg Se/L gave an average recovery of 102.1%. A standard error of ± 0.12 μg was calculated from analyses of 15 standards containing 10 μg Se/L.

12. NOTES ON PROCEDURE

12.1 The analytical method is suitable for the determination of selenium in drinking water, but as little is known about its oxidation state in such waters, analytical modifications may prove necessary in the future. Thermodynamic calculations lead to the prediction that selenate (Se [VI]), selenite (Se [IV]) and selenide (Se [-II]) are stable dissolved forms, but their occurrence is governed by hydro-chemical and geochemical conditions. Microbial reductions to dimethylselenide and other organic selenides have not been extensively studied in fresh waters. The analysis of selenium species in marine waters (Cutter, 1982) indicate that organic selenides are important compounds, suggesting that additional analytical methods may be necessary to quantify them should they account for significant concentrations in drinking water. Most selenium in rain water has been shown to occur as Se [IV] (Suzuki *et al.*, 1981), although river waters may contain only 5–10% of their selenium in this oxidation state (Measures & Burton, 1978).

12.2 Linearity of the calibration graph is not observed with more than approximately 1 µg Se in the final extract (9.5.6). Analysts experienced in Se determinations may require only one Se standard (in triplicate) to construct the calibration graph, provided the Se content of the extract is below 1 µg and thus within the linear range of the method.

13. SCHEMATIC REPRESENTATION OF PROCEDURE

Filter and/or concentrate sample, if necessary
↓
Add 50-mL test portion, containing 0.05 to 1 µg Se, to a 250-mL flask
↓
Add 2 mL of 30% H_2O_2 and boil gently for 10 min
↓
Add 25 mL conc. HCl and boil for 5 min
↓
Adjust volume to ∼75 mL with distilled water and slowly add 20 mL of 7 mol/L ammonia solution. Carry out subsequent steps in diffuse light
↓
Add 5 mL stabilizing solution and adjust pH to 2.0 with dilute ammonia solution
↓
Warm to 50 °C (5 min), add 5 mL DAN reagent, mix and maintain at 50 °C for 30 min
↓
Transfer solution to separating funnel and extract with 10 mL cyclohexane, then with 5 mL cyclohexane
↓
Pool cyclohexane extracts in 15-mL centrifuge tube, make up to 15 mL with cyclohexane and centrifuge for 5 min at 500 x *g*
↓
Measure green fluorescence of Se-DAN complex and quantify by comparison with calibration curve

14. ORIGIN OF THE METHOD

Department of Human Environmental Science
King's College London,
University of London,
Hortensia Road
London SW10 OQX, UK

Contact point: Professor P.J. Peterson

Determination of metals and their compounds in food

METHOD 15 – DETERMINATION OF ARSENIC IN FOODS AND HUMAN TISSUES BY SPECTROPHOTOMETRY

H.A.M.G. Vaessen, A. Van Ooik & J. Zuydendorp

1. SCOPE AND FIELD OF APPLICATION

This method is designed for the determination of total arsenic in foods and biological materials. The limit of detection is 0.15 µg in the test portion.

2. REFERENCES

Dubois, L., Teichman, T., Baker, C.J., Zdrojewsk, A. & Monkman, J.L. (1969) Interferences in the measurement of arsenic by the method of Văsák and Sédivik. *Mikrochim. Acta,* 185–192

Lenstra, J.B. & de Wolf, J.N.M. (1965) De bepaling van arseen in urine. *Pharm. Weekbl., **100**,* 232–238

3. DEFINITIONS

Not applicable.

4. PRINCIPLE

The test portion is digested with a mixture of nitric and sulfuric acids, followed by treatment with perchloric acid and hydrogen peroxide. Arsenic present in the digest is reduced to the trivalent state with potassium iodide and stannous chloride. Subsequently, granular zinc is added to the acidic medium which liberates hydrogen and generates arsine (AsH_3), which is absorbed in a solution of silver diethyldithiocarbamate in pyridine, yielding a pink coloration which is measured spectrophotometrically at 526 nm.

5. HAZARDS

Concentrated hydrogen peroxide is toxic, irritant and a fire and explosion risk. Perchloric acid is a strong irritant and will explode in contact with organic materials or by shock or heat. Pyridine and concentrated hydrochloric sulfuric and nitric acids are toxic and strong irritants. The digestion procedure (9.4) should be carried out in a ventilated fume hood and protective clothing should be worn, particularly face-mask and gloves.

6.   REAGENTS[1]

Unless otherwise stated, all reagents should be of analytical reagent quality. Water must be double-distilled (or equivalent) from an all-glass apparatus of Pyrex or other resistant glass.

Sulfuric acid	98% (w/w), density 1.84 g/mL
Nitric acid	65% (w/w), density 1.40 g/mL (Merck nitric acid tested by dithizone for heavy metals is very suitable)
Perchloric acid	70% (w/w), density approximately 1.67 g/mL
Hydrogen peroxide	30% (w/w)
Hydrochloric acid	36% (w/w), density 1.18 g/mL
Pyridine	Density approximately 0.980 g/mL
Lead acetate [$Pb(CH_3COO)_2 \cdot 3H_2O$]	
Potassium iodide	Neutral
Stannous chloride ($SnCl_2 \cdot 2H_2O$)	
Zinc	Granular or shot. 10 mesh (J.T. Baker or equivalent)
Silver diethyldithiocarbamate [$AgS.CS.N(C_2H_5)_2$]	Fluka A.G. or equivalent
Sodium hydroxide	
Sodium hydroxide solution	Dissolve 350 g of sodium hydroxide in 1 000 mL of water and mix

---

[1] Reference to a company and/or product is for the purpose of information and identification only and does not imply approval or recommendation of the company and/or product by the International Agency for Research on Cancer, to the exclusion of others which may also be suitable.

Potassium iodide solution	150 g/L. Dissolve 15 g of potassium iodide in 100 mL of water and mix. Store the solution in the dark and discard when it has become yellow
Stannous chloride solution	Dissolve 40 g of stannous chloride in a mixture of 25 mL of water and 75 mL of 36% hydrochloric acid
Silver diethyldithiocarba-mate solution	5 g/L. Dissolve 0.5 g of silver diethyldithiocarba-mate in 100 mL of pyridine and mix. Store the solution in a well-closed bottle in the dark cool place. The solution is stable for approximately one month
Absorbent cotton wool im-pregnated with lead acetate	Dissolve 50 g of lead acetate in 250 mL of water. Saturate cotton wool with this solution, drain, tightly press and dry under vacuum in a desiccator over phosphorus pentoxide (P_2O_5)
Arsenic trioxide	
Arsenic stock standard solution	100 mg/L. Dissolve 0.1320 g of arsenic trioxide in 20 mL of sodium hydroxide solution. Add 100 mL of water and (cautiously) 10 mL of 98% sulfuric acid. Make up to the mark with water in a 1000-mL volumetric flask.
Arsenic working standard solution	1 mg/L. Pipette 5.0 mL of the stock solution into a 500-mL volumetric flask and make up to the mark with water.

7. APPARATUS[1]

Glass-ware, including reagent bottles, should be soaked for 24 h in 4 mol/L nitric acid before use, then rinsed twice with distilled water and twice again with double-distilled water before being dried.

Apparatus for controlled decomposition of organic material (Fig. 1)	250-mL round-bottomed flask A, Reservoir B (30 mL) with three-position tap D, Coil condenser, C
Glass beads	Nitric-acid treated and washed with water, as indicated above

---

[1] Reference to a company and/or product is for the purpose of information and identification only and does not imply approval or recommendation of the company and/or product by the International Agency for Research on Cancer, to the exclusion of others which may also be suitable.

Argand burners

Measuring pipettes	1- and 10-mL (Fortuna), with glass piston
One-mark pipettes	1-, 2-, 3-, 4-, 5-, 10-, 15-, 20- and 25-mL
Arsine evolution and absorption apparatus	The apparatus shown in Figure 2 ensures complete absorption of arsine and consists of: conical flask (100-mL) for the evolution of arsine (A); connecting tube to trap hydrogen sulfide (B); absorption tube made of brown glass or wrapped in aluminiumfoil to exclude daylight (C)
Measuring cylinders	50-mL
Water bath	Thermostatically controlled and adjusted to 55 °C
Water bath	Filled with ice-water
Spectrophotometer	
Optical cells	10-mm path-length.

8. SAMPLING

Proceed from a representative sample (preferably 200 g) and homogenize. Food grinders or other homogenization aids used must be checked for arsenic contamination.

9. PROCEDURE

9.1 *Blank tests*

With no test portion in the 250-mL flask, carry out procedures 9.4, 9.5 and 9.6 to determine the reagent blank.

9.2 *Check test*

Not applicable.

9.3 *Test portion*

The portion of sample taken for analysis should contain no more than 25 μg of arsenic and should be weighed to the nearest 0.01 g.

Fig. 1. Apparatus for controlled decomposition of organic material

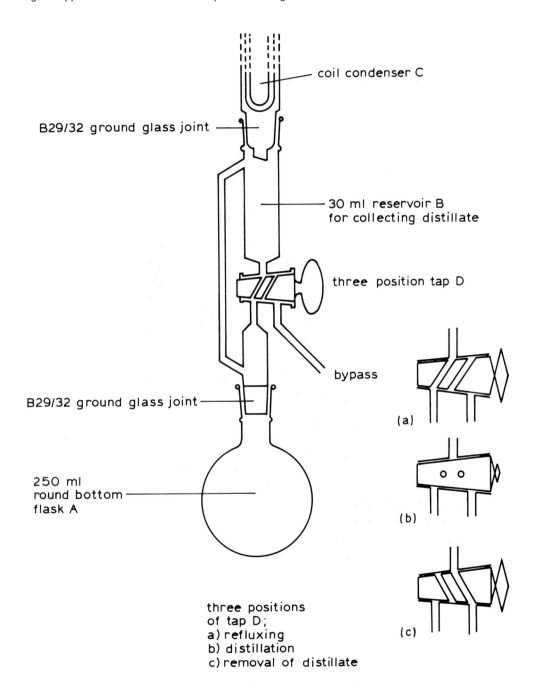

coil condenser C

B29/32 ground glass joint

30 ml reservoir B
for collecting distillate

three position tap D

bypass

B29/32 ground glass joint

250 ml
round bottom
flask A

(a)

(b)

(c)

three positions
of tap D;
a) refluxing
b) distillation
c) removal of distillate

Fig. 2. Apparatus for arsenic determination

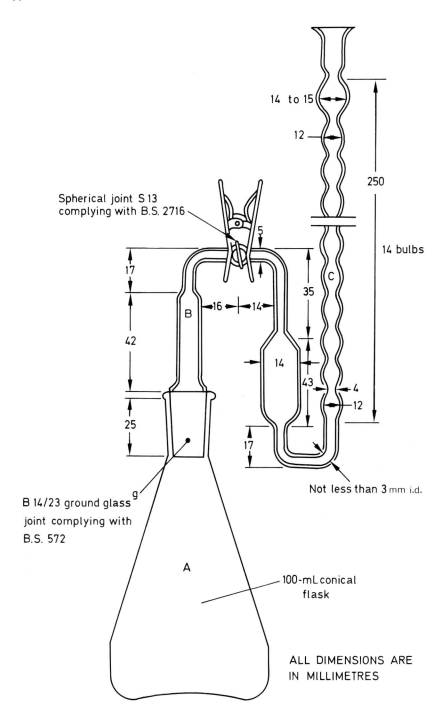

Spherical joint S 13
complying with B.S. 2716

B 14/23 ground glass
joint complying with
B.S. 572

100-mL conical
flask

Not less than 3 mm i.d.

ALL DIMENSIONS ARE
IN MILLIMETRES

9.4 *Sample digestion*

9.4.1   Weigh the test portion (9.3) into a 250-mL flask (Fig. 1)

9.4.2   Add 30 mL of 65% nitric acid and three glass beads. Mix thoroughly. Add 10 mL of 98% sulfuric acid and mix again.

9.4.3   Turn the three-way tap to position (a) (Fig. 1). Heat the flask contents to boiling, using an Argand burner; continue boiling for 30 min.

      NOTE: During steps 9.4.2 and 9.4.3, excessive foaming may occur. This is easily controlled by cooling with tap water. Foaming can be avoided if the flask is left overnight in a fume hood after the addition of nitric acid (9.4.2).

9.4.4   Close reservoir B (Fig. 1) by turning tap D to position (b) and continue the digestion by gentle boiling (all distillate is now collected in reservoir B).

9.4.5   Maintain oxidizing conditions during digestion (9.4.4) by adding small fractions of distillate [tap D in position (a)] whenever the digest turns brown or darkens. (Immediately return tap D to distillation position).

9.4.6   Continue digestion (9.4.5) until all organic matter is destroyed and sulfuric acid fumes are copiously evolved. Stop heating when, 5 min after fuming has started, the solution remains colourless, or only a light straw colour. (If a colour change is observed during this period, step 9.4.5 should be repeated).

9.4.7   Cool and add the distillate in reservoir B to the contents of the round-bottom flask by turning tap D to position (a), then turn tap D to the distillation position and repeat step 9.4.6.

9.4.8   Repeat step 9.4.7 once more, then pass the distillate in reservoir B through the bypass [position (c)] and discard.

9.4.9   Cool to room temperature and disconnect the round-bottom flask. Add 0.5 mL of 70% perchloric acid and re-heat until copious white fumes appear, then cool.

9.4.10   Repeat the perchloric acid treatment, 9.4.9.

9.4.11   Remove the Argand burner and add 1 mL of 30% hydrogen peroxide. Heat to fuming and continue for 3 min thereafter.

9.4.12   Repeat 9.4.11 twice.

9.4.13   After cooling to room temperature, transfer the digest quantitatively into the 100-mL conical flask (Fig. 2), with 50 mL of water.

9.5 *Arsenic reduction and complex formation*

9.5.1   Add 2 mL of potassium iodide solution to the sample solution (9.4.13), mix, add 2 mL of stannous chloride solution and mix again.

9.5.2   Place the conical flask in a water bath adjusted to 55 °C and allow to stand for 15 min.

9.5.3   Cool to 0 °C in ice-water.

9.5.4   Transfer by pipette 3.0 mL of silver diethyldithiocarbamate solution into the absorption tube (C, Fig. 2). Place a plug of lead acetate-impregnated cotton wool in the top third of the connecting tube (B, Fig. 2) and pack lightly. Slightly grease the spherical joint and connect absorption and connecting tube with a spring clip.

9.5.5   After cooling to 0 °C (9.5.3), introduce 3 g of zinc into the conical flask and immediately assemble conical flask and absorption train (B and C, Fig. 2); secure the ground glass joint with a spring clip. Allow the reaction to continue for 60 min at 0 °C.

NOTE: The reaction is carried out at 0 °C in order to prevent concentration of the absorption solution by evaporation of solvent due to violent generation of hydrogen.

9.5.6   Disconnect the absorption tube and tilt the absorber so that the reagent solution flows back and forth between the absorber bulbs to dissolve any red solid and to mix the solution thoroughly.

9.6 *Arsenic determination*

9.6.1   Transfer the solution to the optical cell and measure the optical density (extinction) at 526 nm, using silver diethyldithiocarbamate solution as a reference (the precise wavelength of maximum absorption should be checked for each instrument).

9.6.2   Correlate the extinction (9.6.1) with the total arsenic content (µg) of the test portion (or blank) by means of the calibration curve (9.7).

9.7 *Calibration curve*

9.7.1   Depending on the amount of arsenic presumably present in the test portion, pipette 0, 1, 2, 3, 4 and 5 mL (or 0, 5, 10, 15, 20 and 25 mL) of the arsenic working solution into six 100-mL conical flasks. Bring the total volume to 50 mL with water.

9.7.2   Cautiously add 10 mL of 98% sulfuric acid to each flask and mix.

9.7.3   Continue the analysis as described from 9.5.1 to 9.6.1, inclusive.

9.7.4   Calculate the linear regression (y = a + bx) relating the arsenic content of the standards (9.7.1) in µg (y) to the measured extinction (x). Plot the calibration curve corresponding to the calculated linear regression.

10. METHOD OF CALCULATION

The mass fraction, ω(mg/kg), of arsenic in the sample is given by

$$\omega = (m_3 - m_2)/m_1$$

where

m_3 = amount of arsenic found in test portion in 9.6.2 (µg)

m_2 = amount of arsenic found in blank in 9.6.2 (µg)

m_1 = mass of test portion taken in 9.4.1 (g).

11. REPEATABILITY AND REPRODUCIBILITY

The repeatability of the method has been tested by repeated analysis of standard reference materials obtained from the National Bureau of Standards (USA) and the International Atomic Energy Agency. The results are shown in Table 1.

Table 1.   Repeatability of method

Standard reference material	Code	Mass fraction of arsenic (mg/kg)		
		Claimed[a]	Measured (no. of detn.)	Range
Orchard Leaves	NBS/SRM 1571	10 ± 2	10.2 (4)	10.2 −10.2
Dried Mashed Potatoes	IAEA/V-4	0.026 ± 0.004	0.026 (1)	−
Wheat Flour	IAEA/V–2/1	0.022 ± 0.007	0.023 (3)	0.019– 0.028
Milk Powder	IAEA/A-8	0.013	0.010 (3)	0.009– 0.011
Animal Bone Ash	IAEA/A–3/1	1.16 ± 0.55	1.27 (3)	1.14 − 1.38
Dried Animal Blood	IAEA/A-2	0.296 ± 0.11	0.272 (3)	0.245– 0.253
Sea plant Material	IAEA/SP-M-1	3.3 ± 0.2	2.53 (3)	2.40 − 2.58
Copepod Homogenate	IAEA/MA-A-1	6.7 ± 0.6	8.08 (4)	0.9[c]
Tomato Leaves	NBS/SRM 1573	0.27 ± 0.05	0.279 (2)	0.278– 0.279
Spinach	NBS/SRM 1570	0.15 ± 0.05	0.145 (2)	0.141– 0.148
Albacore Tuna	NBS/RM 50	3.3 ± 0.4[b]	3.01 (5)	0.8[c]
Sea Plant Material	IAEA/SP-M-1	3.3 ± 0.2	2.93 (4)	2.1[c]

[a] NBS-values are certified; IAEA-values are best estimates from statistical evaluations of co-operative trials.

[b] Research Material; provisional value

[c] Relative standard deviation in %

12. NOTES ON PROCEDURE

Not applicable.

13. SCHEMATIC REPRESENTATION OF PROCEDURE

Weigh test portion into 250-mL flask (Fig. 1)
↓
Add 30 mL HNO$_3$ + 3 glass beads and mix;
add 10 mL H$_2$SO$_4$ and mix
↓
Boil under reflux condenser for 30 min
↓
Distill into reservoir, returning portions of distillate
to digest when browning occurs
↓
Continue distillation until organic matter destroyed
and H$_2$SO$_4$ fumes evolved; stop heating when solution
remains colourless 5 min after fumes evolved
↓
Cool, return distillate to digest and distill again
until H$_2$SO$_4$ fumes evolved for 5 min, then discard distillate
↓
Cool, disconnect flask, add 0.5 mL HClO$_4$ and heat until
fumes appear, then cool; repeat
↓
Add 1 mL H$_2$O$_2$, heat until fumes evolve,
continue 3 min then cool, repeat twice
↓
Cool and transfer to conical flask (Fig. 2),
bring volume to 50 mL with water
↓
Add 2 mL KI solution and mix,
then 2 mL SnCl$_2$ solution and mix
↓
Allow to stand 15 min in 55 °C bath, then cool to 0 °C
↓
Add 3 g zinc and assemble flask + absorption train
containing 3.0 mL silver diethyldithiocarbamate solution.
Allow to react 60 min at 0 °C
↓
Transfer solution to optical cell and measure extinction at 526 nm
↓
Calculate arsenic content of sample from extinction
and calibration curve

14. ORIGIN OF THE METHOD

National Institute of Public Health and Environmental Hygiene
PO Box 1
NL-3720 BA Bilthoven
The Netherlands

Contact point: Dr H.A.M.G. Vaessen

METHOD 16 – DETERMINATION OF CHROMIUM IN PLANTS BY ELECTROTHERMAL ATOMIC ABSORPTION SPECTROMETRY (AAS)

E.E. Cary

1. SCOPE AND FIELD OF APPLICATION

This method describes a procedure for interference-free determination of Cr in plant tissues. It has not been tested on meats or dairy products. However, there is no reason to believe that it will not be adequate for many of these types of samples. Numerous interferences generally encountered in the determination of Cr by AAS are eliminated by a simple separation of Cr from the sample and digestion matrix. A set of six test portions and necessary standards can easily be analysed in an eight-hour day. The sensitivity is 1.5 absorbance units/µg Cr and the detection limit is 4 ng/mL. The working range generally used is 0.05 to 1.0 µg of Cr in 8 mL of solution.

2. REFERENCES

Cary, E.E (1985) Electrothermal atomic absorption spectroscopic determination of chromium in plant tissues: Interlaboratory study. *J. Assoc. Off. Anal. Chem.,* **68,** 495–498

Cary, E.E. & Allaway, W.H. (1971) Determination of chromium in plants and other biological materials. *Agric. Food Chem.,* **19,** 1159–1161

Cary, E.E. & Rutzke, M. (1983) Electrothermal atomic absorption spectroscopic determination of chromium in plant tissues. *J. Assoc. off. anal. Chem.,* **66,** 850–852

Zief, M. & Mitchell, J.W. (1976) *Contamination control in trace element analysis.* New York, John Wiley & Sons

3. DEFINITIONS

Not applicable.

4. PRINCIPLE

The test portion is digested in a HNO_3-$HClO_4$-H_2SO_4 mixture. After digestion, it is transferred to a calibrated polyethylene centrifuge tube. The Cr[VI] is reduced by Na_2SO_3 to Cr[III], then Fe is added. Chromium [III] is coprecipitated with Fe, using NH_4OH. After centrifugation, the supernatant is discarded. The precipitate is dissolved in 9.6 mol/L HCl. Iron is extracted into 4-methyl-2-pentanone and discarded. Any silicon present is solubilized with HF. The solution is made to volume and analysed by atomic absorption spectrophotometry (AAS).

5. HAZARDS

Perchloric acid is a strong oxidizing agent when it is hot and concentrated to 70–72% or greater. It can form a number of unstable compounds. It is recommended that users obtain literature from G. Frederick Smith Chemical Co. (PO Box 23214, Columbus, OH 43223, USA) pertaining to the use of this acid. Hydrofluoric acid is an extremely corrosive acid and must be used with extreme caution. Chloroform is considered to be a potential carcinogen.

6. REAGENTS[1]

All reagents must be of analytical reagent quality or of the best quality available. Water must be redistilled from an all-glass apparatus (Pyrex, or equivalent).

Argon gas	99.99% Ar
Sulfuric acid	sp. gr. 1.84 (96%) Ultrex or equivalent (J.T. Baker Co.)
Nitric acid	sp. gr. 1.42 (69–71%). Redistill in glass. Distill approximately 90% of total
Perchloric acid	sp. gr. 1.6 (70–72%). Double-distilled from Vicor [G. Frederick Smith Chemical Co., PO Box 23214, Columbus, OH 43223, USA) No. 230 or equivalent]
Hydrofluoric acid	(48–51%)
Ammonium hydroxide	sp gr 0.9 (28.7% NH_3)
4-Methyl-2-pentanone (MIBK)	Eastman No. 416 or equivalent
Chloroform	

---

[1] Reference to a company and/or product is for the purpose of information and identification only and does not imply approval or recommendation of the company and/or product by the International Agency for Research on Cancer, to the exclusion of others which may also be suitable.

Hydrochloric acid	sp gr 1.18 (37%). Dilute to 9.7 mol/L with distilled water
Sodium sulfite	1 g/100 mL (1%). Prepare fresh daily in distilled water.
Iron solution	Dissolve 10 g of $FeCl_3 \cdot 6H_2O$ in 10 mL of 12 mol/L HCl. Add 0.5 mL of 1% Na_2SO_3 and mix. Extract 3 times with 20-mL portions of MIBK. Combine the organic phases after each extraction. Wash the combined organic phase with 3 mL of 6 mol/L HCl. Extract the organic phase twice with 50-mL portions of distilled water. Save the aqueous phase and dilute to 500 mL with distilled water. Check for Cr using procedure 9.4.4 to 9.5.2, inclusive.
Chromium standard solution	Dissolve 0.3736 g of K_2CrO_4 in distilled water and dilute to 1 L. Dilute the solution to a working concentration of 0.1 µg of Cr/mL in 0.1 mol/L HCl. Commercial atomic absorption standard solutions can also be used.
Methyl red	0.02 g in 60 mL of ethanol (95%). Dilute to 100 mL with distilled water.

7. APPARATUS[1]

Atomic absorption spectrometer	With digital output and graphite furnace (Perkin-Elmer Model 603 with HGA 2100 furnace, or equivalent)
Digestion tubes	Approximately 20 × 175 mm
Polyethylene centrifuge tubes	Calibrated to 15 mL
Polyethylene pipette	Adjustable to 5 mL
Pyrolytic coated graphite tubes	

[1] Reference to a company and/or product is for the purpose of information and identification only and does not imply approval or recommendation of the company and/or product by the International Agency for Research on Cancer, to the exclusion of others which may also be suitable.

Microkjeldahl digestor

NOTE: Clean new digestion tubes and glass or Teflon boiling beads by heating
        with 1.8 mol/L H_2SO_4 for 15 min, then soaking overnight. Soak poly-
        ethylene for 24 h in 1.8 mol/L H_2SO_4. Rinse everything with distilled
        water. Subsequently, it will suffice to wash with distilled water, followed
        by a 1.2 mol/L HCl rinse, then a distilled water rinse. Dry glass and
        polyethylene on polyethylene mesh in a dust-free environment. *Use for
        Cr determinations only.*

8. SAMPLING

See 12. NOTES ON PROCEDURE

Proceed from a representative sample of at least 200 g if possible. Store solid
samples in polyethylene containers in such a way that deterioration and change in
composition are prevented. Store liquid samples in polyethylene bottles, after acidify-
ing to pH 3.5, or less, with HCl.

9. PROCEDURE

9.1 *Blank test*

Analyse three reagent blanks with each set of test portions, but digest (9.4.1,
9.4.2) only two of them. (Digested blanks must be handled exactly as a test
portion. If extra HNO_3 is needed to complete digestion of one or more test
portions, an equal amount of HNO_3 must also be added to *one* of the digested
blanks). The undigested blank should contain all the reagents in 9.4.1, except
HNO_3, and follow the procedure from 9.4.3 to 9.5.2, inclusive.
Reagent blanks should read no more than 0.030 ± 0.001 absorbance units when
a 10 μL test portion from a final dilution volume (9.4.9) of 8 mL is analysed in
the graphite furnace (9.5).

9.2 *Check test*

Most homogenizers and metal grinders contain Cr. It the sample has to be ground
(or homogenized), check for contamination by analysing a test portion which has
not been ground.

9.3 *Test portion*

The size of the test portion will depend on the material to be analysed. No more
than 1 g dry weight can be conveniently wet-ashed in the tubes described. Weigh
the test portion to the nearest 0.01 g or pipette to the nearest 0.01 mL. Weigh onto
a polyethylene boat only, or directly into the digestion tube. (Weighing papers
may contain relatively large concentrations of Cr and should not be used).

9.4 *Sample digestion*

9.4.1   Weigh or pipette the test portion into a digestion tube. Add 2 boiling beads, 0.5 mL of concentrated H_2SO_4 and 5 mL of concentrated HNO_3 per 0.5 g (dry weight) of test portion, then add 1 mL of 70% $HClO_4$. (The acids may be mixed together before adding to the digestion tube. Digestion will be easier if the test portion and tertiary acid mixture are allowed to stand overnight at room temperature.)

9.4.2   Heat slowly on a microkjeldahl digestor until all easily-oxidized material is in solution, then heat to boiling. Continue digestion at least 10 min beyond appearance of $HClO_4$ fumes. If the digest begins to darken just before appearance of $HClO_4$ fumes, *immediately* add 0.25 mL of HNO_3 and continue heating (see 9.1). Repeat if necessary.

9.4.3   Cool the digest to room temperature and transfer it (including particulate matter and boiling beads) to a 15-mL polyethylene centrifuge tube with four 1-mL water rinses, then add 0.05 mL of 1% Na_2SO_3 and mix.

9.4.4   Add 1.0 mL Fe solution and mix, then 2 mL concentrated NH_4OH and mix.

9.4.5   Age the precipitate for at least 10 min, then centrifuge and decant carefully. Discard the supernatant.

9.4.6   Resuspend the precipitate in about 6 mL water. Centrifuge and discard the supernant.

9.4.7   Add 1 mL of 9.6 mol/L HCl and 1 drop of methyl red (as a phase marker) and allow the precipitate to dissolve. Extract twice, first with 5-mL then with 3-mL portions of MIBK, and separate the phases with a clear polyethylene-tipped pipette. Discard the MIBK phase.

9.4.8   Add 1 mL $CHCl_3$ and mix, then centrifuge. If a layer of solids is seen at the $CHCl_3$ water interface, add 0.1 mL HF. Do not mix. Allow this material to dissolve or wait for 2 hours.

9.4.9   Make the aqueous phase to volume, mix and centrifuge. The final volume chosen will depend on the amount of Cr present in the test portion. It can be as little as 1.5 mL if the test portion contains very little Cr, but must be the same for standards, samples (test portions) and blanks. For many plant tissues, standards of 0.05 to 1.0 µg of Cr diluted to a final volume of 8 mL will bracket 0.50 g test portions.

9.5 *Chromium determination by AAS*

9.5.1   The following settings are used on the Perkin-Elmer Model 603 atomic absorption spectrophotometer:

Wavelength:	357.9 nm
Absorbance:	Peak mode

HGA 2100	drying:	110 °C for 20 s
	charring:	1 000 °C for 10 s
	atomization:	2 700 °C for 9 s

Argon flow:	Normal
Flow rate:	40 through Brooks tube, size R-2-15A (CO)

No background correction is necessary.

For other instruments, follow the manufacturer's instructions.

9.5.2   Inject 10 μL of final aqueous digest (9.4.9) or standards into the graphite furnace and record the absorbance.

9.6 *Calibration curve or equation*

9.6.1   Carry three standards and one (undigested) blank through the entire procedure, starting with step 9.4.3. These should contain all the reagents added in 9.4.1, except HNO_3. The concentrations of the standards should be chosen to bracket the concentrations obtained with the test portions (9.4.9).

9.6.2   If the data are linear, prepare a calibration curve for each determination, giving the mass of analyte, m_a (μg), in the chosen volume (9.4.9) *versus* the absorbance, A, corrected for the blank value.

9.6.3   If the data are not linear, generate a second-order polynomial equation, using the absorbance values of the undigested blank and standards and their Cr contents. The equation is

$$m_a = \alpha + \beta A + \gamma A^2$$

where α, β and γ are constants, A = absorbance and m_a = μg Cr in the chosen volume (9.4.9). Set up three simultaneous equations using the values of m_a and A (corrected for blank value) for the three standard solutions and solve for the constants α, β and γ.

10. METHOD OF CALCULATION

10.1 Correct the sample absorbance values by subtracting the absorbance of the digested blank which contained the same amount of nitric acid as the digested sample.

10.2 Using the corrected sample absorbance, obtain m_a from the calibration curve or the polynomial. The mass fraction, ω (mg/kg), of chromium in the test portion is then given by

$$\omega \quad = \quad m_a/m_t$$

where

m_a = mass of chromium in the test portion (μg)

m_t = mass of test portion (g).

If the sample was liquid, the mass concentration, ρ (mg/L), is given by

$$\rho \quad = \quad m_a/V$$

where

V = volume of test portion (mL).

NOTE: The specific gravity of the liquid test portion should be cited.

11. REPEATABILITY AND REPRODUCIBILITY

The coefficient of variation (C.V.) for test portions containing several μg Cr/g dry wt is about 2%. At concentrations near 0.5 μg Cr/g the C.V. is about 15% and at concentrations less than 0.1 μg Cr/g the C.V. is 60 to 80%.

12. NOTES ON PROCEDURE

Many materials, including dust, contain chromium, so that great care must be taken in sampling, sample preparation and sample storage (see Zief & Mitchell, 1976). For dry, nonabrasive samples, good quality chrome-plated or stainless-steel utensils can be used for sampling (Cary & Allaway, 1971). It is preferable, however, to avoid metal-ware. Solutions and moist samples should not contact metal or paper. They may be handled with polyethylene or porcelain ware.

13. SCHEMATIC REPRESENTATION OF PROCEDURE

Test portion

↓

Digest in conc. sulfuric, nitric, perchloric acid mixture

↓

Transfer to polyethylene centrifuge tube

↓

Reduce Cr with sodium sulfite

↓

Add Fe to coprecipitate Fe and Cr[III]

$\downarrow$

Centrifuge and wash precipitate
(discard aqueous supernate)

$\downarrow$

Redissolve Fe–Cr in hydrochloric acid

$\downarrow$

Extract Fe in MIBK
(discard the organic phase)

$\downarrow$

Add $CHCl_3$ and centrifuge

$\downarrow$

Add HF if solids are evident
at $CHCl_3$-H_2O interface

$\downarrow$

Make aqueous phase to volume with H_2O,
mix and centrifuge

$\downarrow$

Determine Cr by AAS.

14. ORIGIN OF THE METHOD

U.S. Plant, Soil and Nutrition Laboratory
USDA-ARS-NER-NAA
Tower Road
Ithaca, NY 14853, USA

Contact point: E.E. Cary

METHOD 17 – DETERMINATION OF NICKEL IN FOODS BY ATOMIC ABSORPTION SPECTROMETRY

Adapted from the Report of the Analytical Methods Committee (1979),
The Analyst, **104,** 1070–1074

1. SCOPE AND FIELD OF APPLICATION

This method is suitable for the determination of nickel in most foods and other organic materials. The digestion procedure described, however, is not satisfactory for fats and oils, for which an alternative procedure is indicated. The limit of detection is approximately 20 µg/kg. The presence of more than about 0.2 mg of copper and/or 2 mg iron in the sample may result in low recoveries.

2. REFERENCES

2.1 Analytical Methods Committee (1960) Methods for the destruction of organic matter. *Analyst,* **85,** 643–656

2.2 Analytical Methods Committee (1976) The use of 50 per cent hydrogen peroxide for the destruction of organic matter (second report). *Analyst,* **101,** 62–66

2.3 Analytical Methods Committee (1979) Determination of small amounts of nickel in organic matter by atomic-absorption spectrometry. *Analyst,* **104,** 1070–1074

3. DEFINITIONS

Not applicable.

4. PRINCIPLE

The organic matter is destroyed by wet oxidation in the presence of sulfuric acid and the nickel is complexed with ammonium tetramethylenedithiocarbamate (APDC). The complex is then extracted into 4-methyl-2-pentanone (methyl isobutyl ketone; MIBK) and the resulting solution is aspirated into the burner of an atomic absorption spectrometer (AAS) for nickel determination.

5. HAZARDS

MIBK is highly flammable and possibly toxic. Mercaptoacetic acid is toxic by ingestion and inhalation and is a strong irritant to tissue. Concentrated perchloric acid will explode in contact with organic materials or by shock or heat. These chemicals, and hot concentrated acids, should be handled in an acid-resistant, ventilated hood. A protective face mask and acid-resistant gloves should be worn.

6. REAGENTS[1]

Highest-quality analytical-reagent grade chemicals should be employed whenever possible.

Nitric acid	Sp. gr. 1.42
Sulfuric acid	Sp. gr. 1.84
Perchloric acid	60% (w/w)
Mercaptoacetic acid	
Acetone	
Water, double-distilled (or de-ionized)	From quartz or glass still
4-Methyl-2-pentanone (MIBK)	
Ammonium tetramethylenedithiocarbamate (APDC) solution	Place ~1.5 g of APDC in a sintered-glass (porosity 4) crucible, wash with 20 mL of acetone and suck dry with a water pump. Weigh 1.0 g of the dried APDC and dissolve in 100 mL of distilled water containing 0.1 g of mercaptoacetic acid. Adjust the pH to between 6 and 7, using aqueous acetic acid or ammonia solutions and a pH meter or indicator paper.
Stock standard nickel solution	1 000 mg/L, commercially available; alternatively, dissolve 1.0 g of pure nickel in 100 mL of 10% (v/v) nitric acid, cool and dilute to 1 L with distilled water.

---

[1] Reference to a company and/or product is for the purpose of information and identification only and does not imply approval or recommendation of the company and/or product by the International Agency for Research on Cancer, to the exclusion of others which may also be suitable.

Working standard nickel solution	10 µg/mL. Dilute stock standard solution 1→100 with distilled water.
AAS calibration solutions	Prepare calibration solutions to cover the required range of nickel contents by adding accurately measured amounts (e.g., 0.1 to 2 mL) of working standard solution to 5 mL of sulfuric acid in a 50-mL volumetric flask and diluting to the mark with distilled water.

7. APPARATUS[1]

Conical flask	500-mL, glass, with B24 neck and a B24 cone to act as a short air condenser (this arrangement may be replaced by a 250-mL Kjeldahl flask)
Separating funnel	100-mL
Volumetric flasks	50-mL, for preparation of calibration solutions
Pipettes	0.1 to 2.0 mL, glass, graduated, and 10.0 mL, with bulb
Hot-plate	
Atomic absorption spectrometer	With air-acetylene burner and nickel hollow-cathode lamp

NOTE: All glass or quartz apparatus must be thoroughly cleaned with sulfuric and nitric acids, then abundantly rinsed with distilled water, just before use.

8. SAMPLING

Consult chapter 12 for sampling and sample preparation and storage procedures.

9. PROCEDURE

9.1 *Blank test*

With each sample, analyse several reagent blanks by following procedures 9.4 and 9.7, but with no sample in the 500-mL flask (9.4.1).

---

[1] Reference to a company and/or product is for the purpose of information and identification only and does not imply approval or recommendation of the company and/or product by the International Agency for Research on Cancer, to the exclusion of others which may also be suitable.

9.2 *Check test*

When working with a particular sample material for the first time, the analyst is advised to carry out a preliminary digestion procedure (9.4.1–9.4.6) on a small scale, to check for possible difficulties. It is necessary to allow the vigorous oxidation of organic matter by nitric acid to subside before the temperature is raised sufficiently to allow the perchloric acid to react. Should darkening due to charring occur, cool, add a further position of nitric acid (2–5 mL) and gradually increase the temperature until smooth oxidation by perchloric acid is complete and a pale yellow or colorless residue results (see Notes on Procedure, 12.1).

9.3 *Test portion*

2.00 g of a homogeneous (well-mixed) sample is usually adequate, but the optimum amount depends on the characteristics of the atomic absorption spectrometer employed and the nickel content of the sample.

9.4 *Sample digestion* (see Notes on Procedure, 12.2, 12.3)

9.4.1　Weigh 2.0 g of sample (see 9.3) into a 500-mL conical flask having a B24 neck and fit a B24 cone to act as an air condenser. (For more reliable results, analyse samples in duplicate).

9.4.2　Reflux carbohydrate samples with 30 mL of 1:1 nitric acid for 30 min. With other types of sample, add 15 mL nitric acid (sp. gr. 1.42), shake to wet sample completely and allow any reaction to subside.

9.4.3　Add 10 mL perchloric acid (60%) and 5 mL sulfuric acid (sp. gr. 1.84), swirling the contents of the flask during addition.

9.4.4　Place the flask on a cold hot-plate and switch to medium heat. (As the temperature rises, the material should dissolve with evolution of brown fumes, which clear to leave a gently boiling solution, with some refluxing taking place in the air condenser. When most of the nitric acid has been driven off, there may be signs of a more vigorous reaction with further evolution of brown fumes. If this occurs, add a few mL of nitric acid and continue heating.)

9.4.5　Finally, heat the solution until white fumes are evolved, then cool.

9.4.6　Dilute the solution with 5 mL distilled water and heat again until white fumes are evolved.

9.4.7　Allow to cool, then dilute to about 50 mL with distilled water.

9.4.8　Transfer solution to a separating funnel (rinsing with a minimum volume of water), add 2 mL of APDC solution, mix and set aside for 5 min.

9.4.9   Add 10.0 mL of MIBK and shake vigorously for 1 min.

9.4.10   Allow the layers to separate, discard all the aqueous layer and filter the organic layer through a small, dry filter paper into a vessel with a tight stopper.

9.5 *AAS operating conditions*

9.5.1   Set up the spectrometer using the manufacturer's recommended procedures and adjust the monochromator to 232.0 nm.

9.5.2   Aspirate MIBK into the flame when setting the zero of the instrument and between all readings. Frequent checks on the zero and the calibration (9.6) should be made when analysing large numbers of samples.

9.6 *Calibration curve*

9.6.1   Transfer each of the 50-mL calibration solutions (section 6) to a separating funnel and carry out steps 9.4.8 to 9.4.10, inclusive.

9.6.2   Aspirate each of the resulting MIBK extracts into the AAS several times and prepare a graph of the mean signal response *versus* the nickel concentration (μg/mL of extract). The graph should be linear up to 2–5 μg/mL of extract.

9.7 *Nickel determination*

Aspirate the MIBK extracts (9.4.10) into the AAS and record the mean signal responses for samples and blanks.

9.8 *Recovery*

The recovery of nickel from the test portion should be determined by analysing spiked samples according to procedures 9.4 and 9.7. Calculate the percentage recovery from the spikes after subtracting the mean nickel content found in the samples as received.

10. METHOD OF CALCULATION

10.1 Determine the mass concentrations, ρ_s and ρ_b (μg/mL) in the sample and media blank extracts, respectively, using the mean signal responses (9.7) and the calibration curve (9.6.2).

10.2 The mass fraction, ω (mg/kg), of nickel in the sample is given by:

$$\omega = 100V(\rho_s - \rho_b)/mR$$

where

V = volume of MIBK extract in 9.4.10 (mL)

m = mass of sample in 9.4.1 (g)

R = percent recovery (section 9.8).

11. REPEATABILITY AND REPRODUCIBILITY

No precise data for foods are available. A limited collaborative study has been carried out with condensed milk and olive oil (see reference 2.3), but the digestion methods employed by the contributing laboratories were not specified.

12. NOTES ON PROCEDURE

12.1 A milder digestion procedure, which avoids the use of perchloric acid, will suffice for some types of food sample. Such a procedure is described in reference 2.1, where the procedure in section 9.4 is also to be found. If the analyst has limited experience of wet oxidation method, references 2.1 and 2.2 should be consulted before proceeding with 9.4.

12.2 For the digestion of finely-divided powders and materials that might react vigorously with nitric acid, preliminary moistening of the sample with a few mL of distilled water is advisable. It is recommended that the digestion procedure be carried out behind a safety screen.

12.3 For the analysis of fats and oils, a generally more satisfactory method of digestion employs sulfuric acid and 50% hydrogen peroxide. See reference 2.2 for description of procedure and safety precautions.

13. SCHEMATIC REPRESENTATION OF PROCEDURE

Place 2 g sample in conical flask with short air condenser
↓
Add 15 mL HNO_3, then 10 mL $HClO_4$ and 5 mL H_2SO_4
↓
Raise temperature slowly until digestion complete (white fumes)
↓
Cool, add 5 mL water and heat until white fumes again evolved
↓
Cool and dilute to ~50 mL with distilled water
↓
Transfer to separating funnel and complex Ni with 2 mL APDC
↓

Extract complex into MIBK (10.0 mL), discard aqueous layer
↓
Analyse MIBK solution by AAS and quantify by means of calibration curve

14. ORIGIN OF THE METHOD

Report of the Analytical Methods Committee (1979),
The Analyst, **104,** 1070–1074

Contact point: C.A. Watson
Metallic Impurities in Organic Matter Sub-committee
The Royal Society of Chemistry
Burlington House
Piccadilly
London W1 VOBN
UK

METHOD 18 – DETERMINATION OF LEAD AND CADMIUM IN FOODS BY ANODIC STRIPPING VOLTAMMETRY

S. Capar, R. Gajan, M. Sanders & J. Zyren

1. SCOPE AND FIELD OF APPLICATION

This method is suitable for the determination of lead and cadmium in a wide range of fresh and processed foods and beverages. In the case of samples with very high fat or oil content, however, it is necessary to verify that acceptable recoveries of added analyte are obtained.

Using a 10-g sample, the method has an estimated quantification limit of 10 µg/kg for lead and 5 µg/kg for cadmium.

Thallium can interfere with the determination of lead, but is not likely to be found in food (see section 12, Notes on Procedure).

2. REFERENCES

Capar, S.G., Gajan, R.J., Madzsar, E., Albert R.H., Sanders, M. & Zyren, J. (1982) Determination of lead and cadmium in foods by anodic stripping voltammetry. II. Collaborative study. *J. Assoc. off. anal. Chem., 65,* 978–986

Gajan, R.J., Capar, S.G., Subjoc, C.A. & Sanders, M. (1982) Determination of lead and cadmium in foods by anodic stripping voltammetry. I. Development of the method. *J. Assoc. off. anal. Chem., 65,* 970–977

Jones, J.W. & Boyer, K.W. (1979) Sample homogenization procedure for determination of lead in canned foods. *J. Assoc. off. anal. Chem., 62,* 122–128

Jones, J.W., Gajan, R.J., Boyer, K.W. & Fiorino, J.A. (1977) Dry ash-voltammetric determination of cadmium, copper, lead and zinc in foods. *J. Assoc. off. anal. Chem., 60,* 826–832

3. DEFINITIONS

ASV   = anodic stripping voltammetry

DPASV = differential pulse anodic stripping voltammetry

LSASV = linear sweep anodic stripping voltammetry

4. PRINCIPLE

Homogenized samples of foods are dry-ashed at 500 °C with potassium sulfate. Residual carbon, if present, is oxidized with nitric acid. The ash is dissolved in dilute nitric acid and diluted to volume with water. Lead and cadmium are determined in a mixture of the sample solution with an acetate buffer, using DPASV or LSASV.

5. HAZARDS

Concentrated nitric and sulfuric acids are toxic and should be handled in a ventilated hood. Acid-resistant gloves and safety glasses should be worn. When diluting concentrated sulfuric acid, always add the acid to the water, not the reverse.

6. REAGENTS[1]

Reagent grade chemicals should be used throughout.

Nitric acid (HNO_3)	Concentrated (<1 ng Pb/mL and <0.5 ng Cd/mL)
Water	Double-distilled or deionized
Nitrogen	Ultra-high purity compressed gas
Potassium sulfate (K_2SO_4)	
Ash-aid solution	Dissolve 50 g K_2SO_4 in 400 mL water containing 10 mL HNO_3. Dilute to 500 mL with water. Clean to <1 ng Pb/mL and <0.5 ng Cd/mL by controlled-potential electrolysis, if necessary
Tartaric acid	
Glacial acetic acid (HOAc)	
Sodium acetate trihydrate (NaOAc · $3H_2O$)	
Sodium hydroxide (NaOH)	1 mol/L
Acetate electrolyte solution	Dissolve 170.0 g NaOAc · $3H_2O$ in 300 mL water. Add 97 mL glacial HOAc and 1.5 g tartaric acid. Dilute to 1 L with water (pH should be 4.7 ± 0.1). Clean to <1 ng Pb/mL and <0.5 ng Cd/mL by controlled-potential electrolysis, if necessary

[1] Reference to a company and/or product is for the purpose of information and identification only and does not imply approval or recommendation of the company and/or product by the International Agency for Research on Cancer, to the exclusion of others which may also be suitable.

Standard lead solution	1.0 g/L. Dissolve 1.000 g Pb (99.99%) in 10 mL HNO_3 in a 1-L volumetric flask. Dilute to volume with water
Standard cadmium solution	1.0 g/L. Dissolve 1.000 g Cd (99.99%) in 10 mL HNO_3 in a 1-L volumetric flask. Dilute to volume with water
Working standard solution	Prepare either separate or mixed working standard solution for Cd and Pb in the range 0.1–10 µg/L by diluting standard solutions with 1% (v/v) HNO_3.

7. APPARATUS[1]

Voltammetric analyser	For DPASV: E.G. & G. Princeton Applied Research Corp., Models 174A; 351A, 303, or equivalent. For LSASV: Environmental Sciences Associates Model 2014, or equivalent, with composite mercury-graphite electrode
Ashing vessels	150–250 mL quartz, Vycor or Pyrex beakers, equipped with suitable glass covers (quartz is preferred)
Drying oven	Controllable within range 50–150 °C with <5 °C variation
Furnace	Controllable within range 100–700 °C with <5 °C variation
Micropipettes	10- to 100-µL (Eppendorf, or equivalent)
Ribbed watch glasses	Fisher Scientific Co.

NOTE: All glassware must be washed in 20% (v/v) HNO_3 and thoroughly rinsed with distilled water.

8. SAMPLING

Consult Chapter 12 for sampling, sample preparation and storage procedures.

---

[1] Reference to a company and/or product is for the purpose of information and identification only and does not imply approval or recommendation of the company and/or product by the International Agency for Research on Cancer, to the exclusion of others which may also be suitable.

Homogenize representative samples with a clean homogenizer-blender to produce a uniform slurry, then store in Pyrex or plastic containers until required for analysis. Canned foods which may contain lead particulates from soldered seams may require a special homogenization procedure (Jones & Boyer, 1979). If blended samples are stored in a freezer, they must be thawed and rehomogenized before analysis. Precautions must be taken to prevent lead and cadmium contamination of the sample from the laboratory and sample preparation equipment.

9.   PROCEDURE

9.1 *Blank tests*

> 9.1.1   Determine a reagent blank prior to sample analysis by following procedures 9.4 to 9.6 (or 9.7), but omitting the test portion in 9.4.1.

> 9.1.2   In the same way, determine three more reagent blanks in parallel with the sample analysis.

9.2 *Check test*

When applying the method to a new substrate, spike at least two samples with standard solutions of the analytes and determine recoveries of added analytes, following procedures 9.4 to 9.6 (or 9.7). The method may be applied satisfactorily if the recoveries obtained are in the range 80–120%.

9.3 *Test portion*

5.0 to 10.0 g of homogenized sample.

9.4 *Preparation of test solution*

> 9.4.1   Weigh test portion into ashing vessel (use 5.0 g for dry materials, such as cereals).

> 9.4.2   Add 5.0 mL K_2SO_4 ash-aid solution and mix thoroughly, using glass stirring rod. If needed, add small amount of water to ensure sample and ash aid are well mixed.

> 9.4.3   Cover ashing vessel with glass cover and heat in 110–120 °C oven until thoroughly dry.

> 9.4.4   Place vessel with cover in cold furnace and slowly raise temperature to 500 °C. Avoid excessive temperature overshoot. Maintain temperature 4 h or more (may be ashed overnight).

> 9.4.5   Remove vessel from furnace, and cool. Ash should be white and essentially carbon-free (brownish-red colour in the ash, possible Fe_2O_3, is

acceptable). If ash is grey or black (carbon particles), follow procedure 9.4.6. If ash is white, proceed directly to 9.4.7.

9.4.6   HNO$_3$ Treatment

9.4.6.1   Wash down sides of vessel with water and add 2.0 mL HNO$_3$. Use glass stirring rod to break up solid particles.

9.4.6.2   Dry thoroughly on hot plate at low setting (if spattering occurs, dry under IR lamp).

9.4.6.3   Return vessel to 500 °C furnace for 30 min.

9.4.6.4   Remove from furnace and cool. If necessary, repeat HNO$_3$, treatments using 1 mL increments of HNO$_3$, until white, carbon-free ash is obtained.

9.4.7   Add 1.0 mL HNO$_3$ and about 10 mL water to vessel and, if necessary, heat on hot plate at low heat until ash is dissolved (small amounts of white, siliceous-like precipitate may remain undissolved).

9.4.8   Cool and quantitatively transfer solution to 50-mL volumetric flask, rinsing with water. Dilute to volume with water and mix well. Let stand to allow any precipitate to settle. Use clear supernatant solution to determine analytes by DPASV or LSASV.

9.5 *Measurement of cadmium and lead by DPASV*

9.5.1   Transfer 5.0 mL aliquot of solution (9.4.8) to electrolysis cell containing Teflon-coated stirring bar and add 5.0 mL acetate electrolyte solution (volumes may be varied as long as 1:1 ratio is maintained).

9.5.2   Purge solution 5 min with nitrogen. Adjust gas inlet to let nitrogen flow gently about and across solution surface.

9.5.3   If hanging mercury drop electrode is used, add fresh drop of mercury to capillary tip with micrometer or similar device, to ensure reproducibility of drop.

9.5.4   Turn on stirrer motor and electrolyse solution at −0.8 V *versus* saturated calomel electrode (SCE) or Ag/AgCl electrode to deposit elements at working electrode. Deposition time may vary with instrument (see manufacturer's instructions).

9.5.5   After deposition, stop stirring and let solution equilibrate for 30 s.

9.5.6   Increase applied anodic voltage linearly. Follow manufacturer's instructions for rate of scan, e.g., 2–6 mV/s.

9.5.7   Record voltammogram and measure wave height at peak potentials for cadmium (-0.62 ± 0.05 V) and for lead (-0.45 ± 0.05 V) *versus* SCE or Ag/AgCl electrodes.

9.6. *Quantification by standard additions*

9.6.1   To the cell solution remaining after step 9.5.7, add known amounts of lead and cadmium from working standard solutions, using appropriate micropipettes. Add sufficient amount of each element to generate peak heights about twice those obtained in 9.5.7. Record voltammogram of cell solution after the addition.

9.6.2   Repeat 9.6.1 with two more similar additions of working standard solutions, recording the voltammogram after each addition.

9.7 *Measurement of cadmium and lead by LSASV*

9.7.1   Transfer 2.0 mL aliquot of solution from 9.4.8 to electrolysis cell and add 3.0 mL acetate electrolyte solution.

9.7.2   Deposit analytes on composite mercury graphite electrode at -0.9 V (*versus* Ag/AgCl) for 30 min. Bubble nitrogen through cell solution during entire deposition period.

9.7.3   Increase applied anodic voltage linearly at 60 mV/s from -0.9 to -0.2 V. Measure peak current (μA) for each analyte.

9.8 *Quantification using conversion factor ($\mu g/\mu A$)*

For each analyte, make standard addition to cell solution (9.7.3) and measure peak current (μA) to determine response per μg added analyte. Repeat periodically to verify stable instrument response.

10. METHOD OF CALCULATION

10.1 DPASV

10.1.1   Using results for each analyte from 9.6, plot mass added (μg) on x-axis *versus* peak height (μA) on y-axis. Extrapolate linear plot to x-axis intercept to determine total amount of analyte in sample (or blank) aliquot (9.5.1). If available, use computer program based on method of least squares to calculate regression line.

10.1.2   The mass fraction, ω(mg/kg), of analyte in the sample is given by

$$\omega = (m_s\text{-}m_b)V_1/V_2M$$

where

m_s = mass of analyte in sample aliquot, determined in 10.1.1 (μg)

m_b = average mass of analyte in blank aliquots, determined in 10.1.1 (μg)

V_1 = final volume of sample solution in 9.4.8 (mL)

V_2 = volume of sample solution aliquot in 9.5.1 (mL)

M = mass of test portion in 9.4.1 (g).

10.2 LSASV

10.2.1   From data of 9.8, calculate conversion factor (μg/μA) for each analyte by dividing the amount added by the difference between the peak currents before and after addition of analyte standard.

10.2.2   Multiply peak currents (9.7.3) by conversion factor to determine mass of each analyte in sample (m_s) and blank (m_b) aliquots (9.7.1).

10.2.3   The mass fraction, ω(mg/kg), of analyte in the sample is given by the equation in 10.1.2,

where

m_s = mass of analyte in sample aliquot, determined in 10.2.2 (μg)

m_b = average mass of analyte in blank aliquots, determined in 10.2.2 (μg)

V_1 = final volume of sample solution in 9.4.8 (mL)

V_2 = volume of sample solution aliquot in 9.7.1 (mL)

M = mass of test portion in 9.4.1 (g).

11. REPEATABILITY AND REPRODUCIBILITY

The AOAC collaborative study of this method was performed on six food commodities. The low fortification levels ranged from 0.03 to 0.08 mg/kg for cadmium and from 0.05 to 0.15 mg/kg for lead. The high fortification levels ranged from 0.12 to 0.28 mg/kg for cadmium and from 0.24 to 0.45 mg/kg for lead. Each commodity was analysed by ten collaborators (Capar *et al.*, 1982).

11.1 *Repeatability*

The overall average coefficient of variation (CV) for repeatability (10 collaborators) was 18.5% for lead and 15% for cadmium at the low levels, and 11.2% for lead and 11.2% for cadmium at the high levels.

11.2 *Reproducibility*

The average CV for reproducibility at the low levels was 24% for lead and 21% for cadmium. At the high levels, the average CV was 18% for lead and 16% for cadmium.

12. NOTES ON PROCEDURE

If thallium interference is suspected, treat as follows: Transfer aliquot of sample solution to electrolysis cell and make basic with 3.0 mL of 1 mol/L NaOH. Determine elements of interest in this solution by ASV as in 9.5 or 9.7. The plating potential is -1.0 V *versus* SCE. Strip deposited elements by anodically scanning from -1.0 to -0.3 V *versus* SCE. In this manner, the cadmium and lead peaks shift to -0.78 ± 0.05 V and -0.73 ± 0.05 V *versus* SCE, respectively. The thallium peak remains at -0.47 V *versus* SCE.

13. SCHEMATIC REPRESENTATION OF PROCEDURE

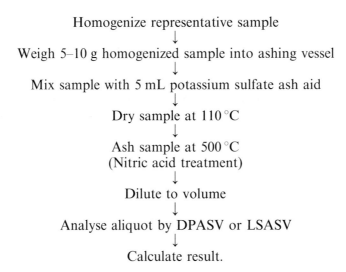

Homogenize representative sample
↓
Weigh 5–10 g homogenized sample into ashing vessel
↓
Mix sample with 5 mL potassium sulfate ash aid
↓
Dry sample at 110 °C
↓
Ash sample at 500 °C
(Nitric acid treatment)
↓
Dilute to volume
↓
Analyse aliquot by DPASV or LSASV
↓
Calculate result.

14. ORIGIN OF THE METHOD

Food and Drug Administration
200 C Street SW
Washington DC 10104
USA

Contact point: Mr S.G. Capar
  Mr R.J. Gajan

METHOD 19 – DETERMINATION OF LEAD AND CADMIUM IN FOODS BY FLAMELESS ATOMIC ABSORPTION SPECTROPHOTOMETRY

K.C. Faul & B.E. Young

1. SCOPE AND FIELD OF APPLICATION

This method is suitable for the determination of lead and cadmium in all classes of raw and processed food products.

The limits of detection range from $\sim 15\,\mu g/kg$ for Pb and $\sim 2.5\,\mu g/kg$ for Cd, using a 5 g sample.

2. REFERENCES

Koirtyohann, S.R., Kaiser, M.L. & Hinderberger, E.J. (1982) Food analysis for lead using furnace atomic absorption and a L'vov platform. *J. Assoc. off. anal. Chem.*, **65**, 999–1004

Young, B.E. & Faul, K.C. (1981) The quantitative determination of lead and cadmium in total diet market baskets by flameless atomic absorption. *FDA Laboratory Information Bulletin no. 2403,* US Food and Drug Administration, 1009 Cherry Street, Kansas City, Mo 64106, USA

3. DEFINITIONS

AAS = atomic absorption spectrophotometry.

A microboat is a rectangular piece of pyrolytic graphite which fits inside a slot in the graphite cuvette device in the flameless AAS instrument.

A L'vov platform is a small curved piece of graphite placed inside the furnace and centered below the sampling part of the flameless AAS instrument.

4. PRINCIPLE

The homogenized sample is treated with 20% sulfuric acid and the oven-dried residue is ashed in a muffle furnace. Nitric acid is added to oxidize carbon particles and the residue is dried and re-ashed in the muffle furnace. The remaining ash is dissolved in nitric acid and diluted to volume so that the final concentration of nitric acid is 0.8% (v/v). Lanthanum in nitric acid is added as a matrix modifier, to give a final La concentration of 0.8 g/L. The solution is then aspirated onto a pyrolytic microboat situated in a pyrolitic cuvette in the AAS furnace. Alternatively, the solution may be pipetted onto a L'vov platform inside a conventional flameless AAS furnace (Koirtyohann *et al.*, 1982). The furnace is then cycled through the atomization cycle and the absorbance is measured. Quantification is carried out by comparison with the absorbance of Pb and Cd standard solutions.

5. HAZARDS

Concentrated nitric and sulfuric acids are toxic and should be handled in a ventilated hood. Rubber gloves and safety glasses should be worn. Dilute sulfuric acid by adding the acid slowly to the water, not the reverse.

6. REAGENTS[1]

All chemicals should be reagent grade, except where noted.

Water	Deionized
Nitric acid (HNO_3)	Concentrated (redistilled, G.F. Smith, or equivalent). For 20% (v/v) solutions, slowly add 200 mL HNO_3, to an equal volume of water, then dilute to 1 L.
Sulfuric acid (H_2SO_4)	Concentrated ('Baker Analyzed' Reagent, or equivalent). For 20% (v/v), slowly add 200 mL concentrated H_2SO_4 to an equal volume of water, then dilute to 1 L.
Lanthanum matrix-modifier solution	50 g/L. Weigh 29.32 g of La_2O_3 (MCB, or equivalent) and transfer to a 1-L beaker. Add ∼50 mL water and stir. Carefully add, while stirring, 40 mL concentrated HNO_3. Cool and transfer into a 500-mL volumetric flask. Dilute to volume with water. Use 0.8 mL of this solution per 50 mL of final sample or standard solution.
Cadmium stock standard solution	1000 mg/L. Dissolve 1.0000 g of 99.99% Cd powder in 100 mL of 20% HNO_3. Heat on a steambath to dissolve. Dilute to 1 L with water.

---

[1] Reference to a company and/or product is for the purpose of information and identification only and does not imply approval or recommendation of the company and/or product by the International Agency for Research on Cancer, to the exclusion of others which may also be suitable.

Cadmium working standard solutions	Prepare working standard solutions in 0.8% (v/v) HNO_3 with Cd concentrations of 0.5, 1, 2, 4 and 8 ng/L, all containing 0.8 mg La/mL.
Lead stock standard solution	1000 mg/L. Dissolve 1.0000 g of 99.99% Pb powder in 100 mL of 20% HNO_3. Heat on a steambath until dissolved. Dilute to 1 L with water.
Lead working standard solutions	Prepare working standard solutions in 0.8% HNO_3 with Pb concentrations of 2.5, 5, 10, 15 and 25 ng/mL, all containing 0.8 mg La/mL.

7. APPARATUS[1]

Analytical balance	Sartorius 1364 MP, or equivalent
Atomic absorption spectrophotometer	Instrumentation Laboratory 951, with the IL CFT 555 Atomizer (Furnace) and the IL 254 Fastac Autosampler, or equivalent.
Furnace cuvette	Rectangular, single piece, pyrolytic graphite, for use with the IL 254 Fastac Autosampler (obtainable from Instrumentation Laboratory, Inc, 1 Burtt Road, Andover, MA 01810, USA).
Microboat	See Notes on Procedure, 12.1. Pyrolytic graphite, for use with furnace cuvetttes. Cuvette life varies with acid and lanthanum concentration and with atomization temperature (obtainable from Instrumentation Laboratory, Inc.).
L'vov platform	See Notes on Procedure, 12.1. For use with conventional flameless AAS. See Koirtyohann et al. (1982) for preparation procedure.
Micropipette	Eppendorf, Gilson, or equivalent
Volumetric flasks	50-mL, 1-L
Vycor or quartz beakers	100-mL
Ribbed watch-glasses	Fisher Scientific Co., or equivalent

---

[1] Reference to a company and/or product is for the purpose of information and identification only and does not imply approval or recommendation of the company and/or product by the International Agency for Research on Cancer, to the exclusion of others which may also be suitable.

NOTE: Before use, wash all glassware in 20% (v/v) HNO_3 and rinse thoroughly with deionized water.

8.   SAMPLING

8.1 Consult chapter 12 for sampling, storage and sample preparation procedures. Precautions must be taken to prevent Pb and Cd contamination of the sample from the laboratory and sample preparation equipment.

8.2 Homogenize representative samples with a clean homogenizer/blender to produce a uniform slurry. Store the blended samples in clean Pyrex or plastic containers until needed for analysis. If blended samples are stored in a freezer, they must be thawed and rehomogenized before analysis.

9.   PROCEDURE

9.1 *Blank test*

Analyse 1 reagent blank per 5 samples, following procedure 9.4–9.6, but omitting the test portion in 9.4.1.

9.2 *Check test*

Check the validity of this method for a new substrate by spiking two samples with known amounts (~ 1 µg) of Pb and Cd. Analyse these and two non-spiked samples as described in 9.4 to 9.6 and calculate the recovery (see 9.8).

9.3 *Test portions*

Sugar, ~ 1 g; fats and oils, ~ 2.5 g; meats, grains, fruits, vegetables, beverages, ~ 5 g. Weigh to nearest 0.01 g.

9.4 *Preparation of sample solution*

   9.4.1   Weigh (to the nearest 0.01 g) a test portion of each item (see 9.3) into clean 100-mL Vycor or quartz beakers. To determine Pb and Cd recoveries, weigh duplicate test portions.

   9.4.2   Spike duplicate test portions of each item with ~ 1 µg of Pb and Cd per 5 g sample, for determination of recoveries (the mass of the spike should at least double the amount of analyte in the test portion).

   9.4.3   Add 25 mL of 20% H_2SO_4 to each sample and mix with a stirring rod (if necessary) until the composite is completely mixed. Keep all samples covered (e.g., with larger beakers) when not in oven, muffle furnace or contamination control hood.

9.4.4   Cover each beaker with a ribbed watch-glass and place in cool oven. Raise the temperature to ~100 °C and leave samples in oven overnight (a charred, viscous sulfuric acid/sample residue remains).

9.4.5   Transfer samples to a cool muffle furnace and raise temperature in 50 °C increments every 2 h until 350 °C is reached. Hold at 350 °C for ~2 h, then increase temperature to 470 °C and hold 12–16 h.

9.4.6   Gradually cool furnace (to avoid cracking watch glasses) and remove cooled beakers. Rinse sides of beakers with water if necessary.

9.4.7   Add 2 mL 20% HNO_3 and slowly evaporate to dryness on a warm hot-plate.

9.4.8   Place samples in muffle furnace and re-ash at 470 °C. Hold for at least 2–3 h (this step can be repeated, if necessary, to remove most of the remaining carbon).

9.4.9   Remove beakers from muffle furnace, store in clean area and allow to cool, then add 0.4 mL 20% HNO_3 and ~10 mL water.

9.4.10   Warm on hot-plate to dissolve residue, then transfer solution to 50-mL volumetric flasks containing 0.8 mL of 50 g/L La matrix-modifier solution. Dilute to volume with water. (If the spiked sample solutions require further dilution, the final solution should contain a concentration of 0.8% HNO_3 and 0.08% La.)

9.5 AAS operating conditions

The instrument parameters given below are specific for an IL 951 Atomic Absorption Spectrophotometer, equipped with an IL CFT 555 Atomizer (fitted with pyrolytic cuvette and microboat) and an IL 254 Fastac Autosampler. If another instrument is used, the optimum parameters must be established prior to conducting sample analysis.

AAS	Channel A (Lead)	Channel B (Cadmium)
Wavelength	283.3 nm (or 217.0 nm)[1]	228.8 nm
Hollow Cathode	Pb (5 mA)	Cd (3 mA)
Background correction	Deuterium	Deuterium
Bandwidth	0.5 nm (1.0 nm)	1.0 nm
Mode	Concentration	Concentration
Integration mode	Peak height	Peak height

[1] See Notes on Procedure, 12.2

Atomizer	*Temperature*	*Time*
Drying cycle	25°C (initial)	Ramp – 0 s
	155°C (final)	Hold – 5 s
Pyrolysis	600°C (initial)	Ramp – 20 s
	650°C (final)	Hold – 5 s
Atomization cycle	2 000°C (initial)	Ramp – 0 s
	2 000°C (final)	Hold – 10 s

Nitrogen flow rate	420–570 L/h (15–20 cubic feet/h)
Integration time	18 s

Auto-sampler	
Delay	7 s
Deposit	12 s (approximately equal to 12 µL, vary as necessary to optimize atomization)
Nebulizer	3.0 L/min
Repeat	2

9.6 *Determination of Pb and Cd*

Measure absorbance of sample, spiked sample and blank solutions from 9.4.10, using the conditions specified in 9.5.

9.7 *Calibration curve*

Using the conditions employed in 9.6, measure the absorbance of the working standard solutions of Pb and Cd. With the IL-951 AAS instrument, the calibration curve itself is obtained and stored (as ng/mL *versus* absorbance) in the IL-951 computer for automatic quantification of analyte levels in sample solutions. If the instrument used does not have this capability, construct a curve of the concentration of analyte in standard solutions *versus* absorbance peak height for a fixed volume (e.g., 12 µL) aspirated.

9.8 *Recovery*

Using the absorbance measurements (9.6) and the calibration curve (9.7), calculate the recovery, R(%), from the equation

$$R = 100(\rho_s - \rho)V/m_s$$

where

ρ_s = average mass concentration of analyte in spiked sample solutions (ng/mL)

ρ =   mass concentration of analyte in non-spiked sample solution (ng/mL)

V   =   final volume of solution in 9.4.10 (mL)

m_s =   mass of spike added in 9.4.2 (ng).

10. METHOD OF CALCULATION

Using the absorbance measurements (9.6) and the calibration curve (9.7), calculate the mass fraction, $\omega(\mu g/kg)$, from the equation

$$\omega = 100\ (\rho - \rho_b)V/RM = \frac{(\rho - \rho_b)m_s}{(\rho_s - \rho)M}$$

where

ρ_b =   mass concentration of analyte in reagent blank solution (ng/mL)

M   =   mass of test portion; in 9.4.1 (g)

and the other symbols are defined in 9.8.

If recovery correction is not applied,

$$\omega = (\rho - \rho_b)V/M.$$

11. REPEATABILITY AND REPRODUCIBILITY

11.1 *Repeatability*

National Bureau of Standards (NBS) Standard Reference Material (SRM) Spinach has a certified mass fraction of 1.2 ± 0.16 mg/kg for Pb and 1.5 mg/kg (non-certified) for Cd. Twelve analyses of the NBS-SRM Spinach over a four-month period gave a mean of 1.05 ± 0.16 mg/kg (coefficient of variation = 11%) for Pb and a mean of 1.41 ± 0.15 mg/kg (coefficient of variation = 11%) for Cd.

11.2 *Reproducibility*

Reproducibility has not been verified.

11.3 *Recovery*

Sixty-eight lead spike recovery determinations (34 different food items) gave a mean result of $94 \pm 12\%$. The mean value for 66 cadmium spike recoveries (33 different food items) was $103 \pm 10\%$. These results were obtained over an approximately one-year period.

12. NOTES ON PROCEDURE

12.1 Lanthanum is used as a matrix modifier and prevents the premature volatilization of either Pb or Cd. However, La will gradually attack the pyrolytic graphite surface of the microboat or the graphite tube wall (if microboat is not used). Thus, the use of microboat (or L'vov platform) is preferred not only because it reduces matrix interferences, but also because of the lower replacement cost of a microboat *versus* a graphite tube.

12.2 The use of the 283.3 nm Pb line is preferred over the 217 nm line (which was originally used to verify the method) because of reduced interferences with certain matrices. For clean, routine samples, the 217 nm Pb line may be preferred because it is approximately twice as sensitive as the 283.3 nm line.

13. SCHEMATIC REPRESENTATION OF PROCEDURE

Accurately weigh (± 0.01 gm) homogeneous sample
into a 100-mL beaker
↓
Add 25 mL of 20% sulfuric acid,
mix if necessary
↓
Dry samples in oven,
transfer to muffle furnace and ash
↓
Oxidize remaining carbon in residue using
20% nitric acid, evaporate slowly to dryness
↓
Dissolve residue in nitric acid and water
↓
Add La matrix-modifier solution and dilute to 50 mL
(final solution, 0.8% nitric acid, 0.08% lanthanum)
↓
Analyse standards, blanks, samples and
spiked samples by flameless AAS

14. ORIGIN OF THE METHOD

Food and Drug Administration
1009 Cherry Street
Kansas City, MI 64106
USA

Contact point: Kent C. Faul (FDA, 721 19th St., Denver CO, 80202)
                   Barbara E. Young

METHOD 20 – DETERMINATION OF SELENIUM IN FOODS AND OTHER BIOLOGICAL MATERIALS BY FLUORIMETRY

R.J. Hall & P.J. Peterson

1. SCOPE AND FIELD OF APPLICATION

The method is suitable for the determination of selenium (as Se[IV]) in biological samples containing less than approximately 7% (w/w) of lipids (i.e., for most plant materials, animal tissues, foodstuffs and body fluids). The wet oxidation procedure should not be used directly for samples rich in natural fats or lipids (full-fat milk powders and egg poweders, creams, cheeses, animal or vegetable oils, oil-bearing seeds, non-extracted bone meals, meat and bone or liver meals). However, most fats contain negligible amounts of selenium and the digestion can be safely applied to samples after removal of the lipids by Soxhlet extraction with a suitable solvent.

The limit of detection is about 5 µg/kg, using a 5 g sample. A set of 20 samples can be analysed in triplicate by a competent chemist in two days.

2. REFERENCES

Hall, R.J. & Gupta, P.L. (1969) The determination of very small amounts of selenium in plant samples. *Analyst, 94,* 292–299

Parker, C.A. & Harvey, L.G. (1962) Luminescence of some piazselenols, a new fluorimetric reagent for selenium. *Analyst, 87,* 558–565

3. DEFINITIONS

Not applicable.

4. PRINCIPLE

Organic material in plant, blood, milk and other food samples is destroyed by wet oxidation with nitric acid, assisted by hydrogen peroxide, then with perchloric acid. All oxidation states of Se are converted to Se[IV] by boiling the digest with hydrochloric acid. The Se in the digest is complexed with 2,3-diaminonaphthalene to form 4,5-benzopiazselenol, which is extracted into dekalin and its green fluorescence is measured in a spectrofluorimeter at 520 nm, or in a filter fluorimeter at 525 nm.

5. HAZARDS

The digestion procedure must be undertaken in a fume chamber having an efficient extractor fan. A perchloric acid-resistant chamber is preferred. Beakers and flasks containing the digestion mixture, together with bottles of acids, should be placed on trays with an acid- and heat-resisting surface. Suitable acid-resistant gloves and safety spectacles should be worn.

The use of boiling nitric and perchloric acids with plant and animal fats can cause explosions. The lipids present in kidney and liver tissues are particularly hazardous in this regard and *must* be removed with chloroform:methanol (2:1, v/v) before digestion of the solvent-free tissue.

6. REAGENTS[1]

'Micro-analytical reagent' grade chemicals should be used.

Water	Re-distilled in an all-glass apparatus
Nitric acid (HNO_3)	Ultra-pure grade, specific gravity 1.42
Hydrogen peroxide solution (H_2O_2)	30% (w/w)
Perchloric acid ($HClO_4$)	70% (w/w), E. Merck
Hydrochloric acid (HCl)	Specific gravity 1.18
Hydrochloric acid	~6 mol/L. Dilute 600 mL of HCl (specific gravity 1.18) to 1 L with water
Hydrochloric acid	~0.1 mol/L. Dilute 10 mL of HCl (specific gravity 1.18) to 1 L with water
Ammonia solution	7 mol/L. Dilute 420 mL of ammonia (specific gravity 0.88) to 1 L with water
Formic acid	50% (v/v)
Chloroform ($CHCl_3$)	
Disodium ethylenediamino-tetraacetate (EDTA)	

---

[1] Reference to a company and/or product is for the purpose of information and identification only and does not imply approval or recommendation of the company and/or product by the International Agency for Research on Cancer, to the exclusion of others which may also be suitable.

Hydroxylammonium chloride reagent	Dissolve 5 g of hydroxylammonium chloride (hydroxylamine hydrochloride) in water. Add 10 mL of HCl (specific gravity 1.18) and dilute to 1 L with water
Stabilizing solution	0.025 mol/L EDTA disodium salt in 25 g/L hydroxylammonium chloride. Dissolve 9.036 g of the disodium EDTA and 25 g of hydroxylammonium chloride in 1 L of water.
Dekalin (decahydronaphthalene)	Obtainable from Aldrich Chemical Co. (Cat. No. 18582-5). If a high blank fluorescence is obtained, it is necessary to redistil the dekalin and use only the fraction distilling at 188–192 °C.
2,3-Diaminonaphthalene (DAN) reagent	Obtainable from Aldrich Chemical Co. (Cat. No. 13653-0). For purification procedure, see Notes on Procedure, 12.1
Selenium (Se)	High purity (Johnson Matthey Ltd)
Charcoal	Decolorizing
Sodium sulfate	Anhydrous.
DAN working solution 2 mg DAN/mL	Just before use and in diffuse light, add 200 mg of purified DAN to 100 mL of hydroxyammonium reagent. Warm to 50 °C for not more than 25 min to facilitate solution.
Se standard solution A	1.0 mg Se[IV]/mL. Dissolve 50 mg of pure Se in 5 mL of warm 70% perchloric acid in a 50-mL volumetric flask. Dilute to the mark with water.
Se standard solution B	2.0 µg Se[IV]/mL. Dilute 2 mL of standard solution A to 1 L with water.

7. APPARATUS

Spectrofluorimeter	To measure green fluorescence (excitation, 366 nm; emission, 520 nm). A spectrofluorimeter is preferred, but a filter fluorimeter with a primary filter (transmission 340 to 380 nm) and a secondary filter (transmission 525 nm) is suitable.
Optical cells (or quartz tubes)	Preferably 10-mm light path, for use in the fluorimeter

Pyrex tubes	Glass-stoppered, graduated, 50-mL and 10-mL capacities
Beakers	250-mL, Pyrex
Volumetric flasks	50-mL, 1-L
Pasteur pipettes	
Buchner funnels	6-cm diameter, sintered glass, No. 1 and No. 3 porosity
Filter papers	Whatman, No. 4, 6-cm diameter
pH Paper	pH range 1–4
Sample grinding equipment	
Electric hotplate	With thermostat
Bench centrifuge	$\sim 1000 \times g$
Digestion flasks	With reflux tubes (see Fig. 1). These are modified Kjeldahl-type flasks of ~ 60 mL capacity, with a bowl volume of 40–45 mL and a ground, flat base of 2.5 cm diameter. The neck is 10 cm in length (including a B19/26 joint), with an internal diameter of 2 cm. An adapter, 15 to 16 cm in length (including the B19/26 socket) is fitted into the neck to act as an air condenser. Appropriate ground glass stoppers are also required. The whole apparatus is made of Pyrex (or other heat-resistant glass) and can be constructed by any competent glass blower. It has been found useful to support the flasks, with adapters, in a stainless-steel wire cage (without floor) made up into sections for individual flasks.

NOTE: Clean all glass-ware by immersion for several hours in very dilute detergent. Rinse with tap water, then with glass-distilled water.

8. SAMPLING

Spread a fresh sample of up to 100 g on a shallow tray (20×25 cm) lined with polythene sheeting and dry at 40–60 °C for 48 h in an oven with a forced air draught.

Fig. 1. Modified Kjeldahl-type digestion flask and adapter

Higher temperatures are to be avoided, since measurable amounts of Se can be lost at this stage. Grind the dry sample in a suitable mill to pass a 1-mm mesh sieve.

9. PROCEDURE

9.1 *Blank tests*

9.1.1   Sample reagent blank:
Carry out procedures 9.4 to 9.6, inclusive, but with no sample in step 9.4.1

9.1.2   Standard reagent blank:
Add 5 mL of 70% $HClO_4$ to a digestion flask and follow procedures 9.4.10 to 9.6, inclusive

9.2 *Check test*

It is advisable to establish a 'standard sample' of material such as grass or brassica, on which 50–100 determinations have been completed and a statistical standard determined. This standard sample should be included in every set of determinations.

9.3 *Test portion*

The analytical procedure is designed for 5 g of dry sample, containing up to 1 µg of Se. See Notes on Procedure, 12.2. Samples containing high levels of fat or oil must be extracted in a Soxhlet apparatus with chloroform:methanol (2:1, v/v) before digestion. The fat content of the sample taken for digestion should not exceed 7% (w/w). Certain liquid samples, such as whole blood or plasma, milk or urine, may be pipetted directly into a digestion flask in step 9.4.1. Take 5 mL of blood, no more than 10 mL of milk or 20–30 mL of urine. Weigh a separate volume of the sample to within $\pm 1\%$.

Where more than 0.2 µg Se per gram of sample is expected (as in oil-seed meals), a smaller weight of sample may be taken (usually 2 g). With Se-supplemented foods, a smaller sample may suffice, or only part of the digested sample may be compexed with DAN.

9.4 *Sample digestion*

9.4.1   Weigh three 5-g portions of dried sample into separate 250-mL Pyrex beakers and spike one of them with 0.10 mL of Se standard solution B, for recovery determination.

9.4.2   When the main reaction has ceased and no more frothing takes place, cover each beaker with a watch glass and return to the hotplate. Boil gently for 30 min, remove the watch glass and boil more rapidly to reduce the volume of the acid to 15–20 mL. Allow the beaker and its contents to cool.

9.4.3   Transfer each digest quantitatively to a separate digestion flask, add a few anti-bumping granules and 5 mL HNO_3, fit the reflux condenser tube and reflux for at least 30 min.

NOTE: Attempts to replace the digestion flaks with 150–250-mL beakers have consistently resulted in poor reproducibility and low recoveries.

9.4.4   Remove the condenser tube and boil to reduce the volume to approximately 10 mL. Remove the flask from the hotplate and allow to cool.

9.4.5   Add 5 mL of 100 vol H_2O_2, 1 mL at a time. (This step must be done very carefully with the flask *off* the hotplate, as a very vigorous reaction occurs which is delayed for several seconds after the addition of each mL of peroxide.)

9.4.6   When the last reaction has subsided, replace the flask on the hotplate and again reduce the volume to 5–10 mL, then allow to cool.

9.4.7   Repeat the addition of 5 mL of H_2O_2 in 1-mL aliquots and reduce the volume to approximately 8 mL. (Use 20 mL of hydrogen peroxide with liquid milk samples.) Remove the flask from the hotplate and cool.

9.4.8   To eliminate remaining HNO_3, add 5 mL of 70% HCl_4 and continue heating until the volume of liquid in the flask is reduced to 4–5 mL, when the $HClO_4$ will start to boil. At this point, a new reaction will take place, with production of brown nitrogen dioxide. A more vigorous reaction then follows, sometimes with charring of the small amount of organic material which may be left.

9.4.9   Gently swirl the contents of the flask as required to dislodge any carbon particles. The digest will rapidly clear and become pale green to colourless, the obvious effervescence subsiding quite suddenly to a gentle simmer of the $HClO_4$, indicated by a heavy white vapour at the top of the digestion flask. Prepare calibration standard (9.7.1) before proceeding to step 9.4.10.

9.4.10   Cool the flask and add 5 mL of H_2O_2, then heat until the $HClO_4$ boils. The digestion is now complete. (It is most important *not* to continue heating after this stage has been reached, or Se may be lost.) Remove the flask from the hotplate and allow to cool.

9.4.11   Add 5 mL of 6 mol/L HCl, return the flask to the hotplate and boil gently for 15 min. Remove the flask from the hotplate and cool.

9.5 *Preparation of Se[IV]-DAN complex*

NOTE: This part of the analysis should be undertaken in diffuse light.

9.5.1   Add 5 mL of formic acid and 10 mL of stabilizing solution to the digests from 9.4.11. Mix.

9.5.2   Add 7 mol/L ammonia solution to obtain a pH of 2.0, using pH paper (in the case of plant samples, ∼ 12 mL is required).

9.5.3   Transfer the flasks to a water bath at 50 °C. After 5 min, add 2.5 mL of DAN reagent and make the volume to approximately 50 mL with water. Maintain the mixture at 50 °C for 30 min.

9.5.4   Remove the flasks from the water bath, allow to cool to room temperature and add 3 mL of dekalin to each. Stopper the flasks and shake vigorously by hand for 1 min.

9.5.5   With a Pasteur pipette, remove the dekalin layer as completely as possible into a dry 10-mL graduated glass tube (avoid removing any of the aqueous phase).

9.5.6   Repeat the extraction of the aqueous phase twice with 2×2 mL of dekalin, adding these extracts to the first. Dilute the pooled extracts to 7 mL with dekalin.

9.5.7   Wash the pooled extract by shaking vigorously for 30 s with 4 mL of 0.1 mol/L HCl. Remove the HCl with a Pasteur pipette and discard. Repeat the washing procedure.

9.5.8   Centrifuge the tubes at ∼1000 × g for 2 or 3 min to clarify the dekalin phase. Retain dekalin phase for fluorescence measurement (9.6).

9.6 *Determination of Se*

With the fluorimeter calibrated as described in 9.7, measure the green fluorescence of the dekalin extracts, 9.5.8.

9.7 *Fluorimeter calibration*

9.7.1   Add 4 mL of 70% $HClO_4$ to a clean digestion flask containing 0.25 mL of Se standard solution B.

9.7.2   Follow procedure 9.4.10 to 9.5.8, inclusive.

9.7.3   Set the fluorimeter to give full-scale deflection for the green fluorescence of the dekalin extract from 9.7.2 (i.e., for 0.5 µg Se).

10. METHOD OF CALCULATION

10.1 The mass fraction, ω(mg/kg), of Se in the dry sample is given by

$$\omega = \frac{m(f_1 - f_2)}{M(f_3 - f_4)}$$

where

   m   =   mass of Se in calibration standard, 9.6.1 (µg)

   M   =   mass of dry test portion in 9.4.1 (g)

   f_1 =   average fluorescence reading for the 2 sample extracts

   f_2 =   fluorescence reading for sample reagent blank (9.1.1)

   f_3 =   fluorescence reading for calibration standard (9.7.3)

   f_4 =   fluorescence reading for standard reagent blank (9.1.2)

10.2 The recovery, R(%), of Se from the spiked test portion (9.4.1) is given by

   $R = 100(m_1 - m_2)/m_3$

where

   m_1 =   Se content obtained for spiked test portion (µg)

m_2 = Se content obtained for sample in 10.1 (µg)

m_3 = mass of Se (spike) added to test portion in 9.4.1 (µg).

10.3 The moisture content of the sample must be determined separately if the results are to be expressed as the mass fraction of Se in the sample as received. This type of correction will also apply to samples which have been extracted for the removal of fat.

11. REPEATABILITY AND REPRODUCIBILITY

The repeatability (n = 10) has been determined using mixed dried grass and dried kale, with the following results:
Mixed dried grass; mean fluorimeter reading = 87.4, S.D. = 5.2.
Dried kale; mean fluorimeter reading = 69.4, S.D. = 2.4

12. NOTES ON PROCEDURE

12.1 For optimum sensitivity, DAN must be purified. It is advisable to carry out the purification process in diffuse light, since DAN is photosensitive.

Prepare a lump-free slurry of 5 g of DAN in 20 mL of chloroform. Transfer, with additional chloroform, to a 1-L flask fitted with a reflux condenser and make the total volume to 360 mL with chloroforom. Add a few anti-bumping granules and reflux gently for 10 to 15 min on an electric hotplate. Remove from hotplate and, when boiling ceases, add a slurry of ~6 g of decolorizing charcoal in 20 mL of chloroform. Continue to boil under reflux for 2 min. Prepare a filter consisting of a 2-cm bed of sodium sulfate loosely packed in a 6-cm diameter sintered-glass Buchner funnel of No. 3 porosity. Place a Whatman No. 4 filter paper on top of the sodium sulfate and heat the assembly in a drying oven to 100 °C. Filter the boiling DAN solution rapidly, under slightly reduced pressure, through the heated filter assembly. Cool the filtrate in cold water while swirling. Keep the filtrate at −20 °C for 2 to 3 h to crystallize the DAN. Filter the crystals through a pre-cooled sintered funnel (porosity No. 1), covered with a Whatman No. 4 filter paper, and wash the crystals twice with 20 mL portions of chloroform, previously cooled to −20 °C. Remove the remaining solvent under slightly reduced pressure and dry the DAN in a desiccator over calcium chloride in the dark. The yield should be about 60%. Store the crystals in a cool place in an amber bottle with an air-tight closure. Except for the most precise work, solutions freshly prepared from DAN purified in this manner may be used for 4–7 days if stored in an amber bottle at 4 °C. Blanks should, however, be checked periodically.

12.2 Selenium levels in foods and feedstuffs vary widely. Cereals usually contain ~0.03 mg Se/kg, but imported seed-cakes, seeds and other by-products may contain 0.4 mg/kg or more. An average figure for grass is 0.06 mg/kg dry weight. Normal cows milk contains ~ 0.01 mg/L (0.08 mg/kg of total solids). Normal cattle and sheep blood contains about 0.07 µg/g of whole fresh sample. Fish meals may have levels of more than 1.0 mg/kg. Cattle and sheep liver may contain more than 0.5 mg/kg dry weight.

13. SCHEMATIC REPRESENTATION OF PROCEDURE

Weigh 5 g of dried, ground sample into 250-mL beaker
↓
Add 50 mL HNO₃, warm slowly,
then concentrate to 15–20 mL by gentle boiling
↓
Transfer to digestion flask, add 5 mL HNO₃
and reflux for 30 min
↓
Remove condenser tube
and boil to concentrate to ~ 10 mL
↓
Cool and carefully add 5 mL H₂O₂, 1 mL at a time,
then concentrate to 5–10 mL by heating
↓
Cool and repeat addition of 5 mL H₂O₂, 1 mL at a time
↓
Cool, add 5 mL HClO₄ and concentrate to 4–5 mL by heating
↓
Cool, add 5 mL H₂O₂, then heat until HClO₄ boils
↓
Cool, add 5 mL of 6 mol/L HCl and boil gently for 15 min
↓
Cool, add 5 mL formic acid and
10 mL stabilizing solution. Mix
↓
Adjust pH to 2.0 with 7 mol/L ammonia solution
↓
Transfer to water bath and maintain at 50 °C for 5 min
↓
Add 2.5 mL DAN reagent and dilute to ~ 50 mL with water;
maintain mixture at 50 °C for 30 min
↓
Cool and extract with 3 mL dekalin for 1 min;
transfer dekalin layer into graduated tube
↓
Repeat extraction with 2 × 2 mL dekalin
and combine extracts

↓
Wash combined extracts with 4 mL 0.1 mol/L HCl; repeat
↓
Centrifuge washed dekalin extract
↓
Measure green fluorescence of Se-DAN complex in extract
↓
Quantify by comparison with calibration standard

14. ORIGIN OF THE METHOD

Ministry of Agriculture, Fisheries and Food
Kenton Bar
Newcastle upon Tyne NE1 2YA
UK

Contact point:　R.J. Hall
　　　　　　　　The Mount,
　　　　　　　　30 West Road,
　　　　　　　　Newcastle upon Tyne, NE20 9SX
　　　　　　　　UK

METHOD 21 – DETERMINATION OF ZINC IN FOODS BY ATOMIC ABSORPTION SPECTROPHOTOMETRY

G. Rogers, J. Jones, R. Gajan, K. Boyer & J. Fiorino

1. SCOPE AND FIELD OF APPLICATION

This method is suitable for the determination of zinc in a wide range of foods of animal and plant origin, such as dairy products, meat, fish, grains, vegetables, fruits, water and beverarges. The method has been collaboratively studied and adopted by the Association of Official Analytical Chemists (AOAC). The present version, however, does not require the use of platinum crucibles for the dry-ashing procedure.

The detection limit is approximately 50 µg/kg, based on a 10-g sample.

2. REFERENCES

Jones, J.W., Gajan, R.J., Boyer, K.W. & Fiorino, J.A. (1977) Dry-ash-voltammetric determination of cadmium, copper, lead and zinc in foods. *J. Assoc. off. anal. Chem.*, **60**, 826–832

Official Methods of Analysis of the Association of Official Analytical Chemists, 13th Ed. (1980), Section 25.150–25.153. Association of Official Analytical Chemists, Washington, DC, p. 412

Rogers, G.R. (1968) Collaborative study of atomic absorption spectrophotometric method for determining zinc in foods. *J. Assoc. off. anal. Chem.,* **51**, 1042–1045

3. DEFINITIONS

AAS = atomic absorption spectrophotometry.

4. PRINCIPLE

The sample is ashed and the residue taken up in acid and diluted to optimum working range. The absorbance of the solution is determined by AAS at 213.8 nm and converted to zinc concentration, using a calibration curve.

5. HAZARDS

Concentrated nitric acid is toxic and a fire risk with organic materials. Concentrated sulfuric acid is toxic and a strong irritant. Hot acids should be handled with care and safety spectacles and resistant gloves should be worn. Both wet washing and dry ashing must be carried out in a well-ventilated hood.

6. REAGENTS[1]

Nitric acid	Analytical Reagent grade, $\sim 70\%$ (w/w)
Nitric acid	20% (v/v) and 5% (v/v). Carefully add 200 mL concentrated HNO_3 to 500 mL water. Cool and dilute to 1 L with water. For 5% HNO_3, dilute 20% HNO_3 $1 \rightarrow 4$ with water.
Sulfuric acid	Analytical Reagent grade, 98%
Sulfuric acid	20% (v/v) and 2% (v/v). Carefully add 200 mL concentrated H_2SO_4 to 500 mL water. Cool and dilute to 1 L with water. For 2% H_2SO_4, dilute 20% H_2SO_4 $1 \rightarrow 10$ with water.
Zinc metal	$> 99.9\%$ pure
Zinc stock standard solution	1000 µg/mL. Dissolve 1.000 g zinc metal in 100 mL 20% HNO_3 and dilute to 1 L with water.
Zinc working standard solutions	Dilute aliquots of stock standard solution with 2% H_2SO_4 to obtain 5 or more solutions within the linear range of the AAS instrument (e.g., 0–10 µg/mL). Prepare working standards daily.

7. APPARATUS[1]

Kjeldahl digestion apparatus	Capable of handling 300- or 500-mL Kjeldahl flasks
Drying oven	Temperature range, 50 to 150 °C, with less than ± 5 °C variation.

---

[1] Reference to a company and/or product is for the purpose of information and identification only and does not imply approval or recommendation of the company and/or product by the International Agency for Research on Cancer, to the exclusion of others which may also be suitable.

Muffle furnace	Temperature range, 100 to 500 °C, with less than ± 5 °C variation. Check temperature control calibration to ensure accurate ashing temperatures. Automatic temperature programming facility simplifies the ashing procedure.
Ashing vessels	a) For wet ashing, 300- or 500-mL Kjeldahl flasks (quartz, Pyrex, or equivalent), b) For dry ashing, 150-mL quartz or Pyrex tall-form beakers, with ribbed glass covers.
Volumetric flasks	100-mL
Atomic absorption spectrophotometer	Capable of operating at 213.8 nm. Equipped with Zn hollow-cathode lamp and air-acetylene (oxidizing) flame.

NOTE: All quartz- or glass-ware should be soaked in 20% HNO_3 and thoroughly rinsed with distilled water before use.

8. SAMPLING

Refer to Chapter 12 for general sampling, sample storage and sample preparation procedures applicable to foods and biological materials.

Homogenize representative samples with a clean homogenizer blender to produce a slurry uniform in appearance. Inherently homogeneous materials such as sugar or clear beverages may not require blending before ashing. Store the blended samples in clean Pyrex or plastic containers until required. If blended samples are stored in a freezer, they must be thawed and homogenized before analysis.

9. PROCEDURE

9.1 *Blank tests*

9.1.1   Test the acids to ensure an acceptably low zinc blank by atomic absorption measurement of 20% acids.

9.1.2   Determine reagent blank in parallel with sample analyses, using the same procedure (9.4, 9.6), but omitting the product being tested. The reagent blank zinc content should be below the detection limit or less than one-tenth of the level found in the sample with the lowest zinc content.

9.2 *Check test*

Verify the validity of this method for new substrates by fortifying samples with a zinc standard solution (see 9.7) and carrying them through the entire analytical method. Recovery of added zinc should be in the 90–100% range for the method to be applicable to the new substrate. When analysing familiar substrates, determine at least one recovery per 10 samples, as described in 9.7.

9.3 *Test portion*

Because of differences in ashing characteristics, the size of the test portion is governed by the water and fat content of the sample. The amounts in Table 1 give roughly the same quantification limit on a dry-weight basis, while minimizing ashing difficulties.

Table 1.   Optimum test portions

Sample characteristics	Test portion (g)
Greater than 50% water and/or less than 25% fat	20
25–50% water or fat	10
Less than 25% water and/or greater than 50% fat	5

9.4 *Sample digestion*

9.4.1   Wet ashing

NOTE: If a dry ashing procedure is preferred, proceed directly to 9.4.2

9.4.1.1 Weigh appropriate homogeneous test portion (Table 1) to nearest 0.01 g into 300- or 500-mL Kjeldahl flask containing several acid-cleaned glass boiling beads.

9.4.1.2 If sample is liquid, evaporate to small volume and cool before adding acids.

9.4.1.3 Add 5 mL 70% HNO_3 and cautiously heat until first vigorous reaction subsides.

9.4.1.4 Add 2 mL 98% H_2SO_4 and continue heating, maintaining oxidizing conditions by adding 70% HNO_3 in 1 mL increments until solution is colourless.

9.4.1.5 Continue heating until dense fumes of H_2SO_4 are evolved and all HNO_3 has been removed.

9.4.1.6 Cool digest, dilute with about 20 mL water and transfer to 100-mL volumetric flask. Wash digestion vessel twice into volumetric flask with 10–20 mL 2% H_2SO_4 and dilute to volume with 2% H_2SO_4. Allow any undissolved siliceous-like residue to settle before withdrawing aliquot for AAS analysis (9.6).

9.4.2   Dry ashing

9.4.2.1   Weigh appropriate homogeneous test portion (Table 1) to nearest 0.01 g into ashing vessel.

9.4.2.2   Add 25 mL of 20% H_2SO_4. Mix each sample thoroughly with clean glass stirring rod to ensure all sample material is wetted by the acid. Rinse the stirring rod into the ashing vessel with water and cover with a ribbed watch glass.

9.4.2.3   Dry the samples in an oven or furnace at $110\,°C \pm 5\,°C$ until a charred viscous residue remains. Usually, 12 to 16 h (overnight) is sufficient.

9.4.2.4   Transfer the ashing vessels containing the dried samples to a cold, clean muffle furnace, which is provided with good external ventilation (fume hood). Ensure samples remain covered during transfer.

9.4.2.5   Set the furnace at $125\,°C$ and increase the temperature hourly in $50\,°C$ increments to $275\,°C$ ($25\,°C$ every 30 min for high-fat, high-solids or high-sugar samples). Hold the temperature at $275\,°C$ for 3 h. Finally, increase the temperature at $50\,°C/h$ to $475\,°C$ and hold for 12 to 16 h (overnight).

9.4.2.6   Remove the covered ashing vessels from the furnace and allow to cool to room temperature in a clean, draft-free area.

9.4.2.7   Add 0.5 mL of water and 1 mL of 95% HNO_3 to the ash in each vessel. Evaporate carefully just to dryness on a *warm* hot-plate in a fume hood. Place the ashing vessels (covered with watch glasses) in a cool muffle furnace, raise the temperature to $300\,°C$ and hold for exactly 30 min. Remove each covered sample ash from the furnace and allow to cool as before.

9.4.2.8   If residual carbon remains, repeat the nitric acid treatment (9.4.2.7) until a carbon-free white ash is obtained. The covered ashing vessels containing the ash may be stored in a desiccator or in a laminar-flow clean hood.

NOTE: Copious carbon residues (i.e., black ashes) after overnight ashing (9.4.2.5) may indicate inefficient or uneven heating within the furnace. If so, recalibration of the furnace temperature is advised.

9.4.2.9   Add 2 mL of 70% HNO_3 and 15 mL water to each cool ashing vessel, then warm gently on a hot-plate at 80–90 °C for 5 to 10 min to dissolve the ash. Proceed as described in step 9.4.1.6.

NOTE: The presence of a precipitate other than the insoluble siliceous-like material in the digest or ash solutions may lead to low or erratic results. Precipitate formation can result from heating samples too long or at too high a temperature after nitric acid treatment of the ash (9.4.2.7).

9.5 *Calibration curve*

9.5.1   Using the 213.8 nm zinc line, determine absorbance of each of the working standard solutions with the instrument set to previously established optimum conditions, or according to manufacturer's instructions.

9.5.2   Plot a calibration curve of absorbance *versus* mass concentration (µg/mL) of Zn in the working standard solutions.

9.6 *Determination of Zn*

9.6.1   Determine the absorbances of the sample ash solutions (9.4.1.6) under the conditions employed in 9.5.1. If an absorbance exceeds the linear portion of the calibration curve, dilute the sample solution to a known volume with 2% H_2SO_4 to obtain absorbances within the linear portion of the calibration curve.

9.6.2   Monitor instrument stability by measuring the absorbance for each working standard solution, both before and after all sample solutions are analysed. In addition, if more than 20 sample solutions are to be analysed, repeat the measurement of standard solution absorbance after each set of 20 sample solution measurements. Aspirate water and check zero point between all standard and sample solution measurements.

9.6.3   Determine the mass concentration (µg/mL) of Zn in the solutions, using the calibration curve and the measured absorbance (9.6.1).

9.7 *Recovery*

9.7.1   Determine at least one recovery per 10 samples analysed, or per batch of samples if fewer than 10 samples are analysed. Fortify a duplicate test portion (9.3) using a Zn working standard solution. The amount of Zn added should be about the same, but not less than the amount of Zn in the unfortified test portion.

9.7.2 Analyse the fortified samples using the procedure employed (9.4, 9.6) for the unfortified samples.

10. METHOD OF CALCULATION

10.1 The mass fraction, ω(mg/kg), of zinc in the sample is given by

$$\omega = (\rho_s - \rho_b)V_s/m$$

where

ρ_s = mass concentration of Zn in sample solution, 9.6.3 (μg/mL)

ρ_b = mass concentration of Zn in reagent blank (μg/mL)

V_s = final volume of sample solution in 9.4.1.6, or 9.6.1 if diluted (mL)

m = mass of test portion in 9.4.1.1 or 9.4.2.1 (g).

10.2 The recovery, R(%), of Zn added to fortified samples is given by

$$R = 100(\rho_f V_f - \rho_s V_s)m_f$$

where

ρ_f = mass concentration of Zn in fortified sample solution (μg/mL)

V_f = final volume of fortified sample solution (mL)

m_f = mass of Zn added to fortified sample in 9.7.1 (μg)

ρ_s = mass concentration of Zn in sample solution, 9.6.3 (μg/mL)

V_s = final volume of sample solution in 9.4.1.6, or 9.6.1 if diluted (mL).

11. REPEATABILITY AND REPRODUCIBILITY

11.1 *Using wet ashing procedure at 5 mg/kg level*

Repeatability: no data available.

Reproducibility: the coefficient of variation has been found to be 12.3%.

11.2 *Using dry ashing procedure at 2.5 mg/kg level*

Repeatability: coefficient of variation = 1.9%.

Reproducibility: coefficient of variation = 11.9%.

12. NOTES ON PROCEDURE

Not applicable.

13. SCHEMATIC REPRESENTATION OF PROCEDURE

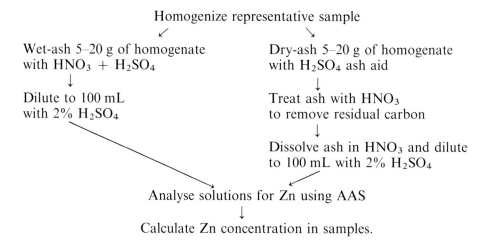

14. ORIGIN OF THE METHOD

14.1 *Using wet-ashing procedure*

Food and Drug Administration
Chemistry Branch
60 Eight Street, NE
Atlanta, GA 30309
USA

Contact point: Grayson R. Rogers

14.2 *Using dry-ashing procedure*

Food and Drug Administration
Division of Chemical Technology
200 C Street SW
Washington, DC 20204
USA

Contact point: John Jones

Biological monitoring

METHOD 22 – DETERMINATION OF ARSENIC IN HUMAN TISSUES AND FOODS BY SPECTROPHOTOMETRY

H.A.M.G. Vaessen, A. van Ooik & J. Zuydendorp

SEE METHOD 15

METHOD 23 – DETERMINATION OF CHROMIUM IN HUMAN TISSUES BY ATOMIC ABSORPTION SPECTROMETRY

C. Veillon & K.Y. Patterson

1. SCOPE AND FIELD OF APPLICATION

This method is suitable for the determination of chromium in biological materials (CrIII), using a graphite furnace atomic absorption spectrometer with a high-intensity background corrector lamp.

Certain matrices require that the method of additions be used. The detection limit is about 0.05 ng/mL for a 25 µL aliquot of the sample digest. This corresponds to a 0.5 g sample containing 1 ng Cr/g, diluted to a final volume of 10 mL.

Since chromium levels in most tissues are low, the most critical aspect of the method is the prevention of sample and blank contamination.

2. REFERENCES

Guthrie, B.E., Wolf, W.R. & Veillon, C. (1978) Background correction and related problems in the determination of chromium in urine by graphite furnace atomic absorption spectrometry. *Anal. Chem., 50,* 1900–1902

Kayne, F.J., Komar, G., Laboda, H. & Vanderlinde, R.E. (1978) Atomic absorption spectrophotometry of chromium in serum and urine with a modified Perkin-Elmer 603 atomic absorption spectrophotometer. *Clin. Chem., 24,* 2151–2154

Kumpulainen, J.T., Wolf, W.R., Veillon, C. & Mertz, W. (1979) Determination of chromium in selected United States diets. *J. agric. Food Chem., 27,* 490–494

Veillon, C., Patterson, K.Y. & Bryden, N.A. (1982) Direct determination of chromium in human urine by electrothermal atomic absorption spectrometry. *Anal. Chim. Acta, 136,* 233–241

Versieck, J., Speecke, A., Hoste, J. & Barbier, F. (1973) Trace-element contamination in biopsies of the liver. *Clin. Chem., 19,* 472–475

Versieck, J., Hoste, J., Barbier, F., Steyaert, H., De Rudder, J. & Michels, H. (1978) Determination of chromium and cobalt in human serum by neutron activation analysis. *Clin. Chem., 24,* 303–308

3. DEFINITIONS

Method of additions: adding increasing, known amounts of the analyte to ali-quots of the sample, plotting the analytical results and extrapolating to zero added-analyte to find the original analyte concentration.

4. PRINCIPLE

Samples are collected and processed under carefully controlled conditions to minimize contamination. They are digested in fused silica tubes, using nitric acid and hydrogen peroxide, then evaporated to dryness, dissolved in hydrochloric acid and diluted to volume. Aliquots are analysed by graphite furnace atomic absorption spectrometry (AAS) with background correction from a high-intensity continuum lamp. Until it is established that the sample matrix does not affect the results, the method of additions is used. Blanks are processed in an identical fashion to monitor contamination.

5. HAZARDS

Human tissue samples almost always present a small but finite risk of transmit-ting diseases, for example, hepatitis. Precautions must be taken to prevent human exposure. Powder-free polyvinylchloride disposable gloves should be worn, as well as protective clothing. Normal safety practices in handling acids and oxidizing agents should be followed.

6. REAGENTS[1]

Nitric acid	16 mol/L. Ultrex, J.T. Baker, Phillipsburg, New Jersey, USA
Hydrogen peroxide	50%. Fisher Scientific, Pittsburgh, Pennsylvania, USA
Hydrochloric acid	1 mol/L. Ultrex, J.T. Baker
Water, demineralized	Milli-Q, Millipore Corp., El Paso, Texas, USA
Chromium standard stock solution	1000 mg/L. Alfa Products, Danvers, Massachu-setts, USA

---

[1] Reference to a company and/or product is for the purpose of information and identification only and does not imply approval or recommendation of the company and/or product by the International Agency for Research on Cancer, to the exclusion of others which may also be suitable.

| Chromium working standard solutions | Prepare three or more working standards in 0.1 mol/L HCl such that 100 µL of working standard contains about 1 to 5 times the content of the test portion (9.3) (e.g., 100, 200 and 500 ng Cr/mL for a sample containing 10 ng Cr) |

NOTE: Check reagents for chromium content prior to their use.

7. APPARATUS[1]

Atomic absorption spectrometer	Perkin-Elmer (Norwalk, Connecticut, USA) Model 5000 with Model HGA 500 graphite furnace, tungsten-halogen background corrector lamp and pyrolytically-coated furnace tubes. Or, a Perkin-Elmer Model Zeeman/5000 atomic absorption spectrometer may be used.
Quartz (fused silica) test tubes	Fabricated from fused quartz tubing (Thermal American Fuzed Quartz, Montville, New Jersey, USA)
Heating blocks	Of appropriate size for quartz tubes (Lab-line Instruments, Melrose Park, Illinois, USA)
Pipettes	Disposable-tip, 10-µL. 25-µL, 1-mL Eppendorf Standard[2] Pipetters (available through major laboratory supply houses). Rinse disposable tips just before use by pipetting demineralized water several times (see 9.5.2)

NOTE: Clean the quartz digestion tubes by gentle boiling in 10% nitric acid for 8 h, letting them soak in this solution at room temperature overnight, then thoroughly rinsing them with deionized water prior to use.

8. SAMPLING

The most critical aspect of sampling is preventing contamination during the collection, storage and handling of the samples. Collect tissue samples by cutting with

---

[1] Reference to a company and/or product is for the purpose of information and identification only and does not imply approval or recommendation of the company and/or product by the International Agency for Research on Cancer, to the exclusion of others which may also be suitable.

[2] In our experience, the all-plastic Eppendorf 'Standard' Pipetters are to be recommended. Other brands and other Eppendorf models contain stainless-steel parts, occasionally leading to serious contamination problems.

a knife consisting of a Teflon handle attached to a titanium blade. Stainless-steel implements are to be avoided. Store samples at $-20\,°C$ in clean plastic airtight containers or sealed bags. Place the latter within a larger sealed plastic bag containing several cubes of ice to maintain 100% relative humidity.

9. PROCEDURE

9.1 *Blank test*

Analyse several blanks with each batch of samples. Treat the blanks in exactly the same way as the samples, using the same quantities of all reagents, but omitting the materials being analysed.

NOTE: For some types of samples, the absence of inorganic sample components in the blanks may lead to matrix effects, i.e., a different instrumental response to the analyte in blanks and in samples. For this reason, when applying the method to a new type of sample, it is advisable to use the method of additions and also to measure the chromium content of pooled test material of the same kind, whose chromium content has been verified by independent means (see Check Test, 9.2).

9.2 *Check test*

When applying the method to a new material, it is helpful to have a large pool of the same material, but of known chromium content. This can be used to verify the accuracy of the determination and can serve as a day-to-day check on the operation of the instrument and the reproducibility of the standards.

Accuracy of the chromium content of the pool material can be established by testing the analytical method on a material of like or similar composition having an established chromium content (e.g., 'Standard Reference Materials' available from the U.S. National Bureau of Standards). Lacking a suitable reference material, the chromium content of the pool material must be established using an independent analytical method (see chapter 12).

9.3 *Test portion*

9.3.1   Take test portions of the samples and the pool material (and/or reference materials) with the same care as sample collection, i.e., minimize contamination. Use one or more aliquots of known weight to determine the moisture content of the samples. This can be done by lyophilization, heating under vacuum at $60\,°C$ or heating at atmospheric pressure at $100\,°C$, as appropriate. Drying should continue until constant weight is achieved.

9.3.2   Weigh to the nearest 0.001 g at least 0.25 g but preferably 0.5 g of the dry material into cleaned quartz tubes.

9.4 *Sample digestion*

9.4.1   Add 1 mL of HNO_3 to the test portion and let the tubes stand (covered) overnight.

9.4.2   Begin heating slowly in heating blocks at 80 °C for several hours (the quartz tubes must be substantially taller than the heating blocks for good reflux action).

9.4.3   Raise temperature to 100 °C, then begin small additions (0.1 mL) of H_2O_2 (if necessary, additional known amounts of HNO_3 can be added if volume has decreased; foaming may occur when H_2O_2 is added to some types of samples).

9.4.4   Continue heating and H_2O_2 additions, raising temperature to 120 °C, if necessary, until sample solution clears.

9.4.5   Raise temperature to 140 °C and evaporate to dryness.

9.4.6   Let samples cool; dissolve residue in 1 mL of 1 mol/L HCl.

9.4.7   Add 9 mL water and mix by 'vortexing' (final volume, 10 mL).

9.4.8   Place at least four 1-mL aliquots of the sample in quartz tubes and spike with increasing, known amounts of chromium, using 10-µL spikes of working standard solutions (leave one aliquot unspiked), and cap the tubes until required for analysis (9.5.2).

9.5 *Chromium determination by AAS*

9.5.1   Establish the following AAS operating conditions:

Wavelength:	357.9 nm
Slit:	0.7 nm (low)
Lamp current:	25 mA
Background corrector:	tungsten-halogen
Mode:	AA-BG, peak height
Recorder:	10 mV full-scale
Expansion:	1- to 10-fold, as needed.

9.5.2   Mix sample aliquot (9.4.8) by vortexing and pipette 25 µL into graphite furnace tube, then start the following furnace programme:

Step	Temperature (°C)	Ramp time (s)	Hold time (s)	Comments
Dry	100	15	20	

Dry	130	10	20	
Char	1 200	15	30	
Atomize	2 700	0	4	Internal flow 50 mL/min
Clean-out	2 700	1	4	

9.5.3   Plot the measured peak heights *versus* the amounts of chromium added to the 1-mL aliquots (9.4.8) (a straight line should be obtained). Extrapolate back through zero Cr addition. The line will intersect the extrapolated added-chromium axis at the Cr content of the unspiked aliquot (method of additions).

9.5.4   Repeat 9.5.2 and 9.5.3 for the blanks from 9.4.8.

10. METHOD OF CALCULATION

The mass fraction, ω (mg/kg), of chromium in the sample is given by

$\omega \quad = \quad m_a V / m_t v$

where

m_a = mass of analyte found in unspiked aliquot, 9.4.8, minus the average blank value (ng)

V = final volume of sample digest, 9.4.7 (mL)

m_t = mass of test portion (g)

v = volume of each aliquot (9.4.8) analysed (mL).

NOTE: Specify whether ω = mg/kg dry weight, or wet-weight, and cite moisture content of sample.

Considering the reproducibility attainable with graphite furnace atomic absorption spectrometry, results should be reported to no more than two significant figures.

11. REPEATABILITY AND REPRODUCIBILITY

Assuming that sample weighing, reagent dispensing, etc., are all controlled to within 1–2% by good analytical techniques, the reproducibility of the method is determined primarily by sample homogeneity (with respect to the analyte) and the reproducibility of graphite furnace atomization.

In practice, with homogeneous biological materials, reproducibilities better than about $\pm$ 10% at analyte levels well above the detection limit are seldom achieved.

12. NOTES ON PROCEDURE

While not essential, the processing of samples in 'dust-free' laminar-flow hoods (*not* constructed with stainless-steel components) greatly increases the chances of successful determinations. Airborne contamination is minimized, increasing reproducibility of the blanks. This becomes increasingly important as the detection limit is approached.

13. SCHEMATIC REPRESENTATION OF PROCEDURE

Weigh 0.5 g samples into quartz tubes
(moisture determined on separate aliquots)
↓
Add 1 mL HNO_3 (let stand overnight)
↓
Heat to 80 °C (several hours)
↓
Heat to 100 °C;
begin additions of H_2O_2 (0.1 mL each)
↓
Heat to 120 °C; continue additions
until solution clears and becomes colourless
↓
Heat to 140 °C; evaporate to dryness
↓
Cool; dissolve residue in 1 mL of 1 mol/L HCl
↓
Add 9 mL H_2O; mix
↓
Take four 1-mL aliquots;
spike 3 with increasing, known amounts of Cr
↓
Analyse 25-µL aliquots of each by graphite furnace AAS
↓
Plot peak height *versus* Cr added;
determine Cr content of unspiked solution
↓
Calculate Cr content of original sample from
dilution factor, sample weight and blank level

15. ORIGIN OF THE METHOD

US Department of Agriculture
Human Nutrition Research Center
Vitamin and Mineral Nutrition Laboratory
Beltsville, Maryland 20705
USA

Contact point: Claude Veillon,
                   Kristine Patterson,
                   US Department of Agriculture
                   Vitamin and Mineral Nutrition Laboratory
                   Beltsville Human Nutrition Research Center
                   Room 215, Building 307
                   Beltsville, MD 20705
                   USA

METHOD 24 – DETERMINATION OF NICKEL IN BODY FLUIDS, TISSUES, EXCRETA AND WATER

F.W. Sunderman, Jr

SEE METHOD 11

METHOD 25 – DETERMINATION OF CADMIUM IN WHOLE BLOOD BY ISOTOPE DILUTION MASS SPECTROMETRY (IDMS)

E. Michiels & P. De Bièvre

1. SCOPE AND FIELD OF APPLICATION

This method is suitable for the determination of the absolute cadmium (Cd) concentration in fresh whole blood or reconstituted lyophylized blood. Essentially the same procedure can be used to assay Cd in other biological matrices such as urine or human tissue (liver, kidney, etc.)

The method is applicable to samples with Cd contents ranging from less than 1 ng/g (< 1 ppb) up to 100 mg/g (10%) or more.

Both the chemistry involved and the mass spectrometric measurement procedure are elaborate and time-consuming. The time required for a complete set of analyses (e.g., 5 samples and 3 blanks) is about one week if a calibrated "spike" solution is available. The technique is thus not suitable for routine assays, but yields "definitive" results with small uncertainties. The inherent accuracy is due to the proven absence of (or correction for) all systematic errors at the indicated precision level.

2. REFERENCES

Barnes, I.L., Murphy, T.J., Gramlich, G.W. & Shields, W.R. (1973) Lead separation by anodic deposition and isotope ratio mass spectrometry of microgram and smaller samples. *Anal. Chem., 11,* 1881–1884

Moody, J.R. & Beary, E.S. (1982) Purified reagents for trace metal analysis. *Tantala, 29,* 1003–1010

3. DEFINITIONS

Not applicable

4. PRINCIPLE

Isotope-dilution mass spectrometry is based on the change in the ratio of two isotopes of the element of interest (Cd) measured when a known amount of the element with an artificially altered ratio of the same isotopes (a "spike") is added to a weighed aliquot of the sample.

Mixing a spike and a sample yields a "blend" with an intermediate isotope ratio. The change induced in the isotope ratio is a direct measure of the ratio of the known amount of Cd in the spike to the unknown amount of Cd in the sample. The unknown amount of Cd in the sample can hence be calculated from the isotope ratio measurements in sample, spike and blend and the known amount of spike added.

Since only isotope ratios are measured, sample treatment or recoveries for chemical separations need to be quantitative once isotopic equilibrium is achieved.

5. HAZARDS

Concentrated nitric acid is toxic by inhalation and a fire risk in contact with organic materials. Concentrated perchloric acid will explode in contact with organic materials or by shock or heat. These reagents should be handled in a ventilated hood and protective clothing, face mask and gloves should be worn.

6. REAGENTS[1]

Use only acids (HNO_3, HCl, $HClO_4$) and water which have been purified by sub-boiling distillation from quartz stills.

Nitric acid (HNO_3)	15.8 mol/L, 4 mol/L, 1 mol/L, 0.3 mol/L
Hydrochloric acid (HCl)	10.5 mol/L, 8 mol/L, 0.5 mol/L, 0.02 mol/L
Perchloric acid ($HClO_4$)	11.6 mol/L
Phosphoric acid (H_3PO_4)	0.25 mol/L
Cadmium-111 spike solution	Dissolve Cd-111 metal (an isotopic enrichment of > 90% is sufficient) in conc. HCl and dilute with distilled water. Assay by reverse isotope dilution. A final concentration close to that of the sample to be analysed is suitable.
Anion-exchange resin	100–200 mesh, strongly-basic (AG-1), 8% cross-linkage

[1] Reference to a company and/or product is for the purpose of information and identification only and does not imply approval or recommendation of the company and/or product by the International Agency for Research on Cancer, to the exclusion of others which may also be suitable.

Silica gel powder	(60 HR, extra-pure, E. Merck, Darmstadt)
Silica gel suspension	Grind ~ 1 g of silica gel powder in a new agate mortar for 2–3 h to produce extremely fine particles, then mix with 15 mL distilled water and shake thoroughly for a few minutes at 2-h intervals during the first day. Allow to settle for 3 days, then carefully decant the supernatant, which is used as the silica gel suspension (Barnes *et al.*, 1973).

7. APPARATUS[1]

Syringes	5-mL, Teflon FEP (or equivalent)
Teflon FEP tubing	For use with 5-mL syringe
Beakers	30-mL, Teflon FEP, with Teflon covers
Hot plate	
Mass spectrometer	Thermal ionization, single-focussing, with 90° analyser tube and magnet pole pieces, thin-lens "Z"-focussing ion source. Ion current measurement by means of vibrating-reed electrometer and digital voltmeter, interfaced to a minicomputer.
Separation column	5-mm i.d. quartz column containing 1 mL of anion-exchange resin. Clean resin by eluting successively with 5 g of 4 mol/HNO_3, 5 g water, 6 g of 8 mol/L HCl and 5 g water. Condition with 2 g of 0.5 mol/L HCl prior to use.
Clean-up column	2-mm i.d. quartz column containing 0.06 mL (height, 20 mm) of anion-exchange resin, cleaned and conditioned as described for separation column.
Clean laboratory	To reduce particulate contamination, the entire chemical procedure is carried out in class 100 clean air hoods inside a vertical-flow, class 100 clean room ("class 100" means < 100 particles, smaller than 0.5 micrometer, per cubic foot).
	All laboratory-ware used is made from Teflon FEP or quartz and must be cleaned rigorously before use.

---

[1] Reference to a company and/or product is for the purpose of information and identification only and does not imply approval or recommendation of the company and/or product by the International Agency for Research on Cancer, to the exclusion of others which may also be suitable.

8. SAMPLING

Samples should be taken and stored in such a way as to avoid contamination by Cd.

9. PROCEDURE

9.1 *Blank test*

Carry out the blank test in parallel with the analysis, using procedures 9.4 to 9.7, inclusive, but omitting the test portion in 9.4.2. Typically, 3 blanks are determined along with 5 or more samples. (The analytical blank for Cd can be reduced to less than 1 ng. Total system blanks of 100 ± 50 pg have been achieved).

9.2 *Check test*

Not applicable

9.3 *Test portion*

Accurately weigh a 2 g test portion into a weighed, 30-mL Teflon FEP beaker

9.4 *Sample spiking and digestion*

9.4.1   Allow the (reconstituted or fresh) blood sample to come to room temperature and draw the sample into a 5-mL syringe, using Teflon FEP tubing.

9.4.2   Weigh, by difference, two test portions into 30-mL Teflon FEP beakers.

9.4.3   Using a 5-mL syringe, add a weighed (by difference) amount of Cd-111 spike solution. (The amount of Cd-111 to be added depends on the approximate amount of Cd in the sample. The latter should not differ from the amount of spike by more than a factor of 2, if possible.)

9.4.4   Add 5 g concentrated HNO_3 + 1 g $HClO_4$ mixture to the beaker.

9.4.5   Cover the beaker with a Teflon cover and put it on a hotplate inside a clean-air fume hood. Heat gently until foaming stops (about 20 min), then raise the temperature to 200–220 °C (almost the melting point of Teflon FEP).

9.4.6   When dissolution is complete ($\sim$ 48 h), take off the covers and evaporate to dryness (white to light-yellow residue; if charring is evident, add HNO_3, then $HClO_4$).

9.4.7   Rinse the walls of the beaker with H_2O to remove excess $HClO_4$ and evaporate to dryness. Repeat two or three times to get rid of as much $HClO_4$ as possible.

9.4.8   Add a few drops of concentrated HCl and evaporate to dryness.

9.4.9   Dissolve the residue in 2 g of 0.5 mol/L HCl.

9.5   *Chemical separation on anion-exchange column*

9.5.1   Pour the sample on a cleaned and conditioned 1-mL separation column.

9.5.2   Wash sample and elute alkalis, Fe, Zn etc. with 7.5 g 0.02 mol/L HCl, then rinse the tip of the column with water.

9.5.3   Elute Cd fraction with 5 g of 1 mol/L HNO_3, into a clean 30-mL Teflon FEP beaker.

9.5.4   Evaporate the Cd fraction to dryness, then add a drop of concentrated HNO_3 to destroy organic material that may be present.

9.5.5   Evaporate to dryness again, then add a drop of concentrated HCl and evaporate to dryness.

9.5.6   Take up the sample in 0.5 g 0.5 mol/L HCl.

9.5.7   Pour on a conditioned clean-up column.

9.5.8   Wash with 0.75 g 0.02 mol/L HCl, one drop at a time (discard).

9.5.9   Elute Cd with 0.5 g 1 mol/L HNO_3, then evaporate to dryness.

9.5.10   Dissolve the residue in a small drop of 0.3 mol/L HNO_3 and retain for IDMS analysis.

9.6   *Sample loading on MS filament*

The entire loading procedure should be performed on a "class 100" bench with vertical laminar air-flow to avoid Cd contamination.

9.6.1   Place a 5-µL drop of the silica gel suspension in the centre of a 0.025 mm × 0.70 mm Re filament. Dry for 5 min using a 1A current through the filament and a heat lamp placed above the filament so that the temperature at the filament surface is 50 °C.

9.6.2   Place a 5 µL drop of the sample solution (9.5.10) on the filament and dry for 5 min with a 1A current and the heat lamp on.

9.6.3   Place a drop of 0.25 mol/L H_3PO_4 on the filament. Dry with a current of 1.5A under the heat lamp for 5 min.

9.6.4   Increase the filament current to 2A and hold for 5 min, keeping the heat lamp on.

9.6.5   Turn off the heat lamp and slowly increase the current until the first appearance of vapours from the filament is noticed. Keep the filament temperature at this level until a white, uniform and dry deposit is observed.

9.6.6   Increase the filament current to obtain a dull red heat, then turn off the filament current.

9.6.7   Place the filament in the ion source of the mass spectrometer.

9.7 *Mass spectrometric measurement procedure*

9.7.1   Using pulse counting (very small sample, < 100 ng Cd)

9.7.1.1 Set temperature at 900 °C using an optical pyrometer. Background may be relatively high, but should decrease rapidly.

9.7.1.2 At t = 5 min, raise the filament temperature to 1000 °C. Check Cd peak shape and baseline. Optimize focusing conditions.

9.7.1.3 At t = 15 min, raise filament temperature to 1050 °C.

9.7.1.4 At t = 20 min, start data collection. (Magnetic field switching and data acquisition are controlled by a programmable calculator). Measure two sets of ratios (A/B) in the sequence 114/111, 112/111, 112/111, 114/111. This permits internal normalization of the data, if that is desired.

9.7.2   Using Faraday cage detection (> 100 ng Cd on the filament)

9.7.2.1 Set temperature at 1100 °C using an optical pyrometer. Locate a Cd peak and optimize beam focusing conditions.

9.7.2.2 At t = 5 min, raise the temperature to 1150 °C.

9.7.2.3 At t = 10 min, raise the temperature to 1200 °C.

9.7.2.4 At t = 20 min, start data collection. Measure two sets of ratios, as in the case of pulse-counting detection.

10. METHOD OF CALCULATION

From the measurement of the isotope ratio, R = A/B, in the blend, calculate the amount, m_t (µg), of the analyte in the test portion using the equation:

$$m_t = m_s \left(\frac{A_s - RB_s}{RB_t - A_t} \right)$$

where

m_s = mass of Cd in spike added in 9.4.3 (μg)

A_s = atomic fraction of isotope A in spike

B_s = atomic fraction of isotope B in spike

A_t = atomic fraction of isotope A in test portion

B_t = atomic fraction of isotope B in test portion.

The amount, m_o, of Cd in the blank is obtained from the above equation when m_o is substituted for m_t and R_o (the isotope ratio in the blank) for R.

The mass fraction, ω (mg/kg), in the sample is given by,

ω = $(m_t - m_o)/M$

where M = mass of test portion in 9.4.2 (g)

and m_t (μg) and m_o (μg) are defined above.

11. REPEATABILITY AND REPRODUCIBILITY

The coefficient of variation for 5 analyses of a blood sample with an average mass fraction of 7.05 ng Cd/g was 0.28%. Somewhat less dispersion than this can be obtained if the correction for the blank is insignificant.

No data are available for the reproducibility of the method.

12. NOTES ON PROCEDURE

Not applicable

13. SCHEMATIC REPRESENTATION OF PROCEDURE

Weigh 2 g test portion into 30 mL Teflon FEP beaker
↓
Add Cd-111 spike and HNO_3 + $HClO_4$ mixture
↓
Heat to complete dissolution, then evaporate to dryness
↓
Rinse beaker walls with water, then evaporate to dryness,
repeat several times
↓

Add several drops HCl and evaporate to dryness
↓
Dissolve in 2 g 0.5 mol/L HCl
↓
Pour onto anion-exchange separation column
↓
Wash with 7.5 g 0.02 mol/L HCl, then elute Cd with 5 g 1 mol/L HNO_3
↓
Evaporate to dryness, add 1 drop conc. HNO_3
↓
Evaporate to dryness, add 1 drop conc. HCl
↓
Evaporate to dryness, dissolve in 0.5 g 0.5 mol/L HCl
↓
Pour onto clean-up column
↓
Wash with 0.75 g 0.02 mol/L HCl
↓
Elute Cd with 0.5 g 1 mol/L HNO_3
↓
Evaporate to dryness, then dissolve in 1 drop 0.3 mol/L HNO_3
↓
Place 5 µL on silica gel-treated Re filament
↓
Heat filament until uniforme white deposit formed, then to dull red heat
↓
Mount filament in MS and measure Cd isotope ratios
↓
Calculate Cd content of test portion

14. ORIGIN OF THE METHOD

Developed by E. Michiels[1] during the tenure of an EC Fellowship at the National Bureau of Standards, Washington, DC, USA

Contact point: P. de Bièvre
                   Commission of the European Communities
                   Joint Research Centre
                   Central Bureau for Nuclear Measurements
                   Steenweg op Retie
                   B-2440 Geel, Belgium

---

[1] CBNM, Geel, Belgium

METHOD 26 – DETERMINATION OF THE MASS CONCENTRATION OF LEAD IN BLOOD BY ATOMIC ABSORPTION SPECTROPHOTOMETRY

J.W. van Loon & P.L. Schuller

1. SCOPE AND FIELD OF APPLICATION

This method is suitable for the determination of the mass concentration of lead in whole blood at levels up to 0.80 mg/L.

2. REFERENCES

Delves, H.T. (1970) A micro-sampling method for the rapid determination of lead in blood by atomic-absorption spectrophotometry. *Analyst, 95,* 431–438

3. DEFINITIONS

Not applicable

4. PRINCIPLE

After partial oxidation with hydrogen peroxide in micro nickel cups, the samples are volatilized into a quartz absorption tube by the air-acetylene flame of an atomic absorption spectrophotometer (AAS). Atomic absorption is measured in the flame at a wavelength of 283.3 nm.

5. HAZARDS

Concentrated nitric acid is toxic and represents a fire hazard in contact with organic materials. Operations involving the concentrated acid should be carried out in a ventilated hood and acid-resistant gloves and safety glasses should be worn.

6. REAGENTS[1]

All reagents must be of recognized analytical quality and in particular, free of lead. The water used must be double-distilled from an all-glass apparatus of Pyrex or other resistant glass.

Nitric acid	65% (w/w). 1.42 g/mL at 20 °C
Hydrogen peroxide	30% (300 g/L)
Lead nitrate [$Pb(NO_3)_2$]	
Lead nitrate standard solutions	
Standard I (200 mg Pb/L)	Dissolve 319.8 mg of lead nitrate in water, transfer the solution quantitatively into a 1000-mL volumetric flask, add 10 mL of 65% nitric acid and dilute to volume with water.
Standard II (10 mg Pb/L)	Pipette 5.0 mL of standard I into a 100-mL volumetric flask, add 1 mL of 65% nitric acid and dilute to volume with water.
Standard III (20 mg Pb/L)	Pipette 10.0 mL of standard I into a 100-mL volumetric flask, add 1 mL of 65% nitric acid and dilute to volume with water.
Standard IV (30 mg Pb/L)	Pipette 15.0 mL of standard I into a 100-mL volumetric flask, add 1 mL of 65% nitric acid and dilute to volume with water.
Standard V (40 mg Pb/L)	Pipette 20.0 mL of standard I into a 100-mL volumetric flask, add 1 mL 65% of nitric acid and dilute to volume with water.
Standard VI (60 mg Pb/L)	Pipette 30.0 mL of standard I into a 100-mL volumetric flask, add 1 mL of 65% nitric acid and dilute to volume with water.
Standard VII (80 mg Pb/L)	Pipette 40.0 mL of standard I into a 100-mL volumetric flask, add 1 mL of 65% nitric acid and dilute to volume with water.

---

[1] Reference to a company and/or product is for the purpose of information and identification only and does not imply approval or recommendation of the company and/or product by the International Agency for Research on Cancer, to the exclusion of others which may also be suitable.

Working standard solutions	0.1, 0.2, 0.3, 0.4, 0.6 and 0.8 mg Pb/L. Pipette 1000 µL of each of the standards II to VII, inclusive, into 100-mL volumetric flasks, add 50 µL of 65% nitric acid to each and dilute to volume with water.
Blank solutions	Transfer 1 mL of 65% nitric acid into a 100-mL volumetric flask and make up to volume with water. Pipette 1000 µL of this solution into a 100-mL volumetric flask, add 50 µL of 65% nitric acid and dilute to volume with water.
Heparin	100 000 units/mg (B.D.H., Poole, U.K.)
Heparin solution	400 mg heparin/50 mL water
Bank-blood	Blood sample with known, low lead content. Store at $\leq -10\,°C$
Quality-control blood	Blood sample with certified lead content. Store at $\leq -10\,°C$
Liquid soap solution	Dilute about 2 mL of concentrated soap solution (e.g., Laviton ●) to 100 mL with water.

7. APPARATUS[1]

Volumetric flasks	100-mL and 1000-mL
One-mark pipettes	5-, 10-, 15-, 20-, 30-, 40- and 50-mL
Finn ● pipettes	5–50-µL
Finn ● pipettes	200–1000-µL
Finn ● tips No. 60	For microlitre pipettes, range 1–250-µL
Finn● tips No. 61	For microlitre pipettes, range 200–1000-µL
SMI ● Micropipettor No. 1075B	10-µL. Before use, assemble and rinse ~6 times with soap solution, empty, wipe outside dry with Kleenex tissue and rinse ~6 times with double-distilled water. To prevent sticking, leave the glass capillary filled with water until required.

[1] Reference to a company and/or product is for the purpose of information and identification only and does not imply approval or recommendation of the company and/or product by the International Agency for Research on Cancer, to the exclusion of others which may also be suitable.

Analytical balance

Vortex ● mixer

| Nickel cups | Before use, place the cups in the flame of the AAS to burn off any residual lead, then cover with a Kleenex tissue until required. |

Electrical hot plate

Sample cup tray

| Micro-sampling system | As described by Delves (1970) |

| Atomic absorption spectro-photometer | Fitted with a lead hollow cathode lamp, a deuterium lamp for background correction and a 3-slot burner head. Acetylene and air are used, the flame should be non-luminous. |

| Recorder | 10 mV full-scale, chart speed, 20 mm/min |

Vinyl examination gloves

Kleenex ● tissues

| Pharbil diagnostic vials | 5-mL, check for contamination with Pb |

| B-D plastic pak syringes | 2-mL, with detachable needles, check for contamination with Pb |

| Steri-swabs | Skin cleanser with 70% isopropanol |

NOTE: The nickel cups, the cup holder and the quartz absorption tube all have a limited lifetime and should therefore be regularly inspected and periodically replaced.

Glass-ware, including reagent bottles, should be soaked for 24 h in 4 mol/L nitric acid and, before use, rinsed twice with distilled water, then twice with double-distilled water. Dry in a dust-proof environment.

8. SAMPLING

8.1 Add 50 µL of heparin solution to a 5-mL Pharbil vial and dry overnight at 40 °C.

8.2 Clean the skin above the vein with a steri-swab and take 1.0–2.0 mL of blood by venipuncture with 2-mL Plastic pak syringe.

8.3 Detach the needle (do not touch lower part of syringe) and discharge the syringe into the vial (8.1).

8.4 Close the vial and mix well by inverting at least 15 times. Store at $\leq -10\,°C$.

8.5 Before analysis, preferably freeze samples and an appropriate amount of bank-blood and quality-control blood at $-70\,°C$ for at least 24 h, then bring to $-10\,°C$ the day before analysis.

9. PROCEDURE

9.1 *Blank test*

Not applicable

9.2 *Check test*

With every four blood samples (in duplicate), analyse one quality-control sample.

9.3 *Test portion*

Ten µL of blood sample pipetted into micro nickel cups according to the following procedure:

9.3.1   Discharge the water from the Micropipettor, take up and discard 10 µL of blood.

9.3.2   Repeat 9.3.1 twice (discarding 30 µL in all).

9.3.3   Pipette 10 µL blood sample into nickel cup.

9.3.4   Rinse Micropipettor 6 times with soap solution, then dry outside of pipettor with Kleenex tissue and rinse 6 times with double-distilled water. Dry outside of pipettor with Kleenex tissue and proceed to 9.3.1 with the next sample.

NOTE: Wear gloves while pipetting samples and protect working space from dust.

9.4 *Preparation and partial oxidation of blood samples*

9.4.1   On the day of analysis, bring test samples, bank-blood and quality-control samples to room temperature and mix on Vortex mixer.

9.4.2   Following the procedure described in 9.3, pipette 10 µL of bank-blood into each of the first 5 nickel cups in the cup tray.

9.4.3   Spike the bank blood in cups 1–5 with 10 μL of working standard lead solutions containing lead concentrations of 0.0, 0.1, 0.2, 0.3 and 0.4 mg/L, respectively[1] (see Diagramm 1). It is not necessary to rinse pipettor with soap and water when passing from one lead solution to the next.

9.4.4   Pipette duplicate-10 μL portions of quality-control blood into cups 6 and 7.

9.4.5   Pipette duplicate 10-μL test portions of four blood samples into the next 8 cups.

9.4.6   Pipette 10-μL calibration samples into the last 5 cups, following steps 9.4.2 and 9.4.3.

9.4.7   Place the sample cup tray on a hot plate at 170–180 °C (the bottom of the cups should be about 7 mm above the surface of the hot plate, not in contact).

9.4.8   When samples reach dryness, add 20 μL of 30% hydrogen peroxide to each cup and continue heating to dryness. The completely dried samples are ready for the AAS measurement.

9.5 *Instrumental conditions*

9.5.1   Align the quartz absorption tube for maximal light throughput after allowing the flame to burn with the tube in place for several minutes. Position the absorption tube so that the aperture is exactly centered over the three-slot burner head.

9.5.2   Set the distance between the nickel cup and the aperture in the absorption tube at about 1.5 mm. Increasing the distance reduces the sensitivity. (Reducing the distance improves the sensitivity, but the smoke peak becomes so large that the background corrector is unable to provide complete compensation.)

9.5.3   To obtain optimum performance, measure four series of working standard lead solutions (0.0, 0.1, 0.2, 0.3 and 0.4 mg Pb/L) at the beginning of each day of analysis.

9.6 *Measurement of absorbance*

9.6.1   Volatilize the dried samples (9.4.8) in the air-acetylene flame by placing them one by one in the holder of the Delves sampling accessory and inserting them in the flame below the entrance hole of the absorption

---

[1] Use higher concentrations when the blood samples contain > 0.4 mg Pb/L.

Fig. 1. Pipetting scheme for determination of Pb in blood

	Standards for calibration curve (9.4.3)					Quality control sample (duplicate) (9.4.4)		Samples to be analysed (duplicate) (9.4.5)								Standards for calibration curve (9.4.6)				
A	1	2	3	4	5	6	7	8	9	10	11	12	13	14	15	16	17	18	19	20
B	10	10	10	10	10	10	10	10	10	10	10	10	10	10	10	10	10	10	10	10
C	10	10	10	10	10											10	10	10	10	10
D	0	0.1	0.2	0.3	0.4											0	0.1	0.2	0.3	0.4

A, micro nickel cup. no.

B, blood volume (μL)

C, working standard solution volume (μL)

D, lead concentration of standard solution (mg/L)

tube. (The speed with which the cup is inserted into the flame is not critical, but it must suffice to prevent any combustion of the sample before it reaches the correct position in the flame.)

9.6.2   Analyse the calibration samples, quality-control samples and unknowns in the order in which they were prepared (9.4.2–9.4.6, inclusive, see Diagram 1). Record the absorbance peak height obtained at 283.3 nm.

NOTE: After passing the complete sample tray, it is advisable to readjust the wavelength for maximum reading on the lamp energy display, in preparation for the next set of samples.

9.7 *Calibration curve*

Construct a calibration curve by plotting the average peak heights *versus* the lead concentration (mg/L) of the working standard solutions used to prepare the spiked calibration samples (9.4.3 and 9.4.6), corrected for the known, low lead content of the bank blood. If the relationship between peak height and concentration is not linear, or if the lead content of the quality control sample at a level of 200 µ Pb/L differs from the certified value by ≥ 30 µg of lead/L of blood, it is necessary to identify and to rectify the source of error before proceeding with analysis.

10. METHOD OF CALCULATION

Obtain the mass concentration (mg/L) of lead in the blood samples, using the average absorbance peak heights and the calibration curve (9.7).

If at levels of 100 µg Pb/L and 800 µg Pb/L, duplicate samples differ by ≥ 20 µg/L and 80 µg/L, respectively, analyse the samples again in triplicate or quadruplicate.

11. REPEATABILITY AND REPRODUCIBILITY

At a level of 0.1 mg of lead per litre of blood, a coefficient of variation of less than 10% should be obtained.

12. NOTES ON PROCEDURE

Not applicable

13. SCHEMATIC REPRESENTATION OF PROCEDURE

Freeze blood samples at $-70\,°C$ for 24 h
↓

Warm samples to -10 °C for 24 h
↓
Warm to room temperature and pipette 10 μL into nickel cup
↓
Evaporate to dryness, add 20 μL 30% hydrogen peroxide
and evaporate to dryness again
↓
Place dried sample in AAS flame and determine absorption at 283.3 nm
↓
Obtain lead concentration from calibration curve, prepared with spiked blood

14. ORIGIN OF THE METHOD

Laboratory for Chemical Analysis of Foodstuffs
National Institute of Public Health and Environmental Hygiene
Bilthoven, The Netherlands

Contact point: J.W. van Loon

METHOD 27 – DETERMINATION OF SELENIUM IN HUMAN TISSUES, FLUIDS AND EXCRETA BY HYDRIDE GENERATION AND ATOMIC-ABSORPTION SPECTROMETRY

K.S. Subramanian

1. SCOPE AND FIELD OF APPLICATION

This method is suitable for the determination of selenium (Se) in human whole blood, plasma, red cells, urine, kidney cortex, kidney medulla and liver. The method can probably be extended to other types of human tissue samples and physiological fluids.

The method is applicable to samples containing 0.05 to 0.5 μg Se/g of wet tissue.

Because of the wide range of apparatus available for applying this family of techniques, the detection limit for Se is highly variable. Using a Perkin-Elmer MHS20 hydride generation system, Llyod *et al.* (1982) obtained a detection limit of 13.5 μg/L for Se in blood and plasma; using an automatic hydride evolution procedure, Subramanian and Meranger (1982) obtained a detection limit of 10 μg/kg for Se in human liver and kidney samples.

2. REFERENCES

Analytical Methods Committee (1979) Determination of small amounts of selenium in organic matter. *Analyst, 104,* 778–787

Clinton, O.E. (1977) Determination of selenium in blood and plant material by hydride generation and atomic absorption spectroscopy. *Analyst, 102,* 187–192

Kneip, T.J., Ajemian, R.S., Driscoll, J.N., Grunder, F.I., Kornreich, L., Loveland, J.W., Moyers, J.L. & Thompson, R.J. (1977) Arsenic, selenium and antimony in urine and air: analytical method by hydride generation and atomic absorption spectroscopy. *Health Lab. Sci., 14,* 53–58

Lloyd, B., Holt, P. & Delves, H.T. (1982) Determination of selenium in biological samples by hydride generation and atomic absorption spectroscopy. *Analyst, 107,* 927–933

Subramanian, K.S. & Méranger, J.C. (1982) Rapid hydride evolution-electrothermal atomisation atomic-absorption spectrophotometric method for determining arsenic and selenium in human kidney and liver. *Analyst, 107,* 157–162

3. DEFINITIONS

The detection limit is defined as the concentration of Se equal to three times the standard deviation of the Se concentration of the blank.

4. PRINCIPLE

The sample is digested with a mixture of nitric, perchloric and sulfuric acids to destroy the organic matter and Se[VI] is reduced to Se[IV] using hydrochloric acid (HCl). Se[IV] hydride is then formed in the acidic solution with sodium tetrahydroborate [III] and is subsequently decomposed in a heated cell, where the Se concentration is measured by atomic absorption spectrometry (AAS).

5. HAZARDS

Selenium is toxic. It is desirable to practice the usual methods of safe handling and disposal of all solutions containing Se. Hot acid digestion mixtures should be handled in a ventilated hood and resistant gloves and face mask should be worn. Concentrated perchloric acid will explode in contact with organic materials, or by shock or heat.

6. REAGENTS[1]

> NOTE: The reagent concentrations given below refer to the hydride generation system used in the author's laboratory. The volume and concentrations of the reagents to be used may vary with the type of hydride generation system employed. Use analytical grade reagents and glass-distilled, deionized water throughout.

Argon

Nitric acid	68–71%, specific gravity 1.42, 'Suprapure' or equivalent, or distil from glass and discard the first and final 10%.
Perchloric acid	72%, specific gravity 1.67.
Sulfuric acid	90%, specific gravity 1.84.
Hydrochloric acid	Approximately 6 mol/L. Dilute 540 mL of HCl (36–38%, specific gravity 1.18) to 1 L with water.

---

[1] Reference to a company and/or product is for the purpose of information and identification only and does not imply approval or recommendation of the company and/or product by the International Agency for Research on Cancer, to the exclusion of others which may also be suitable.

Hydrochloric acid	Approximately 0.5 mol/L. Dilute 50 mL of HCl (36–38%, specific gravity 1.18) to 1 L with water.
Sodium tetrahydroborate [III] solution	10 g/L. Dissolve 10 g of sodium tetrahydroborate [III] (Alfa Inorganics) and 2 g of sodium hydroxide in 1 L of glass-distilled water. Keep refrigerated in a tightly capped polyethylene bottle until ready for use. The solution is stable for at least one week under these conditions.
Standard Se solution A	1 g/L. Dissolve 1.000 g of black Se (purity = 99.9%) in about 10 mL of HNO_3 by warming. Dilute to 1 L with water and mix well.
Standard Se solution B	10.0 mg/L. Dilute 10.0 mL of standard Se solution A to 1 L with 0.1 mol/L HCl.
Standard Se solution C	0.10 mg/L. Dilute 10.0 mL of standard Se solution B to 1 L with 0.1 mol/L HCl.
Bovine liver powder	Standard Reference Material 1577 (US National Bureau of Standards).

7. APPARATUS[1]

Usual laboratory equipment and the following items (Fig. 1):

Atomic absorption spectrophotometer	Many commercially-available instruments are acceptable. (The author used a varian Techtron Model AA-5 atomic absorption spectrometer. More sophisticated versions are now available.)
Se hollow cathode lamp (HCL), or electrodeless discharge lamp (EDL)	Any commercially-available lamp. An EDL is recommended. The HCL may be used with reduced sensitivity. The lamp should emit monochromatic radiation at 196 nm, corresponding to the resonance wavelength of Se.

---

[1] Reference to a company and/or product is for the purpose of information and identification only and does not imply approval or recommendation of the company and/or product by the International Agency for Research on Cancer, to the exclusion of others which may also be suitable.

Atomic reservoir (see Fig. 1)	Preferably an electrically-heated, silica tube furnace. The temperature of the furnace may be regulated by means of an 0–110 V Variac transformer. (The tube furnace may also be heated with an air-acetylene flame.) Satisfactory results may be obtained using a silica tube of approximately 15.0 cm length and 1.2 cm i.d., with a central side-arm (0.4 cm i.d.) for 'hydride' introduction.
Autosampler	
Strip chart recorder	10 mV full-scale
Hydride generation system	Single injection system or continuous evolution system. Automatic continuous evolution systems produce better precision and lower detection limits than single injection systems. See Subramanian and Méranger (1982).
Digestion vessels	Pyrex glass tubes (28 × 133 mm, 50 mL capacity) with a means of heating at a controlled rate (e.g., hot plate). Alternatively, a temperature-programmable aluminium 'block digestor' may be found to be advantageous, particularly when large numbers of samples have to be processed.
Volumetric flasks	Pyrex, 20-mL (see also 9.5.4).

NOTE: Prior to analysis, rinse all glass-ware with hot water, hot $HNO_3:H_2SO_4$ (1:1, v/v), hot tap water and distilled, deionized water. Dry in oven at 110 °C or at ambient temperature in air.

8. SAMPLING

Proceed from a representative sample and store in such a way that deterioration and change in composition are prevented (see Chapter 10, Sampling, storage and pretreatment of biological material).

9. PROCEDURE

9.1 *Blank test*

Carry out a blank test in parallel with the analysis of the sample, using procedure 9.4–9.7, but omitting the sample (9.4.1).

9.2 *Check test*

Carry out a check test by analysing the NBS standard reference material, bovine liver, using procedure 9.4–9.7.

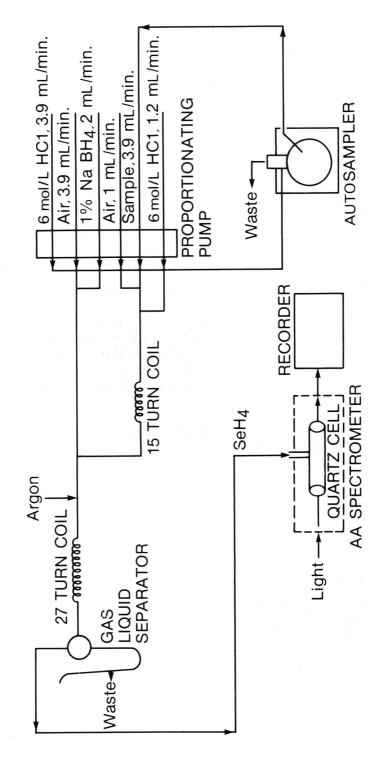

Fig. 1. Schematic representation of autosampler, proportionating pump and atomic absorption spectrometer

9.3 *Test portion*

Weigh accurately 1.00 to 2.00 g of representative tissue sample or measure accurately 0.10 to 5.0 mL of blood or plasma.

9.4 *Digestion of sample*

The digestion procedure given below is that recommended by the Analytical Methods Committee (1979), with slight modifications.

9.4.1   Place duplicate test portions in two Pyrex Tubes (28 × 133 mm).

9.4.2   Add 10 mL of nitric acid and 2 mL of perchloric acid.

9.4.3   Heat cautiously on an electric hot plate (sand-bath) or a block digestor until the initial foaming and bumping subsides, the sample is solubilized and the volume is reduced to about 5 mL. Cool to room temperature.

9.4.4   Add 5 mL of nitric acid and 5 mL of sulfuric acid.

9.4.5   Return the tube to the heater and continue to heat until the solution becomes clear and colourless (or pale yellow), and dense white fumes of sulfur trioxide begin to appear. (Caution: If the digest begins to darken during heating after the addition of nitric acid-sulfuric acid solution, prevent the darkening by the cautious addition of 1 mL increments of nitric acid.)

9.4.6   Allow the solution to cool to room temperature.

9.5 *Reduction of Se[VI] to Se[IV]*

9.5.1   Dilute the solution (9.4.6) to 5 mL with 0.5 mol/L hydrochloric acid.

9.5.2   Add sufficient concentrated HCl to produce a solution approximately 6 mol/L in HCl.

9.5.3   Boil the solution gently for 5 min, then allow to cool to room temperature.

9.5.4   Transfer to a volumetric flask of a suitable volume (which will depend on the Se content of the sample and the sensitivity of the instrument) and dilute to the mark with water. Retain for AAS (9.7).

9.6 *AAS operating conditions*

9.6.1   Allow the atomic absorption spectrometer to warm up and the silica tube furnace to attain thermal equilibrium. The following operating conditions are optimum for the Varian Techtron Model AA-5 spectrometer:

Wavelength	196.0 nm
Band width	0.3 nm
Hollow-cathode (Cathodeon) lamp current	4,5 mA
Damping	maximum (D)
Argon flow rate	400 mL/min
Sample time	1 min
Wash time	2 min
Recorder span	5.0 mV full-scale
Chart speed	0.6 cm/min.

NOTE: The optimum conditions will depend on the particular atomic absorption spectrometer employed. The analyst should determine the optimum operating conditions experimentally for his instrument.

9.6.2   Turn on the argon flow at the pre-determined flow rate.

9.6.3   Insert the Technicon manifold tubes into 6 mol/L HCl and 1% sodium tetrahydroborate [III], as shown in Fig. 1. (Caution: These reagent concentrations may vary with the hydride generation system employed. The analyst is therefore advised to determine his own optimum solution conditions experimentally.)

9.6.4   Start the Technicon proportionating pump.

9.6.5   When the system has attained equilibrium as indicated by the minimal baseline noise on the strip-chart recorder, adjust the atomic absorption spectrometer to zero absorbance.

9.7 *Selenium determination*

9.7.1   Transfer 3–4 mL of the solution from 9.5.4 into a 5-mL disposable polypropylene cup in the autosampler.

9.7.2   Switch on the autosampler and record the Se atomic absorption peak.

9.7.3   Repeat 9.7.1 and 9.7.2 three times and record average absorption peak value for the four measurements.

9.8 *Preparation of calibration graph*

9.8.1   Transfer into a series of Pyrex test tubes (28 × 133 mm) 0.0, 1.0, 2.0, 4.0, 6.0, 8.0 and 10.0 mL of standard Se solution C, each in duplicate.

9.8.2   Add enough water to bring the total volume in each tube to approximately 10 mL.

9.8.3   Proceed as instructed in steps 9.4.2 to 9.5.3, inclusive.

9.8.4   Transfer the solutions from 9.8.3 into 20-mL volumetric flasks and make up to the mark with water.

9.8.5   Transfer 3–4 mL of each solution into 5-mL cup in the autosampler and proceed as in 9.7.2 and 9.7.3.

9.8.6   Plot a calibration graph of absorbance-peak height *versus* concentration of Se (0.0, 5.0, 10.0, 20.0, 30.0, 40.0 and 50.0 ng Se/mL). Prepare a new calibration curve daily.

10. METHOD OF CALCULATION

10.1 *Selenium in human whole blood and serum*

Using the absorption-peak height (9.7.3) and the calibration curve (9.8.6), obtain the mass concentration, $\rho(\mu g/L)$, of Se in whole blood or serum by multiplying the mass concentration of the final solution (9.5.4) by the dilution factor, V/v,

where

V   = volume of solution in 9.5.4 (mL)

v   = volume of blood or serum in 9.4.1 (mL).

10.2 *Selenium in urine*

The Se content of urine is determined as in 10.1, but may be expressed in three different ways: (i) μg of Se/L of urine; (ii) μg of Se/24-h urine (i.e., total volume of urine collected over a 24-h period); (iii) μg of Se/g of creatinine in urine.

When expressing the Se content either as (i) or (ii) above, the use of a correction factor to normalize to an average specific gravity of 1.024 is recommended.

Thus, the corrected μg Se/L or 24-h urine is given by

$$\mu g/L \text{ (or } \mu g/24 \text{ h)} \times \frac{1.024 - 1.000}{\text{sp. gr.} - 1.000}$$

where

sp. gr.   = measured specific gravity at room temperature (The specific gravity may be measured with the use of a calibrated specific gravity meter or urinometer).

10.3 *Selenium in tissues*

The mass fraction, $\omega(mg/kg)$ of Se in tissues may be expressed as mg Se/kg of wet tissue, as mg Se/kg of dry tissue, or as mg Se/kg of ash (in which case the tissue sample will have to be ashed prior to acid digestion; it is important to ensure that no loss of Se occurs by volatilization during ashing).

The mass fraction is given by

$$\omega = \rho V/m$$

where

ρ = mass concentration of Se in final solution, 9.5.4 (mg/L)

m = mass of test portion (wet, dry or ashed) in 9.4.1 (g) and

V is defined in 10.1.

11. REPEATABILITY AND REPRODUCIBILITY

11.1 *Repeatability*

For human liver and kidney samples analysed on the same day, Subramanian and Méranger (1982) obtained coefficients of variation (n = 20) of 21, 12 and 7% at 0.05, 0.10 and 0.20 µg Se per g of wet tissue, using the above procedure.

Lloyd *et al.* (1982) obtained coefficients of variation (n = 20) of 4.5 and 4.0% at 143.8 µg Se/L of whole blood and 120.4 µg Se/L of plasma, respectively, using the Perkin-Elmer Model MHS20 Hydride Generation System.

11.2 *Reproducibility*

No data available.

12. NOTES ON PROCEDURE

Not applicable.

13. SCHEMATIC REPRESENTATION OF PROCEDURE

Sample (1–2 g tissue; 0.1–5 mL blood or plasma)

↓

Add 10 mL HNO$_3$ + 2 mL HClO$_4$

↓

Heat to reduce volume to 5 mL

↓

Cool to room temperature
↓
Add 5 mL HNO_3 + 5 mL H_2SO_4
↓
Heat until the solution is clear and colourless
or pale yellow
↓
Cool to room temperature
↓
Dilute to 5 mL with 0.5 mol/L HCl
↓
Add conc. HCl to obtain concentration of ∼6 mol/L
↓
Transfer 3–4 mL into autosampler cup
↓
Generate the hydride automatically
under optimized conditions
↓
Decompose the hydride, atomize the Se
and measure its atomic absorption signal
under optimized conditions
↓
Determine Se content of sample
by reference to calibration graph

14. ORIGIN OF THE METHOD

Health and Welfare Canada
Health Protection Branch
Environmental Health Centre
Tunney's Pasture
Ottawa, Ontario K1A OL2
Canada

Contact point: Dr K.S. Subramanian

METHOD 28 – DETERMINATION OF SELENIUM IN PLASMA AND SERUM BY ELECTROTHERMAL ATOMIZATION-ATOMIC ABSORPTION SPECTROMETRY

K.S. Subramanian

1. SCOPE AND FIELD OF APPLICATION

This method is suitable for the determination of selenium (Se) in microlitre volumes of human serum and plasma. The detection limit is 2.6 µg/L and the total time required for analysis is about 8 min.

2. REFERENCE

Alfthan, G. & Kumpulainen, J. (1982) Determination of selenium in small volumes of blood plasma and serum by electrothermal atomic absorption spectrometry. *Anal. Chim. Acta, 140,* 221–227

3. DEFINITIONS

The detection limit is defined as three times the standard deviation of the Se concentration in the blank.

4. PRINCIPLE

The serum or plasma sample is diluted ten-fold with a solution containing nickel and nitric acid. The Se content of this matrix-modified solution is then determined by the method of standard addition, using graphite furnace atomic absorption spectrophotometry.

5. HAZARDS

Selenium is toxic. It is desirable to practice the usual methods of safe handling and disposal of all solutions containing Se.

6. REAGENTS[1]

Use the purest available reagents and ultrapure water throughout, except as noted.

Ni[II] solution	2.5% (25 g/L). Dissolve 12.3 g of $Ni(NO_3)_2.6H_2O$ in 100 mL of water. Store in a clean 125-mL Nalgene polyethylene bottle equipped with screw-cap.
Nitric acid	Approximately 0.72 mol/L. Dilute 46.0 mL of nitric acid (68–71%, specific gravity, 1.42, ultrapure grade) to 1 L with water and store in a clean Nalgene polyethylene bottle with screw-cap.
Standard Se solution A	1 g Se/L. Dissolve 1.450 g of Se dioxide (purity = 99.9%) in 1 mL of concentrated HCl (36–38%, specific gravity, 1.18). Dilute to 1 L with water.
Standard Se solution B	1 mg Se/L. Dilute 1.0 mL of standard Se solution A to 1 L with ultrapure water.

7. APPARATUS[1]

Atomic absorption spectrophotometer	Many commercially-available instruments are suitable (e.g., Perkin-Elmer Model 4000 atomic absorption spectrophotometer).
Graphite furnace	Any commercially-available furnace (e.g., a Perkin-Elmer Model HGA-500 graphite furnace).
Background corrector	Deuterium or hydrogen continuum lamp.
Se hollow cathode lamp (HCL) or electrodeless discharge lamp (EDL)	Any commercially-available lamp. An EDL is recommended. The HCL may be used with reduced sensitivity.
Other accessories	Autosampler; printer; recorder. (These are desirable, but not essential).
Micropipettes and pipette tips	Any available brand (e.g., Eppendorf).

---

[1] Reference to a company and/or product is for the purpose of information and identification only and does not imply approval or recommendation of the company and/or product by the International Agency for Research on Cancer, to the exclusion of others which may also be suitable.

Volumetric flasks   1.0-mL, borosilicate glass

Vortex mixer

Nalgene polyethylene   125- and 1000-mL
bottles

NOTE: Prior to analysis, wash all lab-ware with detergent, soak in 10% analytical reagent grade nitric acid for at least 4 h and rinse at least six times
with ultrapure water.

9. PROCEDURE

9.1 *Blank test*

Carry out a blank test in parallel with the analysis of the sample, using procedure
9.4.1 to 9.5.6, but omitting the test portion in 9.4.1.

9.2 *Check test*

Not applicable.

9.3 *Test portion*

100 µL of serum or plasma.

9.4 *Sample preparation*

9.4.1   Pipette 100 µL of serum or plasma into each of five 1.0 mL volumetric
flasks.

9.4.2   Add 100 µL of 2.5% Ni[II] to each flask.

9.4.3   Add 100 µL of 0.72 mol/L nitric acid to each flask.

9.4.4   Add, respectively, 0, 10, 20, 30 and 40 µL of standard Se solution B to
the five volumetric flasks.

9.4.5   Vortex each solution vigorously for 30 s, then make up to 1.0 mL with
ultrapure water and mix thoroughly.

9.5 *Selenium determination*

9.5.1   Inject 20 µL of solution 9.4.5 from the first flask (containing no added
Se) into the pyrocoated graphite tube.

Table 1. Instrumental conditions for the determination of selenium in serum and plasma (wavelength 296.0 nm, spectral bandwidth 0.7 nm, scale expansion 10X, background correction, peak height mode, 20 mL sample)

Step	1 Dry	2 Dry	3 Ash	4 Atomize	5 Clean
Temperature (°C)	70	110	1100	2400	2700
Ramp time(s)	10	30	30	0	1
Hold time(s)	0	20	20	4	2
Internal gas (mL Ar/min)	300	300	300	20	300

[a]From Alfthan & Kumpulainen, 1982.

9.5.2   Atomize the Se under the optimized instrumental conditions given in Table 1 (see 12, Notes on Procedure).

9.5.3   Record the absorbance-peak height.

9.5.4   Repeat steps 9.5.1 to 9.5.3 at least two more times and calculate the mean absorbance-peak height from the three injections.

9.5.5   Proceed as in steps 9.5.1 to 9.5.4 for the second, third, fourth and fifth flask (i.e., for 10, 20, 30 and 40 ng of added Se/mL).

9.5.6   Prepare a linear regression standard addition plot from the above data (abcissa: Se spike concentration, μg/L; ordinate: absorbance-peak height).

NOTE: For a serum sample diluted ten-fold, the method gives a standard addition graph which is linear up to 100 μg Se/L.

10. METHOD OF CALCULATION

Determine the mass concentration (μg/L) of Se by extrapolation of the standard addition graph (9.5.6) and multiplication by a factor of ten to correct for the ten-fold dilution (9.4.5).

11. REPEATABILITY AND REPRODUCIBILITY

11.1 *Repeatability*

A pooled reference serum with a mean Se concentration of 87 μg/L gave a coefficient of variation of 4.4% (124 determinations).

11.2 *Reproducibility*

No data available.

12. NOTES ON PROCEDURE

The optimum operating conditions for every atomic absorption spectrometer-graphite furnace combination may not be the same as those given in Table 1. These parameters must be optimized before attempting to obtain useful measurements.

13. SCHEMATIC REPRESENTATION OF PROCEDURE

100 µL serum or plasma

↓

Add 100 µL 2.5% Ni(II] and 100 µL 0.72 mol/L HNO_3

↓

Mix (Vortex) for 30 s

↓

Dilute to 1 mL with ultrapure water

↓

Inject 20 µL into pyrocoated graphite tube

↓

Measure atomic absorption under optimum instrumental conditions

↓

Determine Se content of sample from standard addition graph.

14. ORIGIN OF THE METHOD

National Public Health Institute
Helsinki 28
Finland

Contact point: K.S. Subramanian
Environmental Health Centre
Tunney's Pasture
Ottawa, Ontario K1A OL2
Canada.

METHOD 29 – DETERMINATION OF SELENIUM IN WHOLE BLOOD AND OTHER BIOLOGICAL MATERIALS BY SPECTROFLUORIMETRY

H.A.M.G. Vaessen, A. van Ooik & P.L. Schuller

1. SCOPE AND FIELD OF APPLICATION

This reference method is suitable for the determination of the selenium (Se) content of human blood, with a lower limit of 10 µg/kg. It has also been shown to be applicable to foodstuffs and a wide range of other biological materials. A set of 5 samples and 3 calibration standards can be analysed in approximately 5 hours.

2. REFERENCES

Hoffman, I., Westerby, R.J. & Hidiroglou, M. (1968) Precise fluorometric microdetermination of selenium in agricultural materials. *J. Assoc. off. anal. Chem., 51,* 1039–1042

Ihnat, M. (1974) Fluorometric determination of selenium in foods. *J. Assoc. off. anal. Chem., 57,* 368–372

Michie, N.D., Dixon, E.J. & Bunton, N.G. (1978) Critical review of AOAC fluorometric method for determining selenium in food. *J. Assoc. off. anal. Chem., 61,* 48–51

3. DEFINITIONS

Not applicable.

4. PRINCIPLE

Organic matter in the sample is digested under pressure at 150 °C in a wet decomposition vessel. The resulting solution is treated with a perchloric acid/sulfuric acid mixture. Perchloric acid is completely expelled and Se is reduced to the tetravalent state by hydrogen peroxide, then complexed at pH 1 with 2,3-diaminonaphthalene, to form 4,5-benzopiazselenol. The piazselenol is extracted with cyclohexane and measured fluorimetrically.

5. HAZARDS

The digestion procedure employs concentrated nitric, sulfuric and perchloric acids and hydrogen peroxide. These should be handled only in a ventilated fume hood and protective gloves and spectacles should be worn.

6. REAGENTS[1]

Unless otherwise stated, all reagents should be of analytical reagent quality. Water must be double-distilled (or equivalent) from an all-glass apparatus of Pyrex or other resistant glass.

Nitric acid	65% (w/w), density 1.40 g/mL. Merck 'Suprapur', or equivalent.
Perchloric acid	70% (w/w), density ∼ 1.67 g/mL.
Sulfuric acid	98% (w/w), density 1.84 g/mL. Merck 'Suprapur', or equivalent.
Hydrogen peroxide	30% (w/w).
Buffer solution	pH 1.00. Merck glycine-hydrochloric acid buffer.
Ammonia solution	25% (w/w), density 0.91 g/mL. Merck 'Suprapur', or equivalent.
Cyclohexane	Spectrofluorimetric quality. Merck 'Uvasol', or equivalent.
Disodium ethylenedi-aminetetraacetate dihydrate	(EDTA)
2,3-Diaminonaphthalene	(DAN) Fluka A.G.
Hydrochloric acid	0.1 mol/L.
Sulfuric acid	2.5 mol/L.
Dilute ammonia solution	Mix 1 volume of 25% ammonia solution and 2 volumes of water. Prepare fresh daily.

---

[1] Reference to a company and/or product is for the purpose of information and identification only and does not imply approval or recommendation of the company and/or product by the International Agency for Research on Cancer, to the exclusion of others which may also be suitable.

EDTA solution

0.01 mol/L. Dissolve 2.1 g of EDTA in 250 mL of water and mix.

DAN solution

Accurately weigh 50 mg of DAN in a 150-mL beaker, add 50 mL of 0.1 mol/L hydrochloric acid and dissolve by warming to 50 °C for 30 min on a water-bath. Purify the solution by extraction with four 5-mL portions of cyclohexane. Discard the organic layers and filter the aqueous phase through a Whatman No. 1 (or equivalent) filter paper. Prepare this reagent immediately before use.

Se dioxide

Se stock solution

100 mg/L. Dissolve 70.3 mg of Se dioxide in water in a 500-mL volumetric flask and make up to the mark with water.

Dilute stock solution

5 µg/mL. Pipette 5.0 mL of 100 mg/L stock solution into a 100-mL volumetric flask, add 2.0 mL of 2.5 mol/L sulfuric acid and make up to the mark with water.

Se working solution

200 µg/L. Pipette 4.0 mL of dilute stock solution into a 100-mL volumetric flask, add 2.0 mL of 2.5 mol/L sulfuric acid and make up to the mark with water.

7. APPARATUS[1]

NOTE: Soak glass-ware, including reagent bottles, for 24 h in 4 mol/L nitric acid and rinse twice with distilled water, then twice with double-distilled water before use. Boil the Teflon decomposition vessels for 1 h in a 1 mol/L hydrochloric acid-detergent solution, rinse with water and boil another hour in 25% hydrochloric acid, then thoroughly rinse with distilled and double-distilled water and dry in a suitable oven at 120 °C.

Decomposition vessels

See Fig. 1 (Uniseal Corporation, Haïfa, or equivalent vessels, are equally suitable). The inner Teflon vessel holds 20 to 23 mL.

Round-bottom flask

250-mL, long neck.

---

[1] Reference to a company and/or product is for the purpose of information and identification only and does not imply approval or recommendation of the company and/or product by the International Agency for Research on Cancer, to the exclusion of others which may also be suitable.

Glass beads	Nitric acid treated and washed with water, as indicated above.
Measuring pipettes	1-, 2- and 5-mL, with glass piston (Fortuna type or equivalent).
One-mark pipettes	5-mL.
Measuring cylinders	5- and 50-mL.
Volumetric flasks	100- and 500-mL.
Separating funnels	250-mL, with Teflon stopcocks.
Argand-burners	
Analytical balance	Accurate to within 0.1 mg.
pH meter	Accurate to within 0.05 pH-units and fitted with a combined pH glass electrode, reserved for the determination of Se.
Oven	Ventilated, thermostatically-controlled at 150 °C (place in a fume hood).
Water-bath	Thermostatically-controlled at 50 °C.
Spectrofluorimeter	Ratio-recording, scanning instrument is preferred (Aminco-Bowman type SPF-500, or equivalent).
Quartz cells	Suitable for fluorimetric measurements, optical pathlength 1 cm.
Finn-pipettes	Adjustable, to deliver volumes of 50 to 250 μL and 200 to 1000 μL, with disposable plastic tips.

8. SAMPLING

Consult Chapter 10.

Homogenize a representative blood sample. If the sample comes into contact with metal parts of the homogenizer, check for Se contamination. Avoid contact with metals by using porcelain whenever possible.

9. PROCEDURE

9.1 *Blank test*

The reagent blank is determined with the calibration curve (9.6), which then provides an automatic blank correction.

Fig. 1. Wet decomposition vessel (all dimensions are in mm)

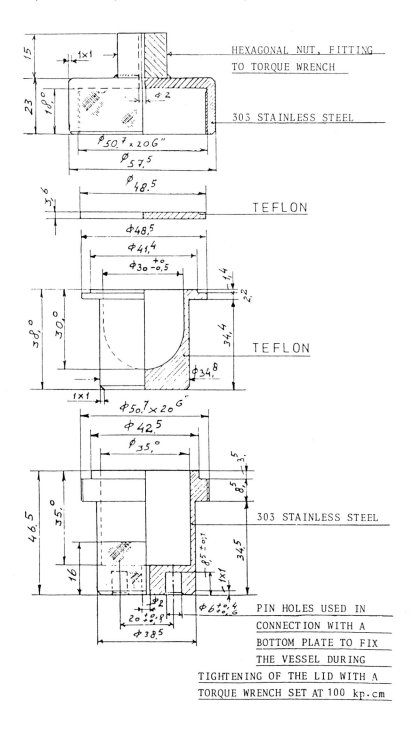

9.2 *Check test*

Not applicable.

9.3 *Test portion*

Weigh, to the nearest 0.1 mg, a homogenized test portion containing not more than 500 ng of Se.

For safety reasons, the test portion in the Teflon decomposition vessel should be restricted to 500 mg (200 mg dry material).

9.4 *Digestion*

9.4.1   Weigh the test portions (9.3) into decomposition vessels (Fig. 1), add 3.0 mL of 65% nitric acid with a measuring pipette, close the vessels and place them in an oven at 150 °C for 10 h. (Close the vessels with a torque wrench set at 100 kp. cm = 4.448×10^3 N.m.)

9.4.2   Allow the digestion vessels to cool to room temperature and transfer the digest to a 250-mL round-bottom flask.

9.4.3   Add three glass beads, 2 mL of 70% perchloric acid and 5 mL of 98% sulfuric acid. Mix.

9.4.4   Heat the mixture using an Argand-burner. The solution will first turn straw-yellow. Continue heating until, after vigorous swirling, the digest remains colourless and dense sulfuric acid fumes appear.

9.4.5   Cool to room temperature, rinse the neck of the flask with 5 mL of water, mix and reheat to fuming.

9.4.6   Allow the digest to cool to room temperature and add 1 mL of 30% hydrogen peroxide. Heat until small gas bubbles are no longer evolved (hydrogen peroxide is completely decomposed) and dense sulfuric acid fumes appear.

9.4.7   Repeat 9.4.6 twice.

9.4.8   Cool the digest to room temperature, rinse the neck of the flask with 10 mL of water and heat to fuming. Continue heating with evolution of fumes for a further 5 min.

9.4.9   Cool digest to room temperature and dilute with 50 mL of water.

9.5 *Formation and extraction of benzopiazselenol*

9.5.1   Add 10 mL of EDTA solution and 7.5 mL of 25% ammonia to the diluted digest (9.4.9). Cool to room temperature and adjust the pH of the solution to 1.0 with dilute ammonia (Use a pH meter).

9.5.2   Add 5.0 mL of DAN solution with a pipette and place in a water-bath at 50 °C for 30 min. Carry out following steps in subdued light.

9.5.3   Cool solution to room temperature and quantitatively transfer to a 250-mL separating funnel, using as little water as possible for rinsing. Add 5.0 mL of cyclohexane.

9.5.4   Allow the layers to separate and discard the aqueous layer. Wash the organic layer with 25 mL of 0.1 mol/L hydrochloric acid (shake vigorously for 30 s), allow the layers to separate and discard the lower layer. Retain cyclohexane extract for Se determination.

9.6 *Calibration graph*

Establish a calibration graph for each series of samples.

9.6.1   Using Finn-pipettes, add to three decomposition vessels amounts of Se working standard solutions containing 0 (blank), 1/2x and x ng Se, where x is the maximum quantity of Se considered to be present in the test portions.

9.6.2   To each vessel, add 3.0 mL of 65% nitric acid. Close the vessels and place them in an oven at 150 °C for 10 h. Cool to room temperature and proceed as described in steps 9.4.2 to 9.5.4, inclusive.

9.6.3   Calibrate the spectrofluorimeter for 0% fluorescence with the instrument dark current. As described in 9.7.1, determine the fluorescence of the cyclohexane extract of the most concentrated calibration solution (9.6.1) and set the instrument to read 100% fluorescence at the fluorescence maximum (522 nm).

9.6.4   With the instrument calibrated as described in 9.6.3, determine the relative fluorescence (%) of the extracts of the other two calibration solutions (9.6.1).

9.6.5   Calculate the linear regression relating the mass, m, of Se in ng to the percent relative fluorescence, F. Plot the corresponding calibration curve, $m = a + bF$.

9.7 *Selenium determination*

9.7.1   Transfer an aliquot of the cyclohexane solution (9.5.4) into a quartz cell and record the fluorescence from 400 to 640 nm, using an excitation wavelength of 375 nm.

The shape of the fluorescence spectrum of the samples should be similar to the spectrum of the standard solutions taken through the entire procedure. If digestion was incomplete, the spectrum will be distorted, especially at about 500 nm.

9.7.2   Measure the relative fluorescence in percent at the fluorescence maximum (522 nm).

10. METHOD OF CALCULATION

Calculate the mass fraction, ω (mg/kg), of Se in the sample using the formula

ω = m/M

where

m   = mass of Se in the test portion, obtained from the relative fluorescence (9.7.2) and the calibration curve, 9.6 (ng)

M   = mass of the test portion in 9.4.1 (mg).

11. REPEATABILITY AND REPRODUCIBILITY

The accuracy and repeatability of the method are indicated in the following table.

Material (code)[a]	Se content[b] (μg/g)	Average Se found[c]	Coefficient of variation (%)
NBS Spinach (SRM 1570)	0.04 ± 0.01	0.036(5)	10.0
NBS Tomato leaves (SRM 1573)	0.05 ± 0.01	0.050(5)	13.1
NBS Rice flour (SRM 1586)	0.4 ± 0.1	0.361(2)	–
NBS Orchard leaves (SRM 1571)	0.08 ± 0.01	0.084(5)	3.0
IAEA Copepod (MA-A-1)	3.0 ± 0.2	3.11(5)	1.6

[a] NBS = National Bureau of Standards, USA
   IAEA = International Atomic Energy Agency
[b] Reference values (NBS) or best estimates (IAEA), dry sample basis
[c] Number of determinations in parentheses.

12. NOTES ON PROCEDURE

Not applicable.

13. SCHEMATIC REPRESENTATION OF PROCEDURE

Add 3 mL 65% HNO_3 to test portion in decomposition vessel
and heat sealed vessel 10 h at 150 °C

$\downarrow$

Transfer cooled digest to 250-mL flask, add glass beads,
2 mL 70% $HClO_4$ and 5 mL 98% H_2SO_4.
Heat until white fumes appear

$\downarrow$

Cool, rinse neck of flask with 5 mL water
and heat to fuming

$\downarrow$

Cool, add 1 mL 30% H_2O_2 and heat to fuming.
Repeat twice

$\downarrow$

Cool, rinse neck of flask with 10 mL water
and heat to fuming (5 min)

$\downarrow$

Cool, add 50 mL water, 10 mL EDTA solution and
7.5 mL 25% ammonia. Adjust pH to 1.0 with dilute ammonia

$\downarrow$

Add 5.0 mL DAN solution and hold at 50 °C for 30 min

$\downarrow$

In subdued light, cool, transfer to 250-mL separating funnel,
add 5.0 mL cyclohexane and shake for 1 min.
Discard aqueous layer

$\downarrow$

Wash organic layer with 25 mL 0.1 mol/L HCl.
Discard acid layer

$\downarrow$

Measure fluorescence of cyclohexane solution
and determine Se content using standard solution calibration curve.

14. ORIGIN OF THE METHOD

National Institute for Public Health and Environmental Hygiene
NL-3720 BA Bilthoven
The Netherlands

Contact point: H.A.M.G. Vaessen
Rijks Instituut voor de Volksgezondheid
Antonie van Leeuwenhoeklaan 9
Postbus 1
3720 BA Bilthoven
The Netherlands

INDEX OF AUTHORS

PUBLICATIONS OF THE INTERNATIONAL AGENCY FOR RESEARCH ON CANCER

SCIENTIFIC PUBLICATIONS SERIES

(Available from Oxford University Press)

SCIENTIFIC PUBLICATIONS SERIES

SCIENTIFIC PUBLICATIONS SERIES

No. 36 CANCER MORTALITY BY
OCCUPATION AND SOCIAL CLASS
1851-1971 (1982)
By W.P.D. Logan
253 pages

No. 37 LABORATORY DECONTAMI-
NATION AND DESTRUCTION OF
AFLATOXINS B_1, B_2, G_1, G_2 IN
LABORATORY WASTES (1980)
Edited by M. Castegnaro, D.C. Hunt,
E.B. Sansone, P.L. Schuller,
M.G. Siriwardana, G.M. Telling,
H.P. Van Egmond & E.A. Walker,
59 pages

No. 38 DIRECTORY OF ON-GOING
RESEARCH IN CANCER EPI-
DEMIOLOGY 1981 (1981)
Edited by C.S. Muir & G. Wagner,
696 pages; out of print

No. 39 HOST FACTORS IN HUMAN
CARCINOGENESIS (1982)
Edited by H. Bartsch & B. Armstrong
583 pages

No. 40 ENVIRONMENTAL CAR-
CINOGENS. SELECTED METHODS
OF ANALYSIS
Editor-in-Chief H. Egan
Vol. 4. SOME AROMATIC AMINES AND
AZO DYES IN THE GENERAL AND
INDUSTRIAL ENVIRONMENT (1981)
Edited by L. Fishbein, M. Castegnaro,
I.K. O'Neill & H. Bartsch
347 pages

No. 41 N-NITROSO COMPOUNDS:
OCCURRENCE AND BIOLOGICAL
EFFECTS (1982)
Edited by H. Bartsch, I.K. O'Neill,
M. Castegnaro & M. Okada,
755 pages

No. 42 CANCER INCIDENCE IN FIVE
CONTINENTS. VOLUME IV (1982)
Edited by J. Waterhouse, C. Muir,
K. Shanmugaratnam & J. Powell,
811 pages

No. 43 LABORATORY DECONTAMI-
NATION AND DESTRUCTION OF
CARCINOGENS IN LABORATORY
WASTES: SOME N-NITROSAMINES
(1982) Edited by M. Castegnaro,
G. Eisenbrand, G. Ellen, L. Keefer,
D. Klein, E.B. Sansone, D. Spincer,
G. Telling & K. Webb
73 pages

No. 44 ENVIRONMENTAL CAR-
CINOGENS. SELECTED METHODS
OF ANALYSIS
Editor-in-Chief H. Egan
Vol. 5. SOME MYCOTOXINS (1983)
Edited by L. Stoloff, M. Castegnaro,
P. Scott, I.K. O'Neill & H. Bartsch,
455 pages

No. 45 ENVIRONMENTAL CAR-
CINOGENS. SELECTED METHODS
OF ANALYSIS
Editor-in-Chief H. Egan
Vol. 6: N-NITROSO COMPOUNDS
(1983)
Edited by R. Preussmann, I.K. O'Neill,
G. Eisenbrand, B. Spiegelhalder &
H. Bartsch
508 pages

No. 46 DIRECTORY OF ON-GOING
RESEARCH IN CANCER EPI-
DEMIOLOGY 1982 (1982)
Edited by C.S. Muir & G. Wagner,
722 pages; out of print

No. 47 CANCER INCIDENCE IN
SINGAPORE (1982)
Edited by K. Shanmugaratnam, H.P. Lee
& N.E. Day
174 pages

No. 48 CANCER INCIDENCE IN
THE USSR Second Revised
Edition (1983)
Edited by N.P. Napalkov,
G.F. Tserkovny, V.M. Merabishvili,
D.M. Parkin, M. Smans & C.S. Muir,
75 pages

No. 49 LABORATORY DECONTAMI
NATION AND DESTRUCTION OF
CARCINOGENS IN LABORATORY
WASTES: SOME POLYCYCLIC
AROMATIC HYDROCARBONS (1983)
Edited by M. Castegnaro, G. Grimmer,
O. Hutzinger, W. Karcher, H. Kunte,
M. Lafontaine, E.B. Sansone, G. Telling
& S.P. Tucker
81 pages

No. 50 DIRECTORY OF ON-GOING
RESEARCH IN CANCER
EPIDEMIOLOGY 1983 (1983)
Edited by C.S. Muir & G. Wagner,
740 pages; out of print

SCIENTIFIC PUBLICATIONS SERIES

No. 51 MODULATORS OF
EXPERIMENTAL CARCINO-
GENESIS (1983)
Edited by V. Turusov & R. Montesano
307 pages

No. 52 SECOND CANCER IN
RELATION TO RADIATION
TREATMENT FOR CERVICAL
CANCER: RESULTS OF A CANCER
REGISTRY COLLABORATION (1984)
Edited by N.E. Day & J.C. Boice, Jr,
207 pages

No. 53 NICKEL IN THE HUMAN
ENVIRONMENT (1984)
Editor-in-Chief, F.W. Sunderman, Jr,
529 pages

No. 54 LABORATORY
DECONTAMINATION AND
DESTRUCTION OF CARCINO-
GENS IN LABORATORY WASTES:
SOME HYDRAZINES (1983)
Edited by M. Castegnaro, G. Ellen,
M. Lafontaine, H.C. van der Plas,
E.B. Sansone & S.P. Tucker,
87 pages

No. 55 LABORATORY
DECONTAMINATION AND
DESTRUCTION OF CARCINOGENS
IN LABORATORY WASTES: SOME
N-NITROSAMIDES (1984)
Edited by M. Castegnaro,
M. Benard, L.W. van Broekhoven,
D. Fine, R. Massey, E.B. Sansone,
P.L.R. Smith, B. Spiegelhalder,
A. Stacchini, G. Telling & J.J. Vallon,
65 pages

No. 56 MODELS, MECHANISMS AND
ETIOLOGY OF TUMOUR PROMOTION
(1984)
Edited by M. Börszönyi, N.E. Day,
K. Lapis & H. Yamasaki
532 pages

No. 57 N-NITROSO COMPOUNDS:
OCCURRENCE, BIOLOGICAL EFFECTS
AND RELEVANCE TO HUMAN
CANCER (1984)
Edited by I.K. O'Neill, R.C. von Borstel,
C.T. Miller, J. Long & H. Bartsch,
1013 pages

No. 58 AGE-RELATED FACTORS
IN CARCINOGENESIS (1985)
Edited by A. Likhachev, V. Anisimov
& R. Montesano
288 pages

No. 59 MONITORING HUMAN
EXPOSURE TO CARCINOGENIC AND
MUTAGENIC AGENTS (1984)
Edited by A. Berlin, M. Draper,
K. Hemminki & H. Vainio
457 pages

No. 60 BURKITT'S LYMPHOMA: A
HUMAN CANCER MODEL (1985)
Edited by G. Lenoir, G. O'Conor
& C.L.M. Olweny
484 pages

No. 61 LABORATORY DECONTAMI-
NATION AND DESTRUCTION OF
CARCINOGENS IN LABORATORY
WASTES: SOME HALOETHERS (1984)
Edited by M. Castegnaro,
M. Alvarez, M. Iovu, E.B. Sansone,
G.M. Telling & D.T. Williams
55 pages

No. 62 DIRECTORY OF ON-GOING
RESEARCH IN CANCER EPI-
DEMIOLOGY 1984 (1984)
Edited by C.S. Muir & G.Wagner
728 pages

No. 63 VIRUS-ASSOCIATED CANCERS
IN AFRICA (1984)
Edited by A.O. Williams, G.T. O'Conor,
G.B. de-Thé & C.A. Johnson,
773 pages

No. 64 LABORATORY DECONTAMI-
NATION AND DESTRUCTION OF
CARCINOGENS IN LABORATORY
WASTES: SOME AROMATIC AMINES
AND 4-NITROBIPHENYL (1985)
Edited by M. Castegnaro, J. Barek,
J. Dennis, G. Ellen, M. Klibanov,
M. Lafontaine, R. Mitchum,
P. Van Roosmalen, E.B. Sansone,
L.A. Sternson & M. Vahl
85 pages

No. 65 INTERPRETATION OF
NEGATIVE EPIDEMIOLOGICAL
EVIDENCE FOR CARCINOGENICITY
Edited by N.J. Wald & R. Doll
232 pages

No. 66 THE ROLE OF THE REGISTRY
IN CANCER CONTROL
Edited by D.M. Parkin, G. Wagner
& C.S. Muir
155 pages

No. 67 TRANSFORMATION ASSAY OF
ESTABLISHED CELL LINES:
MECHANISMS AND APPLICATIONS
Edited by T. Kakunaga & H. Yamasaki
225 pages

SCIENTIFIC PUBLICATIONS SERIES

No. 68 ENVIRONMENTAL
CARCINOGENS — SELECTED
METHODS OF ANALYSIS.
VOL. 7: SOME VOLATILE
HALOGENATED ALKANES AND
ALKENES
Edited by L. Fishbein & I.K. O'Neill
479 pages

No. 69 DIRECTORY OF ON-GOING
RESEARCH IN CANCER
EPIDEMIOLOGY 1985 (1985)
Edited by C.S. Muir & G. Wagner
756 pages

No. 70 THE ROLE OF CYCLIC NUCLEIC
ACID ADDUCTS IN CARCINOGENESIS
AND MUTAGENESIS
Edited by B. Singer & H. Bartsch
(in press)

No. 71 ENVIRONMENTAL CARCINOGENS.
SELECTED METHODS OF ANALYSIS
VOL. 8:. SOME METALS: As, Be, Cd,
Cr, Ni, Pb, Se, Zn
Edited by I.K. O'Neill, P. Schuller
& L. Fishbein
486 pages

No. 72 ATLAS OF CANCER IN
SCOTLAND 1975-1980: INCIDENCE AND
EPIDEMIOLOGICAL PERSPECTIVE (1985)
Edited by I. Kemp, P. Boyle, M. Smans
& C. Muir
282 pages

No. 73 LABORATORY DECONTAMI-
NATION AND DESTRUCTION OF
CARCINOGENS IN LABORATORY
WASTES: SOME ANTINEOPLASTIC
AGENTS
Edited by M. Castegnaro, J. Adams,
M. Armour, J. Barek, J. Benvenuto,
C. Confalonieri, U. Goff, S. Ludeman,
D. Reed, E.B. Sansone & G. Telling
(1985) (in press)

NON-SERIAL PUBLICATIONS

(Available from IARC)

ALCOOL ET CANCER (1978)
By A.J. Tuyns (in French only)
42 pages

CANCER MORBIDITY AND CAUSES OF
DEATH AMONG DANISH BREWERY
WORKERS (1980)
By O.M. Jensen
145 pages

IARC MONOGRAPHS ON THE EVALUATION OF THE CARCINOGENIC RISK OF CHEMICALS TO HUMANS

(English editions only)

(Available from WHO Sales Agents)

Volume 1
Some inorganic substances, chlorinated hydrocarbons, aromatic amines, N-nitroso compounds, and natural products (1972)
184 pp.; out of print

Volume 2
Some inorganic and organometallic compounds (1973)
181 pp.; out of print

Volume 3
Certain polycyclic aromatic hydrocarbons and heterocyclic compounds (1973)
271 pp.; out of print

Volume 4
Some aromatic amines, hydrazine and related substances, N-nitroso compounds and miscellaneous alkylating agents (1974)
286 pp.; US$7.20; Sw.fr. 18.-

Volume 5
Some organochlorine pesticides (1974)
241 pp.; out of print

Volume 6
Sex hormones (1974)
243 pp.; US$7.20; Sw.fr. 18.-

Volume 7
Some anti-thyroid and related sub-stances, nitrofurans and industrial chemicals (1974)
326 pp.; US$12.80; Sw.fr. 32.-

Volume 8
Some aromatic azo compounds (1975)
357 pp.; US$14.40; Sw.fr. 36.-

Volume 9
Some aziridines, N-, S- and O-mustards and selenium (1975)
268 pp.; US$10.80; Sw.fr. 27.-

Volume 10
Some naturally occurring substances (1976)
353 pp.; US$15.00; Sw.fr. 38.-

Volume 11
Cadmium, nickel, some epoxides, miscellaneous industrial chemicals and general considerations on volatile anaesthetics (1976)
306 pp.; US$14 00; Sw.fr. 34.-

Volume 12
Some carbamates, thiocarbamates and carbazides (1976)
282 pp.; US$14.00; Sw.fr. 34.-

Volume 13
Some miscellaneous pharmaceutical substances (1977)
255 pp.; US$12.00; Sw.fr. 30.-

Volume 14
Asbestos (1977)
106 pp.; US$6.00; Sw.fr. 14.-

Volume 15
Some fumigants, the herbicides 2,4-D and 2,4,5-T, chlorinated dibenzodioxins and miscellaneous industrial chemicals (1977)
354 pp.; US$20.00; Sw.fr. 50.-

Volume 16
Some aromatic amines and related nitro compounds - hair dyes, colouring agents and miscellaneous industrial chemicals (1978)
400 pp.; US$20.00; Sw.fr. 50.-

Volume 17
Some N-nitroso compounds (1978)
365 pp.; US$25.00; Sw.fr. 50.-

Volume 18
Polychlorinated biphenyls and poly brominated biphenyls (1978)
140 pp.; US$13.00; Sw.fr. 20.-

Volume 19
Some monomers, plastics and synthetic elastomers, and acrolein (1979)
513 pp.; US$35.00; Sw.fr. 60.-

Volume 20
Some halogenated hydrocarbons (1979)
609 pp.; US$35.00; Sw.fr. 60.-

Volume 21
Sex hormones (II) (1979)
583 pp.; US$35.00; Sw.fr. 60.-

Volume 22
Some non-nutritive sweetening agents (1980)
208 pp.; US$15.00; Sw.fr. 25.-

IARC MONOGRAPHS SERIES

Volume 23
Some metals and metallic compounds (1980)
438 pp.; US$30.00; Sw.fr. 50.-

Volume 24
Some pharmaceutical drugs (1980)
337 pp.; US$25.00; Sw.fr. 40.-

Volume 25
Wood, leather and some associated industries (1981)
412 pp.; US$30.00; Sw.fr. 60.-

Volume 26
Some antineoplastic and immuno-suppressive agents (1981)
411 pp.; US$30.00; Sw.fr. 62.-

Volume 27
Some aromatic amines, anthraquinones and nitroso compounds, and inorganic fluorides used in drinking-water and dental preparations (1982)
341 pp.; US$25.00; Sw.fr. 40.-

Volume 28
The rubber industry (1982)
486 pp.; US$35.00; Sw.fr. 70.-

Volume 29
Some industrial chemicals and dyestuffs (1982)
416 pp.; US$30.00; Sw.fr. 60.-

Volume 30
Miscellaneous pesticides (1983)
424 pp; US$30.00; Sw.fr. 60.-

Volume 31
Some food additives, feed additives and naturally occurring substances (1983)
314 pp.; US$30.00; Sw.fr. 60.-

Volume 32
Polynuclear aromatic compounds, Part 1, Environmental and experimental data (1984)
477 pp.; US$30.00; Sw.fr. 60.-

Volume 33
Polynuclear aromatic compounds, Part 2, Carbon blacks, mineral oils and some nitroarene compounds (1984)
245 pp.; US$25.00; Sw.fr. 50.-

Volume 34
Polynuclear aromatic compounds, Part 3, Industrial exposures in aluminium production, coal gasification, coke production, and iron and steel founding (1984)
219 pages; US$20.00; Sw.fr. 48.-

Volume 35
Polynuclear aromatic compounds, Part 4, Bitumens, coal-tar and derived products, shale-oils and soots (1985)
271 pages; US$25.00; Sw.fr. 70.-

Volume 36
Allyl Compounds, aldehydes, epoxides and peroxides (1985)
369 pages; US$25.00; Sw.fr. 70.-

Volume 37
Tobacco habits other than smoking; betel-quid and areca-nut chewing; and some related nitrosamines (1985)
291 pages; US$ 25.00; Sw. fr. 70

Volume 38
Tobacco smoking (1985)
(in press)

Supplement No. 1
Chemicals and industrial processes associated with cancer in humans (IARC Monographs, Volumes 1 to 20) (1979)
71 pp.; out of print

Supplement No. 2
Long-term and short-term screening assays for carcinogens: a critical appraisal (1980)
426 pp.; US$25.00; Sw.fr. 40.-

Supplement No. 3
Cross index of synonyms and trade names in Volumes 1 to 26 (1982)
199 pp.; US$30.00; Sw.fr. 60.-

Supplement No. 4
Chemicals, industrial processes and industries associated with cancer in humans (IARC Monographs, Volumes 1 to 29) (1982)
292 pp.; US$30.00; Sw.fr. 60.-

INFORMATION BULLETINS ON THE
SURVEY OF CHEMICALS BEING
TESTED FOR CARCINOGENICITY

(Available from IARC)

No. 8 (1979)
Edited by M.-J. Ghess, H. Bartsch
& L. Tomatis
604 pp.; US$20.00; Sw.fr. 40.-

No. 9 (1981)
Edited by M.-J. Ghess, J.D. Wilbourn,
H. Bartsch & L. Tomatis
294 pp.; US$20.00; Sw.fr. 41.-

No. 10 (1982)
Edited by M.-J. Ghess, J.D. Wilbourn
H. Bartsch
326 pp.; US$20.00; Sw.fr. 42.-

No. 11 (1984)
Edited by M.-J. Ghess, J.D. Wilbourn,
H. Vainio & H. Bartsch
336 pp.; US$20.00; Sw.fr. 48.-